SCHOOLING, EDUCATIONAL POLICY AND ETHNIC IDENTITY

The European Science Foundation is an association of its 56 member research councils and academies in 20 countries. The ESF brings European scientists together to work on topics of common concern, to coordinate the use of expensive facilities, and to discover and define new endeavours that will benefit from a cooperative approach.

The scientific work sponsored by ESF includes basic research in the natural sciences, the medical and biosciences, the humanities and the social sciences.

The ESF links scholarship and research supported by its members and adds value by cooperation across national frontiers. Through its function as coordinator, and also by holding workshops and conferences and by enabling researchers to visit and study in laboratories throughout Europe, the ESF works for the advancement of European science.

SCHOOLING, EDUCATIONAL POLICY AND ETHNIC IDENTITY

COMPARATIVE STUDIES ON GOVERNMENTS
AND NON-DOMINANT ETHNIC GROUPS IN
EUROPE, 1850–1940

Volume I

Edited by
JANUSZ TOMIAK
in collaboration with
KNUT ERIKSEN, ANDREAS KAZAMIAS and ROBIN OKEY

European Science Foundation
NEW YORK UNIVERSITY PRESS
DARTMOUTH

© European Science Foundation 1991

Published by
Dartmouth Publishing Company Limited
Gower House
Croft Road
Aldershot
Hants GU11 3HR
England

Published in the U.S.A by
New York University Press
Washington Square
New York, NY 10003

British Library Cataloguing in Publication Data
Schooling, educational policy and ethnic identity. –
(Comparative studies on governments and non-dominant
ethnic groups in Europe, 1850–1940; v 1)
1. Europe. Ethnic minorities. Education, history
I. Tomiak, J.J. (Janusz Jozef) 1924–   II. European
Science Foundation   III. Series
371.97

Library of Congress Cataloging-in-Publication Data
Schooling, education policy, and ethnic identity / edited by J.J.
Tomiak in collaboration with K.E. Eriksen, A. Kazamias, and R. Okey.
    p.   cm. – (Comparative studies on governments and non-
dominant ethnic groups in Europe, 1850–1940; v. 1)
    "Published for the European Science Foundation."
    Includes bibliographical references.
    ISBN 0–8147–8193–4
    1.   Minorities–Education–Europe–History–Case studies.
2.   Education and state–Europe–History–Case studies.
3.   Comparative education.   I. Tomiak. J. J.   II. Eriksen, Knut
Einar.   III.   Kazamias, Andreas M.   IV. Okey, Robin,
V. European Science Foundation.   VI. Series.
LC336.A2S34   1990   90–40501
371.97'0094–dc20   CIP
ISBN 1 85521 082 7

Printed in Great Britain by
Billing & Sons Ltd, Worcester

Contents

List of Tables   vii
List of Maps   viii
Notes on Contributors   ix
Titles in the Series   xii
Series Preface   xiii
Foreword   xix

1   Introduction
    Janusz Tomiak and Andreas Kazamias   1
2   The British State and the Education of Irish Catholics,
    1850–1921
    Richard Vincent Comerford   13
3   Education and Nationhood in Wales, 1850–1940
    Robin Okey   35
4   Norwegian and Swedish Educational Policies *vis-à-vis*
    Non-dominant Ethnic Groups, 1850–1940
    Knut Eriksen   63
5   Educational Policy in Finland under Russian
    Domination, 1850–1917
    Martti T. Kuikka   87
6   Language in Education in Belgium up to 1940
    Maurits de Vroede   111
7   State, School and Ethnic Minorities in Prussia,
    1860–1914
    Manfred Heinemann   133
8   Educational Policy and Educational Development in
    the Polish Territories under Austrian, Russian and
    German Rule, 1850–1918
    Jozef Miąso   163
9   Education of the Non-Dominant Ethnic Groups in the
    Polish Republic, 1918–1939
    Janusz Tomiak   185
10 German Schools in Czechoslovakia, 1918–1938
    Wolfgang Mitter   211
11 The Education of Czechs and Slovaks under Foreign
    Domination, 1850–1918
    Jan Havránek   235

12 Italian Educational Policy Towards National
   Minorities, 1860–1940
   Angelo Ara   263
13 Spanish Education Policy Towards Non-Dominant
   Linguistic Groups, 1850–1940
   José Luís García Garrido   291
14 Education and Modernisation in a Multi-Ethnic
   Society: Bosnia, 1850–1918
   Robin Okey   319
15 The Education of the Greeks in the Ottoman Empire,
   1856–1923: A Case Study of 'Controlled Toleration'
   Andreas Kazamias   343
16 The Education of the Muslim Turks and the Christian
   Greeks in Cyprus, 1850–1905
   Costas P. Kyrris   369
17 Governments and the Education of Non-Dominant
   Ethnic Groups in Comparative Perspective
   *Knut Eriksen, Andreas Kazamias, Robin Okey and
   Janusz Tomiak*   389

   Index   419

List of Tables

5.1 Pupils and elementary schools in Finland, 1870–1900   98
6.1 French language schools in the Flemish part of Belgium   117
6.2 Dutch language schools in the Flemish regions with education in French, 1860–1875   118
6.3 Dutch language schools in the Flemish regions with education in French, 1902 and 1905   118
8.1 Pupils at state and private elementary schools according to the pupils' denomination in Galicia   170
9.1 Nationality (1921) and mother tongue (1931) in interwar Poland according to the censuses of population of 1921 and 1931   186
9.2 Population according to the mother tongue in the eastern and south eastern *voivodships*, as given in the 1931 census of population in Poland   186
10.1 The quantitative educational development of German medium schools in Bohemia, Moravia and Silesia   217
10.2 The quantitative educational development of Czech medium schools in Bohemia, Moravia and Silesia   218
11.1 Population active in, or dependent on others active in, different branches of production in Czech Lands and Slovakia in 1910   237
11.2 Illiterate persons among the older age groups in Prague in 1900   238
11.3 Pupils in Czech *gymnasiums*, *reálkas* and higher schools for girls, 1848–1898   245
11.4 National structure of the population living in the territory of Slovakia in 1880 and 1910   250
11.5 National structure of the population of Slovak towns in 1910 and 1921   251
11.6 Knowledge of reading and writing among the adult population of Slovakia in 1880 and 1910   252

List of Maps

2.1 Roman Catholics in Ireland in 1861 as a percentage of the
    population by counties   33
3.1 Welsh speaking people in Wales   62
4.1 Sapmi and some Sami centres   86
5.1 The Grand Duchy of Finland, 1815–1918   110
6.1 Languages spoken in Belgium up to 1940   131
7.1 Language minorities in the eastern regions of Prussia,
    bordering Austria/Hungary and Russia (1900)   160
7.2 Language minorities in the western regions of Prussia,
    bordering the Netherlands and France (1900)   161
8.1 Polish lands under partitions, 1815–1918   184
9.1 Distribution of minorities in interwar Poland   209
10.1 Dominant languages in Czechoslovakia 1918–1938   233
11.1 Bohemia, Moravia and Slovakia before 1914   261
12.1 Northern Italy, Aosta, Bolzano and Gorizia   290
13.1 Galicia, Catalunya and Basque Country   318
14.1 Bosnia in the nineteenth century   342
15.1 European Ottoman empire before the Treaty of Berlin
    1878   367
16.1 Cyprus under the Turks (before 1878)   388

Notes on Contributors

ANGELO ARA, born 1942 in Stresa, Italy; studied at the Universities of Milan and Naples; 1969–70 Instructor at the State University of New York, Buffalo; 1970–76 Associate Professor at the Universities of Macerata and Parma; 1976–80 Full Professor at the University of Parma, since 1980 at the University of Pavia; amongst his publications are: *Ricerche sugli Austro-Italiani e l'ultima Austria* (Roma 1974); *Trieste. Un'identità di frontiera* (with Claudio Magris) (Torino 1982, 1987); *Fra Austria e Italia. Dalle cinque giornate alla questione Alto-Atesina* (Udine 1987).

RICHARD VINCENT COMERFORD, born 1945 in County Tipperary, Ireland; received his M.A. in 1972 at the National University of Ireland-Maynooth, and his Ph.D. in 1977 at Trinity College Dublin. He is Senior Lecturer in Modern Irish History, St. Patrick's College, Maynooth, Ireland; author of: *Charles J. Kickham: a study of Irish nationalism and literature* (1979); *The Fenians in context: Irish politics and society 1848–82* (1985).

KNUT EINAR ERIKSEN, born 1944 in Sarpsborg, Norway; cand. phil. 1969 at the University of Oslo; Associate Professor from 1970–1; 1975–86 Professor of history at the University of Tromsø; since 1986 Special Advisor, National Archives, Norway; and since 1988 Professor of history at the University of Oslo; his publications include: *The Norwegian Labour Party and NATO: The Internal Struggle about Alliance Policy 1948–49* (Oslo 1972); (together with E. Niemi): *The Finnish Menace: Security problems and minority policy in the north 1860–1940* (Oslo/Bergen/Tromsø 1981); together with T. Halvorsen: *Norway at War: Liberation*, vol. 8 (Oslo 1987).

JOSE LUIS GARCIA GARRIDO, born 1937 in Azuaga, Spain; Doctor in Philosophy and Pedagogy; Professor of History of Education and Comparative Education at University of Madrid, Spain; Past President of Comparative Education Society in Europe; Consultant of UNESCO; his publications include: *Primary education on the threshold of the XXIst century* (Paris 1983); *Sistemas educativos de hoy* (Madrid 1987); *Fundamentos de Educación Comparada* (Madrid 1986).

JAN HAVRANEK, born 1928 in Teplice, Czechoslovakia, studied history at Charles University Prague; 1955–70 Lecturer in Modern Czechoslovak History, Charles University; since 1960 researcher at the Institute of University History, since 1970 in the Archives of Charles University; published textbooks and studies on the history of universities, historical demography and social history; *Stručné dějiny Univerzity Karlovy* (ed. F. Kavka 1964); *Dějiny Československa III (1781–1918)*, (with J. Butvin 1968).

MANFRED HEINEMANN, born 1943 in Lippstadt, Germany; studied at the universities of Münster, Hamburg and Bochum; in 1971 Dr. phil. Ruhr-University Bochum; 1971–79 *Wissenschaftlicher Assistent*, Ruhr-University Bochum; since 1979 Fu!l Professor of education at the University of Hannover; amongst his publications are: *Schule im Vorfeld der Verwaltung* (1974); *Landschulreform als Gesellschaftsinitiative* (1975); *Veröffentlichungen der Historischen Kommission der Deutschen Gesellschaft für Erziehungswissenschaft* (ed.).

ANDREAS KAZAMIAS, born in 1927 in Cyprus, 1948 B.A.(Hons) in History and English Literature, University of Bristol; 1958 Ph.D. in Comparative Education, Harvard University; since 1964 Professor of Educational Policy Studies, University of Wisconsin, Madison, USA; since 1987 also Professor of Comparative Education, University of Crete, Greece; amongst his publications are: *Tradition and Change in Education: a Comparative Study* (1965); *Education and the Quest for Modernity in Turkey* (1966); *Politics, Society and Secondary Education in England, 1985–1926* (1966).

MARTTI TAPANI KUIKKA, born 1939 in Polvijärvi, Finland; 1970 received Licenciate in Theology; Doctor in Philosophy in 1973; 1973–74 Rector in teacher training college; 1974–78 Associate Professor at the University of Joensuu, since 1978 at the University of Helsinki; his publications include: *Religious Instruction in Teacher Training College for Primary Schools in Finland 1863–1895* (1973); *Die Erforschung der Geschichte der Erziehung in Finnland 1945–1975* (1979); *Society and Development of an Elementary School System in Finland 1866–1968*.

COSTAS KYRRIS, born 1927 in Lapethos, Cyprus; received his B.A. Hons. in 1952 at the University of Athens and M.A. in 1961 at the University of London; 1962–76 Researcher, 1976–81 Senior Researcher and 1981–87 Director at the Cyprus Research Centre; amongst his publications are: *History of Secondary Education in Famagusta 1191–1955* (Cyprus 1967); *History of Cyprus* (Cyprus 1985); *Turkey and the Balkans* (Athens 1986).

JOSEF MIĄSO, born 1930 in Witkowice, Poland; graduated in 1955 from the University of Warsaw and received his Ph.D. from there in 1959; Professor from 1973; since 1955 research worker at the Institute of History of Science, Education and Technology at the Polish Academy of Sciences in Warsaw; also Professor at the University of Warsaw; amongst his publications are: *Vocational Education in the Kingdom of Poland* (Wrocław 1966); *The History of the Education of Polish Immigrants in the United States* (Warsaw 1977); *Vocational Schools in Poland in the Years 1918–1939* (Wrocław 1988).

WOLFGANG MITTER, born 1927 in Trautenau, Czechoslovakia; studied at the University of Mainz 1948–53; Doctoral promotion at the Free University of Berlin in 1954; 1954–64 *Gymnasium* teacher in Kassel; 1964–72 Professor of Education at the *Pädagogische Hochschule* at Lüneburg; since 1972 Head of Department of General and Comparative Education at the *Deutsches Institut für Internationale Pädagogische Forschung* at Frankfurt am Main (1978–81 and since 1987 Director of the Institute); since 1974 teaching at the University of Frankfurt am Main; published *Education for all* (Paris 1985); *Schule zwischen Krise und Reform. Zur Theorie und Praxis der Vergleichenden Bildungsforschung. Gesammelte Aufsätze* (Köln/Wien 1987); together with Leonid Novikov: *Pädagogische Forschung und Bildungspolitik in der Sowjetunion* (Weinheim/Basel 1978).

ROBIN OKEY, born 1924 in Cardiff, Great Britain; studied history at Jesus College and Nuffield College, Oxford; since 1966 Lecturer and then Senior Lecturer in the History Department of the University of Warwick; author of *Eastern Europe 1740–1985; Feudalism to Communism* (2nd edition London 1986).

JANUSZ TOMIAK, born 1924 in Krotoszyn, Poland; studied in Poland, Germany, USA and England; received his B.Sc. in 1953 and M.A. in 1965 at the University of London; 1966 Lecturer, since 1984 Senior Lecturer in Comparative and Russian/Soviet Education, University of London; amongst his publications are: *The Soviet Union* (World Education Series) (1972); *Soviet Education in the 1980s* (ed.) (1983); *Western Perspectives on Soviet Education in the 1980s* (ed.) (1986).

MAURITS DE VROEDE, born 1922 in Mechelen, Belgium; received his B.A. in 1943, Ph.D. in 1957 and *Agrégation supérieure* in 1970; he was a Professor at the *Katholieke Universiteit* Leuven until he retired in 1987; published books and articles on the Flemish movement: *The history of the press; Cultural history; The history of education, 18th-20th centuries.*

Comparative Studies on Governments and Non-dominant Ethnic Groups in Europe, 1850–1940

Titles in the Series

Schooling, Educational Policy and Ethnic Identity
Edited by *J.J. Tomiak* in collaboration with *K.E. Eriksen, A. Kazamias* and *R. Okey*

Religion, State and Ethnic Groups
Edited by *D. Kerr* in collaboration with *M. Breuer, S. Gilley* and *E. Suttner*

Ethnic Groups and Language Rights
Edited by *S. Vilfan* in collaboration with *G. Sandvik* and *L. Wils*

Governments, Ethnic Groups and Political Representation
Edited by *G. Alderman* in collaboration with *J. Leslie* and *K. Pollmann*

Ethnic Groups in International Relations
Edited by *P. Smith* in collaboration with *K.K. Koufa* and *A. Suppan*

The Formation of National Elites
Edited by *A. Kappeler* in collaboration with *F. Adanir* and *A. O'Day*

Roots of Rural Ethnic Mobilisation
Edited by *G. von Pistohlkors* in collaboration with *D. Howell* and *E. Wiegandt*

Ethnic Identity in Urban Europe
Edited by *M. Engman* in collaboration with *F.W. Carter, A.C. Hepburn* and *C.G. Pooley*

Series Preface

This series of eight volumes represents the results of the first major project in historical research to be undertaken by the European Science Foundation. The project's title, adopted also for the series, was carefully constructed to convey with precision the subject matter, and approach, of the enquiry; for the specialist, the lawyer, the diplomat, or the politician there are crucial differences between 'ethnic groups' and 'nationalities' and between 'non-dominant ethnic groups' (which may well be majorities) and 'ethnic minorities'. In plain language, however, and ignoring a multitude of qualifications, this is a study of some of the characteristic historic (as distinct from twentieth-century extra-European immigrant) non-dominant ethnic groups of Europe (usually minorities) and the ways in which their lives, their survival, and their development were affected by governments and the institutions of the state. The aim is strictly historical, to study what has happened in the past and try to understand and explain it. But the existence of ethnic minorities, their aspirations and their problems, is never far below the consciousness of every country in Europe, and they have contributed to many of the most dramatic and significant events in the remaking of the European scene in 1989 and 1990. The strength of deeply-rooted distinctions of religion, language, and culture in determining current political actions has been repeatedly demonstrated; and the apparently unsuspected existence of minorities within minorities, like so many Russian dolls, has continually startled Western press and television reporters. The past definitely does not predict the future: but it does give rise to the present. These volumes are, therefore, essential to the understanding of one of the most fundamental as well as most complex dimensions of contemporary Europe.

The problem addressed in these volumes can be defined as the problem created by imposing the concept of the nation–state on a mosaic of frequently intermingled peoples of differing religion, language, and culture, whose geographical distribution and pattern of settlement simply did not conform to the abstract specifications assumed by the concept. The idea of the nation as a large, supra-local, community of people with certain characteristics and purposes in common, and of the state as the legitimate embodiment of judicial, coercive, and military power, were far from new in the nineteenth century. The fusion of the two ideas, however, owed much to the French Revolution and the Napoleonic Wars; and multiple aspirations for forming new nation–states were the main driving force of the 1848 Revolutions. In spite, and often because, of the reality on the ground, the ideal of one nation, one state commanded increasingly general acceptance, outside some dynastic and aristocratic circles; it was widely believed that no nation could achieve full expression of its distinctive identity unless it was embodied in a state, and that no state could have legitimate authority over its people unless those formed a single nation.

These principles were patently and glaringly contradicted by the great multi-national empires of the nineteenth century, the Habsburg, the Russian, the German, and the Ottoman. It was less noticed that the United Kingdom also belonged to this group, perhaps because it was more liberal, and more unified in language although not in religion, perhaps because the dominance of the English was of such long standing that the existence of the other three nations had become all but invisible to the rest of the world. While most of the other European sovereign states could plausibly claim, for external purposes, to fit the nation–state model, there was scarcely one whose territories did not contain minorities with aspirations for recognition, autonomy, independence, or union with a mother country. France, Spain, Italy, Belgium or Sweden, for example, fit such a description; while the Swiss, uniquely in Europe a nation which was multi-lingual and federal, did not escape minority issues.

The First World War was a power struggle, a struggle for mastery, not a war of nationalities, but as the fighting went on it became increasingly like that as governments sought to sustain popular commitment to the war, or to undermine the unity of their enemies. Its conclusion, for a mixture of practical and idealistic reasons, saw the not too blatantly partisan application of the principle of self-determination to the map of Europe in the treaties of Versailles and Trianon. The multi-national empires, apart from the United Kingdom, fell apart or were dismembered. A new multi-national state, Yugoslavia, was created; and Europe came as close as it has ever been to appearing as a collection of independent sovereign nation–states.

Some of the successor states, such as Poland or Lithuania, were revived after years or centuries of oblivion, while others, such as Czechoslovakia, were new creations. In all of them the previously non-dominant groups gained control, and promptly found themselves faced with minorities within the new borders, consisting chiefly of the former masters. In western and Mediterranean Europe there was no similar *bouleversement*, aside from the withdrawal of southern Ireland from United Kingdom, and the identity of non-dominant groups remained unchanged throughout the whole study period. Minorities certainly did not cease to exist or to be important in 1940; the Second World War, however, started a markedly different phase in their history, which has lasted for fifty years. During the war several minorities were treated with unsurpassable and previously unthinkable savagery and inhumanity; grievously depleted, they survived. Then, through the years of the Cold War, in some countries minorities were driven underground, marginalised, and virtually deprived of any official, public, existence; minority questions, along with nationalist issues, largely disappeared from the agenda of European international relations; and several western European countries became for the first time countries of large-scale immigration, hosts to new, non-historic, minorities. Europe seemed to have changed irrevocably, to have left history behind, to have jettisoned old minority problems and acquired new ones. Then in 1989 and 1990 the Europe of 1939, or something with a passing resemblance to it, came rushing back to life, and there was more than a hint that elements of the pre-1914 world were re-awakening. All of a sudden it became clear that historians dealing with the events of 1850 to 1940 were, in effect, also throwing light on current affairs.

In the long, and open-ended, continuum of the history of minorities in European countries the period between roughly 1850 and 1940 thus has a distinct unity; the sharp discontinuity of 1914 was, in this perspective, the hinge around which aspirations for national independence were converted into reality. Such was the general context for the proposal by the Norwegian historian John Herstad that the European Science Foundation should mount a major collaborative study of minorities, or more specifically of governments and non-dominant ethnic groups. This proposal was developed into a research programme by a planning committee chaired by Gerald Stourzh, of Vienna, consisting of members from ten different countries, including the late Professor Benjamin Akzin (Jerusalem) and the late Professor Hugh Seton-Watson (London). This programme then ran for the five years 1984-8, with an overall steering committee chaired by myself. The aim of the project was not to produce a narrative or descriptive history of each and every minority or non-dominant ethnic group in Europe, nor to produce an exhaustive, and exhausting, history of the policies and actions of each government towards its minority groups. The aim was at once simpler, more limited, and more demanding: to undertake a number of case studies on a selection of well-defined themes providing different angles of approach to the central topic, and lending themselves to comparative evaluation. From a much larger number of possibilities, eight themes were chosen, and these furnish the eight volumes of the series: Schooling; Religion; Language Rights;

Political R presentation; International Relations; Formation of National Elites; Rural Settlements; Urban Settlements.

John Herstad's original idea was that studies in depth of minority groups in particular, sometimes quite small, localities could reveal much about group survival strategies, the most significant and tenacious characteristics of ethnic identities, the most important influences on assimilation, the actual impact and effect of legislation and administrative practices, and many other features which tend to get lost or obscured in the generalisations and rhetoric of national histories. This call to employ local history as a methodology has been followed where the nature of the material permits, especially in the rural and urban volumes. The claim is not that the particular villages and towns chosen for study necessarily merit intense international attention for their own sakes, but that they are microcosms of the larger world in which more general features of ethnicity, culture, custom, and law can be observed in action in the lives of individuals and families. In other chapters and other volumes the emphasis is necessarily on larger regions, and states, whose educational systems, laws and institutions, judiciaries and bureaucracies, ecclesiastical organizations and economic and social structures, set the framework within which direct interaction between non-dominant ethnic groups and the long arm of government took place. In both types of case study the selection of localities, regions, and countries is representative of the variety of different situations, different levels of economic and social development, and different forms of govern-ment which were to be found in Europe; but it does not set out to be comprehensive in its coverage, and that is not necessary to the achievement of the objective of writing a thematic, comparative, history.

That objective was pursued by assembling eight teams of experts drawn from 18 countries and a wide range of disciplines: history, law, theology, education, sociology, anthropology, and geography. More than 90 scholars took part in the project, and although all of them had extensive previous research involvement in the field, they de-veloped, deepened, and extended their personal research in order to tackle the specific formulation of issues in the project and in order to put their own material into thematically comparable form. More preparation and research went into this task than can appear in these volumes, whose chapters in many cases are distillations and sum-maries of larger pieces of work. Several of the individuals who have taken part hope to publish separately longer and more complete versions of their work, especially when it was originally written in a language other than English. The decision to have a single language publication, in English, was made after much discussion and heart-searching. It goes against many long-held traditions of European scholarship in the humanities, but for a science foundation it is clearly the right decision and the one best calculated to make the results of the project most widely accessible. Hence many of the contributions are translations, and while the sense has not been altered the loss of some of the finer points of argument and subtleties of style is regrettably unavoidable.

The working programme of each group was arranged by a co-ordinator, assisted by the collective efforts of his team; and the co-ordinators, assisted by small editorial teams drawn from their colleagues, have been the editors of their individual volumes. Each group has been fully European, multi-national, multi-cultural, and multi-lingual; the co-ordinator–editors have performed difficult feats of academic organization and intellectual discipline with much tact, and with a success which can be judged in these volumes. Each group, and hence each volume, has a different structure, and the significance of the separate contributions and the conclusions to be drawn are excellently handled by the volume editors; it is not the province of this general preface either to anticipate or to summarise them. One general feature of the enterprise, so obvious that it can easily be overlooked, does however deserve emphasis. The humanities work within national cultures and languages in a way that is not true of the natural or experimental sciences. In this project researchers brought up in many very different scholarly traditions have learned each other's ways, and while continuing to speak in many tongues have adopted a common 'language' for identifying the problems for intellectual enquiry and the methods for investigating them. This is the key to successful international cooperation in the humanities, and to have come so far towards achieving it in this project is a major innovation in the methodology of European scholarship. Without sacrificing any of the particularity and individuality of specific circumstances and situations in different places at different times, which are fundamental to the historical method, the varieties of experience of non-dominant ethnic groups have been approached and analysed in a common way which for the first time has made wide-ranging comparative assessment based on firm empirical evidence possible and meaningful.

In an enterprise of this size and complexity many friendships have been formed and many individuals and institutions have given their help. Above all, everyone who has participated in the project would wish to have recorded their appreciation of the incomparable contribution made by Christoph Mühlberg, Secretary of the Humanities Committee of the European Science Foundation throughout the major part of the programme, whose skill in administrative organization has been matched only by his grasp of the intellectual challenges of the theme and the soundness of his suggestions for meeting them. In addition, unknown to the majority of the authors, Dr Judith Rowbotham has made a vital contribution to the consistency of these volumes in the very demanding work of adding the finishing touches of painstaking sub-editing, which is the more successful the more unobtrusive it seems.

F.M.L. Thompson
Institute of Historical Research,
University of London

Foreword

In selecting the theme of 'Governments and Non-dominant Ethnic Groups in Europe, 1850–1940', the European Science Foundation chose, true to its objectives, a topic of very considerable international significance for a comparative analysis. No one living in the closing years of the twentieth century can have any doubts that such phenomena as nationalism, domination, modernisation lie at the very heart of the rapid social, cultural, political and economic change which is taking place everywhere today, and was taking place in the past.

Within the larger framework of the project, a group of several European scholars, including both historians and comparative educationists, was able to meet regularly between 1984 and 1988. The group focused its attention upon the dominant governments' educational policies *vis-à-vis* the non-dominant ethnic groups in a significantly large number of European states in the second half of the nineteenth and the first forty years of the twentieth century. The meetings proved most exciting and thought-provoking encounters, in which a whole range of issues linked to the formulation, legitimation and execution of educational policy were hotly debated and examined with due academic rigour. They provided an ideal ground for testing a variety of hypotheses as well as formulating, challenging and reformulating tentative conclusions. Information which as a rule was only available to experts in command of particular minority languages could be exchanged, juxtaposed and compared. No doubt the historical and comparative perspectives of all those who participated in these exciting encounters were both deepened and broadened. For all the participants, this was a unique and unforgettable experience. Its concrete result is the present volume.

The editor of the volume has additional debts of gratitude to express. The substance of both the introductory chapter and the concluding chapter are the result of hard work by the editorial board, who devoted many days of concentrated effort to the task of summing up the results of the research pursued by the members of the group. The difficult task of editing the volume and finalising the conclusions was greatly facilitated by the editor's opportunity to work on it in November–December 1988 in the Rockefeller Foundation Conference and Residential Study Centre at Bellagio, Italy, for which he is most grateful to the Foundation. This may, indeed, be taken as an irrefutable proof that the way to better understanding and scholarly achievement is through good will and effectively organised international cooperation.

Janusz Tomiak

1 Introduction

JANUSZ TOMIAK AND
ANDREAS KAZAMIAS

This collection of case studies examines the interrelationships of states, societies and schools involving non-dominant ethnic groups in a number of European countries from approximately 1850 to 1940. The socio-political formations that are dealth with include large and diverse polyethnic, polyglot and multi-religious, multi-cultural empire–states (for example, the British, the Austro–Hungarian or Habsburg, the Prussian, the Russian and the Ottoman) and relatively smaller polyethnic 'nation–states', such as Belgium, Norway, Italy, Poland, Spain and Czechoslovakia. The non-dominant groups within these governing state units stretch over a wide and diverse ethnic spectrum: the Welsh, the Irish, the Turks and the Greeks in the British Empire; the Serbs and the Czechs in the Habsburg empire; the Poles and the Finns in the Russian empire; the Greeks and the Serbs in the Ottoman empire; the Samis and Kvens in Norway; the Catalans, Basques and Galicians in Spain; the Ukrainians, Byelo-russians, Germans and Jews in Poland; the Flemings in Belgium; and the Sudeten Germans in Czechoslovakia.

The focus of each study is on schooling; namely, the institutional-isation of education as a purposive/intentional socio-cultural process, or in E. Gellner's term as 'exo-socialisation',[1] entailing a formal apparatus of administration, supervision/control and support, special cultural agents (for example, teachers), codified forms of communication and knowledge (for example, language and pro-grammes of study), and pedagogical practices and means (for example, text books, and methods of instruction). Schooling is examined at the policy and institutional levels, namely, the educa-tional intentions and courses of action of the politically dominant governments towards the non-dominant ethnic minorities, and, in turn, the educational reactions and activities of the latter, within the dynamics of state–ethnic group relations as well as intra-group conflicts and concerns. Given the availability of sources, the studies presented here emphasise more the development of policies and institutions and the related motives of government and non-dominant group actions, and less the grass root implementation of

1

classroom experience. The specific aspects of schooling that are emphasised by each author vary, depending on the idiosyncracies of each individual case. But we all sought to consider at least the following aspects: educational provision (compulsory and/or voluntary), language or languages of instruction, curriculum (explicit and 'hidden'), types of teachers and their training, and existence or not of 'public' and/or private schools.

All the contributions in this volume are self-contained historical case studies, dealing as such with particular sets of circumstances, institutions, processes and factors. But the analysis and interpretation of each are organised on the basis of a common, albeit loose framework, and make use, to a degree more or less, of more generalised concepts, gleaned from the literature available. This combination of the particular with the general helped provide a conceptual focus to look at and interpret past events, while allowing, at the same time, for comparative analysis and synthesis. The latter is presented in the concluding chapter. It would be appropriate, therefore, to refer here to the main features of the common framework and to the main guiding concepts and procedures.

In the conceptualisation and characterisation of patterns of state policy regarding schooling, the contributors considered a wide range of plausible concepts or ideas applicable to their particular case, such as assimilation, segregation, domination, integration or *laissez faire*. At the same time, they tried to indicate the character and intensity of the means and the specific measures each government used to pursue or operationalise state actions at the national, regional and local levels. The heuristic value of generalising concepts is also present in the explanatory aspects of the case studies. In the all-important quest for explanation of particular patterns of policy and measures of implementation, contributors were asked to consider and assess the relative weight of ideological, socio-economic, political and other factors. In particular these were to include nationalism, imperialism, Social Darwinism, cultural differentiation, modernisation (economic, political, social), the nature and structure of the state and its constituent institutional mechanisms, supra-national forces, national security and foreign policy considerations, intra-group power relations and the like.

A guiding framework was also considered in the examination of the attitudes, reactions, and more generally, the educational activities of the ethnic minorities. It was suggested that the degree of consensus and/or conflict within both the dominant and non-dominant segments be taken into account. As to the non-dominant ethnic elements, we sought to conceptualise their reaction in terms of such categories as acceptance, apathy/indifference, manifest or latent opposition and alignments or antagonisms with other groups (for example, with the opposition among the rulers or other non-dominant segments). Likewise, we sought to cast the interpretative rationale for the reactions and activities of the ethnic minorities in a multi-dimensional explanatory mould with ideological as well as socio-economic and political parameters such as anti-imperialism, cultural pluralism, political federalism, social justice, power relations and the nature and structure of the state, interstate relations and supra-national factors, as well as socio-economic structures.

In the conceptual framework outlined above, it is clearly implied that each case sought to approach educational policies, institutional developments and pedagogical practices as arenas of social and ideological conflict and debate upon which impinged a constellation of external forces and factors – local, national and supra-national. Schooling as a socio-cultural system ramifies into other sectors of the broader social context as a reproductive but also a productive agent, and cannot be adequately examined or understood independent of the social (which also includes the political, the economic and the ideological) *milieu* in which it is situated. Here again there are particularities in the social *milieu* of each case study, and all contributors sought to bring them out, as is documented in the chapters that follow and in the synthesising concluding chapter at the end. But in introducing this collective undertaking it might help to outline in broad, and perhaps over-simplified, terms the social landscape of Europe during the period under consideration. Such a contextual backdrop to the substantive issues of schooling that are analysed could also act as a helpful prism through which to see each individual case in relation to others, that is, in a comparative perspective.

In the general historical literature on this period, certain inter-related contextual non-educational factors whose relevance is investigated in the several studies, have been conceptualised in different ways, but one that we have found especially useful, is the dynamic concept of modernisation. Modernisation is an ambiguous, protean and controversial concept, and as sometimes used, it has also been replete with teleological, ideological and ethnocentric (mostly western) assumptions. Yet, it can be of considerable methodological value if it is employed as a concept to refer to certain *historical* processes of socio-economic and political change rather than to universal and timeless processes and to historicist laws or theories of unilinear development. In our framework, modernisation serves to summarise at least two constellations of historical phenomena:

● The socio-economic transformations attendant upon the increased industrialisation and the concomitant application of science and technology to the means of production in the nineteenth and twentieth centuries, conditions which were associated with the expansion and transformation of European capitalism into an imperialist world economic system, and

● the politico-ideological transformations attendant upon the emergence of liberalism, nationalism, a constitutional nation–state and societies of citizens, during the same period.

Some of the phenomena of modernisation were structural and pertained to the transformation of the socio-economic and demographic infrastructure of western Europe. Specifically, by the First World War most characteristics of a modern and advanced capitalist 'world economic order' had become quite visible. A corporate organisation and management, a pluralist world order and international competitive mass markets, a technological revolution, differentiated and hierarchical social structures with an expanded public and private tertiary sector, and what Eric Hobsbawm has described as 'the growing convergence between politics and economics, that is to say the growing role of Government and the public sector'[2] are all discernible. The essence of this emerging world economic system was captured well by L. S. Stavrianos when he wrote that 'Europe by 1914 had become the banker as well as the workshop of the world'.[3] The dynamism of western European capitalist expansion extended and impinged upon the economies, social structures, and cultures of central and eastern Europe, including the economically cloistered and predominantly agrarian Balkan peninsula and the Ottoman empire.

An intrinsic structural characteristic of the new social order was the expansion and rise to political, commercial and cultural prominence of a bourgeois 'middle class' consisting of 'capitalists' or businessmen, bureaucrats, intellectuals and free professionals. In addition to expansive capitalism and economic imperialism, with the rise of the bourgeoisie and the consolidation of bourgeois society there also developed a bourgeois 'ethos', a bourgeois 'culture', and, one may interject here, a bourgeois system of education, as well as certain epochal political ideologies or social movements. Two such developments are especially significant in framing the historical context of most of the ensuing case studies. One was 'liberalism' and the other 'nationalism'.

Liberalism and nationalism during the nineteenth century, as R. Okey, one of the editors and a contributor to this volume, has observed in another source, had different connotations in western as opposed to eastern Europe. In the western core countries of its origins ('industrial England, ex-republican France and politically divided Germany'), Okey elaborates:

> liberalism was the creed of the middle classes . . . whose numerical and economic strength led them to demand political power and the reorganisation of society according to individual rather than inherited distinctions.[4]

In its heyday during most of the second half of the nineteenth century, bourgeois liberalism denoted individualism, property, progress, a constitutional nation–state composed of 'citizens' who possessed certain basic political and legal rights, and a rather limited state in the sphere of social policy (including education). By the end of the nineteenth century, liberalism as a policy generating political creed, as a programme and as an ideology had lost its earlier rather united and consistent identity and had moved in different, and often contradictory, directions – from left to centre to right – in the western core countries. It is in these countries, it should be remembered, that imperialism, a movement not easily reconcilable with liberalism, gained ascendancy, while in Germany and Italy the right wing versions of nationalism also showed their illiberal faces.[5]

In central and eastern Europe (Austria, Hungary and Poland) liberalism, unlike its counterpart in western Europe, was an upper class rather than a middle class movement. It was, to paraphrase Okey, enlightenment from above rather than from below, for a middle class bourgeoisie, comparable to that of the western industrial countries, was small and weak. East European liberals were not a revolutionary class pushing aggressively into the un-known, but the spokesmen of a fairly small, educated stratum, usually members of the privileged order they condemned and often linked to it still by ties of sentiment and interest. Their key theme for reform was 'for a timely piece of social engineering', and their key call was for law 'as the linchpin of a new civil society'. Hence, Okey adds, 'the East European liberals' preoccupation with another aspect of classical liberalism which above all seemed calculated to guarantee that "community of interests" they craved – the idea of nationality.'[6]

Among other things, the nineteenth century and the pre–First World War years of the twentieth that politically and socially are classed with it, has been called the age of 'nationality' and 'national-ism'. The genesis of nationalism, and the related concepts of national identity, national consciousness and their relation to state and nation building in Europe and the Balkans during this period, is a subject of debate among historians and other social analysts, but clearly beyond the scope of our analysis here. Suffice it to say that in the context of a combined set of relations (political, socio-economic, intellectual, cultural, territorial and others) a powerful and assertive emotional force of belonging to a community of people, an 'ethos', emerged, which had far reaching effects on European history.

Post–1848 nationalism, as Hans Kohn has reminded us, 'had its good and its evil aspects'.[7] Perhaps more so than liberalism, with which it is often associated, its connotations have oscillated on the politico-ideological pendulum from left to centre to right, or, para-doxically, in all directions simultaneously. Whatever its source of origin or its politico-ideological colouration, nationalism, as well as the associated concepts of national identity and national consciousness, inspired as it was in large part by the writings of romantic intellectuals such as Johann Gottfried Herder, acted as a powerful kinetic force for political independence, self-government and nation building, or for protest and maintenance of ethno-cultural distinctiveness among subjugated ethnic groups, especially in the empire–states of the period. This generally positive contribution of nationalism, combined with liberalism, implied, to a degree, the assertion and extension of basic political, social and human rights. But in the hands of dominant ethnic groups as in Italy, Norway and the Russian and German empires, state nationalism was used negatively as an instrument for the promotion of racialist and discriminatory policies, for the restriction of basic rights, and for the purpose of assimilating the non-dominant groups into the dominant ruling culture, that is of 'denationalising' them.

There were other developments of importance for our project during this period of study, which can also be viewed from the perspective of modernisation. There was an uneven growth in secularising tendencies and a corresponding decline in religious convictions noticeable everywhere. The influence of religion and the Churches was in a steady decline and their power was inevitably curtailed in a wide range of culturally and socially significant activities, though the differences in the rate of change between the various countries were in this context as significant as the general trend and there were exceptions to this rule, particularly in central and eastern Europe. Most important, the concept of the state and its role in society was also undergoing constant and very fundamental changes.

The case studies, as indicated earlier, deal with subject minorities in socio-political formations that can be classified in two broad categories: empires and nation–states. But although such categories imply certain differentiating state structures, patterns of authority and state roles, obviously they obscure variations between and within each of them, and they do not fully bring out intra-state changes. Among those classified as empires, for example, there was the 'liberal' constitutional and, by the 1920s, 'liberal democratic' English metropolis of the British empire; the constitutional, 'pluralist' but undemocratic Habsburg empire; the similarly constitutional and highly authoritarian federal German empire controlled by an emperor and the *Junkers* (land owning aristocracy); the autocratic and absolutist empire of the Romanovs; and the politically discriminatory, theocratic Ottoman empire.

Lastly and most pertinently for our purposes here, the historical period we have chosen, especially the nineteenth century, was characterised by fundamental changes in institutionalised education. In the core industrial countries of western Europe (Britain, France and Prussia) there was a considerable expansion of popular education, and the foundations of national systems of education – supported and controlled by state agencies – were laid. 'In educational terms', Hobsbawm has asserted, 'the era from 1870 to 1914 was above all, in most European countries, the age of the primary school'.[8] Among other things, this entailed the extension of the state into a socio-cultural sphere, which had hitherto been the purview mainly of the Church and of other voluntary agencies.

State involvement in education did not mean that all schooling had become completely 'nationalised', in the sense that its provision at all levels and in all types had shifted and become the exclusive responsibility of the state. Different concordats involving the state, the Church and other sectors of civil society were negotiated in the respective countries, and different public–private patterns emerged. But, for several reasons, the rather strict *laissez faire* liberal doctrines of the classical economists (for example, Adam Smith) had gradually given way, as noted above, to more 'collectivist' ideas, even to the adumbration of a democratic welfare state. This development was especially visible in the area of education, one of the first arenas of public policy to reflect the gradual transformation of the west European concept of the bourgeois state.

Increased interest in education, both on the part of the states but also of civil societies, was observed in practically all areas of Europe and the Ottoman empire. The development of 'national' or 'quasi-national' systems of education was an inseparable process from the other macro-social and political changes whose main parameters were outlined above. Industrialisation and bourgeois capitalism exposed the limitations of fragmented voluntaryism in educational provision, and in due course, of classical humanistic learning which was so prevalent in the secondary and higher reaches of the educational systems (the grammar schools, the *lycees* and the *gymnasiums* that is, the classical secondary schools, and the universities). The different modes of production and capital accumulation attendant upon economic modernisation and developing capitalism created new educational imperatives (extension of educational provision and functional literacy, scientific and 'modern' programmes of study, and technical and vocational training).

The impetus given to educational reform was reinforced by the other, more politically and ideologically relevant initial conditions or processes, namely, liberalism, nationalism and nation building. Constitutional government and liberal democracy presupposed the extension of the social rights of citizenship, which included the right to education. In the industrial capitalist states, pressures for educational expansion and reform came from all social strata: the socially and politically entrenched elites, the status conscious and increasingly powerful middle classes, and the disenfranchised but slowly assertive working classes. As the Liberal politician Robert Lowe, urged in the English parliamentary debate on the Elementary Education Bill of 1870, and just after the passing of the Second Reform Bill (1867) which had extended the right to vote to greater segments of the English people, 'Now we must educate our masters'.

The historical interconnections of the political with the educational (both in the broad meaning of the cultural and the narrower one of schooling) spheres were also germane to most nationalist movements, as noted by several social historians, students of nationalism, and comparative educators. Generally speaking, such associations have referred to state nationalist educational policies (that is, to policies of dominant governments) as well as to nationalist aspirations and educational activities of non-dominant ethno-religious or ethno-linguistic minorities, the two dimensions of particular relevance to our study here. To Gellner, for example, 'cultural homogeneity' and 'the school transmitted nature of culture within each political unit', or 'exo-socialisation' was a functional imperative of nationalism and a concomitant of industrial society.[9] Similarly, according to Hobsbawm:

> What made state nationalism even more essential was that both the economy of a technological era and the nature of its public and private administration, required mass elementary education, or at least literacy . . . From the state's point of view the school had a further and essential advantage: it could teach all children how to be good subjects and citizens.[10]

Anthony Smith, in turn, considers the role of secular education as 'paramount' to the genesis of nationalism and the formation of nations. Indeed, he avers that 'in one sense the "nation" itself is the institutionalisation of secular education'.[11] To others, for example, the historian Hugh Seton-Watson and the comparative educator Nicholas Hans, language – an important aspect of schooling – was a crucial factor in the formation of national consciousness/identity and national character.[12]

It has been generally recognised, therefore, that schooling in all its cultural aspects was an inextricable component of modernising societies in the nineteenth century, and in its language aspect particularly, of paramount instrumental value in state nationalism, nationalist movements and nation building. Yet one is struck by the paucity of documented analyses and by conspicuous *lacunae* in the literature, both the theoretical and the historical–empirical. Scattered references are often made as to how states, especially the liberal democratic states, through education, sought to disseminate the benefits of culture and enlightenment to wider segments of society: to extend human rights and to mobilise populations for purposes of greater economic efficiency and social justice and for the general improvement of human welfare. But there is also a tendency among writers to treat all members of society as collective entities or as cohesive groups, and to assume that state policies applied equally and without discrimination to all subjects or 'citizens'.

Clearly, this was not always the case. Relatively little, if any, attention has been given to the fact that interventionist states often interpreted concepts such as nation, nationality, citizenship and the like narrowly and differentially so far as their polyglot, polyethnic and multi-religious subjects were concerned. The doctrines of liberalism, even of the radical quasi-leftist variety, were noticeably restrictive and exclusionist as regards minorities when translated into programmes of social action such as education. State nationalism, in some cases, was sought through school policies that aimed at the assimilation of the different ethno-cultural groups into the dominant culture. This, if successful, would, in essence, result in the 'denationalisation' of the ethnic minorities, something which non-dominant groups did not always look at with favour.

Several of the case studies in this volume seek to illuminate this rather neglected aspect of modern European comparative socio-educational history. The discriminatory nationalist policies towards ethnic minorities, the conflicts they engendered and their success or failure, as evidenced by overt or clandestine reactions to them, are examined especially in the chapters dealing with Italy under the Fascist regime, Poland during the period of autocratic Russian domination and liberal democratic Norway, indicating the wide range of the phenomenon under investigation.

There is another angle of vision regarding the interrelationship of states, societies and ethnic minority schooling that, we feel, has not been adequately addressed in the extant comparative historical scholarly literature. This has to do with the educational activities of the non-dominant ethnic groups themselves in response to the policies of the dominant groups, assimilative or otherwise, or in the context of the contemporary matrix of socio-economic and politico-ideological processes and relations mentioned above.

While in virtually all states, dominant groups perceived education as a means of political socialisation, social control or, at worst, an unavoidable suspension of the right to study in the mother tongue, the non-dominant ethnic groups considered education to be of cardinal importance in promoting national identity, ensuring cultural–ethnic cohesion and creating or reviving ethno-nationalist aspirations. Against the social and political background of the times, ethno-nationalist awareness also led to political demands and actions which conflicted with the intentions of the states. Virtually all non-dominant ethnic groups perceived education as a mechanism of political emancipation or liberation and the creation of 'nations'. Of course, there were variations in the educational policies and activities of the two groups – the rulers and the ethnic subjects – particularly in the teaching of the mother tongue, and these are carefully examined in each case study.

Yet, the difficulties inherent in presenting a truly comprehensive and, at the same time, a reliable picture of the existing patterns in this respect should not be underestimated. A number of studies under-taken from the standpoint of non-dominant ethnic groups which are available tend to be isolated and confined in focus, that is, confined to the individual countries concerned. This collection of papers permits the attempt to delineate the principal lines of development on a larger European scene in respect of the intricate character of educational policy *vis-à-vis* non-dominant ethnic groups in a number of countries in a very important period of European history. Of course, far from being a final word on the subject, this volume should be seen as a contribution to the ongoing debates concerning both educational policies and nationalism and, particularly, as a document revealing with some precision the role of education in the growth of national-ism and the parallel processes of political expansion and modernis-ation.

The enormous importance attached to education by both the dominant as well as the non-dominant groups in all countries in the period 1850–1940 is, from the evidence provided in the pages which follow, quite plain. This is understandable in the socio-political climate of rapidly changing circumstances under which these groups then lived, which made the creation of new civic consciousness so desirable. Late twentieth century scholars, including many educationalists, have been more cautious in their judgement and have tended to accept that no single mechanism of the institutional kind like the school, can by itself mould human perceptions and understanding according to those who are in power. These studies, therefore, while examining the existing educational objectives and the associated policy measures pursued by the dominant ethnic groups in respect of the non-dominant ones in the years gone by, also reveal the limitations of schooling as an instrument of social policy and thus, hopefully, help to shed light on what is, and what is not, realistically attainable in the complex world of human affairs.

Notes

1. Gellner defines 'exo-socialisation' as 'the production and reproduction of men outside the local intimate unit', to differentiate it from education as 'a cottage industry, when men could be made by a village or clan'. See Gellner, p. 38.
2. Hobsbawm, pp. 50–4.
3. Stavrianos p. 145.
4. Okey, pp. 68–9
5. Hobsbawm, pp. 9–10; 22; 188–9.
6. Okey, pp. 74–5.
7. Kohn, p. 12; also see Hobsbawm, pp. 142ff.
8. Hobsbawm, p. 150.
9. Gellner, pp. 39–40.
10. Hobsbawm, p. 155.
11. Smith, p. 37.
12. Seton-Watson, pp. 9–10; Hans, pp. 9–11.

Select Bibliography

Gellner, E. (1983), *Nations and Nationalism*, Basil Blackwell, Oxford.
Hans, N. (1949), *Comparative Education*, Routledge and Kegan Paul, London.
Hobsbawm, E. (1989), *The Age Of Empire, 1875–1914*, Vintage Books, New York.
Kohn, H. (1967), *The Age of Nationalism*, Collier, New York.
Okey, R. (1982), *Eastern Europe, 1740–1985: Feudalism to Communism*, Hutchinson, London.
Seton-Watson, H. (1977), *Nations and States*, Methuen, London.
Smith, A. (1979), *Nationalism in the Twentieth Century*, Martin Robertson, Oxford.
Stavrianos, N. (1985), *The Balkans since 1453*, Holt, Rinehart and Winston, New York.

2   The British State and the Education of Irish Catholics, 1850–1921

RICHARD VINCENT COMERFORD

From 1 January 1801 Ireland was joined with Great Britain in the United Kingdom, and its parliament was merged with that at Westminster. Ireland had just 100 seats in the House of Commons, out of a total of over 600. There was little change in these figures down to 1921. As the population of Britain grew dramatically throughout the period while that of Ireland declined steadily from the 1840s onwards, the smaller country, initially underrepresented, came to be strongly overrepresented. Like the rest of the United Kingdom Ireland saw its electoral system 'democratised' by stages from 1832 onwards with the result that members of parliament became more amenable to the impulses of popular feeling in the constituencies, especially from the mid 1880s. However, since laws for Ireland were enacted by parliament as a whole, the legislative influence of Irish members and Irish opinion was limited. Besides, the House of Lords retained until 1911 an absolute power of veto and Irish representation there was meagre. In any case the shape of legislation was largely determined by government initiative and not many Irishmen reached the high ministerial levels at which such initiatives were formulated.

The United Kingdom was not a unitary state. Scotland, Ireland and (to a lesser extent) Wales possessed various distinctive institutions. Thus, Ireland continued to have its own body of law which was augmented and modified by laws made for the entire United Kingdom as well as measures enacted for Ireland alone. Central Irish administration was not transferred to London but remained at Dublin Castle until 1922. At the head of this administration were the Lord Lieutenant and the Chief Secretary, both usually senior English political figures and the latter normally a member of the Cabinet. Major Irish policy matters were discussed and decided by the Cabinet on the basis of papers prepared by the Irish law officers and other

Dublin Castle bureaucrats under the direction of the Chief Secretary and his Undersecretary.

To the end of the century and beyond, local government in Ireland was fragmented and weak. The county grand juries, consisting of leading landowners, operated independently of the partially elective boards of Poor Law Guardians established by an act of 1838, and of the municipal authorities, which from 1841 were fully elective. A system of county councils established in 1899 superseded the grand juries and brought greater democracy and coherence but nevertheless failed to acquire the weight and importance of local authorities in England or most European countries. The weakness of local government (together with the deficiencies in social cohesion that were to blame for it) encouraged a degree of centralisation and state intervention in Ireland that would not have been acceptable in England. In the 1830s Ireland acquired a state financed Board of Public Works, a centralised state financed police force, and a national system of primary education.

While the country as a whole can be seen as subject to British rule, this chapter looks primarily at Irish Catholics as a non-dominant minority within the United Kingdom. The first regular Irish census to record religious affiliation, that of 1861, numbered Catholics as constituting 78 per cent of the population (of 5.8 million); they were at 74 per cent (in a total of 4.4 million) by 1911. For historical reasons the preponderance of Irish landed property in the early nineteenth century was in the hands of Protestants. Until 1870 the Anglican Church of Ireland (to which 12 per cent of the population belonged in 1861) was the established Church of the land and its members – or the more privileged of them – constituted a social and political establishment that retained certain advantages even when its legal privileges had been abolished. Catholics were indeed well established in commerce but their progress into the upper middle class was inhibited by the lateness of their admission to the professions – 1792 in the case of the legal profession. The history of Ireland in the century before 1920 was dominated by the endeavours of Catholics to achieve economic, social and political status to match their numerical position. The best known episode of this was the campaign for 'Catholic emancipation' (actually the right to sit in parliament and hold certain public offices) that achieved its objective in 1829, thanks to a popular mobilisation under the leadership of Daniel O'Connell that had few contemporary parallels.

Irish Catholicism had a crucial ethnic dimension. The objective basis for the ethnic distinctiveness of Irish Catholics is a complex question and need not detain us here. What matters is that they saw themselves as the indigenous inhabitants of the island – 'the people of Ireland' – possessed of a national identity and deprived of hegemony in their own country by 'invaders' who could be identified with the English government or the Irish Protestants. As a consequence of the ethnic dimension, Irish Catholics saw themselves not simply as a deprived minority within the United Kingdom but as a suppressed nationality. They tended to alternate between seeking more favourable terms within the United Kingdom and demanding self-government for Ireland. The pressing of the latter demand resulted in the disruption of the union, and the partition of Ireland, in 1921–2.

Throughout the period of the union most English people who adverted to the subject at all did, also, tend to see the Catholics as the 'native' population and to acknowledge the distinctiveness of the country. It was a cardinal point in British policy throughout the nineteenth century that control of Ireland was a *sine qua non* for the security of the empire. Thus it was seen as essential that Ireland be integrated into the United Kingdom and, spoken or unspoken, this objective underlay all policy towards the country. The extent to which the assimilation of Irish culture and society with those of England was envisaged is somewhat less certain. There was no sustained effort in that direction. Yet it was assumed that the progress of civilisation – whether through education or otherwise – rested on the adoption of certain English *mores* and attitudes.

The National School System

The government's entry into the arena of education was affected in Ireland and in England by the same factors; namely, growing demand for elementary schooling, poisonous rivalry between the religious denominations, and a utilitarian urge towards initiative in conflict with deep *laissez faire* prejudice against state intervention. That intervention came first in Ireland was a reflection of obviously greater financial need there, but also of the greater scope enjoyed by the central executive. Beginning in the eighteenth century, parliamentary funds had been allocated to certain voluntary societies providing schools and schooling. From 1818 support was concentrated on one of these, the Kildare Place Society. When that, in the course of time, proved unsatisfactory more direct state provision was resorted to, and a national system along lines that had been mooted for many years previously was introduced.

Avoiding the great debate that would have been provoked by an attempt at legislation on the subject, Edward Stanley, Chief Secretary for Ireland, announced in 1831 the institution of a 'board for the superintendence of a system of national education in Ireland'.[1] Generally referred to as the Commissioners for National Education, the Board of Education, or, simply, the Commissioners, this body began as a group of prominent personages willing to lend their time and their prestige to unremunerated public service. Soon a paid full time commissioner was added and a bureaucracy grew up at the Dublin headquarters that created the impression of a regular civil service operation.

Funding was provided by an annual parliamentary grant. Yet the Irish national education system did not come under direct government control. The Commissioners were not under the day-to-day direction of any minister of state. Parliamentary pressure or government decision could lead a Lord Lieutenant and his Chief Secretary to use their informal (if very real) influence with the Commissioners, but this was obviously a cumbersome business. Formal government influence was confined to the need for the Lord Lieutenant's approval of changes of rules, and his power to appoint and dismiss individual Commissioners. None ever was dismissed, but over and above normal replacements additional appointments were made on a number of occasions, with a view to changing public perception of the balance of interests on the board.

Just as the Commissioners were at arms length from the state, the 'national schools' retained much autonomy *vis-à-vis* the Commissioners. The Commissioners might meet most of the costs of building, monitor the curriculum, closely enforce a system of inspection, and pay the bulk of teachers' salaries, but they were not the proprietors of the schools. They dealt with each through its locally appointed manager, who was not in any sense their servant.

If the national education system was shaped by a desire to minimise direct state involvement, an even more weighty factor in determining its character was the problem of confessional conflicts. In Ireland as in England, the perceptions of many churchmen suggested that large numbers of people seeking education for their children were not highly concerned about the specifically religious content of education and so were potential converts to the faith of their educators. The resultant animosity between Protestant denominations in England was as nothing compared to the emotions stirred up in Ireland when privately funded missionaries set out to win souls away from Rome through schooling and other means.

The government had concentrated support on the Kildare Place Society in 1818 precisely because it was endeavouring to maintain neutrality as between the confessions, and abandoned the society in 1831 when it was perceived to have failed in this. The Commissioners of National Education set out with instructions that one of their main objects should be 'to unite in one system children of different creeds' and that local applications for new schools coming jointly from Protestants and Catholics should be especially encouraged. The

Commissioners' early regulations for the conduct of schools that had been admitted to their system made elaborate arrangement to separate in every school the literary (or 'regular') instruction that would be common to all, from the religious instruction that would be specific to the requirements of each denomination for its own adherents and given by the ministers of the various faiths.[2] Reading of the Bible would be confined to the period of specifically religious instruction, although a selection of biblical extracts approved by the Commissioners might be used during the period of common, literary instruction.

Richard Whately, Church of Ireland archbishop of Dublin, was a key supporter of the national system and one of the original Commissioners. However, the great majority of Anglican church-men were strongly opposed to it. They resented the studiously professed neutrality of the new system, claiming that government was obliged to favour the Protestant state Church. They found the attempt to draw a distinction between religious and secular education particularly reprehensible. Following unavailing efforts to crush or alter radically the national system through political pressure, the Church of Ireland in 1839 initiated the Church Education Society to support its existing schools and establish new ones on a voluntary basis. After years of striking success this experiment began to falter in the 1850s and over subsequent decades most Church of Ireland schools were forced by financial considerations to attach themselves to the national system. This did not, however, amount to total surrender, for the national system as originally conceived had by then been modified in the direction of denominationalism, a develop-ment which answered some, if by no means all, of the Anglican objections.

It was the Presbyterians who first obtained a modification of the Commissioners' regulations concerning religion. Making up 9 per cent of the total population in 1861 (and 10 per cent 50 years later) the Presbyterians were concentrated in the north east. They were ready to coalesce with Anglicans in political opposition to Catholic mobil-isations in favour of Irish self-government, but Presbyterians other-wise maintained a very distinct collective existence, marked by a strong tendency towards internal dispute. As on so many other matters, they had divided opinions about the national school system.

In the early years scores of Presbyterian ministers became managers of national schools or joined in signing local applications to the Commissioners. However, the national school issue was taken up by a conservative evangelical faction as a convenient new weapon for the pursuit of a continuing warfare against moderates and other backsliders. The national system was denounced on the grounds that it purported to separate education from reading of the Bible and that it gave legal recognition to the inculcation of 'Romish errors' (albeit among Catholic children). A Presbyterian school system was formed in 1834 and subsequently severe pressure was directed against schools under Presbyterian management remaining in connection with the national system. But resources to maintain the independent system were limited and, on the other side, the Commissioners were anxious not to lose the main block of Presbyterian schools – especially after the secession of the Anglicans in 1839.

An accommodation with the Presbyterians was achieved in 1840 when the Commissioners allowed a modification of their rules in respect of those schools classified as 'non-vested' (which usually indicated that they had been built at local expense prior to affiliation with the system). In such a school clergymen of denominations other than that of the manager would not, in future, have the right to enter for the purpose of teaching religion (though they might have children of their own faith in the school come to them elsewhere for instruction at the appropriate times). In non-vested schools there would, in future, be no obligation to exclude children of other faiths when religious instruction was being given unless their parents positively requested such exclusion.

The Presbyterians could now join the national system and, with their schools classified as 'non-vested', conduct them along lines distinctly more denominational than those originally set out by the Commissioners and which still applied in the majority of schools.[3] The Commissioners had made concessions under pressure. Nevertheless, they had not abandoned the principle of a 'united' system, and in particular they stood by the axiom that no pupil attending a national school would be required against parental wishes to attend religious instruction in a faith other than his (or her) own.

Catholics stood to gain more than anyone else from evenhanded state funding of primary education. A great demand for initiation in the three 'Rs' had been demonstrated in the decades before 1831 and had produced a profusion of 'pay-schools' throughout the country. These were unreliable, unstable institutions dependent on the availability of accommodation, of individuals willing to try their hand at teaching, and of parents willing and able to pay them enough. As a consequence, provision, though plentiful, was haphazard, unevenly spread, and extremely variable in quality. The national system did not offer an end of school fees (at least until 1892), but it did offer reliability, continuity, suitable accommodation and standardisation. The Catholic priests were particularly attracted. They had a strong professional interest in education and were keenly aware of the lack of resources that had prevented the Church from organising a satisfactory system.

The national system also largely cancelled out the financial advantages hitherto enjoyed by evangelical Protestants in their search for converts. From the point of view of the churchman as from that of the statesman, there was great comfort in having an institutional framework that could monitor the curriculum and teaching personnel. Many of the pay-school teachers were of a dislocated, peripatetic and radical seeming type, and were feared to be purveyors of ideas and attitudes subversive of the reigning political and moral order. By organising local applications to the Commissioners, Catholic priests were able to become managers of national schools and so take in charge an area of parochial life hitherto difficult to control. The paucity of Protestants over much of the country, together with the efforts of the Church Education Society to maintain its own system, served to ensure that a great many national schools were preponderantly or even exclusively Catholic in their clientele. The attraction of the national school system for Catholics was highlighted by the presence of Archbishop Murray of Dublin on the Board of Commissioners. The concession of equality to Catholics in the area of education was a profoundly significant acknowledgement – long denied – of the legitimacy of their collective status in the land.

Notwithstanding the symbolic importance and the practical advantages of the national schools for Irish Catholics, Murray's acceptance of the system betokened a readiness to compromise which others in other circumstances might not share. Like the Protestant Churches, the Catholic Church was susceptible to the more rigorous movements of the religious spirit of the age. The tractarians' (high Anglican) sense of the autonomy of the ecclesiastical, and the Evangelicals' uneasiness about concession to 'error', both of which stances menaced governmental initiatives in Britain and Ireland alike, resembled attitudes never far below the surface of Catholicism. Purists could readily find grounds on which to condemn the national schools as unacceptable to Catholics. Indeed, it might be very difficult to compose a theoretical defence of them that abstracted from the particular circumstances of the time.

By 1850 changing fortunes and attitudes permitted the episcopal body – invoking the ideal of Catholic education as a seamless web of spiritual and intellectual formation – to demand modification of the system in the direction of denominationalism. Much was conceded during subsequent decades to Catholic pressure and Catholic sentiment. From 1859 onwards, half of the Commissioners were Catholics. They combined with most of the Protestant members to create a large majority in favour of concessions to denominationalism.

Teacher training provides a striking case in point. With a view to providing at least a minimum of teacher training, the Commissioners had set up a 'model' school in Dublin in the 1830s. In the late 1840s a series of such model schools was announced for various provincial centres. The model schools, being under the direct management of the Commissioners, were conducted along the unadulterated 'mixed' or 'united' undenominational lines originally envisaged for the national system. On the grounds that they posed an unacceptable threat to the faith of Catholic trainee teachers and pupils, the bishops proceeded in the early 1860s to denounce the model schools and effectively to end Catholic participation in their work. Extension of the model school network was abandoned by the Commissioners, and in 1863 they began to finance teacher training in some of the larger national schools attached to convents. Twenty years later there followed the logical step of funding denominationally controlled training colleges. By 1900 the Catholic bishops were prepared to admit that over most of the country the national school system was as denominational as they could wish.

Nevertheless, it would be too harsh a judgement to condemn the national system as an undenominational endeavour that failed. True, Catholics and Protestants were for the most part separated even where demography and geography would have allowed for mixing such as was envisaged in 1831. In the circumstances of time and place, however, such mixing was probably unachievable. The system evolved from 1831 onwards to resolve in unpredicted form some of the principal political (as distinct from educational) concerns behind the 1831 initiative. These can be summarised as follows: first, the achievement of evident evenhandedness in the state's treatment of Catholics and Protestants; second, the control of interconfessional struggle for souls at school level. The Commissioners never abandoned the principle that no child in a national school should be *required* to attend instruction in a faith other than his or her own.

One of the blessings enjoyed by the national system was that it never became the subject of extended conflict between the British political parties. This was partly a matter of luck but it also reflected an awareness at Westminster of how much was at stake.

Secondary Schools and Universities

Secondary education presented a rather less happy picture from the Catholic viewpoint. The upper class and gentry made a fashion of sending their sons to English public schools, which had the effect of siphoning off a large proportion of the private wealth potentially available for new developments.[4] The motley collection of schools of old endowment that the country possessed were Anglican insti-tutions (though not necessarily exclusively Church of Ireland in their clientele) and remained so after 1871. They prepared middle class youths for the public service and university, many of them with conspicuous success. In addition to these institutions, Catholic efforts, entirely voluntary, built up a series of colleges from the late eighteenth century onwards.

It was the Conservatives, less squeamish than their Liberal opponents on the question of ecclesiastical establishments, who found an acceptable method of aiding the finances of Irish Catholic secondary schools. By an act of 1878 an Intermediate Education Board was instituted, resembling in many respects the Board of National Education. However, the Intermediate Board did not initially receive any money directly from the exchequer. Its funding came from the annual interest on part of the surplus remaining on disposal of the property of the former established Church. Out of the income thus available to it, the Board had a wide brief. It had to seek its own running expenses, conduct a system of public examinations for under-16s, under-17s and under-18s, bestow prizes on the most successful candidates and, most importantly, pay fees to the managers of schools (irrespective of denomination) according to the numbers of successful students they had entered for the examinations. The Board's influence over schools was of a purely external nature. Schools could choose to respond to the opportunities offered by the Board's examinations and awards, but the Board had no function with regard to management, or to the employment or qualification of teachers, much less school construction or ownership.[5]

Thanks largely to the equalising effects of the national school system, Catholic participation rates in primary education were by 1861 already almost on a par with that of Protestants. By contrast a Protestant was still three or four times as likely as a Catholic to be attending a secondary or an intermediate school. However the decennial census figures demonstrate the progress of Catholic participation at secondary level a generation later. By 1911 Catholics were only slightly behind Anglicans and were actually achieving participation rates greater than those of Presbyterians. The Intermediate Education Act of 1878 was not the sole cause of this breakthrough but it was a very great help.

The foundation and funding of Maynooth College by act of parliament of 1795 was an event of great importance for the Irish Catholic Church, but, after some early experimentation with the idea of a lay college, Maynooth developed exclusively as a seminary. Catholics could graduate at Trinity College Dublin (founded in 1592) from 1794, and numbers did so in subsequent decades, but while Trinity might serve individuals of all faiths it remained a stronghold of Anglican interests. To remedy the consequent sense of grievance of Catholics and Presbyterians, the government established the Queen's University with colleges in Belfast, Cork and Galway by an act of 1845. This new system of colleges was thoroughly un-denominational. In 1850 the Catholic bishops declared it unsuitable for their flock and decided to launch a university of their own for which they hoped to obtain a charter and government money. Except for its medical school, however, the Catholic University wilted for want of support, but the bishops maintained their demand for state funding. There was one British politician likely to be sympathetic to Irish Catholic demands. This, at least from 1865 onwards, was William Gladstone. However the radical wing of his Liberal party had grave objections to the endowment of ecclesiastical institutions. These radicals were delighted to support him in disestablishing the Church of Ireland (with effect from 1 January 1871) but they tied his hands when he came to tackle the Irish university question. The result was the defeat of his Irish university bill in 1873.

A similar formula to that employed in secondary education was applied to university education by an act of 1879. This act instituted the Royal University, a purely examining body which could grant fellowships and other prizes to institutions presenting students for its examinations. The Catholic University (which in 1882 became University College, before passing to Jesuit management in 1883) could compete for these awards with the Queen's Colleges. The allocation of fellowships to members of the teaching staffs of the Queen's Colleges and University College was technically the prerogative of the Royal University authorities, but was in practice determined by extensive behind-the-scenes political and ecclesi-astical manoeuvrings. These fellowships enabled University College to provide for a growing stream of students coming up from the by now expanding Catholic secondary school sector.[6]

The very success of University College served to highlight the anomalies of Irish university arrangements and the inadequacy of a purely examining institution. After lengthy efforts a new regime was established by an act of 1908. Trinity College was left undisturbed: all religious tests and barriers had been abolished there in 1873 but it was still viewed on all sides as having a distinctly Anglican ethos. Queen's College Belfast became Queen's University, formally undenominational but certain to be predominantly Presbyterian. Queen's College Galway, Queen's College Cork, and University College became constituent bodies of the new National University of Ireland, again formally undenominational, but expected by all to become almost exclusively Catholic in ethos and personnel. The government allowed itself no more than minority representation on the controlling bodies of the National University of Ireland so that the new institution became, in effect, an expression of collective Catholic autonomy. The university settlement of 1908 has survived 80 years of political and social upheaval: it has been augmented but not dismantled.

The Irish Language

If the twentieth century brought a settlement in the university area, it witnessed new strains emerging at the lower levels. The greatest task of the national system in the nineteenth century, from the political viewpoint, had been to cope with the demands of a Catholic collectivity possessing great political weight and growing socio-economic ambitions. However, the ethnic dimension of Irish Catholicism had not proved to be a problem. Textbooks designed to avoid interconfessional controversy – especially those composed by the Commissioners themselves – equally avoided questions of racial origin and distinctive identity. As time went on the Commissioners, responding to demand, did authorise the use of textbooks that were more 'racy of the soil', but they were always concerned to avoid controversial material such as history, and most treatments of Irish history were seen as controversial. The intermediate system did give some scope for the study of Irish history, one of the examination subjects listed by the act of 1878 being 'the language, literature and history of Great Britain and Ireland'. However it was not Irish history but the Irish language which eventually forced on the educational authorities decisions about the curricular handling of Irish ethnic identity.

Until the final quarter of the nineteenth century the Irish language question was a pedagogical problem without a political dimension, and therefore one that educational authorities could ignore. It has been estimated that for at least 28 per cent of those born in Ireland between 1831 and 1841 (the first decade of the national school system) Irish was their first language. For six counties on the western and southern seaboards the figure was more than 65 per cent.[7] The implications of this for the national education system were not what might appear at first sight.

The Irish language had been in rapid decline since the late eighteenth century and there was great popular demand for schooling in Ireland both before and after 1831 partly because so many Irish speaking parents wished their children to learn English. Only 13 per cent of the cohort born 1861–71 acquired Irish. Native Irish speakers were preponderantly Catholic, but cultivation of the language was not an objective of the Catholic–ethnic Irish nationalism of the early and middle nineteenth centuries. Very few individuals dissented from the consensus view that acquiring mastery of English was one of the means by which the Irish Catholic could secure a respected place in the world. There was no debate about the place of Irish in the new national schools because it was assumed to have none. Large numbers of children for whom Irish was the language of the home were sent to the national school in order that they might learn English. An occasional voice questioned the humanity or pedagogical good sense of schooling young children entirely in a strange language, but little attention was paid to such considerations until other factors were added.

The two factors which, in the last quarter of the century, came to supplement pedagogical and humanitarian considerations were, first, the developing appreciation of the value of Celtic and other peripheral languages and, second, the adoption of the Irish language as a hallmark of Irish nationality. Responding in 1878 to a petition arranged by the recently formed Society for the Promotion of the Irish Language, the Commissioners of National Education agreed to permit the teaching of Irish as an additional subject outside of normal hours. At this time a payment-by-results system was in operation and Irish was now admitted as an optional subject examinable for results payments on the same basis as Latin or Greek. A regulation made in 1883 permitted teachers to use Irish in the classroom as a help in putting Irish speaking children through the normal (English) courses. That could be a boon if the teacher as well as the pupils knew Irish, but many teachers in Irish speaking areas were monoglot anglophones.

The intermediate education system was introduced just in time to be influenced by the new appreciation of things Celtic. Parliament added Irish to the list of modern languages examinable by the new board, putting it in the same category as French and German. The status of Irish in the intermediate examinations was to be the subject of recurrent argument in subsequent decades, thanks partly to the work of the Gaelic League – founded in 1893 and keenly devoted to the promotion of what it described as the national language. With the emergence of the Gaelic League and its *cadres* of young urban middle class language revivalists, the question of Irish in the schools was no longer simply a matter of how to deal with monoglot Irish speaking pupils.

By the opening years of the twentieth century the Gaelic League had persuaded the Catholic–nationalist collectivity to accept the ideal of a restoration of Irish. By way of reaction most Protestants came to regard the language as a symbol of the Catholic nationalism that threatened to submerge them. So, the place of Irish in the educational system was now a political issue of some importance. It became the subject of questions and resolutions in the House of Commons. These put pressure on the Chief Secretary for Ireland who, in turn, endeavoured to influence the Intermediate Education Board and Commissioners of National Education. Their response could set the cycle going again. The challenge to the Commissioners was a variant of the confessional problem that they had been coping with since 1831 and their response was along the by now familiar lines. The opposing parties were given considerable scope to go their own ways while being retained within the one comprehensive system.

For those schools that wished to have it, Irish was made more attractive. A new national school curriculum introduced in 1900 was more child centred and activity oriented and permitted more practical language work. Irish could now be taught within the normal school day or as an additional subject after normal hours. In 1904 a bilingual programme was approved for use in schools in predominantly Irish speaking districts. By 1906, the Commissioners of National Education were subsidising the Gaelic League's summer schools for the instruction of teachers in Irish.

In 1899 just 105 national schools had presented pupils for examination in Irish. Thanks to Gaelic League agitation (and the enthusiasm it generated), and to the Commissioners' cooperation, more than 2500 national schools (or 31 per cent of the total) were teaching Irish in 1912. Expansion at primary level facilitated the promotion of the language in the secondary schools. Up to 1900 approximately 5 per cent of candidates for the Intermediate Board's examinations were accustomed to take Irish; in the decade of 1910–19 that figure exceeded 60 per cent. The achievements of the Gaelic League in the field of educational politics reached a high point in 1910 when the National University of Ireland prescribed Irish as an essential subject for matriculation from 1913 onwards, thus paying a tribute (whether merited or not) to the level of Irish language studies in the schools of Ireland.[8]

The Challenge to Clerical Dominance

The Irish Catholic collectivity that was such a prominent political entity within the United Kingdom was under the leadership of the clergy and also of a series of lay elites. Laymen provided parliamentary representation and almost the entire central or national leadership of political, cultural and agrarian movements, though in all of these fields they had to allow for clerical interest and power. In the realm of education, however, the Catholic priests had things very much to themselves. With the exception of the National University, almost every concession to Irish Catholics set out above was an enhancement of specifically clerical (or episcopal or religious) power and influence. Even though the laity might have a majority on the institutions of the new university, there was ample scope for clerical membership: Archbishop Walsh of Dublin was elected the first Chancellor. Catholic secondary schools were owned and controlled almost exclusively by religious orders or congregations, or diocesan clergy. Even when, from 1879 onwards, they came to be recipients of public money through the Intermediate Board, they continued to be wholly private institutions. They hired lay teachers insofar as they were needed to do work for which no priest or religious teacher was available, and were free to dismiss them at convenience.

The position of the lay teachers in the national schools was somewhat better and from 1873 they even enjoyed some contractual rights. An *esprit de corps* also existed, as evidenced by the formation of the Irish National Teachers Organisation in 1868, and the national teacher enjoyed some esteem in his locality. Nevertheless, national teachers were subordinate in the clearest manner to the managers who hired them and could fire them. (The Commissioners in 1851 had surrendered the right to block managerial dismissal of teachers.) The typical Catholic national school had the local bishop as patron and the parish priest as sole manager.

The single manager system had emerged by default and, from an early stage, the desirability of management by committee was canvassed. In England and Wales state assistance carried with it the requirement that management be in the hands of committees, and that applied to Catholic schools from the initiation of government funding for them in 1847.[9] The Powis Commission which investigated Irish primary education from 1868 to 1870 made a firm recommendation in favour of mandatory management committees, but in vain.

The Education act of 1870 gave locally-levied rates a key role in the financing of education in England and Wales. The act of 1902 took this a stage further, by giving the elected local authorities throughout the land responsibility for funding and overseeing the provision of schooling, including the funding of denominational schools. In Ireland the raising of a local school rate had long been suggested before an act of 1875 endeavoured to give it effect. It was a limited attempt that proved a serious disappointment in practice. However, in the early years of the twentieth century, with Ireland falling behind England, Wales and Scotland in its level of educational funding, a local school tax was an attractive proposition for many. Not, however, for the Catholic clergy, who saw that rate support was in practice inseparable from a new form of control of one kind or another.

The levying of local rates for education was achieved in Ireland at the turn of the century, but only in respect of technical schooling. Acts of 1898 and 1899 permitted the country councils to raise money by taxation for the support of technical education, and gave Ireland a Department of Agriculture and Technical Instruction that directed and coordinated local provision of such education.[10] The Department performed creditably against great odds, but to the Irish public mind technical education was peripheral.

In the domain of what was seen as mainstream education, civic intervention, either central or local, was successfully resisted. In Britain the proprietors of denominational schools, Protestant and Catholic, had welcomed the 1902 act as a great financial rescue operation which still left their institutions with a distinctive identity and some control over their own affairs. For the same reasons Nonconformist and secularist opponents of denominational schooling had denounced it. That the Catholic clergy could see the proposed enactment of similar measures for Ireland as a grave threat is an indication of just how satisfactory existing arrangements were from their point of view.

That such a threat existed seemed to be confirmed in September 1902 when W.J.M. Starkie, Resident Commissioner of National Education, publicly advocated co-ordination of primary and intermediate schooling on the basis of rate aid and elective local control. For good measure he went on to denounce national school managers for widespread incompetence and to deplore the lowly status of lay teachers in Catholic intermediate schools.[11] An English expert, sent to examine the national system in 1903, essentially supported Starkie's proposals and added a recommendation for a regular department of education to replace the mainly amateur Commissioners.

The creation of a Department of Education was one feature of a projected devolution of power to Dublin proposed in a government bill of 1907. By comparison with the existing Boards, the proposed Department would be under more direct political control and would give a consultative role to elected local politicians, who would make up 75 per cent of the membership of a departmental council. Catholic churchmen, motivated by fear of such innovations, contributed handsomely to the groundswell of opinion that rejected the proffered devolution and renewed the demand for a full measure of Home Rule.

Since the 1880s, the Irish Catholic majority had been represented at Westminster by a nationalist party dedicated to winning Home Rule, an ill-defined objective but with an Irish parliament as its most definite feature. The Church was allied to the party in various informal ways. With the accession of the Liberal government of 1906 however churchmen began to show signs of positively yearning for Home Rule, in order that the educational arrangements countenanced by nineteenth century British politicians could be saved from the depredations of their successors. The new government endeavoured (unsuccessfully as it turned out) to change the 1902 act to the disadvantage of denominational schools. This did not affect Ireland directly, but Irish nationalists joined in the parliamentary opposition because of their need to please Catholic ecclesiastical opinion. Although a number of them would have wished it to be otherwise, the Home Rule politicians slid into acceptance of the proposition that the educational rights of Irish Catholics were synonymous with the existing system, and so with exclusive clerical control.

Irish Protestant political opinion was by this time represented in parliament almost exclusively by supporters of continuing political union between Britain and Ireland. As is the way with polarising politics, the Unionists emerged as advocates of change in the Irish educational system that the nationalists were committed to upholding. It was not that the Protestant Churches had ceased to desire denominational education, although some Presbyterians had indeed followed English and Welsh Nonconformists in that direction. Rather, the stubborn opposition of the Catholic priesthood to change induced many Protestants to welcome it, while at the same time not expecting it to go beyond what they themselves could comfortably tolerate.

If the Irish education question divided Irish politicians, it did not divide the British parties. They might be polarised by English education, or by the issue of Home Rule for Ireland, but on Irish social questions and especially education they had settled into a concensus. For some years from 1908 onwards, government attention was directed to part of the Irish education system that greatly offended the consensus – the circumstances of the lay secondary teacher. By 1912 the Chief Secretary was able to offer an increase of £40 000 in the annual sum disbursed in the form of examination premiums to the secondary schools, but only if the schools accepted changes that would ensure the extra money went in higher salaries to an increased number of lay teachers. The key was the requirement that schools should employ a minimum ratio of lay teachers, and at rates of pay well above the levels prevailing in Catholic schools; registration of teachers and minimum notice of dismissal were predictable corollaries.

The bishops and the headmasters of Catholic schools put up strong resistance to the government's terms, arguing that they constituted state interference reminiscent of the behaviour of contemporary anti-clerical regimes in France and Portugal. Lengthy negotiations having failed to produce an agreement, the government proceeded to legislate in 1914, making one significant change in its proposals. The required ratio would be demanded not in individual schools but in nationwide sectoral groupings of schools. In other words all Catholic schools would be assessed as a unit and so would Protestant schools. In the following year the Catholic authorities accepted the *fait accompli*, and the lot and status of the secondary teacher was considerably improved, with no real loss to school management.

Home Rule for Ireland, enacted in 1912, was due to come into effect in 1914 but was deferred on the outbreak of the First World War. As the war ended, government and bureaucrats began a determined move to place the Irish education system on a new footing. The work of two commissions of investigation set up in 1918 led to the introduction of a major Irish education bill at Westminster in 1919. A large increase in funding was proposed, and this would be handled by a Department of Education having a council with a high proportion of elected members and controlling primary, secondary and technical schooling. Central funding would be supplemented by a local rate to be collected and allocated by committees including elected local politicians and school managers. No interference with existing school management was proposed and there were explicit guarantees of denominational rights. Nevertheless, the Catholic bishops waged a strenuous campaign against the bill.

By 1919 Ireland's constitutional prospects were in flux. At the general election of 1918, the Home Rule nationalists had been replaced by the more extreme *Sinn Féin* (Ourselves Alone) party that was demanding not mere self-government within the United Kingdom, but an independent Irish republic. Accordingly, the Church could look to a not too distant time when legislation for Irish education would be in the hands of a government representing the Irish Catholic majority. In education, as in other areas, the push for Irish independence can be seen as an endeavour to protect the *status quo* against the momentum for social change evident in early twentieth century Britain. Episcopal denunciation of the 1919 bill (which continued until the measure was dropped in 1920) cemented a political *rapprochement* with *Sinn Féin*. Thus not only were the British prevented from tampering with the system in their last days ruling Ireland, but, even more significantly, clerical and proprietorial prerogatives in education were further sanctified and even more closely identified with Irish national rights. In the Irish Free State that took shape in 1922 the Commissioners of National Education and the Intermediate Board were replaced by a government Department of Education, and the Irish language was given greatly increased status in the curriculum. However, the pre–1922 system was untouched in its essentials and remains largely so to the present day.

What Catholics and Nationalists opposed in 1919–20, Protestants and Unionists, predictably, supported. The clash on the Education bill was an instance of that mutual incapacity for compromise that marked the wider debate about Irish self-government and led to the territorial partition of 1921 by which Northern Ireland, consisting of the six north-eastern counties forming a territory with a clear Protestant majority, was given a large measure of self-government within the United Kingdom. In 1923 the parliament of Northern Ireland passed an act creating local education authorities and establishing undenominational schools, which, it was well known, would not be acceptable to the large Catholic minority. With the island's interconfessional problems now largely bottled up in Northern Ireland, educational policy was one of many sources of grievance, but by no means the major one.

Conclusion

It is a commonplace that the approach of British rulers and administrators in the nineteenth century to matters of government and empire was characteristically 'off the cuff' and lacking in farseeing design. Indeed, they made a virtue of 'muddling through', contrasting themselves with the supposedly theorising French and the allegedly regimented Prussians. Certainly, the handling of Irish education was an instance of the predominantly pragmatic approach. This is not to minimise either its significance or its success.

The single key measure was the institution of the national scheme in 1831, made necessary by the government's wish that the state should cease its long association with voluntary Protestant school movements. In turn that followed from a new found willingness to accept that the Catholic collectivity was a permanent feature of the Irish socio-political landscape which would not disappear through coercion and could not be ignored. Integrating this large and politically aware body into the United Kingdom and the empire was an obvious necessity. The national system was calculated to do this in the obvious ways, and also by helping to control conflict between Catholics and Protestants in Ireland. The more thorough embrace connoted by 'assimilation' would be another matter. There being no clearcut national identity, it was not certain what outsiders might be assimilated to. Englishness? Britishness? If individual motivation is probed too far, it fragments. Thus, Richard Whately, government appointed Church of Ireland archbishop of Dublin, and enthusiastic promoter of the national schools, secretly hoped (or so he claimed for the information of another Protestant divine) that by providing reading extracts from the Bible the new system would demolish the spirit of popery in young Irish Catholic breasts (although the extracts had been vetted and approved by the Catholic archbishop and would be presented by Catholic teachers!).

With Stanley's successors alternating pragmatic initiative and pragmatic inertia, educational matters were not to blame to any great extent for serious disaffection among Irish Catholics down to the end of the nineteenth century. Of course, any system of elementary education predisposes a population over a generation or more to easy mobilisations in the interest of nationalism. That, though, would scarcely have been a problem for British power in Ireland if they had been as successful, or as fortunate, in all other aspects of policy as they were in education. From the turn of the century, things were becoming more difficult as the Catholic authorities resisted proposed changes that they identified with the spirit of bureaucratic 'statism'. But if, in 1920, Catholic nationalists were drawn up in bitter conflict against Protestant unionists over an educational measure, that was merely the symptom of much wider collapse, and not an indication that the breakdown had been caused either by a particular educational dispute or by the effects of long-term educational policy.

Notes

1. Akenson, p. 392.
2. Ibid., pp. 157–61.
3. Ibid., pp. 161–87.
4. Flanagan, pp. 27–43.
5. Coolahan, pp. 62–5.
6. Morrissey, pp. 89–221.
7. Fitzgerald, p. 127.
8. Ó Buachalla, pp. 75–92.
9. Murphy, pp. 35–6.
10. Coolahan, pp. 85–92.
11. Titley, p. 17.

Select Bibliography

Akenson, D. H. (1970), *The Irish educational experiment: the national system of education in the nineteenth century*, London.
Atkinson, Norman (1969), *Irish education: a history of educational institutions*, Dublin.
Coolahan, John (1981), *Irish education: its history and structure*, Dublin.
Corish, Patrick J. (1985), *The Irish Catholic experience: a historical survey*, Dublin.
Dowling, P. J. (1961), *History of Irish education*, Dublin.
Fitzgerald, Garret (1984), 'Estimates for baronies of minimum levels of Irish speaking among successvie decennial cohorts, 1771–81 to 1861–71', in *Royal Irish Academy Proceedings*, series C. xxxiv, no. 3, pp. 118–53.
Flanagan, Kieran (1984), 'The shaping of Irish Anglican secondary schools, 1854–78', in *History of Education*, xiii, no. 1, pp. 27–43.
Hyland, Aine (1983), 'The Treasury and Irish education, 1850–1922: the myth and the reality', in *Irish Educational Studies*, iii, no. 2, pp. 57–82.
Hyland, Aine and Milne, Kenneth (eds) (1987), *Irish Educational Documents*, vol. 1, Dublin.

Kerr, Donal (1982), *Peel, priests and politics: Sir Robert Peel's administration and the Roman Catholic Church in Ireland 1841–46*, Oxford.

McElligott, T. J. (1966), *Education in Ireland*, Dublin.

Miller, David (1973), *Church, state and nation in Ireland, 1898–1921*, Dublin.

Morrissey, T. J. (1983), *Towards a national university: William Delany, S. J. and an era of initiative in Irish education*, Dublin.

Murphy, James (1971), *Church, state and schools in Britain 1800–1970*, London.

Norman, E. R. (1965), *The Catholic Church and Ireland in the age of rebellion, 1859–73*, London.

ŌBuachalla, Seamus (1984), 'Educational policy and the role of the Irish language from 1831 to 1981', in *European Journal of Education*, xix, no. 1, pp. 27–43.

Titley, E.B. (1983), *Church, state and the control of schooling in Ireland, 1900–44*, Kingston.

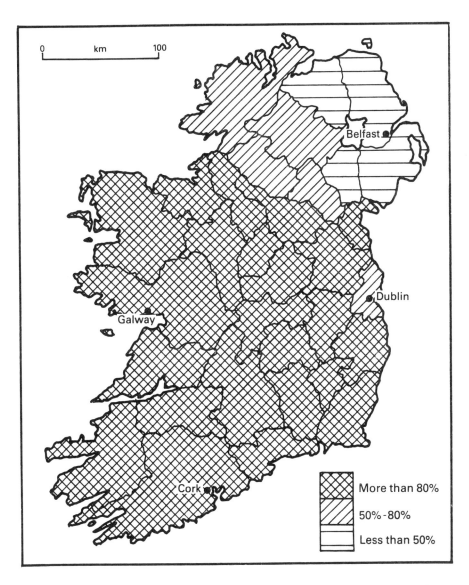

Map 2.1 Roman Catholics in Ireland in 1861 as a percentage of the population by counties
Source: Census of Ireland

3 Education and Nationhood in Wales, 1850–1940

ROBIN OKEY

At the outset of our period of study the Welsh were clearly one of many non-dominant ethnic groups then living within the framework of a larger state. By its end they had neither moved towards political autonomy nor undergone the assimilation of the failed ethnic group. The difficulty of categorising the not uneventful process that had taken place lends the Welsh case perhaps, a peculiar interest for comparative purposes.

In 1851 the 13 counties of the principality of Wales had a population of just over 1 150 000. Unlike Scotland or Ireland, she no longer had a separate constitutional status apart from England. Her independence had ended in 1282 and, following the administrative union of England and Wales in 1536, the last specifically Welsh institution, the Court of Great Sessions, had been abolished in 1830. Nonetheless, Wales was markedly distinct in culture; slightly more than four-fifths of the population belonged to various nonconformist religious denominations and slightly less spoke Welsh, a Celtic language, in great majority as their only tongue. The English speakers were localised descendants of medieval colonies, or more recent migrants to the developing iron industry, particularly in Monmouthshire, or anglicised border farmers in mid Wales and, everywhere, landowners, despite their mainly Welsh origins. Bilingualism was significant only in the towns, though not among the urban lower class in the north or west.

Welsh was a literary language of long standing, whose medieval norms had been recodified in the sixteenth century, when it became the liturgical language of the state Anglican Church, while losing all role in administration and the courts. In the eighteenth century, 1300 books appeared in Welsh, some 3500 were published in the first half of the nineteenth century, and 5500 appeared from 1850–1900. The wide literacy in the mother tongue that this presupposed was provided in the so-called Sunday Schools run by the churches for the reading of the Bible and attended by a quarter of the entire population according to the religious census of 1851. Between 1820 and 1840 13

Welsh educative periodicals appeared aimed at Sunday School readers, and the regular circulation of all Welsh language journals was estimated at 120 000 in 1866 and 270 000, 22 years later. For all this activity, an atmosphere of cultural nationalism along East European Herderian lines was largely absent. Welsh historical awareness certainly existed, but it was *sui generis*.

The 13 surveys of Welsh history published between 1810 and 1826 alone continued an ancient tradition of reflection on the loss of the 'sovereignty of Britain' to the Anglo–Saxons many centuries before. Medieval prophecies of Celtic resurgence had, however, been remoulded; Welsh sufferings were now held to have been redeemed by the spiritual blessings of Protestantism. In a constitutional age the Welsh were called upon to vindicate their nationhood in moral and religious excellence. This approach owed much to the religious revivalism endemic since the eighteenth century which, in some ways, played the mobilising role of linguistic/national revivals on the continent. However, since the Nonconformist sects that emerged from this revivalism were organised on an all-Wales basis and used Welsh more exclusively than the state Church supported by the anglicised landowners, religious disputes often had an ethnic undertone. The oscillations of national feeling that existed in these circumstances are well illustrated in the comments of a north Wales Anglican vicar in an essay of 1840:

> The natives of Wales have a strong feeling of nationality. Tracing their descent from the remotest antiquity, and conscious of their divine right to the country as first heirs of the soil, a feeling of exultation pervades the whole mass. To exist after so many and persevering attempts at their extinction, and to retain the vernacular use of their primitive, nervous and enchanting language are facts in which they will ever glory; . . . it must, however, be confessed that many of our countrymen set too high a value upon these things. It is truly amusing to hear some of our rustic wise ones . . . tell of what the ancient Britons have been . . . forgetting altogether our present insignificant position among the nations of the globe, and inducing those who will not enquire into the merit of our claims to remind us of a certain Emperor in Africa, who dines . . . under one of the trees in the forest, after which he commands his herald to proclaim, with the sound of trumpet, that all the kings of the earth may take their dinner![1]

The cultural isolation of which thoughtful Welshmen like the Reverend Jones were becoming uneasily aware was perpetuated by a rudimentary educational system. Some 100 000 pupils attended – briefly and intermittently – three kinds of primary school. These consisted of the grant-aided 'voluntary societies', the Anglican National Society and non-denominational British and Foreign

Schools Society; the works schools founded by employers in industry and mining; and the so-called private adventure schools held by old dames, former sempstresses and milliners, one-time mariners and domestic servants, that is, anyone who, in life, had acquired a smattering of English. For by contrast to the Sunday Schools and the eighteenth century Circulating Schools movement, English was the only medium of instruction in the day schools. For the sons of tradesmen and prosperous farmers, a couple of dozen vegetating old grammar schools of Anglican stamp and a much larger number of private schools, sometimes run by clergymen, produced post-primary education; there were still only 4000 pupils in these in 1880.

The absence of an organised educational system reflected the *laissez faire* traditions of the British state. From the Enlightenment, state education in Central and Eastern Europe had been an important factor in governments' bids to mobilise sluggish societies to catch up with the west. Both the national intelligentsias produced by this process and the sheer scale of the ethnic problem obliged them to formulate strategies for the education of non-dominant groups. Neither consideration applied to the Anglo–Welsh relationship. The British state saw its task as smoothing the path of the most dynamic economy in Europe. Not till 1833 was a Committee of the Privy Council set up with power to give grants to the two voluntary education societies mentioned above; not till 1870 did the state undertake to provide primary education for all. In Ireland, where the ethnic problem existed in force, state education was indeed initiated earlier, in 1831. However the effect of this, by accelerating the ongoing transition from Irish to English (95 per cent of Irish people could speak English in 1851), only reduced the saliency of linguistic difference in the state as a whole, and made the Welsh situation more anomalous. But in English eyes it was an anomaly more bizarre than dangerous. The modern Welsh education movement was not a response to the innovations of a centralising state.

The Commission of 1846–7 and the First Phase of the Welsh Education Movement

The importance for the education movement of the Commission on the State of Education in Wales (1846–7) might seem to contradict this view. A case could be made that British government, increasingly interventionist after the social reforms of the 1830s, now turned its hand to an exercise of social engineering in Wales. In setting up the enquiry, which was to explore ways of getting Welsh workers to learn English, the Home Secretary linked the Welsh Chartist disturbances of 1839 with popular ignorance in the principality. However, it was a

Welsh member of parliament who provoked the government action, by bringing a motion on its neglect of Welsh education, and introducing the theme of Welsh unrest. This Commission was a catalyst for a movement which was already under way, and its establishment reflected British government practice of responding to social tendencies rather than initiating them. In this case the tendencies were the stirrings in Wales on behalf of educational reform and, at a deeper level, the economic pressures which had induced them. The prime mover in Wales was the powerful English capitalism which had packed 250 000 people into the iron and coal rich valleys of Monmouthshire and Glamorgan and whose railways looked set to penetrate a countryside already unsettled by population pressure, poverty and the Rebecca riots.

The role of the Commissioners' reports (the so-called Blue Books) was to highlight the issues and crystallise attitudes towards them, both Welsh and English. Three young Anglican lawyers without previous experience in Wales, working with assistants, produced a devastating picture of educational deficiency. The 1800 or so day schools were mostly fleeting affairs, held in teachers' living rooms, in chapel vestries, even church towers. Most teachers were paid less than agricultural labourers, which meant they were drawn from the lowest ranks of society. Only an eighth of them had received training of any kind and they were, on average, 30 years of age on beginning their work. Pupils attended usually for less than two years. They made little progress because the teaching technique consisted mainly in reading from an English text, often the Bible, without any formal attempt to teach the children English or explain to them the meaning of what was being read. Since the enquiry had to communicate with some teachers through interpreters, this was hardly surprising.

It was, however, the Commissioners' comments on Welsh society and culture which provoked the greatest controversy. In the words of Lingen, cleverest of the three, south Walian society exhibited 'the phenomenon of a peculiar language isolating the mass from the upper portion of society'.[2] 'Rude and primitive agriculturists living poorly and thinly scattered' were constantly changing places with 'smelters and miners wantoning in plenty and congregated in the densest accumulations'. But the change of scene did not change their social position. 'They are never masters . . . ; [their] language keeps [them] under the hatches.' Cut off by a 'brass wall' from his superiors, who were 'content, for the most part, to ignore his existence, in all its moral aspects', the Welshman devoted his mental energies to theological speculation in his Sunday Schools. These represented

the most characteristic development of native intellect, and the efforts of the mass of the people, utterly unaided, to educate themselves upon their own model. . . . They gratify that gregarious sociability which animates the Welsh towards each other. They present the charms of office to those who, on all other occasions, are subject; and of distinction to those who have no other chance of distinguishing themselves.

They also satisfied the urge to self-expression which made the Welsh worker so much more the master of his language than was the English worker of English, and so correspondingly humiliated when forced to communicate haltingly in an alien tongue. Here was the rub. The Welshman's recognition of the necessity of knowing English, and the inadequacy of the Sunday School for general education, clashed with the powerful social bonds and 'affection' which maintained the older tongue. A 'not inconsiderable nor uninfluential number of the clergy, both established and dissenting', admitted Lingen, wished Welsh to be both taught and used as medium in the day schools. But the attempt to expand its use to secular spheres was doomed by its indelible association with the 'peculiar moral atmosphere' which it wove round the population, thereby keeping it in thrall.

This, in many ways penetrating, analysis was vitiated both in Lingen's report and those of his colleagues by a repetitive insistence on 'the unreasoning prejudices and impulses', the 'social and moral depravity' which linguistically induced isolation was believed to have produced in Wales. 'It is not easy to overestimate its evil effects,' wrote Commissioner Symons of Welsh. The balance of witnesses (232 Anglicans; 79 Nonconformists) was plainly awry, and only helped to confirm the distaste for Welsh Nonconformity prevalent in the majority community. Thus the Reports' stresses of the shadow side of Welsh religiosity – the hypocrisy, excess, the 'strange and abnormal features of [evangelical] Revival' was common coin, just as their insistence on the unfitness of Welsh to be the vehicle of modern, *practical* culture had been foreshadowed in the parliamentary debates setting up the Commission and was to be reiterated in later educational enquiries. Above all, the Commissioners reflected, with all the arrogance of youth, the immense self-confidence of their imperial society when in contact with other cultures. Indeed, their emphasis on the need for an exclusively English language education for Wales can hardly be called a policy of assimilation, since that implies the merging of a clearly existing alternative culture. In the Commission's view, however, Welsh was so out of touch with the modern world that it could not come into consideration in this respect. The policy recommended was one of integration; for, on the oft-stated premise that the language of law and administration was English, the Welsh could only spare themselves misery by acquiring it. Besides, 'what share in the notions which constitute our national existence can a lad have who calls the capital of England Tredegar', Lingen asked indignantly. Integration equalled development, the escape from poverty to join the 'march of society', so far proceeding above the Welshman's head.

On the Welsh side the 'Treason of the Blue Books', as it came to be known, fed long lasting feelings of resentment and injustice which prompted the politicisation of a once conservative peasantry and quietist religious dissent in directions hostile to landlord and (state) Church. There was an outpouring of protest in prose and verse. It was the charges of immorality and of the low level of religious knowledge of children questioned in English which rankled most. The tone of the remarks on Welsh was strongly resented and the exclusively religious bias of Welsh periodical literature rightly denied. The response to the Blue Books, however, also showed up the ambiguous attitude of the emerging democratic majority in Wales to its national tongue. This ambiguity ensured that the educational movement that now gathered pace in ostensible reaction to the Commissioners' strictures in fact achieved very much the results that they had desired.

This movement had three main characteristics in its opening phase. It was based, first and foremost, on sectarian competition between the Anglican National Society and the Nonconformist-backed British and Foreign School Society, spurred into action by their respective Welsh bodies, the Welsh Education Committee (1845) and the Cambrian Educational Society (1846). The Anglican Church with its superior resources and landlord backing was at this time massively in the lead. When in 1843 the London Welshman Hugh Owen issued his famous 'Letter to the Welsh People' apprising Nonconformists of the procedure for founding government aided British Schools there were only two such schools in north Wales. With appointment of organisers in north Wales in 1844, and south Wales in 1855, the British and Foreign School Society had increased this number by 1870 to 97 in the north and 302 in the whole of Wales, by which time, however, the National Society claimed nearly 1000. National Schools were repugnant to Nonconformists because they entailed use of the Anglican catechism and attendance at the parish church. Government policy, that is, that of the Committee of Council of Education, claimed to be to refuse a National School where Nonconformists were in a majority, and to grant permission where they were fewer only if a 'conscience clause' released non-Anglicans from those obligations. In practice, Anglican wealth and the conscience clause, which Nonconformists disliked both in theory and practice, meant that very many places in a predominantly Non-conformist country had only National Schools. The field was open to endless recriminations, during which successive official enquiries concluded that ordinary people generally found accommodation, but the rising generation of Welsh Nonconformist politicians could use the question to win their spurs.

The problem, of course, was not just religious; it was also social, ethnic and party political. Anglican landowners frequently prevented prospective British schools from obtaining a site, and insisted on their Nonconformist tenants attending National Schools. From 1710 to 1870 no Welsh speaking Welshman had been appointed an Anglican bishop in Wales. The Anglican Church in Wales was not a wholly English institution. While it included the most vociferous critics of the Welsh language it had long had an able, patriotic wing in the lower clergy who, with their theory of *Ecclesia Cambrensis* (the Welsh Church) and their superior education, numbered some of the most explicit advocates of Welsh nationality and culture. But English leadership of the Church cut the ground from under this party's feet. The three most active proponents of the National School movement in Wales, Dean Cotton (1780–1862) in the north, and Bishops Thirlwall (1797–1875) and Ollivant (1798–1882) in the south, were also Englishmen. Though all learned Welsh and were favourably disposed to it, the damage had been done. The British Society's supporters were able effortlessly to wrap it in the mantle of Welsh patriotism. Moreover, as Welsh Nonconformists entered politics, led by their ministers and an emerging commercial and professional elite, they did so uniformly as Liberals, opposed to a Church which was seen as 'the Tory [Conservative] party at prayer'.

The Liberal Education act of 1870, which ordered the election of rate backed local School Boards to organise non-denominational education whenever the voluntary societies had failed to make provision, therefore played into the hands of the Welsh Nonconformist majority. Between 1870 and 1902 the ratio of non-denominational to denominational schools in Wales reversed from 41:59 to 71:29. By this time 267 000 pupils were receiving schooling, for an average of seven years. Teachers to cope with these swelling numbers were prepared initially in National Society Training Colleges in Carmarthen (1848) and Caernarfon (1849), and British colleges in Bangor (1858) and Swansea (1872). From 1890 they were also prepared in departments attached to the university colleges in Wales. Sectarian tension remained. Lloyd George, whose first public action as a Baptist pupil in a National School had been to organise a strike against recital of the Apostles' Creed in the annual diocesan inspection, led the 'Welsh revolt' against the Conservative party's 1902 Education Act which transferred public funding of denominational schools from central government to local authorities. The Welsh local authorities refused to implement the act and were saved from forfeiting their educational powers only by the Liberal party's return to power in 1906.

The second feature of the developing educational movement was that for its Nonconformist wing, at least, it aimed at an integrated system of primary, secondary and higher provision in Wales, such as would enable Welsh youth to play a role in the expanding Victorian empire. The marginality of the Welsh alongside the English and Scots in the 'battle of life' was a preoccupation of Welsh periodicals. By contrast, the Anglican educational priority had been the revivification of the state Church. As this religious motivation was sapped by the creeping secularism of government policy, the failure of clerical inspection to ensure a systematic religious education even in Church schools, and realisation of the deep seated nature of Nonconformity's appeal to the Welsh people, the flagging Anglican programme yielded to the more dynamic and contemporary vision of Nonconformity.

Central to this was provision for the emerging Welsh-speaking middle class. Hugh Owen, a London-based civil servant and Calvinistic Methodist (1804–81), exemplified this trend. 'I will never rest until the Welsh Educational appliances have been perfected', he once remarked. His main achievements were the founding of the Bangor Normal College (1858) and the University College in Aberystwyth (1872). In Welsh tradition, the latter was financed by the 'pennies of the poor' from Chapel collections. He also presided over the setting up of the Aberdare Commission on Intermediate and Higher Education in Wales in 1880. Its report laid the foundation for the Welsh intermediate Education Act of 1889, which established a system of rate supported county secondary schools several years ahead of England.

The hiatus between primary education for the working class and secondary education for their betters had always been a notorious feature of English education. Owen had found that the primary schools were too elementary and the Welsh grammar schools too anaemic and Anglican in spirit to produce youths for Aberystwyth University College. The Aberdare Report provided a more thorough going solution to what he called 'the need of an educational ladder in a national system' than the North Wales Scholarship Association he had previously founded. In 1896 the Central Welsh Board was set up to co-ordinate the counties' implementation of secondary education. In 1893 government-funded university colleges in north and south Wales were amalgamated with Aberystwyth into the federal University of Wales. Sir Hugh Owen (he was knighted for services to Welsh education in the year of his death) was also the architect of the Social Science Section of the National Eisteddfod (1861) and the National Eisteddfod Association (1880), which gave this premier

Welsh cultural festival the secure base on which it exists today. Well has he been dubbed a Welsh positivist.[3]

Owen's career also exemplifies the third main feature of the Welsh education movement in this period – its silence concerning the Welsh language. This silence is remarkable not only in a comparative European context but with regard to the stress of the 1847 Reports on the language problem. Effectively, Welsh educationalists adopted the Commissioners' solution – exclusive use of English – but without confronting the great practical difficulties which the Commissioners themselves had recognised this involved.

Did this tacit decision reflect a bowing to superior force, to the inflexible anglocentrism of the state? In fact, the state's far from monolithic educational apparatus had no rigid language policy for Wales. Despite the 1847 Reports, the Secretary of the Committee of Council, Kay-Shuttleworth, argued in 1849 that improved English in Wales could be achieved only by the general introduction of 'efficient bilingual teaching'. He approved the appointment of a National Society inspector for south Wales in that year, largely on the strength of his knowledge of Welsh. During the 1850s a £5 bonus was available from the Committee to teachers qualified in Welsh working in places where the Committee deemed Welsh necessary. Welsh was taught in all training colleges in Wales and in the British Schools' central training college in London. The Committee were also willing to help fund 'duoglott' books (which, together with the use of Welsh explanations of English lessons, was what was understood as bilingual instruction in the parlance of the time). A series of National Society inspectors in Wales and the Anglican Welsh Education Committee echoed these themes, perhaps from a certain paternalism the Church felt for those it tended to see, more than the utilitarian Nonconformists, as passive peasants. Indeed, Bishop Thirlwall in his opening charge to his clergy in 1842 had warned against an 'erroneous impression' that the cause of English in Wales was served by excluding Welsh from the schools. 'It would have done you good' he wrote to a Welsh friend after a visit to Queen Victoria, 'to hear the warmth with which she expressed her feeling of recoil from the idea of an old language becoming extinct'.[4] At the Queen's request, he selected a set of Welsh books to be sent to her daughter's Welsh maid and checked the proofs of the translation of her Highland journal into Welsh!

For all this support in unlikely places, the weight of pragmatic English opinion lay rather with editorials of 1848 and 1866 in *The Times*, dismissing Welsh as a useless anachronism. Ironically, in view of Welsh preference for the British Schools, their inspectors were much cooler than the National inspectors towards Welsh. The archbishop of Canterbury, reading the Aberdare Report's statement that 70 per cent of the people of Wales habitually spoke Welsh, growled that it seemed the language would have to be put up with for another century. Lingen, the 1847 Commissioner, succeeded Kay-Shuttleworth as the Committee of Council secretary in 1851. But pressures from the majority community were not so united that Welsh educationalists could not have found a niche for Welsh in the schools had they chosen, at least till the 1862 Revised Code omitted Welsh from the list of grant aided subjects in the curriculum. The matter was alluded to frequently in Welsh periodicals in the late 1840s and 1850s, usually with endorsement of bilingual instruction. But no organised body responded to the call of the Congregationalist *Diwygiwr* in 1848 for a society to publish books on every branch of useful knowledge in Welsh.

Four reasons may be adduced for this. First, the energies of many of the most energetic and pro-Welsh public leaders in south Wales were committed primarily to the lost cause of voluntaryism, that is, opposition to any state support for education, a stand which could be traced to traditional Welsh remoteness from the state, as well as a *laissez faire* principle. Second, and again a matter of priorities, the need to compete on equal terms with '60 million of the most enterprising people who ever walked the earth'[5] in the words of the Methodist minister, Kilsby Jones, made the acquisition of English appear more important than the means by which it was done. Ultimately, too, most teachers seemed happier with the simpler techniques of unilingual instruction they were used to. As Kilsby Jones also said, 'the locomotive cannot talk Welsh' and people feared a countryside flooded with English railway officials, taking the bread out of native mouths. Besides, Welsh, it was felt, was already taught in the Sunday Schools, though usually not Welsh writing. Third, the absence of a linguistic ideology comparable to continental Herderianism left language patriots floundering glumly in elusive rhetoric rather than confidently seeking practical solutions.

> Hallowed by religion and rich with the magic of genius and associations of home, [the Welsh language] cannot be otherwise than dear to our hearts. . . . If die it must, let it die fairly, peacefully, and reputably. . . . But no sacrifice would be deemed too great to prevent its being murdered . . .[6]

So spoke the head of Brecon Congregational Academy to the 1847 commission. A member of the Newcastle Commission on Education in 1861 fairly remarked on the 'confusion of thought' on the Welsh language, and the failure to get to grips with the mechanics of bilingual instruction.[7] Fourth, it is plain that many Welsh public figures, faced with the overpowering influx of English ideas and English speakers into Wales, felt it was Welsh religion rather than the

Welsh language that could and should be defended. In the words of
the influential Reverend Thomas Rees in 1867,

> If the day is to come – may it be very distant, when the Welsh language
> shall be no more spoken in the valleys and on the hills of Wales! May
> that dark day never come when evangelical Nonconformity shall cease
> to be the religion of the majority of its people.[8]

This extra dimension of Welsh ethnicity, together with the fact that
the Welsh had a deep sense of historic identity, meant that the oft-
mooted demise of the Welsh language was much less often seen as
presaging the end of Welsh nationality. After all, the Scots and Irish
spoke English. Opening up links with the majority community
therefore entailed for most Welsh reformers no existential question,
just as nineteenth century Jewish Neologs did not envisage the
extinction of Judaism. Thus the formative phase of the Welsh
education movement bore a dual aspect. Sociologically speaking, it
was entirely Welsh, but ideologically it disclaimed a narrowly ethnic
goal. As a statement on behalf of the projected Welsh University
College assured in 1863, the work was not 'to foster a merely Welsh
nationality and promote in any degree the separation of the inhabitants from the English community . . . her people should in
reality, as well as politically, become an integral part of the United
Kingdom'.[9]

The Welsh Language Question and the Second Phase of the Welsh Education Movement

The 1880s saw a quickening of the pace of change throughout
Europe. The British Parliamentary Reform act of 1884 accelerated the
disintegration of the Conservative party's landowning grip on parliamentary representation in Wales which had begun in the election of
1868. By 1906, none of the 34 Welsh members of parliament was a
Conservative party member. With the democratisation of local
government in 1888, Liberal party supporting Nonconformists,
largely Welsh speaking, also dominated the newly elected county
councils. By 1900 there were 1310 students in the University of Wales;
between 1903 and 1910 the number of pupils in the Welsh Intermediate Schools rose from 8799 to 13 729, in 99 schools. In the
ascendant Nonconformist middle class, which did not lack even big
capital, Welsh Nonconformity began to be valued as a national
religion, revelatory of the national genius – a process common, A.D.
Smith has argued, in the emergence of modern nationalisms.[10]
  The evolution was facilitated by a higher degree of cambrophilia in

the dominant community in the period 1880–1920 than has ever existed, before or since. At least till the 1880s the authorities had assumed that the same regimen could achieve the same social goals in Wales as in England. There was no realisation, for example, that the 1868 Taunton Commission's three way grading scheme for secondary schools according to social class of pupils could not be applied to the simpler, more egalitarian society of most of Wales. Neither was there a realisation that the view that secondary education for the lower middle classes should have a technical rather than a humanistic bent did not accord with the ambitions of this sector of Welsh society, locally more important and more self-confident than its English counterparts. Here bureaucratic routine played as big a part as ideology. In terms of the latter, government attitudes mixed a general utilitarianism (practical value of the English language) with varying degrees of imperialism or cultural pluralism according to taste. With the enhanced consciousness of Welsh individuality which set in towards the end of the nineteenth century it was naturally English liberals who led the way, with Gladstone telling the National Eisteddfod in 1873 how he became aware of Welsh nationality and orating on the slopes of Snowdon in advanced old age. His Majesty's Inspector (for schools) Thomas Darlington wrote in 1912, 'Welsh nationality is a real thing with a clear and definite meaning. The national language is an essential element in this nationality'.[11] Alfred Zimmern, first Professor of International Affairs at Aberystwyth University College, spoke of 'the wonderful material that passes into the schools of Wales, the remarkable and distinctive endowment that a teacher recognises at once in the Welsh people' and commented feelingly on 'the poison of the sense of inferiority, of a sense of dependence, of inner bondage, of slavery . . . such as comes of great qualities unused or misused'.[12]

Of course, cambrophilia was made all the easier by the modesty – for English liberals, at least – of 'Welsh national aspirations', which were wholly compatible with dawning cultural pluralist ideals of a progressive empire. Disestablishment of the Anglican Church in Wales (achieved in 1920), educational reform and cultural institutions (National Museum and National Library, 1907) were always more popular in Wales than the call for home rule briefly launched by the *Cymru Fydd* (Young Wales) movement of the 1890s. *Cymru Fydd*'s decline began in 1895 when the young Lloyd George was shouted down in anglicised south Walian Newport by opponents of 'the dominance of Welsh ideas', a sobering reminder to Welsh patriots of the demographic changes industrialisation was beginning to effect in this period.

Nonetheless, the natural result of the developments of the period as a whole was a more positive attitude to national–cultural motifs in the Welsh education movement, specifically, an upgrading of the role of the Welsh language. Inevitably, not everything changed at once. The goals of the Welsh Language Society founded by the schools sub-inspector D.I. Davies in 1885, in association with the *London Society of Cymmrodorion* and the patriotic Anglican Archdeacon John Griffiths, were still extremely modest and reflected, ostensibly, the utilitarian values that had previously guided educational reforms. Capitalising, however, on the democratising trends of the time, which were giving ordinary workers more say in the appointment of foremen, colliery doctors and technical personnel, Davies argued that bilingualism was an economic asset to the Welshman. 'Is it or is it not true that a feeling is springing up in Wales in favour of having bilingual public servants?'[13] Parents should not throw away the only weapon Providence had given their children in the battle of life which the Englishman did not possess. The Language Society campaigned only to have Welsh recognised as a 'specific subject', which could be examined and grant aided, and as a 'class subject', which would permit the systematic study of Welsh texts, grammar and translation as an aid to the teaching of English. Its Nonconformist members – less so the irascible and patriotic old Archdeacon – swore to the Cross Education Commission in 1887 that their concern was not the preservation of Welsh for its own sake, but the interests of a more efficient education. Fear of arousing English suspicions, of course, also played a role here.

The new movement was not, then, so far removed from the spirit of the generation of Sir Hugh Owen and Kilsby Jones. D.I. Davies believed Welsh should be the second language of the schools of Wales; and a fellow witness to the Cross Commission argued, under close questioning from a clearly surprised Commissioner, that ultimately the interests of the 80 per cent who did not really need English should be subordinated to those of the bright minority who needed English to get on. The Language Society's objectives, which were granted in the school codes of 1889 and 1893 (together with concessions on the teaching of Welsh songs, history and geography), were little more than the 'bilingual method' so widely approved, in principle, in the 1850s. Yet Davies's frenetic energy and the emotional tone of the hundreds of letters and scores of articles he wrote before his early death in 1887, as well as of the response they evoked, suggest that a chord was being touched that was not merely utilitarian. The Language Society's work was 'opening our eyes as a nation to the violence and oppression we have ignored, or suffered, to our shame'.[14] It is likely that only this emotional drive gave his movement the tenacity so lacking 30 years earlier, and that broader demands would have met opposition both from Welsh people and English interlocutors, as critical references by some Cross Commissioners to a 'separate' Welsh nationality suggest. There was, too, a wholly new element in the Language Society's unspoken agenda. While its emotional appeal rested on the image of Welsh monoglots struggling with an unknown tongue – and there were still half a million of these according to the first language census of 1891, including three quarters of the population of the five western and northern counties – Welsh as a 'specific subject' seemed directed rather at integrating the children of English migrant workers with the native population. D.I. Davies's headquarters were in cosmopolitan Cardiff.

By the new century the element of cultural nationalism was unmistakable. It found expression in the Welsh Department of the Board of Education, set up in 1907 after the House of Lords had rejected proposals for a Welsh National Council for Education. Its Permanent Secretary, Alfred Davies, an enthusiastic proponent of Welsh, had direct access to the President of the Board. It was, however, the Department's Chief Inspector, Owen Morgan Edwards, who provided the inspirational role. With O.M. Edwards (1858–1920), the university trained son of a peasant and former Oxford history tutor, the romantic concept of the nation and its culture finally arrived in Wales. Through his notion of the unique qualities of the Welsh 'cultured common man', his mystic sense of the unity and continuity of Welsh history, his voluminous publications as author and editor, Edwards succeeded in implanting a flattering self-image in Welsh speakers that remains at the popular level the stock-in-trade of the Welsh language movement to this day.

The advocacy of Welsh which with Edwards' influence was shared throughout the Department had three prongs. First, because of Welsh literature's 'wealth of romance and lyric' it was 'peculiarly adapted', to the education of the young.[15] Second, bilingualism sharpened the mind; it was, in fact, 'an educational weapon for elementary training denied to elementary schools in other parts of the kingdom'. Third, in the words of an inspector's report on schools in an increasingly anglicised area:

> The best teachers know that the highest aim of the teaching of Welsh in a Welsh school is a moral one; the Welsh child must be taught to love his country and his language, and to admire the heroes of past history. This will increase self-respect and self-reliance and furnish a potent motive for making him a worthy member of a noble nation.[16]

This philosophy found expression in the Welsh Code of 1907. The school curriculum should always include Welsh history and geography and, 'as a rule', Welsh. Where conditions made it desirable, any subject could be taught through Welsh. Welsh should be the medium of instruction of Welsh speaking infants. The Welsh Department energetically extended its competence to all educational activity connected with Wales. In its own publication series and circulars it sought to engage local interest in its work, sending copies of area inspection reports to every school – the Department had its own inspectors, who, unlike their English counterparts, were not subject specialists. Major legislation, like the 1918 Education Act, generally led to the appointment of a departmental committee to consider the implication for Wales, and afforded a chance to press local authorities to extend provision for special Welsh circumstances. On certain topics, parallel commissions were appointed to enquire separately into conditions in England and Wales. The dropping of questions on Welsh history from the Teachers' Training Certificate syllabus in 1920 led Sir Arthur Davies to complain to English colleagues that the Board of Education 'should not be hampered by a suspicion of lack of sympathy on this point with Welsh aspirations in Education'. History should not be taught from an English or Welsh, but a British point of view.[17]

The zeal did not go unchallenged. The Director of the Board's Publications Department ridiculed 'the huge educational fallacy' that all school subjects required special treatment in Wales and mocked Davies' proposed pamphlets, particularly 'The Civil Service as a Career for Welsh boys', with a degree of snobbery – 'I should like to discuss the possibilities of this pamphlet, but I won't'.[18] But with the Welsh Department vigorously exploiting Lloyd George's name it was difficult to put down. 'I hope', Davies greeted one new President of the Board, 'that your attitude will not be one whit less favourable to Welsh than that shown by your six immediate predecessors'.[19]

There were limits. The Department was prevented from pushing an opt-out rather than opt-in scheme for the teaching of Welsh in Cardiff primary schools where parents had voted against compulsory Welsh. But all in all it benefited from a tolerant sympathy for what must have seemed its harmless enthusiasm. The Department missed no chance to capitalise on whatever cambrophilia existed. It laboured long, for example, on orchestrating a ten day programme in Wales for the wartime President, the famous historian H.A.L. Fisher. He duly recorded in his autobiography the happy memories that remained of 'a land so foreign to me . . . the Welsh were exuberant in their enthusiasm for education. It was a pleasure to speak to them'.[20] The Welsh were, after all, a pleasing blend of the exotic and the loyal. Davies and Edwards participated in the imperial Conference on Bilingualism in 1911, and Davies liked to see himself as big brother in Mauritian eyes. A national ego so easily satisfied was worth indulging a little.

Cross-currents: the Welsh Education Movement in the Balance

In Wales after 1918, then, the element of educational autonomy which had been won acted as a surrogate for the political autonomy to which other non-dominant groups increasingly laid claim. Education carried a special charge. 'The Welsh people' wrote Davies' successor in Whitehall in 1932, 'seem to have something akin to a religious belief in education'.[21] The previous year a Welsh County Director of Education affirmed that Wales had made more and faster educational advances over the previous half century than any country in Europe – 'the record of the progress made reads like a romance'. Essential to such claims was the belief that the educational movement had given Wales in a real sense, control over her own destiny. 'The future of Wales will depend largely on [your] response', the Welsh Department wrote to the Welsh Local Education Authorities in asking them to submit schemes for the implementation of the Education Act of 1918. This control was to be exercised in the interests of the best things in the national life, 'bringing the educational system into line with Welsh ideals of culture and civilisation', in the words of a Welsh Departmental Committee of 1919. These ideals, roughly speaking, were held to be 'enlightened Patriotism', community concern and enrichment of the life of the 'cultured common man', as opposed to the education for leadership of hierarchical England. They were a distillation, as Welsh leaders saw it, of the successful movement of social and ethnic emancipation of the Welsh common people since the mid nineteenth century, by which they had demonstrated their commitment to the cause of liberty and progress.

Influential as this vision has been in Wales, it was, of course, patriotic myth: more specifically, the legitimising myth of the triumphant liberal Nonconformist bourgeoisie. As national myths go, it was doubtless more out of tune with reality than most. The interwar Welsh Department was hardly as significant as the Estonian or Latvian Ministries of Education. The decline of Liberalism and Nonconformity in Britain and Wales (in 1922 the Labour party already held a majority of Welsh seats); the anglicisation of industrial south Wales; all this already in our period posed question marks against the successful synthesis of Welsh nationhood with the British democratic state that Welsh educational reformers believed they had achieved. The patriotic myth was vulnerable at three points: the natural radicalism and progressiveness of the Welsh common people, their devotion to their national tongue and their unity of national purpose.

How far did Welsh people correspond to the view of them held by liberal Nonconformity? Recent research on the school boards of the North Wales county of Caernarfonshire between 1870 and 1902 reveals three kinds of situation at the grass roots.[22] By far the best attendance records and most generous educational expenditure came from the quarrying areas represented by a Welsh speaking lower middle class in close touch with the workers. These areas showed both the greatest enthusiasm for the learning of English and for Welsh cultural activities (local newspapers, literary societies, progressive politics). They, at least, approximated to the self-image of radical Welsh Nonconformity in its heroic age. But in the coastal towns these boards were dominated by upper middle class, linguistically mixed and fairly self-interested elements, among whom Nonconformists had a slight edge over Anglicans. In the rural Boards cheeseparing Nonconformist farmers dominated a largely apathetic population. A study of Anglesey tells a similar story of the rural population; nearly half the school boards there in the 1870s had to be compulsorily formed because of indifference and fear of expense. As late as 1901, just over a quarter of the county's primary school children were reported to be permanently absent.[23]

The conclusions that might be drawn about a section, at least, of the rural population, might be uncomfortably close to the charges of the 'Blue Books'. In 1915 a collection of satirical short stories entitled *My People*, the first significant work of Anglo–Welsh literature (though the author's mother tongue was Welsh), painted a grotesque picture of bigoted, hypocritical, lecherous and tight-fisted Cardiganshire peasants. It created an outcry and was burnt by Aberystwyth University students. Yet O.M. Edwards himself, as Chief Inspector of the Welsh Department, had polemicised against the Central Welsh Board for the philistinism, examinationitis and indifference to his Welsh cultural ideals of the secondary schools it administered. It was the secondary schools, mainly set up under the Welsh Intermediate Education Act of 1889, the pride of Welsh educational autonomy, which most disappointed sensitive Welsh observers. True, the number of secondary school pupils had risen to 51 624 by 1939, a quarter of the age group, 69 per cent of whom held free places in 1934 and 95 per cent of whom came direct from elementary school – all figures far higher than in wealthier England. Yet there was ample evidence that behind this democratic trend was the desire, for many Welsh parents, that the secondary schools should prepare bright children for profitable employment in England. Welshness was incidental. Indeed, whereas primary school teachers by the late nineteenth century were overwhelmingly Welsh, the first batch of Intermediate School headmasters was half English.

The language issue was the sorest point. In-migration to the south Wales coalfield and ports meant that already, by the first language census of 1891, only 54 per cent of the inhabitants of Wales were Welsh speaking. Though the absolute number of Welsh speakers continued to rise till 1911, falling slightly thereafter, the percentage figures went from 43 per cent in 1911 to 37 in 1931. This trend conflicted so much with the national ideal that it was denied in the very appeals for remedies that it provoked. Thus 17 Welsh members of parliament petitioning the President of the Board of Education in 1907 to make Welsh a compulsory subject for all Welsh students in Welsh training colleges could write 'Welsh remains the mother tongue of the people, and the language of the home and the services of religion'.[24]

Privately, Welsh Department officials conceded that 'it must be largely a matter of opinion in the case of some districts in Wales if one would describe them as Welsh speaking districts or not'.[25] A convention developed of dividing Wales into Welsh speaking, English speaking and mixed areas. All presented difficulties. Not one school in Welsh speaking Anglesey had made Welsh a 'class subject' under the Cross concessions by 1902. Though by the 1920s such areas had all adopted the O.M. Edwards philosophy on paper ('The Elementary School will be a centre for diffusing Welsh culture and enriching Welsh intellectual life' – the Cardiganshire scheme in response to the 1918 Education Act), fear for the children's English, which was still required to reach the same standards, inevitably limited what could be done and led to cries of Cinderella treatment of Welsh. The use of Welsh as a medium in secondary schools, permitted by the 1907 Code, but not seriously considered till the 1920s, raised problems of textbooks. In English speaking towns like Cardiff, Barry and Newport ambitious schemes brought Welsh teaching into every school before 1914. Inspectors' reports were enthusiastic, but though many teachers did speak Welsh, their lack of training in teaching it, repetitive and stereotyped methods, and continuing public controversy over the subject between pro- and anti-Welsh factions made the introduction of Welsh in this area a Pyrrhic victory. Far sharper and more disappointing for the Department's Welsh policy, however, were Inspectors' reports from 'mixed' districts like the south Wales coalfield, where Welsh speaking parents were ceasing to speak Welsh to their children.

As awareness of these difficulties mounted, language patriots bombarded the Welsh Department with appeals for action. The Department responded that its powers (as by the British tradition) were ultimately only advisory and that the responsibility lay with the local authorities. Sir Arthur Davies wrote in 1923

It is fairly certain that no Government Department, within the British Empire, or indeed any Central Government has ever given such warm encouragement to the use of the Mother Tongue as is to be found in the . . . advice which has issued during the last sixteen years from the

Welsh Department. Probably what is now needed in the way of a stimulant is a little hostility and less benevolence towards the native language on the part of the Central Authority.[26]

Multifarious factors, however, led to the appointment of a commission by the Board of Education in 1925 to suggest ways of advancing the study of Welsh language and literature in the Welsh educational system. Davies strongly opposed an 'impartial' composition of the commission, in the sense of including opponents as well as proponents of the use of Welsh and the bilingual idea, and its report 'Welsh in Education and Life' (1927) duly reflected the thinking of its *bien pensant* membership. The English monoglot majority was declared to be a lagoon cut off from the great ocean of the national life and past, and 72 recommendations were made to systematise as much as increase provision for Welsh. However, Wales was about to enter a period of intense depression which saw the emigration of nearly a fifth of her population. In industrial Glamorgan, where many schemes, both county and local, had been formulated already before the 1927 Report (deputing of certain schools as Welsh medium schools, bilingual teacher supply and so on) these withered in the new atmosphere. The one effect of the 1927 Report was to generalise Welsh medium instruction, not only in the infant but also in the higher elementary classes, in Welsh speaking Wales and to increase its use in teaching subjects like Welsh history and scripture at the secondary stage.

A recent socialist critic of the language movement in Welsh education has argued that the Welsh language commission episode reveals the interwar Welsh educational bureaucracy to have been an elite out of touch with public indifference to Welsh, and unwilling, therefore, to expose its linguistic goals to the test of democratic sanction.[27] This seems more plausible than fair. Whatever Davies's patriotic motives, his opposition to an 'impartial' enquiry into the merits of bilingualism was based on the common sense of the practical bureaucrat. As he pointed out, national cultures do not allow themselves to be argued out of existence. Likely consequences of an allegedly objective exercise would be to inflame political passions. Here, it was the more radically minded pro-Welsh faction rather than their opponents that Davies feared. On the other hand, to take at face value Davies's charge of apathy on the part of the Welsh public to his Department's language policy is to forget the almost insurmountable difficulties which faced local authorities in trying to implement it. These lay in the complexity of the language situation and in the contradictions of the Department's bilingual policy itself. To stress the supreme value of Welsh culture, yet continue to maintain the nineteenth-century assumption that a Welsh child could only succeed in the battle of life if he knew English as well as an English child was almost to invite the symbolic treatment of Welsh which aroused complaint.

Here the picture must be rounded off with reference to the position of the Welsh Department in Welsh political life. It had been created as a sop to Welsh feelings after the House of Lords' rejection of the proposed National Council of Education for Wales. The Central Welsh Board, which had seen the National Council as a natural extension of itself, remained bitterly resentful of the Whitehall based Welsh Department, which, in a polemical view, had 'operated as an instrument for moulding the system of education in Wales in accordance with English ideas' and, in its anti-Central Welsh Board stance, 'to rob the Principality of the only piece of autonomy that it possesses'.[28] It was not difficult for an able administrator to puncture the Central Welsh Board's continuing calls for a Welsh National Education Council. As Davies blandly briefed the President of the Board of Education before one such Welsh deputation, it would suffice to ask the National Council enthusiasts what were their *concrete* proposals. How, for example, would they reconcile the call for 'complete' Welsh educational autonomy with the need for parliamentary accountability, had they besides reached agreement between rural and industrial counties over the precise financing of the Council, and so on?[29] Davies's successor was to oppose moves to devolve Welsh administration to a Welsh Secretary of State with a Welsh Office in Cardiff, because this would detach Wales from the corridors of power. Yet he had not been able to maintain a really distinctive Welsh educational stance. His proposals in 1929 for effectively comprehensive secondary schools to solve the problems of thinly populated Welsh rural areas foundered on London's preference for post-primary schools differentiated by academic type; and he implemented government cuts in the numbers of free places in secondary schools despite massive protests in Wales.

It would be wrong to suggest that any Machiavellianism was involved, but in view of the above it is clear that the particular pattern of government provision for Welsh education that developed operated as an admirable instrument of divide and rule. The Central Welsh Board, the Welsh Department and Local Education Authorities, the often passionate Welsh speakers and the more numerous but less passionate English speakers, all were contained within a framework which kept each in a constant state of modest frustration. No doubt as far as the Welsh language, the core issue, was concerned, this was the only way to prevent an insoluble problem from becoming truly intolerable for any of the parties concerned. For the bleak tone of some previous comments should not suggest that stresses and strains had become intolerable. The Welsh patriotic consensus still held. True, the Welsh Nationalist Party had been founded in 1925, but its electoral performance remained dismal between the wars, though its intellectual influence grew (its Welsh paper had 7000 subscribers in 1939), and it had a special appeal to teachers. A nationalist oriented National Union of Teachers of Wales was founded in 1940.

The labour movement, by contrast, was much more powerful, but the old liberal myth of the common man was congenial to it, and in many cases the transition from Liberal to Labour was more a matter of generation than of ideology. Nor did the declining proportion of Welsh speakers affect the credibility of the national myth as the bare figures might lead one to suppose. The bulk of the English speakers were congregated in certain populous corners of Wales, among the young, and among low status immigrant workers. In rural areas the language border changed little in our period and there were more native speakers of Welsh in 1940 than in 1850. Besides, considerable *pietas* remained to the old language; English speakers often continued to attend Welsh language chapels. For such people, the teaching of Welsh history, geography and language in the schools remained popular, even if they never mastered Welsh. At the end of our period the Welsh education movement still counted itself a success story.

Conclusion

The Welsh education movement was a complex phenomenon, successively assimilating religious, democratic and linguistic/ethnic motifs. Its high self-valuation has been dented with the decline of the liberal Nonconformist ideology which formed its core, and appears even more questionable if comparison is made with the experience of the small nations of eastern Europe, say Slovenia, for example, a society closer to nineteenth-century Wales in area and population than any other. Yet how far is the comparison in order? The conventional view among east European scholars is that west European ethnic groups lost any meaningful independent existence either before, or during, the bourgeois age, surviving only as vestigial, vegetating communities. Discussion of a Welsh nationhood in the modern epoch is to them a puzzle.

Nonetheless, comparison can be helpful, and not just to puncture Welsh self-importance. The crucial features of east European ethnic evolution can be cast in higher relief, for these too were specific and should not necessarily be taken for a universal case. Implicitly, this generalising of east European experience has occurred, however, in the influential work of the social philosopher Ernest Gellner, born in Prague. In this functionalist interpretation, the nation and nationalism are born in circumstances of industrialisation and uneven development. Group B, arriving at the workplace later than Group A, who have already established their language and culture as the norm of communication, seek to escape from under-dog status by mobil-ising their own ethnic traits into a rival 'high culture'.[30] Gellner acknowledges that not all traditional ethnic groups succeed in the modern period in evolving into fully-fledged nations in this way, but his functionalist framework does not really promote explanations as to why this is so. In the Welsh case, where industrialisation brought together Welsh and non-Welsh on a large scale, Group A and B differentiation, leading to a language based separation, did not occur.

The reasons were two-fold. The British state was prestigious and attractive; strong, therefore, not in the sense of bureaucratic inter-ventionism, but through its social roots in a dynamic capitalist culture. The question of major upheaval, into which national demands could be inserted, was not on the agenda, as it always was in the east European empires of the nineteenth century. At best, the brief proposal for 'Home Rule all round' at the time of the Irish crisis immediately before and after the First World War (that is, a federal solution involving Wales and Scotland) offers an analogy. Second, the continental ideology of romantic nationalism was, till late in the day, absent in Wales, largely because it was absent in dominant but somewhat insular England. In eastern Europe these ideas were all transmitted to non-dominant groups initially in German language universities. Yet the intellectually isolated people among whom the Welsh educational movement began to germinate in the mid nine-teenth century did have an ideology – it was Nonconformity. Nonconformity, with its individualist stress on personal salvation and rejection of traditional folk culture, was brought by Welsh people with them into the industrialising situation, just as workers in east European towns often found Herderian minded school teachers waiting for them:

> Here I find myself a stranger
> And my native country lies
> Far beyond the ocean's danger
> In the land of paradise

as the eighteenth-century Methodist hymnist Williams Pantycelyn wrote. Gellner's assumption that pre-industrial, non-dominant societies were mere repositories of peasant lore is incorrect. It follows that the idea of a turning point between traditional and modern society, in which national communities had either to become fully fledged nations or stagnate as ethnic groups, is overdrawn. The Welsh case helps to show how state structures and relatively autonomous ideologies could interact with processes of social change to produce a variety of patterns of evolution of non-dominant groups which fell between these poles.

No doubt the starker alternatives were more pressing in eastern Europe, where the ethnic problem became the central question for the polities concerned. The Welsh case was characterised by peripherality – without a strategic aspect – which, while entailing intellectual isolation and weakness *vis-à-vis* the state, lessened the need for state regimentation. In western Europe peripherality has taken many forms. Wales and the Spanish Basque country present intriguing parallels, in that heavy industrialisation, mass immigration and the minoritisation of the native tongue occurred in both. Yet the state background was quite different. In Spanish politics provincial privileges lasted until the nineteenth century, so that ethnic issues have had in modern times a constant, though not a dominant, place. Within the United Kingdom itself, in the nineteenth century, there were many parallels between the three Celtic territories: expansion of an industrial enclave in each, together with rural depopulation; religious and linguistic divergence; peasants of conservative life style but increasingly radical politics. But the population of Ireland fell sharply during the century; that of Wales trebled and Scotland more than doubled. Ireland's proportion of the British national product fell from 2/17 to 1/20; that of Scotland and Wales greatly increased. This dramatic difference in the benefits received from Britain's economic advance by the Celtic countries must surely be part explanation of why with education Gaelic Highlanders and Welshmen drew closer to the British state, but not Irishmen. The cultural nationalism which finally reached Wales via the neo-Hegelian atmosphere of Oxford in the 1880s was half a century later than in eastern Europe, in a society which had industrialised half a century sooner. It was correspondingly muted.

However, integration was not conflict free, and did not fully correspond to a simple political diffusion model of centre–periphery relations. The American sociologist Hechter, in his *Internal Colonialism: the Celtic Fringe in British National Development*, has argued statistically that the unequal pattern of Anglo–Welsh relations, established by conquest and institutionalised by a cultural division of labour in the English favour, has not been made good by subsequent 'development', including industrialisation. Hechter's views have been criticised by theoreticians but they seem to find corroboration in the picture of Welsh society presented by Lingen in 1847; while the idea of the continuing legacy of exploitation accounts well for that residue of reserve, of schizophrenia towards the English, that subterranean vein of Welsh emotion which could suddenly surface, after a generation's absence, in the Welsh Language Society movement of 1885–7. H.A.L. Fisher wrote interestingly of O.M. Edwards as 'a man of genius [who] seemed to embody the im-memorial melancholy of an aggrieved people'.[31] If this unreconciled element in Welsh people's character was one reason why economic integration with England did not dissolve a separate Welsh identity, another was that, as Lingen showed, they already existed as a people, with a collective mentality, before the education movement opened a way towards the majority community. The ideology of Sir Hugh Owen's generation may have been utilitarian individualism, but it was an individualism *collectively* embraced. The common experience necessary for nationhood therefore remained.

It was at this point, not earlier, that English government, as opposed to English society, became relevant to the nascent Welsh movement. Welsh Nonconformists found understanding among their English coreligionists and, therewith, the Liberal party, with which they largely associated. An alliance was forged between the Welsh people and the British left. There was a certain irony in this. The traditionalism and historicism which is an important part of ethnic maintenance was more to be found in the Conservative camp, particularly the Anglican Church, including its Welsh branch. However, religious differences ruled out any possibility of an alliance with clerical conservatives such as ushered in the modern Slovene nation, for example, in eastern Europe. In the struggle over dis-establishment of the Anglican Church in Wales before 1914, it was English liberals who argued for the Welsh case on grounds of nationality and English conservatives who saw the Welsh as an ethnic group, whose wishes could have no constitutional signi-ficance. However, once the Church question had been settled, in favour of Wales, in practice the attitude of Conservative politicians to Wales came to resemble that of the left. Sir Percy Watkins, Secretary of the Welsh Department of the Board of Education from 1925 to 1933, spoke of his Conservative party President Lord Eustace Percy as 'deeply interested in our Welsh questions' and possessing 'a very clear realisation of the point of view of a minority nation'.[32] Hence the stability of the educational framework which had emerged by the interwar years, a stability based on a measure of success. Though more contentious calls for universal bilingualism were not heeded, the education service played a major, and widely popular, role not just in sustaining the Welsh language in rural areas – village Breton survived these years without support, after all – but in strengthening national consciousness there, so producing a constant flow of patriotic recruits to the teaching profession, who helped to maintain a Welsh identity in anglicised parts of the country. All this was acceptable to government.

Of course, it could be said that no English politician had reason not to cooperate with an ethnic group which challenged no important postulate of the state. The Welsh had, after all, accepted the fundamental premise of the Blue Books of 1847 that a knowledge of English was essential for successful functioning in British society. This was a crucial step. It met the barely articulated requirement of most English people that while the Welsh might have a nationality of their own, this should not, somehow, be too 'separate' from the dominant British identity. For all situations where the non-dominant ethnic group was not, or is not, prepared to take the equivalent step, the Welsh case may have little relevance or interest. For the increasing number of situations where minority groups do recognise a need to know the main language of the state in which they live, the Welsh experience, and the flexibility shown in its course by government and non-dominant elements, may merit attention.

Notes

1. W. Jones. p. 69.
2. *Reports of the Commissioners* Pt. I., p. 2 and pp. 3, 4, 7, 28, 32 (Lingen); Pt. II., p. 66 (Symons).
3. G.A. Williams, p. 164.
4. Stanley, p. 23.
5. J.V. Morgan, p. 117.
6. *Reports of the Commissioners*, Pt. II., p. 115.
7. Ll.M. Rees, p. 154.
8. T. Rees, p. 19.
9. B.L. Davies, p. 563.
10. A.D. Smith, pp. 230–54.
11. G.A. Jones, p. 193.
12. Ibid., p. 209.
13. J.E. Hughes, p. 56.
14. Ibid., p. 126.
15. Introductory note to the Code of Regulations for Public Elementary Schools in Wales (1907), cited in E. Evans, p. 82.
16. Public Record Office, London. Education Department (hereafter PRO ED) 91/13, W 62/1911. *General Report on the Teaching of Welsh in the Elementary Schools under the Pontypridd Education District*, (1910).
17. PRO ED 93, WS 2419, A.T. Davies – *History Committee*, 22 Nov. 1921.
18. L.W. Evans (1974), p. 312.
19. G.A. Jones, p. 222.
20. Fisher, p. 102.
21. Watkins, p. 193.
22. H.G. Williams.
23. Pretty, pp. 176; 217.
24. PRO ED, 91/13. Welsh MPs petition n.d.
25. PRO ED, 91/13, W 2/911, T.G. Roberts to O.M. Edwards; 19 January, 1911.
26. PRO ED, 91/57; A.T. Davies, *Memorandum*, 17 January, 1923.
27. C. Williams.
28. PRO ED, 35/7129, enclosing letter of J.C.Davies, Secretary of the Central Welsh Board, printed in the *Liverpool Post and Mercury* of 27 February, 1926.

29. PRO ED, 91/45W 148/1917; A.T. Davies, *Memorandum*, September 1917.
30. Gellner.
31. Fisher, p. 100f.
32. Watkins, p. 126.

Select Bibliography

General Background

Coupland, R. (1954), *Welsh and Scottish Nationalism*, London.
Fisher, H.A.L. (1940), *An Unfinished Autobiography*, Oxford.
Gellner, E. (1983), *Nations and Nationalism*, London.
Jones R. Brinley (ed.) (1972), *Anatomy of Wales*, Peterson super Ely.
Morgan, J. Vyrnwy (n.d.), *Kilsby Jones*, (in Welsh), Wrexham.
Morgan, Kenneth (1981), *Rebirth of a Nation: 1880–1980*, Oxford and Cardiff.
Pretty, D.A. (1977), *Two Centuries of Anglesey Schools*, Llangefni.
Rees, Rev. T. (1867), *Miscellaneous Papers on subjects relating to Wales*, London.
Smith, A.D. (1971), *Theories of Nationalism*, London.
Smith, D. (ed.) (1980), *A People and a Proletariat*, London.
Stanley, Rev. A.P. (ed.) (1881), *Letters to a Friend by Connop Thirlwall, late Lord Bishop of St. David's*, London.
Watkins, Sir Percy (1944), *A Welshman Remembers*, Cardiff.
Williams, David (1950), *A History of Modern Wales*, Cardiff.

Educational Surveys and Key Official Reports

Barnard, H.C. (1961), *A History of English Education from 1760*, 2nd edn.
Curtis, S.J. (1967), *History of Education in Great Britain*, 7th edn.
Reports of the Commissioners into the State of Education in Wales (1847), London.
Southall, J.E. (1888), *Bilingual teaching in Welsh Elementary Schools, or minutes of evidence of Welsh witnesses before the Royal Commission on Education in 1886–7*, Newport.
Welsh in Education and Life (1927), Report of Department Committee, H.M.S.O.
Williams, Jac L. (ed.) (1966), *Ysgrifau ar Addysg: Addysg i Gymru* (Essays on Education: Education for Wales), Cardiff.

Monographs Relating to the History of Welsh Education

Evans, Ellen (1924), *The Teaching of Welsh: an investigation into the problem of bilingualism*, Cardiff.
Evans, L.W. (1971), *Education in Industrial Wales 1700–1900*, Cardiff.
Evans, L.W. (1974), *Studies in Welsh Education: Welsh Educational Structure and Administration 1880–1925*, Cardiff.
Hughes, J. Elwyn (1984), *Arloeswr dwyieithedd. Dan Isaac Davies 1839–87* (Pioneer of Bilingualism. Dan Isaac Davies 1839–87), Cardiff.
Jones, G.E. (1982), *Controls and Conflicts in Welsh Secondary Education 1889–1944*, Cardiff.
Jones, W.R. (1966), *Bilingualism in Welsh Education*, Cardiff.

Key Unpublished Theses and Papers

Davies, B.L. (1979), *A Reassessment of the Contribution of Sir Hugh Owen to Education in Wales*, 2 vols, Ph.D., University of Wales.

Jones, Gwilym Arthur (1978), *Dysgu Cymraeg rhwng 1847 a 1927*, (The Teaching of Welsh between 1847 and 1927), Ph.D., University of Wales, Bangor.

Jones, T.P. (1967), *The Contribution of the National Society to Welsh Education, 1811–70*, External Ph.D., University of London.

Jones, Rev. W. (1841), *A Prize Essay in English and Welsh on the Character of the Welsh as a Nation in the Present Age*, London.

Rees, Ll. Morgan (1968), *A Critical Examination of Teacher Training in Wales, 1846–98*, Ph.D., University of Wales, Bangor.

Webster, J.R. (1959), *The Place of Secondary Education in Welsh Society, 1800–1918*, Ph.D., University of Wales, Swansea.

Williams, T. (16 Nov. 1984), *English and Welsh in the Schools of Wales*, unpublished paper given at the University of Warwick.

Williams, H.G. (1973), *The History of the School Board Movement in Caernarvonshire, 1870–1902*, MA, University of Wales, Bangor.

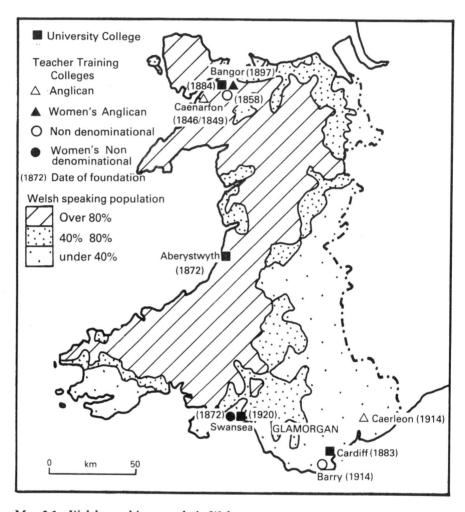

Map 3.1   Welsh speaking people in Wales

4 Norwegian and Swedish Educational Policies *vis-à-vis* Non-dominant Ethnic Groups, 1850–1940

KNUT ERIKSEN

Introduction and Summary

In the period of 1850–1940 the northern parts of the Scandinavian peninsula could be described as containing a multi-ethnic society. There were four distinct ethnic groups: Norwegians, Swedes, Samis (Lapps) and the Finnish speaking population found along the Fenno–Swedish border (Norrbotten) and in the northern provinces of Norway (Finnmark and Troms). The minority group of Finnish stock in northern Norway was usually called Kvens. Certain major political changes took place in the period. The Swedish–Norwegian Union created in 1814, was dissolved in 1905. In 1918, in the wake of the Bolshevik revolution the former archduchy of Finland, established in 1809, also won full independence.

The Samis were during this period citizens of four countries: Norway, Sweden, Finland and the Russian empire/Soviet Union. Around 1850, according to the official censuses, there were approximately 15 000 Samis in Norway, 6000 in Sweden and 1000 in Finland. There is no census for northern Russia, but probably there were less than 1500 Samis in the Kola district. These censuses up to 1940 do show a remarkable stability in the number of Sami speaking people in all three Nordic countries, even though one should not take these figures too literally: it is generally assumed that the figures are somewhat too low. According to anthropologists there are today about 40 000 Samis in Norway; 20 000 in Sweden; 5000 in Finland; and 2000 in the Soviet Union. Rather more than 50 per cent of them speak a Sami language or dialect.[1]

Around 1700 the immigration of Kvens to northern Norway really got under way. By 1850 there were approximately 3000 Kvens in northern Norway. Immigration peaked in the second half of the nineteenth century: according to official statistics between 1875 and 1930 there were about 10 000 Kvens in Norway. After this date their number declined sharply, and in following censuses the authorities did not think it worthwhile even to register the Kvens.[2] There were more Finnish speaking people in Sweden than in Norway. When Finland was ceded to Russia by Sweden in 1809, fewer than 10 000 Finnish speakers were left on the Swedish side of the border. However, their number increased swiftly during the nineteenth century due to high birth rates and immigration. In addition, censuses in the interwar period showed that more than 70 per cent of this stock, that is about 30 000, still had Finnish as their mother tongue.[3]

The complex ethnic situation of Fenno–Scandia is thus conducive to a comparative approach, analysing how the modern state affected small minority groups. The focus here will be on the educational policies pursued by the authorities in Norway and Sweden *vis-à-vis* the Samis and the Finnish speaking people, on the basis of a discussion of the extent to which these authorities argued and acted on similar lines as regards the two groups. Using Norway as the main case study, we can ask whether an indigenous people were, in fact, dealt with in the same way as an immigrant group. In addition, special emphasis will be given to a broader comparative perspective: the extent to which similar aims towards these groups were pursued in both Norway and Sweden, with explanations of any differences.

Until 1850 the impact of the Norwegian and Swedish cultures on ethnic minorities in the north was modest. However, in the second half of the nineteenth century, a more deliberate assimilation policy gradually developed. The explanations traditionally given for this fall into three main groups: political, ideological and economic. Security considerations – the need to defend the border areas against foreign infiltration and expansion – played a decisive role. In this paper attention will focus upon the role and effects in this assimilation process of schooling.

Realpolitik or Ideology?

Although *Realpolitik* probably constituted the most important basis and motive for policies of assimilation, especially towards the Finns (Kvens), this explanation has to be somewhat modified. An ethnic policy was defended on fundamental ideological grounds of such force that they cannot be ignored in any discussion of cause and background. The most important ideologies in the Scandinavian context are nationalism and racism.

As far as one can judge, to some extent policies of norwegianisation and swedification probably had a Social Darwinist basis which gave authorities a 'scientific' legitimacy for their policies. The aim was the assimilation of so-called 'primitive' groups that had not yet reached a 'civilised level'. Primitive and semi-nomadic ways of life were doomed to die: inferior races had to be absorbed into the greater community or else Nature would 'solve' the problem. A policy of assimilation was thus aimed at shortening their death agony and at spreading enlightenment among these races – in other words a Nordic edition of 'the white man's burden'. This classification applied particularly to the Sami elements, but the Finns were also included to a certain extent.[4]

The development of a 'Sami should remain Sami' philosophy in Sweden around the turn of the century was also greatly influenced by Social Darwinist thinking. It was a widespread notion that Samis were well suited for survival in the primitive reindeer economy of the Arctic. Other Samis, however, were regarded as losers in the internal struggle, and consequently even less fitted to cope with the challenge of modern, 'civilised' ways of life. Assimilation was their only road to true cultural and material progress.

Together with Social Darwinist thinking, nationalism provided clear grounds for ousting the Sami and Finnish languages and cultures so as to make way for the homogeneous national state. Nationalism expressed by ethnic groups excited alarm. It could split nations and involve governments in territorial disputes with hostile neighbouring states. Equally, European nationalism provided the Norwegian and Swedish authorities with models and ideological legitimacy for an assimilationist minority policy. In Norway particularly, a vigorous nationalism developed in connection with the dissolution of the union with Sweden. Internally this nationalism was directed towards the destruction of separate Sami and Finnish culture and identity, or as one Norwegian author put in 1902: 'Near the border one has no right to be either a conservative or a liberal: here one can only be Norwegian'.[5]

Economic motives tended to strengthen a policy of assimilation in both Norway and Sweden. Several writers claim to have discovered a certain parallel between the new economic imperialism, as expressed in the colonial policy of the west, and the Scandinavian minority policy in the Arctic.[6] The national states supported the cultivation of new land and industrialisation. The Samis have traditionally exploited the natural resources of Fenno–Scandia, mainly as reindeer herders. Rurality and nation building of the Nordic states had had important consequences for the Sami people, forcing them, for instance, to become citizens of one specific country on the basis of location of their winter pastures. In the twentieth century, in conflicts between Sami reindeer herders on the one side and farmers and capitalist mining companies on the other, state authorities regularly supported the allegedly more 'civilised' forms of production. This meant the loss of traditional pastures and other natural resources to the Sami people. Discriminatory economic measures and the modernisation process had thus a clear assimilative effect in both Sweden and Norway.

Bureaucratic considerations with educational implications were also put forward by Norwegian and Swedish officials. One common language would simplify administration and reduce costs, some argued. Bilingual education in schools was impractical, time consuming and prevented learning of the main language. Cultural uniformity was the prerequisite for economic progress, industrialisation and social mobilisation. With the help of a single common language all inhabitants could easily communicate with the authorities. The modern society thus required a mobile, literate and technologically equipped population provided through a mass, public, compulsory and standardised education system.

An examination of the assimilation policies in their totality, the means used, the geographical patterns and the concrete arguments, demonstrates that neither ideology nor imperialist theory provide a comprehensive answer. The security factor is also needed to explain why the border areas were given special attention in implementing assimilation policies and why such policies in both countries were pursued more rigorously vis-à-vis the Finnish-speaking people than the Samis. In both school and church, cultural pressure was slightly harsher on the former. Sami organisations were allowed to function but attempts to mobilise the Finns were thwarted and kept under close surveillance. Free weeklies and radio sets in the 1930s, as part of the process of national consolidation, were available to the Finns, but not to Samis. Practically, only Finnish speakers were subject to close surveillance by Norwegian authorities.

Moreover, the formulation of an ethnic policy was only partly discussed openly at the parliamentary level or in the press. In Norway in particular one must have recourse to secret documents on the departmental level to study minority policy. Likewise, secret boards served as important tools for the promotion of new ideas and measures. The contents of the documents provide rich evidence of persistent Norwegian and Swedish fears of losing the borderland to expansionist neighbouring states exploiting the 'foreign' ethnic groups in the north.[7]

Before 1850: A Policy of Ambivalence and Non-discrimination

The efforts of the nation states to establish control over Samiland had other farreaching implications. The various means employed, including education, missionary work, colonisation and trade, dealt a severe blow to the traditional Sami way of life and culture. Central and local authorities promoted a policy of permanent settlement at the expense of the Samis semi-nomadic existence. Sami society was gradually integrated into the respective national states, first and foremost legally and administratively. Moreover, the Samis were converted to Christianity and, at an early date, were given an organised school system as a result of increased missionary activities by the church. Up to 1850, however, there was no express aim in favour of assimilation by the state, although some officials favoured such a policy. The main objective was the securing of political control of the northern areas.

Any more profound assimilationist process was, moreover, counteracted by an ecclesiastical struggle over language policy dating back to the end of the seventeenth century. Policy was shifting in Norway, but many clergymen there preferred to evangelise and educate the minorities in their own language. Their attitude in this respect was in accord with the Lutheran tradition and was additionally defended by humanitarian, cultural and pedagogical arguments. In Sweden a new language law of 1723 enabled a similar policy for the Swedish Samis. In practice, however, there were several districts in which this principle was never implemented.

The cultural impact of Norway and Sweden on Finnish speakers, welcomed by authorities before 1850 for their farming skill, was even more restricted. In fact, the two states had yet to formulate a distinct and uniform ethnic policy, and few churches, schools and courts existed in the north. To a large extent, the attitude of the authorities may be described as one of *laissez faire* and formal non-discrimination.

The Period of Moderate Assimilation 1850–80

The first examples of a policy of more deliberate norwegianisation and swedification came in the decades following 1850. In Sweden the first influential political opposition to Finnish cultural dominance in the borderland could be seen around 1860. In the 1870s, state schools were established in Tornedalen and Swedish soon replaced Finnish as the language of education. A similar policy of assimilation was introduced for the Samis. In Norway a coalition of liberal politicians and some influential church leaders began to criticise sharply the pro-Sami language policy of the majority of local clergymen in the north. In 1851 the Norwegian parliament decided that the language policy of the state was to 'encourage the knowledge of the Norwegian language' in mixed language areas where possible and reasonable. Money was granted for various purposes such as schools, teacher training, wage bonuses for teachers and textbooks. These annual grants (the so-called Finns Fund) were increased, and continued until the 1920s.

Although this new line meant a definite departure from the language policy advocated before 1850, especially by the clergy, it was in many respects a moderate policy. In a circular concerning language instruction issued by the Norwegian authorities in 1862, both Sami and Finnish were accepted as natural secondary languages. School children were to get a certain amount of instruction in reading and writing their native tongue, and the teaching of religion was to take place in either Sami or Finnish. Teachers were ideally to know both languages, and instruction was consequently given in Sami and Finnish at the teacher training college in Tromsø. Bilingual textbooks were still preferred, and only the mixed language areas were at first included in these efforts of assimilation of the minorities. Assimilation was the long term objective, but a moderate and flexible strategy was adopted.[8]

The Introduction of Strict Norwegianisation and Swedification 1870–1900

The new language directives of 1880 and 1898 in Norway (and the corresponding one of 1888 in Sweden) adopted a more rigorous and ambitious language policy. Education was, from the outset, to be mainly in the Norwegian language. All Sami and Kven children were to learn to read, speak and write Norwegian. Previous provisions that they were also to learn their own native language were dropped. The Sami and Finnish languages were to be used only when absolutely necessary. Even religious instruction was now normally to be given in Norwegian. Bilingual textbooks disappeared completely before the turn of the century. Even during breaks between classes Sami and Kven schoolchildren were forbidden to use their mother tongues. Similar measures were introduced to eradicate Finnish nationalism and culture in Norrbotten, and to assimilate Samis here and elsewhere in Sweden.[9]

This policy was complemented by economic measures directed at teachers as well as parents. To encourage Sami or Kven schoolchildren to learn Norwegian, the brightest among them were given grants. Their parents, too, could receive extra money if they encouraged them to learn Norwegian quickly. On the other hand, the teacher had to prove to his superiors that his Norwegian instruction bore fruit or risk severe sanctions. If he failed, the teacher lost a salary supplement amounting to about a quarter of his total income. Swedish teachers were also given financial incentives in Norrbotten.

There was a complex political and ideological background behind the hardening of assimilation policies in both countries. Between 1850 and 1940, many Norwegian and Swedish authorities feared that Russia–Finland, and later the independent Finnish state, aspired to obtain ice free harbours in northern Norway and rich mining and forestry districts in Norrbotten. The ethnic minorities were regarded as potential fifth columnists. Officials feared that the resident Finnish speaking population, and to a lesser degree the Samis, would side with Russia or Finland in a military or political conflict or, at the very least, remain neutral.[10]

There were two main reasons for the sudden emergence of a concern about this 'menace'. Finnish nationalism, and the development of the Greater Finland movement, resulted in Greater Finland supporters becoming deeply concerned about the fate of the Finnish speaking peoples, their kith and kin in northern Norway and Sweden. A second factor was that the Finnish immigration into these latter areas reached alarming proportions in the eyes of Norwegian and Swedish authorities, especially as the new wave of immigrants settled in the most exposed borderlands, where they soon came to constitute a majority. These two developments increased Norwegian and Swedish fears that Russia–Finland would argue, or possibly even fight, for a new border that took greater account of the principle of nationality. Leading politicians drew a parallel between Finnmark/Norrbotten and the fate of Schleswig–Holstein in the German–Danish war of 1864. A firm assimilation policy was seen by both countries as the best means of defending the borderland against foreign infiltration. In such a policy schools were to play a key role.[11]

1900–40: The Zenith of the Assimilation Policy in Norway: New Signals in Sweden

In Sweden, a somewhat ambiguous and shifting minority policy developed from the start of the twentieth century. A policy of segregation competed with the traditional policy of assimilation, where the declared objective of the former was the protection of the culture and economy of the Sami reindeer herders. A demarcation line was established in the last decades of the nineteenth century between farmland and reindeer pastures, and so-called nomad schools were set up to enable the reindeer herders to maintain their traditional way of life. The majority of Samis, as well as the Finnish speakers, were, however, to be assimilated.[12]

In Norway, by contrast, a new stiffening of the assimilation policy occurred in the years before and after 1905. A mounting wave of nationalism stirred Norwegian opinion, and a homogeneous national state became the explicit political aim. Increased efforts were thus made to assimilate the ethnic minorities. A more developed and industrialised Norwegian state could also now finance more easily new measures for extinguishing non-Norwegian languages and cultures. In order to increase the percentage of Norwegians in the border areas, and thereby facilitate the assimilation process, land distribution now became explicitly discriminatory against Samis and Kvens. Ability to speak, write and read the Norwegian language became the main provision for land-holding under the Land Sales act of 1902. In practice the edict on land sales was less strictly enforced by local authorities than the government had expected. It is also worth noting that similar measures were not adopted in Sweden.

As before, special emphasis was attached to schooling and language policy. A Director of Schools was appointed by the government in 1902 to promote and control school policy in Finnmark – the only area at this time with such a post. In subsequent years, the Director of Schools initiated several new measures to ensure the speeding-up of the assimilation process. Education in the Sami and Finnish languages at the teachers training college in Tromsø was ended. Norwegian teachers were now preferred in Finnmark, in contrast to Norrbotten, where teachers and clergymen of Finnish stock were still welcome. The few teachers of Sami and Finnish descent in Norway were discriminated against economically and encouraged to leave the northern provinces. Thus nationalist minded teachers came, more and more, to dominate school life. At the same time, any moderate clergy (two of the northern bishops were opposed to the new language instruction) more or less lost their influence on the schools.

The Director of Schools was convinced that if the primary school system was to achieve its purpose, more schools had to be built, and school attendance had to be extended. The favourite scheme, however, was the building of new boarding schools financed by the state. Apparently, Swedish policies were the inspiration. Similar schools had recently been established in Norrbotten. Through boarding schools established at a distance from home areas, he hoped to reduce the influence of Sami or Kven parents over their children. The children were to remain under the influence of a purely Norwegian cultural environment for as long as possible. National authorities decided to build the first boarding schools to counteract the Kven 'colonies' along the north eastern border. Although the new school policy in the north also had social and modernising functions, national security considerations took a high priority. The philosophy of the Director of Schools was never to lose sight of the goal of a steady assimilation: it would take time to fulfil it, but success would come, if the goal was persistently pursued in the schools, and if other state institutions took a more enthusiastic part in the fight for national consolidation.[13]

In the interwar period the assimilation policy in the schools continued without any fundamental changes in aims or means. The economic crisis and the shortage of qualified teachers prevented new reforms. The effect of the assimilation process was, therefore, not increasing. It was, rather, more an age of consolidation in this respect. However, while the central authorities still considered schools to be an important factor in the assimilation process, more weight was also now given to other factors. A successful realisation of the assimilation process, said many Norwegian (and Swedish) officials, would now depend first and foremost on economic conditions and communications in the northern periphery. If these requirements were satisfied, the Samis and the Kvens could easily be integrated into the nation.

Some new elements, however, were introduced in the school policy *vis-à-vis* the ethnic groups. Most important was the new, and extended, role of the teacher. During the interwar years a fairly comprehensive and complicated network of supervision took shape. The bishop of Tromsø and the Director of Schools in Finnmark played a crucial part in this system, and were in close contact with the general staff of the army and with the county governor in Finnmark. Particular attention was paid to the Kvens in the border regions and to the religious communities known as Læstadians. Teachers were told to send reports to their bishop about possible 'unnational activities' in their region, and they complied.

The Role of the School in the Policy of Assimilation

Between 1850 and 1940 schools continued to be regarded by the authorities in both Sweden and Norway as the main instrument in the 'civilisation' of the minorities. School was seen as influencing all young Finnish speakers and Samis, and also as setting cultural standards for the older generations. In fact, schools and church buildings near the border were regarded as national symbols and just as important to the security of the country as the establishment of garrisons. Cultural measures and military projects were two sides of the same coin.

The specific significance of schools in the assimilation process is difficult to evaluate, but as long as there were very few schools and teachers and the duration of the education was limited to only some weeks a year, its impact was probably minor. This view actually found support in the many school reports from Finnmark and Norrbotten in the nineteenth century, complaining of the meagre results from educational policies. In fact the Church rather than the school was probably the official institution with which both Samis and Finns had most contact at that time. In the twentieth century this picture changed. A modern elementary school system was developed, and more effective educational measures were employed in both countries. Schooling played a more decisive role as one of many institutions and resources aimed at assimilating the minorities.

Some educational theorists, however, have recently disputed this view. They claim that the Sami children and their parents, especially in the reindeer districts, saw no relevance to their future occupation in the school curriculum. School, therefore, influenced their way of life only to a very limited extent. These researchers argue that a policy of assimilation often had the opposite effect of what was intended: that it provoked a revolt among many Sami children, and that in various ways the Norwegian and Swedish teachers were isolated and obstructed.[14] While this may be an accurate description of the situation in some of the isolated Sami communities, generally, and in the long run, the schools, even in the Sami districts, tended to assimilate the younger generation.

However, Norwegian, as well as Swedish, authorities were rapidly convinced that the language and cultural work, although important, was not sufficient. A more effective policy would be one that would influence other sections of society as well. Briefly, it can be said that in the 1800s the range of measures was less extensive than in the 1900s. From having been first and foremost a cultural education policy, the policy of assimilation now also embraced policies on colonisation, establishment of industry and development of communications. Coordination was the key word.

Education in the Context of Other Assimilation Measures[15]

All in all the aim, several of the means and the motives of the ethnic policy in the schools and elsewhere remained the same in Sweden and Norway in this period. But some new measures were introduced in Norway after 1905. In Sweden the policy vis-à-vis the Samis was partly changed after 1900 and that vis-à-vis the Finns in Tornedalen was later gradually modified.

The existence of an independent Finnish state from 1917 aggravated the border problem, particularly for the Norwegian authorities.

To counter the 'Finnish menace' the Norwegian government had plans for an extension of its borders in the north in the period of 1918–24. In practice, these plans were brought to nothing when, early in 1920, Finland occupied Petsamo, and a little later, forced Soviet Russia to cede the entire border area. The Norwegian government was thus faced with a *fait accompli*. It then attempted to achieve a minor border revision through bilateral negotiations with Finland, but to no avail. By 1924 Norwegian dreams of territorial expansion in the Kola peninsula had definitely come to an end.

The breakdown of these expansionist plans resulted in strategies to reduce contact between Finland and the minority groups in Norway. Border trade, for instance, was reduced to a minimum. This policy also had cultural consequences. Visits by Finnish clergy and politicians and the spread of Finnish literature were greatly restricted in the interwar period. In addition, the state supported the establishment of new settlements in the border areas more actively than before, in order to increase the Norwegian part of the population. Even in recruitment to industry and public office Samis and Kvens were discriminated against in the border regions. The interwar period also saw high priority being given to the development of communications linking isolated Finnish and Sami speaking communities with the rest of Norway and Sweden. In Sweden, too, the authorities wished to attract Swedes as settlers in the border provinces, especially in Norrbotten, but apparently by means of less formal discrimination.

The last group of measures aimed more directly at developing and strengthening Norwegian or Swedish identity among the ethnic groups. Here the language policy in the daily work of the school, and the Church, played a crucial role. In Norway the conscious use of national symbols was also important, including the distribution of portraits of the king and queen and the use of 'Norwegian Romanticism' in the architecture of schools and churches. There was also a free distribution of Norwegian weeklies, and the establishment of libraries and folk high schools, as well as the erection of a radio transmitter in the Kven 'capital' in east Finnmark (Vadsø).

In Norrbotten neither state supported Swedish colonisation nor a screening policy seem to have played any major role. In contrast to Norway, formal job regulations to a certain extent favoured Finnish speaking applicants, if they were equally well qualified. Instead more emphasis was laid on schools, churches and libraries in the swedification process. In the educational context particularly, language policy was regarded as essential. In the 1920s, for instance, the use of Finnish in schools in Norrbotten was ended.[16]

Church Opposition and Loyal Teachers

Until 1900, overt opposition to an assimilation policy came mainly from representatives of the majority community. In Norway the institution that represented the most marked continuity in this respect was the Church. Many clergymen, including some bishops, protested against attempts to make the Church and religious education an instrument of state interests. They argued that the Church had its own goals. The main purpose of the Church was to save souls, not to norwegianise Samis and Kvens. Like Luther, they emphasised the necessity of addressing people in their own language. Such clergymen regarded the Samis as northern Norway's first inhabitants and considered that the state had a special responsibility to protect the interests of a weak indigenous people. While this ethnic group survived they should be entitled to retain their own language. 'It was a question of mitigating their evening hours', said one Church leader.[17] From both a historical and a humanitarian point of view it would be a mistake to force them to abandon their own language and culture. Assimilation ought to be a gradual and more or less natural process. In the religious sphere especially the Samis should be entitled to be educated in their own language.

Yet very few people showed any concern for the Kvens. They were immigrants, not indigenous, and even voices in the Church that aimed to protect the Samis, generally accepted the prevailing attitude that they constituted a menace and had therefore to be norwegianised as soon as possible. On pedagogical and tactical grounds, however, some clergymen argued for a moderate policy of assimilation towards Kvens. As supervisors of education, they knew the pedagogical problems of a brutal norwegianisation policy. 'It was a caricature of education', reported a bishop in the 1930s, and he regretted that the Director of Schools would not change the language policy.[18] In terms of policy towards both Samis and Kvens, some also warned that harsh measures could have the opposite effects from those expected by the authorities. Instead of strengthening national identity, one could risk throwing the two groups into the arms of the neighbouring states, which would create a real security problem.

Another tactical argument concerned the Church more directly. From about 1850, the clergymen had seen that the Samis as well as the Kvens often preferred their own religious assemblies. The Læstadians (a movement named after its founder, a well known Swedish minister and natural scientist) were critical of the clergy and were led by laymen usually speaking in their own language. Through most of this period the Norwegian clergy regarded this movement as a threat both to a united Church and the promotion of Norwegian cultural values. To counteract this Læstadian movement many ministers advocated a more liberal use of Sami and partly also Finnish in school and church services.

The ecclesiastical opposition in Norway reached a peak at the turn of the nineteenth century. The Director of Schools thereafter succeeded in reducing the influence of the Church in school affairs, and also managed to prevent the appointment of a bishop strongly opposed to a policy of norwegianisation, despite the fact that the candidate was supported by the majority of the clergy. Responsibility for this lies with both the teachers of Finnmark and the Director of Schools who, in a personal letter to the Minister of Education warned against 'anarchy in school' and threatened to resign if the priest was elected.[19]

In the interwar period the Church supported norwegianisation more loyally. One bishop's attempt to moderate slightly the methods on pedagogical and tactical grounds failed because, he complained, it proved impossible to prevail over the combined opposition of the school and defence establishment. These groups advocated an even harsher policy of assimilation. Swedish clergymen and bishops initiated and eagerly supported a policy of swedification in schools throughout. Even in Norrbotten, however, church services were frequently held in the mother tongue of the congregation, and several clergymen as well as teachers were of Finnish stock.[20]

All in all in both Sweden and Norway the Church as an institution functioned as an instrument of an official policy of assimilation, especially in the school sector. But many of the Church leaders and ministers had moral reservations, particularly on behalf of the Sami people. Norwegianisation and swedification were therefore not pursued by the Church with the same eagerness and vigour as by the schools. Church attitudes form an interesting contrast to the role of teachers, who constituted a category from which a certain measure of opposition might have been expected. After all they witnessed at first hand the pedagogic shortcomings and the social and personal tragedies that could result from assimilation policies. The fact that teachers in both Sweden and Norway either remained silent or expressed their eager approval of the policy was probably due both to their national liberal–ideological background and to the sanctions that might have been invoked against them.

Party Consensus

An almost astonishing degree of agreement existed among both the central administration and the different political parties, especially in Norway. In Sweden the conservatives and the Agrarian party were generally the strongest supporters of a consistent policy of assimilation while some liberals, and later on also some socialists, argued for moderation and ethnic group rights. One might perhaps have expected strong protests from within the labour movement due to its internationalism and its traditional defence of weak and oppressed groups, but that was not the case. The socialists in Norway and Sweden were generally no champions of the cause of the minorities; most of them were not even interested in ethnic problems.

Although it was easier for members of the ethnic groups to make a political career within the Labour party, the socialists generally supported norwegianisation and swedification, and in conflicts between Sami reindeer herders and Norwegian fisher-farmers over pastures they generally sided with the latter. Even socialists were influenced by the ruling ideologies of the time – nationalism and social Darwinism. No change of policy occurred when a Labour government came to power in Norway in 1935. In Sweden, however, a social democratic government modified the language policy in Norrbotten in the 1930s.[21]

In the interwar years we have to go to the small Swedish Communist party and to a Norwegian socialist group at Oslo University (called 'Mot Dag') to find an opposition within the majority population based entirely on pluralist cultural ideas, which took both Kvens and Samis into consideration.

Ethnic Opposition and Mobilisation

Opposition to a policy of assimilation among Samis and Kvens was never either vigorous or well organised. However, the sources on which this conclusion is based, are naturally flawed. The minorities had few opportunities to organise any resistance. All the odds were against them. They faced language difficulties and lacked proper organisation and social status. Very few of them went to secondary schools. Nevertheless, it can be documented that even in the latter half of the nineteenth century several individual Samis and Finnish speakers did protest against the repression of their language in school and church and that some parents also withheld their children from education.

Around 1905, some Sami associations appeared both in Norway and Sweden, to the surprise of the authorities. This Sami mobilisation could be considered a reaction against the discriminatory policies and nationalism of the majority population in order to protect both their cultural and economic interests. Their spokesmen were often teachers fighting vigorously for the survival of Sami culture as well as for the protection of reindeer breeding against the expansion of modern agriculture and industry. Such demands met with little understanding from the majority population. But one remarkable aim was achieved. In 1906 the Sami movement succeeded in getting a Sami socialist elected to the Norwegian parliament with the slogan, 'Norway, be just to the Samis'!

It is interesting that in Sweden many of the Sami leaders protested vehemently against the primitive nomad schools because they offered the Sami children less teaching than the ordinary primary school. Swedish was also normally the dominant or sole language of instruction. Many Sami leaders also opposed government efforts to split the Sami people into different categories and treat them differently. From the beginning, influential Sami leaders argued on the basis of a pluralist culture. Some of them were well acquainted with similar minority problems in other parts of Europe. It may safely be said that they were ahead of their time, with ideas that are in focus today. However, there were also Sami leaders and groups that recommended restraint and more moderate cultural claims.

In Norway some Sami leaders even presented plans for a completely independent Sami school system where the administrative and teaching personnel had to be of Sami stock, and the teaching of all Sami children was to be in the mother tongue. They should be taught Norwegian only from the age of 12 and then as a foreign language. Ideas promoted by Sami leaders were thus based on ethnic equality, a certain right to self-determination and justice. It should come as no surprise that Norwegian school authorities attacked and ridiculed such radical plans. 'The Samis were too weak', commented the Director of Schools in the 1920s.[22] It can fairly be said that indifference was a normal Sami reaction. Extreme poverty, conflicting economic interests (reindeer against farming interests) and severe organisational problems made it difficult to mobilise a genuine grass roots movement. Indeed after 1925 the Sami movement almost disappeared from the political scene and no new mobilisation took place until the 1960s.

Even less is known about Finnish resistance, apart from the fact that in both countries some Finnish speakers protested vehemently against suspicions that they nourished unnational attitudes. Neither in Sweden nor Norway did any 'pro-Finnishness' exist in the form of separatist aspirations. There was little contact with the Greater Finland movement. Leading Finnish speakers dissociated themselves openly from its ideas and they seemed greatly concerned to demonstrate their loyalty to their host country. Those who expressed an opinion on this matter mostly accepted the process of gradual and considerate assimilation. Finnish speakers also never organised themselves to protect their economic and cultural interests, except on a religious basis in the Læstadian movement. Finally, the official nightmare of a joint Sami and Finnish cultural and political protest never materialised. Their backgrounds and interests were too different. The relatively limited opposition must also be considered in the light of the countermeasures instigated by the authorities. It was, as one clergyman bitterly commented to a friend in the Foreign Ministry in the 1930s, 'almost dangerous to discuss the policy of norwegianisation'.[23] He was himself spied on and castigated by the Director of Schools in Finnmark.

Outcomes and Effects[24]

An important impact of the coordinated offensive to assimilate the minorities, particularly during the interwar years, can be seen through regional development. There is every reason to believe that the most 'exposed' border areas in Sweden and Norway enjoyed a more generous share of state funds for schools and churches, as well as communications, colonisation, border supervision and defence than they would otherwise have received. In Norway most of the Kvens, as well as many of the Samis along the coastline, were more or less assimilated by the end of the 1930s. Thus the Norwegian example clearly demonstrates that a minority policy can contribute to the dissolution as well as help to protect and develop a culture. The Finnish language and culture in Norway died to a certain extent. In Sweden the Finnish and Sami languages were also on the defensive, but in Tornedalen the larger Finnish speaking group was more resistant to a swedification policy. Moreover the measures taken in Sweden were never so consistent and severe as in Norway.

By contrast, the position of Sami culture generally appeared to be different. It proved to be considerably more resistant than the authorities ever expected, in particular in the inner parts of Finnmark and in the main reindeer districts of northern Sweden, even though elsewhere in Sweden Sami culture often lost ground, as the authorities had intended. The Sami resistance might partly be attributed to the fact that throughout the period the policy of assimilation was focused on the Finns. Some consideration had to be shown to a weak indigenous people that apparently represented less of a security risk than the Finns. Norwegian and Swedish impact was also more restricted in the main Sami areas, where both Norwegians and Swedes represented a small and partly isolated upper class. Few state institutions existed apart from some scattered schools and churches. Another important difference is found in the fact that the Finns were more integrated into the Norwegian and Swedish economy and way of life than the Samis. Although only a small Sami minority can be identified with reindeer breeding, this traditional occupation was still very important for preserving and developing Sami culture.

The precise role of the school in the assimilation process is difficult to evaluate and is also a controversial issue in the scholarly debate. It is difficult to separate schooling from other factors influencing the ethnic situation and to distinguish between short term and long term effects. On the whole, state authorities in both Sweden and Norway tended to overestimate the possibilities and benefits of schooling in the assimilation process. In the nineteenth century, school and church were in many places the only state institutions in a position to influence the Sami and Finnish speaking populations. Yet the restricted teaching and curriculum offered, the many unqualified teachers, the shortage of relevant and efficient schoolbooks and the low school attendance all contributed to reduce the influence of primary education. From the end of the nineteenth century, however, more attention was paid to developing the school sector. A modern and extended compulsory school system was now introduced, new state boarding schools were built in the peripheral borderlands and school administration was strengthened and secularised. This development necessarily offered new opportunities for influencing and controlling the assimilation process. It is, however, reasonable to consider that the total effect of the modernisation process, including education, was to accelerate the assimilation of the Samis and Finns. Undoubtedly the effects of education on schoolchildren and their parents were greater in the twentieth century than before. In relative terms, however, the efforts of the schools to continue the assimilation process probably diminished through time.

Also, on the deficit side one should not forget that a more assimilative educational policy tended to provoke more resentment. After all, an expansion of schooling advanced the opportunities for talented Sami and Finnish speaking pupils to complete higher education and some of the educated Samis and Finns later became spokesmen for extended minority rights. When studying educational policies *vis-à-vis* ethnic minority groups it is therefore necessary to distinguish sharply between the policy making and what actually happened at the local level and in the classrooms. It must not be forgotten that many Samis and Finns failed at school. They had no social reference and were unable to learn both their own and the Norwegian or Swedish language properly. The result was the development of semi-lingualism. Sustained cultural oppression, in and out of schools, resulted in many Samis and Finns developing a tendency to conceal their own identity. Overall, therefore, more research into the educational experience is needed.

Summary: Nordic and European Perspectives

Right up to the time of the Second World War Norwegian and Swedish minority policy may appear rigorous and highly discriminatory. This policy becomes more comprehensible, however, in the context of the European scene: it was the child of the ideology and *Realpolitik* prevailing in a definite historical epoch. Nevertheless, it may sound surprising that it proved possible to carry out a policy of assimilation so consistently over a period of a century, making few, if any concessions to the new European thinking on minority problems. Norway and Sweden were members of the League of Nations, and often championed the cause of minorities in this forum. Yet, neither of them admitted that they had minorities within their own boundaries and that the minority rights of Samis and Finns were set aside. The few who tried to implant new ideas were in their own generation crying in the wilderness.

The ethnic policies of Russia and Finland towards the Samis were not so precisely defined. In the sparsely populated border areas of north-western Russia a minority policy of non-intervention and indifference was dominant in the tsarist epoch. In fact, most Russian Samis were illiterate well into the interwar period. Partly due to increasing colonisation, the first primitive schools on the Kola peninsula were erected by the Orthodox Church in the last decades of the nineteenth century, with the primary aim being to produce faithful subjects and believers. Education was in the Russian language up to the 1920s. At that time the new Bolshevik regime started partly to spread Marxism–Leninism to the national minorities in their mother tongues, and the Sami culture and language were now to some extent supported by 'socialist' educational policies. On the other hand, reindeer keeping was collectivised and nomadism was brought to an end. Many Russian Samis, however, still speak a Sami dialect and possess a distinct culture today.[25]

In northern Finland, too, increasing colonisation made it difficult for the Samis to maintain the traditional ways of life. Gradually the Samis were forced northwards by Finnish settlers, and nomadism came to an end. Reindeer breeding was opened for other groups in contrast to the Swedish and Norwegian preferential treatment of the Samis in that respect. The assimilation process was also supported by educational policy. The Finnish language and Finnish speaking teachers dominated schools in the Sami regions. However, especially in the districts of Utsjok and Enare, where the Samis constituted a major group, Sami was used as the language of instruction in the lower grades or, more usually, as a supporting language. Language policy changed slightly from time to time, from district to district and from school to school according to the knowledge and attitudes of local teachers and clergymen and their regional superiors. In the interwar period some limited efforts were undertaken to educate Sami speaking teachers and to prepare Sami textbooks.[26]

Taken as a whole, Swedish and Norwegian minority educational policies were fairly similar up to the turn of the century – until the dissolution of the union in 1905. From then on they went different ways. The swedification policy *vis-à-vis* the Samis was now considerably modified. Several 'nomad schools' were opened with Sami subjects, even though Sami was the language of instruction to a limited extent. However, Samis that left Samiland or entered other occupations were still to be assimilated into the Swedish nation. The result was that in Sweden an assimilationist policy competed with a mildly segregationist one.

The policy pursued by the Swedish state *vis-à-vis* the Finnish speaking population in Tornedalen, the area bordering on Finland, for a long time revealed many parallels with Norwegian policy *vis-à-vis* the Kvens. A policy of swedification was initiated at about the same time and special emphasis was put on schooling. This intensified and culminated around the turn of the century. In Sweden, as in Norway, defence policy was probably the main consideration. Measures aimed at countering the Russian–Finnish and later the Finnish 'menace' were more or less the same, that is, a definite language policy in the schools and the efforts to modernise and integrate the periphery areas by means of improved communications and industrial development.

But despite similar educational practices, Swedish policy towards the Finnish speaking population never became as rigorously comprehensive and coordinated as the Norwegian. Furthermore, a number of Norwegian measures existed for which no parallel was found on the Swedish side. In Sweden there was no discrimination against the Finnish population in the allocation of land and jobs. In fact, to some extent Finnish speakers were given preference. Even though the Church played an important role in swedification in the schools, its religious activities were organised along the lines of the Lutheran tradition. In 1902 it actually insisted that the clergy in the border areas should be able to speak Finnish. One other change that took place in Swedish educational policy in the 1930s, under a Labour government, was not followed up in Norway. In 1935, despite strong local opposition, the Swedish government facilitated the use of Finnish as an optional subject in secondary schools and in 1937 Swedish and Finnish foreign ministers agreed on the principle of bilingualism in Tornedalen. All in all, the continuity in Norway's minority policy, including education, in the north is remarkable in the light of the farreaching national and political changes during this period. Three changes of regime occurred in Norway. In 1884 parliamentarism was introduced; in 1905 full independence was achieved; and in 1935 the first Labour government came into power.

How are the differences between the two countries to be explained? Firstly it is necessary to bear in mind that Norway and Sweden had separate governments under the union and therefore separate policies, even though differences in the minority policy of the two countries were limited, until the termination of the union. The most important explanation for the more relaxed Swedish approach both before and after 1900 must be that militarily and economically Sweden was in a stronger position than Norway. The more rigorous Norwegian policy can also be seen in the light of the dissolution of the union and the wave of nationalism sweeping the country before and after 1905. On the domestic level, this nationalism was directed against 'foreign' nationalities. Besides, Swedish authorities had long maintained closer political and cultural contacts with Finland than had Norway. This meant that Swedish authorities generally were in a better position to undertake a realistic appraisal of the Finnish policies, and in particular of the influence of the Greater Finland movement. This goes a long way to explaining the harsh Norwegian policy towards the Kvens. Although Norwegian authorities feared the neutrality, even the disloyalty, of a majority of the Sami in case of a border conflict, the policies towards this minority group had other and presumably more important motives, including Social Darwinism and nationalism. The road to survival and progress was through Norwegian culture.

Security motives alone cannot offer a satisfactory explanation of assimilation policies directed at both ethnic minority groups. In Sweden such policies had to compete with a 'humanitarian' policy of segregation after the turn of the century. A reasonable theory would be that without the Russian and Finnish 'menaces' the policies of norwegianisation and swedification *vis-à-vis* the Sami people would not have been pursued rigorously over such a long period. On the other hand, experience shows that it was often difficult to discriminate between Finns and Samis in the ethnic and cultural sense such as many clergymen and also some politicians wanted. This was due, among other things, to such factors as intermarriage, bilingualism, common places of habitation, and so on.

After 1945, Norwegian and Swedish minority policies have in many respects changed fundamentally due to developments on both the international and national scene. The problem of securing the border no longer appeared to have played any role in the context of the minority policies. After Hitlerism and the holocaust, racist ideologies were totally discredited. The idea of a pluralist society has gradually established itself. The post-war period thus shows a change in favour of support of Sami and Finnish culture in the two countries, not least in the school system. However, there are still many political and practical problems to be overcome.

Notes:

1. Aarseth; Nickul (1977).
2. Eriksen and Niemi, pp. 30–33.
3. Slunga, pp. 16–30.
4. Eriksen and Niemi, pp. 324–8, 347.
5. *Morgenbladet*, 10 May 1902.
6. Otnes, pp. 23 f.; Gjessing (1973), p. 103.
7. Eriksen and Niemi, p. 331.
8. *Ibid.*, pp. 317–50.
9. Niemi and Salvesen, pp. 63–7.
10. *Ibid.*, pp. 67–72.
11. Slunga, pp. 33–57; 61; 65; 86–7; 130–40; 151–3; 173; Eriksen and Niemi, pp. 37–8; 86; 347–9; Jaakkola, pp. 40–3.
12. Ruong, pp. 185–8.
13. Eriksen and Niemi, p. 59.
14. Hoem (1976a); Hoem (1976b).
15. Eriksen and Niemi, pp. 333–8.
16. Slunga, pp. 173–80.
17. Eriksen and Niemi, p. 325.
18. *Ibid.*, p. 266.
19. Norwegian Public Record Office (Oslo), KUD. A. Kontoret for kirke og geistlighet. Bispevalg. Pk. 326.
20. Slunga, p. 175.
21. *Ibid.*, pp. 135–6; Eriksen and Niemi, pp. 279–305.
22. Lind Meløy, p. 103.
23. Eriksen and Niemi, p. 261.
24. *Ibid.*, pp. 341–3.
25. Eidlitz; Grannes.
26. Nickul (1977) p. 54; Nickul (1952).

Select Bibliography

History and Historiography (in English or with an English summary)

Aarseth, B. (1973), 'Language Minority Problems in Education', in *Interscola*, Alta.
Barth, F. ed. (1970), *Ethnic Groups and Boundaries*, Bergen-Oslo-London.
Eidheim, H. (1974), *Aspects of the Lappish Minority Situation*, Oslo.
Eriksen, K.E. and Niemi E. (1981), *Den finske fare. Sikkerhetsproblemer og minoritets-politikk 1860–1940* (The Finnish Menace, Security Problems and Minority Policy in the North 1860–1940), Oslo-Bergen-Tromsø.
Gjessing, G. (1954), *Changing Lapps*, London.
Jernsletten, R. (1986), 'The Land Sales Act of 1902 as a Means of Norwegianization', in *Acta Borealia*, A Norwegian Journal of Circumpolar Societies, no. 1.
Minde, H. (1985), 'The Sami Movement, the Norwegian Labour Party and Sami Rights', in *XVIth International Congress of Historical Science*, Stuttgart.
Nickul, K. (1952), 'Report on Lapp Affairs', *Fennia*, 76:3, Helsingfors.

84   SCHOOLING, EDUCATIONAL POLICY AND ETHNIC IDENTITY

Nickul, K. (1977), *The Lappish Nation*, Bloomington.
Niemi, E. (1980), 'Immigration from Northern Finland and Sweden to Northern Norway in the 19th century', in *Siirtolaisuus – Migration*, 1.
Salvesen, H. (1980), 'Tendenser i den historiske sameforskning – med særlig vekt på politikk og forskning', ('Trends in historical Sami Research – with special emphasis on Politics and Research'), in *Scandia. Tidsskrift for historisk forskning*, 1.
Thuen, T. (ed.) (1980), *Samene – urbefolkning og minoritet* (The Samis – Indigenous People and Minority), Oslo-Bergen-Tromsø.

History and Historiography (only in Norwegian or Swedish)

Bjørklund, I. (1985), *Fjordfolket. Fra samisk utkant til norsk utkant 1550–1980* (The Fjord People. From Sami Periphery to Norwegian Periphery 1550–1980), Oslo.
Dahl, H. (1957), *Språkpolitikk og skolestell i Finnmark 1814 til 1905* (Language Policy and Schooling in Finnmark 1814 to 1905), Oslo.
Eidlitz, K. (1979), *Revolutionen i norr. Om sovjetetnografi och minoritetspolitik* (The Revolution in the North. About Soviet Anthropology and Minority Policy), Uppsala.
Gjengset, G.H. (ed.) (1981), *Samisk mot – norsk hovmot* (Sami Courage and Norwegian Arrogance), Oslo.
Gjessing, G. (1973), *Norge i sameland* (Norway in Samiland), Oslo.
Grannes, A. (1974) 'Samane i Sovjetunionen' (The Samis in Soviet Union'), in *Syn og Segn*, 9–10, Oslo.
Hirsti, R. (1980), *Samisk fortid, nåtid, fremtid* (Sami Past, Present and Future), Oslo.
Hansegård, N.E. (1968), *Tvåspråkighet eller halvspråkighet?* (Bilingualism or Confusion of two Languages?), Stockholm.
Hoem, A. (1976), *Makt og kunnskap* (Power and Knowledge), Oslo.
Hoem A. (1976), *Yrkesfelle, sambygding, same eller norsk?* (Occupation, Fellow Villager, Sami or Norwegian?), Oslo.
Homme, L. (ed.) (1969), *Nordisk nykolonialisme* (Nordic Neo-Imperialism), Oslo.
Jaakkola, M. (1973), *Språkgransen. En studie i tvåspråkighetens sociologi* (The Language Border. A Study of Bilingual Sociology), Stockholm.
Klockare, S. (1972), 'Norrbotniska språkstriden 1888–1958' ('The Struggle about Language in Norrbotten 1888–1958'), in *Finska språket i Sverige* (The Finnish Language in Sweden), Stockholm.
Küng, A. (ed.) (1970), *Samemakt! Välfärd till döds eller kulturellt folkmord?* (Sami Power. Welfare to Death or Cultural Genocide?), Stockholm.
Lind Meløy L. (1980), *Internatliv i Finnmark. Skolepolitikk 1900–1940* (Boarding Schools in Finnmark. Educational Policy 1900–1940), Oslo.
Niemi E. and Salvesen H. (1987), 'Samene og kvenene/finnene i minoritetspolitisk perspektiv' ('The Samis and Kvens/Finns in Minority Political Perspective'), in *Rapporter til den XX nordiske historikerkongress*, vol. II, Reykyavik.
Otnes, P. (1970), *Den samiske nasjon* (The Sami Nation), Oslo.
Ruong, I. (1975), *Samerna* (The Samis), Stockholm.
Svensson, T.G. (1973), *Samernas politiska organisation* (The Political Organisation of the
Samis), Stockholm.
Schwarz, D. (ed.) (1971), *Identitet och minoritet. Teori och politik i dagens Sverige* (Identity
and Minority. Theory and Politics in Present Sweden), Stockholm.
Slunga, N. (1965), *Staten och den finskpråkiga befolkningen i Norrbotten* (The State and the Finnish speaking Population in Norrbotten), Luleå.
Svonni, L. (ed.) (1974), *Samerna – ett folk i fyra lander* (The Samis – A People in four Countries), Uppsala.
Tanner, V. (1929), *Skolt–lapparna* (The Skolt–Samis), Helsingfors.

Tønneson, S. (1972), *Retten til jord i Finnmark* (The Right to Land in Finnmark), Bergen-Oslo-Tromsø.

Uppman, B. (1978), *Samhallet och samerna 1897–1925* (The Society and the Samis 1897–1925), Umeå.

Vorren Ø. and Manker E. (1976), *Samekulturen* (The Sami Culture), Oslo.

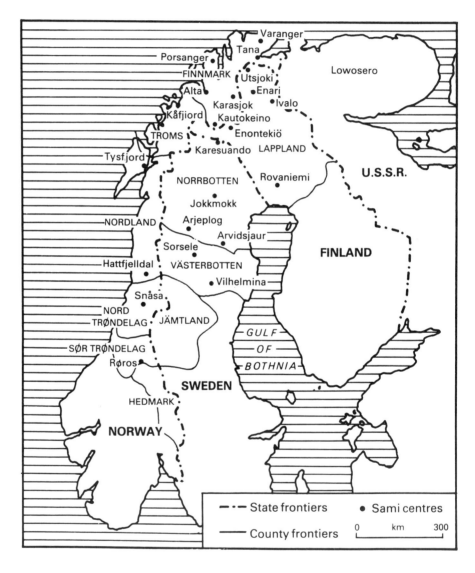

Map 4.1 Sapmi and some Sami centres
Source: Nina Hveen Carlsen 1988

5 Educational Policy in Finland under Russian Domination, 1850–1917

MARTTI T. KUIKKA

Introduction

In examining school policy in Finland between 1850 and 1917, one has to remember that the country was linked to Sweden until 1809, so that Swedish and Finnish school policies developed on similar lines. However, it was during this Swedish period that Finland had first begun to establish her own educational system, with the Lutheran Church being responsible for public instruction from the Reformation onwards. The country's first university had been established in Turku in 1640 but was later moved to Helsinki in 1828. The first grammar schools had been founded in the Middle Ages, but it was only during the eighteenth century that a network of such schools began to develop.

When Finland eventually became connected with the Russian empire in 1809, she retained many Nordic features and both her laws and culture were greatly influenced by those of the Scandinavian countries. In 1809 the tsar undertook to keep intact earlier Swedish legislation. Gradually a central administration took shape, the central organ of which was the senate, although in 1809 Finland was also given her own *diet*, the members of which were to be allowed to make proposals for the development of different aspects of society. However the tsar did not actually convene this *diet* until 1863 and it was only then that it began to function regularly.

As the map shows[1] Finland's boundaries remained more or less constant between the years 1850 and 1917, but during that period many Finns could also be found in the other Nordic countries as well as in Canada, the USA and Russia itself, especially in Russian Karelia.

Though Finland, like other Nordic countries, is relatively homogeneous linguistically, during the time of autonomy under the tsar (1809–1917) there were three official languages, Swedish, Russian and Finnish. There would still be two official languages – Finnish and

Swedish – even after the gaining of independence. In 1870 there were 1.9 million Finns, of whom 88 per cent were Finnish speakers and 11 per cent Swedish speaking. Other language groups have always been extremely small. In 1920 the Sami people of Lapland, for example, numbered only 3000 (see the chapter by Knut Eriksen). Finland has three religious groupings. Most of the population are members of the Lutheran Church. In 1870 its membership stood at 1.8 million (98 per cent of the population) while 18 437 were Orthodox (0.9 per cent) and 566 Catholics (0.02 per cent). By 1920 the numbers were Lutheran 98 per cent, Orthodox 1.7 per cent and the Catholics 0.01 per cent.

In this article I shall concentrate on educational policy in Finland between 1850 and 1917; that is, the latter part of the period of autonomy before Finland gained her full independence from Russia in 1917. Naturally, educational policies formed only one part of the general development of Finnish society and it should be borne in mind that other aspects of Finnish history have been analysed from other viewpoints by colleagues taking part in the ESF project. (See the contributions by Tore Modeen, Max Engman, Risto Alapuro, Osmo Jussila.) The most important sources for this article are to be found in Finnish archives, especially the National Archive. This means that the picture given here is one based on Finnish sources. Documents in the Leningrad archives would, no doubt, provide a rather different view of events but I have not had an opportunity to consult them.

The Period before 1850 – Static Conservatism

The new administrative system that grew up after 1809 meant that the development of educational policy was in the hands of the Senate and its office. At the same time, much depended also on the actions of the governor general and on how proposals were actually presented to the tsar in whose hands any final decision on educational matters rested.

The educational policies of the senate between 1809 and 1855 were predominantly conservative, and the period saw not merely the development of the senate itself but also of the central administrative boards. Indeed, this was later to be referred to as the period of bureaucratisation, a period during which the officials and the tsar had similar aims and wished to cooperate in making political decisions without involving the *diet*. During the 1820s and 1830s the senate effectively prevented any educational reform. During this period Finland was still a static society, reflecting a long established set of social divisions, and it was the senate's intention that each 'estate' in society should arrange its own educational affairs relatively independently. Moreover, all developments in Finland had to be related to the general policies of the Russian empire in which defence, internal security, foreign policy, opinion control and the repression of revolutionary tendencies all played a prominent role.

Discussion of school policy revived in Finland during the 1830s and continued until the events of 1848. The growing revival of interest in Finnish culture required open discussion. The Finnish Literature Society was founded in 1831, and the first publication of the national epic 'Kalevala' took place in 1835. Policies for public education, vocational education and teacher training were all matters for keen public discussion. An influx of ideas from foreign countries was manifest in Finnish newspapers. One particular influence was scandinavianism. Cultural contacts with Scandinavia were close, while pedagogical ideas came from Germany and Switzerland. Russian civil servants were well aware of the effects of scandinavianism on the development of political ideas in Finland, given her earlier connections with Scandinavia, and of the fact that they reflected the aim of eventually separating Finland from Russia.

Such ideas were met by a firm conservatism. During the time of Tsar Nicholas I (1825–55), Russian universities were kept under strict control and regulation. The Christian faith and the predominating social system were the cornerstones of public education.[2] This conservatism reached its peak following 1848. Censorship was instituted in 1850 and a further ominous sign appeared in 1853 when a committee recommended that public education should be placed under the control of the police authorities.

The Period of Liberalism

The concept of liberalism has many meanings in the history of Finland. Liberalism in a political sense began to spread in 1848 – and especially among the students of Helsinki University – once the news of the February revolution reached Finland, while later influences came from Britain. Liberalism gained followers and a newspaper, *Helsingfors Dagblad* (Helsinki Daily) became their organ. During the 1860s, while followers of liberalism did not establish their own political party, they tried to exert an influence through the various social estates in the *diet* and the senate. These liberals had as their slogan, 'One nation, two languages'. Their social aim was to turn the *diet* into an institution that was convened regularly and exerted some authority. They hoped they could develop, by this means, a greater degree of local self-government and could liberate the country's economic life from government control. During the 1860s, liberalism found support among both language groups but not among the so-called *Fennomen* (the Finnish speaking nationalist party) who saw in the language question a major issue of social importance.

Educational policies in Finland had undergone a major change in 1856 when the new Tsar Alexander II visited Finland and presented the senate with a major development programme for society as a whole. One section of this concerned public education. The programme had been prepared by Finnish civil servants who understood both the tsar's ideals and the nature of Finnish society. It was seen in Finland as a manifestation of liberalism, stressing the importance of unrestricted economic activity and the education of the individual.[3]

Plans for elementary education advanced quickly in the years 1856–1858. The senate began by seeking the opinions of the chapters in the various dioceses and then sought the views of citizens generally on the question of public education. On the basis of these investigations, the senate made proposals and the tsar accepted these Guidelines for Public Education in 1858. According to the new law, elementary education was the responsibility of the parents and the home. The local parish was to be responsible for organising schools, or Sunday Schools, where the home could not provide such basic teaching. The aims of public education were: to develop morality; to promote general welfare, a good rounded education and an amount of useful knowledge. This law had many liberal characteristics: the local administration of elementary schooling, for example, was to be autonomous.

This meant that each commune would decide independently how elementary schools should be established, and the move formed part of a general reform of local government that took place in 1865. At the same time, each elementary school was given its own Board, and would thus have a chance to make decisions on its own internal affairs. The 1858 act had already provided for the founding of a National Board of Education as the central organ of administration. By such means, overall control of both elementary and grammar school education was to be transferred from the Church to the state, thus involving a reformulation of the Church/state relationship in Finland. It meant that the state accepted responsibility for ensuring that elementary education was provided. The law also directed that before any final decision was made on the shape of Finnish elementary education, a person should be designated who would make himself familiar with foreign models and would draw up a proposal for the establishment of a system of public education in Finland. In other words, this meant opening a door towards Europe.

The pedagogical reform of teacher training had already begun at the beginning of the 1850s, and in 1852, a chair in pedagogy and didactics, directed especially towards the training of grammar school teachers, had been established in the University of Helsinki, the first professorship of its kind in any Nordic university. The law of 1858 had also provided for the foundation of a teacher training system for elementary teachers in Finland. The senate chose a clergyman, Uno Cygnaeus, to be the planner required by the act, and in accordance with his commission, he visited Sweden, Prussia, Switzerland and Austria, investigating their educational systems and exploring pedagogical trends. His tour took place in 1858–59 and his proposals for the organisation of Finnish elementary education were made in 1860. These proposals clearly display the extent to which his pedagogical and religious thinking was influenced by liberalism. The ideas of Pestalozzi, Froebel and Diesterweg were much in evidence in his proposals, which a committee of the senate studied before drawing up a bill on elementary education and teacher training which was eventually passed in 1862, a bill clearly based on the values to be found in Finnish society and culture.

The tsar accepted the law dealing with teacher education in 1863 and that dealing with public education in 1866.[4] The latter showed evidence of having been influenced by many aspects of liberal politics. The language of instruction, for example, would be chosen independently in each locality so that Finnish and Swedish speaking populations would both have their own elementary schools. The only obligatory language at the primary stage was to be the mother tongue, while the teaching of the other national language remained optional. The Russian language was not to be taught at that stage. Each school in rural areas would have its own Board which would make decisions about, for example, the curriculum of the school and could select its own teachers.

During the 1860s, liberalism also manifested itself in Finland in a number of other ways. The development of the grammar schools, for example, took a new turn. Finnish speakers, hitherto forced to seek such education in Swedish speaking institutions, now demanded their own schools and in 1859, the first such Finnish speaking grammar school was opened in Jyväskylä. As early as the 1840s, the teachers in such schools had asked permission unsuccessfully to found their own professional union. In 1860 they were allowed, for the first time, to call a general meeting of the profession every three years, and the first such meeting proved a success. It decided to establish a pedagogical association and to launch a pedagogical journal. In a statement on educational policy, the teachers emphasised the need for truly independent grammar schools and separation from the Church. Such meetings of teachers became more common during the 1860s. Uno Cygnaeus also made himself familiar with meetings of elementary school teachers in Switzerland, and clearly considered them very important events. In his initial proposals, in 1860, he had incorporated the idea of regular teachers' meetings and in 1867, he helped to organise the first meeting dealing with primary education, bringing together teachers from both the training colleges and the elementary schools.[5]

Liberalism was also apparent in the way the administrative system developed, and a regulation of vital importance was that of 1863, which made Finnish an official language. However, the implementation of this measure aroused the opposition of Finnish speakers. According to the act of 1863, grammar schools were to have two teaching languages but the school committee of 1865 opposed this on pedagogical grounds. Each school, they believed, should have only one teaching language, Finnish or Swedish. As far as the elementary schools were concerned each commune could decide which language, depending on the dominance of any particular one in the locality, provided the general meeting of teachers agreed. The *diet* also intervened, proposing the establishment and development of Finnish language grammar schools. The tsar decided, in 1870, to establish a committee to investigate the matter. Its brief was to discover whether the Finnish language had developed to a sufficiently high level to make it a suitable vehicle for advanced scientific teaching.

In Finland there was astonishment among Finns, who saw that the tsar's decision indicated some change in political direction. The committee included representatives of both the *Fennomen* and *Svecomen* (Swedish speaking nationalist party). In the event, the National Board of Education and later the senate, accepted the opinion of the *Svecomen* and in an act of 1871, it was decreed that the teaching language in elementary schools should be that of the majority of the local inhabitants but that the senate would decide on the teaching language in grammar schools and *Realschulen* (non-classical commercially-orientated secondary schools). However in such schools there was to be only one teaching language, either Finnish or Swedish.[6]

One important sign of liberalism was the decision of the tsar to convene the Finnish *diet* in 1863. In that *diet* the estates had two important aims: to augment their own privileges and to reinforce the special position of Finland. An important aim was the reinforcement of the independence of local communities, and this eventually was achieved by the law on Local Administration, which the tsar accepted in 1865, so far as rural communes were concerned, and in 1873 for the towns.

Another important sign of liberalism was the new Church law of 1869 which changed the position of the Lutheran Church. No longer was it to enjoy a monopoly as the only recognised Church in the state. Other denominations were also to be officially tolerated. On the other hand, the Lutheran Church was given its own administrative organ, the Church Assembly, in which laymen had significant represent- ation alongside the clergy. It brought with it a new conception of the Church involving the transfer of the control of schools to the state.

At the same time, many restrictions were also being swept away in the economic sphere. In the economic history of Finland, this period is referred to as the period of modernisation, during which the aim was to remove limitations of mercantilism. For example, the guild system was abolished in 1868. Freedom of trade and industry was further decisively extended in 1879. This positive economic develop- ment accelerated in the 1870s, and the sawmill and paper industries in particular grew quickly as exports were more and more directed towards central Europe. However, industrialisation proceeded rather differently in Finland when compared with Sweden and other parts of western Europe. Development was relatively slow, and Finland remained a predominantly agricultural country. At the end of the nineteenth century the number of wage earners was still continuing to increase at the same rate in both industry and agriculture.

Even so, these new economic developments had many effects on Finnish society and its hitherto static structures underwent a change. This economic freedom also had an effect on the workings of Finnish democracy. For instance, a culture that had been based on the differences between the old groupings of society began to break down. Money and property were the new criteria for evaluating social status. In the towns, the status of the bourgeoisie was thus continually rising. In the countryside, the economic position of the independent farmers was consolidated, and they were given fresh chances to influence educational, cultural and political affairs. In addition, political developments wiped out the earlier distinction between the four estates on which Finnish society had been based. According to Heikki Ylikangas, it was the reform of economic legislation that accelerated these changes; reform that was greater in that sphere than in other areas of the national life between 1856 and 1879. The mercantile system was swept away, to be replaced by an emphasis on the rights of the individual. Liberalism emphasised private ownership, the freedom to make contracts, the independent activity of individuals, freedom of movement and private enter- prise.[7]

Throughout this period of political development the actual number of elementary schools increased very slowly and, during the 1860s, very few schools were founded. It seems that the founding of such schools was greatly affected by the availability of financial resources. Communes were very cautious about accepting state assistance, which was seen as likely to infringe communal independence and the commune's right to make its own decisions. When, in the 1867 *diet*, the appropriations for elementary schools were debated, the representatives of the farmers and the clergy were among those suggesting cuts. Because the communes proved cautious, it was, in fact, common for the establishment of schools to be initiated by private individuals and it was only at a later stage that they became the responsibility of the commune as such. Such individuals included clergy, farmers and factory owners, while in some areas groups of individuals came together to form school associations in order to foster the establishment of a school. One explanation for the tsar's liberal policies in Finland lay in political developments elsewhere in Europe. He no doubt wanted not only to pacify the Finns but also to make Finland a political 'showcase' to impress western Europeans worried by the measures he had taken in Poland during the 1860s.

Slavic Policy versus Finnish Nationalism

The first signs of an end to liberalism began to appear at the end of the 1870s. The spirit of liberalism had led to the development of a number of political movements both in Russia and in central Europe. The events of 1863 in Poland and later, in 1865, an attempt on the life of the tsar had changed the political climate and resultant practices. The new Minister for Cultural Affairs, D. Tolstoy, emphasised that henceforth cultural policy was to form part of security policy in Russia. This had an immediate effect in Finland, for it meant that the fair wind of liberalism was coming to an end. The Russian empire and its administration no longer looked favourably on the way Finnish autonomy had been developing. One reason for this change in the political situation was the development of the Slavic movement, one of the many national romantic movements then sweeping Europe, which had had its beginnings in the mid century. Its aim was to base the further development of the Russian empire on a close adherence to Slavic tradition. It stressed the importance of uniformity within the empire and that meant the promotion not only of one language, but also of one religion. The supporters of the Slavic movement revered the Orthodox faith and religion because it seemed to correspond most closely to their own national characteristics. The Slavic and the Orthodox mentalities were believed to be close to one another.

Later, the aims of the movement expanded. It aimed not only at integrating the Slavic world itself but also at extending the Slavic culture to the peoples who lay outside it, that is to foreign 'tribes'. It had in mind particularly those territories that were politically linked with Russia. Their population had to be fully integrated into the Russian culture, and cultural minorities were to be more fully integrated into the empire. In 1869, for example, it was decreed that in Russian Poland the Russian language would henceforth be the language in schools and in official business. In the 1880s many sanctions were also introduced in the Baltic states whenever the Slavic programme appeared to be failing in its objectives. All forms of self-government there were brought to an end. The school systems, the police forces and the courts were all 'Russified' and attempts were made to hinder public activities in the local language. Orthodox priests were actually punished when the local population showed a desire to return to the Lutheran churches. In such ways, an attempt was made to extend the Slavic programme to all sectors of social life – to religion, to cultural activities, to politics, to education, to the judicial system and administration generally.[8]

Tension between this Slavic ideology and Finnish nationalism increased considerably during the 1880s and 1890s. The Finns were unanimously opposed to these Russian policies, though they saw their own internal political problems in quite different terms. Particularly important issues were those of language and of what actually constituted the nation, questions which now began to dominate politics and to divide the members of the *diet* in a new way. Gradually quite new political boundaries began to separate its members.

Whereas in 1869 there had been two main groups, liberals and conservatives, after 1872 new groupings emerged, based on linguistic divisions. The party of the *Fennomen* had many members among the clergy and the farmers, and they aimed at establishing the Finnish language as the language of culture and administration throughout Finland. Such a change, they hoped, would reinforce the feeling of national unity and help to even out differences between the social classes. The *Svecomen* were closer to the old liberals. Most of the leaders of industry and business life were Swedish speaking, and a later development led to the main part of the liberals joining the *Svecomen*. Support from the nobility and the burgesses in the *diet* was very important for this group, and it adopted a quite different language policy from that of the *Fennomen*. They believed that a Finnish state should be allowed to emerge and develop freely and they did not wish to give any special status to the Swedish language as such. Their aim was to keep alive skills in Swedish and other European languages until the Finnish language became a clearly viable vehicle for teaching at university level.

From the point of view of the *Fennomen*, this meant that a conservative Russian government and the Finnish liberals seemed to have much in common so far as language policies were concerned and this led to open conflict. Certainly, there were great differences between the two parties in Finland so far as education was concerned. The Finnish liberals emphasised the study of practical subjects and new languages. For example, an experimental *Realschule* was established, a manifestation of the view of life held by the liberals, for whom private endeavour played a central role. From the point of view of the *Fennomen* such liberal policies seemed actually conservative and repressive, for they meant that those speaking only Finnish could not proceed to higher education – to the university, for example. The grammar schools, which provided the only road to university, had been designed for Swedish speakers, so that Finnish speaking people had usually to be satisfied with a lower level of education. However, the *Fennomen* aimed at providing the same opportunities for the social development of all citizens, the overall aim being the creation of an intellectually and materially independent, self-supporting nation. The school system had a central role to play in this process.[9]

Heikkilä's research suggests that behind all this there lay a different concept of the nation. The *Fennomen* wished to emphasise that a nation is not merely the sum of its members. A nation has its own peculiar national spirit which emerges as an organic totality by way of its language and its history. Therefore, for the *Fennomen*, the concept of the nation had to involve a national language. This concept was especially supported by the farmers and also, in part, by the clergy. The *Fennomen* wished to increase educational opportunities for Finnish speakers so that they could eventually take over the dominant role in national life from the Swedish speaking people, in a way that the census evidence on the relative size of the two language groupings would appear to justify. All this presupposed an improvement in the position of the Finnish language, so as to encourage the development of a body of Finnish speaking civil servants and citizens, all playing their part in the economic life of the country, and including the conversion by education of the lowest, non-landed classes into a body of independent farmers. The Finnish liberals' aims were different. For them, the nation consisted of all those who wished to belong to it. For them, the concept of a fatherland was based on laws and institutions. For them, instead of language, Finland's national identity was to be based on the social system and structures inherited from Sweden.

Alongside these two groupings, *Fennomen* and liberals, a third grouping emerged later, the constitutionalists, who drew their support from among members of both language groups. They shared the view that it was its laws and institutions that formed the basis of Finnish society. It was these that had to be so protected that neither the Russian government nor any political movement emanating from the lower classes could change them. These constitutionalists found their support not only among leading Swedish speaking civil servants, but also among the Swedish–Finnish nobility and the middle classes of the coastal areas.[10]

In the 1870s Russian policy followed the Slavic ideology and this manifested itself in many ways in Finland. When the National Board of Education was established in 1869, a Russian general, Casimir von Kothen, was appointed as its first head. This caused great surprise in Finland, and three years later he was removed from the post. In addition, decision making became more and more centralised. For example, the business of deciding what language should be used by teachers in a particular grammar school was moved from the local level to the senate. During the reign of Tsar Alexander III (1881–94), simple Slavic policies were brought to an end to be replaced by what could be called panSlavic or even panRussian policies which aimed at binding all the Slavic nations into a single political entity under the leadership of Russia. During this period, the tsar did not want to institute any reforms which might cause unrest. The main aim of this policy was to maintain public order and discipline. Thus Russia began increasingly to take on the character of a police state. The aim was to create a political unity whose cornerstones would be Russia, the Orthodox faith and autocracy. The outlying nations were all to be integrated into the same unity, and in Finland, the guardian of the policy was the governor-general.

From 1881 onwards Governor General Heiden attempted to achieve the tsar's aims by adopting a policy of divide and rule. Thus he sided with the *Fennomen* in many of his political decisions by, for instance, offering them official positions and giving recognition to their language programme. His favouring of the Finnish language was explained by the Russian desire to weaken the position of the Swedish language, along with Finland's links with Sweden and the rest of Scandinavia. Despite this, however, the Finns attempted on important issues to maintain a united front against Russia and this, in turn, led to an even greater political tension exacerbated by events abroad. In the 1890s, in reaction to a dramatic increase in Germany's political influence, Russia entered into a military alliance with France. She considered Germany to form a threat to her border states; to the coastal areas of southern Finland for instance. Russia did not necessarily trust the Finns either, but she aimed at keeping them under tighter control than in previous years, especially when it came to military matters.

The economic progress of Finland led to the establishment of many more schools. The number of elementary schools increased continuously from the 1870s onwards as the following table indicates.

Whereas there were in all 109 rural communes without elementary schools in 1886, this number had fallen by 1891 to 54, and by 1898 to seven. However, local circumstances could still provide obstacles to

Table 5.1: Pupils and elementary schools in Finland, 1870–1900 (according to the language of instruction)

	Finnish	Swedish	Finnish and Swedish	Russian	Total
Schools					
1871–2					
a	39	23	7	–	69
b	154	20	2	1	177
1880–1					
a	91	62	3	1	157
b	373	76	7	1	457
Pupils					
1890–1					
a	13 458	5 778	–	30	19 356
b	29 235	5 835	–	117	35 187
1900–01					
a	21 892	7 236	–	23	29 151
b	70 430	12 184	–	–	82 614

Note
a = in towns
b = in the countryside

such a generally favoured development.[11]

One important question concerned the curriculum guidelines for the elementary school. Uno Cygnaeus, the father of the Finnish elementary school who had drawn up the 1860 proposals for an elementary school system, placed great emphasis on the importance of a good general education on the Swiss model. An alternative approach would have taken a more immediately practical line stressing vocational education in the elementary school. In the 1860s and 1870s there was no general elementary school curriculum. Its local shape depended in the countryside on the laymen elected to the board of a particular elementary school, while in the towns it was the responsibility of the municipal school council, also consisting of elected laymen. Nevertheless, in both town and country there was, as a rule, an emphasis on general education as advocated by Cygnaeus. In 1881 the National Board of Education put forward so-called model courses for the elementary school, but these only provided a detailed syllabus for each subject and did not spell out general aims. At that time neither the senate nor the *diet* decided matters of curriculum, leaving such matters for final decision at the local level, a further indication of their liberalism.[12]

As the number of pupils in the elementary schools steadily increased, the schools changed from being single sex to being coeducational establishments. Thus the idea of coeducation came to fruition first in the elementary sector, reaching the grammar school sector only in the 1880s.

The role of the Lutheran Church in society also began to change during the 1870s, following the Church act of 1869. Under this act, despite its new administrative body, the Church Assembly, the Church lost its direct connection with the schools following the separation of the Church and general schooling. This change manifested itself first of all in relation to its administrative role. The clergy had earlier acted as district inspectors of the elementary schools in addition to their religious duties, although a committee in 1882 noted that this arrangement ran contrary to the original principle of community controlled elementary education. Gradually the inspection of elementary schools was transferred from the clergy to a new, specially appointed body of inspectors.

The second change occurred in relation to elementary teaching. The leaders of the Church began to view with some suspicion the work of the teacher training colleges, and of the elementary schools, especially insofar as religious instruction was concerned. They believed that non-Christian liberalism had begun to have a greater effect on elementary teaching. The Church therefore began to develop its own education system, by setting up schools and supporting the training of teachers for those schools. During the 1880s and 1890s, the number of elementary schools increased considerably as well as the number of pupils in both Church and non-Church schools. In fact, the number of pupils in the Church's peripatetic schools was higher than in the communal primary schools, and one interesting detail is that most of the Church schools were established in areas with a majority of Swedish speaking people.[13] At the same time small teacher training establishments were also founded as a support for the Church's peripatetic schools.

The language question also had an effect on teacher training for the elementary schools. The first college, established in 1863 at Jyväskylä was intended for Finnish speaking students. Initiatives for the provision of Swedish speaking colleges were taken only in the senate: the *diet* was not involved. The first initiatives envisaged two colleges, one for women and one for men. Tsar Alexander II accepted this proposal in 1871. At the same time the provision of a further college for Finnish speakers also became a topic of discussion and caught much public attention, because the *diet* as well as the senate and many civil servants were eventually involved in this debate. It was finally decided to establish the new college at Sortavala, a small town in eastern Finland. One reason for this decision was that siting the college there would have a considerable effect on the development of Orthodox culture, not only in the east of the country, but also in other parts of Finland. Until 1880 the official language of the Orthodox Church in Finland was Russian and its services were in that language. Now Finnish Orthodox believers began to demand teaching and schools using Finnish as well as religious services in that language. The establishment of a teacher training college in Sortavala would mean the thwarting of Russian attempts to russify the Orthodox people and the whole territory of Karelia. Teaching there did in fact take place in Finnish and many of the students were Orthodox, thus providing a teaching force for the Orthodox children of Karelia.[14]

As the Russian policies came to be more and more strictly applied in Finland, the *diet* decided to convert elementary education from a voluntary system into a compulsory one. In 1898 they passed an act to this effect and the tsar approved it in the same year. Under the new act the rural communes were obliged to divide the area under their jurisdiction into school districts, so that every child of school age would have the opportunity to be educated in his or her mother tongue. In dual language communities at least one school would have to be set up for the minority language. From the point of view of school policy this act was very important. It increased the opportunity for communities to develop a real municipal school system at the local level.[15]

This new act of 1898 reflected the fact that the Finns aimed at reinforcing their national identity by means of the elementary school. As a result of the act, the number of pupils was likely to increase considerably, and four new teacher training colleges for the elementary sector were established in the 1890s, all for Finnish speaking students. They were situated in small towns in various parts of Finland and became, like the earlier colleges, a key educational factor in Finnish nationalism.

The Policy of Assimilation

Russian policy continued to tighten in Finland throughout the 1890s. This reflected the needs of both internal and foreign policy. In the eyes of the Russian national movement Finland had been given too much autonomy. Meanwhile Finland, in its development, followed the models of western Europe more and more. Economically she had good trade relations with that part of the world, and was not dependent on the Russians, who naturally tried therefore to strengthen their hold on her by other means. The panSlavic movement became increasingly imperialistic, concentrating its attention particularly on south eastern Europe. In her foreign policy, Russia began to emphasise a military approach, and showed less flexibility in her approach to all sorts of issues. Tensions continued to mount in Finland. In Finnish history, indeed, the years 1898 to 1917 are now known as the period of Oppression. It has been analysed in different ways. It was the period of the policy of assimilation, when Russia attempted more and more to assimilate Finland in a political sense. On the other hand, it is also known to Finns as the period of russification, because the Finns felt that the Russian government's measures would gradually lead to Finland losing all her legal safeguards and to her becoming totally Russian.

The decades 1898 to 1917 can be divided into two sub-periods. The first lasted from 1898 to 1906. A new governor general, Nikolai Bobrikov, attempted in every way possible to put into effect an administrative programme which was considered by the Finns to amount to one of russification. Its principles were embodied in what was known as the February Manifesto, promulgated by the tsar in 1899. This affirmed that:

> The Finnish military was to be assimilated into the Russian army. The State Secretariat of Finland was to be abolished. All legislation applying to the rest of the empire was to apply also to Finland. The Russian language was to become the official language of the Finnish senate and of all public offices in Finland and to figure in relevant qualification requirements. The separate Finnish customs system was to be fully assimilated into the Russian administrative system. Finland's separate currency was to be withdrawn. The University of Helsinki and the grammar schools were to be brought under strict control. Official Russian newspapers were to be established in Finland.

One of the means by which assimilation could most readily be brought about was an effective language policy and indeed the next measure was the Language Manifesto of 1900. Under its terms the Russian language was to be used as the administrative language in all public offices in Finland. To bring this about the teaching of Russian was to be expanded to all Finnish grammar schools. The history of Russia and its geography were also to be taught in Russian. The teaching of Russian was not provided in elementary schools, however. There it remained a voluntary activity.[16]

The russification policy naturally provoked considerable Finnish opposition. All Finns were unanimously against such measures as a matter of principle. Even so, they reacted in different ways. Those of a more compliant disposition believed that because Russia's aims apparently remained limited, it might be possible to have discussions with the Russians and to achieve a compromise. In the *diet*, the clergy and the farmers favoured such a policy of compliance. An alternative reaction was that of passive resistance or the constitutionalist line. Its supporters believed that the February Manifesto was merely one manifestation of a systematic policy for the whole Russian empire which might well, in the end, lead to the ruin of Finland. They thought that legal measures should be taken to thwart it. They fought to maintain the constitution of Finland, and thus to keep the control of the senate and of public positions in their own hands. In reaction to the February Manifesto, Finnish attitudes changed, breaking up the pattern of previous political groupings based on language and on the estates of the *diet*, causing new political divisions to emerge. The more conservative elements among the *Fennomen*, the so-called Old Finns, were the main supporters of the compliant line while passive resistance found its main support among the Swedish speaking party, the liberal wing of the former *Fennomen*, the so-called Young Finns and in the newly established Labour party.[17]

What happened in the area of education? The Finns tried more and more actively to develop all areas of their educational system. An important starting point was the feeling embodied in J.V. Snellman's words: 'We cannot accomplish anything with violence; Finland's security is based on Finnish culture'. In protest against the oppression many new grammar schools were founded in the countryside, where the mother tongue and the cultural inheritance of western Europe had a central place in the curriculum. The *Fennomen* made efforts to establish new Finnish language *lyceums* (secondary schools) in large towns, pursuing their aim of producing a Finnish speaking educated class and body of officials. All Finns were encouraged to participate actively in the affairs of society. Folk high schools were established, and the first Workers' Educational Institute began to function in Tampere in 1899. Many societies, such as the Women's Association, aimed at awakening women both culturally and politically. University students did effective work, giving lectures on the history of Finland and on cultural and political questions.[18]

The assimilation policy became even stricter in 1904 by which time Bobrikov had already gained the powers of a dictator. Schools were more directly controlled than in earlier times. The activities of teachers were investigated and some were dismissed because of their beliefs. Censorship became stricter and pressure was put on newspapers. Tension was considerably increased when, in June 1904, Bobrikov was murdered in the senate building, an event which meant that there was now an open confrontation with the Russians. The tsar then changed his political line and appointed a committee with the task of solving the legislative problems of Finland. In January 1905 all expulsions were rescinded and exiled citizens returned to Finland.

Why did this change of policy occur? One answer lies in foreign policy. Russia had adopted an imperialistic policy in Asia but had suffered a serious defeat at the hands of Japan in the war of 1904–5. This had a great effect throughout the empire, giving rise to new political movements and much unrest. The tsar was confronted with a new political situation. He had to decide between imposing a military dictatorship or pursuing a constitutional line. He opted for the latter, and at first this had a positive effect in Finland. The tsar issued a new manifesto, sweeping aside the regulations imposed under the February Manifesto of 1899 and, as a liberal statement, this prepared the ground for a new form of *diet* which finally came into being in 1906. The old four estate body was now replaced by a unicameral parliament and thus the country was accorded a truly modern governmental system. This was indeed, the biggest step towards the creation of a genuinely democratic society to be taken during the period of Finnish autonomy. The real extension of democracy involved could be seen most clearly in the much increased number of citizens now entitled to vote. In the parliamentary elections of 1906 that number was 1 273 000; whereas earlier the number entitled to vote had been a mere 126 000. Moreover, Finnish women were now given the right to vote, the first women in Europe allowed to do so in elections to a national parliament. In addition to granting universal and equal suffrage, the *diet*, in August 1906, also passed a law safeguarding rights of expression, assembly and association. It thus provided for new forms of political activity on a far bigger scale than previously.[19]

Instead of four estates the new Finnish parliament had six political parties: the Young Finns (26 members); the Old Finns (59); the Agrarian Union (nine); the Swedish People's party (24); the Social Democratic party (80) and the Christian Labour Union (two): a total of 200 members. In accordance with this new parliamentary system, the senate was now responsible to the elected house, and this was recognised during the years 1906–9. The members of the new parliament set about the development of Finnish society with enthusiasm and were especially interested in the further development of elementary schools and teaching. Questions of compulsory education and cooperation between the elementary and grammar schools were also of importance.[20]

The Finns naturally expected these parliamentary developments to continue, so that their disappointment was great when the tsar eventually seemed to be putting a brake on the proposed reforms. In fact the Governor General was clearly intent on regaining full control over Finland and reinforcing the power of the tsar. Thus a new period, dominated by policies aiming at assimilation, began in 1908 and did not end until 1917. The short constitutional era was over. For example, the selection of members of the Finnish senate had been greatly influenced by the opinions, first, of the *diet* and, later, of the parliament. From 1909 onwards however, the Governor General appointed to the senate only such members as would cooperate with Russia.

One reason for this renewed assimilation policy was the international situation in Europe. Russia had continued to cooperate with France in spite of the defeat she had suffered in the Japanese war, and later entered into a form of alliance with Britain so that all three were united against Germany. The arms race became more and more real, and as a result, the Russians concentrated on the protection of all parts of their empire. They did not trust the Finns, and therefore felt the need to increase their control over Finnish society.

The policy of assimilation certainly had an effect on school legislation, given that all the plans of the Finnish parliament for school reform remained at a standstill during this period. For example, in 1914 parliament had proposed that schooling should be made compulsory in every commune on lines to be decided locally, but the proposal made no progress. The Governor General did, however, try to take some practical steps in pursuance of his own policies. In particular, the teacher training college at Sortavala received his attention. He wanted to move this college to another place and to establish a Russian speaking college in Sortavala, the alternative being to close the place completely. Behind this lay a Russian plan for the whole of Karelia. The administration wanted to ensure the russification of this area by establishing a network of Russian schools with Russian teachers. These plans succeeded to only a limited extent, because of the opposition of the National Board of Education, of the town of Sortavala, and of the Finnish speaking nationalist elementary teachers. Nevertheless pressure continued in other directions. The teaching of Russian became compulsory in all teacher training colleges in 1916, when a new curriculum came into force. According to this plan, schooling was extended to five years instead of the earlier four, to allow for 22 hours a week of Russian teaching in order to ensure its success. Yet though the teaching of Russian was the subject of much inspection, the actual results remained very poor.[21]

Why was the assimilation policy limited in its effect on Finnish school policy? One reason yet again lay in the foreign policy sphere. The Finns always made sure that news of fresh political developments in Finland spread to the Nordic countries and to central Europe. There was a strong Finnish national presence at the 1908 Olympic Games in London as well as at the 1912 Games in Stockholm, and the athletic successes of the Finns aroused international attention. Although Finland was not geopolitically important in Europe as a whole, Russia did not press assimilation unduly because it wished to maintain good relations with Britain and France.

A second reason lay in the complex and highly bureaucratic administrative system of Finland. The Finnish parliament exploited this fact, to delay many proposals while protesting against Russian policy. Parliament was united in its opposition to the growing Russian influence even though the opinions and courses of action proposed by the various political parties differed widely. Moreover, the central offices of the administration itself, in particular the National Board of Education, often thwarted the proposals of the Governor General in all possible legal ways and attempted to justify their attitude on pedagogical grounds.

A third reason lay in the actions of the Finns themselves. An active national opposition movement came into being, and Finnish schoolboys and young men went secretly to Germany for military training from 1915 onwards, their aim being to return and share in the liberation of their native land. Such actions on the part of Finns proved necessary for the strengthening of the nation's position once the February revolution of 1917 began. In May of that year, a new curriculum for teacher training colleges was accepted, and Russian language teaching was removed from the curriculum of the grammar schools. The October revolution of 1917 finally destroyed the power that had been wielded by the tsars. The political developments thus began which led out of the period of autonomy to the period of Finland's total independence. The assimilation policy was now dead.

Outcomes and Effects

The development of educational policy in Finland falls into three distinct but complex periods between 1850 and 1917. During the period from 1850 to 1870 conservatism was replaced by a liberal Russian policy towards Finland. During that time the autonomy of the country was reinforced. The Finnish *diet* began to be convened regularly from 1863 onwards, and local autonomy was made a reality by the new legislation of 1865. In the spirit of such liberalism, several laws on education were accepted by the tsar, such as the law on teacher training of 1863 and the law on public education of 1866. School teachers were given permission to hold assemblies and changes in economic legislation had a positive effect, for when the limitations of mercantilism were removed, the resultant economic freedom had an important effect on the process of establishing new elementary schools.

This liberal line gave way to a Slavic policy from 1870 onwards. This meant that the tsar gave priority to the enforcing of a Slavic uniformity on the whole empire by administrative means. The post of Governor General of Finland was regularly filled by generals of the Russian army, who tried to pursue a policy of divide and rule so as to break the unity of the Finns. The Governor Generals favoured the Finnish speaking nationalists, and gave permission for the establishment of Finnish language elementary and grammar schools. In turn this Slavic policy gave way to a panRussian policy in the 1890s, which took on an imperialist complexion when, at the beginning of the twentieth century, Russia turned her attention towards Asia, a change of focus reflected in her internal policies. As stricter control became necessary, Russia turned into a police state and the Russian nationalist movement attempted to assimilate all the minority nations of the empire. This assimilation period in Finland (1899–1917) was filled with conflict. Attempts were made to put an end to the country's special status, while Finnish schools and the university were placed under the control of Russia's own Ministry of Public Education. Once the imperialist policy began to fail, a short period of greater democracy was launched in Finland. The old four estate representative body was replaced by a unicameral parliament and this formed an important part of a general process of modernisation. However this period of greater democracy was cut short when the tsarist authorities returned to their assimilation policies. All school legislation and reforms were halted. In pursuance of the new policy, the acquisition of a knowledge of Russian history and geography was positively encouraged, and these subjects were taught in the Russian language, though it is interesting to note that at the same time, the Finnish and Swedish languages also began to be taught in Russian schools so as to prepare Russian officials for service in Finland. In fact, the assimilation policy did not achieve many of its objectives because of active opposition by the Finns.

Nordic and International Perspectives

The Finns formed a very small minority group in the Europe of last century, a mere part of the vast Russian Empire like so many other small nations. Therefore, any measure that served to reinforce the national identity assumed a great importance. One important element in this was the development of an elementary school system from the 1860s onwards. International political developments also had a direct effect on Finland. Many international ideas found their way there and gained supporters. Liberalism, manifesting itself politically, economically and culturally, affected many sectors of national life. It had a decisive effect on the development of school education, especially in the elementary schools. It is worth bearing in mind, however, that such liberal ideas were only tolerated when they suited Russia's political aims in Finland, when the tsar wished to make the country a showcase for the eyes of western Europe. Political conditions elsewhere in the Russian empire were very different. However Russian nationalism in Finland in the shape of the Slavic movement with its emphasis on cultural unity, soon began to display panSlavic features. Whereas earlier liberal policies had reinforced the autonomy of Finland, the panSlavic movement began to weaken and erode this special status, with the ultimate aim of full assimilation.

Yet Finland also had close links with the other Nordic nations throughout this time, in the shape of scandinavism. This involved both political and cultural aspects and, as a political movement, its emergence can be discerned in the newspapers of the 1860s. While its main ideal, the essential unity of Scandinavia, did not survive for long, scandinavism did nevertheless have an effect on Russian policy. It made the Slavic enthusiasts in the administration of Finland very suspicious of Swedish speaking liberals and the supporters of Swedish speaking nationalists. They were afraid that such people wished to reinforce Finland's political contacts with other Nordic countries and such a suspicion still remained alive at the beginning of this century, with the consequent impact on Russian policy. Governor Generals tended to counteract this by favouring the Finnish speaking nationalists in various areas, including education.

Notes

1. See Map 5.1, p.110; Hanho pp.140–65; Jutikkala and Pirinen pp. 166–73.
2. Jutikkala and Pirinen pp.180–90; Halila, 1949, pp. 173–90.
3. *Senaatin yleisistunnon pöytäkirja,* Valtionarkisto 24.3.1856.
4. *Keisarillisen Majesteetin Armollinen julistus* 17.3.1863; *Keisarillisen Majesteetin Armollinen julistus* 17.5.1866.
5. See Halila (1949) pp. 364–9.
6. *Keisarillisen Majesteetin Armollinen asetus,* 30.11.1871. Somerkivi, pp.42–3.
7. Alapuro pp. 67–70; Tuominen, pp. 378–80; Ylikangas pp. 112–22.
8. Koukkunen, pp. 125–33.
9. Heikkilä, pp. 14–15.
10. See Heikkilä, pp. 15–16. Jussila, pp. 18–21.
11. *Statisk Årsbok för Finland 1903,* pp. 287–95.
12. *Koulutoimen ylihallituksen kirje* 3.3.1881. See Halila (1949), pp. 233–5.
13. Kuikka (1973), pp. 235–49. *Statisk Årsbok för Finland 1903,* pp. 287–93.
14. Tuominen pp. 602–3; Kemppinen pp. 10–12.
15. *Keisarillisen Majesteetin Armollinen asetus* 24.5.1898. See also Tuominen, pp. 602–3.
16. Polvinen, pp. 91–2. Paasivirta, pp. 321–8. Juva, pp. 20–5.
17. Paasivirta, pp. 332–40.
18. Karjalainen, pp. 86–93; Polvinen, pp. 211–12.
19. Laki 20.8.1906; Paasivirta, pp. 356–66; Puntila, pp. 76–80.

20. Kuikka (1981), pp. 15–17.
21. Kemppinen, pp. 166–7; Halila (1950), pp. 80–4; Kuikka (1978), pp. 23–4; Kiuasmaa, pp. 202–9.

Select Bibliography

Alapuro, R. (1985), Yhteiskuntaluokat ja sosiaaliset kerrostumat 1870–luvulta toiseen maailmansotaan; in Tapani Valkonen-Risto Alapuro-Matti Alestalo-Riitta Jallinoja–Tom Sandlund, (eds), *Suomalaiset. Yhteiskunnan rakenne teollistumisen aikana*, Juva.

Halila, A. (1949), *Suomen kansakoululaitoksen historia* (A History of the public school system in Finland), II, Turku.

Halila, A. (1950), *Suomen kansakoululaitoksen historia* (A History of the public school system in Finland), IV, Turku.

Hanho, J.T. (1955), *Suomen oppikoululaitoksen synty* II (The rise of secondary school in Finland), Porvoo.

Heikkilä, M. (1985), 'Kielitaistelusta sortovuosiin' (From language disputes to oppression), History of the Senate's Department of Ecclesiastical Affairs, in the *Ministry of Education*, volume III, Pieksämäki.

Jussila, O. (1979), 'Nationalismi ja vallankumous' (Nationalism and Revolution), *Historiallisia tutkimuksia*, 110, Helsinki.

Jutikkala, E., and Pirinen, K. (1985), *A History of Finland*, Espoo.

Juva, E. (1967), 'Tie itsenäisyyteen ja itsenäisyyden tie' (A way to Independence and the Independence's way) in *Suomen kansan historia*, V, Keuruu.

Karjalainen, E. (1970), *Suomen vapaan kansansivistystyön vaiheet* (The phases of free public education in Finland), Tapiola.

Keisarillisen Majesteetin Armollinen asetus 24.5.1898, 30.11.1871.

Keisarillisen Majesteetin Armollinen julistus 17.3.1863, 17.5.1866.

Kemppinen, L. (1969), *Sortavalan seminaarin historia* (A History of the teacher training college in Sortavala), Helsinki.

Kiuasmaa, K. (1980), *Oppikoulu 1880–1980* (The secondary school 1880–1980), Helsinki.

Koukkunen, H. (1980), 'Uudenkaupungin rauhasta nykypäiviin' (From the Peace of Uusikaupunki to our day) in *Ortodoksinen kirkko Suomessa*, Lieto.

Koulutoimen ylihallituksen kirje 3.3.1981.

Kuikka, M.T. (1973), *Uskonnonopetus Suomen kansakoulunopettajasemi-naareissa vuosina 1863–95* (Religious education of teacher training college for primary schools in Finland in the years 1863–95). Helsingin yliopiston käytännöllisen teologian laitos. Uskonnonpedagogiikan julkaisuja A 5/1973.

Kuikka, M.T. (1978), *Kansakoulunopettajankoulutussuunnitelmien kehitys Suomessa vuosina 1917–1923* (A development of plans for teacher training for primary schools in Finland in the years 1917–1923). Joensuun korkeakoulu. Kasvatustieteiden osaston julkaisuja No 4. Joensuu (with English summary).

Kuikka, M.T. (1981), 'Society and the Development of an Elementary School System in Finland, 1866–1968', *Scandinavian Journal of History*, 6, pp. 7–28.

Laki 20.8.1906.

Paasivirta, J. (1978), *Autonomiankausi ja kansainväliset kriisit* (The period of autonomy and international crises), Helsinki.

Polyginen, T. (1984), *Valtakunta ja rajamaa. N.I. Bobrikov Suomen kenraalikuvernöörinä* (The Empire and the Borderland. N.I. Bobrikov as Governor General of Finland 1898–1904), Juva.

Puntila, L.A. (1963), *Suomen poliittinen historia* (A political history of Finland), Keuruu.

Senaatin yleisistunnon pöytäkirja 24.3.1856. Senaatin arkisto. Valtionarkisto.

Somerkivi, U. (1979), 'Kouluhallitus ja koulutoimen kehittyminen' in Somerkivi. U., Cavonius, G. and Karttunen M.O., (eds), *Kouluhallitus-Skolstyrelsen*, Vantaa.

Statisk Årsbok för Finland 1903 (Statistical Year Book of Finland), Helsinki.

Tuominen, U. (1981), 'Valtiopäivien osuus kulttuuripolitiikassa' (An interest of the *Diet* in culture policy), in *Suomen kansanedustuslaitoksen historia II*, Helsinki.

Tuominen, U. (1981), 'Uuden valtiopäiväjärjestyksen alkukausi' (The early period of the new *Diet*), in *Suomen kansanedustuslaitoksen historia II*, Helsinki.

Ylikangas, H. (1986), *Käännekohdat Suomen historiassa* (Turning points in the History of Finland), Juva.

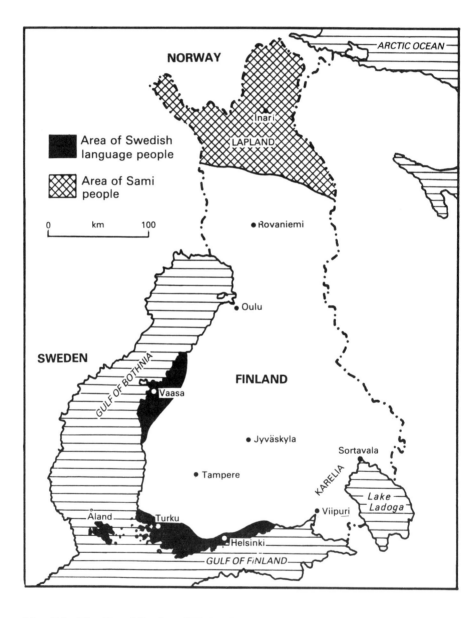

Map 5.1   The Grand Duchy of Finland, 1815–1918

6   Language in Education in Belgium up to 1940

MAURITS DE VROEDE

This paper concentrates on the place of language in education in the Flemish part of Belgium, rather than the actual supply of schooling. We have chosen this approach, taking the specific character of Belgian situation into account, for two reasons. In dealing with government policies, one has to bear in mind that Belgium, from its birth in 1830, has been a liberal state, where private initiative in the field of education had every chance to develop. In the second place, in speaking of a minority group, one has to note that the Flemings were as numerous as the Walloons, but nevertheless took inferior positions in economic, social and cultural life. Until the Second World War, the problems caused by these circumstances appeared mainly in the field of language use. So the question really is, which factors played a decisive role in this respect: the government's policy or other influences?

The Linguistic Communities

A linguistic border runs through Belgium in virtually a straight line from west to east. It separates the Dutch speaking regions (the provinces of West Flanders, East Flanders, Antwerp, and Limburg and the northern part of the province of Brabant) from the French speaking areas (the provinces of Hainaut, Namur, Liège, and Luxemburg and the southern part of the province of Brabant). These regions have been called Flanders and Wallonia since the nineteenth century. The linguistic border in Belgium is a part of the line running from Aachen to Calais, separating the zones of the Germanic and Romance languages from each other. How precisely this border originated has yet to be clarified fully. What is certain is that it dates from the early Middle Ages and that it has remained unchanged through the centuries in spite of many territorial shifts and changes in the political fate of this part of Europe.

The Belgian state was founded only in 1830. Its territory consisted of areas that had belonged to different principalities since the Middle Ages. Most of them had been under the rule of the Habsburgs since the sixteenth century: first the Spanish and then, in the eighteenth century, the Austrians. In addition, the prince–bishopric of Liège had been an independent state. In the French period (1794–1814), all of the principalities of the southern Low Countries and Liège had been annexed to France as *départements* (regional administrative areas), and later, in the kingdom of the Netherlands (1815–1830), they had formed the southern provinces. In 1830 they came together to constitute the independent state of Belgium.

This state numbered slightly more Flemings than Walloons, but in its centre French was the dominant language. The Flemish population was itself not an homogeneous linguistic entity. In Flanders, there was another linguistic border, not territorial but social. The broad mass of the people were Dutch speaking, but the upper layer of society used French as the language of high culture. The members of the leading class even pretended – as Baudelaire noted during his stay in Belgium in 1864/5 – that they did not know Dutch, though they did use it to scold their servants. This upper layer had gradually become frenchified after the middle of the eighteenth century. In Brussels, part of the reason for this was the influence of the central administration established there. While the Austrian government did not have a language policy, it used French itself and thus contributed to its spread. That French became the language of the aristocracy, the higher clergy, and – to a certain extent – of the middle class in the Flemish regions cannot be explained without noting the pervasive influence of French culture. The same phenomenon also occurred elsewhere in Europe. The use of French was both a status symbol and a means of differentiation from the lower social classes.

The frenchification process in the Flemish regions, however, did not stop at the end of the eighteenth and the beginning of the nineteenth century as it did in other European countries. Rather, it intensified. The French Governors assumed that the linguistic assimilation of the population of the annexed area could be of service to their political hegemony. Thus, they intentionally implemented a language policy, the aim of which was frenchification with French as the only official language. The new generation from the upper level of society was thus educated in French. Moreover, direct contact with Frenchmen facilitated frenchification. The Flemish middle class was also frenchified to a large extent.

An analogous language policy was applied by the Dutch government between 1815 and 1830, but in the reverse direction: it used Dutch as the state language and tried to promote it. However, this policy failed and the use of French seemed to expand rather than decrease. The already French speaking leading class rejected dutchification. The language question was one of the reasons for opposition to the government.

After 1830

The success of the revolution of 1830 stimulated Belgian national consciousness. Men of letters and historians, Flemish as well as Walloon, lauded the new fatherland and tried to trace the historical routes that ultimately led to its creation. Around 1850, a Walloon popular poet wrote a poem in which he said that 'Walloon' and 'Flemish' were merely the given names of people who all bore the family name of 'Belgian'. This phrase, much cited later, was a typical expression of a unitary perception of the two linguistic communities. Development of a Belgian national consciousness was critical for the consolidation of the new state.

The French speaking dominant class held political power in this state because of the censitairian system. This class was convinced that a modern nation had to be based on a monolingual centre and that this centre would, obviously, be French. For the new Governors, language, in this case French, was a very important instrument in the construction and consolidation of a Belgian nation. But what was to happen to Dutch? The new regime was a liberal regime. Together with other freedoms, the freedom of language was also written into the constitution. *De facto*, this gave the opportunity for an un-hampered, further frenchification of the Flemish regions, where the local administration was free to use French. Moreover, for all the constitutional freedom, only one language was official everywhere in the country: French. It was the language of laws and decrees, of the central and provincial administrations, of the courts and of the army. Should it not also become the language of education, for was not education the best means to assimilate the linguistic communities under the flag of Belgian nationalism? For the Flemish regions, this meant assimilation within a French language identity.

The liberal regime of 1830 also introduced freedom of education, guaranteed by the constitution. This meant that not only the authorities (national, provincial and municipal), but also private individuals or associations could organise schools without being hampered in any way. Extensive use was made of this right. In the supply of schooling, private persons or associations actually played a bigger role than the state. It was only in the field of higher, general secondary and teacher education that the central authorities organ-ised schools themselves. It is worth noting that in doing so, they made no distinction between the Flemish and the Walloon part of the country. In 1835, one of the two state universities was located in

Wallonia (Liège), the other one in Flanders (Ghent). In 1842, two state normal schools were founded, again one in each of the two regions. The act of 1850 distributed the state secondary schools over the different provinces equally.

However, what language was used in all these institutions? The two state universities used only French, and so, for that matter, did the two private ones (Louvain and Brussels). In the state secondary and normal (teacher training) schools, French was also the only language of instruction. In the Flemish area of the country, the study of Dutch was prescribed, but this regulation long remained a dead letter. Moreover, Dutch was generally taught in, and via, French. In the private institutions, and particularly in the schools organised by the bishops or religious orders, the situation was no different. By the 1830s, they had already switched over to French as the medium of instruction. Students were even forbidden to speak Dutch in the playground. In view of the dominance of French as the language of the Belgian centre, and of the establishment in Flanders itself, the use of this language as the medium of instruction in secondary and higher education is not surprising. What was important was assimilation of both the upper and the middle classes, from which the students at these educational levels generally originated. But what was the situation in primary education, which was intended for the broad mass of the population?

Regulations Concerning Primary Education

In the following pages we will concentrate on primary education, for if the authorities had intended to plan the frenchification of the lower classes in Flanders, the elementary school should have been the main instrument of so doing. In this respect one has to stress two elements. First, that the central authorities did not act as the organising power in that field. Primary schools were set up either by private or public bodies, but the latter were the municipalities, not the state. While Belgium was a centralised state, the municipal administrations still enjoyed a certain amount of autonomy. They were, for example, empowered to organise education. As far as primary education was concerned, they did this within the context of the organic law of 1842.

The government subsidised the municipalities and the legislators designed the framework within which education had to be given. The municipalities had control over their own schools, including the private schools they adopted to function as municipal schools. Both the municipal and adopted schools also fell under the supervision of the state inspection apparatus. The completely private schools, however, had no supervision, not even over language usage. Thus, understandably, there is no statistical material on these private schools. The data that are given below – taken from the government *Rapport triennal sur la situation de l'instruction primaire en Belgique* (Triennial Reports on the Development of Primary Education in Belgium) – thus concern only the schools organised and/or inspected by the public authorities. It should be stressed, however, that information regarding language education in these schools will apply at least as much to private schools. Provisions for the free education of poor pupils were, by law, only made for the public schools. The private schools did provide free education for some, but one may assume that the number of paying pupils was relatively higher in such schools. These pupils were the children of parents who stood higher in the social hierarchy. The pressure of frenchification, to be discussed further later, was directly proportional to the place one occupied on the social ladder.

In the second place, what was prescribed by legislators in relation to language use? The law of 1842 stipulated that French and Dutch, or German had to be taught in the public primary schools to meet the needs of the area where the school was located. This stipulation was maintained in the laws on primary education of 1879, 1884, and 1895. The last law remained in force until 1914. These laws permitted the obligatory minimum curriculum to be expanded at will. Up to the First World War, it was thus possible to use French as the language of instruction in Flemish primary schools or, if Dutch was the language of instruction, to have French taught as the second language. The extent to which this was the case will be examined next.

French as the Language of Instruction

The phenomenon of French as the language of instruction in the primary school was to be found primarily in Brussels and its suburban municipalities. The population of the capital in the middle of the nineteenth century was still 60 per cent Dutch speaking. Nevertheless, by the 1830s, the municipal schools had already switched from Dutch to French as the language of instruction. Although it is difficult to describe the linguistic situation with precision, it is obvious that French remained the language of instruction in general until the end of the 1870s. The result of this kind of education for Flemish children was criticised by contemporaries for obvious reasons. These children spoke a dialect and still had to master Dutch as a cultural language, but they had no opportunity to do so. On the other hand, they learned French mechanically, without grasping the meaning of what they read. For pedagogical reasons, therefore, another language regime was introduced that took into account the mother tongue of the pupils. This took place under Charles Buls, the Alderman for Education from 1879 to 1881, and then Burgermaster from 1881 to 1899.

The new language regime was based upon dual medium model. It consisted – at least these were the regulations – in placing the Dutch native speakers, that is, the vast majority, in Flemish classes for the first two years, in which Dutch was the language of instruction but where French was also taught. In the subsequent two years of study education would be given in the two languages. This was to make the transition to the last two years of study possible, during which French was the only language of instruction. In practice, Dutch was used in this system to bring the Flemish pupils to use French, which remained the dominant language. The aim was replacement bilingualism, that is, the mother tongue was to be replaced by a second language.

However, this system was never implemented in full. It encountered opposition from the teaching staff and, after the 1880s, from the municipal councils. Thus, it was pushed back to the third year of study, while the study of French was intensified from the second year on. Very few Flemish classes were organised and, in the 1890s and early 1900s, they even decreased in number. In 1911, the Buls system was completely dropped. Instead, Flemish or French classes would be organised for all six years intended for pupils with Dutch or French respectively as their mother tongue. What the mother tongue was would no longer be determined by the teachers, as it was under the Buls system, but by the head of the family. The pressure for frenchification was by then already so great that no more Flemish classes were created. On the eve of the First World War, the municipal educational system had six Dutch and 405 French classes.

In the suburbs of Brussels, where in the middle of the nineteenth century the population was with a few exceptions, even more predominantly Dutch speaking than in Brussels itself, an analogous development occurred in the language regime in primary education. At first it became purely French, then a transmutation system was introduced that resulted again in purely French language instruction. In 1914, Dutch as the language of instruction in suburban municipalities like Elsene, Etterbeek, Sint-Gillis, and Sint-Joost-ten-Node had virtually disappeared. In others, like Anderlecht, Molenbeek, and Laken, there were still Flemish schools or schools with Flemish and French divisions, but here French was predominantly or exclusively used as the language of instruction in the upper grades.

Outside the Brussels agglomeration, Dutch as the language of instruction in the primary school was dislodged by French to only a limited extent: in the Chief Inspectorate of Brussels (Flemish cantons), this was the case in 22.5 per cent of the schools in 1902 and

22.7 per cent in 1905. The Chief Inspectorate of Leuven included both Walloon and Flemish cantons. In the latter, French was the language of instruction, according to official information, in the upper classes (seventh and eighth years) of the municipal schools in Leuven and in one school in Tienen. For the other Chief Inspectorates in the Flemish region, the situation at the beginning of the twentieth century is given on Table 6.1.

Table 6.1: French language schools in the Flemish part of Belgium (%)

Chief Inspectorate	1902	1905
Antwerp	0	0
Mechelen	0	0
Bruges	0	0
Kortrijk	11.9	11.7
Aalst	0	0.2
Ghent	1.9	2.2
Hasselt	4	4.1

The figures for 1902 are taken from a survey that the Ministry conducted after a prominent Flemish association had submitted a complaint at the end of 1900 about the use of French as the language of instruction in numerous Flemish schools. These figures were not correct. For example, it was not stated that French was the language of instruction in Antwerp in the municipal schools for paying pupils as well as in the biggest division of schools in the neighbouring municipality of Berchem. Also not included were the schools in which the subject matter was first taught in Dutch and then repeated in French. But the figures are indicative. The striking percentage in the Kortrijk area is largely due to the situation prevailing in a number of municipalities near the French border. This was an argument used by the Minister to claim that there were no abuses: if French language education was given, then this was to meet the local needs or the desire of the heads of family.

French as the Second Language

For education in French as the second language in the Flemish schools, the picture is different. Table 6.2 shows what the situation was in 1860 and how it developed in the 1870s.

The gradual increase, taken globally, is clear, and so is the fact that the provinces of East and West Flanders were catching up with the others. The high percentages indicate that education in French was

Table 6.2: Dutch language schools in the Flemish regions with education in French, 1860–1875 (%)

Province	1860	1863	1869	1872	1875
Antwerp	86	100	91	89	90
Limburg	89	91	91	93	95
East Flanders	51	53	54	77	80
West Flanders	55	59	66	79	83
Total	64	69	73	82	86

not limited to the cities, but also had become the fashion in the village schools, albeit to a somewhat lesser degree. In 1872, it was found in 82.1 per cent of the village schools as opposed to 87.1 per cent of the city schools: in 1875, the respective percentages were 85 per cent and 92.7 per cent.

During the last quarter of the nineteenth century, French lost no ground as the second language in Flemish primary schools, as is shown by Table 6.3, which gives the situation in the beginning of the twentieth century.

Table 6.3: Dutch language schools in the Flemish regions with education in French, 1902 and 1905 (%)

Chief Inspectorate	1902	1905
Antwerp	82.4	90.1
Mechelen	70.5	89.3
Brussels	91	93.5
Leuven	95.2	61.8 ?
Bruges	98.3	99.2
Kortrijk	100	98.6
Aalst	86.8	98.8
Ghent	99.1	100
Hasselt	82.3	84.1
Total	89.8	91.1

These data concern only the presence of second language education and say nothing about the classes it was given in or how much time was devoted to it. A distinction must be made in this regard between city schools and village schools.

For the cities, let us take two examples: Ghent and Antwerp, the two largest Flemish cities. In Ghent, central evening schools were established at first (in 1835 for boys, in 1837 for girls) where pupils of the highest class of the municipal schools could learn French. They operated until 1858. Thereafter, second language education was programmed in the day schools themselves; first after the ordinary school hours, but by the 1860s, within them. French rapidly came to be taught in all the classes: in the lowest two for one hour per day; in the middle two for two to two and a half hours per day, and in the highest classes for half the day. In the Antwerp city schools, second language education in the 1840s was not yet strongly developed: it was taught in the highest two classes. Afterwards, it was extended to the middle division (third and fourth years), and even to the second year. In the 1860s and 1870s, one hour per day was devoted to French. In 1899, the situation began to change in the opposite direction: beginning the study of French was shifted from the second to the third year. In 1900, this study was begun in the fourth year and, in 1910, only in the second semester of it. In addition to the free municipal schools intended for pupils from the working class, municipal schools for paying pupils were also established in Ghent and Antwerp. Here, French was given a larger place. Although these schools were officially Dutch language schools, French predominated *de facto* as the language of instruction.

Sufficient information about the situation in the village schools is lacking. On average, around 1890, about a half an hour per day was spent on French as opposed to an hour in the city schools. The higher the grade, the more French was taught. Doubtless, there were local variations, but this is a matter for further research. It should be noted that the village schools had fewer teachers than the city schools, and that the conditions under which the pupils attended school in most of the villages may have obliged the teachers to limit themselves to the essentials, the elementary skills.

The objectives *and* the results of education in French in the Flemish schools thus varied. In Brussels, the objective was to switch the pupils from the use of their mother tongue to the use of French, and this goal was largely achieved. The number of monolingual Dutch speakers in the capital declined from 59 per cent in 1880 to 23 per cent in 1910; the number of bilingual speakers rose from 23 per cent to 50 per cent; and the number of monolingual French speakers rose from 18 per cent to 27 per cent. Bilingualism, therefore, led to monolingualism in Brussels. While it was there still a matter of complementary bilingualism in the first generation, that is, the second language was habitually used for clearly defined functions, the following generation switched over completely to French. Apparently, this phenomenon did not occur in the other Flemish cities, or at least only to a very limited extent. In the social context, the number of French speakers was less than 5 per cent. Nevertheless, there was a general striving to learn French, to achieve complementary bilingualism, or at least supplementary bilingualism, that is, the ability to be able to use French on an occasional basis outside the normal routine. How can this be explained?

Why Bilingualism?

The first factor is the enhanced value that French had acquired over Dutch as a cultural language. Even before 1830, Dutch as a spoken language had degenerated into a number of dialects in the Flemish regions. As a written language, it gave access to a literature of only limited significance. Flemish philologists set out to reconstruct standard Dutch in Flanders, but this took a great deal of time. Flemish writers were producing an expanding body of literature for their own people, but how could this withstand comparison with the French? Moreover, French remained the language of science. As late as 1906, the Belgian bishops declared that a university education in Dutch was inconceivable.

French not only gave access to a culture that was assigned higher prestige, but it was also the language of the national centre, the official language. Obviously, that centre influenced the periphery. Participation in the political decision making process required knowledge of French, and this language also dominated in the administration, the army and the courts. Judges in Flanders were not even required to know Dutch.

The powerful position of French was also supported by the economic relations in the country. The industrial centre of gravity was situated in Wallonia, which had coal and iron ore, so the attention of the banking system and the government was focused on it. In Flanders, the traditional flax industry collapsed in the 1840s. Around 1850, Ghent, with its mechanised cotton industry, was almost an industrial island in the middle of a predominantly agrarian area. Antwerp was a commercial centre, a harbour, but not an apex of industrial growth. The shippers spoke French, the dock workers Dutch. Bruges was described as a dead city. In Flanders, there were too few jobs. Hundreds of thousands of Flemish people emigrated to Wallonia. When industry and trade also developed in Flanders, which was the case toward the end of the nineteenth century, the modernisation process increased the need for knowledge of French, which also dominated the business world.

With a view to both public and private life, those Flemish who tried to climb the social ladder were thus obliged to know French. Also the burden of learning a second language was placed on them alone, and not on the Walloons. In spite of their numerical superiority in the country, sociologically the Flemish constituted a non-dominant group. In Flanders itself, Dutch very definitely was a second class language. The middle class regarded Dutch disparagingly and made use of its social, economic, and political power to promote frenchification. The attitude of the clergy is also illuminating. The higher clergy supported the use of the mother tongue for parochial work and religious education in the schools, but otherwise preferred French. At the beginning of the twentieth century, the bishops still declared themselves in favour of bilingual primary education in Flanders. Of course, they did not aim at a total dutchification of even secondary education, let alone the higher level. On the other hand, among the lower clergy, at work in the colleges of education and the parishes, a large number of priests favoured the Flemish cause and so supported the Flemish Movement.

The Flemish Movement in the Nineteenth Century

Reactions against frenchification can already be noted even at the end of the eighteenth century. These reactions received a fresh impulse in the years between 1815 and 1830. Thereafter, a movement developed that initially was more like the activity of a general staff without soldiers, as it consisted of middle class intellectuals. Gradually, it acquired more support from this class, but it had not developed into a broad popular movement by 1914. It also lacked the support of the bourgeoisie in Flanders. Another difference with the classic national movements in the nineteenth century is that one notes that the Flemish Movement did not strive for self-government or the creation of a new political structure. Up to the First World War, its supporters made no headway against the Belgian state. Flemish national tendencies grew only after 1914.

The *Flamingants* (Flemish nationalists) just worked for reforms within the existing state structure, and specifically, for the recognition of the language rights of the Flemings. Under the influence of Romanticism, they developed a mystique based on the mother tongue, which was expressed in the slogan '*De taal is gans het volk*' (the language is the people). Language, it was said, gave the members of a community their own identity, an identity which was lost if the language was yielded. Frenchification was thus seen as a threat to the very existence of the Flemish people. Flanders could, therefore, no longer suffer frenchification. In practice, this was translated into the efforts of the *Flamingants* to establish the use of Dutch in Flanders alongside French. This use was to be regulated in the official sector by language laws, for it was believed that, in the relation between the weak and the strong, freedom oppressed and the law liberated. Obviously, the *Flamingants* also championed the right to education in the mother tongue.

How could these *Flamingants*, however, obtain such language laws? Laws had to be voted in parliament, and this was dominated by the French speaking and francophile elite. Could the *Flamingants* carry on a campaign through a political party of their own? Quite rapidly this hope turned out to be a failure, for two reasons, mainly. To many *Flamingants* the ideological controversies between Catholics and liberals were more important than their Flemish convictions and, under the censitairian system, politically they had little representation as a group. So, from the 1860s on, they started acting inside the existing political parties separately, hoping to gain as much influence as they could.

In the Liberal party, dominated by francophones, these efforts were unsuccessful. The Flemish liberal pressure groups lacked the power to change the anti-Flemish character of their party. In the Catholic party, leadership was in hands of the conservative bourgeoisie, which was no more Flemish minded than the liberal one. However, a faction of Christian Democrats gradually emerged, and they actually combined Flemish and democratic objectives. Around 1900, the strongest political support for the Flemish programme came from this side. The Belgian Workers' party was founded in 1885, but although it was not anti-Flemish, it only gave a little support to the Flemish cause. The *Flamingants* belonged mainly to the middle class and, in socialist eyes, they paid too little attention to social problems. Their influence upon the socialists thus remained small. The socialists themselves aimed almost exclusively at the improvement of the material circumstances of the workers. Besides, it was Wallonia and Brussels, that became the centres of gravity of their party.

Because of the censitairian system, unchanged until 1893, and the political constellation in general, the outcome of parliamentary debates about language laws depended upon contemporary circumstances and these laws never brought quite what the *Flamingants* wanted.

The work of the *Flamingants* did lead to the language law of 1883 with its implications for secondary education. Thereafter in state institutions, modern languages and at least two other subjects had to be taught in Dutch. Dutch also became the medium of instruction in the preparatory divisions of these institutions. The application of this law was certainly not perfect. Moreover, it did not apply to private education, which was quantitatively the most important. In the Catholic schools, the language regime was adapted to a certain extent, but it was 1910 before they received a system like that of the state institutions. By that time, the forces of the *Flamingants* were focused on the dutchification, in whole or in part, of the state University of Ghent, an objective they were unable to achieve before the First World War.

Insofar as the primary schools were concerned, the *Flamingants* agreed that the mother tongue of the Flemish pupils had also to be the language of instruction. Other arguments in addition to the pedagogical ones were enlisted. Instead of frenchifying the children of the working class, the leading classes had to use the language of the people in order to play a civilising role. This position, however, did not mean that French had to be banned in primary schools. Education in French, as the second language, had been accepted for decades by almost everyone, although opinions did differ about exactly when it was best to begin it. It was often stated that this must not be done too soon – not before the foundations of the knowledge of the mother tongue were established – but when was that? Should it be deferred to the upper grades or introduced in the middle years? No consensus on the matter emerged.

In the 1890s, however, an entirely different notion caught on: French could still be taught in the large cities outside the normal school hours, but elsewhere this language did not belong to primary education in Flanders. This idea gained supporters, though it was certainly not accepted generally. For example, in the discussions conducted in the Permanent Commission for Education established in 1900 by the Royal Flemish Academy for Linguistics and Literature and charged with the promotion of education in and through the mother tongue, opinions were divided. According to some, the study of French in primary schools was not justified; others held that it was very desirable to introduce it in the fifth and sixth grades or even earlier.

The opponents of second language education used several arguments, nationalistic, pedagogical, and pragmatic. To have working class children learn French meant the penetration of frenchification to that part of the population that had still remained Flemish. The specific character of the people, which was based on the mother tongue, was thus further threatened. To try to teach two languages in primary school was pedagogical nonsense. It could only lead to faulty knowledge of both. The study of French did not promote the intellectual development of Flemish children but rather hindered it. It stood in the way of a sound acquisition of Dutch as a standard language that the pupils, who spoke dialect, had to master. Moreover, study of French was useless. Not only did the results not justify the effort, but in a social context, 95 per cent of the pupils had no need of it in view of the small number of French speakers in the Flemish regions.

Against this, the supporters of second language education stressed the social need for it. In general, not only was a person who knew more than one language better equipped for life, but in Belgium, knowledge of French was a necessity for anyone who came in contact

with the public sector in commerce as well as in public administration. Anyone from the working class who wanted to climb the
social ladder had to learn French. Even getting an ordinary job in
Belgium or abroad could depend on it. This situation might be
regretted, but it was a fact. French thus had to be given the necessary
attention in primary education. Schools that failed to do so would not
attract any pupils. Knowledge of French was, of course, required for
anyone who wanted to study further after primary school.

This sharpening of positions on primary education emerged in
Flamingant circles in a period during which their movement entered a
new phase. From the 1890s, several factors had come together to
improve the Flemish position. The demographic situation had
worked in favour of the Flemish, and, with the second industrial
revolution, the process of economic modernisation had also got
under way in Flanders. The workers' movements, both socialist and
Christian-Democrat, gained in significance. In 1893, a plural
universal franchise was introduced. Although this was to the
advantage of the conservative minded, the common man did receive
a say in political affairs. This was not without importance for the
language in which he had to be addressed in Flanders. The ranks of
Flamingants expanded, and new ideas emerged. It was argued that
the struggle was no longer only for the language rights of individual
citizens; it was not only for language laws – which, moreover, were
often poorly applied; but it was for the broad cultural, economic,
and social development of the Flemish part of the population.

Spiritual interests, those involving the use of language among
them, were interwoven with material ones. On the question of use of
language, the slogan was now Flanders Flemish instead of Flemish in
Flanders. Inevitably, this involved the rejection of the essentially
francophone character of the Belgian nation state. The state had
instead to be founded on a dual linguistic ethnicity with equality for
both parts. Opposition now arose on the Walloon and French
minded Flemish side against the efforts of the *Flamingants*, whose
opposition to the up to then purely French speaking centre became
seen as a threat to the Walloon position. In 1898, and not without
difficulty, an equality law was passed that recognised Dutch as an
official language alongside French. However, this measure, like
previous language laws, did not mean the end of frenchification in
Flanders, which was due to the striving for upward mobility and the
attraction that continued to be exercised by Brussels. A regionalist
ideology was not yet generalised among the *Flamingants* and they
were not yet strong enough to impose it. This is shown, for example,
by the unsuccessful attempts to have it introduced in primary
education.

In 1895, in the parliamentary debate over a new primary education law, a *Flamingant* member of parliament for Brussels proposed that education in the Flemish municipalities be given in Dutch. This proposal was rejected, however, after the government had made its objections known. The rights of the French speakers in Flanders had to be respected. In Brussels, Dutch language schools were completely impossible. The municipalities still had the authority to specify the language used in the schools depending on local needs.

The Act of 1914

In 1914, the time was not yet ripe for adopting the principle of territoriality of the language of instruction. Nevertheless, *Flamingants* did introduce it in an amendment to the new primary education law of that year. Only for Brussels did they maintain the principle of personality: mother tongue = language of instruction. French, moreover, was not to be banned from schools in Flanders, but it was not to be taught before the fifth grade. In view of the actual situation and of the varying opinions that *Flamingants* held on the matter, it was not to be expected that parliament would exclude French. The law of 19 May 1914 stated that the mother tongue (or the usual language) of the pupils in all municipal, adopted, and adoptable schools (that is, private subsidised schools of the same level as the others, but which had not been adopted by the municipalities) had to be the language of instruction. It was for the head of the family to indicate the mother tongue. For the Brussels agglomeration and for the municipalities on the linguistic border, the minister could grant mitigated application of the proposed principle; in other words, allow the use of a language other than the mother tongue. The law did not give any details. Further, it placed no restrictions on second language education in the Flemish schools. No stipulations were made regarding its commencement or duration. Thus, the law of 1914 did not prevent the existence of French language schools or divisions in Flanders. It did not apply to the completely private schools, and municipal authorities could also organise French language education. Around 1930, there were still more than 200 French language municipal or subsidised private schools in addition to an unknown number of non-subsidised schools. The number of pupils, children from the middle class, that they had amounted to about 1.5 per cent of the total school population.

In Brussels, the law of 1914 was violated continuously and on a large scale. The parents were supposed to indicate the mother tongue of their child and on this depended whether their child was placed in a French or a Flemish class. In practice, the parents were asked what language of instruction they wanted for their child. They generally chose French language education. There was a very distinct lack of Flemish classes. The municipal authorities rarely requested the mitigated application of the principle of mother tongue equals language of instruction – during the 1920s this only happened four times – and they acted as they liked. Abuses were not stopped. Only Minister Camille Huysmans made an attempt to do so, in 1925–7, but with little success. In fact, the situation that existed before 1914 was continued after the First World War. The results were anything but negligible. In 1930, the number of monolingual French speakers in Brussels came to 43 per cent of the population, while the number of monolingual Dutch speakers dropped to less than 20 per cent. The number of bilingual people also declined.

Developments in the capital after 1918 were affected by the repercussions of the events of the war. A number of *Flamingants*, the activists, had then collaborated with the Germans to obtain strict implementation of the language laws. The German occupying forces had also made Dutch the language of Ghent University in 1915. The Flemish movement suffered from adverse reactions to these events after 1918; for after the armistice, Belgian patriotism reigned un-challenged. But the war also had another effect. At the front, it had been mainly the Flemish who had served as soldiers in the Belgian army, but they had been commanded in French. In their ranks had grown, first openly but then clandestinely, the so-called Front Movement, in which *Flamingant* intellectuals and ordinary young men came to terms. After the war, this movement developed into the Front party, which was formed to defend Flemish interests. The party took more radical positions than the pre-war *Flamingants* had done, for its objective was self-rule for Flanders in one or another form, and it tried to put pressure on the *Flamingants* within the traditional political parties. These politicians revived pre-war demands in what was called a minimum programme that provided for, among other things, the dutchification of the state University of Ghent in the near future. The execution of this programme, however, was no simple matter. With the implementation of the simple universal franchise in 1919, political power relations became differ-ent from those before the war. Only coalition governments could be formed. Thus, the Liberal party, although weaker than the Catholics and the socialists, played a relatively important role. It supported the French speaking minority – and French language education – in Flanders, while the *Flamingants* advocated integration into the Flemish cultural community. From the pro-Flemish point of view, the 1920s were thus a period of defective language laws. No significant changes took place in the language regime in secondary and primary education.

The Territoriality Principle and Bilingual Brussels

In the meantime, the demographic, economic, and cultural significance of Flanders grew within the context of the Belgian state. As
a result of this, on the Walloon side, the notion arose – already
articulated before 1914 – that bilingualism could not be made the basis
for Belgian national unity. The Walloons wanted to secure their own
identity in a monolingually French Wallonia and also backed Dutch
monolingualism in Flanders and so abandoned the French speaking
minority there at the end of the 1920s. The first result of this in
education was the total dutchification of the state University of Ghent
in 1930. The private university in Leuven, for its part, organised
parallel Dutch language education alongside French language
education. Secondary and primary education in the Flemish regions
were then converted to Dutch by the law of 14 July 1932.

Looking at the situation created by this law, we note that its
significance must be qualified. A distinction must be made between
the rule that was applied for Brussels and the linguistic border
communities and that for the Walloon and Flemish regions. The law
stipulated that the regional language, that is, the language of the
region in which the school was located, had to be the language of
instruction. In Wallonia, therefore, only education in French was
provided, and in Flanders, only in Flemish. This regionality principle
was however, not absolute. Theoretically, it applied to all children,
including those from the linguistic minority; in other words, the
French speakers in Flanders. However, the right of these children to
education in their mother tongue was recognised. Thus, there came
the pragmatic solution that allowed the municipal authorities or
private school administration to organise special classes with
education in French. From the third year on, however, education in
the regional language also had to be given in such a way that the
pupils would be capable of continuing their studies after primary
education in the language of the region. These special classes,
therefore, were called transmutation classes.

One may thus state that the new law was an important step to the
complete dutchification of primary education in Flanders. Totally
private schools could still organise French language education, but in
public and subsidised education, this was no longer possible, except
in the transmutation classes. These classes were not intended for
Flemish children. In fact, however, pupils were admitted that did not
belong there. Only in exceptional cases did pupils with French as
their mother tongue continue their studies after primary school in
Dutch. Thus, under the guise of the transmutation system, French
language education was, in fact, maintained. The number of transmutation classes actually increased. French did not disappear from

primary schools in Flanders with the introduction of the territoriality principle. The law permitted the study of this language to be included in the curriculum from the fifth grade on. Most of the municipal authorities and private school administrations did make use of this facility, which had a long tradition behind it and it continues to the present day.

For the Brussels agglomeration and for the bilingual municipalities on the linguistic frontier (municipalities where at least 30 per cent of the inhabitants spoke a language different from that of the majority), a special regulation was devised. Here the mother tongue (or the usual language) of the pupils had to be the language of instruction, as was the case before 1914. Second language education was obligatory there from the third grade on (minimum of three and maximum of six hours per week). With permission granted by royal decree presented in the ministerial council and published in the Belgian *Monitor*, second language education could even begin earlier and be expanded with review exercises. In municipalities with a linguistic minority of 20 per cent (according to the last census), the municipal authorities or the administrators of private schools could begin the teaching of the second language in the second grade. This could, in practice, apply for municipalities near the capital that did not belong to the Brussels agglomeration.

Thus, in Brussels, in contrast to Flanders and Wallonia, a bilingual regime was maintained. The school structure underwent no fundamental changes. French and Flemish classes had to exist alongside each other, but there were very few of the latter. The pupils were assigned to a French or a Flemish class on the basis of their mother tongue, and what the mother tongue was indicated by the head of the family. Theoretically the correctness of such a declaration had to be examined by the head of the school, but that generally did not happen. Consequently the heads of families submitted false declarations on a large scale and they gave preference to French language education for their children even though Dutch was their mother tongue. This preference, together with the indifference or anti-Flemish attitude of the heads of schools caused the school population of the Dutch language system to decline constantly in spite of the continuing Flemish immigration into Brussels. Two language inspectors were charged with the supervision of the implementation of the law. They noted countless violations and reported them to the authorities, but no sanctions followed. Indeed, none had been provided in respect of the declarations of the heads of families.

The most important explanation for the lack of honesty in the application of the language law in the Brussels agglomeration is certainly the socio-economic pressure that had long been operative on the Flemish. The Flemish wanted to see their children advance in the world by means of their mastery of French. It was for this reason, and not out of a spirit of opposition to the law, that false declarations were made. The law of 1932 thus had little significance in the Brussels context: it did not stop the shift from Dutch to French.

The language regulation of 1932, therefore, can hardly be considered a positive attempt to create a new structure that would resolve all the educational problems. It was much more a forced concession to the Flemish demands. On the periphery, both languages were now equal. A plural monolingualism was established in the country whereby Dutch and French formed the basis of, respectively, Flemish and Walloon cultural identity. In the centre of the nation–state, however, French continued to maintain its dominant position. The Flemish had been able to prevent assimilation, to establish a Flemish sub-nation in Belgium, and to push through a regionalist ideology, but they could not yet set the tone of the central state apparatus. Moreover, the socio-economic pressure in Brussels turned out to be stronger than the law, leaving more than enough ground for conflict.

It was only after the Second World War that the demographic and economic situation in Belgium developed to the benefit of the Flemings. The change to Dutch in the educational system now proved effective. Among the upper social classes the Dutch speakers moved into important positions and took some of the levels of command into their own hands. The social barrier constituted by language lost its former significance. The linguistic legislation was completed, and for the younger generation, 'normal' conditions were created. From the linguistic struggle, the Flemish movement extended the front to all domains of social life. On the other hand, in Wallonia the outlook became increasingly dreary. The Walloons lost their traditional preponderance. This caused a broader than linguistic problem. The relations between the two communities deteriorated, which ultimately led to the adaptation of the present state structure. In cultural and economic matters, the responsibilities of the central government were partly transferred to regional bodies.

Select Bibliography

Aelvoet, H. (1957), *Honderd vijfentwintig jaar verfransing in de agglomeratie en het arrondissement Brussel, 1830–1955* (125 years of frenchification in the agglomeration and the district of Brussels), Brussels.

Boon, H. *Enseignement primaire et alphabétisation dans l'agglomération bruxelloise de 1830 à 1879* (Louvain, 1969. University de Louvain, Recueil de travaux d'histoire et de philologie, 4e s., 42).

Clough, S.B. (1930), *A history of the Flemish Movement in Belgium*, New York.

De Vroede, M. (1975), *The Flemish Movement in Belgium*, Antwerp.

Elias, H.J. (1963–65), *Geschiedenis van de Vlaamse gedachte, 1780–1914* (History of the Flemish thought), 4 vols, Antwerp.

Elias, H.J. (1969), *25 jaar Vlaamse Beweging 1914/1939* (25 years of the Flemish Movement), 4 vols, Antwerp.

Fishman, J.A., (ed.) (1978), *Advances in the study of societal multilingualism*, The Hague.

Fishman, J.A. (1972), *Language and nationalism. Two integrative essays*, Rowley, Mass.

Haugen, E. (1972), *The ecology of language*, Stanford.

Lorwin, V.R. (1969), 'Belgium: religion, class, and language in national politics', in Dahl, R.A. (ed.), *Political oppositions in Western democracies*, New Haven.

Mallinson, V. (1963), *Power and politics in Belgian education 1815 to 1961*, London.

Ruys, M. (1973), *The Flemings. A people on the move. A nation in being*, Utrecht.

Van Haegendoren, M. (1965), *The Flemish Movement in Belgium*, Antwerp.

Van Velthoven, H. (1981), 'Taal en onderwijspolitiek te Brussel 1878–1914' (Language and educational policy in Brussels), in *Taal en sociale integratie*, vol. IV, Brussels.

Willemsen, A. (1969), *Het Vlaams-nationalisme. De geschiedenis van de jaren 1914–1940* (The Flemish nationalism. History of the years 1914–1940), 2nd edn., Utrecht.

Zolberg, A.R. (1975), 'Transformation of linguistic ideologies: the Belgian case', in Savard, J.C. and Vigneault, R., (eds) *Les États multilingues. Problèmes et solutions* (Multilingual political systems. Problems and solutions), Québec.

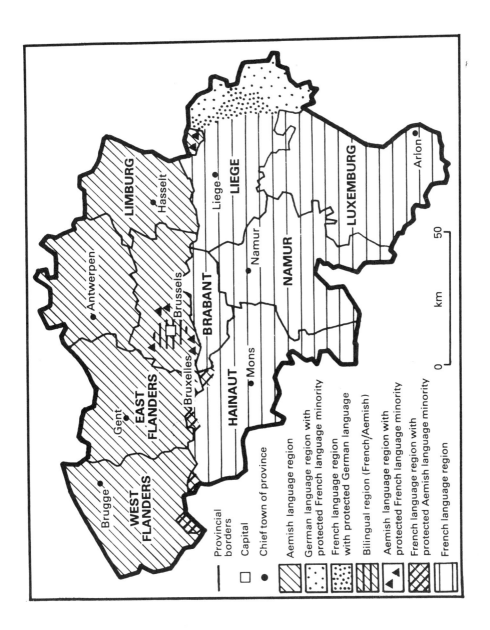

Map 6.1 Languages spoken in Belgium up to 1940

7 State, School and Ethnic Minorities in Prussia, 1860–1914

MANFRED HEINEMANN

Education and Cultural Assimilation

The relationship between the Prussian state, schools and minorities has always been controversial. From the seventeenth century onwards there have been great differences in Prussia's policies towards the different minority groups: religious groups were treated differently from language minorities. Invited Protestant minorities were more welcome than those immigrants, Catholics or Jews[1] for example, who arrived under pressure. The French reformists who in the late seventeenth century settled in Berlin under the legal provisions of the Potsdam edict of 1685 were granted the privilege of running a special educational system for instance.[2] In the nineteenth century while this system was absorbed into the national stream of school development it still was respected and retained the privilege of using French as teaching language in the *Französisches Gymnasium* (French grammar or classical secondary school).

The Case of the Jews

After settling in Brandenburg in 1671, the Jews as a minority were harshly treated by special legislation. It was not until 1812 that the *Emanzipationsedikt* (edict of emancipation) offered them Prussian citizenship and positions in society. This offer was reduced in its substance some years later. In 1822 access for Jews to positions such as teaching at *gymnasiums* ceased. From 1835 onward Jews were allowed to take the qualifying examination for teaching in grammar schools but there was no hope of further training. This changed in 1872 when local circumstances led to Jewish teachers being accepted in Wrocław (*Breslau*) under an order of the Minister of Culture, Falk.[3] Some years later they were teaching at *gymnasiums* in almost every

133

province of Prussia. They were even permitted to teach history and German. In 1930 Jewish religious studies were accepted as a subject in examinations for teachers at *gymnasiums*.

Positions at universities had been opened to the Jews earlier. Under the law of 23 July 1847 Jews were permitted to teach medicine, mathematics, science, geography and languages even though they were excluded from holding chairs and performing functions as deans, senators and rectors.[4]

On 15 May 1824 a law demanding elementary education for Jewish children in Prussia came into force, with the exception of the province of Rhineland, where during Napoleonic occupation French law establishing the principle of public education for everyone had been introduced.[5] Legally, the Jews were seen as Prussian residents and therefore like all other residents subject to the *Allgemeines Landrecht* (general country law) of 1794. Parents were responsible for ensuring their children's education, but the state controlled it. This was in itself a threat to Jewish education.[6] The state would always prefer its own system and deny a special need for Jewish Hebrew (orthodox) education. Hesse-Darmstadt, a neighbouring state, prohibited Jewish elementary schooling in 1804. The opposite policy was followed by Hesse–Nassau (incorporated into Prussia in 1866) where the state took over the school finances of Jewish schools. In no case was the Christian control of elementary schooling ever suspended in Germany. Priests were still supervising Jewish schools in the Prussian provinces of Westphalia and Poznań (*Posen*) at the turn of the twentieth century.

Jews could make use of private schools where they existed and of Christian elementary schools where private Jewish teaching was not available. After the order of 1824, Jewish elementary education was supervised by the state. In private or public schools the state was demanding trained, certificated teachers, which necessitated special Jewish teacher seminaries. The aim of this act was primarily to encourage Jewish communities to organise a separate school system. In cases where Jewish communities were unable to do so (or liberal Jews wanted to follow a policy of assimilation or wanted to avoid anti-semitism) Jewish children were to attend public community based schools making special provision for religious teaching.

Under the law of 23 July 1847 Jews obtained the right to organise Jewish religious education and were at least enabled to ask for the creation of special school districts within an elementary Jewish public school system and make their own provision for religious education.[7] After the order of 18 May 1888, elementary religious education had to be granted for a minimum of twelve children. Statistics of 1901 show that in such courses only 3530 children participated out of 17 085.[8]

Christian *gymnasiums* were open for Jews where they were admissible. In 1859 the Ministry decided that Jewish religious education was not compulsory at the *gymnasiums* and therefore had to be paid for as an extra. A decline in interest resulted. Statistics of 1863 show Jewish school attendance at *gymnasiums* in every province with the exception of 21 institutions. Maximum figures were reached in Silesia and Brandenburg (including the city of Berlin). Minimum school attendance was counted in the provinces of Saxony and Westphalia.[9] In 1880 nearly 10 per cent of students at classical *gymnasiums* and in 1886 nearly 6 per cent of the students at universities were Jews; effectively seven times more than Christian Germans. In 1907 nearly 8 per cent of the Jewish work force had an academic background compared with 6.2 per cent of the rest of the population.[10] A special section among these students was formed by the massive concentration in Berlin of Polish students of medicine. In 1911/12, 307 out of 431 foreign students of medicine there were Polish. Jewish students were the youngest among the students and passed their examinations earliest. They were often successful in the competition for jobs and this led to widespread opposition of an anti-semitic character from other students. The assimilation of Jews was more and more hampered by its own success. Anti-semitism and the beginning of racism were adding to the controversies. The role of a *völkische Bewegung* (folk movement) became noticeable in reducing the Jewish influence in society, but it was the new elites of Prussia which started to disseminate hatred against *die Judenfrage* (the Jewish influence) in society.[11]

A cultural assimilation of the Jews can be ascribed to the impact of the *Kulturkampf* (cultural campaign), when Bismarck tried to separate the state from the Churches. The decline of Christianity in society, economic progress of the era of the *Reichsgründung* (foundation of the empire) made it much easier than ever before to assimilate, to change Jewish family names and to gain full citizenship.[12] In consequence, *gymnasiums* accepted Jewish teachers. This was permitted first in 1872 at Piła (*Schneidemühl*) in Poznań province. Prussia, with her new territories, was confronted with the existing Jewish *gymnasiums* with different traditions. The inclusion of the city of Frankfurt into Prussia in 1866 brought highly developed Jewish private *gymnasiums* under the control of the Prussian administration.[13] In Berlin in 1907, 15 per cent of Jewish children attended lessons in Christian religious education at *gymnasiums*. The figure for all Prussia was 9 per cent. So Jewish Orthodoxy with its few schools remained a minority influence and liberal tendencies among the Jews prevailed.[14]

In response to the demand to professionalise elementary teacher training the *Marks Haindorf Foundation* in Münster in Westphalia province was established in 1825. At the end of the century Jewish seminars with small numbers of students were in existence in Münster, Kassel, Berlin and Hanover.[15] In the Weimar republic the school situation for the Jews remained as it had been before the First World War. The 1920 school statistics show there were nearly 10 per cent of Jewish students at the classical *gymnasium*: 5047 out of 54 802.[16] At the *Realgymnasien* (classical and commercially orientated secondary school) there were 3566 Jewish students out of a total of 51 038; and at the *Oberrealschulen* (extended commercially orientated secondary school), 1918 out of 43 106. At *Realschulen* (commercially orientated secondary school) the proportion was only 1606 out of 27 360. Male Jews still preferred the higher levels obtainable at *Gymnasien*. Female students at institutes of higher education for women numbered 12 237 out of 138 211.

The language policy of the Prussian Ministry of Education towards the Danish or Polish language minorities at the turn of the century provided a sharp contrast to the policies of moderate assimilation made possible by a system based on religious tolerance. Attempts through educational policy to integrate these national minorities was a total failure. Schools in the east and in the north of Prussia became battlefields of cultural oppression. The *Volksschule* (elementary school) became its most sinister exponent because it pursued the one and only German *Volkserziehung* (national education) in respect of national minorities.[17]

Minorities in a Nation–State

During the first half of the nineteenth century Prussia was neither a culturally nor a regionally uniform state; nor was it totally centralised. But it had always pursued a nationalist policy, trying to assimilate and mould its population into 'Prussians'. The state organised cultural matters on a federal basis from 1815 until the revised constitution was passed in 1850. Cultural centralisation became the political aim in Prussia from 1871, when Bismarck's Prussia came to lead the *Reich*, itself a federation. Yet considerable differences between provinces, regions and towns remained, let alone the differences between urban and rural situations.

After 1815, schools were put under the severe pressure of a unifying administrative reorganisation. But the regional traditions remained important even after 1871 when the administration tried several times in vain to set up a school law respecting the basic principles of the constitution of 1850. The administration acted as if there existed constitutional demands for a unifying Christian education for each Prussian. Until the establishment of the Weimar Republic all attempts to pass such a common school law failed. Therefore, in education, unresolved conflicts between the administration and the traditional forces beneath the surface of centralised policy making could always be found. Additionally, lack of money for public education led to various special arrangements. By law, public education including public elementary schooling, was still a secondary consideration, the primary one being parental responsibility for teaching their own children. Parents could make use of public schools organised by local school societies, or later by communes, but they were not under an obligation to do so. Children of the wealthier classes avoided attending public elementary schools and attended special preparatory classes before entering a *gymnasium*, exempt from ordinary regulations. It was only in the long run that the Prussian state was able to undermine this structure and to replace it by modern arrangements. It was only during the period of the Weimar Republic that the first four years of schooling became compulsory for everyone and it was only in 1938 during Hitler's Third *Reich* that compulsory school attendance was fully organised to cover all children of school age.

In the early nineteenth century the aim of elementary education was the building up of schooling free of tuition fees for every Prussian child regardless of its family background, religion, financial resources and abilities: a real common education for a new civil society. The philosophical ideals of *Allgemeinbildung* (general education) as formulated in the reform era after the Napoleonic defeat by such reformers as Privy Councillor Wilhelm von Humboldt and other state officials were to make teaching more or less free from the preoccupation with everyday needs and to overcome the tradition of *cuius regio eius religio* (the religion of the king is the religion of the people) in schooling. The responsibilities in education of the king as *Landesvater* (father of the people) and as the first bishop was to be fully taken over by the administration. Parochial traditions of teaching, education exclusively for a religious life, paying little regard to civic needs of local communities and of the nation–state were to be abandoned. The influence of the state on schooling, scholarship, science and (in later years) industry was developed to promote this idealistic Prussian concept of a unicultural citizenship.

The ensuing prussification conflicted with traditional society in general. *Staatspädagogik* (official pedagogy) was developed as a form of nationalisation through schooling. It was based on *hochdeutsch* (the High German language). Aside French and Latin for the educated classes, the clergy and the nobility, the use of Luther's translation of the Bible for the standardisation of the German language had introduced standard German as a second language in dialect speaking Protestant areas. But these connections between language and religion remained relatively harmless until the modern state and its idealistic planners discovered High German and began to use it to promote easier communication among its citizens. Lutherans, Reformists, Mennonites[18], Catholics, Jews and others could make use of this language for better communication instead of their own languages or Latin or French as used in administration, commerce or courts. But it was in the era of the Enlightenment that a broader use of High German was accepted by Frederick the Great and by the Prussian intellectuals as the official language to unify the Prussian collection of states and nations to form a new European power.

The *Allgemeines Landrecht* of 1794, the basic code of a citizens' state, was written in High German. It claimed that the institutions of the school and university were a public responsibility, operating for the benefit of the new society, the *bürgerliche Gesellschaft* (middle class society). This code made full use of education as the principal means for bringing to an end both the society based on estates as well as the dominance of the Churches in public education. After the Napoleonic defeat of Prussia the use of High German was rapidly expanded through the educational institutions to cover all levels of schooling and the universities. In the years around 1830 bilingual elementary education could still be found in multilingual areas. Thirty years later all subjects at the *Volksschule* were taught in High German only, except for religious education.

High German was made a teaching subject at *gymnasiums*. Regional languages or dialects and traditional Church orientation in teaching in elementary schooling began to decline following the introduction of modernised elementary teacher training in the 1870s. The expansion of *Volksschullehrer-Seminare* (teacher training seminaries) to fully meet the needs of the 1870s and 1880s, affected the language training of teachers of Polish, Danish, French and Latin adversely; these languages could only be taught as *Bildungssprachen* (educational languages) where wanted for improving *Allgemeinbildung* (general education). Many elementary teachers were transferred from their regions, as they mostly spoke dialects. Local languages were officially allowed to be used only to communicate with school beginners and in teaching religion.

Religious education became the last resort of non-German language teaching at elementary schools. It was taught frequently by priests and therefore tolerated. Protestant and Catholic Churches defended the use of local languages to the utmost against the orders from Berlin. But eventually even religious education was undermined by laicism and a modernising society using High German, leaving only some dialect enclaves in the countryside. In Prussia, the introduction of new science subjects such as *Naturgeschichte* by the *Allgemeinen Bestimmungen* (general school order) of 1872, changed the central function of religious education to a marginal one. In general, Church related teaching was superseded by state related contents not respecting regional language needs.

Gymnasiums respected Polish or Danish only as a special subject until the era of *Reichsgründung*. By order of 24 May 1842, it was settled that for Poznań province the Polish language could be used for up to one third of the teaching time devoted to the study of language. This order reduced the use of the Polish language in the upper grades of *gymnasiums* with students mostly of Polish nationality, but still left religious education fully to Polish, respecting the fact that most of the students subsequently studied theology at university.[19] The Polish language teaching examination could be taken only in Wrocław (*Breslau*). Optional languages taught at *gymnasiums* in 1863 were Wendian for the Sorbian minority at the *gymnasium* in Cottbus, Bohemian at Głubczyce (*Leobschütz*), Lithuanian in Tilsit (now *Sovetsk*). But this was not a compromise which minorities were willing to accept. The Prussian policy *vis-à-vis* the Sorbs already followed germanisation lines.[20]

With the help of appropriate measures affecting teacher training, selection and placement of teachers, the administration made schools follow the official lines of national education. The idea of a unified Germany as a world power inspired the *Volksschule* until Germany's collapse following the First World War. Germany was not alone in this. All European powers dreamt of national power. Prussians with mother tongues other than German had to be integrated. Territories with a high percentage of non-German speaking population which had been gained in 1815 (the Grand Duchy of Poznań) or by the war of 1864 (the duchy of Schleswig)[21] were to be integrated by prussification and germanisation. In 1855 in Schleswig, of approximately 396 000 inhabitants 170 000 spoke local Danish, 153 000 local German, 45 000 both languages and 27 000 Frisian.[22]

To be successful in creating the new *Staatsbürger* (Citizen) the power of the Churches had to be broken first. In 1872 the *Schulaufsichtsgesetz* (school supervision law) abolished the classroom control by the Churches which had started the *Kulturkampf* there. It paved the way for an increasing and modernising influence of the state and of the local communities on internal matters of the school. New curriculums and textbooks were introduced. Laws in the 1880s regulated and reduced the fees paid by elementary school pupils to help reduce illiteracy. Higher salaries and better pensions for teachers softened the conflicts with the traditional school autonomy. Better trained teachers, supported by the state, attained higher social prestige. The Prussian school system came to be held in high esteem by foreign visitors while teachers willingly adopted a national role in the state, acting as assimilators of non-German youth, so they became Prussian and German nationals.

As a next step, the state authorities decided to eliminate influence from all remaining social forces opposing change in the school system. As the local boards were rejecting or hampering state interference, the 1906 law on financing the *Volksschule* (and its related institutions at the lower levels of schooling) removed the traditional school boards still in existence in the countryside according to the provision of the *Allgemeines Landrecht* of 1794. In 1906 the influence of parents was replaced by school commissions attached to local or city government under full control of the state.

From 1906, following a *Schulkompromiss* (school compromise) among the parties in the Prussian *diet* the *Volksschulen* became the principal agencies of a state controlled prussification. They were now organised according to the denomination of the majority of their pupils as Catholic or Protestant institutions. Mixed schools for pupils from different religions remained exceptional. This gave rise to new problems facing religious minorities and atheists. The non-religious schools and the *Weltanschauungsschule, Freie Schulen* (free school movement) tried to escape this religious affiliation of elementary schooling but for the great majority of pupils denominational schooling existed throughout the existence of the Weimar Republic.

Nationalsprache versus *Kultursprache*

Conflicts over schooling within the modern industrial society of the Wilhelmian period were unavoidable. The problems resulting from a mass immigration of about 2 000 000 persons (including, in 1910, 250 000 people speaking only Polish) into the industrial areas in the western parts of Prussia from the 1880s onward had to be dealt with not simply by assimilation in elementary schools. Prussia's industrial areas in the Ruhr were the target of a cultural attack that turned them into melting pots of germanisation for these immigrant workers from all over Europe. The rapid growth of both the labour movement and the unions, the fear of unrest and social conflict, the emergence of new nationalistic and radical beliefs resulted in the Prussian administration developing its school policy alongside a very rigid policy of social control. In addition the administration strengthened its policy through a barrier system in higher education, created to ensure its exclusive use by the members of the elites. This system, the *Berechtigungswesen* (officially certified entitlement system), was effective in preventing the minority leaders from holding prestigious positions in the state. Only totally acculturated and assimilated students could advance culturally and socially.

The *gymnasium*, in particular, played an important role in this process. Since 1825, the influence of the Churches on this type of school had been reduced and was now nearly extinguished. State supervisors in the *Provinzialschulkollegien* (provincial school supervisory boards) replaced *Konsistorien* (church administration). In 1834, the *Abitur* (final secondary school examination), introduced in 1788, became the university entrance examination at a time when the *gymnasiums* were still aiming at classical education on eighteenth century lines. Nevertheless, they were engaged in the nation building process and were reorganised as Prussian or German institutions. Subjects like German history and German language were introduced and classical studies reduced in less prestigious branches of the *gymnasiums*. In 1871 the foundation of the *Reich* paved the way to extending *gymnasium* schooling into a nationwide system. The study of classics was left to a minority. The old elites were content to let others enter business and industry. This system seemed to guarantee both Prussian leadership based upon classical education *and* a national industrial elite. But *Bildung* (education) became merely an instrument of advancement through the *Berechtigungssystem* (officially certified entitlement system). Nationalism and business displaced the old European cultural perspective.

Bürgerliche Bildung (civic education), formerly aimed at freeing citizens from old traditions and regional loyalties, now stressed its exclusive function in the creation of a unified state elite. Barring members of the working class, those of non-Prussian background and those who were minority leaders all helped to forge a one nation society. The members of the old Prussian nations like Westphalians, Saxons, Rhinelanders, Hanoverians, Pommeranians, east and west Prussians and others were thus educationally unified. They were merged into Prussians and Germans. After 1871 this process was widened to embrace the whole of the new German Empire, at a time when every European nation was preparing for imperialism and colonialism.

In Prussia, all school curriculums and textbooks followed such orientation. The political perspectives of a world power in the Bismarck era forced upon the masses several kinds of unifying systems. The new legal system of the *Reich*, the new unifying measurement system, the new communications and railway systems, the social security system for the working people, etc. were an overwhelming success and of national influence. People were made to feel that to be Germans was to be part of the great and heroic history of a Nordic culture. Schools in general were under pressure to partake in this strategy to create a powerful German *Reich* and *Volk* (people), withstanding the Slavs and the French. Popular culture organised these ideas within the limits of its own primitive notions of Darwinism and of history on heroic lines.

At the beginning of the nineteenth century, state and nation were used as a formula to make minorities accept prussification. This was followed by nation building concepts based on either *grossdeutsch* (a greater German empire); or *kleindeutsch* (a smaller German empire excluding Austria). Bismarck's foundation of the German *Reich* in

1871 seemed to end cultural federalism. Austria was effectively excluded from concepts of nation building as a result of the war of 1866. German as a *Kultursprache* (civilised language) in a *Kulturnation* (civilised nation) remained politically unfulfilled. But for the intellectuals this concept of a culturally united German nation survived even its nationalistic perversions during both world wars. The idea of moulding the national character of the German people which forced the minorities to be totally germanised culminated in Hitler's concentration camps and in the occupied *Reichsgau Wartheland* and *Generalgouvernement Polen*, where Hitler's elites exterminated the Jews and the Polish intelligentsia.[23]

The Grand Duchy and Province of Poznań under Germanisation

The foundation of the German *Reich* in 1871 was a turning point, after which the language policy of the Prussian state became aggressive. Until 1870 in Poznań province, which had been incorporated into Prussia as *Grossherzogtum Posen* under the decision taken at the Congress of Vienna in 1815, bilingual education was permitted by the state. On 24 May 1842, the Minister of Culture, von Eichhorn, signed an instruction about the use of Polish *and* German language, complying with the theory about the importance of the mother tongue for the development of the Polish nation under Prussian government. The main language used at school was to be the one used by the majority of pupils in a school. This was to be the case in the countryside, while the pupils in the upper grades in the urban areas were to be taught in the German language to prepare the older pupils to meet the needs of commerce.[24] Nevertheless the chances for the minority to reach the *Abitur* were low, because of the lack of secondary schools there compared with other provinces of Prussia.

As Rudolf Korth has pointed out after the examination of many documents, such a mixed language education led to very unsatisfactory results from schooling, from the German point of view.[25] The Polish minority was able to acquire a sound knowledge of German, while the German students were polonised by their comrades. However, this aspect was not the focus of criticism until school policy was placed at the core of germanising activities from Berlin. To make this point more firmly studying at German universities had been a long tradition for the numerically limited Polish elite. But the Polish middle class began to discover that career patterns in Prussia were changing more and more against their children. Attempts in 1843 and 1845 by Wojciech Lipski to found a university in Poznań was a failure.[26] Other attempts in 1851, 1853, 1854 and 1855 by August Cieszkowski and in 1872, 1885 also failed. The later foundation of the

Königliche Akademie (King's Academy) in 1903 was a result of the German influence.

In 1832 German became the official language of the province,[27] though until 1842 Polish district officials remained in office. After 1864 Polish judges were transferred to other parts of Prussia.[28] Patriotic reactions to such moves in the 1840s, which are documented by the police as democratic reactions against the *Deutschtum* (German character) included the foundation as early as 1841 of the *Towarzystwo Pomocy Naukowej* for the advancement of students in Poznań province.[29] This society, later named after its founder Karol Marcinkowski (1800–1846),[30] existed until 1939. After a vigorous start with more than 296 grants awarded before 1844,[31] it financed 4335 students in the first 50 years, but reduced its grants to about ten in the late 1870s, resuming its influence towards the end of the century with about 30 grants. At that time it extended its influence to the western provinces of Prussia to offer grants for theological studies mainly.

Barring the Polish minority from higher education became one of the main aims of the repressive policy of the last decades of the nineteenth century. It was the period when the parliamentary system gave Polish political leaders a chance to put issues of minority policy on the agenda of parliamentary discussion and thereby draw them to the attention of the public. Overheated state reaction led to the closure of a *gymnasium* in Trzemeszno following participation in the 1863 uprising. The increase in fees made schooling more expensive; the reduction of Polish teaching staff[32] reduced career opportunities. Statistics show the decline in numbers of teachers of Polish background at the *Maria Magdalena gymnasium* in Poznań.[33] In 1870 about 70 teachers were teaching in the province, but by 1918 only eight were left (mostly teaching religion). The proportion of Polish pupils there was also reduced, from more than 90 per cent in 1870 to about 50 per cent in 1890 and in the following years.[34] While the number of Polish *Abiturienten* (candidates for the final secondary school examination) increased steadily, the majority of pupils were Germans. The *Realgymnasium* in Poznań in 1873 was transformed into a German school.[35] From 1874 the textbooks in history and geography were in German.[36] The library for the *alumni* of the *Maria Magadalena Gymnasium* was closed. Only a few parents with money were able to escape this process of germanisation, by sending their sons to schools in Galicia.

After the foundation of the German *Reich* Prussia under Bismarck went ahead with sharpening an aggressive policy against Russia and the language question was made a key issue in the debates. In connection with the first and very effective law on school supervision in 1872 Bismarck announced his intention to foster the use of the German language in further administrative acts.[37] On 16 October

1872, came the first administrative order through which German was introduced into religious education in secondary schools[38] thus launching the *Kulturkampf* against the Polish intelligentsia. The archbishop of Poznań, Count Ledóchowski, responded by ordering his priests to conduct religious education in Polish in the first four grades even for German pupils. This was answered with the dismissal of all staff accepting the orders of the archbishop. The effect was that most posts in religious education remained vacant during the next decade until Ledóchowski's successor, Dinder, rescinded his order in 1887 and accepted religious education in German. By an order of 27 October 1873, the *Oberpräsident* (provincial governor) von Gunther made German the language of instruction in the province with some exceptions for children of Polish background in religious education and lessons for church music. Somewhat surprisingly, this order left the Polish language as a subject for Polish children for five hours a week in the lower grades, and three hours a week in middle and higher classes. The number of hours for German were: eleven, ten and eight in one classroom schools and eleven, eight and eight in other elementary schools. In itself, this imbalance in language teaching aimed at germanising the schoolchildren, but it had the effect of depriving Germans of a chance to study Polish, which could benefit them in business life.

Similarly, forceable measures on germanisation were taken by the authorities in Silesia, even though some concessions were made to the Polish speaking minority. Using a non-German language remained legal for the lower grades in elementary school; it was accepted as an aid in the middle grades; but it was forbidden in the higher grades of schooling. Schools with more than 25 per cent of children of German language background were seen as pure German schools in which religious education in general had to be carried on in German. Similar regulations were put into effect in West and East Prussia as from 24 July 1873. The Polish and Lithuanian languages were restricted to the lower levels of schooling but were not totally excluded from the higher grades insofar as they were needed as a starting point of instruction. This was not the case in the majority of the German schools.

The aim of all such regulations was to foster the use of the German language. The aspect most open to criticism was the direct interference with religious education of the Catholic Polish speaking minority. Also, from the economic standpoint the restrictions on Polish did damage even to the interests of the German population. One comparison is possible: the Masurians of East Prussia, as Protestants, were treated with much greater consideration despite the attachment to their mother tongue.[39]

'Polenpolitik' in the East

The façade of Prussian *laissez faire* with its expectations of a silent assimilation of the Polish population was abandoned in 1872 and 1873. From then on the authorities used all the administrative tools at their disposal to reduce the Polish influence in schools. Teachers of German background were imported from other Prussian provinces. Such elementary teachers were now trained in the typical seminar fashion. They were given little or no assistance to cope with the problems of Polish speaking children and their parents. The advice they received was simply to speak German. Elementary education at this stage in general was problematic and ineffective.

Battles in the Prussian *diet* and public unrest followed. Government measures were named Darwinistic by Bishop Stablewski in 1883 but the Minister of Culture, von Gossler, defended his policy, rejecting accusations of germanisation by claiming to be introducing Polish children to the Prussian state language and arguing that the minority would otherwise be excluded from full participation in the state and the new *Reich*.[40] This argument seemed acceptable but other restrictions in religious education soon followed.[41] The new orders in 1883 stressed the importance of the use of German as early as possible to exclude the influence of the minorities' cultures on the German children. The conflict between the concept of two national educations was heating up. By 1886 provincial authorities were demanding the exclusion of the use of minority languages altogether though this was rejected by the Ministry. There was, however, a gradual restriction of the use of minority languages to the lower grades only, which was implemented by the school supervisors with great effect.

On 7 September 1887, Minister of Culture von Gossler was able to present a royal order which demanded the exclusion of the Polish language from the *Volksschulen* in the Poznań Province. This order was supplemented by the reduction of Polish language training in teacher training seminaries, now only available for the German students. The Polish opposition rejected such measures as unworthy of the life of Polish speaking families and religious education in general. The authorities in Berlin replied by calling for a fuller assimilation of the minorities into the life in Prussia and the *Reich*. From 1886, in the Poznań province nothing but German was permitted as an official language of state. The use of minority languages in public affairs in Prussia in general was marginalised. Polish could no longer be used officially in court or in business, due to the *Geschäftssprachengesetz* (law for the use of German as the official language) of 28 August 1876. People of Polish nationality felt themselves without a tongue, which caused opposition in their ranks, especially regarding religious education.[42] Some minor administrative concessions, tolerating private language training, were granted in 1891 but that meant no return to previous conditions. The following years saw the Prussian *Polenpolitik* (Polish policy) develop further along these lines. At the turn of the century only in the area of religious education could the mother tongue be used. In a climate of the ongoing attempts of German nationalistic organisations such as the *Ostmarkenverein* (Eastern Marches Society) and the radical *Hakatisten* to heat up the confrontation, popular Polish conventions answered by demanding freedom of language use in religious education; Polish as a school subject; and the right of parents to educate their children in Polish privately.[43]

It was under Minister of Culture, von Studt, that official policy went further still starting the decisive battle. In Poznań province in July or August 1900 the order was given that German be introduced as the language of religious education to 'upgrade' those schools still using Polish. The city of Poznań was the first to resist this attempt.[44] A dozen children were kept at home, causing enormous public outcry and protest actions in Berlin by Polish social democrats. In the Prussian *diet*, Polish members demanded as a right that religious education be left to the Churches. The administration, however, rejected every attempt to discuss its position. Though the protests may have caused it to slow down its policy for all German education, this was a purely tactical matter, as can be seen from the further restrictions on private language teaching. These prohibitions mostly hit the minority national cultural societies or priests. The latter were fined, while teachers were jailed and made heroes. The Polish press did its best to make every prohibition public. This policy resulted in a strike against germanisation in Września (*Wreschen*). It was a determined, if desperate form of protest. Pupils were brutally forced to use German in their religious education which resulted in a parents' appeal to Kaiser Wilhelm II. In 41 public meetings around the city of Września the minority reacted more and more heatedly. Corporal punishment of children was answered with a public riot. The offenders were heavily fined by court in Gniezno (*Gnesen*); some were sentenced to two-and-a-half years' imprisonment. Photographs of the beaten children were distributed. However the families of those imprisoned were kept alive by the support of their neighbours. In addition, the leaders were forced to leave the country, causing more international attention to focus on the matter, which included sympathy and support from the part of Poland under Russian occupation. The ground was being prepared for the great strikes of 1905–6 because approximately 85 000 out of 250 000 children of Polish background were taught purely in German.[45]

In the context of the school reform of 1905 in the Russian occupied part of Poland, which restored elementary education in Polish and allowed Warsaw University to introduce the Polish language in studies, the way seemed open for a Polish school system in Poznań province. The Polish population aided by Archbishop Stablewski prepared a nationwide strike. More than 40 000 children went on strike in November 1906 in the province. In addition, about 6500 children in West Prussia and more than 60 000 in Upper Silesia followed suit. The Prussian administration received the sharpest rebuff it had ever had to its germanisation policy. It lost its battle for *Deutschtum*. It was the same in economic development and in cultural policy. The cultural awakening of Polish theatre and literature was remarkable.

Polish Migrant Labour in the West of Germany

The concept of denationalisation of minorities resulted in increasing measures against all attempts to present a non-German identity in public. This was especially the case when Polish workers migrated to the coal mining areas of the Ruhr. Here, as in other areas, even symbols of the minorities were suppressed. The Westphalian provincial government changed the official colours of the provincial flag from red and white to black and white because the police had tricks played on them by Poles. Prejudices with racial undertones increased. The often mentioned Polish character thus became interpreted as the very opposite of the aims of German education. Being sluggish, idle, dirty, drunk and so on had been the stereotype of the Polish working class since its emergence in greater numbers in the nascent industrial period of the 1880s when the surplus of Polish speaking agricultural labour started migrating to the industrial west. Clashes in behaviour, attitudes and education were not seen as a normal outcome of the migration of an improverished rural population across the *Reich* but as an expression of bad national character, demanding a security response.

After the reorganisation of agricultural techniques in the 1870s and 1880s the rural estates in the eastern Prussian provinces were in great need of seasonal labour. Thousands of cheap male and female Polish or Russian workers were hired for the harvest period. An increasing number remained and provoked a debate about the polonisation of the agricultural districts.[46] Bismarck himself warned against Russia expanding westwards. In 1885 he ordered about 40 000 people to be expelled from the four eastern Prussian provinces, including Poles married to Prussian women.[47] Such a dramatic decision was heavily criticised in the Prussian *diet*, not from a humanistic point of view but simply as a political error. Yet it opened the way for intensive population displacements. The landowners had expected an increasing germanisation of their seasonal workers through their approach of encouraging them to settle but now they found themselves without cheap labour. The industrial barons in the west were similarly interested in ways of getting what they also needed – cheap labour. At reduced military transport rates the railways carried thousands of seasonal workers, even whole villages, to the west to settle in the new areas.[48]

As the proportion of families with children remained low in this period, the problem of bilingual education did not manifest itself at first. There was no need for elementary education, only for elementary language knowledge for safety reasons in the coal mines. This changed dramatically in the following decades, when the first generation of itinerant workers married. The proportion of children with a non-German mother tongue grew rapidly. The immigrants and the non-German speaking minorities from other European backgrounds changed this part of Prussia into a multi-lingual society. The population statistics of 1900 disclosed that nearly ten per cent of the population of Prussia was non-German speaking, a total of 3 676 079 out of which 3 027 603 were only Polish speaking. 141 860 spoke Masurian; 115 702 Danish or Norwegian; 103 231 Lithuanian; 100 201 Kassubian; 60 686 Wendish; and 61 004 Bohemian.[49] Thus the largest language minority was composed of Polish speaking Prussians.

The growth of population in the area of the Ruhr, where coal mines and steel factories offered jobs around the turn of the century, was enormous. The statistics of the main industrial areas of the provinces of Westphalia and Rhineland show the highest increase in foreign immigrants between 1895 and 1910; the actual numbers nearly doubling every five years. In this context, the percentage of the Polish speaking minority in the provinces, in the three districts composing the *Regierungsbezirke* (districts) Düsseldorf, Arnsberg and Münster, increased, reaching 6.3 per cent in Münster in 1910. Seven cities had Polish speaking populations over ten per cent (the highest being 21.6 per cent in the town of Herne). Including unofficial residents, some communities in that period may have contained non-German elements, representing several nationalities, exceeding 50 per cent. Even the majority of Germans there did not generally speak High German but local and regional dialects instead.

Assimilation of the Polish Labour Force Through Control and Germanisation of Children

The living conditions in such rapidly growing localities were similar to those in American gold rush communities. The flow of working population increased the problems as the new towns changed their population twice or three times a year. The anxiety of the Prussian administration grew corresponding to the increasing size of the labour force because of the new potential afforded to social democrats and other organisations that were, in political terms, nonconformist. The Catholic Polish speaking minority also ran into conflict with the dominant German Catholic groups. The confessional traditions of these groups were different, and Polish demands for Polish speaking priests were rejected by the administration. Bishops and local churches took several years to accept the special religious needs of such a minority. Secret discussions between the *Oberpräsident*, the archbishop of Paderborn and the bishop of Münster illuminate the compromise eventually struck between state and Church, and the extent to which it was within the narrow bounds set by a policy of assimilation.[50] The pastoral side was accepted: the Polish national influence was not. With German priests being acceptable to the Polish minority, the state had eventually to compromise on priests of Prussian Polish background. Such priests were returned to the eastern provinces, if local police accused them of fostering the Polish national movement among the minority.

An additional form of control lay in a monopoly over the postal newspaper service. This was the easiest way to detect persons of Polish nationality. In addition, control over societies was rigorously exercised. All politically orientated associations were strictly forbidden. However, the minority reacted by founding religious associations and private entertainment organisations. Within a few years after 1900, the number of children of non-German speaking families exploded, as there were often five or more children in one family. As school statistics show, Polish speaking children at secondary schools went up from below one per cent in 1891 to ten per cent in 1912 in the *Regierungsbezirk* of Münster. It has been estimated that more than half the population in cities like Dortmund consisted of migrants of Polish background.

Such general statistical trends were exceeded in the centres of Polish migration. In 1910 in several *Kreise* (counties) Polish speaking children made up one fifth to one third of elementary schools. Special classes were organised where more than one third came from this language background, but bilingualism was not officially accepted. No teacher was prepared to teach two languages. Importing Polish textbooks for additional private or secret language training was prohibited by the administration. There was no other policy than the promoting of the German national interest through full assimilation, a term officially used by the Minister of Culture. No other European state accepted bilingualism in schools for labour migrants: Why have it in the Ruhr? But programmes and reports of the administration need to be considered carefully. They exaggerated the state of affairs in order to get additional money for schooling. In the district of Arnsberg only 26 special classes for the Polish speaking minority were available in 1905. Funds fell short of the nationalistic demands which were made.

The situation of the Polish minority only varied a little from that of the dominant German groups and other foreigners. Most of the German workers had migrated from nearby, and they all had language problems, as they spoke many different dialects. The social situation of all these groups was similar. At work all were forced to work together under the tough labour conditions. Living in newly created communities – *Kolonien* (colonies) as they were called – every newcomer experienced severe problems. Money was always short. Alcohol abuse was popular. Many were forced to accept overnight guests. It was not rare for the poorest workers to have to share one bed in shifts. Schooling in general was not effective and was never highly regarded by the workers, in spite of all the demands made by organised labour.

A time lag is visible before the emergence of a lower middle class among the Polish minority in the Ruhr. However shopkeepers, clerks and craftsmen appeared after a while, and it was their sons and daughters who aspired to higher education. But the barrier system was effective. There were almost no students from either the working class in general or from the east in the rare grammar schools of the Ruhr, or at the nearby universities at Bonn or Marburg or further away in Berlin. Out of the first generation of migrants only a few studied to become elementary teachers, and they were offered positions in the east. Not to expand the higher levels of education according to the growth of the population was a strategy designed to exclude the working class in general and the minorities in particular from advancing. If, in exceptional cases, a gifted child was accepted by a *gymnasium* headmaster there were orders to test his or her ability by means of effecting comprehensive germanisation. The great mass went through eight years of school without any training in their mother tongue. This left the children more or less germanised. To speak High German with a Polish accent was by no means unique since all other migrants and immigrants similarly spoke German with an accent of some kind.

Within the centrally prescribed curriculums the didactic side of germanisation started with ancient German and cultivated respect for 'king' and 'fatherland'. The induction into German culture was in itself a political training which stressed the leading role of German culture in the world. This concept was applied to every school child regardless of his or her denomination and regional background. Any opposition to such a domination had faded since the unification of the *Reich*. From 1872 onward the bishops had lost their influence on schooling under the law concerning school supervision therefore the battle for cultural identity. They entered into a long running appeasement process in order to salvage some influence on society. A new fight for the rights of minority groups was without any chance of success. The increasing influence of social movements and unions on the minority labour force turned towards new and more pressing fields of social conflict. The strikes of miners and steel workers were much more shocking to the province than language problems. In 1889 the Governor had to use military force to calm down the riots. It was the same Dr von Studt who, as head of the Ministry of Culture later, was responsible for the school strikes in the east. He was a character typical of those during the Wilhelmian era who applied military thinking to domestic 'battlefields'.

The Struggle Against Danish in Schleswig–Holstein

In Schleswig–Holstein, on the Danish border, a region in which a German aristocracy had long been dominant, schools in the *Kaiserzeit* (Kaiser's era) were organised in general as instruments of germanisation. Germany's neighbours acted similarly. Danification of Schleswig started around 1820 and was fostered under circumstances made difficult by doubtful Danish rights of succession to the province. When, in 1851, Denmark successfully integrated both Schleswig and Holstein under its government the German *Bund* (Union) answered in 1863 with a proclamation of war.[51] From 1865 Schleswig was under Prussian rule and Holstein was ruled by Austria, though only until the Austro-Prussian War of 1866. Prussia's victory in that year also led to the incorporation of the kingdom of Hanover, the city of Frankfurt, and the territories of Kurhessen and Nassau. This ended the separation of territory between Berlin and the western provinces.

The Danish–German conflict was effective first in destroying the ancient tradition of German schooling. In 1845, in Kolding, near the border with Schleswig, the Danish government set up a new *gymnasium* for its people near the border. In 1851, in Schleswig, direct control of school supervision was put under the control of Copenhagen, resulting in an order to respect both languages while introducing four hours of Danish in the southern part of the province with a German population. Sermons were to be given alternately in German and Danish. This regulation caused resistance among the Germans.

After the Prussian occupation in 1864 most of the Danish teachers left Schleswig. Control now passed to the Prussian commissioner.

The *gymnasiums* in Haderslev (*Hadersleben*) and Husum had been downgraded after 1850 into *höhere Bürgerschulen* (upper middle schools), taking on a Danish character after 1851. They had to alter their character back from Danish to German after 1864.[52] Higher education opportunities for the German majority in general had also been drastically reduced earlier under the old Danish rule,[53] and elementary schooling followed these changes. The general school order of 1814 for both duchies signed by King Frederick VI of Denmark had in fact specified the use of German only for the traditional German areas. Teachers to serve the Danish minority were then recruited from Danish teacher seminaries or the seminar in Tønder (*Tondern*), offering both German and Danish training. After 1864 some of them migrated to Denmark.

The Prussian administration's first steps were taken with great care. Responding to a proposal from the *Bezirksregierung* (regional government) in Schleswig for the introduction of three or four hours of German in Danish elementary schools, Minister of Culture von Mühler recommended caution in his order of 17 December 1869. Only 201 out of 348 teachers were able to use German as a teaching language. In consequence the Prussian administration terminated the recruitment of teachers from Denmark in 1869. From 1870 onward, as demands for germanisation grew, the Prussians purged schools of local Danish teachers.[54] On 22 June 1870, von Mühler established as a minimum the ability to read a German textbook at the end of schooling. An order of 17 August 1871 instituted six hours of German language in schools per week. The population could still opt for German citizenship until 1871.

In 1875 the district government in Schleswig was confronted with the question of resolving the 'anomaly' of the Danish sections of teacher training seminaries in Haderslev and Åbenrå. While no final decision was taken at that point, germanisation of the seminaries was strengthened, causing thereby a shortage of teachers. Additional money and other financial assistance from Berlin in the 1880s were spent on German teachers and Danish teachers were offered training in German.[55] The idea of Dr Schneider, Prussia's leading elementary school administrator, was simple: to overcome the traditional backwardness associated with local languages and schooling through introducing the educational philosophy of the *Allgemeine Bestimmungen* (General Order) of 1872, with its related textbooks, all written in High German. In 1877, the instruction was criticised as ineffective by Minister of Culture Falk. German from then on was to be used in every subject except religious education.[56]

Following secret negotiations with Austria in 1879 Prussia suspended article V of the Peace of Prague. This abolished the right of the Danish minority to return to Denmark by popular vote. Germanisation for all inhabitants was legalised.[57] The Danes reacted by increasing their resistance and by founding many societies. Conventions were held on Danish soil. Free places at Danish institutes of higher education were offered to Danish students from Schleswig. An attempt to create a private Danish *Realschule* in Haderslev was turned down by the Prussian administration in Schleswig in 1881,[58] while the costly German *Realklasse* (commercial stream) in Haderslev was saved,[59] even though only a few parents sent their sons to it.

In 1871 German lessons were introduced in Danish elementary schools in the northern parts of Schleswig. In 1878 the teaching language was partly German, partly Danish. Berlin instructed that the order of 18 December 1888 should state explicitly that from then on, German was to be the exclusive teaching language, except for religious education in areas where preaching was conducted in Danish. Danish was only permissible where beginners were unable to speak German.[60] The Danish minority reacted by sending children to Denmark for advanced studies. A school society organised financial assistance for more than 2000 students sent across the border.[61]

According to the statutes, however, German as a teaching language still had to be introduced with the free consent of the local school board. A petition to save the local language was handed over to the Minister of Culture in Haderslev in 1885. Again, 10 000 people petitioned the Prussian *diet* in 1889. In following years numerous appeals from Lutheran Church conventions demanded retention of Danish at local levels for the benefit of religious education, but the order of 1889 remained in force. In 1887 one; in 1888 two; in 1889 eight; and in 1890 ten schools were germanised.[62] In parliament Minister of Culture von Gossler declared himself unable to 'cultivate' High Danish in German schools.[63]

The Schleswig government retained some interest in the Danish language in order to recruit loyal teachers from the minority, but it hardened its line under *Oberpräsident* Köller at the turn of the century. Deportation orders were made against political *deutschfeindliche* (anti-German) demonstrators from among the 100 000 to 150 000 Danish nationals who had still not opted for German citizenship. Their children were brought up without any citizenship until 1907. Local Germans increased nationalist feelings by founding a German Society for Northern Schleswig in 1890. Other Germans reacted by founding a peace movement. Some Danish parents sending their children to schools in Denmark after 1897 were deprived of their right to educate their children in Schleswig through a decision of the *Kammergericht* (Berlin High Court).[64] Yet, despite all this, germanisation remained relatively ineffective in the final analysis. In 1912, in Danish areas about 20 000 children received religious education in

German. The authorities considered this a success. Only about 10 000 continued to receive it in Danish.[65]

The Weimar Republic. An Outlook

The changes in the *Sprachenfrage* (language question) when the Wilhelminian period ended in 1918 were slow. Under the threat of an *Volksabstimmung* (plebiscite) in the border areas of Schleswig, Poznań province, and Upper Silesia, the Berlin administration accepted early teaching in the mother tongue plus the foundation of private schools for minorities. Public elementary schooling and the acceptance of language training and examinations for the teachers was a different case. Article 113 of the Weimar constitution called minorities *'fremdsprachige Volksteile des Reiches* (foreign speaking subjects of the *Reich)'*. It offered free use of the mother tongue and no hindrances to participation in public life, but the old regulations remained in power. They were not explicitly suspended in 1918, as in Schleswig[66] and in the districts of Gdańsk (*Danzig*), Kwidzyn (*Marienwerder*) and Opole (*Oppeln*).[67] Polish nationalism took its revenge by expelling after 1918 large numbers of German nationals from the regained territories. The figures for 1921 in Poznań province reveal that the German population had been reduced by between 50 to 70 per cent when compared with 1910 figures. Thus germanisation was answered by *Entdeutschung* (degermanisation). Similar reductions in the German population took place in other cities in various former provinces, such as districts like Toruń (*Thorn*) and Grudziądz (*Graudenz*) where the new administration was aiming at a total polonisation of new territories.

When the Prussian government, and the *Reich* (in the case of Upper Silesia under the Geneva treaty in 1922) restarted a conscious minority policy, government had to balance and restrict its wishes in order to take account of the policies of neighbouring states towards the remainders of their German or Polish or Danish population. As only small numbers of students were to be provided with schools on the German side[68] extension of minority rights could be resumed officially as 'harmless' and of 'no danger for the German *Volkstum*' (racial character).[69] In 1927/8 only 603 students of Danish private and public schools and about 500 in Polish minority schools in Upper Silesia were not considered to be dangerous. In no case was there a political discussion to grant cultural autonomy.[70] In the Ruhr the Polish population was reduced to about 15 000 whose mother tongue was Polish and to 7700 whose language was German and Polish by migration to Belgium or return to Poland. 'Great consequences are not to be feared.' Thus a joint society of all language minorities founded in March 1924 was ineffective. At least the social democratic Prussian administration in 1928 was able to incorporate private schooling into the public system for a minimum of forty children, equivalent to 5 per cent of the school population of a school district.

Even these compromises were washed away by Hitler's *Machtergreifung* (assumption of power) in January 1933. The occupation of Poland in 1939 following the revival of *Auslandsdeutschtum* (German settlers abroad) started the most sinister revenge in history aiming at the extermination of Polish and Jewish culture on formerly German soil. The holocaust ended the assimilation of Jews which in the 1920s had opened to Jews full participation in the new democracy at the price of increasing anti-Semitism. The assimilated Jews reaching their most visible participation in culture, scholarly and scientific life were after 1933 deprived step by step of their rights, reduced to minority status of long forgotten times, thrown out of schools and at the end left without any public or private schooling before being transported to the gas chambers. The German occupation of Denmark and Norway restarted germanisation in schools under the new aims of racism and National Socialism by influencing the text books, teacher training and cultural life. The old liberal or scholarly traditions of enlightened Prussian education in a European context were never reawakened. Germanisation and assimilation as concepts to deal with minorities in 1945 ended in the total collapse of hitherto called German culture.

Notes

1. Cf. Jersch-Wenzel 1981, pp. 486–506.
2. Cf. Muret, 1978; Jersch-Wenzel 1978.
3. For details of Jewish population in Silesia see: Jersch-Wenzel 1987, pp. 191–209.
4. See Wiese 1869, pp. 28–9.
5. See Neigebauer 1934, p. 290.
6. See Breuer, p. 81.
7. von Bremen, p. 556.
8. Breuer, p. 97.
9. Wiese, pp. 444–5.
10. Kampe, p. 78, 80.
11. See Jochmann.
12. See Strauss, pp. 107–36; Rürup, pp. 174–99.
13. See Galliner, chapters about *Frankfurter Philanthropin* and *Samuel-Raphael-Hirsch-Schule*, pp. 53–82; Kurzweil.
14. Cf. Breuer, pp. 101–12.
15. Braun, pp. 47–54; von Bremen, p. 196. As example of a teacher's memoirs: Lazarus.
16. See Handbuch 1920, Appendix p. 44.
17. See as outline Broszat 1963.
18. See Jersch-Wenzel, Minderheiten, pp. 499–501.
19. *Ibid.*, pp. 24–5.

20. Cf. Jersch-Wenzel, Minderheiten, pp. 502–3, with further references.
21. Not to forget the small minority of Frisians, see Petersen, pp. 69–75.
22. Trap, pp. 54–6.
23. See Pleśniarski.
24. Instruction cited in: Rönne, p. 117.
25. At this period heavy clashes between the school authorities and the Polish minority took place and may have influenced the official interpretation of Cultural-Minister Studt of 1906.
26. See Burchardt, pp. 147–64.
27. Details about the leadership see: Molik; for school policy: Truchim.
28. Molik, p. 157.
29. See Jakóbczyk, pp. 72–9.
30. See W. Jakóbczyk, Poznań 1981.
31. Molik, p. 53; Cf. also Molik (1981), p. 161.
32. Molik, p. 33 stated a shortage of 127 elementary teachers in 1869.
33. See Klanowski.
34. *Ibid.*, p. 58.
35. *Ibid.*, p. 45.
36. *Ibid.*, p. 48.
37. See Korth, p. 40.
38. Schneider/ von Bremen, Vol. III, p. 476f.
39. Cf for this chapter: Korth, pp. 40–4.
40. *Ibid.*, p. 44f.
41. See Brandt.
42. Korth, p. 49.
43. See Korth, pp. 59–61
44. *Ibid.*, p. 64.
45. *Ibid.*, p. 121.
46. Cf. Herbert, pp. 15–81. Also Bade, vol. 1, pp. 444–85.
47. *Ibid.*, p. 18.
48. Details Kleßmann.
49. Broesicke, p. 100.
50. Details Heinemann.
51. See Bracker.
52. Details see Achelis, pp. 70–1.
53. Wiese, II, 1869, pp. 338–43.
54. See: Holz; Kopitzsch 1979.
55. See Landesarchiv Schleswig-Holstein (LAS): 301–2860.
56. See LAS: 301–2774.
57. Sievers, p. 11.
58. See Achelis, pp. 98–100.
59. See documents in LAS: 301–2899 & 2901.
60. Wiese, II, 1869, p. 653.
61. See Skoleforening, p. 276.
62. See LAS: 301–2876.
63. See LAS: 301–2875.
64. Sievers, pp. 92–3.
65. See Japsen 1983.
66. *Ibid*.
67. Landé 1933, pp. 1075–1076.
68. In the province of *Grenzmark-Westpreussen* in 1931, 1 216 children were educated in private Polish minority schools. There was no public school for Polish. See Esebeck, p. 163. (Results of a two year research study just before the emergence of the Third *Reich*.)

69.   See Fiedor 1973.
70.   See Pieper, pp. 134–5; Broszat 1968; Bessel 1978.

Select Bibliography

Achelis, Th., O. (1934), *Deutsche und dänische Schulen einer Schleswiger Grenzstadt im Wandel der Jahrhunderte*, Hadersleben.
Bade, K.J. (1984), *Auswanderer, Wanderarbeiter, Gastarbeiter* (Bevölkerung, Arbeitsmarkt und Wanderung in Deutschland seit der Mitte des 19 Jahrhunderts), Ostfildern.
Bessel, R. (1978), 'Eastern Germany as a structural problem in the Weimar Republic', *Social History*, 3, p. 199–218.
Bracker, J. (1972, 1973), 'Die dänische Sprachpolitik 1850–1864 und die Bevölkerung Mittelschleswigs', *Zeitschrift der Gesellschaft für Schleswig-holsteinische Geschichte*, vols 97 and 98.
Brandt, H. J., (ed.) (1988), *Die Polen und die Kirchen im Ruhrgebiet 1871–1919* (Quellen und Studien. Veröffentlichungen des Instituts für kirchengeschichtliche Forschung des Bistums Essen, Bd. 1), Münster.
Braun, S. (1962), '*Die Marks-Haindorfsche Stiftung*', in Hans-Chanoch Meyer (ed.), *Aus Geschichte und Leben der Juden in Westfalen*, Frankfurt.
Bremen, E. von (1905), *Die preußische Volksschule* (Gesetze und Verordnungen), Berlin.
Breuer, M. (1986), *Jüdische Orthodoxie im Deutschen Reich 1871–1918*, Frankfurt.
Broesicke, M. (1904), *Rückblick auf die Entwicklung der preußischen Bevölkerung von 1875 bis 1900* (Preußische Statistik, 188), Berlin.
Broszat, M. (1972), *Zweihundert Jahre deutsche Polenpolitik*, Munich, 2nd ed, Frankfurt.
Broszat, M. (1968), *Außen- und innenpolitische Aspekte der preußisch-deutschen Minderheiten in der Ära Stresemann. Politische Ideologien und nationalstaatliche Ordnung. Festschrift für Theodor Schieder*, pp. 393–445, Munich.
Burchardt, L. (1981), 'Hochschulpolitik und Polenfrage: Der Kampf um die Gründung einer Universität in Posen', in Main, Ekkehard, and Waetzoldt, Stephan (eds), *Kunstverwaltung, Bau- und Denkmal-Politik im Kaiserreich*, Berlin.
Buszko, J., and Paczyńska, I. (eds) (1984), *Universities during World War II*. (Universitas Jagellonica Acta Scientiarum Litterarumque DCXLIII, Schedae Historicae Fasciculus LXXXII: Universitates Tempore Belli Mundialis Secundi etc.), Warsaw.
Esebeck, H.G. Freiherr von (1933), 'Die Gefahrenzone Ostpreußen', in Kries, Wilhelm von (ed.), *Deutschland und der Korridor*, Berlin.
Fiedor, K. (1973), *Antypolskie organizacje w Niemczech 1918–1933*, Wrocław.
Fischer, P. (1931), *Das Recht und der Schutz der polnischen Minderheit in Oberschlesien*, Berlin.
Galliner, A. (1987), *The Philanthropin in Frankfurt*, Leo Baeck Institute Year Book III (1958), p. 169–86.
Handbuch (1920), *der Preußischen Unterrichtsverwaltung mit statistischen Mitteilungen über das höhere Schulwesen*, Berlin.
Heinemann, M. (1975), *Die Assimilation fremdsprachiger Schulkinder durch die Volksschule in Preußen seit 1880*, Bildung und Erziehung 28, p. 53–69.
Herbert, U. (1986), *Geschichte der Ausländerbeschäftigung in Deutschland 1880 bis 1980*, Bonn.
Holz, Cl.-P. (1979), 'Untersuchungen zur regionalen Mobilität schleswig-holsteinischer Volksschullehrer 1791–1900 am Beispiel der Absolventen des Lehrerseminars Tondern; in Brockstedt, Jürgen (ed.), *Regionale Mobilität in Schleswig-*

Holstein 1600–1900. (Studien zur Wirtschafts- und Sozialgeschichte Schleswig-Holsteins, vol.1), Neumünster.

Jakóbczyk, W. (1966), *Karol Marcinkowski (1800–1846)*, Poznań.

Japsen, G. (1983), *Den fejlslagne germanisering*, Åbenrå.

Jersch-Wenzel, St. (1978), *Juden und 'Franzosen' in der Wirtschaft des Raumes Berlin/Brandenburg zur Zeit des Merkantilismus.* (Einzelveröffentlichungen der Historischen Kommission zu Berlin, Bd. 23), Berlin.

Jersch-Wenzel, St. (1981), 'Minderheiten in der preußischen Gesellschaft' in Büsch, Otto, and Neugebauer, Wolfgang (eds,), *Moderne Preußische Geschichte 1648–1947. Eine Anthologie.* (Einzelveröffentlichungen der Historischen Kommission zu Berlin, Bd. 52, 1), Berlin and New York.

Jersch-Wenzel, St. (1987), 'Die Juden als Bestandteil der oberschlesischen Bevölkerung in der ersten Hälfte des 19. Jahrhunderts', Jersch-Wenzel, Stefi, *Deutsche – Polen – Juden.* (Einzelveröffentlichungen der Historischen Kommission zu Berlin, vol. 58), Berlin.

Jochmann, W. (1988), *Gesellschaftskrise und Judenfeindschaft in Deutschland 1870–1945*, Hamburg.

Kampe, N. (1988), *Studenten und 'Judenfrage' im Deutschen Kaiserreich.* (Kritische Studien zur Geschichtswissenschaft, vol. 76), Göttingen.

Klanowski, T. (1962), *Germanizacja Gimnazjów w Wielkim Księstwie Poznańskim i opór Młodzieży Polskiej w latach 1870–1914*, Poznań.

Kleßmann, Chr. (1978), *Polnische Bergarbeiter im Ruhrgebiet 1870–1945.* (Kritische Studien zur Geschichtswissenschaft, vol. 30), Göttingen.

Kopitsch, W. (1979), 'Untersuchungen zur Binnenwanderung von Volksschullehrern in Schleswig-Holstein im Kaiserreich, Brockstedt, Jürgen, (ed.) *Regionale Mobilität in Schleswig-Holstein 1600–1900.* (Studien zur Wirtschafts- und Sozialgeschichte Schleswig-Holsteins, vol. 1), Neumünster.

Kurzweil, Z.E. (1987), *Hauptströmungen jüdischer Pädagogik in Deutschland*, Frankfurt.

Landé, W. (1933), *Preußisches Schulrecht.* (Special edition of: Max von Brauchitsch (ed.), Verwaltungsgesetze für Preußen, vol. VI, 2), Berlin, p. 1099–1101.

Lazarus, M. (1967), *Erinnerungen*, ed. by Hans Chanoch Meyer, Dortmund.

Miąso, J. (1988), *Szkoły zawodowe w Polsce w latach 1918–1939*, Wrocław.

Molik, W. (1979), *Kształtowanie si, inteligencji polskiej w Wielkim Księstwie Poznańskime (1841–1970)*, Warsaw.

Molik, W. (1981), 'The Policy of Prussian Authorities towards the Polish Intelligentsia in the Grand Duchy of Poznań in 1848–1914', *Polish Western Affairs*, Nos 1–2,1981.

Muret, Ed. (1985), *Geschichte der Französischen Kolonie in Brandenburg-Preußen, unter besonderer Berücksichtigung der Berliner Gemeinde*, Berlin.

Neigebaur, J.F. (1834), *Das Volks-Schulwesen in den Preußischen Staaten*, Berlin.

Petersen, Chr. (1979), 'Der Friesischunterricht in Vergangenheit und Gegenwart aus der Sicht des Schulamtes', in: Walker, Alastair, and Wilts, Ommo (eds), *Friesisch heute.* (Schriftenreihe der Akademie Sankelmark, N.F. 45/46), Sankelmark.

Pieper, H. *Die Minderheitenfrage und das Deutsche Reich 1919–1933/34* (Darstellungen zur Auswärtigen Politik, vol. 15), Hamburg.

Pleśniarski, B. (1980), 'Die Vernichtung der polnischen Bildung und Erziehung in den Jahren 1939–1945', in Heinemann, Manfred (ed.), *Erziehung and Schulung im Dritten Reich.* (Veröffentlichungen der Historischen Kommission der Deutschen Gesellschaft für Erziehungswissenschaft, vol. 4, part 1), Stuttgart.

Rönne, L. von (1855), *Das Unterrichtswesen des deutschen Staates*, vol. 8 of: ibd.: Die Verfassung und Verwaltung des Preußischen Staates, Berlin, pt. 1.

Rühlmann, P. (ed.) (1926), *Das Schulrecht der deutschen Minderheiten in Europa*, Breslau.

Rürup, R. (1968), *Judenemanzipation und bügerliche Gesellschaft in Deutschland*, Ernst Schulin (ed.), Gedenkschrift Martin Göring, Wiesbaden.

Schneider, K. and Bremen, E. von (1886/87), *Das Volksschulwesen im Preußischen Staate*, Berlin.

Sievers, K.D. (1964), *Die Köllerpolitik und ihr Echo in der deutschen Presse 1897–1901*, Neumünster.

Sønderjydsk Skoleforening 1892–1942 (1942) Kolding.

Strauss, H.A. (1966), *Pre-Emancipation Prussian Policies toward the Jews 1815–1947*, Leo Baeck Institute Year Book, vol. 11.

Trapp, J.P. (1864), *Statistik-topographisk beskrivelse af Hwertugdømmet Slesvig*.

Truchim, St. (1968), *Historia Szkolnictwa i Oświaty polskiej w wielkim Księstwie Poznańskim 1815–1915*, Two vols, Łodź.

Wiese, L. (1864), *Das höhere Schulwesen in Preußen*, Berlin.

Wiese, L. (1869), *Das höhere Schulwesen in Preußen*, vol. II, Berlin.

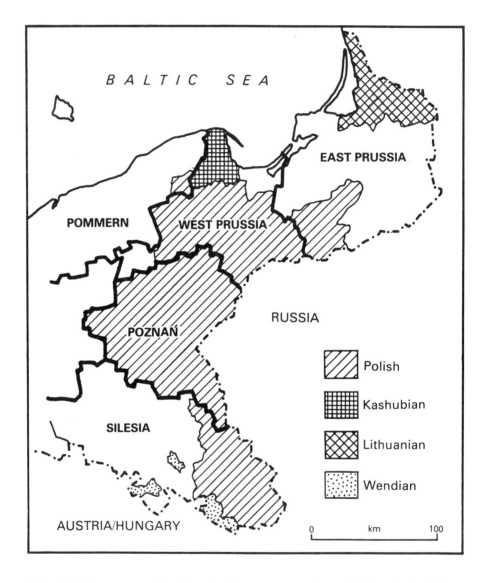

Map 7.1 Language minorities in the eastern regions of Prussia bordering Austria/Hungary and Russia (1900)

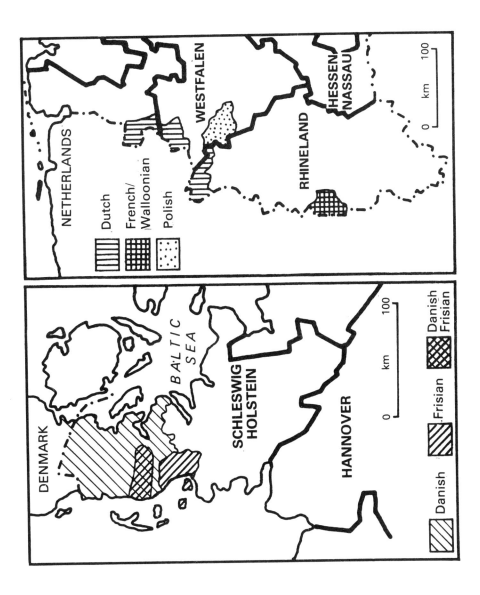

Map 7.2 Language minorities in the western regions of Prussia, bordering the Netherlands and France (1900)

8 Educational Policy and Educational Development in the Polish Territories under Austrian, Russian and German Rule, 1850–1918

JOZEF MIĄSO

Introductory Remarks

In the years 1772–93, neighbouring powers carried out a partial partition of Poland, depriving her of vast territories. As a result of a third partition in 1795, Poland ceased to exist as a state and her lands were finally completely partitioned. Russia took for herself 62 per cent of Poland's territory, with 45 per cent of the population, among which the Poles made up only a small minority. The majority was made up by Byelorussians, Ukrainians and Lithuanians. Prussia occupied 20 per cent of the area, with 23 per cent of the population, including Great Poland with Poznań and Bydgoszcz, Gdańsk Pomerania, and the Mazowsze region with Warsaw. These were, economically, the most developed areas. Austria took 18 per cent of the country, with 32 per cent of the population.[1] Her sector embraced the southern provinces of the former Polish commonwealth, together with Cracow and Lvov (Lviv), called by the Austrians Galicia.

That division lasted till 1807, when Napoleon, having defeated the Prussians, formed a small substitute Polish state, closely linked to France, called the duchy of Warsaw. This included a portion of the territories occupied previously by Prussia, with Warsaw and Poznań, and from 1809, also a part of Galicia and Cracow. This small state ceased to exist with the fall of Napoleon. Following decisions taken at the Congress of Vienna in 1815, the territories of the duchy of Warsaw were divided into three separate Polish state areas, closely linked to the three powers participating in the partitions but enjoying a measure of autonomy. These were: the Kingdom of Poland, linked to Russia; the free City of Cracow; and the Grand Duchy of Poznań, as an integral part of Prussia. As time went by, political freedom in these areas was continually and steadily restricted. In 1846, the Free City of Cracow was liquidated and put under Austrian occupation. The Kingdom of Poland and the Grand Duchy of Poznań were also in the process of losing their rights of autonomy. In the second half of the nineteenth century, these areas suffered severe pressure resulting from policies of russification and germanisation respectively.

Here, we are concerned with only a small portion of the former, pre-partition Polish commonwealth, covering the territories of the former duchy of Warsaw, from which, in 1815, the Grand Duchy of Poznań and the Kingdom of Poland had been created, and also Galicia, occupied by Austria in the first partition in 1772. Many Poles continued, however, to live in the lands which were declared integral parts of Russia or Prussia (Byelorussia, the Ukraine, Lithuania, Latvia, Pomerania and East Prussia). There was also a strong Polish ethnic group in Silesia, which had been conquered by Prussia in the first half of the eighteenth century.

At the time of her fall, Poland had been one of the biggest European states, numbering 12 million inhabitants, the majority of whom were Polish. So, until she regained her independence in 1918, Poland was the largest European country under foreign rule. In addition whereas the Irish, Finns, Greeks or Slovaks each remained under the dominion of a single European power, the Poles had to live in a country divided among three different states.

The loss of independence did not interrupt the process of national identification, because the Polish nation belonged, according to Otto Bauer's typology, to the category of 'historical nations', that is those which had formed their own social structure and their own national culture.[2] As a result, a national political movement manifested itself immediately after the loss of independence. It expressed itself in numerous armed uprisings, the first of which took place as early as 1794, and the last one in 1863. The absence of a state of their own was felt acutely by the educated classes, especially by the lay and ecclesiastical intelligentsia. The former was deprived of careers in state government and administration; the latter lost its position as the most privileged class in the state, and it also suffered economically.

As a result of the partitions, the Catholic Church was no longer a dominant element in the state, becoming instead, subordinate to systems in which the dominant denominations were the Orthodox (Russia) or the Protestant (Prussia) ones. Only in Galicia did the Church find itself within a Catholic state, Austria, but even there it remained under strict control, because of Josephine policy. In the Prussian sector, the Church lost its vast estates, income therefrom being replaced by government salaries for the clergy. The Church in the Russian sector met with a similar treatment after 1864. After the January uprising of 1863, numerous monasteries were liquidated and clergy rights were restricted. For example, the clergy was removed from teaching in elementary schools. Persecution on identical lines became a feature of the treatment of the Catholic Church in the Prussian sector in the 1870s, at the time of the *Kulturkampf* (cultural campaign). Only in Galicia did the Church enjoy considerable liberty, especially after the signature of a concordate with the Holy See in Austria in 1855. The most difficult situation for the Church was that which existed in the Russian sector. Only the *ukas* (official decree) issued by the tsar at the time of the 1905 revolution improved conditions for the church in respect of development of Church institutions and religious life in general. In spite of all these restrictions, however, the Catholic Church remained the only three sector institution linked to the old Polish state which was functioning legally, and with the right to bring people together for the purpose of religious worship. It was, therefore, in a position to play a major role in sustaining national traditions and patriotic feelings.[3]

The period under discussion (1850–1918) was a very important one, because it was during this period that a modern Polish nation was evolving, ready subsequently to assume independent statehood in 1918. In those years, farreaching changes were taking place in social, economic, political and cultural spheres. The Springtime of Nations in 1848 initiated the collapse of feudalism in the country. Between 1848–64, the abolition of serfdom and the enfranchisement of peasants was carried out in all three sectors by the occupying powers. This act favoured a further development of capitalism and increased feelings of national identity amongst the most numerous class, the peasantry. The growth in national consciousness resulting from the social and political emancipation of the peasants expressed itself, first, in the way they defended their native language and their land, and then in their struggle for an independent state, one in which the peasantry would play an appropriate role.

In the second half of the nineteenth century an industrialisation process was taking place in the Polish territories, leading to the development of towns and internal migration, which, in turn, changed the structure of society. The development of capitalism created new social relationships and a new mentality, thereby contributing to the formation of a new class and a fully developed national identity. The most industrialised area of the former Polish state was now the Kingdom of Poland. Galicia was still a rural area with a backward agrarian structure. The Grand Duchy or Poznań also maintained an agrarian character. Industry was insignificant there and it was handicrafts and small trade that prevailed in the towns.

The Polish territories under discussion were covered by three different political systems. Austria and Prussia were constitutional states, which enabled the Poles to look after their national interests by recourse to the law. Poles in Galicia and the Grand Duchy of Poznań had their deputies in the parliaments of the occupying powers. The situation was worst in the Kingdom of Poland, which remained under an autocratic government. The position in Galicia was the most liberal, as this sector had been granted a level of autonomy within the Habsburg monarchy in the 1860s which made it possible to entirely polonise the schools. Yet, at the very time that Galicia obtained the autonomy, the remaining Polish sectors were losing the remnants of their national liberties, and being forced to become integral parts of the occupying powers. This even found expression in their very names. The Grand Duchy of Poznań began to be officially called the Poznań province; and the Kingdom of Poland, the Vistula land. After the January uprising of 1863, inhabitants of the Kingdom of Poland were deprived of basic civil rights. Until 1905 they were not allowed to hold public meetings or demonstrations. Neither were there any political parties, trade unions, cultural and scientific organisations that were permitted to function legally. The only exceptions were charity associations. Full civil rights were enjoyed only in Galicia, which came to be called the Polish Piedmont.

In the years 1850–1914, the population of the three occupied sectors increased more than two-fold, from 10.7 to 23.7 million.[4] In all the territories, population of Polish nationality was in a majority, while in the Kingdom of Poland it was, decisively, the dominant element. In the Duchy of Poznań, the proportion of Poles grew during that period from 55 per cent to almost 62 per cent of the inhabitants. In second place were the Germans, whose number decreased from 42 per cent to 38 per cent, mainly due to migration to the industrialised areas of Germany and to a lower birth rate among Germans than among Poles.[5] The number of Jews there decreased by over three times, mostly owing to emigration and assimilation with the German population. In 1914 the Jews made up 1 per cent of the population of the Duchy of Poznań.[6] In Galicia Poles constituted 45.9 per cent of the population that grew overall from 4.5 million to 8.02 million between 1850 and 1910. Galicia was a multi-national land, and almost equally numerous were Ukrainians at 45.4 per cent, who were uniformly to be found in the eastern parts of that area. By 1900, however, the Ukrainian proportion had declined. The percentage of Jews increased from 7.5 per cent to around 10 per cent, while Germans comprised less than one per cent. Both the German and the Jewish population levels were affected by assimilation and emigration.

The nationality profile of the Kingdom of Poland was different. Poles there made up over 70 per cent of the population, and Jews 15 per cent. The remaining 10 per cent was made up by Germans, Russians, Ukrainians and Lithuanians. In the Kingdom of Poland, as in the Prussian sector and Galicia, Jews enjoyed equal civil rights (from 1862), as a result of which they could live in towns and buy landed property without any restrictions. They had no such rights in Russia proper.

In the second half of the nineteenth century, when the process of the search for a national identity was intensifying, especially among the Slav nations, two of the occupying powers began the process of realising their concept of a national state by means of a policy of germanisation and russification. It was the Russian government which initiated this when, after the fall of the 1863 insurrection, it liquidated the remnants of the separate identity of the Kingdom of Poland.

Galicia

Galicia was an agricultural area where the peasantry constituted about 80 per cent of the total population. Even towards the end of the nineteenth century only 18.1 per cent of the population lived in towns. Industry, which began to develop only in the late nineteenth century, engaged less than 10 per cent of the inhabitants. In the countryside small peasant holdings prevailed, which for the most part could hardly secure a decent living. The backward structure of these holdings, as well as the high birth rate, were among the main causes of a massive emigration of Galician peasants to the USA, Brazil, Canada, Germany and France.

The dominant religion was Roman Catholicism, although the Roman Catholics, at 45.8 per cent of the population in 1900, were not an absolute majority in Galicia. Greek Catholics comprised 42.4 per cent; Jews made up 11 per cent; and Protestants and others only 0.6 per cent. These proportions did not change till 1918. Ukrainians formed a distinct majority in eastern Galicia, that is in the area east of the river San.

The social and occupational make up of the three main ethnic groups differed somewhat. Over 90 per cent of Ukrainians were peasants or farm labourers. The parochial Greek Catholic clergy found itself between the peasantry and the intelligentsia, yet it was the families of that clergy that came to constitute the first generation of a Ukrainian intelligentsia. The Ukrainian nobility had been completely polonised back in the sixteenth and seventeenth centuries.

The social make up of the Polish population was more diverse. Most numerous were the peasants. At the same time, the majority of nobles, civil servants and the intelligentsia were also Poles. The social make up of the Jewish population was different again. In 1910, 53.3 per cent of them made their living in trade, transport and innkeeping; 24.6 per cent in industry and handicraft; and 10.7 per cent in agriculture and forestry. The civil service, army and professions took up 11.4 per cent.[7] A trend towards assimilation among the Jews began to weaken at the turn of the century under the impact of the Zionist movement. Part of the Ukrainian population was also assimilated, namely those who had looked for work in towns, and thus found themselves in the Polish *milieu*. At the same time, a portion of the Polish peasants in eastern Galicia were converted to Greek Catholicism and assimilated into the Ukranian population. This was particularly the case in those areas where Roman Catholic parishes were very rare.

From 1772 till 1848, the period when Galicia had been under the direct absolute rule of central authorities in Vienna, and the official language had been German, the whole school system had been germanised. Consequently, schools, especially the secondary ones, had entered a period of stagnation. The political system had also obstructed any activity aiming at awakening feelings of national identity among Polish as well as Ukrainian peasants. The position of the Ukrainians was even worse than that of the Poles, because of their lack of an upper class. In fact, the Greek Catholic hierarchy had been mostly polonised.

The November uprising of 1830 in the part of Poland ruled by Russia, also contributed to the awakening of national consciousness in Galicia. Indeed, inhabitants of Galicia took part in it, and the numerous independence plots that were organised in Galicia after the fall of that uprising also attracted Ukrainian students, seminarists and peasants. In the 1830s, the Ukrainian students of Lvov University began working on the development of their native language, collecting, among other things, folk songs and popularising new poetry in their language. These activities contributed to the awakening of a feeling of Ukrainian national identity. The Austrian government tried to use such Ukrainian feeling to counteract Polish efforts to regain their country's independence. In 1846 however, the Austrian authorities largely failed in attempts to set Ukrainian peasants against the nobles who were preparing an uprising.[8]

From 1860 on the Galician landed proprietors sought to reach complete agreement with the Austrian government and, once having proved their loyalty, they obtained full control over Galicia in return for their support of the Vienna government. From 1860 till 1915 the position of the Viceroy of Galicia was invariably held by a Pole. The major autonomous institutions were the *Sejm Krajowy* (provincial *diet*) in Lvov and the *Rada szkolna krajowa* (Provincial School Board), the latter's activities having started in 1868. In 1869 the Polish language was restored in the spheres of the administration, law courts and schools. In 1872 the Universities of Lvov and Cracow were also polonised and the Academy of Learning was launched in Cracow.

In the mid nineteenth century there were 2280 elementary schools with 93 860 pupils in Galicia. These catered for no more than 16 per cent of school age children. The Provincial School Board controlled primary and secondary schools, while the central Austrian authorities looked after the universities and also retained the prerogative of appointing directors and teachers of secondary schools. The School Board contributed greatly to the increase in the number of elementary and secondary schools as well as of the teachers' training colleges. An educational bill passed by the Galician legislature in 1873 provided for the setting up of an elementary school in each commune. It also stated that education would be free and uniform, with identical curriculum both in the countryside and town. In addition education was made compulsory for children aged from six to 12, thus shortening it in comparison with the all-Austrian bill of 1869. Schools were to be maintained by the communes and landed proprietors. Teaching was to be done in the children's native language, with the decision in this respect to be taken by the commune administrations.

As a result of the efforts of the School Board the network of elementary schools was steadily growing. In 1900 there were 4090 of them with around 646 000 pupils, in 1914 – 6151 schools with over 1.3 million pupils,[9] though there were still communes without a school. The prevailing school type was a one form school with a six year course of teaching. In 1900 there were 2366 one form schools, mostly having only one teacher, while there were 284 four form ones. As a result, the extent of illiteracy was diminishing only very slowly. In 1900 illiterates over nine years of age made up 64 per cent of the population and in 1910 – 41 per cent. The highest rate of illiteracy was among the Ukrainians.[10]

In 1858, there were 4585 pupils, including 2650 Poles; 1260 Ukrainians; 336 Germans; 316 Jews; and 23 others in all Galician secondary schools. Secondary school pupils came from the families of Polish nobility, Greek Catholic clergy, German bureaucracy and wealthier Jews. During the next 50 years, the number of secondary school pupils increased by more than six times. In 1911 there were 33 172 pupils in the *gymnasiums* (classical secondary schools) and *Realschulen* (non-classical commercially orientated secondary

Table 8.1: Pupils at state and private elementary schools according to the pupils' denomination in Galicia[11]

	1890	1900
Roman Catholic	238 801	348 058
Greek Catholic	173 845	249 163
Jewish	50 291	78 466
Protestant	5 948	6 783
Others	789	461

schools), including 18 369 Roman Catholics; 7615 Jews; 6898 Greek Catholics; 244 Protestants; 33 Orthodox; and 13 of other denominations.[12]

The Ukrainian elementary schools were mostly one form schools, though in the early twentieth century the organisation of many of such schools was improved. In 1911–12 there were 2420 schools in which teaching was done in the Ukrainian language. Of the 15 teachers' training colleges, eight were bilingual.[13] In the period from 1873 to 1911, ten secondary schools were founded with Ukrainian as the teaching language, of which five were state ones. Apart from that, in two state secondary schools parallel sections existed in which the teaching language was Ukrainian. At Lvov University there were several Ukrainian chairs.[14]

Until almost the end of the nineteenth century it was the Conservative party which determined the educational policy. The Conservatives were trying to restrict any further development of education in the countryside and limit the range of teaching in the schools situated there. Their aim was to use the school network in order to preserve the existing social set-up. The Conservatives also determined the ethos dominant in the schools, their purpose being to inculcate loyalty to Austria and the nobility.

The educational policy of the Conservatives, supported at the turn of the century by the nationalistic Bourgeois party, discriminated against the Ukrainian schools. But it did not manage to halt the growing educational aspirations of the Ukrainian people, who at that time were quite distinctly becoming a separate nation. Many Polish pedagogues and liberals pleaded for the Ukrainians to have their own national schools. Joint appeals were made by Polish and Ukrainian liberal organisations, peasant and socialist parties. Towards the end of the nineteenth century their influence increased in both the provincial and Vienna parliaments, and from then on, the conservatives began to lose a strong grip on educational policy. In the early twentieth century powerful organisations of primary school teachers appeared, and the changing political set-up began to exercise a beneficial influence over the development of education in the period preceding the First World War.

The autonomy granted to Galicia favoured not only the development of Polish learning and culture. It also had a similar effect on Ukrainian culture, such as was not possible in either Russia or Hungary. In tsarist Russia, the teaching of Ukrainian, as well as the publishing of books in that language, were both prohibited, whereas in Galicia not only were schools founded, but also various cultural institutions, which greatly contributed to the emergence of the national awareness amongst Ukrainians. Many Ukrainian writers also wrote in Polish (I. Franko, M. Pawlik). From 1868, an educational society, *Proswita*, had been active, setting up schools for adults, libraries and reading rooms. In 1891 an Ukrainian Pedagogical Society was founded, which established numerous schools in the country. It also published several educational journals. Of particular significance for Ukrainian culture was the founding in 1873 of the T. Szewczenko Society, which developed in time into a national institution of learning.[15]

The extent to which national education and cultural growth progressed was demonstrated by the growth of a Ukrainian press and its circulation. In 1881 its global circulation amounted to 411 000 copies, and in 1910, to 4.5 million.[16] During the First World War, Galicia became a war area, which brought about immense losses in population and resources. During the Russian occupation of eastern Galicia, both Ukrainian culture and the Greek Catholic Church suffered. All Ukrainian schools were closed, only to be reopened in 1918 after eastern Galicia found itself within the boundaries of a restored Polish state.

The Kingdom of Poland

The number of inhabitants of the Kingdom of Poland grew during the period 1860–1910 from 4 840 000 to 12 129 000 and, as has been said, Poles constituted an overwhelming majority of that number. According to official statistics, their number increased from 64.9 per cent in 1870 to 71.85 per cent in 1900, and 72.2 per cent in 1910. In reality, however, that percentage was higher. Official Russian statistics relied on the criterion of religious denomination to establish nationality. Consequently, assimilated Jews, Germans, Ukrainians and Russians, and the Uniats in particular were not included as Poles. According to the Warsaw Statistical Committee in 1904, Catholic Poles made up 73.5 per cent of the Kingdom's inhabitants; Catholic Lithuanians 2.7 per cent; Jews 14.29 per cent; Orthodox Russians (not including the military), Byelorussians and Ukrainians 3.52 per cent; and Protestants, both Poles and Germans, 5.1 per cent.[17]

After the failure of the 1863 January uprising, all Polish central offices and institutions were abolished. Russification of the area included the areas of administration, jurisdiction, and schooling (even the private institutions). The educational system lost its autonomy and was subordinated to the ministry of education in St Petersburg. Schools were reorganised according to the educational rules compulsory in Russia and Russian was, increasingly, becoming the language spoken in them. Personnel recruited in Russia proper were introduced into offices, secondary and higher schools. In 1869 the Polish Main School in Warsaw was replaced by a new Russian University. Between 1869–85, Russian became the official language for the teaching of all subjects, with the exception of the Catholic religion, in schools.

After 1864 Russian authorities favoured the establishment of primary schools, and supported the initiative of the inhabitants in the countryside as well as in towns in this field. However, these schools had to be maintained mainly by the local population. Funds from the central budget would be assigned, first of all, for the maintenance of schools existing in the areas inhabited mostly by an Orthodox or Uniat population. During the years 1865–9 the number of Polish schools grew from 929 to 1560; while that of Uniat and Orthodox ones grew from 132 to 316; that of German ones from 221 to 222; and that of Jewish ones from 12 to 29. In subsequent years the numbers of government schools doubled, yet because of the considerable growth of population, admission to schools was becoming more and more difficult. The following data confirm this statement: in 1873 there were 1993 inhabitants for one primary school, in 1900 there were 2679; and in 1905 there were 2818. As a result, only 18 to 20 per cent of children of school age (7–14 years old) could attend primary schools. The ratio was much more favourable in the European part of Russia, where in 1894 there were 1580 inhabitants for one school.[18]

Government primary schools were divided into the one form category (offering three years of schooling), and the two form category with five year long teaching. The two form schools were not numerous (only 96 in 1900), and embraced no more than 7.5 per cent of primary school pupils. So 92.5 per cent of all the primary school pupils completed their education after three years of schooling and quite often even earlier. The primary school, having no organisational or curricular links with secondary schools, was intended first of all for the children of peasants and poor town dwellers. In 1895 peasant children made up 73.5 per cent of all the pupils; and those of lower town classes, 24.6 per cent; while the children of the gentry and civil servants accounted for 0.9 per cent. The national composition in 1904 was as follows: Poles 73.96 per cent; Russians, Byelorussians and Ukrainians 11.39 per cent; Germans 10.67 per cent; Jews 2.22 per cent; and Lithuanians 1.44 per cent. The very small percentage of Jewish pupils was due to the fact that Jews generally educated their children in private schools, usually the denominational *cheders* (religious schools).[19]

In 1885 primary education became completely russified. From then on the teaching of all subjects was performed in Russian. An exception was made for teaching the Polish language and religion in Polish. However, lessons in the Polish language, to which only two hours weekly were allotted, were not given in all schools. The real purpose of these lessons was very often to improve the children's knowledge of Russian. The fact that children were taught in an alien language did not stimulate their educational interests. The teaching, restricted to the mere memorisation of knowledge, did not prepare pupils for further studies. As a result of russification of the primary school, Polish society as a whole was growing increasingly reluctant to learn Russian and even showing open hostility towards it. The dissatisfaction of that society with government primary schools led to the spread of private teaching, both legal and clandestine.

The Orthodox Church parish schools, which began to be founded from 1876 and were under the supervision of the Holy Synod, were charged with an important assimilatory mission. They were active mainly in the eastern *gubernyas* of the Kingdom (those of Lublin and Siedlce) and were intended for the Polish and Ukrainian population, especially those belonging to the Greek Catholic denomination, the so called Uniats, who from 1875 on had been forced to accept the Orthodox religion. In 1884 there were 12 Orthodox Church parish schools in the Kingdom and by 1912 their number had grown to 363, with over 13 000 pupils.[20]

Even more independent of the authorities were the Protestant and Jewish schools. The Protestant *cantorates*, being private establishments, remained under the control of the Evangelical consistory in Warsaw. In 1864 there were 205 such schools; in 1900 325; and in 1912 221. They were active mainly in the *gubernyas* of Kalisz, Warsaw, Piotrkow and Lublin. However, many *cantorates* did not cope adequately with their teaching tasks, especially in teaching Russian, or were struggling against financial difficulties, and were eventually turned into government schools.[21] The *cheders*, which were generally small in size, were supported exclusively by Jewish religious communities. Any attempt to put them under control failed as a rule. Only a very few of them taught Russian, for instance. In the nineteenth century their number fluctuated between 2000 and 3000. It was not until after 1905 that private Jewish primary schools began to be founded. There were 3544 of these in 1910 with 74 745 pupils.

To train teachers for primary schools, nine colleges with a three year course of study had been established, of which two were for the

Greek Catholic population, and one each for the Germans and the Lithuanians. Initially, trainees were taught in their native language. Then, the basic task of the colleges became the training of these future teachers for teaching in Russian and the instilling in them of loyalty and submission to the authorities. Those teaching in the colleges were, as a rule, recruited in Russia proper, and instructors from the Kingdom were very few in number indeed. Candidates admitted to the colleges were mostly of peasant origin. The authorities acted on the assumption that peasant students could be expected to be more loyal and would, in future, accept as their material and social status, one similar to that of the peasant population. However, in fulfilling their duties, teachers would often come into conflict with the local *milieux*, especially in the countryside. Consequently, they would either break the rules and teach the children in the native tongue after all or give up teaching altogether.

This growing russification process made people reluctant to send their children to the government schools, which gave rise to an emergence of home teaching. This became widespread in towns, but was also practised by many families in rural areas. Such clandestine teaching was increasingly common from the 1870s. Home teachers included not only trained pedagogues, but also students and secondary school pupils, civil servants, clergymen and organists, wives of landowners, craftsmen and, quite frequently, peasants themselves. Towards the end of the nineteenth century special organisations were set up to coordinate this clandestine teaching. Special publications also began to appear, designed for pupils in these underground schools. A brutal policy of russification on the one hand and clandestine teaching on the other, accelerated a maturing of national and social awareness among the lower classes of Polish society. According to data gathered at the end of the nineteenth century, 33 per cent of the Kingdom's inhabitants who could read and write owed these skills not to a government school but to clandestine teaching. The studies of this problem made so far indicate that between 1864–1914 there were over 3100 underground schools operating in the Kingdom. Apart from the Polish underground schools there were similar ones for Jewish and German pupils.

As well as awakening national awareness, clandestine teaching was also helping to reduce existing levels of illiteracy. According to the census made in the Russian empire in 1897, illiterates made up 69.5 per cent of the Kingdom's population. In the towns the level of illiteracy (54.5 per cent) was a little lower than in the countryside (75.6 per cent). Fourteen years later the literacy level among men grew to almost 60 per cent, and among women to about 42 per cent.[22]

During the revolution of 1905, the general school strike embraced not only the academic and secondary establishments, but also the primary schools. It represented a climax in the long standing struggle for a national character of schools, and for granting the right to have its children taught in their native tongue to each nationality within the Kingdom. As a consequence of this revolution, the Russian government was forced to agree to an increased role for the Polish language in primary schools and to give its consent to the setting up of private schools where the national language could be used in teaching. This concession made it possible for private primary schools to become more numerous. In the years 1905–12 their number grew from 586, with 37 866 pupils; to 999, with 86 887 pupils. At the same time, over 500 private schools were established by the Jewish and German populations. Private schools made up in 1905 a quarter of all primary schools in the Kingdom.

The process of russification of secondary schools took the following course. From 1864 the already existing Polish secondary schools began to be transformed into Russian, Polish, Lithuanian, German and mixed (that is for Jewish youth) schools. Some of the *gymnasiums* (classical secondary schools) were transformed into *Realgymnasiums* (non-classical commercially orientated secondary schools), technical or trade schools, not for any particular practical reasons, but in order to diminish the influx of Polish youth into universities. The fees for tuition were also raised, except for Russian and Orthodox youth. Separate secondary schools for different nationalities did not last long. In 1869 all of them were transformed into Russian ones, and from then on Russian became the official teaching language. Polish remained as an optional language but it was taught in Russian, the study being mostly restricted to the translation of a Polish text into Russian.

In 1872 there were no more than 47 secondary schools in the Kingdom, including 29 for boys and 18 for girls. By 1904 their number had grown to 54. They were mainly established in the *gubernya* towns. Around one hundred towns in the Kingdom had no secondary schools at all. The *gymnasiums* were primarily intended for the children of the gentry, civil servants and the rich bourgeoisie. In 1900, in the male *gymnasiums* the sons of the gentry and civil servants made up exactly half of all the students; those of the rich bourgeoisie 37.8 per cent; those of peasants 8.8 per cent; and those of clergymen 2.1 per cent. The denominational make-up of these government *gymnasiums* for boys was as follows: Catholics 64.8 per cent; Orthodox 20.7 per cent; Jews 10.1 per cent; and others 4.5 per cent. Under the terms of a decision by the Education Minister in 1887, students of Jewish origin could not exceed 10 per cent of those admitted to *gymnasiums*. This limitation did not apply to schools for girls. In the early twentieth century girl students of Polish nationality in female *gymnasiums* made up 36.2 per cent; those of Russian nationality 33 per cent; Jews 26.9 per cent; Germans 3.6 per cent; Lithuanians 0.1 per cent; and those of other nationalities 0.2 per cent. A much greater percentage of Jewish youth attended secondary commercial and technical schools.[23]

As a result of the revolution of 1905 and the school strike of that year, the teaching of the Polish language in Polish was eventually allowed in government schools, as well as the setting up of private schools with Polish as the teaching language for all subjects with the exception of Russian, history and geography. By 1913 247 private secondary schools with 50 079 pupils had been established. These educated more than double the number of youth in the government secondary schools.

The Grand Duchy of Poznań

For almost half a century Prussian educational policy in the Duchy was relatively liberal. As a result of the increasing number of elementary schools, almost 85 per cent of children of obligatory school age (from six to 14) were by the mid nineteenth century receiving school education. In those schools where the majority of pupils were Polish, the teaching was done in their native tongue. A number of secondary schools were also Polish in character. The obligatory teaching of German in schools did not yet mean the germanisation of pupils. As a result, schools were at that period, important modernising factors in economic terms as well as in socio-cultural aspects of life.

Soon after the unification of Germany Prussian educational policy changed radically. The main mover behind the new policy was the Chancellor, Bismarck. In his view germanisation was not a question of mere psychological and political assimilation. Its real purpose was to suppress any independent national spirit by, among other things, restricting the influence exercised by the Polish nobility and Catholic clergy on the Polish masses. Germanisation aimed to change the working people into politically passive Polish speaking Prussians, who would obediently follow the leadership of the German upper classes. Bismarck was convinced that bringing up those masses in a spirit of loyalty towards the *Reich*, and making them speak German, would bring them under the influence of government propaganda, thereby weakening the Polish national movement.[24] In achieving this purpose the major role was assigned to schools. So, from 1872, a programme of germanisation of the whole educational system was carried out, and was done in a manner which was even more drastic than that in the Russian sector of partitioned Poland.

In the first place the teaching of the Polish language was forbidden, being replaced by German in both elementary and secondary schools. Polish still remained a school subject for a dozen or so years. Then, in 1887, it was completely removed from elementary schools. It remained an optional subject in secondary schools till 1900. Only religious teaching, including church singing, could be done in the native tongue of pupils. In 1901 even that concession was restricted to the junior forms of elementary schools: in senior forms, religion was to be taught in German. Schools attended by Polish children were, as a rule, ill equipped and the classrooms overcrowded. The fact that children were taught in German, a language that they did not speak at home, meant that their education could not contribute to the widening of their knowledge and the kindling in them of greater cultural aspirations. The germanised elementary and secondary schools completely ignored the Polish cultural heritage or presented it in a distorted way, one disparaging to a pupil's sense of national dignity.

In order to facilitate the germanisation of schools, most teachers of Polish origin were transferred into Germany proper and in their place German teachers were brought into the Duchy of Poznań. German also became the obligatory language of the administration and the judiciary. The names of many localities were germanised as well. There was a prohibition on the singing of the Polish patriotic hymn *Boże coś Polskę* (God save Poland) in churches and the celebration of services on national anniversaries. In 1908, the Polish language was banned at public meetings with the exception of electoral ones for the Prussian parliament.[25]

In spreading an anti-Polish atmosphere, and in propagating the necessity for further germanisation, a major role was played by an all-German organisation called *Ostmarkenverein* (Eastern Marches Society). It was a kind of propaganda agency and a sort of lobby that exercised pressure on political parties and the Prussian government. It called on Germans to defend themselves against alleged polonisation, and aimed to spread a negative image of the Pole in society. But it did not win overwhelming support even among the German population living in the Duchy of Poznań. It was mainly made up of immigrant officials, teachers, some of the Protestant clergymen and a group of landowners.[26]

As germanisation progressed, the number of schools increased, as a result of which the entire younger generation was covered by obligatory schooling. Consequently, by 1914 illiteracy in those territories had been almost completely eliminated. At the same time, however, progress made in secondary education was not so rapid. In 1873 there were 13 secondary schools; and in the early twentieth century nine secondary schools, three *Realschulen* (non-classical commercially orientated secondary schools) and five training colleges as well as 24 *Mittelschulen* (urban secondary schools) with courses lasting six to eight years. As germanisation progressed, the admittance of Polish youth to secondary schools was made more and more difficult. In the years 1902–8, the number of Polish pupils in secondary schools decreased from 26.8 to 25.1 per cent. In training colleges Poles made up 60 per cent in 1898; and in 1908 barely 10 per cent.[27]

The germanisation of schools and other spheres of public life went together with other decisions by the government aiming at a restriction of Polish property in the economic sphere. In the 1880s tens of thousands of people were expelled into the Russian sector and into Galicia because they did not have Prussian citizenship. A Colonisation Commission was set up, financed by the government, the purpose of which was to buy land from Poles and sell it to German settlers. At the same time it was made difficult for Poles to buy land and set up new farms. The number of Poles admitted to work in the administration and enterprises of various kinds, including the railways, was drastically reduced.

Poles fought against this policy, not only by means of official protests, for example in the Prussian *diet* and in the *Reichstag*, but also by organising protest meetings in various towns, appealing to international public opinion, and above all, by establishing a network of their own economic, social and cultural organisations. Numerous agricultural 'circles' were formed, to which thousands of farmers belonged, which taught not only modern farming methods, but also disseminated knowledge about Poland, strengthening national identity thereby. Tens of banks, cooperatives and industrial societies also contributed to the development of Polish agriculture, handicrafts and trade, and so consolidated the economic foundations of national existence. Indeed, all such organisations contributed greatly to the changing of the disparate masses of Polish people into a coherent modern national society.

An important role in this process was played by educational organisations. Founded in 1841, the Society for Educational Assistance granted scholarships for youths attending higher, secondary and professional schools. The Society for Popular Reading Rooms, in existence since 1880, had, by 1914, set up around 1500 reading rooms which made readers familiar with Polish books. Children were taught Polish by a clandestine women's society, *Warta*. The activities of all these organisations stimulated the processes of integration, developed and strengthened national solidarity, despite any social or political divisions among the Polish population.

When, in 1901, the Prussian authorities decided to introduce the teaching of religion in German in secondary schools and senior grades of elementary schools, this was met with violent protests from parents and pupils, which found its expression in massive school strikes. They were inspired by parents, mainly farmers and workers. These events, combined with physical ill-treatment of the children by teachers, and court sentences pronounced against the parents, met with condemnation not only in the other two Polish sectors, but also throughout Europe.[28] The Polish people, especially farmers, re-garded the restrictions on the teaching of religion in their native language as an attack against the confessional unity which had been the mainstay of the linguistic–ethnic identity. Thus drastic forms of germanisation resulted in very definite defensive reactions. These frustrated Bismarck's plans for winning over the Polish masses, and, instead, accelerated a process of growth in Polish people's national consciousness, setting them against the Prussian government.

This reaction also resulted in a deepening rivalry between the Polish and German inhabitants, which led in turn to an economic boycott as well as, occasionally, to social isolation. Evidence of this is provided, among other things, by a decrease in the number of mixed marriages and an increase in the number of those prepared to declare in a census that the Polish language was their native tongue. According to the Prussian census of 1846, of 1 338 529 inhabitants, those speaking Polish only comprised 50.7 per cent; those speaking both Polish and German 21 per cent; those speaking only German 28.3 per cent. A similar census of 1910 indicated that of 2 099 831 inhabitants, those speaking Polish only comprised 60.9 per cent; those speaking both Polish and German 0.6 per cent; and those speaking German only 38.4 per cent. Those using other languages numbered 0.1 per cent.[29]

Conclusions

It is usual to think of the school as an institution stimulating the growth of national identity. The educational policy of Prussia and Russia aimed at something quite opposite. The purpose of school was then to bring about integration through assimilation. Still, in spite of its denationalising tendencies, the elementary school spread edu-cation among the population. Religious instruction in Polish meant teaching children to read in their native language, so that they could make use of a Polish catechism, Polish hymn and prayer books. As there was no provision for teaching Polish literature and history in the curriculums of secondary schools, pupils had to acquire the essential knowledge of their national heritage through self-education, usually sponsored by illegal patriotic organisations. Indeed, the educational policies of the partitioning powers brought about a widespread clandestine education movement which covered all classes of Polish society. It was most intensive in the Kingdom of Poland, where, till 1905, no cultural–educational associations were allowed.

It was the nature of Polish culture that contributed so greatly to the growth of national identity, as, during the nineteenth century, it had become enriched by major works in the fields of literature, music, painting and learning. Works of literature and history had a particularly strong social impact, by evoking the past and strengthening national tradition. A magnificent example of this is provided by the major historical novels of a famous writer and Nobel prizewinner, Henryk Sienkiewicz.

In the process of shaping Polish national identity among peasants in particular, the role of the Catholic Church was of great significance in both the Duchy of Poznań and the Kingdom of Poland. Churches were not only the places where divine services were held, but also those where religion and patriotic notions were taught. That teaching was not subject to governmental control. Russian authorities, which had, in 1864, removed priests from elementary schools and charged lay teachers with the teaching of religion, were obliged to admit at the turn of the century, that 'a priest is more dangerous outside the school than in it'. In the Duchy of Poznań, Catholic priests played an important role in both social life and the economic sphere, being initiators of agrarian and industrial cooperative organisations and banks, all of which formed a basis for the economic prosperity of the Polish population. Persecution of the Church resulted in the strengthening of ties between the Poles and Catholicism. This, in turn, led to an overt manifestation of religion in which traditional rites came to the fore, with a ceremonial full of national and emotional elements, regarded as an important part of Polish cultural heritage.

The educational policy of the Prussian and Russian governments proved utterly unsuccessful. It did not succeed in denationalising the Polish population, neither did it help to assimilate it in terms of language and culture. At the most, it increased the number of those who became bilingual. The processes of denationalisation were a normal phenomenon in nineteenth century Europe. Those who yielded to them were mostly individuals or linguistic–ethnic groups living in a diaspora. National groups living close together in a particular area, leaning on their own religious, social, cultural and economic institutions did, on the whole, preserve and strengthen their national identity.

Notes

1. Kieniewicz, p. 13.
2. Chlebowczyk, pp. 16–20.
3. Kloczowski, pp. 240–7.
4. Krzyżanowski and Kumaniecki, pp. 5–7.
5. Jakóbczyk, pp. 361–3; Hagen, p. 217.
6. Schiper, p. 553.
7. See Schiper (ed.), pp. 401–6.
8. Wereszycki, pp. 65–70.
9. Gomolec and Miąso, pp. 830–8.
10. Najdus, pp. 48–9.
11. Buzek (1904), p. 201.
12. See Buzek (1909), p. 3; Lehnert, p. 71.
13. Lehnert, pp. 10 and 27.
14. Grabiec, p. 86.
15. See: Feldman; Wasilewski; Hornowa; Markovits and Sysyn.
16. Łojek, p. 137.
17. See Trudy.
18. Staszynski, p. 48; Miąso, p. 103.
19. Staszynski, p. 104.
20. Kucha, p. 70.
21. Ibid.
22. See Miąso.
23. Staszynski, p. 106.
24. Of the vast literature on this subject particularly noteworthy are: Feldman; Trzeciakowski; Hagen.
25. See Jakóbczyk; Truchim; Stasierski; Buzek (1909).
26. Poles called that organisation *Hakata* after the initials of its founders: E. Hausemann, H. Kennemann, and H. Tiedemann. This appellation has become common in historiography. See Pajewski.
27. Truchim, p. 75; Jakóbczyk, p. 464; Hagen, p. 193.
28. Grot, pp. 76–122; see also Korth.
29. Jakóbczyk, pp. 69 and 363; see also Buzek (1903).

Select Bibliography

Bujak, F. (1908), *Galicja* (Galicia), Vol. I, Lvov.

Buzek, J. (1903), *Proces wynarodowienia w świetle nowszej statystyki narodowościowej państw europejskich* (The Process of Denationalization in the Light of the Recent National Statistics of European Countries), Lvov.

Buzek, J. (1904), *Studia z zakresu administracji wychowania publicznego. Szkolnictwo ludowe* (Studies in the Educational Administration. Country schools), Lvov.

Buzek, J. (1909), *Historia polityki narodowościowej rządu pruskiego wobec Polaków. Od traktatów wiedeńskich do ustaw wyjątkowych z r. 1908* (The National Policy of the Prussian Government Towards Poles. From the Vienna Treaties Till the Emergency Laws of 1908), Lvov.

Buzek, J. (1909), *Rozwój stanu szkół średnich w Galicji w ciągu ostatnich lat 50, 1859–1909* (The Development of Secondary Schools in Galicia During the Last 50 Years – 1859–1909), Lvov.

Chlebowczyk, J. (1975), *Procesy narodotwórcze we wschodniej Europie środkowej w dobie kapitalizmu* . . . (The Processes of Nation-building in the Eastern Part of Middle Europe in the Capitalistic Era – from the late 18th to the early 20th century), Warsaw.

Feldman, J. (1947), *Bismarck a Polska* (Bismarck and Poland), Cracow.

Feldman, W. (1902), *Na posterunku* (On Guard), Lvov.

Gomolec, L. and Miąso, J. (1972), 'Szkolnictwo, oświata, myśl pedagogiczna' (Schools, Education, Pedagogical Thought) in Kormanowa, Z. and Najdus, W. *Historia Polski* (History of Poland), Vol. III, Part II, Warsaw.

Grabiec, J. (1912), *Współczesna Polska w cyfrach i faktach* (Contemporary Poland in Numbers and Facts), Cracow.

Grot, Z. (ed.) (1964), *Wydarzenia wrzesińskie* (The Events in Września), Poznań.

Hagen, W.W. (1980), *Germans, Poles and Jews. The Nationality Conflict in the Prussian East 1772–1914*, Chicago.

Hornowa, E. (1968), *Ukraiński obóz postępowy i jego współpraca z polską lewicą społeczną w Galicji* (The Ukrainian Progressive Camp and its Cooperation with the Polish Left in Galicia – 1876–1895), Wrocław.

Jakóbczyk, W. (1973), *Dzieje Wielkopolski, 1793–1918* (History of Great Poland, 1793–1918), Vol. II, Poznań.

Kieniewicz, S. (1983), *Historia Polski 1795–1918* (History of Poland: 1795–1918), Warsaw.

Kloczowski, J. (ed.) (1980), *Chrześcijaństwo w Polsce. Zarys przemian 966–1945* (Christianity in Poland. An outline of Transformations 966–1945), Lublin.

Korth, R. (1963), *Die preussische Schulpolitik und die polnischen Schulstreiks. Ein Beitrag zur preussischen Polenpolitik der Ära Bülow*, Würzburg.

Krzyżanowski, A. and Kumaniecki, K. (1915), *Statystyka Polski* (Poland's Statistics), Cracow.

Kucha, R. (1982), *Oświata elementarna w Królestwie Polskim w latach 1864–1914* (Elementary Education in the Kingdom of Poland in the Years 1864–1914), Lublin.

Lehnert, S. (1924), *Szkolnictwo w Małopolsce* (Schools in Little Poland), Lvov.

Łojek, J. (ed.) (1976), *Prasa polska 1865–1918* (Polish Press 1865–1918), Warsaw.

Miąso, J. (1981), 'Education and Social Structures in the Kingdom of Poland in the Second Half of the Nineteenth Century', in *History of Education*, No. 2.

Markovits, A.S. and Sysyn, F.E. (eds) (1982), *Nationbuilding and The Politics of Nationalism, Essays on Austrian Galicia*, Cambridge, Mass.

Najdus, W. (1958), *Szkice z historii Galicji 1900–1904* (Some Outlines on Galicia's History 1900–1904), Warsaw.

Pajewski, J. (ed.) (1966), *Dzieje Hakaty* (The History of Hakata), Poznań.

Schiper, J. (ed.) (1932), 'Żydzi pod zaborem pruskim' (Jews in the Prussian Sector) in *Żydzi w Polsce Odrodzonej*, (Jews in Poland after Independence), Vol I, Warsaw.

Stasierski, K. (1967), *Kształcenie nauczycieli szkół ludowych w Wielkim Księstwie Poznańskim w latach 1815–1914.* (Training of Country School Teachers in the Grand Duchy of Poznań in 1815–1914), Bydgoszcz.

Staszyński, E. (1968), *Polityka oświatowa caratu w Królestwie Polskim. Od powstania styczniowego do I wojny światowej* (The Russian Educational Policy in the Kingdom of Poland. From the January Uprising to World War I), Warsaw.

Truchim, S. (1968), *Historia szkolnictwa i oświaty polskiej w Wielkim Księstwie Poznańskim 1815–1915* (History of Polish Schools and Education in the Grand Duchy of Poznań 1815–1915), Vol. II, Łódź.

Trudy Varschavskogo Statisticzeskogo Komiteta (Works of the Warsaw Statistics Committee), (1907), Vol. XXVIII, Warsaw.

Trzeciakowski, L. (1970), *Kulturkampf w zaborze pruskim* (Kulturkampf in the Prussian Sector), Poznań.

Trzeciakowski, L. (1973), *Pod pruskim zaborem 1850–1918* (Under the Prussian Rule 1850–1918), Warsaw.

Wasilewski, L. (1925), *Ukraińska sprawa narodowa w jej rozwoju historycznym* (The Ukrainian National Cause and its History), Warsaw.
Wereszycki, H. (1986), *Pod berłem Habsburgów. Zagadnienia narodowościowe* (Under the Habsburgs. National Problems), Cracow.

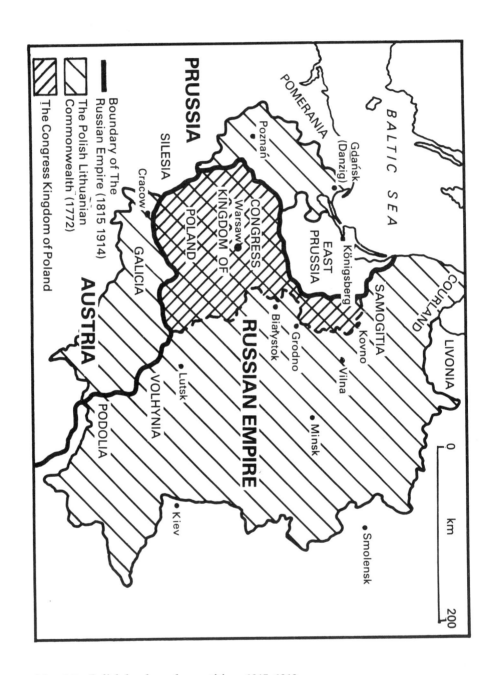

Map 8.1   Polish lands under partition, 1815–1918

9 Education of the Non-Dominant Ethnic Groups in the Polish Republic, 1918–1939

JANUSZ TOMIAK

The Polish Republic of the interwar period (1918–39) was a multi-national state. Some two-thirds of its total population were of Polish nationality. The remainder included (in order of size) the Ukrainians, Jews, Byelorussians, Germans, Lithuanians, Russians, Czechs, as well as much smaller groups of members of other nationalities (Table 9.1). The non-dominant ethnic groups identified above were distributed very unevenly within the republic. The official figures based upon the 1931 census of population revealed that the largest numbers of inhabitants with their mother tongue other than Polish lived in the south eastern and eastern parts of the state. In fact, again, according to the official figures, in three out of the four south eastern and central eastern *voivodships* (administrative regions), over three quarters of the inhabitants gave as their mother tongue, languages other than Polish in the 1931 census (Table 9.2).

The local situation often differed greatly, depending upon the degree of urbanisation and industrialisation, the geographical position of the locality and its history. The degree of concentration or dispersal of the particular ethnic groups, as well as their cultural and socio-economic characteristics had, obviously, repercussions in terms of what could be envisaged in terms of realistic facilities which were to be considered as appropriate for each group, though these were not necessarily the most important considerations. It should also be noted that in conducting both the 1921 and 1931 censuses of population, ambiguities as to what should be understood by nationality or the mother tongue may have very well played a role in certain areas. It is equally clear that the overall structure of population according to nationality or the mother tongue was not necessarily the same as the structure of the school age population based upon the

Table 9.1: Nationality (1921) and the mother tongue (1931) in interwar Poland according to the censuses of population of 1921 and 1931 (in thousands)

Nationality Mother tongue	1921		1931	
	Number	%	Number	%
Poles	18 814,2	69.2	21 993,0	68.9
Ukrainians	3 898,4	14.3	4 441,6	13.9
Jews	2 110,4	7.8	2 732,6[a]	8.6
Byelorussians	1 060,2	3.9	989,9	3.1
Germans	1 059,2	3.9	741,0	2.3
Lithuanians	68,7	0.3	83,1	0.3
Russians	56,2	0.2	138,7	0.4
'Local' popul.[b]	49,4	0.2	707,1	2.2
Czechs	30,6	0.1	38,1	0.1
Others	29,2	0.1	50,3	0.2
Total	27 176 7[c]	100.0	31 915 8[d]	100.0

a) Population with Yiddish and Hebrew as mother tongues
b) Population unable or unwilling to declare their nationality (1921) or mother tongue (1931)
c) Approximate figures for Upper Silesia and for the Vilno region according to a census taken in 1919
d) Excluding the armed forces
Source: Mauersberg S. *Szkolnictwo powszechne dla mniejszości narodowych w Polsce w latach 1918–1939*, Ossolineum, PAN, Wrocław, 1968, p. 13.

Table 9.2: Population according to the mother tongue in the eastern and south eastern *voivodships*, as given in the 1931 census of population in Poland

Voivodship	Total population	Population with Polish mother tongue (%)	Population with mother tongue other than Polish (%)
Vilno	1 275 300	59.9	40.1
Nowogródek	1 056 800	52.6	47.4
Polesie	1 131 400	14.5	85.5
Volhynia	2 084 800	16.5	83.5
Lvov	3 127 800	57.9	42.1
Stanisławów	1 476 500	22.5	77.5
Tarnopol	1 603 300	49.5	50.5

Source: Mauersberg S. *Szkolnictwo powszechne dla mniejszości narodowych w Polsce w latach 1918–1939*, Ossolineum, PAN, Wrocław, 1968, p. 14.

same criteria. It is, nevertheless, obvious that the very size of the non-dominant ethnic groups was bound to affect, in a very profound way, the national politics of the republic, its inner stability, its relations with the neighbouring countries and its general image in world politics.

From the political point of view, interwar Poland was a unitary state in which regular parliamentary elections played their role, and in which there existed numerous political parties, whose pro-grammes were based upon very different ideologies. The Polish government's policy towards the schooling of non-dominant ethnic groups living in the republic was subject to change through time, depending upon precisely who exercised political power in a particular period. The major political orientations which were of consequence here can, however, be identified, though, for obvious reasons, not described and analysed in greater detail.

On the right of the political spectrum, and of great significance, was the *Narodowa Demokracja* (National Democratic Party), which in the years immediately following the end of the First World War, either alone or in alliance with the *Chrześcijańska Demokracja* (Christian Democrats), and later, with a faction of the *Polskie Stronnictwo Ludowe – Piast* (Polish Popular party) played a very important role in national politics. As from 1928, the National Democratic party adopted the name of the *Stronnictwo Narodowe* (National party). Its leader and the chief exponent of its philosophy was Roman Dmowski (1864–1939). In 1926 he founded *Obóz Wielkiej Polski* (Camp of Great Poland). In his *Myśli Nowoczesnego Polaka* (Thoughts of a Modern Pole) he developed his basic political convictions which assumed that the state and the nation were essentially concepts which were inseparable. He viewed the national minority movements based upon linguistic distinctions as hostile, by their very nature, to the Polish nation-state, though he believed that they would gradually, but inevitably succumb to Polish cultural influence.

Another prominent member of the National Democratic party was Stanisław Grabski (1871–1949) who argued, quoting the Ottoman empire and Austria–Hungary as obvious examples, that multi-ethnic states were not viable political structures and that the consciousness of national distinctiveness must necessarily evolve with time into the demand for political independence. From this he drew the con-clusion that the new Poland should become a nation-state and ensure a definite supremacy throughout the whole country of those who considered themselves to be Polish and whose mother tongue was Polish. Yet another influential writer, Jędrzej Giertych, maintained in his book *O program polityki kresowej* (The Policy Programme in Respect of the Eastern Borderlands) that the Poles had a historic mission to accomplish in these territories. The Poles had brought there –

according to him – the blessings of western civilisation and the Ukrainians, Byelorussians and others living there should be assimilated and, ultimately, become part of the Polish nation.

The attitude of the National party towards the Jewish minority was generally dominated by the conviction that Jewish religious, cultural and linguistic distinctiveness made assimilation impossible, as the Jews constituted a minority whose faith, history, tradition, customs and language differed greatly from those of the Polish majority. Since these socio-cultural features evidently constituted the key elements in forging national consciousness, separation and not assimilation was advocated by the leaders of the National party in respect of the Jews in Poland, and the party favoured Jewish emigration to Palestine. Exaggerated national pride promoted by some right wingers involved, however, dangers of an additional kind: it led to outbursts of anti-Semitism which tended to adversely affect Polish–Jewish relations.

On the left of the political spectrum were several political parties, some of which went through complicated processes of internal dissent and consequent splits and reorganisation. The most important ones can be summed up as follows: the *Polska Partia Socjalistyczna* (Polish Socialist party); the two factions, namely *Wyzwolenie* and *Lewica*, of the *Polskie Stronnictwo Ludowe* (Polish Peasants' party); the *Stronnictwo Chłopskie* between 1926 and 1931 and *Stronnictwo Ludowe* from 1931 (Peasants' party) and the *Komunistyczna Partia Polski* (Communist party of Poland) the latter dissolved by the *Komintern* (Communist International) in 1938. Their attitudes towards the education of the non-dominant ethnic groups in Poland covered a range of positions, but they tended to defend, often very emphatically, the right of the minorities to education in the mother tongue, and to support their struggle for a fuller autonomy. The left wing of the Polish Socialist party, *Lewica*, in particular, supported the efforts of the minority groups to establish their own schools and protested against the Polish government's overt and covert attempts at assimilation. Pronouncements showing respect for the rights of minorities also came from Joseph Piłsudski (1867–1935), and not only in the earlier period of his career when he was a member of the Polish Socialist party, but also later on in his life, when he severed his links with it.

The Communist party of Poland demanded secular schools for national minorities, and financial support for such schools by the state, but it went much further in demanding also for the minorities the right for self-determination, including breaking away from the Polish state. The Communist party of Poland also backed the action for state supported Jewish secular schools with Yiddish as language of instruction, but tended to oppose the efforts of the *Bund* (Jewish

Socialist Workers' Union) which was fighting for a greater measure of personal and cultural autonomy.

In between the right and left of the political spectrum the dominant role in national politics was played by the *Bezpartyjny Blok Współpracy z Rządem* (Non-aligned Bloc of Cooperation with the Government), established in 1928 and dissolved in 1935. Its place was then taken by the *Obóz Zjednoczenia Narodowego* (Camp of National Unity), popularly known as *OZON*, which came into being in 1937. Both represented the supporters and, later, the followers of Jozef Piłsudski, who dominated the political scene from the 1926 *coup d'etat* until his death in May, 1935. Piłsudski's close associates, Janusz Jędrzejewicz (1885–1951) and Sławomir Czerwiński (1885–1931), elaborated the concept of *'wychowanie obywatelskopaństwowe'* (education for state citizenship). This aimed at inculcating into all citizens, irrespective of their nationality, positive attitudes towards the state, the willingness to cooperate with all the other citizens, and the determination to defend the republic against 'all inner and outer destructive forces'.

One writer, Władysław Gałecki, pursuing the same idea in a book *Wychowanie państwowe (Education for the State)* stressed that the national character of education was by no means rejected by those who advocated education for citizenship; what they did reject was nationalistic or chauvinistic education. Jędrzejewicz's educational reform of 1932, which he introduced as Minister of Education, stressed the need for teaching in those schools using Polish as the language of instruction, some aspects of the histories of the different minorities and their cultures and awakening an interest in, as well as a respect for, these in pupils. However, the line of distinction between what could be considered as the principal features of the Polish state on the one hand, and the Polish culture and Polish nationalism on the other, was inescapably a blurred one. Many of the representatives of non-dominant ethnic groups saw a veiled attempt to promote Polish nationalism in education for state citizenship and so opposed it.[1]

Formally apart, but practically very much linked to the political parties, were a number of professional and other associations which were involved and intimately interested in the educational issues in the country. The *Związek Nauczycielstwa Polskiego* (Polish Teachers' Union), uniting in its ranks most of the primary and secondary school teachers in Poland, was as such chiefly interested in the educational provision, quality of education and teachers' pay in the country as a whole. An important, and very vocal, left wing of this Union conducted, however, a prolonged and determined struggle for a democratisation of education and for education in the mother tongue for all children. One of its principal exponents was Stefania Sempołowska (1870–1944), a teacher and a writer, whose book *Z tajemnic Ciemnogrodu (From the Secrets of Darktown)* portrayed the negative results of an education of children which denied the opportunity to learn in the mother tongue.

A major proponent of minority rights was Rafał Praski (alias Marian Falski, 1881–1974), who for years consistently demanded a better deal for the Ukrainian, Byelorussian and Lithuanian children. In his brochure *Walczmy o szkołę (Let Us Fight for the School)*, published in 1936, he pleaded for separate schools with different mother tongues for children and adolescents in the republic. Demands for the latter also came from the teachers who were members of the *Towarzystwo Oświaty Demokratycznej* (Society for Democratic Education), the *Komitet Towarzystw Oświatowo–Kulturalnych i Związków Zawodowych* (Committee of Educational–Cultural Societies and Trade Unions), and the various organisations associating members of the non-dominant ethnic groups which are identified later. The writings of Jan Baudouin de Courtenay (1845–1929), a distinguished university professor, linguist and progressive thinker, were no less important. He raised his voice to plead for a fair deal for the different minority groups inhabiting the country, particularly in the field of education.[2]

The legal obligations arising out of the post–1918 peace treaties and the different international agreements concerning national minorities were of great importance. According to the treaty concluded between Poland and the allied and associated powers on 28 June 1919, Poland undertook to assure protection of life, liberty and the free expressions of their religion to all inhabitants, without distinction of birth, nationality, language, race or religion. Polish citizens belonging to racial, religious or linguistic minorities were given the right to establish and control religious and social institutions and schools at their own expense, and to use their own language and exercise their own religion, using that language. In particular, while Polish might be taught as an obligatory language in the minority schools within the public education system, wherever there was 'a considerable proportion' of non-Poles, they were to enjoy primary school instruction in their own language and receive 'a fair share' of state, municipal, etc. grants (articles 8 and 9). The above obligations were incorporated into the Polish constitution of March 1921 and again into the constitution of April 1935.

To avoid the interference of the great powers into internal affairs of the countries which were a party to the treaty, the duty of ensuring that its provisions were observed was entrusted to the Council of the League of Nations. The Polish government endeavoured for many years to extend the obligations arising out of the treaty to all countries. As these efforts were not successful, the Polish Minster of

Foreign Affairs, Joseph Beck (1894–1944) declared in a session of the League of Nations in September 1934, that Poland would no longer cooperate with international bodies exercising control over the protection of minorities. The latter were thus deprived from then on of the opportunity of appealing to the international bodies against the decisions and actions of the authorities. This was bound to lead to problems.

Quite apart from the treaty of 1919, the Polish government signed two other treaties of great consequence for the protection of certain national minorities in Poland. The treaty of Riga, signed on 18 March 1921, stipulated the right for the Ukrainian and Byelorussian population in Poland to cultivate their mother tongues, open their own schools and develop their own cultures, in exchange for similar rights for the Polish population in Russia and the Ukraine. The second treaty constituted the Geneva Convention of 15 May 1922. This defined the legal obligations for the Polish and German state authorities *vis-à-vis* the respective minority groups inhabiting the divided territory of Upper Silesia, which included, among other provisions, the right to establish public schools at all levels of education.

Within the wider socio-economic context, it is important to keep in mind that the period 1918–39 was by no means characterised by stable conditions. The devastation of a very large part of the interwar Poland, brought about by years of fighting which only ended in November 1920, was largely responsible for the difficulties in providing universal compulsory education throughout the country in the years immediately following the cessation of hostilities. Recovery was slow and progress rendered difficult again by the great depression which had as great an effect on Poland as on other countries. The political frontiers of the Polish state, ultimately determined and agreed upon in the years 1920–2 did not correspond either to the historical borders of pre-partitions Poland, or to the lines of ethnic divisiveness which were, in any case, difficult to determine because of the mixed population in numerous regions and districts. Traditional animosities and tensions between the different groups, often deepened by the conflicting economic interests and sometimes fuelled by actions sponsored from outside, also played a considerable role.

As both the government's policies *vis-à-vis* the non-dominant ethnic groups, and the reactions of the groups themselves to such policies, varied, depending upon the background, size and composition of the given group, it is useful to examine the situation in respect of each group separately. Unfortunately, the limited length of the presentation makes a detailed analysis of all the issues involved impossible. Interested readers will, hopefully, find the sources included in Select Bibliography at the end of this chapter informative and illuminating and gain from them further insights into the problem.

The Ukrainians

In all probability some four to four and a half million Ukrainians inhabited the south eastern part of interwar Poland. The exact figure cannot easily be stated, as the data provided by the census of population have been seriously challenged by a number of people and declared unreliable. What was certain, however, was the fact that by 1914 Ukrainian national consciousness was well developed and the Ukrainians were more and more determined to establish an independent state of their own. However, the course of history towards the end of the First World War and following it decided otherwise.

Three years before the outbreak of the First World War, in eastern Galicia, then under Austrian rule, there were 1590 elementary schools with Polish as the language of instruction and 2420 elementary schools with Ukrainian as the language of instruction.[3] Only in districts with mixed populations was it obligatory for the children in schools with instruction in Polish to study the Ukrainian language as a subject, and for the children in schools with instruction in Ukrainian to study the Polish language as a subject. Teachers for elementary schools with Ukrainian as the language of instruction were trained in one of four state teachers' seminaries, operating upon a bilingual basis, or in one of four private teachers' seminaries with Ukrainian as the language of instruction. In the districts inhabited by the Ukrainians, school councils often consisted exclusively of Ukrainians.

After the incorporation of eastern Galicia into Poland, in 1921–2, that is, in the first year of peaceful work, in the *voivodships* of Lvov (L'viv), Stanisławow and Tarnopol there were 2247 elementary public schools with Polish, and 2426 schools with Ukrainian, as the language of instruction,[4] a considerable change compared with the pre-war situation. In the areas formerly under Russian rule, Volhynia and Polesie, where before 1914 there had been no schools with Ukrainian as the language of instruction, a number of such schools had been formed by Ukrainian initiatives under Austrian occupation towards the end of the First World War, even before these territories became part of the Polish republic.[5]

While, during the first six years of the interwar period, the Polish government's policy lacked a definite line, a number of Ukrainian leaders, including members of the *Sejm* (parliament), protested against the tendency to expand the number of schools teaching in Polish in the areas where there were substantial numbers of Ukrainians. The situation became more problematic when the Polish authorities began to sponsor the settlement of ex-members of the Polish army in the south eastern part of Poland, a process which very greatly intensified the existing tensions between the two nations and turned them into an open antagonism.

The 1924 educational reform of Stanisław Grabski instituted a very definite policy. Its fundamental principle was the promotion of 'a common school, preparing the children of Polish and non-Polish nationalities to be good citizens of the state, respecting each other's national characteristics'.[6] However, the reform also stipulated the conditions under which elementary public schools teaching in non-Polish languages could be established. These required that in a *gmina* (local administrative unit) where at least 25 per cent of population was of a given minority nationality, parents of at least 40 children of school age in a school district could formally demand teaching in the mother tongue. If there were fewer than 40, children were to be taught in the official language, that is, in Polish. On the other hand, if there were, in a given school district, at least 20 children whose parents demanded teaching in Polish, irrespective of the number of children of any other nationality, the children were to be taught in two languages. If there were fewer than 20, the minority language was to be the language of instruction. Separate schools offering instruction in Polish and any other language were to be reorganised, whenever possible, into one single school teaching in both languages.

The end result of the measures introduced was a substantial decline in the number of schools teaching in Ukrainian and a substantial increase in the number of bilingual schools. While this phenomenon could, at least in part, have been due to the natural desire to acquire a good knowledge of both languages, many Ukrainian nationalists saw in it a growing threat to Ukrainian national consciousness, and a sign of danger of polonisation, and protested vigorously. In 1928 the Ukrainian deputies in the *sejm* belonging to the Ukrainian Club sought to defend their interests by organising a joint action with the Ukrainians, Byelorussians and Lithuanians living in Poland to promote education in the mother tongue.[7]

The government defended its policy by arguing that creating bilingual schools enabled the authorities to establish larger, more viable schools, with several teachers and thereby improve the quality of education. Many Polish deputies in the *sejm* defended the bilingual schools as positive institutions aiming at the establishment of better relations between two nations. On the other hand, there were school inspectors of Polish nationality who expressed their own criticism of bilingual education for educational, as well as social, reasons and called for its cessation.

Meanwhile, the Ukrainian population in south eastern Poland in general, and the Ukrainian organisations in particular, began a bitter struggle for the preservation of Ukrainian schools with Ukrainian as the language of instruction. Petitions for the retention of such schools in the period 1925–30 were, however, frequently rejected by the school authorities. The result was that in reality the number of schools teaching in Ukrainian decreased further and that of schools with simultaneous bilingual instruction increased.

This process caused a gradual growth in the number of private elementary schools teaching in Ukrainian. They were sponsored by *Ridna Skola*, a society offering support for such schools with the help of voluntary contributions coming from both the Ukrainians living in Poland and those living abroad, mainly in America. As a result, the number of private elementary Ukrainian schools increased from 21 in the school year 1925–6 to 33 in the period 1929–38. It was, however, a small number, when compared with over 3000 bilingual Polish-Ukrainian public schools with some 470 000 pupils and 420 public elementary schools with Ukrainian as the language of instruction with over 52 000 pupils in the school year 1937–8.[8]

The general situation was very much worsened by the acts of terrorism against government officials initiated by the Ukrainian Military Organisation, and acts of sabotage and destruction of property belonging to persons of Polish nationality in the south eastern part of the country. The government responded by repression and arrests on a large scale, which in turn led, inevitably, to a further deterioration in Polish–Ukrainian relations.[9] The late 1930s saw some relaxation of tension, due to the efforts of a more liberally inclined Polish premier, Marian Kościałkowski-Zyndram (1892–1946), and some representatives of the *Ukrainskie Narodno–Demokratychne Obiednanie* (Ukrainian National Democratic Union). Most of the Ukrainians living in south eastern and eastern Poland seemed, however, to be convinced that their attempts at teaching Ukrainian children in their mother tongue were meeting with strong resistance from the Polish government, while bilingual schools did, in practice, little to cultivate Ukrainian culture or promote Ukrainian national identity.

The Jews

In 1921, 2 110 400 persons declared themselves as being of Jewish nationality in the Polish republic. In 1931, 2 732 600 gave Yiddish or

Hebrew as their mother tongue. However, the number adhering to the Jewish religion was greater: 2 800 000 in 1921 and 3 114 000 in 1931. Most of them lived in Warsaw and Łódz and in the larger and smaller towns of central, as well as eastern and southern, Poland. Two-thirds of them worked in trade, commerce and insurance, or as craftsmen.[10] Politically, the Polish Jews were split into numerous orientations, ranging from orthodox traditionalism, through Zionism and Folkism, to socialism and communism. The Jewish movement aiming at assimilation and gradual acceptance of the Polish language as the mother tongue was not insignificant.[11]

Political and ideological divisions had direct educational consequences. Jewish schools teaching in Hebrew were favoured by orthodox Jews and Zionists. Folkism, through its two political organisations, the *Yidishe Folks–Partai in Poilen* (Jewish People's party in Poland) and the *Yidishe Demokratish–Folkistishe Partai in Poilen* (Jewish People's Democratic party in Poland), demanded publicly supported Jewish schools teaching in Yiddish, as did the *Bund* (All-Jewish Workers' Union) and the Jewish socialists, organised through *Poalei Sion*. Some others favoured sending their children to schools teaching in Polish, which was likely to be of an advantage in entering secondary schools and higher education establishments. The laws, rules and regulations concerning the education of Jewish children were, as a result, equally diversified.[12]

In those public schools and classes attended exclusively by Jewish children with Polish as the language of instruction, Saturdays and Jewish festivals were free from work, but lessons could take place on Sundays. Schools of this kind had a curriculum which was identical to the one for children of all backgrounds in public schools, except that the Jewish religion was taught for two periods per week. In schools of this kind, the majority of the teachers were, however, non-Jews. Such schools had an attendance of 34 200 pupils in the school year 1922–3, that is, some 15 per cent of all Jewish children attending public elementary schools in the country.[13] The rest of Jewish children who attended public schools attended schools for the children of all denominations, with teaching exclusively in Polish, except for a small proportion of pupils who attended schools teaching in Polish as well as in one of the other minority languages (German, Ukrainian, Byelorussian or Lithuanian) or in German or Ukrainian only. Demands that Jewish children be taught in Hebrew in public elementary schools were rejected by the authorities.

As time went on, the number of public elementary schools teaching in Polish attended exclusively by Jewish children declined, and their pupils began to attend the public schools catering for the children of all backgrounds. While the pressure for this kind of action came from the state authorities, arguing that this would promote social cohesiveness and also a greater rationalisation of the school network, the process was opposed by at least a section of the Jewish population, as well as by the more nationalistically orientated Polish circles which very much preferred cultural separation.

Faced with the fact that the state authorities refused to provide public elementary schools teaching in Yiddish or Hebrew, those of the Jews in Poland who wanted to see their children taught in either of the two languages had to establish an extensive network of private schools. This, inevitably, reflected the divisions within the Jewish community itself. Taking into consideration first the language of instruction, initially the majority of such private schools taught in Yiddish, though nearly as many taught in Hebrew, and a small number in both these languages and a few in Polish and Yiddish or Polish and Hebrew. As time went by, the relative importance of the schools teaching in Hebrew increased, as did that of the schools teaching in both, Polish and Hebrew or Polish and Yiddish, while the relative importance of the schools teaching in Yiddish only declined.

The private elementary schools attended by Jewish children also differed in character in respect of religious education. The traditional, orthodox *cheders* and *Talmud–Torahs*, controlled by school organisation *Horev*, differed greatly, depending upon whether they were located in larger or smaller towns or settlements.[14] Support for these schools came from *Agudas Israel*, a worldwide Jewish movement seeking to preserve an orthodox Jewish religious outlook. The government attempted to ensure that, in addition to the teaching of religion, Talmud, Hebrew or Yiddish, the curriculum also included mathematics, geography, history, nature study and the Polish language. Attending *cheders* reformed on these lines was considered to be equivalent to attending a public elementary school. However, many *cheders* in small towns or settlements were not reformed, and the authorities were exerting pressure either to include secular subjects into the school programmes of such schools, or else to transfer the children attending them to the ordinary public element-ary schools.[15] Statistical information concerning the number of *cheders* and reformed *cheders* is not available. According to some estimates about 100 000 Jewish boys attended this type of school. Most were aged five to 12 and they came from many different social backgrounds.

Over 34 000 Jewish children attended 183 private elementary schools founded in 1918, and controlled by the organisation *Tarbut* in the school year 1934–5. This number represented about a third of all children attending private Jewish elementary schools. Their growth in the decade 1925–35 was quite pronounced, being linked to the hopes of a return to Palestine. The language of instruction there was Hebrew, the schools promoted a Zionist spirit and rejected the study of Yiddish. Most of these schools also had an officially acceptable adequate standard of education.[16]

Schools remaining under the control of the *Tsentrale Yidishe Schul Organizatsie* (Central Yiddish School Organisation), backed mainly by the *Bund*, were of a religious character, with a socialist, or as their critics often argued, a communist attitude towards education. They offered instruction in Yiddish, but the curriculum included also the study of Polish language. Stress was put upon education through work. They enjoyed a high reputation due to a high level of instruction. In 1925, 16364 pupils attended 91 elementary schools affiliated with the Central Yiddish School Organisation.[17]

In 1931 some 5700 Jewish children attended schools run by *Mizrachi–Yavneh*; these were schools which were trying to attain a synthesis between the traditional *cheder* and a modern school, by stressing both the religious and national aspects of education. Hebrew was the language of instruction in studies relating to the Jewish religion and history, and Polish in the study of the Polish language, history and geography. Other subjects tended to be taught in Hebrew in eastern Poland and in Polish in central Poland. A lesser role, relatively speaking, was performed by the few schools belonging to *Shul–Kult*, aiming at the promotion of an awareness of a close association between modern Jewish aspirations and ancient sources of Jewish culture. The language of instruction there was Yiddish, but great importance was attached to the children also becoming proficient in Hebrew. Pupils attending schools belonging to *Shul–Kult* were mainly recruited from the urban artisan and working class background. Increasing unemployment among industrial workers, and the resulting poverty, placed schools of this kind in a different financial situation in the 1930s, which caused a decline in their number (from 25 in 1930 to 10 in 1935).[18]

Faced with such a diversity of schools, of the orientations they were trying to promote, and of levels of instruction and attainment, the Polish government pursued a policy of neutrality, but consistently refused to offer financial support to Jewish schools teaching in Hebrew and Yiddish. This led to numerous protests and criticism of the authorities by the Jewish members of the *sejm*. They argued that the Jewish population should enjoy the same rights as other ethnic minorities which possessed public schools teaching in the mother tongue. The Jewish member of parliament, Schiper, declared in 1922 during a debate on the subject in the *sejm* that 'the government acted towards the Jewish schools and, particularly, towards the schools teaching in Yiddish not as a patron. . .but. . .in the same way as once did the occupants in respect of (the education) of Polish children'.[19]

The Byelorussians

The population census of 1921 listed 1 060 200 persons who declared themselves to be of Byelorussian nationality. At that time there were also nearly 50 000 persons who failed to declare their nationality and who, it was maintained, because of the areas they were living in, might have in fact been Byelorussians. In the census of 1931, which used the mother tongue as the criterion, 989 900 persons living in north eastern Poland declared that their mother tongue was Byelorussian, but as many as 700 000 persons declared their language as the 'local' one. The above data indicate the nature of the problem concerning national consciousness and national identity of the large numbers of people inhabiting that part of interwar Poland. There also remains the suspicion that this kind of data might have been open to manipulation for political purposes.

In the Russian empire there had been no schools teaching in Byelorussian, but during the First World War the German administration had allowed and, indeed, supported the opening of Byelorussian schools in the areas occupied by the German army, intending thereby to weaken the Russian and Polish influence there. Directly following the war many schools teaching in Byelorussian continued their existence and a teachers' seminary was opened. In 1922–3, a year after the area was finally formally incorporated into Poland, there were 32 public elementary schools with Byelorussian as the language of instruction, with nearly 1900 pupils in existence.[20]

The reform of 1924 resulted in a decline of the number of such schools, most of them being changed into schools teaching in both Byelorussian and Polish. The majority of the Byelorussian children living in the north eastern part of Poland attended, however, schools teaching in Polish. A number of Byelorussian cultural activists and members of the *sejm* protested against this, and the government allowed the opening of more schools teaching in Byelorussian in the late 1920s. In the 1930s, though, the opposite tendency prevailed and in the school year 1937–8 public elementary schools of this kind ceased to exist. The teaching of Byelorussian continued, however, in the bilingual Byelorussian/Polish schools. In the school year 1936–7 there were 13 such schools with 1566 pupils, but in 1937–8 only 5 with 766 pupils. In 44 schools with Polish as the language of instruction, some 8200 pupils could still take the Byelorussian language as a subject in the school year 1936–7.[21]

The Byelorussian cultural organisations, such as the Society for Byelorussian Schools and the Byelorussian National Committee pleaded in vain for the existence of schools teaching in Byelorussian which would correspond proportionately to the numbers of Byelorussians living in the country. From the official sources it is clear

that, in any case, there were large numbers of children of Byelorussian nationality who did not attend school at all.

The decline of schools teaching in Byelorussian brought about the
creation of clandestine schools or classes in the late 1920s, largely due
to the activity of the Byelorussian radical organisation *Hramada*
(community). This was, however, under the influence of the illegal
Communist party of western Byelorussia, and the authorities spared
no efforts to eliminate it, as being politically subversive. Although the
population of Byelorussian nationality living in north eastern Poland
remained passive on the whole, refraining from large scale protests,
an inquiry into the matter undertaken by a Polish sociologist in the
late 1930s revealed a preference for public schools teaching in
Byelorussian among some 40 per cent of population of that
nationality.[22] Yet the Byelorussians were themselves not united on
the issue, and some, at least, seemed to prefer sending their children
to schools with Polish as the language of instruction, while maintaining the use of Byelorussian at home, keeping in mind that fluency in
Polish greatly facilitated access to secondary schools and establishments of higher education.

The Germans

Over one million persons declared themselves to be of German
nationality in the 1921 census of population in Poland. An overwhelming majority of them lived in western Poland, which, up to
1918 had been part of the German *Reich*. The one million Germans
who chose to remain represented, however, only about half of the
total number of Germans living in this area before the First World
War. Following the gaining of independence by Poland in November
1918, and the subsequent redrawing of the country's western
frontier, nearly a million Germans left Polish territory for Germany in
the period 1919–27, most of them from *Wielkopolska* (the Poznań
region) and Pomerania, preferring to abandon their homes rather
than live in Poland. Some 100 000 Germans also left the region of
Polish Upper Silesia, mainly in the years 1921–7. Those who
remained were conscious of the fact that their secure position as a
dominant group in the past would be reversed within the newly
constituted Polish state, where they would form a minority, albeit a
powerful one. The Poles saw in their new state a hope for redressing
the injustice caused by the partitions of Poland back in the eighteenth
century. Some tension between the two groups would be, therefore,
difficult to avoid.

The policy of the Polish government towards the German minority
tended primarily to reflect two considerations. One was the desire to

maintain correct German–Polish relations. The other was the fact that there were also substantial numbers of Poles living in Germany. In addition, the fact that in Poland the Germans constituted culturally and economically a very significant minority was not unimportant.[23] In consequence, the Germans could claim the highest proportion of children of all the minorities in Poland, who attended schools teaching in the mother tongue.

The legal basis for German schools in interwar Poland was not of a uniform kind. In the territories that had remained under German rule until 1918, that legal basis was the Little Versailles Treaty of 1919, reflected in the Upper Silesian Geneva Convention of 1922. In other parts of Poland, schools for the children of German settlers were established or continued on the basis of an earlier decision of the Council of Ministers of the republic to satisfy the existing demand for education in the mother tongue. The overall number of public elementary schools teaching in German was, however, declining over time. According to Polish sources, this was largely due to the continuing emigration of Germans to the *Reich*, particularly in the early 1920s. According to the German view, this tendency was due to Polish policy aiming at reducing opportunities for German children to attend schools teaching in German.[24]

There were, altogether, 1039 elementary schools (901 public and 138 private) in Poland teaching in German in the school year 1923–4; 699 in 1925–6 (apart from 292 teaching in Polish, which had classes with German as the language of instruction); 394 in 1937–8 (including 160 public and 234 private). An overwhelming majority of these schools were located in the western *voivodships* of Poznań, Pomerania and Silesia, but 25 public elementary schools teaching in German operated in the central and north eastern, and six in the south central and south eastern parts of Poland. German settlers in Volhynia had at that time 26 private elementary schools which were attended by over 2000 children in the school year 1934–5.[25]

The issue of elementary schools for the German minority in Poland was, however, becoming a very contentious matter with the passage of time. There were several reasons for this. One was that in regions such as Silesia there were many individuals whose nationality was not clear, even to themselves. There were, for example, children from mixed marriages, germanised Poles as well as polonised Germans. There was the question of whether 40 was an appropriate number of children in a school area to demand a school teaching in German. There also was a demand coming from the *Deutscher Volksbund zur Währung der Minderheitsrechte* (German National Association for the Protection of Minority Rights) for a completely autonomous system of German schools in Poland, which was rejected by the Polish government.[26]

In the 1920s there were numerous complaints to the League of Nations by Germans living in Poland, as well as by Poles living in Germany, in connection with the difficulties experienced by parents in sending their children to schools teaching in the mother tongue. There were conflicts concerning the help that was forthcoming from the *Verband für das Deutschtum im Ausland* (Union for (the Defence of) German Culture Abroad) in Germany for the German schools in Poland, for example over textbooks, which the Polish authorities declared as unacceptable. There were also dissentions among German teachers in Poland: the anti-Polish agitation promoted by the *Landesverband deutscher Lehrer and Lehrerinnen* (Union of German Teachers), made some teachers leave this organisation and start the *Verband deutscher Lehrer beim deutschen Kultur- und Wissenschaftsbund* (Union of German Teachers at the German Association for Culture and Science), which was loyal to the Polish state.[27]

The non-aggression pact between Poland and Germany signed in 1934 and the 1937 bilateral declarations concerning the protection of minority rights in both Poland and Germany, offered a hope of a reasonable basis for removing the causes of frequent disputes. However, according to German sources, even in the school year 1937–8, nearly 43 per cent of German children of compulsory school age in the Poznań region, 43.5 per cent in Volhynia, 61 per cent in central Poland and in Silesia and 19 per cent in south eastern Poland could not study at school in their mother tongue.[28]

The actions taken by the Nazi regime in preparation for an armed conflict in the late 1930s, such as, for example, the promotion of intensive anti-Polish and pro-Hitler sympathies through the German schools with the help of teachers often trained for this purpose in Germany increased, however, the existing tension. Reports from local police and administrative authorities which reached the regional and central organs of state administration contained information on the illegal formation of detachments of *Hitlerjugend* (Hitler Youth) in German secondary schools. As a result, the central authorities took the decision seriously to reduce the number of schools teaching in German in the summer of 1939.[29] Before this could be implemented, however, the Second World War broke out on 1 September 1939.

Looking in retrospect at the policy of the Polish government towards the Germans living in Poland in the field of education in the interwar period as a whole, one can discern a policy aiming at a cautiously conducted gradual assimilation, tempered by the fact that the Germans constituted a minority whose interests were defended by a powerful state which was Poland's neighbour. The Polish government's actions were also influenced by the fact that there was also a very sizeable Polish minority in Germany, which the Polish government did not want to expose to germanisation. The defensive actions taken by the German minority to protect their right to teaching in the mother tongue owed much to the efficient organisation of their local and regional communities, and to their political representatives, as well as to their economic strength and a considerable and consistent support forthcoming from the *Reich*.

The Lithuanians

In the census of population of 1921, 68 700 individuals declared themselves to be of Lithuanian nationality. In the 1931 census, 83 100 persons declared that the Lithuanian language was their mother tongue. Some 55 000 of them lived in the *voivodship* of Vilno (Vilnius), the rest in the *voivodships* of Białystok and Nowogrodek. After the formal incorporation of *Litwa Środkowa* (central Lithuania) into the Polish republic in 1922, there were, altogether, 52 public, and 40 private, elementary schools with Lithuanian as a language of instruction in the school year 1922–3. Two years later, the number of public elementary schools teaching in Lithuanian had decreased to 39, but that of private schools supported by a Lithuanian society *Rytas*, increased to 98. At the same time, there were 11 schools teaching in both Polish and Lithuanian. In the school year 1925–6 the number of public elementary schools teaching in Lithuanian decreased to only seven, while that of the bilingual schools increased to 39, following the changes initiated by the Grabski law of 1924.

In the next decade, however, the number of public elementary schools with Lithuanian as the language of instruction increased (45 in 1936–7), while that of private schools decreased (20 in 1936–7) and that of the bilingual ones rose to 49. Rapid deterioration in Polish–Lithuanian relations caused a drastic reduction in the number of public elementary schools teaching in Lithuanian in 1937–8, to only nine, and the private ones to only 14. There were, however, 102 public elementary schools teaching in Polish, but also offering instruction in Lithuanian language on the eve of the Second World War.[30]

The fluctuations in the number of schools teaching in Lithuanian were due primarily to the changes in Polish–Lithuanian relations in general. The Lithuanians accused the Poles of persecuting the Lithuanians living in Poland; the Polish government did the same in respect of the Poles living in Lithuania. Both minorities living in the two states suffered as the result of it. The fact that both the Poles and the Lithuanians were ardent Roman Catholics had no positive influence on Polish–Lithuanian relations. The representatives of the Lithuanians living in Poland even appealed to the Vatican to intervene on their behalf in Warsaw, but the situation did not change until just before the outbreak of the Second World War, when the Ministry of Education recommended the opening of seven public elementary schools with Lithuanian as the language of instruction.

The Czechs

According to the 1921 census of population there were some 25 000 Czechs living in Volhynia, the descendants of settlers who had arrived there in the middle of the nineteenth century. These Czech colonists had established their own schools with Czech language of instruction long before the rebirth of the Polish state in 1918. Thanks to the fact that the colonists lived in closely knit communities, schools teaching in the mother tongue could embrace a substantial pro- portion of the children of settlers in the interwar period. The traditional attachment to Czech culture was responsible for the fact that, in particular, the Czech language, literature, history and geography were eagerly studied by the pupils in their mother tongue. The subjects taught in Polish, namely the Polish language, history and geography of Poland were studied less enthusiastically, which caused problems for the pupils intending to continue their education in secondary schools.

Schools with the Czech language of instruction tended to be public elementary schools to begin with, but as time moved on, the number of private elementary schools teaching in Czech showed a tendency to increase. There was just one school of the latter kind in 1924–5, seven in 1926–7, 11 in 1928–9 and 13 in 1937–8, while the number of public elementary schools teaching in Czech decreased in the same period from 19 to five. The growth in the number of private elementary schools was facilitated by the conclusion of a Polish– Czech agreement of 23 April 1925. This, in turn, reflected the Polish government's desire to ensure a *quid pro quo* deal for the Poles living in Teschen Silesia under the Czech rule.

The total number of children learning in Czech public elementary schools did not exceed 1000, except in the years 1926–30. In the 1930s four public bilingual Czech–Polish schools existed also, catering for fewer than 300 pupils. Private schools with Czech as the language of instruction were maintained by *Matica Česka*, with its centre in Łuck in Volhynia. Most were found in the three towns of Łuck, Dubno and Równe. Just over 600 pupils studied in private schools in the school year 1937–8. The teachers teaching in Czech schools in Volhynia were trained in special courses organised for them by the Czechoslovak Ministry of Education in Prague.[31]

Concluding remarks

It is obvious that in a short chapter dealing with a very difficult problem such as the vexed question of education of non-dominant ethnic groups in a country, it is quite impossible to present in a satisfactory way the full complexity of the issues involved. Government policy pursued in this respect by the ruling party was often bitterly criticised and resented by the opposition and it did not represent the views of the whole Polish nation.

The Polish government's policy towards the non-dominant ethnic groups in Poland in the interwar period was subject to change, and was by no means always consistent. In the period immediately following the reestablishment of independent Poland, the government's policy reflected for a while the views of the parties of the left and showed a genuine desire to offer a fair deal to the different minority groups inhabiting the country. To begin with Joseph Piłsudski himself favoured a set-up under which Poland, Lithuania, Byelorussia and the Ukraine would form a federation respecting all the cultural and linguistic rights of the inhabitants. However, as neither the Ukrainians, nor the Lithuanians and the Byelorussians entertained any desire for forming a federation with Poland, the idea was bound to come to nothing and had to be abandoned.

Yet, when the new eastern frontier of the Polish state was finally decided, large numbers of Ukrainians, Byelorussians and Jews as well as some Lithuanians found themselves within the reconstituted Poland in the interwar period. An alternative political programme, defined as 'incorporationist', began to prevail in the middle 1920s, originally favoured by the parties of the right, and later on also by Piłsudski's followers. Under this programme, definite assimilationist measures were introduced for a number of minority groups, particularly the Byelorussians, Ukrainians and Lithuanians. Rather than allowing the process of assimilation to run its natural course, the government sought to speed it up by educational measures.

The principal one among these was the growing pressure for a gradual reduction in the number of public schools teaching these non-dominant ethnic groups in the mother tongues and replacing many of them by bilingual schools in the areas inhabited by the Ukrainians and by schools instructing exclusively in Polish in the areas inhabited by the Byelorussians. Closing down small schools teaching in the mother tongue was, at the same time, reinforcing the process of rationalisation of the school network and it was favoured by the authorities also for that reason. However, the most important consideration behind this policy was the desire to promote internal cohesion for political reasons, even if some politicians believed in the 'mission' of the Polish state to act as an agent of acculturation *vis-à-vis* certain minority populations inhabiting the eastern part of the country.

The policy of the Polish government towards other non-dominant ethnic groups in the country was largely based upon other considerations and resulted in different kinds of measures. The Germans represented a well organised and disciplined minority which enjoyed a two-fold source of support for its cultural and educational activities: the relatively high standard of material welfare within its own ranks as well as effective support from the motherland. The cumulative effect of both these factors was the ability to resist assimilation, even if the number of schools with German as the language of instruction showed a clear tendency to decline. Complaints received by the League of Nations indicated that the Germans in Poland were convinced that this was mainly due to numerous rules and regulations which discriminated against them, and argued accordingly. The Polish authorities took the view that, increasingly, with the passage of time, revisionist tendencies supported by German nationalists from outside came to dominate many German schools and constituted a direct threat to legitimate Polish national security interests. Measures were, therefore, taken to ensure stricter control over German schools and to close some of them in the late 1930s, which led to accusations of unfair treatment and reinforced the growing tension between the two nations. The fact that there were both Catholics as well as Protestants among the Germans living in Poland in no way modified or mitigated the conflicting language and national interests of the two groups, reflecting the dominance of nationalistic over religious considerations.

The educational policy aimed at the Jewish population in interwar Poland was based upon the decision to permit unhampered existence of private Jewish elementary schools teaching in Hebrew or Yiddish, but to reject the demand for elementary schools for Jewish children teaching in these languages, to be maintained by public money. This was considered as unfair discrimination by many Jewish people, who never gave up the struggle for Jewish public schools, though this produced no concessions from the government. The determination to communicate to their young the distinctive Jewish religious and cultural heritage permitted continued existence of hundreds of Jewish private elementary schools teaching in Hebrew or Yiddish. Though many Jewish children attended schools teaching in Polish, thousands rejected it. Educational distinctiveness reinforced social divisiveness and, regrettably, offered little opportunity for a better understanding and closer contacts between Poles and those Jews who tenaciously held on to their own language, values and convictions.

The effectiveness of the resistance to the policy of assimilation which came from the non-dominant ethnic groups depended upon a number of factors. The Ukrainians in particular, very conscious of their own identity, resisted the government's intentions to undermine their national distinctiveness with great vigour. The Byelorussians offered less resistance, being less inclined to engage in a difficult struggle. The Lithuanians tended to struggle for a fair deal, despite their lesser numerical strength. There is no evidence that the policy of assimilation, or of enforced assimilation as many would have it, brought about any lasting positive effect in improving cultural or political relations between the majority and the minority groups involved.

Notes

1. Bartnicka, pp. 61–132.
2. Baudouin de Courtenay p. 15.
3. Mauersberg, p. 61.
4. *Ibid.*, p. 61.
5. Iwanicki (1975) p. 133.
6. *Ibid.*, p. 140.
7. Mauersberg, p. 82.
8. *Ibid.*, pp. 90–1.
9. Iwanicki (1975), pp. 155–61.
10. Bronsztejn, pp. 113–25; Tomaszewski (1985a), pp. 96–120; Mauersberg, pp. 52–8; Tomaszewski (1985b), pp. 176–96.
11. Lichten, pp. 106–29.
12. Scharfstein, pp. 160–80; Hoffman, pp. 96–8.
13. Mauersberg, p. 163.
14. Iram, pp. 278–80.
15. Kornecki, pp. 13–15.
16. Iram, pp. 278–9; Mauersberg, pp. 178–9.
17. Iram, p. 280.
18. *Ibid.*, pp. 280–1.
19. Mauersberg, p. 188.
20. *Ibid.*, p. 107.
21. *Ibid.*, p. 113.
22. *Ibid.*, p. 114.
23. Tomaszewski (1985b), pp. 220–7.
24. Bierschenk, p. 158; Heike, pp. 142–4.
25. Mauersberg, pp. 129–31, 150–3.
26. Ręgorowicz, pp. 39–62.
27. Mauersberg, p. 156.
28. Bierschenk, p. 172.
29. Mauersberg, pp. 157–8; Iwanicki (1978), p. 152.
30. Mauersberg, p. 116; Tomaszewski (1985a), pp. 153–8.
31. Mauersberg, p. 123; *Sprawy*, pp. 576–607.

Select Bibliography

Bartnicka, K. (1972), 'Wychowanie państwowe' (Education for the state), in *Rozprawy z dziejów oświaty* (Scientific Papers on History of Education), Vol.XV, Warsaw.

Baudouin de Courtenay, J. (1923), *W kwestii narodowościowej* (On the question of nationalities), Warsaw.

Breyer, R. (1955), *Das Deutsche Reich und Polen, 1932–1937*, Würzburg.

Bierschenk, T. (1954), *Die Deutsche Volksgruppe in Polen (1934–1939)*, Würzburg.

Bronsztejn, S. (1963), *Ludność żydowska w Polsce w okresie międzywojennym, Studium statystyczne* (Jewish Population in Poland in the Interwar Period. A Statistical Study), Ossolineum, Wrocław.

Federowyc, K. (1924), *Ukraiński skoli w Halyczyni w świtli zakoniw i praktyki* (The Ukrainian Schools in Galicia in the Light of Laws and Practice), L'viv.

Falski, M. (1928), *General Information Concerning the State of Elementary Schools in Poland in School Year 1925–26*, Ministry of Religious Cults and Public Instruction, Warsaw.

Falski, M. (1960), 'Walczmy o szkołę' ('Let Us Fight for the School'), in Ługowski, B. and Rudziński, E., (eds), *Polska lewica społeczna wobec oświaty w latach 1919– 1939*, (The Polish Left Wing and Education in the Years 1919–1939), PZWS, Warsaw.

Grabski, S. (1929), *Państwo narodowe* (A National State), Lvov.

Heike, O. (1955), *Das Deutschtum in Polen, 1918–1939* (Das deutsche Schulwesen), Bonn.

Hoffman, Z. (n.d.), 'Schulwesen', in Fuchs, M. et. al. *Polnische Juden, Geschichte und Kultur*, Interpress, Warsaw.

Iram, Y. (1985), 'The persistence of Jewish ethnic identity: The educational experience in inter-war Poland and Lithuania, 1919–1939', in *History of Education*, vol. 14, no.4.

Iwanicki, M. (1975), *Oświata i szkolnictwo ukraińskie w Polsce w latach 1919–1939* (Ukrainian Education and Schooling in Poland in the Years 1919–1939), Wyższa Szkoła Pedagogiczna, Siedlce.

Iwanicki, M. (1978), *Polityka oświatowa w szkolnictwie niemieckim w Polsce w latach 1918–1939* (Educational Policy in the German School System in Poland in the Years 1918–1939), PWN, Warsaw.

Kornecki, J. (1929), 'Szkolnictwo dla mniejszosci narodowych w Polsce' (Schooling for National Minorities in Poland), in *Oświata Polska* (Polish Education), vol.6, no.1, Warsaw.

Lichten, J. (1986), 'Notes on the assimilation and acculturation of Jews in Poland, 1863–1943', in Abramsky, C., et al. (eds), *The Jews in Poland*, Basil Blackwell, Oxford.

Ługowski, B. (1961), *Szkolnictwo w Polsce 1929–1939 w opinii publicznej* (Schools in Poland in Public Opinion, 1929–1939), PZWS, Warsaw.

Mauersberg, S. (1968), *Szkolnictwo powszechne dla mniejszości narodowych w Polsce w latach 1918–1939* (Primary Schooling for National Minorities in Poland in the Years 1918–1939), Ossolineum and PAN, Wrocław.

Ręgorowicz, L. (1961), *Wykonanie polsko-niemieckiej Górnośląskiej Konwencji zawartej 15.05.1922 w zakresie szkolnictwa* (The Implementation of Polish-German Upper Silesia Convention Concluded 15.05.1922 in Respect of Schooling), Śląsk, Katowice.

Scharfstein, Z. (1945–9) *History of Jewish Education in Modern Times*, 3 vols, New York, vol. III.

Scherer, E. (1942), *Polska i Żydzi* (Poland and the Jews), New York.

Sprawy narodowościowe (Nationalities' Affairs), (1927–39), Instytut Spraw Narodowościowych, bi-monthly publication, Warsaw.

Tomaszewski, J. (1985a), *Ojczyzna nie tylko Polaków* (Not only the Poles' Motherland), MAW, Warsaw.

Tomaszewski, J. (1985b), *Rzeczpospolita wielu narodów* (The Republic of Many Nations), Czytelnik, Warsaw.

Zielinski, H. (1982), *Historia Polski* (History of Poland), Ossolineum, Wrocław.

Map 9.1   Distribution of minorities in interwar Poland
Source: H. Zielinski, page 268

10 German Schools in Czechoslovakia, 1918–1938

WOLFGANG MITTER

Introductory Remarks

The history of German education and schooling in the 'first' Czechoslovak republic between 1918 and 1938 must deal with facts, developments and problems which have no direct connection with the present. It is true that there still is a very small German minority in the Czechoslovak republic today. In view of quantitative and qualitative criteria, however, it would be erroneous to suggest that there is a continuity which, in fact, does not any longer exist.

Before trying to outline the socio-political framework of the theme, let me give a few remarks about the conceptual approach and its underlying considerations. In retrospect, we become aware, first of all, of the catastrophic end of the Germans as an ethnic group who had lived for centuries in Czechoslovakia and its predecessor territories. As we focus on this catastrophe, we may be tempted to look at the history of the 'Sudeten Germans' in general, and their schools in particular, between 1918 and 1938 in a fatalistic manner. Furthermore, their demise, while only final in 1945, had actually been caused by Hitler's seizure of power in Germany in 1933 and his subsequent destruction of the 'first' Czechoslovak republic. In retrospect, the disappearance of the German schools there may seem to be self-evident, the more so as Hitler's aggressive policy toward Czechoslovakia benefitted from conflicts which the two groups concerned, namely the 'dominant' Czechs and the 'non-dominant' or minority Germans, had not been able to resolve themselves. The impact of those conflicts on the educational scene must be neither denied nor obscured, since they constitute a part of the history of that time.

Even a rough examination of available sources, however, gives a

211

far more complex picture, which shows that hostility and destruction, though of great consequence in 1938–9 and again in 1945, are not the whole history. Rather, the search for historical truth necessitates the disclosure of documents presenting the constructive approaches, too, which were made, on both sides, for the sake of solving conflicts and developing genuine coexistence. It is my intention to examine the history of German education and schooling in Czechoslovakia, with its hopes and attempts to maintain its objectives, as well as its destructive elements and its definitive failure, as a paradigm of how education can influence socio-political developments; while, on the other hand, educational idealism can be perverted into doctrinairism and inhumanity when involved in counteracting processes on the 'big' political scene.

As regards the terminology, we will speak of 'Germans in Czechoslovakia', using the term 'Sudeten Germans' only with reference to quotations and specific emphasis. Nonetheless, a brief clarification may be useful. Before the foundation of the 'first' Czechoslovak republic, the terms *Sudetendeutsche* (Sudeten Germans) and *Sudetenland* were only used in respect of the Germans living in northern Moravia and Silesia (where the 'Sudeten', a chain of medium height mountains, are situated). In regard of the Germans living in Bohemia, people spoke of 'German Bohemians'. It was only in the course of the 1920s that the term 'Sudeten Germans' came into use for the whole German ethnic group in Bohemia, Moravia and Silesia. In addition, the term *Karpatendeutsche* (Carpathian Germans) was being applied to the Germans living in Slovakia, which had been part of Hungary before 1918.

The Socio-political Framework

With regard to the inextricable involvement of education and schooling in the overall occurrences and developments, a reference to the socio-political framework, brief though it must be in the present context, seems to be legitimate. It can be summarised through the following five points:

First, the new Czechoslovak republic inherited the multi-national character of the shattered Habsburg empire, though on a smaller scale. The census of 1921 produced this picture: 64.4 per cent Czechs and Slovaks; 22.9 per cent Germans; 5.5 per cent Hungarians; 3.4 per cent Ruthenians (Ukrainians); 1.3 per cent Jews; 0.5 per cent Poles; 0.2 per cent others; and 1.8 per cent foreigners.[1] Considered a 'minority', the German proportion was fairly remarkable, reinforced by the fact that most of the Germans lived in the densely settled areas of the border districts of Bohemia, Moravia and Silesia. As regards relations between Germans and Czechs, they had had a century long history. The last period had been characterised by the birth of modern nationalism, which was accompanied by two important phenomena. On the one hand, the two groups had changed their political positions: that is, the Czechs having been non-dominant became dominant; the Germans having been dominant or, at least, having claimed a privileged status found themselves in the position of a non-dominant group. On the other hand, the scope and the intensity with which the two groups experienced the revolutionary change of October 1918, was significantly different. In this respect the Czechs were also in a better position, because they had achieved their independence as the result of a long process of developing national self-awareness leading to the role of 'liberated victors'. The situation in which the Germans found themselves after 1918 was very complicated. Even in the old Habsburg empire, they had lost their former dominant position, which had weakened their allegiance to the state and their emperor. Nonetheless, they had never expected to find themselves in the position of a 'non-dominant' group.

Secondly, the Austrian-Hungarian heritage into which the new Czechoslovak republic entered also had the legacy of the legal and practical problematics of a 'nationality state'; that is, a state composed of several ethnic groups claiming the status of 'nationalities'. These problematics were transferred from the constitutional monarchy of the 'old' Habsburg empire to the parliamentary democracy of the 'new' republic. The 'first' Czechoslovak republic was constituted as a democratic state, with all its constituent elements, such as individual rights and duties, and proportional representation in the electoral system as well as a division of powers. These fundamental principles safeguarded equality between the dominant Czechs and Slovaks and the non-dominant minorities, with regard to civil and public law as well as compulsory school attendance and conscription, to mention two essential socio-political areas. The new republic also adopted the characteristics of a 'nation–state' in its political practice. It did this in spite of the fact that the dominant sector actually consisted of two, closely related, ethnic groups, namely the Czechs and Slovaks, and that the minorities totalled more than one third of the entire population. This manifested itself in particular in the installation of the 'Czechoslovak' language as the exclusive official medium at the central level of politics and administration. Therefore, the new republic was, from its start, burdened with a tension between the democratic principle based upon individual rights, and the claim of the non-dominant minorities to be acknowledged as corporate bodies with specific collective rights. It must be added, though, that in spite of this unsolved problem, the German minority in fact enjoyed rights which generally exceeded those of the German minorities in other countries. The rights included, for instance, the usage of the mother tongue (especially at the local level), the organisation of political parties and, as will be described later, the maintenance of a highly developed education system.

The relation between Czechs and Germans must be seen as being considerably influenced by the economic structure of the three (later two) provinces of the Czechoslovak republic (Bohemia, Moravia, Silesia; the latter two united to form the province of Moravia–Silesia 1 December 1928). In the nineteenth century the Czech populated parts of the centre had remained predominantly agricultural, whereas in the less fertile regions of the border districts, a great variety of industries had been established, which made northern Bohemia the most industrialised region of the Habsburg empire. This development had entailed, among other factors, such a strong immigration of Czechs to the new industrial areas, in particular the mining districts of north west Bohemia, that in some local communities the Czech population had become the majority. Where this was not the case, the new Czech minorities had suffered from the resistance or reluctance of the German majorities there to let them participate in local decision making, and to establish Czech medium schools (since the local authorities were responsible for the materials budget of their schools). Another serious problem then emerged in the late 1920s, when the overall economic recession resulted in the demise of industrial firms and disproportionately higher unemployment in the German districts than in the Czech ones.

While the aforementioned conditions were based on objective facts and developments, our analysis must also pay attention to the subjective aspect of what defines a 'non-dominant' group. Wherever dominant and non-dominant groups are in conflict about the definition and implementation of legal and administrative rights, the subjective aspect plays a great role, since it affects loyalty to the common state. The Czechoslovak situation was concerned with this problem to a particularly great extent because the Germans had to overcome their objections to accepting their status as a 'second class people'. One should not be surprised by the enormous impact of this problem on the education issue.

The Italian educationalist, Francesco Lunetta, in an article about the educational situation of the minorities of present day Italy, has drawn attention to the problem of how they can maintain their ethnic identities through education and schooling. This depends, he says, to a great extent on how their claims are supported 'from abroad'. Lunetta thinks principally of the positive impact that the existence of a 'mother nation' abroad can have on the social and educational development of ethnic minorities.[2] In the case of the Sudeten Germans, however, our appraisal should be rather cautious. J.W. Brügel who has thoroughly investigated the relations between Czechs and Germans in the 'first' Czechoslovak republic, has made the comment that at the end of 1919, the German population in Czechoslovakia was far from being in 'a mood' to be called 'embittered, nationalistic or hostile to Czechs'.[3]

Irrespective of how one regards this comment, in view of its plausibility one has to take into account that, at that time, the political parties of the German minority shared the refusal to acknowledge the new republic as 'their' state. Since the middle of the 1920s, the democratic German parties which, until 1935, represented 'an overwhelming majority of the Sudetenland populace', gradually reconciled themselves to the Czechoslovak state.[4] This change of political attitudes was evident in the fact that, between 1926 and 1938, the Czechoslovak government included representatives of the democratic German parties, namely the Agrarians (continuously), Christian Socialist party and the Social Democrats (the latter two for most of that period). Thus the period between 1926 and 1933 (and, in fact, even until 1935), as a result of the so-called 'activist' policy pursued by these three parties, indicated a chance of integrating the Sudeten Germans into the Czechoslovak republic. However the impact from the 'mother country' turned out to be profoundly detrimental, once the Nazis had taken over power in Germany in 1933.

How did the representatives of the Czech group look at the 'nationality problem'? In spite of the wide range of viewpoints arising out of the differences in political and ideological outlooks among historians, there seems to be widespread agreement about the fact that the history of the 'first' Czechoslovak republic presents itself as a series of lost opportunities, as regards official policies. Practice never kept pace with the great stress which leading policymakers, above all Thomas G. Masaryk, laid on the nationality problem. Thomas Masaryk, founder of the 'first' Czechoslovak republic, took a continuous interest in this problem. Let us quote, as an example, some passages from the speech he made on the occasion of the tenth anniversary of the republic in 1928:

> Above all we have to realise that we are a state which is nationally and linguistically mixed. It is true there are other states, properly speaking all states, having national minorities, but in this country the minorities are of different nature. For solving the minority problems there is no uniform pattern, as each majority is characterised by its specific and particular problem. In this country, the focus has to be laid on the relationship between the Czechoslovak majority and our German co-citizens. This problem having been solved, the rest of the linguistic and

national problems will be easily solved. Fate has created the fact that there is a significant number of Germans in our state beside Czechs and Slovaks . . . Moreover, our German co-citizens enjoy a high cultural and economic standard . . . In our policy we have to exclude any chauvinism, though on both sides. Not only our Germans, but likewise also the members of other nationalities are our co-citizens and, therefore, should enjoy democratic equality. In a democracy the representation of the minorities is a necessity. In any case it is the duty of the majority which, according to the democratic majority principle, imprints its character on the state, to win the minorities for the state.[5]

The present outline of the socio-political framework has confined itself to developments in the western part of Czechoslovakia which, with reference to this theme, was a real 'problem area'. The situation of the Carpathian Germans was totally different. Above all, the Carpathian Germans were a small ethnic group living in linguistic enclaves. During the Hungarian dominance, like all the other minorities, they had suffered from the policy of 'magyarisation'. Up to 1918 all children of German descent attended Magyar medium schools. In view of this experience the founding of the Czechoslovak republic effected a change for the better which, among other improvements, led to the establishment of a German medium school system. This development continued throughout the existence of the independent Slovak state (1939–45) and ended in 1945.

Structural and Curricular Features of the German Medium School System

The German schools were entirely integrated into the educational system of the Czechoslovak republic. This system was organised as a centralised one and followed the preceding Austrian pattern with regard to structures and syllabuses. As regards this aspect of continuity, the Czechoslovak school system preserved the Austrian heritage to a far greater extent than the other successor states to the Habsburg empire, including the Austrian republic. As a representative contemporary spokesman, the Czech educationalist, Otakar Kádner, has commented: 'Our present elementary school (and actually the 'middle school' too) has properly remained that old Austrian school with all its bright lights and shadows'.[6] It was based upon an eight year compulsory school attendance. The Slovak school system, descending from the Hungarian one, was broadly adjusted to that of Bohemia, Moravia and Silesia (later Moravia–Silesia).

The organisational structure consisted of the following sectors:

- The *Volksschule* (elementary school): attendance for five years in certain places where a *Bürgerschule* (non-selective secondary school) existed; otherwise attendance of eight years' duration;
- the *Bürgerschule* (non-selective secondary school); attendance lasting for three years as part of the compulsory system, and one additional voluntary year (grade 4);
- the selective secondary system consisting of the *Gymnasien* (classical secondary schools of different types) with attendance for eight years; *Realschulen* (non-classical commercially orientated secondary schools) with attendance for seven years; and the *Lehrerbildungsanstalten* (normal or teacher training schools) with attendance for four years;
- the highly diversified and developed system of *Fachschulen* (full time technical, commercial and vocational schools);
- the highly diversified system of part time *Fortbildungsschulen* (vocational schools) linked with apprenticeship schemes;
- the higher education level grouped round universities and *Technische Hochschulen* (higher technical colleges).

Let us now turn to the impact of the nationality problem on the school system, with its individual types and levels. The following data, taken from official statistical sources, helps to illustrate the quantitative educational development in Bohemia, Moravia and Silesia.[7]

Table 10.1: The quantitative educational development of German medium schools in Bohemia, Moravia and Silesia

Schools			
	1914/26	**1921**	**1935**
Volksschulen	3 595	3 284	3 165
Bürgerschulen	396	420	441
	1913/14	**1920/21**	**1935/36**
Gymnasien/Realschulen	101	96	70
Lehrerbildungsanstalten	24	17	10
Pupils			
	1914/16	**1921**	**1935**
Volksschulen	579 569	419 219	315 581
Bürgerschulen	61 559	64 241	84 277
	1913/14	**1920/21**	**1935/36**
Gymnasien/Realschulen	22 744	22 094	26 066
Lehrerbildungsanstalten	1 783	1 965	1 559

To enable a comparison to be drawn, the figures concerning the corresponding development of the Czech medium schools in the three provinces are given in Table 10.2.

Table 10.2: The quantitative educational development of Czech medium schools in Bohemia, Moravia and Silesia

Schools			
	1914/16	1921	1935
Volksschulen	5 547	6 359	7 117
Bürgerschulen	582	1 016	1 119
Gymnsasien/Realschulen	128	157	168
Lehrerbildungsanstalten	29	33	32
Pupils			
	1914/16	1921	1935
Volksschulen	996 415	943 497	728 009
Bürgerschulen	97 112	182 566	287 646
	1913/14	1920/21	1935/36
Gymnasien/Realschulen	34 896	52 687	77 116
Lehrerbildungsanstalten	3 338	4 428	4 871

Before explaining the 'crucial' issues in regard of the nationality problem, the following essential trends to be derived from these data must be pointed out:

1   In both sectors there was a significant decline of pupils in the *Volksschulen*;
2   The *Bürgerschule* found itself in an exceptional position in both sectors due to its expansion in towns at the cost of the upper grades (grades six to eight) of the *Volksschulen*;
3   The *gymnasium* population was characterised by a significant increase in the Czech medium sector, while the German medium sector indicates, after overcoming a slight regression, a trend toward consolidation;
4   The overall development at the elementary and secondary levels was characterised by a decline in the number of pupils by 16 per cent between 1914/16 (1913/14) and 1935 (1935/36), due to the overall decline in the birthrates. In the context of the present analysis it seems to be worthwhile looking at the relevant age groups born in 1900–8, 1907–15 and 1921–29 (in 1000s): 2856, 2527, 2043, which comes up to a regression by about 30 per cent. Unfortunately, these data, derived from the *Population Atlas* (1962), did not include any information on infant mortality which had decreased significantly during that period;
5   When looking at the development at the elementary and secondary levels *in toto*, one discerns a significant shift against the German medium sector with regard to the proportion of pupils in German medium schools: from 37 per cent in 1914/16 (1913/14) to 28 per cent in 1935 (1935/36). Within this framework,

there was a shift between 1914/16 (1913/14) and 1921 (1920/21), *viz.* from 37 to 30 per cent, which deserves particular attention;

6   Despite the declining trend, the German medium sector as a whole maintained its core, consequently one has to take into particular account that the closing down process concerned schools within a Czech environment, especially in towns in central Bohemia and Moravia;

7   With special regard to the situation of the *Volksschulen* in 1921, one has to take into account, that the German medium sector covered 34 per cent, whereas the proportion of its pupils within the overall *Volksschule* population was only 30 per cent. Until 1935, this disproportion had been 'harmonised' (in favour of the Czech medium sector).

Summarising the changes which can be discerned from the above data one cannot but find as the most probable explanation of the aforementioned shifting, in particular between 1914/16 (1913/14) and 1921 (1920/21), an internal migration from German medium to Czech medium schools. However, this shifting predominantly concerned children of Czech nationality,[8] whereas an insignificant shift was caused by a certain growth of interest in the attendance at Czech medium schools among bilingual and linguistically mixed families. Taking this explanatory framework into account the problem area to be explored is not so much related to the proportions of pupils in regard to nationality as such, but rather is dominated by the conditions of formal education and schooling.

The school administration was generally inherited from its Austrian predecessor. Within this overall framework the German school system enjoyed a considerable degree of autonomy. Supervision of the German schools was exercised by German civil servants in the Provincial School Councils; they were recruited, as a rule, from teachers of the respective school sectors. This supervision also related to the vocational educational institutions within the direct competency of the Ministry of Education. In Bohemia and Moravia–Silesia, the Provincial School Councils, while being chaired by (Czech) presidents, consisted of separate divisions for Czech and German schools. In this form, they again followed the Austrian pattern, although one must add that the responsibilities of the presidency had been strengthened. As regards official languages, the German division had to use the Czech language, too, when communicating with individual schools. They, however, were entitled to submit their reports and applications in German. There was no leading civil servant of German descent in the Ministry of Education: during the 1920s only a few Germans were appointed in subordinate positions; in 1927–8 among the 120 ordinary civil servants, there were only five of (probably) German descent.[9]

Let us end this section by giving an overview of the curricular situation. Generally speaking, changes were as moderate as in the structural area. Attempts to reform the syllabuses, especially those initiated in the years 1930–3 by Minister Ivan Dèrer, a leading member of the Czech Social Democratic party, produced only partial results, because the parliament was not able to reach any legislative decision. As regards the German schools, two problems have to be articulated. First, at the beginning of the 1920s, the study of the Czech language was made obligatory in all *Gymnasien* and *Realschulen* as well as in *Bürgerschulen*, and at the beginnng of the 1930s it became the first 'foreign' language in all types of the *Gymnasien* and *Realschulen*. These measures could be regarded as a necessary corollary to the political change of 1918. On the other hand, it must be stressed that the Czech authorities also favoured the expansion of German as a foreign language in Czech schools, which was instituted as a rule in *Bürgerschulen* as well as in *Gymnasien* and *Realschulen*. In this way favourable conditions had been created for the expansion of bilingualism, and that to a much greater degree than had been the case in the Austrian period, when neither of the two languages had officially been an obligatory language in the schools of Bohemia.

The second curricular problem was posed by the problematics of civic education. Although there was no special subject called civics (except in the uppermost grades of *Gymnasien*, *Realschulen* and *Bürgerschulen*), the subjects of history, geography and also German were necessarily involved in the tension caused by the task of educating German youngsters to become loyal citizens of the Czechoslovak republic, while on the other hand they should have also been tied to the contents and values of German culture.[10] In this context let if suffice to remark that this problem was never solved in a way that was satisfactory to both sides. As this problem concerns the level of overall educational policies, we will come back to it in subsequent sections.

Apart from the specific problems concerned with ethnic relevance, there was a remarkable degree of inter-relations between Czech and German educators in the pursuit of innovations – an educational area which has not yet been investigated and, therefore needs to be expanded upon. From a comparative point of view this observation should not come as a surprise, because the innovators in both ethnic communities were stimulated by the *Reformpädagogik* (international reform movement) and *l'Education Nouvelle* (progressive education) in which they wanted to take part. Moreover, the identical or, at least, significantly similar innovative approaches resulted from their common origins in the heritage left by the Austrian educational policy and the inherited structure of the school system.

The Educational Policy of the Czechoslovak Government

As has been indicated already, the Czechoslovak republic came into existence as a nation-state with both the Czechs and Slovaks claiming the privilege of the 'state nation', although the constitution had not legitimated such a position. In terms of educational policy, this fundamental criterion manifested itself, above all, in the structure of the school administration, characterised by the predominance of the centralising authority of the Ministry of Education in its central steering role. On the other hand, autonomy at the level of the Provincial Councils offered some scope to the German schools, in respect of their participation in the appointment of teachers, the selection of non-mandatory subject matter and also the conduct of examinations.[11] This balanced network of formal and semi-formal opportunities was supported by the traditional freedom Austrian teachers, in particular those at *Gymnasien* and *Realschulen*, had enjoyed since the middle of the nineteenth century over the choice of instructional methods and teaching materials. Since this tradition was not abandoned under the political conditions of the Czechoslovak republic, teachers had ample opportunity for shaping their individual lessons, taking into particular consideration the fact that this freedom included the interpretation of literary texts as well as of historical sources and events. It is true that a borderline of tolerance had been drawn by the constitution, and by two laws enacted in 1918 and 1920, concerning the civil servants' loyalty to the new republic. Compared to analogous issues in other European nation–states with minority problems, the supervision exercised by the governmental and administrative authorities here was characterised by remarkable flexibility.

In regard to overall development, educational policy was ambivalent over reducing the numbers of German schools on the one hand, and on the other the Ministry's continual efforts to include the representatives of the German community, in particular the teachers' associations, in its reform activities. The period between 1929 and 1934 above all bears witness to the noteworthy, though partial, success of this cooperation orientated policy, which was aimed to provide the minorities with 'school and cultural autonomy', thus resuming an unsuccessful attempt started by Milan Hodza, as Minister of Education, in 1926. Ivan Dèrer's legislative activity resulted in a bill which intended the extension of the competencies of the *Ortsschulräte* and *Landesschulräte* (Local and Provincial School Councils) to be based on the principles of linguistic separation and independence from the authorities responsible for general administration. This bill was proposed at the end of 1932, but was never passed by the parliament.

The history of that period did coincide with the 'activist' initiatives of the democratic German parties at the highest level, marked by the cooperation of the prominent German political parties with the governmental policy. However it also paralleled Thomas Masaryk's political philosophy quite closely, a philosophy which the first President and founding father of the Czechoslovak republic had repeatedly defined. It must be added that this philosophy seems to have been accepted by the German teachers' associations. The problematic nature of this acceptance, with special regard to its 'democratic' substance, will be dealt with later. Suffice it to remark, in this context that the German teachers' associations maintained their communications with the state authorities far into the 1930s, even into the catastrophic year of 1938, so far as this has been documented by their representative organs. This judgement is also supported by the programme of the Sudeten German Pedagogic Meeting held at Reichenberg (Liberec) from 30 January to 1 February 1938. Beside the papers read by Sudeten German scholars and educators, that programme included, on the one hand, a paper by the prominent German educationist, Eduard Spranger, and, on the other, papers by Czech university professors J.B. Kozák (Prague) on the theme The European mission of the Czech nation, and Josef Tvrdý (Bratislava), on The importance of people and state for the whole of education. Tvrdý died as a Nazi victim in the concentration camp Mauthausen in 1942.[12]

However, the reason why reference to this meeting is made here is this: The Head of the President's Office had sent a letter of greetings, whose full version was read to the plenum on behalf of the President of the Czechoslovak republic, Edvard Benes. Additionally, ten days later, that is, on 10 February 1938, Gottfried Preissler, the Chairman of the *Kulturausschuss der Sudetendeutschen Lehrerverbände* (Cultural Committee of the Sudeten German Teachers' Associations), and in broader terms one of the teachers' leading figures, was given a one hour audience by the President himself. The meeting was devoted to an exchange of thoughts and arguments, and ended by the President's declaration that the German population should be given the same rights in the education system as the Slovak population.[13] Forty years later, in his memoirs, Preissler judged that declaration to have been a somewhat oracular statement,[14] probably remembering the entirely different position of the Slovaks as a constituent element in the two state nation. Ultimately, history cannot offer any further evidence of how the President's pronouncements might have been transferred into legislation and political practice, because eight months after the audience, that chapter reached its end.

Attitudes and Reactions Among Germans

Before considering the attitudes and reactions among Germans, one should take into account that the vast majority on both sides were widely dedicated to their ethnic concerns, whereas there were controversial attitudes as regards the relationship to the 'other' group. The range extended from reserve, or even hostility, to the search for tolerance and mutual understanding. The aforementioned developments in general policy have already brought to light the need to pay special attention to periodisation in the history of the 'first' Czechoslovak republic. The first period, lasting up to the middle of the 1920s, was dominated by articulated tensions between the two ethnic groups. It proved to be detrimental to all attempts at reconciliation by the government, cautious as they were. The subsequent period (between 1926 and 1935, which ended with Henlein's 'Sudeten German party' winning 63 per cent of all German votes in a national election), was dominated by the aforementioned 'activism' of the democratic German parties and a readiness to cooperate prevailed. The latter period was marked by a return and growth in tension and hostility on the one hand, and ongoing efforts to reconcile the German medium school sector with the state on the other. Interpretation of this period will be delayed until the concluding section.

Let us now focus our attention on attitudes and reactions within the German community, as mirrored by Sudeten German publications and teachers' associations. Remembering that the founding of the Czechoslovak republic occurred without the support of, and in spite of the averse views of, most Germans and the leaders of opinion amongst them, we can conclude that the start was not at all easy.

In the first period there was substantial agreement among all three of the German parties, that is, the democratic and the two right-wing parties, that Czechoslovak educational policy discriminated against German medium schools. This attitude was linked with the repudiation of the viewpoint taken by the government and the majority of the Czech parties, that Czech medium schools must be given special attention in order to overcome the underprivileged position they had been in during the Austrian–Hungarian era. In a series of controversial debates, the borderline between objectivity and distortion of fact was crossed more than once. For instance, it is worth quoting Franz Spina, chairman of the German Agrarian party. In a statement he made in 1925 on behalf of four German parties in the Czechoslovak parliament, he said:

> Thousands of [German] schools and school classes have been closed in recent years; thus the educational opportunities of our people, in

particular in those social classes which are dependent upon elementary education, have been reduced to a minimum. On the other hand a
great number of unnecessary Czech medium schools have been
established in the German populated region at public expense, and
German children have been enrolled in these schools by various
coercive measures.[15]

This statement cannot be ignored, particularly as some months
later, Franz Spina entered the government as Minister of Public
Labour, thus paving the way toward the 'activist' policy period.

Throughout the era of the 'first' Czechoslovak republic, that is,
including the 'constructive' period between 1926 and 1935, one can
observe four principal conflict areas between the German representatives and the state authorities. First of all, the closing down of many
Volksschulen, *Gymnasien* and *Realschulen* (but not of *Bürgerschulen*),
documented by the statistical data, was considered a means of
discriminating against the German group as a whole. At the beginning of the 1930s, this complaint was coupled with accusations
against the government for neglecting the evil of unemployment,
which affected the industrialised German speaking districts to an
exceptionally high degree indeed.

Secondly, the *Minderheitsschulgesetz* (Minority School act) of 3
August 1919, one of the first legislative activities of the young
republic in the area of educational policy, was the target of considerable criticism throughout these years. This law created the
category of 'minority schools' They were elementary and secondary
units situated in local catchment areas with majorities of different
ethnic descent. The 'minority schools' were exempted from the
normal supervision of the *Ortsschulräte* (Local School Councils) and
the *Bezirksschulausschüsse* (District School Commissions). Instead,
they were directly under the Ministry of Education as regards
supervision and material maintenance. Since, in most cases, it was
the Czech medium schools in the German environment that
benefitted from this change, the Minority School act was denounced
by the Germans as an important element in the strategy of Czech
penetration of the German territories and diluting their closely
settled areas.

Considering the controversial nature of Czech educational policy,
it is not easy to give due weight to both sides in this significant area of
conflict. The Czech government could argue that it was not responsible for the immigration of Czech workers to the mining
districts of north west Bohemia which started long before the
founding of the Czechoslovak republic. Moreover, German complaints could be contradicted on two grounds; first by the inclusion of
German medium schools, in particular in Bohemia, in the implementation of the Minority School act; second, and more generally,

by a statement that the entire legislative measure had been initiated to liberate the local communities from the burden of maintaining 'minority schools', and to pave the way toward the transformation of individual schools from private to state status (from which, however, only Czech schools profited). Finally, in this context, one must be reminded of the progress of the *Bürgerschulen*, in which the German schools fully participated. This development was legally consolidated by the *Sprengelbürgerschulgesetz*, an act of 20 December 1935 concerning the catchment areas of the *Bürgerschulen*.

The third area of conflict dealt with the 'autonomy' issue. The division of responsibility within the Provincial School Councils was criticised as being unsatisfactory. Instead, the German teachers' associations wanted German schools to be provided with full autonomy, as urged by Eduard Rohn at the aforementioned Sudeten German Pedagogic Meeting. They wanted the Ministry to be divided into departments according to the nationality principle. Furthermore, the members of the nationality bound departments within the Provincial School Councils were to be elected by the respective ethnic constituencies.[16] The demand also included an adoption of the nationality principle by the Local School Councils and District School Commissions, which would have consequently led beyond Hodza's and Dèrer's unsuccessful initiatives. This third area will be discussed further in the conclusion.

The fourth area of conflict refers to a crucial problem, in that it questioned the integrity of the Czechoslovak republic as such. Why did the last conflict area affect the integrity of the state? This issue has to be traced back directly to the overall economic and political circumstances at the beginning of the 1930s. As a result of the economic crisis, with its strong impact on the industrialised German speaking areas in north Bohemia, the two German right wing parties, namely the *Deutsche Nationalpartei* (German National party) and the *Deutsche Nationalsozialistische Arbeiterpartei* (German National Socialist Workers' party), gained ground. The result was that teachers became an exceptionally vulnerable target group. The reaction of the Czech authorities mainly consisted of disciplinary actions against 'unreliable' teachers which often led to 'penalty transfers'.

This policy was aggravated in 1933, the year of Hitler's victory in Germany, when the first shadows were cast over the border. On 12 July 1933, the Czechoslovak parliament enacted a law which set the framework for prosecution for actions directed against the state among civil servants in conjunction with the dissolution of the two German right wing parties. Though it was a minority (between 700 and 1000) among the 13 653 teachers who were involved in those disciplinary actions, the complaints about the sanctions as such also gained support not only among a significant group of right-wing 'sympathisers', but also among the 'moderate' teachers, who reacted in a way well known from similar socio-psychological phenomena in comparable historical situations. The founding and rapid expansion of the *Sudetendeutsche Partei* (Sudeten German party), exacerbated the conflict, though Konrad Henlein, the party leader, ostensibly took the view of 'autonomy' and not yet that of the 'return into the *Reich*', even after the *Anschluss* of Austria in March 1938.

Let us leave this issue of conflict areas and complaints, which clearly demonstrates the connection between educational and general policies, and turn our attention to the sources testifying that, in spite of the rapidly approaching storm, negotiations and the search for compromise continued well into the first months of 1938. The German side was represented by the teachers' associations, which are worth introducing at this point. As in other countries, they were structured according to the existing school types:

- The *Deutscher Lehrerbund im Tschechoslowakischen Staate* (German Teachers' Association in the Czechoslovak State), the largest organisation of teachers at *Volksschulen* and also at *Bürgerschulen;*
- the *Reichsverband der Deutschen Bürgerschullehrerschaft* (*Reich* Association of German *Bürgerschule* Teachers);
- the *Verband der Lehrer an Gewerblichen Staatsanstalten* (Association of Teachers at Technical–Vocational Schools);
- the *Verband Deutscher Handelsschullehrer* (Association of German Teachers at Commercial Schools);
- the *Reichsverband Deutscher Mittelschullehrer in der Tschecho-slowakischen Republik* (*Reich* Association of German Teachers at Academic Secondary Schools in the Czechoslovak republic.

The spectrum was completed by the *Zentralverein der Deutschen Lehrerinnen* the all-embracing association of female teachers.

The associations organised individual and joint meetings, as well as in-service training in the form of summer courses. In this context, the reciprocal activities of Czech and German teachers' associations in organising summer courses for German and Czech language teachers must be mentioned. The climax of the efforts at coordination among the teachers' associations was the founding of the *Kulturaus-schuss der Sudetendeutschen Lehrerverbände* (Cultural Commission of the Sudeten German Teachers' Associations) with Gottfried Preissler as chairman. It started with the edition of a monthly journal, the *Pädagogische Rundschau* (Pedagogic Review), which was published in 1937 and 1938 by the Czechoslovak state publishers in Prague. It also initiated the publication of a *Handbuch für die deutschen Schulen in der Tschechoslowakei* (Handbook for the German schools in Czecho-slovakia) and organised the Sudeten German Pedagogic meeting at Reichenberg (Liberec) in January/February 1938. While the teachers' associations focused their activities on representing those aims of their group concerned with school development 'from within', it was the *Deutscher Kulturverband* (German Cultural Association) and the *Deutsche Pestalozzi–Gesellschaft* (German Pestalozzi Association) which acted as sponsoring agencies. The description of these multifarious activities resulted in a picture which indicates the consolidated power of the German teachers' community, which was apparently widely supported by the public and, even at the beginning of 1938, seemed to be intact enough to pass *Leitsätze für die volks- und staatsbürgerliche Erziehung* (Guidelines for the people and state bound civic education), a paper which aimed at the harmonisation of the two loyalties with which German pupils were confronted.

Concluding Remarks

Let us begin our concluding remarks by quoting from an article written by Gottfried Preissler. It was devoted to 'Development and structure of the Czechoslovak education system with special regard to the Sudeten German school', and it was published in the German journal *Die Erziehung* in Leipzig in December 1937. This article continued the basic idea of Preissler's concept of civic education; at the same time, however, it is worthwhile taking it into particular consideration, because the author puts forth his concept within the wider historical framework of the educational history of the 'first' Czechoslovak republic. The article included the following comments:

> The most urgent tasks the school administration had to tackle can be described as follows: At first the whole school system of the republic had to be adjusted to the new educational idea which symbolised the democratic republic, in order to turn it into reality . . . The changed psychological attitude that was decisive in the success of such efforts, was easy to achieve with the young generation of the Czech people of the new state . . . who had been educated to maintaining a certain distance from and showing a certain reserve towards the old Austrian state and its educational ideas in the pre-war and war periods. The situation was more difficult in the schools of the other ethnic groups in the republic. However, the school administration gave these schools time to develop corresponding educational and instructional forms for coping with the pedagogic problems posed by these difficulties. During the last few years the school administration has become aware of the particular problem of how mutually to promote and coordinate *volks-und staatsbürgerliche Erziehung* (people bound and state bound civic education) in the non-German schools (which rests in the need to educate children of other ethnic descent as citizens of the Czechoslovak nation state) . . . The *Kulturausschuss der Sudetendeutschen Lehrerverbände* (Cultural Committee of the Sudeten German Teachers'

Associations) at Reichenberg . . . has submitted a programme dealing with the solution of this educational question to the state school administration. The Ministry of Education has announced a joint discussion concerning the principles of this proposal orientated towards the solution of the problem.

This passage seems illuminating for several reasons. It is part of an article which, from the today's vantage point, was written on the eve of the fatal year 1938 in a German pedagogic journal, apparently with the intention of informing German educators in the *Reich* of the peculiarities of the Sudeten Germans' school problems. What kind of picture does the author want to present to his readers? First of all, he emphasises his committee's willingness to contribute to the development of an educational concept orientated to the reconciliation of *Volk* (people) and *Staat* (state) as the two dichotomic values of civic education (in its widest meaning). Moreover, the Ministry's response is considered as constructive, in line with the President's meeting with the author of this article on 10 February 1938. Finally, the author, when trying to summarise the development of the past twenty years, articulates an attitude of apparent satisfaction with the school administration's patience in its policy of adjusting the syllabuses of the German medium schools to the new democratic ideals.

A historian is bound to notice that this document was written in a tone of reconciliation and constructiveness. One realises that it echoes Thomas Masaryk's concept and responds to it positively. The following questions should be added: Why had those involved not agreed on a reasonable solution earlier, considering the preceding ten years of ongoing negotiations? To what degree did the search for an agreement on both sides of the educational scene mirror, on the one hand the adversaries' substantial hopes for success and, on the other, people's expectations beyond the educational scene? Instead of answering these questions which necessarily might lead to speculative considerations, the following remarks are directed toward reexamining the range of problematics that the present paper has dealt with. It seems that the discussion can be said to have resulted in essentially three conclusions.

First, one becomes aware of a remarkable continuity with regard to the contacts and negotiations between representatives of the Czechoslovak government, in particular the Ministry of Education, and the leading functionaries of the Sudeten German teachers' associations. These contacts certainly can be traced back to the middle of the 1920s and, what raises greater astonishment, can be observed until the beginning of 1938. Obviously, the government recognised these associations as serious partners.

Secondly, the available sources, including those which take an appreciative view of the position held by the government, admit that the various attempts to solve the minority problem in the area of educational policy by achieving some satisfactory form of 'school autonomy' failed. In retrospect one cannot but regret that Ivan Dèrer, starting his initiatives in the 'constructive' period of cooperation between the democratic parties on the Czech and German sides, was not after all successful.

Finally, the teachers' associations representing a vast majority of Sudeten German teachers, conceived and practised their activities as a contribution to improving the school system at its various levels. On the other hand, one has to recall the susceptibility, if not allegiance, to right wing ideologies of a significant group of teachers. The process of infiltration continued steadily between 1933 and 1938. How many adherents or, at least, sympathisers of Henlein's Sudeten German party were among the participants at the Sudeten German Pedagogic meeting? Probably no small number.

In this context, the theme of this paper widens, opening to the 'big' political scene again. Comparing the rapid growth of the Sudeten German party between 1933 and 1938 with the 'cooperative' climate that can be deduced from the aforementioned events and documents, one can conclude that the rhetoric used by the functionaries of the German teachers' associations should be denounced as camouflage. Such an answer, referring to a professional group *in toto*, seems, however, to be too simplistic to explain the complexity of the Czech–German relations and, in particular, the situation in the educational area. Instead, it may be helpful to consider what Josef Mühlberger has called a 'blindness' to 'dictatorial nationalism':

> . . . most Germans were blind to what had obviously come to light [in Germany] in the years between 1933 and 1935, namely dictatorship, although there was an unhampered flow of information; forming a judgement, therefore, would easily have been possible. The democratic conviction [of most Sudeten Germans] had shrunk to a minimum . . .

With respect to the overall development between 1933 and 1938, Mühlberger qualifies this comment by stating that the question concerning democratic or dictatorial nationalism was left aside.[17] Provided one accepts Mühlberger's interpretation, which can certainly claim plausibility, one has to enter into the debate of how 'democracy' was perceived in the period between the two world wars and take into account the concepts which were typical of the debate in the whole of central Europe, rather than being limited to the Sudeten Germans.

In order to relate these considerations – necessarily fragmentary in the context of this paper – to the educational scene, we should refer to an illuminating passage in the paper which Ernst Otto, Professor of Education at the German University in Prague, gave at the Sudeten German Pedagogic meeting. The paper was entitled 'People – State – School'. Otto made a distinction between the 'liberal party system' and *Ganzheitssystem* (the authoritarian system of totality). While the former represents freedom and equality of all human beings, peoples, sexes and denominations, the latter:

> asserts the inequality of human beings, sexes and peoples. The totality is greater than the member, that is, the community of the people (in other words the state) has priority over the person. Both systems have . . . a common core: both of them must be recognised as democracies, as long as they are willing to ensure the people's interests; that is, liberalism must not be perverted into arbitrariness, nor authority into coercion . . .[18]

This is a crucial statement. When that happens, he said, then democracy and liberalism are confounded, which frequently occurs.

Finally, it is worthwhile quoting from the passage, where Otto switches his wide reaching reflections to the relation between state and school:

> In the liberal state the organisation of the education system can be influenced only by the elected legislature . . . In the *Ganzheitsstaat* (totalitarian state) the aims and ways of the education system, its external organisation as well as its *weltanschaulich* (philosophic) orientation, are not sought in rational discourse and criticism, but are fixed in an intuitive way. The essence of *Führertum* (genuine leadership), according to this idea, is rooted in the charisma of the guidelines which have been formulated by a reliable instinct. However woe to the people when the *Führung* (leaders) fail.[19]

The development of the argument of the whole paper indicates that the speaker's sympathies were in favour of the 'authoritarian' version of 'democracy'. Moreover, it remains open why he did not continue his sequence of thoughts to ask a question which has remained real enough until today and was, in those years, of gruesome relevance: Is there any chance for an inner coherence of a state which is composed of nationalities which feel substantially committed to divergent values – provided one is prepared to accept Otto's interpretation of the 'authoritarian' system as 'democratic', which provokes fundamental doubts of semantic and philosophical nature?

Anyway, the history of the German schools in the 'first Czechoslovak republic presents itself as a multi-dimensional and complex one. Beyond the open questions within the 'inner circle' of the education system, as well as beyond it, in the 'outer circle' of the overall socio-political network marked by the tension between conflict and search for cooperation, there remains the question: Provided that the adversaries in the area of educational policy had succeeded in achieving a satisfactory solution, could the catastrophe of 1938/39 have been prevented? Here again, and to a far greater degree, fundamental doubts remain, since the role of education, though certainly important, was distinctly circumscribed by what was happening on the 'big' political scene; in this case, the growing aggressiveness and compulsive power of a totalitarian system.

Notes

1. Stencl, pp. 5–8. The term 'foreigners' includes permanent residents with a foreign citizenship, mostly of Poland, Austria, Germany and Hungary.
2. See Lemberg, pp. 160–3: Lunetta, pp. 355–63.
3. Brügel, p. 182.
4. Korbel, pp. 118–19.
5. See Masaryk. Cit. from Brügel, p. 191.
6. Kádner, p. 9.
7. Cit. Keil, pp. 556–60, 564–6. This omnibus volume contains detailed statistical data which derived from the records (*Mitteilungen*) of the State Statistics Office of the Czechoslovak republic.
8. Cit. Atlas obyvatelstva, pp. 39–40; Cf. Oberschall, in particular pp. 9–15 (in regard to 'Volksschulen').
9. This information has been given to me by Jan Havránek (Charles University, Prague).
10. Cf. Preissler (1936).
11. Keil, pp. 88–92.
12. *Mitteilungen aus dem hoheren Schulwesen*, 37 (1938) 3/4, pp. 14–20; 37 (1938) 5/6, S. 39–44; Preissler (1979), pp. 47–8. The information on Tvrdy's death at Mauthausen was given to me by Jan Havránek.
13. Note in: *Mitteilungen aus dem höheren Schulwesen* (Reichenberg); 37 (1938) 3/4, p. 23. – In this context reference has to be made to President Benes's official visit to Reichenberg on 19 August 1936. In his speech he pleaded for open discussions between Czechs and Germans and offered his services as mediator. Report in: . *Freie Schulzeitung*, No. 30, 10 September 1936.
14. Preissler (1979), pp. 48–9.
15. Cited in Mühlberger, p. 238.
16. See Rohn, p. 19. In his juridical doctoral thesis (submitted to the University of Giessen, Germany) Ewald Schäfer, after thoroughly analysing the juridical components of German medium elementary schools in Czechoslovakia (and relying, in a one sided way, on Sudeten German sources which articulate the detrimental effects of the Czechoslovak policy), ends (in 1936) with a plea for 'national school autonomy', which 'apparently seems to be in accordance with the interests of the Czech state too'. See Schafer, pp. 63–5.
17. Mühlberger, p. 242. In this context it should be added that most of the functionaries of the Sudeten German teachers' associations (including Gottfried Preissler) were active in the school administration during the Nazi period and – soon after arriving in West Germany – continued their activities in

different positions of the school administration in a number of *Länder*. This phenomenon is worth noting since it is symptomatic of the attitude and self-awareness among many Sudeten Germans.

18. E. Otto, 'Volk – Staat – Schule', prepared for and printed: *Pädagogische Rundschau* (Prague) 5 (1938), but not published (The journal ended with its fourth number), pp. 66–67. A brief version was published in *Mitteilungen aus dem höheren Schulwesen*, p. 15.

19. E. Otto, p. 69.

Select Bibliography

Atlas obyvatelstva CSSR, (1962), Praha.

Brügel, J.W. (1980), 'Die Deutschen in der Vorkriegs-Tschechoslowakei' in Mamatey, V.S. and Luza, R. (eds) *Geschichte der Tschechoslowakischen Republik (1918–1948)*, Vienna.

Kàdner, O. (1931), *Skolstvi v Republice Ceskoslovenskè*, Praha.

Keil, Th. (ed.) (1967), *Die Deutsche Schule in den Sudetenländern. Form und Inhalt des Bildungswesens*, Munich.

Korbel, J. (1977), *Twentieth-Century Czechoslovakia, The Meaning of its History*, New York.

Lemberg, E. (1986), 'Ein Leben in Grenzzonen und Ambivalenzen', in Seibt, F. (ed.) *Eugen Lemberg 1903–1976*, Munich.

Lunetta, F. (1985), 'Die ethnisch–sprachlichen Minderheiten in Italien unter dem Aspekt der Identitätswahrung in Gesellschaft and Schule', in Mitter, W. and Swift, J. (eds.) 'Education and the Diversity of Cultures', *Bildung und Erziehung*, Beiheft 2/I, Vienna.

Masaryk, Th.G. (October 28th, 1918), 'on occasion of the 10th anniversary of the Czechoslovak Republic', in *Prager Tagblatt*, 30 October 1928.

Mühlberger, J. (1978), *Zwei Völker in Böhmen, Beitrag zu einer historischen und geistesgeschichtlichen Struktur analyse*, Munich.

Oberschall, A. (1922), *Das deutsche und tschechische Schulwesen in der Tschechoslowakischen Republik*, Reichenberg.

Otto, E. (1938), 'Volk – Staat – Schule' in *Pädagogische Rundschau*, unpublished, Prague.

Preissler, G. (1936), 'Kulturpolitische Grundfragen unserer Schule', in *Freie Schulzeitung*, No. 30.

Preissler, G. (1979), *Geschichte meines Lebens aus der Sicht des 85. Geburtstages (1979)*,Frankfurt.

Rohn, E. (1938), 'Die nationale Selbstverwaltung der Deutschen Schule', in *Mitteilungen aus dem höheren Schulwesen*, 37, 3/4, Reichenberg.

Schäfer, E. (1936), *Die Berücksichtigung des Deutschen in der Volksschule der Tschechoslowakei*, Giessen.

Stencl, K. (1925), *Republika Ceskoslovenská. Statisticeský prehled stavu populacniho hospodàrskèho a kulturniho*, Praha.

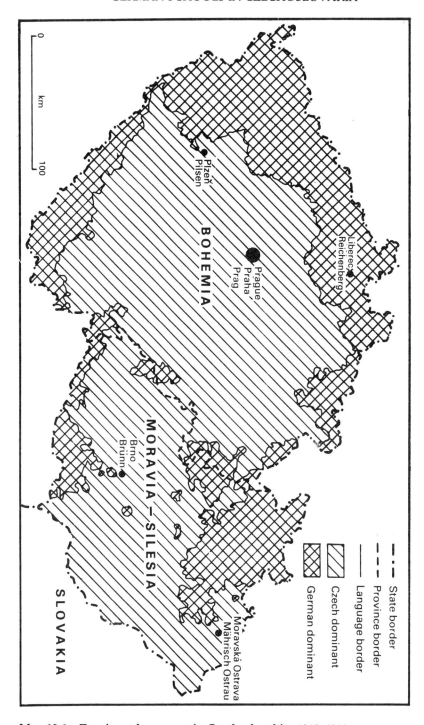

Map 10.1 Dominant languages in Czechoslovakia, 1918–1938

11 The Education of Czechs and Slovaks under Foreign Domination, 1850–1918

JAN HAVRÁNEK

The Czechs and their Schools under the Habsburg Monarchy: 1850–1918

Introductory Remarks

The Czechs inhabited three lands in the north western part of the Habsburg monarchy; Bohemia, Moravia and Silesia. In 1850 6.9 million inhabitants lived there, 63 per cent of whom were Czech and 36 per cent German. This proportion had changed in favour of Czech nationals by 0.8 per cent by 1910. The highest proportion of Czech population in 1910, 71 per cent, was in Moravia; in Bohemia it was 64 per cent; in Silesia, within its 1910 borders, it was 22 per cent. Of the inhabitants in Silesia 33 per cent were of Polish nationality.

The line dividing the nationalities in the agricultural areas was stable and changed little, but it was watched by nationalists from both sides with great attention. The national character of towns in inner Bohemia, including its capital, Prague, changed because of persistent immigration of workers and craftsmen from the countryside during the period of industrialisation between 1830 and 1880. Immigration into Prague and its suburbs changed proportions of Czech and German inhabitants of the metropolitan area to 86:14 by 1880.

The fact that the Prague city government since 1861 had been in the hands of a Czech majority was very advantageous for Czech education, as the Prague City Council put up many buildings for Czech schools and paid teachers relatively well. The situation was similar in other Bohemian towns like Plzeň, Pardubice, Chrudim, Roudnice, etc. In Moravia, the German upper and middle classes retained control in the cities of Brno and Olomouc up to 1918, even if they were surrounded by the predominantly Czech working class suburbs. The City Councils of smaller Moravian towns like Kroměříž, and Uherské Hradište were in the hands of rich German minorities up to the end of the nineteenth century. In Silesia, the Czech position in local government was even weaker. The changes in the national composition of population in the north west Bohemian coal district (Most) and in Vienna in the last third of the century were due to the immigration of Czech miners and workers, apprentices and home servants, but they could not influence the local government, which ran the elementary school system.

There was a division of responsibility in the supervision of the educational system. The parliament and government in Vienna edited laws regulating the whole structure of schooling and its relations to the Churches and controlled the universities. The Land Committees in Prague, Brno and Opava were responsible for the *gymnasiums* (classical secondary schools) and, to some degree, for offering support to the local authorities which financed the elementary and *Bürgerschulen*, or *měštanske školy* (non-selective secondary schools) for children aged between 11 and 15. Local authorities decided on the policy towards the teachers. The fact that the Czechs controlled the local governments in inner Bohemia and parts of Moravia and, together with the conservative nobility, the Bohemian Land Committee in Prague, enabled them to build up a well functioning system of elementary schooling and – first in Bohemia and later on also in Moravia – of vocational schools for agriculture, industry and commerce.

When studying the school system of any state and the school policy of any government, we have to bear in mind that they must be evaluated according to the results they achieve in raising the cultural level of the population. The latter, of course, is difficult to measure statistically, but there are some factors that can be gauged accurately. The first of these is the knowledge of reading and writing, and the second is successful completion of the different levels of education: elementary, secondary and higher. The first can be calculated by using the results of the Austrian and Hungarian population censuses in 1900 and 1910, which also provide the data concerning those who only mastered the simpler of the two basic skills, that is reading. Statistics for higher education are to be found only in the 1961 and 1970 censuses. Both of these were arranged according to decennial groups and so we are now in a position to follow through the levels of schooling of some 50 years before. Even if the statistics cannot be accepted uncritically, other researches made by the author of this paper seem to support their reliability.[1]

According to the official Austro–Hungarian statistics, the degree of literacy among the Czechs was extraordinarily high. In Bohemia, in

1900, only 2.6 per cent of Czech adult population was illiterate, compared with 3.5 per cent of German.[2] The illiteracy rate for Moravia and Silesia was only one point higher. In the period down to 1910 the situation improved a little, and it can be compared with that prevailing in respect of other nationalities in the Austrian half of the monarchy. According to the census of that year, 61 per cent of Ruthenians, 60 per cent of Rumanians, 27.3 per cent of Poles, 13.6 per cent of Slovenes and 10.3 per cent of Italians were illiterate, whereas among the Germans the rate was 3.1 per cent and among the Czechs 2.4 per cent.[3]

Some explanation is needed concerning this curious situation where one of the dominated nations had a lower rate of illiteracy than the ruling nation, even though the difference was not particularly great. The explanation lies in the economic, social and political development of the Czech lands. At the end of the period we are examining, only a third of the population in the Czech lands was agrarian. This was in contrast to the position in Slovakia, which in 1918 joined the Czech lands to make up the new Czechoslovak state. In Slovakia nearly two-thirds of the population depended upon agricultural production, as is illustrated by the following table:

Table 11.1: **Population active in, or dependent on others active in, different branches of production in Czech lands and Slovakia in 1910 (%)**

	Agriculture	Industry	Trade and transport	Public services, liberal professions and persons without a specific profession
Czech Lands	34	40	11	15
Slovakia	63	18	8	11

Source: Statistická Příručka, 2, 82–3

It is clear that the non-agrarian, in contrast to the agrarian, population needed not merely a knowledge of reading and writing but also all the other skills and training they could acquire in the course of their education. Economic and social change connected with industrialisation put greater demands on the cultural level of the agrarian population also. The enlightened absolutist policy of the Austrian government in the second half of the eighteenth century developed an effective system of elementary schools in towns and villages. Data from the 1900 census in Prague and its suburbs demonstrate how illiteracy varied with age group as well as with nationality:

Table 11.2: **Illiterate persons among the older age groups in Prague in 1900 (%)**

Nationality	Age group 50–59	Age group 60–69	Age group 70–79	Age group over 80
Czechs				
totally illiterate	4	5	7	11
reading knowledge only	1	3	3	4
Germans				
totally illiterate	1	1	3	4
reading knowledge only	0	0	0	1

Source: Rauchberg, 2, 187

The overwhelming majority of Prague Germans at that time belonged to the upper and middle classes and most of them had been born either in Prague itself or in other towns. On the other hand, the Czechs who constituted 90 per cent of Prague's population included few families belonging to the upper classes, but made up the majority of the middle classes and comprised almost all the workers and poorer craftsmen. In addition, most of them had migrated from villages directly to the city. We may, therefore, conclude that the difference in the ratio of literacy between the Prague Czechs and the Prague Germans was related to their social position. Yet, even among those Czechs who had been born before 1820, 85 per cent were literate.

The Educational Background

The school reforms of the 1770s and 1780s associated with Empress Maria Theresia and Emperor Joseph II, and especially with their advisers, Ferdinand Kindermann and Ignaz Felbiger, were particularly successful in Bohemia. School attendance was declared obligatory for children between the ages of six and 12, and in 1787, 60 per cent of children in this age group actually attended school. In 1797 the percentage reached 70 throughout Bohemia, with important local (rather than nationality) differences. Thus in the rich Žatec region school attendance was 90 per cent, whereas in the poor mountain region of Prácheň and České Budějovice only 40 per cent of the children were registered as taking their elementary schooling.[4] Political changes in subsequent decades did not alter the trend towards universal elementary education. In 1834, 500 000 pupils attended elementary schools in Bohemia, that is, 93 per cent of the age group. Of course, their schooling was not intensive. A mere 5400 teachers were employed, that is one teacher for every 90 pupils. Older children attended school only in those winter months when their labour was not needed on the farms. Nor can it be said that teachers were anxious to reduce the size of their classes, since they obtained special allowances on top of their poor salaries when the classes they taught numbered more than 100 pupils.

The dense network of elementary schools, where the language of instruction was Czech in Czech villages and German in German villages, was the real explanation for the high degree of literacy in the Czech lands in the first half of the nineteenth century. The idea of the Emperor Joseph II and his administrators had been to enable peasants and textile home spinners and weavers to read books, instructions and newspapers in order to be able to develop more profitable production, pay more taxes and strengthen the state. As a result, the Czech schools in the first decades of the nineteenth century educated a whole generation of peasants, craftsmen and shopkeepers in villages and small towns. However, having become accustomed to reading the newspapers, they also willingly followed the *Národni noviny* published in 1848–9 by Karel Havliček, an influential Czech politician and journalist, and became enthusiastic supporters of Czech national politicians. It was not accidental that the picture painted by Karel Purkyně, called 'Kovář Jech', showing the village smith and farrier Jech reading Czech patriotic news in his workshop, became one of those colour prints that decorated many inns in Czech towns and villages.

School policy in the towns of the Czech part of Bohemia and in Moravia before 1850s was different. Their population was Czech, apart from a small German speaking elite. Nevertheless, in all towns and cities, in most elementary schools and all schools above the elementary level, instruction was entirely in German. A knowledge of the language of the state administration was demanded from all craftsmen who wished to pass the examination required for the title of the master, which was obligatory for all owners of workshops. This policy was to some degree successful. In the first generation of Czech political leaders active in the revolutionary years 1848–9 we find few artisans and merchants, but many millers, brewers and their sons.

At the top of the Josephine educational system, in so-called *normálni škola*, or *Normalschule* (normal or teacher training schools), which provided teacher training in short courses of three or six months' duration, the language of instruction was, again, German. Originally, the *gymnasiums* (classical secondary schools), which provided an education through the medium of Latin for those young people who were going to pursue university studies, were in the hands of the Jesuit and Piarist Orders. However, they were secularised by Joseph II, and German became their language of instruction as well. The same change was introduced in the University of Prague in 1782. However, since about that time, approximately 5 million people in the Czech lands spoke Czech, courses in the language were introduced at university level, first of all at the Military Academy in Wiener Neustadt, then at the Univesity of Vienna and, finally, in 1793 at the Carolo–Ferdinandea University in Prague. Catholic seminaries, of course, had always conducted courses on pastoral theology in Czech. Originally, participation in the new courses in Czech at the University in Prague was high, but it waned later. Similarly, Czech language courses which started in the *gymnasiums* in 1816, attracted a lot of interest, some 2800 pupils taking part in them in the first few years, though numbers declined later.

It is reasonable to conclude that the educational system introduced in the 1780s promoted a rapid increase in literacy among the Czech population of the villages and, partly, of the towns. On the other hand, contemporary literature is full of complaints about Czech children learning German texts by heart without being able to understand what they were memorising. In 1837 the increasing demand for Czech education in the towns, and especially in Prague, led to the foundation of a private school, called *Budeč*. On the eve of the 1848 revolution, the interest of the Czech public concentrated particularly on the need for an education in Czech required by industry. The *Jednota pro povzbuzeni prumyslu v Čechách* (Union for Industrial Progress in Bohemia) which was founded by a group of nobles but controlled by young Czech intellectuals, began publishing a technical journal in Czech in 1837. In the 1840s, under the leadership of Jan Perner, the man responsible for building the railway line between Prague and Olomouc, it organised collections for the creation of a Czech industrial school in Prague. However in April 1847, when the necessary capital had been brought together, the authorities would not permit the foundation of the school because, ultimately, the campaign to raise funds took an openly political character.

The revolutionary year of 1848 also revealed, in the field of education, how important were the social changes that had taken place in the first half of the nineteenth century. In a textbook for the study of the Czech language, published in 1798, František Martin Pelcl, the first Professor of Czech Language in the University of Prague, tried to persuade his students that Czech was a useful language by putting it to the would be officers of the Austrian army that this would be a way to win the sympathy of their subordinates, so that 'your soldiers will willingly sacrifice their lives for you, if they see in you their compatriots'.[5] At that time Czech was almost exclusively the language of the peasant. In 1848 Czech industrialists and intellectuals saw the introduction of Czech into higher education as an important instrument in accelerating their own social advance. On the other hand, the increasing Czech self-confidence resulting from literacy should not be underestimated.

Equal rights for both nationalities and both languages were demanded by the 'citizens and inhabitants' of Prague in the revolutionary meeting at Svatováclavské Lázně on 11 March 1848. Doctors and students of the university similarly demanded equal rights for Czech and German in their own institutions at their meetings four and five days later. On 18 March the consistory of the Catholic Church also supported the idea. When the Ministry of Education was established in Vienna on 23 March 1848 Pavel Josef Šafařik, the Slavonic philologist, became one of its senior officials. Czech lectures were permitted at the university, Czech became the language of instruction in the Academic *gymnasium* in Prague, and in the *gymnasiums* in six other Czech towns, as well as in most Prague elementary schools. The demand for a Czech pedagogical faculty was not granted, though a Czech teacher training college at the secondary level was set up in Prague along with a German one.

Education in the Second half of the Nineteenth Century

The defeat of the revolution and the introduction of neo-absolutism in Austria in the 1850s not only retarded the development of Czech as a language of instruction but also produced setbacks in both the university and the *gymnasiums*. The reintroduction of German as a language of instruction in the Academic *gymnasium* in Prague in 1853, and the suspension of a number of Czech professors of this school, were seen by the Czechs as a serious defeat of the Czech national movement. This change was brought about by the bureaucratic administration, which saw in the increase in the intensity of instruction in Czech the danger of disintegration of the multinational monarchy.

The dominant position of bureaucracy in the neo-absolutist interlude in Austria (1851–60) was oriented towards the reintroduction of German as the language of instruction in all *gymnasiums* in Bohemia. In Moravia they were all German up to 1867, when two Czech *gymnasiums* were opened. One year earlier, Czech *gymnasiums* were reopened in Bohemia, originally eight of them. The *gymnasiums* – as well as the universities – were state schools and the professors were paid by the Austrian Ministry of Education, but allocated to different schools by the school authorities in Prague and Brno. In the Czech *gymnasiums* in Bohemia, German language was only an optional subject right up to 1918, because the Germans tenaciously opposed any attempt to introduce Czech as an obligatory subject into German *gymnasiums*, where it had been compulsory between 1861 and 1868 (though in many cases only in theory). In the latter year, the German dominated Bohemian *diet* in Prague abolished the *Sprachenzwang-gesetz*, the law enforcing the learning of what was considered by the Germans to be a useless language. The effectiveness of optional teaching of Czech in German *gymnasiums* (except in Prague) was minimal, but the knowledge of German achieved by many Czech pupils in the *gymnasiums*, where nearly all of them attended optional lessons of this language, was not very good either.

The establishment of new Czech *gymnasiums* was one of the goals followed by the Czech politicians, because of the need for qualified specialists and for reasons of national prestige. In the 1870s the city councils of Czech towns founded Czech *gymnasiums*, built impressive buildings for them and started to pay their teachers. Then, in the 1880s, after the Czech representatives had taken part in the 'Iron Ring' coalition supporting the Taaffe government, these schools were taken over by the state. By then, however, there was quite a dense network of such schools; in 1877 there were 26 Czech *gymnasiums* in Bohemia.

The existence of a large number of Czech *gymnasiums* prepared the way for the division of the Prague *Polytechnic* and the university. Up to the division both institutions had been bilingual *de iure* (in law), but predominantly German *de facto*. The governor of Bohemia at the time, Philip Weber, argued against the proposed foundation of the Czech university as a measure unavoidably leading to the disintegration of the Habsburg empire in his memorandum sent to the Prime Minister on 21 January 1881. He concluded his warning against the foundation of the University with Czech as language of instruction with the words:

> For the state the results of the Czechisation of the university would be fatal . . . Too much has already been done for the Czechisation of the education of the youth in Bohemia, more would be disastrous. It is necessary to cry: *Hannibal ante portas* (Hannibal at the gates)![6]

The German speaking state bureaucracy tried to delay the expansion of Czech schools at secondary and higher rather than elementary level. This policy was, for a relatively long time, successful in Silesia, where the first and only Czech *gymnasium* was founded in Opava as a private school in 1883 and became a state school in 1889. The autonomous Land Committee succeeded in preventing the foundation of other Czech secondary schools in the crownland. The Czechs studied, of course, in the schools in neighbouring Moravian towns, especially in Moravska Ostrava. The situation in Moravia, where the

German liberal party, together with liberal aristocracy, controlled the Land Committee was different. The Czech *gymnasiums* were founded later. In 1877 only six schools of that type existed there, but just before the war there were 32 such schools for the 1.6 million Czech inhabitants of Moravia. This number was generally considered by Czech public opinion as satisfactory. Nevertheless, it was small in comparison with the 36 German *gymnasiums* in Moravia for its 700 000 German inhabitants. However, the German politicians in Moravia did not allow the foundation of a Czech university in Moravia during the existence of the Habsburg Monarchy. There was only a Czech *polytechnic*, which had been in existence in Brno since 1899, alongside the German one, founded in 1849. In Prague, the real centre of Czech national life, a Czech *polytechnic* had also existed since 1869, alongside the German one. All the lectures and examinations in the two *polytechnics* and in the Czech University in Prague, were from 1882 in Czech. The only exception was the state examinations at the Czech faculty of law, which had to be taken partly in German because Emperor Franz Joseph demanded the knowledge of the language of state service from all potential state officials.

Elementary Education

Since the elementary and secondary schools were financed by the local authorities, the language of instruction there was also determined by them. Up to 1919, local authorities were not obliged to establish special schools for national minorities, although this was demanded by Czech minorities in German towns and villages in north western Bohemia, Silesia and Vienna. The law of 1919, however, put communities under an obligation to establish minority schools wherever there were at least 40 children of a respective nationality living in a given town or village.

From 1890 the minority schools became a subject of fervent national struggle. On the one hand Czech local authorities in inner Bohemia tried in their towns to abolish German schools that had existed there since the late eighteenth century, as schools for children from the families of nobles, officers, officials and Jews from the time when the magistrates of the towns had come under the control of the German speaking bureaucracy. After 1880 fewer and fewer pupils attended such schools, as Jews in inner Bohemia began to prefer sending their children into Czech schools. On the other hand, German local authorities in northern and western Bohemia resisted opening Czech minority schools.

An elementary education system based on interconfessional

schools requiring eight years of compulsory attendance was introduced in Austria in 1868. With it came an improvement in the social
position of teachers. The system also diminished the influence of the
Catholic Church in education, and it was therefore accepted by Czech
teachers, even though it was introduced by a German liberal
government which was strongly opposed by Czech political
representation. Only a few private religious schools (Catholic and
Jewish) were still active in the 1870s and they gradually disappeared
soon afterwards. The state schools had a good reputation, were free
of charge and, therefore, were attended by 99 per cent of children.

Even when there existed equal opportunities for Czech children in
schools in Bohemia and Moravia, in the last decades before the First
World War, some problems connected with the position of the
Czechs as the non-dominant nation existed right down to 1918. One
such problem was particularly acute in Prague and in Moravian
towns, where some of the Czech families sent their children to
German elementary schools. Prague city statistics for the year 1889
recorded the presence in Czech elementary schools, and in the
secondary schools, of some 13 249 pupils, among whom 14 gave
German as their mother tongue (0.1 per cent). In German schools, the
presence was recorded of 3837 pupils, among whom 1545 indicated
Czech was their mother tongue (40.3 per cent).[7]

In trying to explain why one tenth of the Czech children in Prague
still attended German schools in the 1890s, on the eve of a strong
explosion of fervent Czech nationalism, we first have to inquire into
their religious adherence. Half of them were Jewish and the Jews in
the Czech lands were, with few exceptions, bilingual. Thus, for
example, Franz Kafka's father registered his firm under the name
Heřman Kafka and declared his nationality to be Czech, though he
knew that German schools opened wider opportunities for a professional career in Austria–Hungary as well as in Germany. The other
half of the people concerned were Czech Catholics, who preferred
German schools as offering a better start for their children, since
German was the language of the army, the bureaucracy, the postal
service, the railways and of the overwhelming majority of industrial
and commercial enterprises.

Secondary Education

The *reálka* or *Realschule* (non-classical commercially orientated
secondary school) held special position among Czech schools of
gymnasium type. It was the school that was intended to prepare its
pupils for industry, business and studies in the polytechnic. Such
schools also existed in other parts of the monarchy, and in Bohemian

lands there were even some with German as a language of instruction. But their strong representation among Czech schools was linked with highly developed industry and modern agriculture there. In Bohemian and Moravian towns, important sums were invested in new school buildings and there was a keen competition between Czech and German towns. In 1907 36 Czech *gymnasiums* and 23 *reálkas* existed in Bohemia; in Moravia there were 16 Czech *gymnasiums* and 16 *reálkas*, with one Czech *gymnasium* in Opava.[8] The increase in the number of pupils in Czech schools of *gymnasium* type – in which category the Prague higher school for girls and, from 1890 *Minerva*, the *gymnasium* for girls in that city also belonged – was significant for the cultural emancipation of the Czechs.

Table 11.3: **Pupils in Czech *gymnasiums, reálkas* and higher schools for girls, 1848–1898**

	1848	1860	1870	1880	1890	1898
Boys in Prague	680	1005	1519	2772	3177	3072
Bohemia (except Prague)	2267	3730	5657	9565	10 360	11 500
Moravia	–	–	235	2954	3258	5808
Silesia	–	–	–	–	296	284
Girls in Prague	–	–	312	254	494	634
Total	2947	4735	7723	15 545	17 585	21 298

Source: Šafranek, Školy 2, 171, 172

The pupils of *gymnasiums*, together with their teachers were at the centre of Czech public life, especially the cultural life of Czech towns. On leaving school they joined the ranks of the Czech intelligentsia which, in the absence of a Czech aristocracy, played a disproportionately important role in the life of the nation. Among the pupils at such schools, with few exceptions, no aristocrats were to be found. 5 per cent were of bourgeois origin; 25 per cent came from peasant families; 20 per cent were children of officials and clerical workers; 5 per cent were the children of Protestant clergy and *gymnasium* teachers; 20 per cent were sons and daughters of elementary school teachers; 25 per cent came from artisan families; and 5 per cent were the offspring of workers. The proportion of children of peasants was surprisingly large, though this can be explained by the relatively high economic and cultural standard of prosperous Czech peasant families, as well as by the dense network of *gymnasiums*.

The reasons for attending this type of school varied. In the poorer districts of Bohemia (Domažlice) and, to an even greater extent, of Moravia (Třebíč and Valašské Meziříči) most of the pupils subsequently continued their studies in Catholic seminaries. Down to the 1890s Czechs from Bohemia and until even later from Moravia, were overrepresented in the theological faculties and the diocesan schools. Later, their interests changed radically, and all regions followed a strong preference for studying at the faculties of law and at technical universities, a preference that was already common among the students from Prague and central Bohemia in the 1870s. The number of new Czech *gymnasiums* founded in small towns was so high that, in the 1880s, Franz Joseph himself intervened to oppose the establishment of such a school in the Moravian town of Uherský Brod, warning against the danger of overproduction of intellectuals drawn from families with a low social status, since they were the potential bearers of revolutionary ideas. In spite of his intervention, however, the school later came into existence.

When the Czech secondary school system in Bohemia reached approximately the same level as the German system, both the Czech public and its political representatives became anxious to extend the use of Czech language at Prague University. Even though Czechs and Germans had formally enjoyed an equal status there since 1848, the number of lectures given in Czech was much smaller than that given in German and, of more importance, German was the language used in the examinations. This meant that all students were forced to attend lectures in German and to study with the help of textbooks in that language. Even outstanding Czech students, such as Konstantin Jirecek and Bohuslav Rieger, both of whom later became university professors (the latter at the University of Vienna), were afraid that, despite their thorough knowledge of German, their examiners might use the examinations as a means of taking revenge for their fathers' political activities. From the 1860s onward, Czech professional organisations and local government representatives, as well as the students themselves, increasingly demanded a real equality in the use of the two languages.

The first success came in 1869 with the division of the Prague *Polytechnic*, but the most important Czech political success came with the division of the old Carolo–Ferdinandea in 1882. When most of its existing staff moved over to the German University, the new Czech University drew in fresh young and active professors, Czech by nationality, who subsequently assumed leading positions in Czech cultural and political life. Seven of them were later on ministers in Austrian governments and one, T.G. Masaryk (1850–1937), became the first President of the Czechoslovak republic. His successor, Edvard Benes, was also a professor of this university, and 12 professors were deputies of the Revolutionary National Assembly of Czechoslovakia in 1918–20.

Even if the Czechs in Moravia did not succeed in establishing a second Czech university, by the first decade of the twentieth century a complete educational system with Czech as a language of instruction existed in the Czech lands. This can be confirmed by information dating back to 1908, showing that, in the Czech University in Prague and in the Czech Polytechnic, 6470 of their students, or 92 per cent, were Czechs, while the remaining 8 per cent was made up by Croats, Slovenes, Serbs and Poles.[9] Only 157 Czech students studied at the German University in Prague, and they constituted 6 per cent of the total student enrolment. The number of Czech students in Vienna was higher than in the Prague German University and Polytechnic. However, 90 per cent of the Czechs who graduated in the last years before the outbreak of the First World War came from Czech schools of university level. Once the Czechs had their own school system, it was possible for an independent Czechoslovak state to emerge and improve that system still further.

Nevertheless, under the conditions of fervent national struggle in the Austrian half of the monarchy, the problems of schools in general, and of the language of instruction in particular, remained one of the central areas of dispute. The fights between German and Czech university students in Chuchle near Prague in 1881, when the final negotiations for the division of the old university were in progress, provoked a new outburst of nationalist feelings in most German universities and led to the foundation of *Der deutsche Schulverein* (the German School Association), an organisation supporting German minority schools in Czech districts. The organisation founded some German schools in the suburbs of Prague, but also tried to save a Jewish school in Kosova Hora, in central Bohemia, where German was the language of instruction. The Czechs replied by establishing the *Ústřední Matice Školská* (Central Educational Society) which, in ten years, founded 36 private schools, mainly in the coal mining districts of north west Bohemia. These private schools were particularly directed towards the poorer population and were, therefore, free of charge. Meanwhile, the *Schulverein* schools in Prague began to serve free lunches to their pupils. The publicity given by both sides to these activities for their own political purposes led, in the end, to an overestimation of the true importance of private schools in the educational system.

Education in the Early Twentieth Century

The assimilation tendency, represented by the attendance by Czech pupils of German schools, still had some importance in the early twentieth century in Moravia and Silesia. Among a series of laws connected with the *Mährischer Ausgleich* (the nationality compromise) of 1905, the Moravian *diet* agreed to a so-called *lex Perek* forbidding the admission to respective national schools of children without prior knowledge of the language of instruction. However, it was not so much this law, as the growing national consciousness among the Moravian Czechs, that brought to an end the practice of sending Czech children to German schools in Moravian cities and towns.

This practice, however, remained common in Vienna where attendance at German schools had a considerable effect in germanising many Czech immigrants. About half a million people had come to Vienna from the Czech lands between 1850 and 1910, from both Czech and German districts. In 1900 and in 1910, some 100 000 inhabitants of Vienna declared Czech to be their everyday language. However Czech private schools in Vienna operated under unfavourable circumstances, due to legal obstacles placed in their way, administrative persecution and the tendency of the Czech immigrants there to assimilate. Although, after 1918, the legal position of Czech immigrants in Vienna improved, they found little encouragement to continue their use of Czech for employment reasons, as most of them were workers, so the interest in Czech private schools in Vienna declined. Yet Czech minority schools, including a *gymnasium*, persisted as an important part of the minority educational system in the Austrian republic down to 1938.

The fact that Josephine absolutism had built up a very dense network of elementary schools in Bohemia and Moravia was of great importance for the Czechs as an underprivileged nation. Books in Czech – primers, readers, elementary instructions for breeding cattle, bee-keeping, etc. – came into villages in the last decades of the eighteenth century, at the time when Czech books were rare in the libraries of Prague burghers. The originally close collaboration of educated, enlightened priests with teachers, who mostly were former non-commissioned officers with short training courses behind them, did not outlive the 1848 revolution. After it, and especially in the 1860s, most Czech teachers became fervent nationalists, supporters of the Young Czech party; whereas Catholic priests, if active in national politics, remained loyal Habsburg subjects, and supported the dignified, conservative Old Czech party, led by F.L. Rieger. When defeated in the elections to the Bohemian *diet* in 1889, Rieger saw the principal reason for his defeat in the radical agitation of teachers. It was the teachers who organised the distribution of Czech nationalist journals in towns and villages, especially of *Narodni Listy*, and who organised amateur theatres all over the country. However, these activities were stronger in Bohemia, where the clerical influence in local government was weak, than in Moravia, where Catholicism was strong among the peasants.

The teachers were, naturally, frequently torn between two loyalties – to the emperor, state and Church on the one hand and the liberal and, gradually, more and more anti-Catholic Czech nationalism on the other. In the decades between 1848 and 1914 national loyalty came fully to overshadow loyalty to the dynasty, and the behaviour of Czech teachers had many features common with that of the famous Josef Švejk. The syllabuses, those in Czech language and history especially, were very much at loggerheads with a Czech political programme resting on the continuity of the legal existence of the kingdom of Bohemia. Books by Alois Jirásek celebrating the Hussite revolution became obligatory reading in Czech *gymnasiums* a few years after their publication. The most popular history textbook for *gymnasiums* in the last pre-war decade – Josef Pekař's *History of Our Empire* – was *de facto* Czech national history. With the *addendum* dealing with the First World War and Masaryk's struggle for independence, it was subsequently reedited many times as *Czechoslovak History*.

Conclusions

In the light of the above evidence, the policy of the Austrian government towards the Czech people in the realm of education could be said to be characterised by the following features: The reforms of Joseph II introduced elementary education in Czech in the villages and, partly, in towns throughout the territory inhabited by Czechs. On the other hand, all higher education was in German, as in the universities the German language replaced Latin. In the revolutionary year 1848, the Czech language was introduced in higher schools including the universities. The neo-absolutist government tried to reintroduce the *status quo ante* and was not entirely unsuccessful in its efforts, but the constitutional reforms in the 1860s ensured that the local communities came to exercise an important influence on education and opened the way for language equality between Czech and German schools, first in Bohemia and, later, also in Moravia. Problems were still posed by the Czech schools in Silesia and in communities with a dominant German influence in local government. On the other hand, German continued to exist even where there were few German pupils and local government was in Czech hands. Only under such circumstances, it could be argued, did the unequal position of the Czechs as a non-dominant nation continue in the educational provision until 1914.

The Education of the Slovaks under the Hungarian Rule (1850–1918)

Introductory remarks

The Slovak population in 1847 was, according to data given by Elek Fenyes, a Hungarian statistician, 1 722 000 and 91 per cent of them lived in the territory of Slovakia, with the rest in other parts of Hungary. An overwhelming majority of Slovaks were peasants or agricultural workers. The importance of the urban population in Slovakia was relatively small. As late as 1910, only 21.5 per cent of the whole population of Slovakia lived in communities with more than 2000 inhabitants, and many of these were either of semi-agrarian character or were artificial administrative units of large size consisting of many small settlements. The predominantly agrarian character of the country can be illustrated by the occupational structure of the population of Slovakia. In 1910, 63 per cent of the inhabitants derived their income from agriculture; 18 per cent from industry and building; and 8 per cent from trade and transport. The percentage of agrarian population among Slovaks was over 63 per cent.[10]

The towns in northern Slovakia, inhabited by Slovaks, were small. The somewhat larger towns in southern, central and eastern Slovakia were in the hands of German and Hungarian middle and upper classes, with Slovaks living there being mostly servants and workers. Some, however, were craftsmen. Around 1850, 83 per cent of Slovaks were Roman Catholics; 15 per cent belonged to the Lutheran Church, and the rest were Calvinists or Greek Catholics. The Slovaks had the highest percentage of adherents of Reformed Churches among all the Slavic nations.

In the second half of the nineteenth century, Slovakia was inhabited by a number of different nationalities, even if the Slovaks constituted a majority in the population. However, as Table 11.4 indicates, the Slovak majority significantly declined in the three decades between 1880 and 1910. The causes of this phenomenon will be discussed later.

Table 11.4: **National structure of the population living in the territory of Slovakia in 1880 and 1910 (%)**

Nationality	1880	1910
Slovak	61.2	57.7
Ukrainian	3.2	3.4
Polish	0.4	0.4
Hungarian	22.2	30.3
German	9.1	6.8
Other	3.9	1.4

Source: *Československe dějiny v datech*, p. 649

The great changes in the national structure of the population between 1880 and 1910 were principally due to political, rather than economic, reasons, even if emigration overseas in the first quarter of the twentieth century played an important role in the northern districts of Slovakia. There were a number of factors for the politically induced changes. Strong pressure existed on Slovak nationals to declare Hungarian as their nationality. This reached its peak in the first 18 years of the twentieth century, despite some Czech support for the Slovaks, which was particularly important in the western part of Slovakia. Hungarian policy was supported by many influential persons in the hierarchy of both the Catholic and Protestant Churches, while there was a strong opposition to it among a part of the lower clergy, supporting the Slovak national movement. Whereas the families of Lutheran pastors played a great role, especially in the early phases of Slovak national movement, there were some Catholic parish priests who were fervent political speakers on national rights in the last pre-war decades.

In towns the magyarisation had ostensibly been successful since the 1880s, and reached its peak in the first decade of the twentieth century. But it was superficial, and many 'new Magyars' who registered as members of the ruling nation in 1910 declared their nationality as Slovak under the new conditions 11 years later. This can be clearly seen from Table 11.5, which shows great changes in respect of the nationality of inhabitants in towns in the second decade of the twentieth century. By 1921, the dominant nationality was Slovak. Some change was caused by the fact that people who so wished could register their nationality as Jewish in 1921. That

Table 11.5: National structure of the population of Slovak towns in 1910 and 1921 (%)

Town	Slovaks		Magyars		Germans	
	1910	1921	1910	1921	1910	1921
Bratislava	14.9	42.3	40.5	23.7	41.9	29.5
Banská Bystrica	40.7	79.4	48.8	8.4	8.2	7.3
Banská Štiavnica	54.9	90.8	41.8	5.0	3.0	2.3
Komárno	3.4	14.3	89.2	80.5	5.6	4.3
Košice	14.8	62.3	75.4	22.1	7.2	4.2
Levice	7.1	29.0	90.5	65.5	2.1	2.1
Lučenec	13.0	46.7	82.2	43.8	3.3	4.5
Nitra	30.0	79.6	59.4	10.9	10.0	3.9
Nové Zámky	5.9	40.9	91.4	50.0	2.3	1.2
Prešov	39.8	70.4	48.9	11.3	8.6	4.7
Ružomberok	68.1	89.9	14.2	0.9	8.4	5.0
Spišská Nová Ves	48.5	70.1	33.2	10.4	17.0	16.1
Trenčín	47.1	87.7	38.4	3.3	11.9	3.3
Trnava	53.0	77.4	30.3	8.0	15.0	5.2
Žilina	54.0	83.3	25.5	3.8	15.9	6.5

Source: *Československá statistika*, vol. 9, p. 62

possibility had not been given in 1910, when even people using the Yiddish language in their daily life (who were not very numerous in Slovakia) had only the choice of German, Magyar or, possibly, some other non-Jewish nationality. In most towns in 1921 3 to 8 per cent of inhabitants declared Jewish nationality. The percentage was higher in larger towns: 9.3 in Trnava; 10.4 in Košice; and 11.0 in Prešov. Jewish nationality was unimportant only in Komárno (0.8 per cent).

Educational Background of the Population

The adult population of Slovakia was still predominantly illiterate in 1880, and the increase in literacy rates in the following decades, though stable, was not very fast. The differences in literacy rates between the various nationalities and the different parts of the country were considerable. The highest illiteracy rate in 1910 was in the north eastern districts of Užhorod (47 per cent) and Šaryš (42 per cent). The lowest was in two southern districts, Gemer and Hont, and one south western district, Bratislava, where only 19 per cent of the adult population were registered as illiterate. However, these three districts belonged to those Slovak areas where the share of the Slovak population was relatively low; there the Slovaks represented only 40 per cent of the inhabitants. Among the four districts with the highest proportion of Slovak population in 1900 (90 to 95 per cent), two belonged to the districts with a high illiteracy rate (Trenčin, 38 per cent and Orava, 32 per cent); and two were among those with average illiteracy (Liptov and Zvolen). In this context the religious background of the population seems to have been important. The districts with high numbers of Protestants had a lower illiteracy rate than districts inhabited exclusively by Catholics. The situation was even worse in the districts where the Greek Catholics prevailed.

Table 11.6: Knowledge of reading and writing among the adult population of Slovakia in 1880 and 1910

| Nationality | Percentage of adult population according to the results of the census of | | | |
| | 1880 | | 1910 | |
	able to read and write	able to read only	able to read and write	able to read only
Slovaks	32	5	57	5
Ukrainians	8	2	26	2
Magyars	44	2	69	2
Germans	61	3	71	2

Source: *Statistická Příručka* 2, p. 32 and 80; *Slovenská vlastiveda* 3, p. 294

The relatively high illiteracy rate in Slovakia in 1910 demonstrates that the system of education in elementary schools in the country was not effective enough in the course of the nineteenth century. A more sustained progress in this respect cannot be traced before 1920. The main reason for this was that many children did not attend schools: as late as 1907 the percentage was as low as 20 per cent throughout Hungary.[11] This situation was in sharp contrast to the school system in the neighbouring Czech and Austrian areas, where universal school attendance had dominated the scene since 1800.

The school system in Slovakia was complicated. The elementary schools were run by the Churches, state or municipal authorities and private persons. In 1899, in the 16 districts in which Slovaks lived (the territory about 5 per cent larger than the Slovakia of today), there were 4086 elementary schools: 2014 (49 per cent) of them were operated by the Roman Catholic Church; 410 (10 per cent) by Greek Catholics; 596 (14 per cent) by Lutherans; 351 (9 per cent) by Calvinists; and 114 (3 per cent) by Jewish communities. Of the rest 342 (8 per cent) were state schools, 190 (5 per cent) municipal and 69 (2 per cent) private schools. The language of instruction in the schools was as follows: Hungarian 2076 (51 per cent), Slovak/Hungarian 1189 (29 per cent), Ruthene/Hungarian 142 (3 per cent), German/Hungarian 117 (3 per cent), Slovak 519 (13 per cent), Ruthene 35 (1 per cent) and German 5 (negligible in percentage terms).

The overwhelming majority of schools were in the hands of the Churches. Teachers were paid by them and the teachers' second – and sometimes even first – duty was to take care of church music. Up to the 1880s, no systematic long term training of would-be teachers existed in seminaries. There were only preparatory courses and 16 per cent of active teachers did not possess any professional training. The professional level of teachers did improve in the years following 1889, but quality of education of non-Magyar children became worse in most schools, as more stress was put on training in Magyar. Without a satisfactory knowledge of the language of instruction, the Slovak children mostly only memorised the contents of their lessons without a real understanding.

Educational Policy and the Pressure for Magyarisation

The pressure for magyarisation developed by Hungarian represent-atives in the administrative centres of different Churches was strong, but resistance to it was offered for some time by Slovak and German representatives in the Lutheran Church. In 1900, 1 258 860 persons were registered as Lutheran religious adherents in Hungary. Of these 37 per cent were Slovaks; 33 per cent Germans and only 29 per cent Magyars.[12] But even the resistance within this religious community was broken in the campaign led by the state against the Slovak *gymnasiums*, which were accused of being centres of pan-Slavist agitation and closed in 1874. The Magyar language was introduced as an obligatory subject into all Lutheran schools and, from 1894, this Church was subject to a policy of full magyarisation and those teachers who opposed this policy were dismissed. Other occasions for dismissal lay in the examinations that tested for an adequate knowledge of Hungarian, which was obligatory for all teachers. From 1902, the minimum of hours per week in which instruction had to be in Magyar was 18. This process found its final expression in the Apponyi laws of 1907, which declared that the aim of the elementary school system was for all non-Magyar pupils to be able to express themselves in Hungarian both orally and in writing by the end of the fourth year of school attendance.

The Apponyi laws strongly prohibited any involvement of the teachers in Slovak national activities. Even earlier, measures of an administrative character were taken to counter any contacts by teachers with the nationalist movement. In 1895, when some 2800 teachers were still Slovaks, only 128 of them subscribed to the pedagogical journal in Slovak *Domov a škola*.[13] In the census of 1910, 409 elementary school teachers in Slovak districts declared their nationality as Slovak, compared with 5672 teachers of Magyar nationality. In *gymnasiums* and secondary schools 11 teachers were Slovaks and 828 were Magyars.[14] This was the result of the great pressure exerted upon the schools by the Hungarian government.

In 1909, the Apponyi law was supplemented by a ministerial instruction, introducing Magyar as the obligatory language of religious instruction in all schools. Official statistics indicated that the magyarisation campaign following Apponyi law was a success. In 1907, 526 Slovak primary schools with 725 Slovak teachers existed, in comparison with 519 Slovak and 1189 Slovak/Hungarian schools in 1899. In 1913, 365 Slovak schools with 593 teachers existed; in 1918, only 276 teachers taught 30 118 pupils in 276 Slovak primary schools. This represented a mere 13 per cent of Slovak children aged between six and 12 years.[15] Even if this extremely sad picture of the decline of Slovak schools and the speedy progress of magyarisation is somewhat exaggerated, it is certain that Slovak schooling was not far from extinction in 1918.

The fate of Slovak primary schools was pre-determined by the fate of Slovak *gymnasiums*. At the time when neo-absolutism was abolished in the Habsburg monarchy, in 1860, Slovak political representation demanded the foundation of seven Slovak *gymnasiums* and a law academy. In the following years Slovaks succeeded in building three *gymnasiums* – one Catholic and two Protestant. In these schools, Slovak was the language of instruction, but the schools found themselves under attack through the administrative measures taken in 1874. The Lutheran Church tried to save the *gymnasium* in Turčiansky Svetý Martin at least, but without success. The Hungarian government, politically controlled by the Liberal party, saw a danger of panSlavism in the strengthening of the Slovak national position in education and cultural life and was determined to prevent it. The Slovak role in the elementary schooling system was at that time at least tolerated.

The importance of teachers in Slovak national life was not as great as in the life of the neighbouring nations. To some extent it was even smaller than the role of teachers in the national activities of a small German minority in Slovakia in Spiš. When in 1913 the Hungarian Ministry of the Interior completed the list of active Slovak national-ists, the 'Black Book of panSlavists', of the 513 persons included in it, only 14 per cent were teachers – as many as bank officials.[16]

Enforced or Voluntary Assimilation?

The reasons behind the really catastrophic position of elementary instruction of Slovak pupils in their mother tongue were the subject of many discussions by politicians before 1914, and are still a subject of polemics between Slovak and Hungarian historians today. The earlier polemics of considerable interest are, going back to the end of the 1870s, between M. Potemra who published an important article on the school policy of Hungarian governments around 1900, and his Hungarian opponents, P. Hanak and I. Dolmanyos.[17] The key problem was whether the reasons that more and more Slovak children learning in Hungarian were to be sought in the state policy of magyarisation, or in the tendency towards voluntary assimilation in the Slovak population.

It could be argued that the number of people affected by assimi-lation in the nineteenth century was not very high, but many of them belonged to the potentially leading stratum of Slovak society. The Slovak speaking gentry, who had played an important role in the Slovak national life up to 1867, largely disappeared, apart from very few individual exceptions, in the following decades as a result of voluntary magyarisation. However, towards the end of the nine-teenth, and early in the twentieth century, when the number of Slovak schools was declining, the numbers of Slovak industrialists and tradesmen was growing. To some extent they were supported by their Czech neighbours and by their own countrymen living in America. Yet an overwhelming majority of the Slovak population was peasants and a minority was artisans, small shopkeepers, etc.

Were these people interested in a voluntary assimilation to Magyar national community? Were they to be willing adherents to Hungarian state patriotism?

As these people were the parents of children attending primary schools, we should ask whether they sent their children to schools with Magyar as language of instruction in order to facilitate their path towards voluntary assimilation. Clearly, they were forced to do so because school attendance was obligatory and no other schools existed in their towns and villages. Nevertheless, we could find some parents who wanted their sons to be able to speak and write in the language that enabled them to apply for employment in the state service, the post office or the railways in Slovakia and, indeed, throughout Hungary. Some looked towards working in Budapest where their knowledge of Hungarian was likely to open for them improved professional opportunities. Hungarian was the only language of higher education in the country, and all who wished to study in a *gymnasium* or in the universities had to possess a faultless knowledge of Hungarian.

For those who wanted to advance in life along this path, in 1910, Slovakia possessed 33 *gymnasiums*, six technical *gymnasiums* and six *lycees* (secondary schools) for girls. In 1881, 1700 pupils were registered in Hungarian *gymnasiums* who recorded their mother tongue as Slovak. That number went up slightly, on average, in the period 1901–5, but it declined in the years 1906–10 to 1530, and even further, to 1380, in the period 1911–4. It was a very low number. Only about 175 boys from a year's intake attended the schools that prepared pupils for university. In 1900, there were some two million Slovaks in Slovakia and, therefore, a particular year's intake of those between ten and 19 years of age numbered approximately 40 000.[18] Thus, only 0.4 per cent of young Slovaks born between 1885 and 1905 attended a school which could prepare them for university study.

According to the estimates made by Anton Stefanek, a sociologist and politician with a thorough knowledge of the relevant material, only about half of them were nationally conscious Slovaks. The figure of 1380 Slovak *gymnasium* pupils constituted only 2 per cent of the total number of pupils studying in *gymnasiums* in Hungary in the last four pre-war years, whereas people of Slovak nationality made up 11 per cent of the inhabitants of Hungary.[19] Thirty years earlier, the situation of Slovak youth was, in this respect, much better: in 1885, the Slovak *gymnasium* pupils had constituted 4.6 per cent of the country's total. Some Slovaks also studied in Czech *gymnasiums* and professional schools in Bohemia and Moravia; in 1913 there were 133 of these. In addition, between 30 and 40 Slovaks graduated from the Czech University and Polytechnic in Prague at that time. However, the Slovak intelligentsia was, at that time, so scanty that the Slovak writer Jozef Gregor-Tajovsky could state in his memoirs: 'Before 1918, I knew all the members of conscious Slovak intelligentsia'.[20]

Teachers, even when they were employed by the Churches, were strictly controlled by the state. The Apponyi laws further strengthened state supervision over them, and the regulatons were applied very strictly. In just one of the districts in Slovakia, Liptov, of the 161 Slovak teachers employed there at the beginning of the century, 17 were dismissed in 1907 for insufficient knowledge of Hungarian, 18 because they were accused of panSlavic activities by the authorities and 23 were admonished for unsatisfactory results made by their pupils in the study of Hungarian language. The Slovak teachers were, indeed, in a difficult position. Even if their social position and prestige were much lower than the status of primary school teachers in the Austrian and Czech lands, they still could live much better than the peasants in their respective villages. Dismissal from their teaching posts was likely to be a disaster for them and their families. So, most of them yielded to the pressure of district school authorities. After all, Catholic and Protestant Slovak clergy were, at that time, under a similar pressure. However, the clergy's social position was somewhat stronger and some priests were politically active. In 1906, four of them (three Catholic and one Lutheran) were among the seven Slovaks who were elected to the parliament in Budapest. These seven deputies were, in fact, the largest ever political representation of Slovaks in the Hungarian parliament. The next election, in 1910, saw their number reduced to three.

The Slovak position in the districts was even weaker. Local government was completely in the hands of the landowners, rich burghers and bureaucracy and the Slovak influence was, therefore, minimal. The protests from abroad, from Slovak emigrants in the USA, from the Czech slovakophile movement, and from influential writers such as B. Björnson or historians such as Robert Seton-Watson, could not influence for the better the difficult situation of the Slovaks in public and cultural life of their country. The position of the Slovak children in the primary schools was extremely weak. In the last year of the old monarchy, only 17 per cent of them attended schools where, beside the Hungarian curriculum, reading and writing in Slovak were taught.

Why did this oppressive policy from the Hungarian government against Slovak schools and the teaching of Slovak language in schools appear to have been successful? The reasons must be sought in the economic and social weakness of the Slovaks and the fact that constitutional rights in the state, districts and communities were limited to taxpayers rather than being the same for all. This deprived the Slovak people of the possibility of finding any support in governmental institutions. It also affected the Churches, especially the Church hierarchy and leaders, while the local clergy who supported the Slovak nationals were not strong enough to bring about changes in teaching in the Church schools. The Slovak population was too poor to afford private schools. All these factors combined to result in the inherent weakness of the Slovak position within the Hungarian state, and were largely responsible for the psychological complex of the 'little Slovak people', especially in the towns. When they saw that it was only a good knowledge of the Magyar language which would enable their children to advance in life, they did not oppose their education in schools which were ensured a good knowledge of the state language, even if it meant neglecting the mother tongue of the children at the same time.

The Epilogue

The foundation of the Czechoslovak republic in 1918 completely changed the position of the Slovak language in the school system. Even if the *l'udove školy* (primary schools) were still linked with the Churches, the status of the teachers and their income came to equal those of their colleagues in the Czech lands. This was particularly reflected by the increase in the teachers' salaries. It was a necessary change, because many Czech teachers from Bohemia and Moravia came to teach in Slovak schools, especially in *gymnasiums* and secondary schools established after 1918. In primary schools, the number of Czech teachers was not very high, because in these schools, after 1918, as well as the 800 Slovak teachers who had declared their Slovak national adherence even before that year, there were also those teachers who had belonged to the category of 'covert Slovaks' before the war. In other words, they were the individuals who, although being Slovak, had accepted Magyar nationality under pressure and taught in Hungarian before independence. Their number was estimated at some 3000.

Schooling in Slovakia remained a political problem even after 1918, despite a general improvement in its position in the following years. Conflicts between the Czechoslovak state and the Catholic Church, between young Slovak graduates and the Czech teachers and professors in *gymnasiums* and the University of Bratislava, were an important political development in the late 1920s and in the 1930s. In 1938 many of the Czech teachers and professors had to leave Slovakia, and were replaced by those who had completed their education in the Slovak *gymnasiums* and the Czechoslovak University of Bratislava within a relatively short period of 20 years, 1918–38.

Notes

1. See the author's study of the Omladina trial in Prague in 1894, which showed that among the hundreds of testimonies which were produced, only one had to be signed by three crosses.
2. Rauchberg, 2, p. 181.
3. *Statisticka příručka*, pp. 32 and 45.
4. Šafránek (1897), pp. 37–8.
5. Havránek (1985), p. 51.
6. Havránek (1982), p. 67.
7. Rozvoj, p. 52.
8. Šafránek (1913–1918), p. 138.
9. *Statistická příručka*, p. 168.
10. *Československé dějiny*, pp. 646–9.
11. *Slovenska vlastiveda III*, p. 294.
12. *Ottův slovnik*, 26, pp. 122–3.
13. Bokes (1946), pp. 315–18.
14. *Statistická příručka*, p. 166.
15. Bokes (1955), p. 375.
16. *Slovenska*, p. 137.
17. *Historický Časopis*, 16 (1978), pp. 497–536.
18. *Atlas obyvatelstva*, p. 43.
19. Johnson, p. 33.
20. *Ibid.*, p. 36.

Select Bibliography

The Czech lands

Havránek, J. (1982), 'Česká univerzita v jednání rakouských úřadů do roku 1881', *Acta Universitatis Carolinae. Historia Universitatis Carolinae Pragensis*, 22, 1.
Havránek, J. (1985), 'Temno očima osvícence Pelcla', *Acta Universitatis Carolinae. Historia Universitatis Carolinae Pragensis*, 25, 1.
Kadner, O. (1931), 'Školství v republice Československé', *Československá vlastivěda*. X, *Osvěta*, Prague.
Rauchberg, H. (1905), *Der nationale Besitzstand in Böhmen*, vol. 2, Leipzig.
Šafránek, J. (1913–1918), *Školy české. Obraz jejich vývoje a osudů*, 2 vols, Prague.
Šafránek, J. (1897), *Vývoj sustavy obecného školství v králostí Českém, 1769–1895*, Prague.
Srb, J. (ed.) (1889), *Rozvoj školství v královském hlavním městě Praze*, Prague.
Statistická příručka Království Českého (1913), vol. 2, Prague.

Slovakia

Atlas obyvatelstva ČSSR (1962), Prague.
Bokes, F. (1946), *Dejiny Slovákov a Slovenska*, Bratislava.
Bokes, F. (1955), 'Príspevok k uhorskej školskej politike v rokoch 1848–1918 so zretel'om na Slovákov', in *Historický časopis*, 3.
Československá statistika (1924), sv. 9. Scitani lidu 15.2.1921. Prague.
Československé dějiny v datech (1986), Prague.

Historická statistická ročenka ČSSR (1985), Prague.

Johnson, O. (1985), *Slovakia 1918–1938. Education and the Making of a Nation*, New York.

Kadner, O. (1931), 'Školstvi v republice Československé', *Československá vlastivěda*, vol. X, *Osvěta*, Prague.

Ottův slovnik naučný, Prague.

Potemra, M. (1978), 'Školska politika maďarských vlád na Slovensku na rozhraní 19 a 20 storoči', in *Historický časopis*, 26.

Slovenska vlastiveda III (1944), Bratislava.

Statistická příručka republiky Československé (1925), II, Prague.

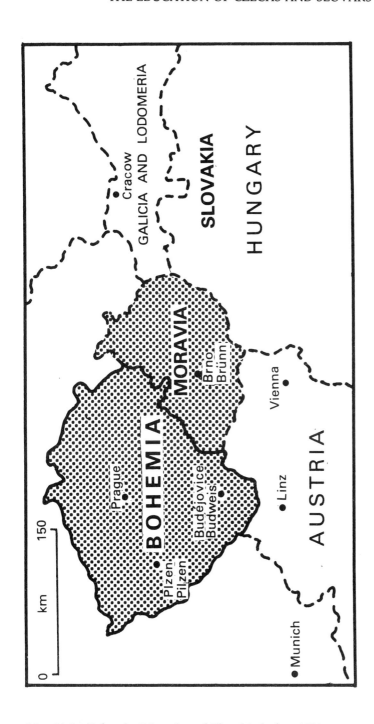

Map 11.1 Bohemia, Moravia and Slovakia before 1914

12 Italian Educational Policy Towards National Minorities, 1860–1940

ANGELO ARA

Introductory Remarks

It was only at the end of the First World War, with the annexation of south Tyrol (Upper Adige) and Julian Venetia, that a real problem of national minorities, with important political and demographic dimensions arose in Italy. From this moment on, about 200 000 Germans and 400 000 south Slavs, Slovenes and Croats came to be included into the kingdom of Italy. Apart from the substantial numbers involved, the importance of the problem was mainly due to the 'fact that these populations adopted a hostile attitude towards Italy and were concentrated in well defined geographical areas, located next to the Italian borders and contiguous to the 'mother nations' they belonged to. Moreover, until then, they had lived within a multi-national state, the Habsburg monarchy and, subsequently, they tended to seek solutions to the problems of minorities in Italy which would be similar to the ones adopted earlier on in Austria.

Before taking into consideration the period after 1918, on which the main emphasis will be laid in this paper, it is necessary to focus on the situation before 1918, characterised by a less marked ethnic pluralism, though still not destitute of some interesting aspects relevant to our inquiry. The linguistic frame of the Italian peninsula, even before political unity was achieved, had been characterised (apart from a very high percentage of illiteracy and a poor knowledge of 'high Italian' among the non-educated classes) by an absolute preponderance of Italian speaking people, among whom dialect differences were more marked than today. There were, however, some linguistic units, the so-called 'ethnic islands' – Greek, Albanian, Croatian, Catalan, Franco–Provençal and others – spread all over the country and particularly in the south plus a strong compact French area concentrated in the continental part of the kingdom of Sardinia.[1]

Already during the first half of the nineteenth century the small linguistic units had been heavily exposed to the danger of losing their ethnic and linguistic identity, due to their rural character, their economic marginality, and the trend within their elites to join the then emerging Italian ruling class, which, at a national level tended towards the modernisation of Italian society and its political structure.

As mentioned before, within the kingdom of Sardinia there were two very compact areas, the valley of Aosta and Savoy, separated by the chain of the Alps, and both inhabited by a French speaking population, which gave the Savoyard kingdom the character of a bilingual state, although with an Italian majority. In both provinces, the language of the administration, the judicial organisation, and the school system were French. The constitutional regime introduced in 1848 gave the members of parliament elected in the towns and villages where French was used the right to express themselves in their own language in the parliament in Turin.

National Minorities after the Unification of Italy

It was precisely the attitude evolving towards the French group which represented the first consistent example of the policy of the unitary state towards national minorities.[2] The condition of the French speaking population deteriorated after the unification of Italy, due above all to the change in its relative strength within the new state. Weakened by the annexation of Savoy to France and inserted into a much broader political structure, the French group turned from a strong national minority within the kingdom of Sardinia into an insignificant percentage of 0.49 within the kingdom of Italy. In 1861, Giovenale Vegezzi-Ruscalla, a Piedmontese scholar, expressed the first worries about the Aosta valley being really a part of the French linguistic area, and about the possible development of an irredentist feeling. He urged a linguistic, administrative, economic, educational and religious policy of italianisation, on account of the geographical position of the valley within the natural borders of Italy, and expressed the fear that the new kingdom might otherwise also be forced to grant particular rights to the other small minorities living within it. He also recalled the denationalisation policy adopted by France against her own minorities.[3]

Vegezzi-Ruscalla's proposals provided important evidence of a new attitude towards the Aostan problem in the light of the ideological values and political interests of a unitary state. In the decades from 1861 to the First World War this climate affected government policies in the Aosta valley and particularly the school policy. Soon after the annexation of Savoy to France, and still before the proclamation of the kingdom of Italy, Italian took the place of French as a teaching language in the Aosta lower *gymnasium* (classical secondary school). Moreover, the union of the valley with the province of Turin gave the authorities the opportunity to abolish the Aosta upper *gymnasium*, in compliance with the law dated November 1861, which envisaged the existence of only one secondary school in each province. A private denominational school, the episcopal *gymnasium* of Aosta, therefore became the centre of French linguistic resistance: the number of students enrolled in this school increased in reaction to the pressure of italianisation.

The Church came to the aid of French in order both to defend the traditions of the rural population and to stand against the lay and anticlerical Italian state. Indeed, during the first half of the nineteenth century, the Catholic Church had already defended Aostan identity, whereas the liberals had worked to subdue its particularism and force it into becoming part of the Italian national movement. To the pressure upon the secondary school system, was added pressure upon the primary school system. In 1883, the Provincial School Council of Turin made provision for the introduction of Italian as a teaching language in the primary schools of Aosta. Public opinion in the valley reacted and managed to obtain the acknowledgement, albeit a token one, of a parity between the two languages by appealing to the ancient Piedmontese law safeguarding the French speaking areas.

In 1911, the Credaro law, named after the Minister of Education Luigi Credaro, was passed, having validity throughout the national territory. This had deprived municipalities of the right to appoint teachers and assigned this right instead to the Education Department. This decision aimed at establishing rational criteria for appointing teachers and avoiding influence from municipalities and the Church upon such appointments. In the Aosta valley, its consequence was that many classes were left without teachers, as the Ministry of Education could not find people with the necessary requirements who would be willing to teach in small villages in a mountainous area and, in some cases, teachers were appointed who were technically qualified, but had no knowledge of French. This constituted a step backwards at a time when the Aostan willingness to defend their language had strengthened.

In 1909 a *Comité pour la protection de la langue française dans la Vallée d'Aoste* (Committee for the protection of the French language in the Aosta Valley) had been created which, at a later time, took the name of *Ligue Valdôtaine pour la defense de la langue française* (Valdotaine League for the Defence of the French Language). The position of French was more favourable in small villages where the number of children was too low to have regular schooling and where 350 village schools operated. The latter were schools created in small villages or isolated clusters of houses, and supported by municipal administrations of local communities, whose task was to provide the children with the basic elements of primary education. There, the so-called 'adjoined teachers' were employed, who often had no regular teaching degree, but all of whom were at least Aostan and therefore bilingual.[4]

The other major example of the Italian government's attitude towards national minorities is provided by the case of about 35 000 Slovenes in the Natisone valley, the 'Slavia Veneta', which had become part of the kingdom in 1866.[5] There, the authorities pursued an assimilationist policy with regard to an ethnic group which was completely loyal to the state to which it belonged. The use of the mother tongue in school was forbidden. The diffusion of Slovenian textbooks and catechisms was prohibited. Authorities even rejected the proposal of a Slovenian teacher, Antonio Podrecca, that a bilingual textbook he had prepared in order to help Slovenian children to learn Italian be adopted. Only the teaching of religion was allowed in Slovenian. This was taught in the so-called parish schools, where children came to learn the catechism, but were sometimes given language tuition also.

The Italian state also paid little regard to the small linguistic units mentioned earlier. In 1861 the authorities acknowledged the existence of some minorities in the census of population taken in that year, yet they made no move towards allowing them to develop their own identity. Nor were the distinctive cultural features of the inhabitants of Friuli and Sardinia taken into consideration by the government. In these cases, as in those of the linguistic 'islands', the government's attitude was made easier by the already mentioned phenomenon of the asssimilation of the elites. This arose out of the attraction exercised on the peripheral ruling class by the liberal foundations of the new state, its policy of modernisation, and the potential for safeguarding the economic interests of the landed classes. The state, therefore, exercised a levelling and unifying influence over the different groups dwelling within its borders.

The effectiveness of the school system as an instrument of italianisation was, of course, still limited by the poor distribution of schooling and education among the people and this also constituted, without doubt, a great obstacle to the preservation of non-Italian languages and cultures. Government policy in this respect could be ascribed to a complex series of reasons: the almost sacred concept of a unitary and national state which developed during the *Risorgimento* and constituted a fundamental element in Italian political thought; the implementation of the unification process which led to a shaky centralism; the idea that the state should necessarily be based on a linguistic and cultural monolithism. This brief reconstruction of the Italian government's behaviour before 1918 can be useful in explaining the origins and the reasons for the later post-war attitudes.

Italian Schools within the Habsburg Monarchy

Within the Habsburg monarchy two national conflicts arose at a local level: one between Italians and Germans in Tyrol and the other between Italians and south Slavs along the Adriatic coast. These conflicts reappeared in a more severe form in Italy after 1918. Public opinion in Italy was very sensitive to the problems of Italians in Austria. This played a significant role in the Italian policy of that period, whereas reactions to the very rapid denationalisation process carried out by the French in Nice were very rare. The national rights of the Italians living in Austria, particularly those concerning language and education, were fully safeguarded by the *Staatsgrundgesetz über die allgemeinen Rechte der Staatsbürger*, dated 21 December 1867. As a 'historic nation' Italians enjoyed a very efficient and well developed system of education.[6] The only source of dissatisfaction was connected with the university, and the question of the establishment of a faculty of law to be precise, always rejected by the imperial government, which thus gave the question a greater political rather than cultural relevance.[7]

The problem of Italians in the Habsburg monarchy assumed different features in the Trentino and on the Adriatic coast. Trentino, part of a crownland Tyrol, with a German majority, was denied the political and administrative autonomy it requested. The clear-cut separation of the two ethnic groups, on the other hand, made a solution of the school problem easier. In the Italian areas and in the Ladin district of Ampezzo, Italian was the official language of instruction. However, some consequences of the broader national and political contrast between Italians and Germans could also be seen in the educational field. In the Italian schools, subject to the *Schulaufsicht* (supervisory authority) of Innsbruck, teaching of Italian history and culture was poor, to the extent that the feeling was created that it was a *school in Italian* rather than an *Italian school*.[8] The quality of textbooks, prepared by bureaucrats worried about political problems, was unsatisfactory. Moreover, the Italians constantly protested against the activities of the German *Schutzvereine* (Defence Associations) and the presence of state German schools in Trento. These served the bureaucratic and military German settlement in the city, but were also attended by Italian pupils, whose parents wanted to give their children a thorough knowledge of the state language of the monarchy. These schools were perceived as a threat to the Italian make-up of the city.

The situation on the Adriatic coast, where the two ethnic groups, the Italians and the south Slavs, lived next to each other in a climate of high tension, rendered harsher by the overlapping of national and social contrast was more complicated and strained.[9] The Italian group, historically dominant in this area, reacted aggressively to the national awakening of the Slovenes and the Croats, the 'nations without history' as they became publicly known. In the period 1871–1910, as far as primary schools were concerned, a remarkable balance between the number of Italian and Slav schools was discernible in the provinces of Gorizia–Gradisca and Istria. This was easier to achieve in Gorizia, where a geographical separation existed to some extent between the two groups, and where the prevalence of a rural population reduced the harshness of the national conflict. It was different in Istria, where the intermingling of the two groups was stronger and where the Italian municipal authorities often opposed the creation of Slovenian and Croatian schools.

The heart of the conflict, however, was Trieste, where the Italian municipal authority, in order to stress the Italian character of the town, allowed the creation of public Slovenian primary schools only in the outskirts and in the rural districts of Trieste. As elsewhere, the Italians wanted to assert in the educational field their argument that the Slovenian presence in Trieste was merely a suburban and rural feature. In the city centre, therefore, there was only room for private Slovenian primary schools, financed by the Society of Cyril and Methodius. A three year private commercial school, created in 1910, was the only Slovenian secondary school in Trieste. An acceptable Slav secondary school network existed in Gorizia, whereas in Istria the number of these schools was much lower. On the whole, the atmosphere in these regions was characterised by an open national conflict, and schools provided one of the most significant areas for expression of this tension. Slovenes and Croats attempted to undermine Italian supremacy while the Italians were determined to preserve their superiority in such a vital field as education.

The weight given to culture as an instrument of national defence and of national penetration was confirmed by the enormous amount of money the Italian municipality of Trieste invested in secondary schools. These were all, except for the technical and vocational ones, municipal and not state schools. On the other hand, in Dalmatia, where the number of Italians was declining even though they still exercised a considerable economic power and cultural influence, they possessed state schools only in Zara and for the rest had to rely on private institutions financed by the National League. In such an atmosphere, schools became, as the Austrian journalist Claus

Gatterer observed, not just education centres, but also 'national bulwarks'.[10] Even on the Adriatic coast, and still more in Trentino, German schools carried a remarkable weight. A widespread German school network existed in Gorizia, a Julian town where the German element was more firmly rooted, and in Trieste, which was an influential commercial and bureaucratic German centre. These schools exercised a strong influence, even on the non-German environment. In Trieste, in particular, they were attended by both Italians and Slovenes.

The attendance of German schools by Italian pupils, generally belonging to families from within the entrepreneurial and commercial classes, was an object of criticism for the Italian political leadership. That leadership feared the possibility of their own denationalisation not so much from the linguistic, as from the cultural and political point of view. To the Slovenes, on the other hand, the attendance of German schools represented one consequence of the insufficiency of their own primary school network and the total lack of secondary education in their own language. German schools, where some classes included the teaching of Slovenian, represented for them, therefore, a way to avoid the pressure of italianisation. In 1910, the German primary school in Trieste was attended by 829 German, 845 Italian and 668 Slovenian children, whereas in the secondary school there were 171 Germans, 142 Italians and 197 Slovenes. The presence of German state schools in Gorizia and in Trieste with a centripetal political function, was a fact that made the national problem even more complicated and the linguistic and educational conflict in Julian Venetia more acute, right up to 1918.

Liberal Italy after World War I

The history of developments in the school system of the multilingual territories of the Habsburg monarchy, destined to become part of the Italian kingdom after 1918, as well as information concerning the treatment of minorities in the peninsula before 1918, is essential to an understanding of Italian policy towards minorities after that year. During the First World War, foreseeing that in case of victory, Italy would have to cope with new ethnic minorities, the government recognised an ethnic minority problem for the first time, and gave some indication of its intentions for the future. In the Aostan primary schools French survived only as an extra-curricular subject; French teaching was reintroduced as part of the normal school schedule. On the other hand, at the same time, Giorgio Pitacco, an Italian member of parliament for Trieste in the *Reichsrat* in Vienna, then an exile in

Rome, made a statement in threatening terms for the future. He said that Italy, as a single national state, should never try to extend to her future Slav citizens the linguistic and educational rights they had enjoyed in multi-national Austria.[11]

At the end of the First World War the Italian government had to deal with new and delicate problems of national minorities, when even the problem of the French population in the Aosta valley seemed to assume a different aspect within the new political framework.[12] The seizure of power by the Fascists a few years later doubtless represented a turning point in the attitude towards minorities. It is therefore advisable to examine first the Liberal government's policies in the period 1918–22, and then those of the Fascist government, although it is necessary to stress that there was also some continuity between the two phases.[13]

The first statements of the Italian politicians and of the king, Victor Emmanuel III, were rather reassuring to the minorities, as these authorities promised to respect their rights and defend their identity.[14] But soon afterwards the contrast between what the government considered to be the correct meaning to be assigned to the concept of autonomy in the so-called 'new provinces' and what the representatives of the minorities thought, became evident.[15] This contrast was particularly striking in the case of the almost entirely German south Tyrol, where the possibilities for defence of minority rights were much greater, as a consequence of its geographical isolation from the Italian speaking area, and of its strong and well established elite, composed of the old aristocracy, the landowners, and the intellectual and commercial bourgeoisie of the urban centres.

South Tyroleans demanded administrative and political autonomy on the pattern of that existing within the Habsburg multinational state; whereas even the more open minded Italian politicians did not intend to go beyond a form of administrative decentralisation which they considered consistent with the nature of the Italian national state. Julius Perathoner, German mayor of Bolzano, declared during the visit to the town by Victor Emmanuel III that with the annexation of the new provinces Italy had ceased to be a national state. No other statement better expresses the gap between the two points of view. In the view of Italian public opinion, the national state had been strengthened as a result of the accomplishment of unity and the achievement of the 'natural boundaries'.

In this political climate, which created misunderstandings between even the more moderate elements in Italian public opinion and the national minorities, nationalist and Fascist pressures surged to the fore. For some politicians, any agreement with minorities re-presented a threat to Italian 'sacred' interests and a national betrayal. Furthermore, the regions close to the borders were affected by both new and old conflicts between the groups living there. National tensions and the centralist tradition that was so characteristic of the Italian state thus prevented a positive solution to the problem of autonomy even before 1922. In the short liberal period preceding the Fascist seizure of power, individual rights were fully granted – at least at a theoretical level – to citizens belonging to national minorities, though no solution was offered to the problem of their collective and corporate rights.

As far as the educational system was concerned, the Italian authorities made a promise to respect the right of minorities to be educated in their own language, but at the same time they integrated their schools into the Italian school system, and tried to extend Italian cultural and linguistic penetration in the territories inhabited by minorities. In south Tyrol, this policy was carried into practice by the opening, first of all, of new Italian schools next to the German ones, both in the few multi-lingual areas and in the areas until then exclusively inhabited by Germans, where an influx of Italians was then taking place.[16]

On the other hand, Italian policy aimed at reshuffling Slovenian and Croatian schools in Julian Venetia, where all German schools had been shut down immediately after the end of the war.[17] According to the official statistics for 1918–19, the number of Slav schools was smaller than that reported by the last Austrian official census of 1913: 149 primary schools had been closed, whilst 392 kept working. All private schools financed by the Cyril and Methodius Society were abolished. Many of the suppressed Slovenian and Croatian schools were transformed into Italian establishments. Starting with the school year 1919–20, Italian taught by Italian teachers was introduced as a compulsory subject in Slav primary schools. The logic followed by the authorities was to reduce drastically, if not eliminate alto-gether, the educational structures of the minority in the most important urban centres of the region (Trieste, Gorizia and Pola), as well as in the Istrian coastal towns, which were predominantly Italian, and in the bilingual areas of inner Istria. This line of action was clearly visible in the decision to eliminate all but one Slovenian primary school in the urban area of Trieste.

The logic of the Italian attitude showed itself even more clearly in the secondary school field. The schools in Trieste, Gorizia, Pola, Zara, Pisino and Abbazia–Volosca were closed, whilst the technical school at Idria was kept working. To replace the schools which had been closed, a lower *gymnasium* and a normal (teacher training) school for teachers at Tolmino were created. Slovenian secondary schools were thus 'exiled' to two small towns in totally Slovenian districts in the interior of Julian Venetia, and reorganised as vocational schools. The Italian authorities more and more tended to give a rural character to Slovenian and Croatian settlements, and to reduce the Slav community to playing a rural role.[18] The echo of the harsh conflict of the past between Italians and south Slavs was thus reflected in the Italian government's policy in Julian Venetia: a liberal system could not deny its Slav citizens the right to an education in their mother tongue, but it stressed simultaneously the marginal position of the Slav group.

If, on the one hand, a marked difference could be seen between the Italian attitude in Julian Venetia and that in Upper Adige, on the other, some common elements did exist also. Soon after Italian troops entered the new provinces, the supreme military authority introduced changes in the syllabuses of primary schools.[19] History and geography had to be taught with particular reference to Italy. In teaching history, the dominant emphasis had to be upon the period of the Italian *Risorgimento*. Teachers were requested to introduce individual tuition programmes in compliance with these provisions. In schools where a minority language was taught, provisions were made for the compulsory introduction of Italian as a second language. Even in Upper Adige, where the Italian policy was not as harsh as in Julian Venetia, tensions arose between public authorities and local public opinion.

The state organs aimed at compulsory introduction of bilingualism among the minorities through the school and at 'rescuing' the 'denationalised' Italians; that is, at national reintegration of those who had earlier on succumbed to the Habsburg monarchy's denationalisation policy. This reitalianisation policy was developed from a single case: that of the village of Laghetti (Laag), where social pressures by certain German landowners had effectively overcome the Italian population. The post-war provincial authority decided to open an Italian primary school instead of the German one after ascertaining that children belonging to families which had declared themselves German actually knew only Italian. Similar cases, although less striking, can be found in other villages in the southern part of Upper Adige (Unterland), where, in the past, Italians had preferred to merge with the numerically and socially stronger ethnic group. However Italian policy was to replace German schools with Italian ones throughout the Unterland and in the Ladin valleys, the inhabitants of which were automatically considered to be Italian.

In August 1921, an explicit general legislative rule, the Corbino law, named after the Minister of Public Education Mario Orso Corbino, stipulated that all Italian children had to attend Italian schools.[20] Their nationality was, however, ascertained in a somewhat debatable way. In the Unterland, Italian family names were automatically held to be a sign of belonging to the Italian ethnic group, and Ladin names were considered Italian. As a result, a considerable number of German primary schools (49 schools with 115 classes, to be precise) were changed into Italian schools, whilst Italian primary schools were put next to the German ones in any village in Upper Adige where there were at least 12 Italian children of school age. In the newly established Italian schools, German was taught in extra hours as an additional subject.

Local public opinion considered the Corbino law to be a first attempt to change the ethnic physiognomy of the region, and also considered it an infringement on parents' rights to choose a school for their children. However, the educational policy of liberal Italy cannot be equated – as must be stressed very firmly – with that of the Fascist regime. Notwithstanding the Corbino law, Germans in South Tyrol kept most of their schools, including all the secondary ones which were consistent with the Italian school system. In Julian Venetia, the blows dealt to the minorities' educational institutions were certainly not soft, but at least insofar as primary education was concerned, the school network was not fundamentally affected.

There are, doubtless, some aspects of the period which tend to make the difference with the Fascist period which followed less marked. There was, for instance, the national character given to school syllabuses; the tendency to consider the presence of minorities in Italy as an anomalous factor and, therefore, as an exceptional and transitory stage; the centralisation of the school system, a logical consequence of the overall political and administrative centralism. No structural and formal autonomy was granted to the German and Slav schools, in spite of the fact that special provisions for the new provinces, and the respect for their educational peculiarities and traditions, were requested not only by the minorities, but also by some Italians like the writer and secondary school teacher, Giani Stuparich.[21] Thus the belief that the goal of a national state should be the assimilation of the minorities became a widespread notion.

In the eyes of the Fascists, this process was to be accomplished rapidly and violently, while for the moderate politicians, it needed to be done in a painless way that retained respect for the minorities. In this context, voices like that of Giovanni Ferretti, the head of school administration for the new provinces, who was in favour of introducing teaching the mother tongue of minorities all over the peninsula, both in the new provinces and the linguistic islands, were rather isolated.[22] According to Ferretti, a general provision dealing with the teaching of minority languages could have reduced the ugly character of the debate over the school problem in the new provinces. It is necessary to emphasise that the logic of unification of the school system also affected a minority such as the Aostan one, whose loyalty towards the state was not in doubt. A decree of 6 July 1919 objected to the existence of village schools, while offering salaries equal to those of the teachers in public schools to their teachers. This made it difficult to find local teachers who spoke French, and imposed financial burdens they could not afford upon the small villages. Benedetto Croce, Minister of Education under Giovanni Giolitti at the time, tried to reduce the negative effects of this provision, but his efforts became an empty gesture with the fall of government.[23]

The Fascist Period

Suppression of minority schools and dismissal of alloglot teachers were to figure even more prominently in the years to come. Fascism, which, after a brief transitional interlude, was to become an open dictatorship in 1925, represented the third stage in the periodisation of Italian governmental policy towards national minorities. It came after the liberal experience of the pre-war years, characterised by the growth in national consciousness and striving for national unity, and after the weak liberal governments of the post-war period, which were unable to cope with the tense and explosive political climate of those years. The coming to power of Fascism did not promise a rosy future to national minorities, as the fascist movement represented the most radical wing of Italian nationalism. In the previous years, it had violently criticised the Liberal cabinets, charging them with excessive softness towards alloglot populations, who had been the object of open Fascist violence, especially in Julian Venetia, but also in Upper Adige. The myth of a 'mutilated victory' itself, which was one of the basic themes of Fascist propaganda, had both an international and a domestic relevance. In fact, not only did it criticise the 'insufficient fruits' obtained by Italian diplomacy at the peace treaty of 1919, but also attacked the unwillingness of the Liberal cabinets to nationalise rapidly the new provinces.

Yet, despite these precedents, the initial attitude of minorities towards Fascism was a 'wait and see' one. There was a sense of relief when an end was made of that separation between formal authority and effective power which had characterised the period of the last Liberal cabinets. Mussolini, for his part, showed a cautious realism and avoided exacerbating the situation. As far as schools were concerned, strong pressures were exerted for an italianising thrust, especially in south Tyrol, where Italian penetration had been slow in previous years. This, at least, was the gist of the accusations that came from a fanatical nationalist from Trentino, Ettore Tolomei, and also from the Prefect and the local Director of Education in Trento. Both officials maintained that Italian behaviour must not be affected by the existence of a minority group, but that it should be guided by the principle of the unitary character of the state.[24] As a consequence of this pressure, German speaking school officials were forced to use Italian only in their official correspondence, and four more German primary schools in bilingual areas were closed. In these schools, German could survive only as 'a language of comparison'.[25]

In fact, at the beginning, Mussolini paid more attention to the Aosta valley, suggesting the abolition of the extra hours of French in the schools of the region, as a countermeasure to the repeal of the guarantees the Italians had enjoyed in Tunis and the denationalisation policy which had always been pursued in Nice and Corsica. Thus, the question of the Aosta valley began to get some attention within the context of Franco–Italian relations (a first hint of the interconnection between foreign policy and the attitude towards national minorities which was to be a constant feature of the Fascist period), and Mussolini linked the case of this ancient and loyal minority to that of the newly constituted ethnic minority groups. The Minister of Education, the philosopher Giovanni Gentile, at first managed to oppose pressure from both local authorities in Venezia Tridentina and those of the *Duce*. Confronted, however, with a powerful intervention by Mussolini, who stated that 'in Italy Italian must be spoken', he was compelled to bow to the will of the *Duce* and to sanction the abolition of the extra hours of French in Aostan primary education.[26]

The attitude of the Italian authorities that then prevailed towards alloglot schools can be deduced from a note dated 21 August 1923, from the Directorate General for primary and popular education in the Ministry of Public Education.[27] In this document, which was mainly devoted to the 'rescue' of the Italians in the Unterland begun under the Corbino bill, some statements of general intent were also contained. Italian policy, it was stated, must not take into account demographic ratios, but base itself upon the principle of the 'unitary character of our national body'. The liberal conception of a school policy, which was to seek a compromise between the interests of the state and those of the small groups of alloglot people, was therefore rejected. On the contrary, it was seen as necessary to subdue particularist interests to the superior goal of the development of a national civilisation embracing all Italy. For the first time, the *Leitmotiv* of the whole school policy of the Fascist state was affirmed: school, the place where the cultural preparation of the new generations was accomplished, was to be the fundamental instrument of the policy of assimilation.

Less than a year after the Fascist seizure of power, the fate of minority schools was definitely decided, not by means of specific measures designed for this purpose, but within a more general provision of the Italian school reform. The bill, introduced by Minister Gentile and therefore known as the Gentile reform, confirmed Italian as the only language of teaching in the schools of the kingdom.[28] Rejecting his previous position in favour of linguistic liberalism and freedom of teaching, the Sicilian philosopher now considered the nation as a unitary and organic community which could not allow any particularist deviations. Gentile, however, introduced the bill as consistent with a philosophical trend, according to which the realisation of each individual personality could be reached only through the state. On the other hand, in the name of an educational and not a mechanical concept of teaching, the Minister underlined the need to find space for the study of dialects and local traditions. The provision concerning dialects constituted, at least for a few years, a way of preserving in schools, a limited presence of the languages of the major non-dominant groups.

The Gentile law envisaged a single national school, with a gradual abolition of the minority schools. From the year 1923–4 on, Italian became the only teaching language in the first grade of primary school. Children who had already begun their studies in their mother tongue were, however, allowed to follow and finish primary education in their own language. In the second, third and fourth grades, however, pupils had to attend five hours a week of tuition in the 'state language' Italian. This was increased to six hours in the fifth. The suppression of alloglot primary schools was to be accomplished in five years' time.

In this context, it is needless to stress that history and geography were taught without any reference to the peculiarities of the national minorities. These two subjects were, on the contrary, considered as a means of inculcating an Italian national consciousness into the alloglot children, and to persuade them of the superior value of Italian culture and civilisation. No room was left for local elements, folk traditions or popular songs. The italianisation process was basically accomplished by 1927–8, when only 35 post-primary German school classes survived and even these were to be abolished within the next three years. In these classes some subjects were already taught in Italian anyhow. The Gentile reform affected the fate of 444 Slovenian and Croatian schools (with 842 classes and 52 000 pupils) and 324 German primary schools (with 593 classes and 30 000 pupils) which were operating in 1923. In secondary schools, Italian was to have been introduced in non-Italian schools from 1927–8 onward. In fact, the italianisation process was accomplished much faster, with the immediate abolition or transformation of several German, Slovenian and Croatian schools into Italian teaching establishments.

Primary schools were among the first to be closed. This fact is to be seen on the one hand as a logical consequence of the process of italianisation of primary education, and on the other, as an indication of the significance attached to the problem of training the future primary school teachers. On 10 May 1927, Gentile's successor as Minister of Education, Pietro Fedele, could announce triumphantly to Mussolini that Italian was the only teaching language in public secondary schools in Julian Venetia and Upper Adige. Only some German private schools run by religious orders survived.[29] Attendance at state secondary schools was made easier by the fact that it was declared free, and that special provisions were made for the pupils and their families.

Dialects and local traditions were taught all over the country at primary school level, mainly in the first years after the approval of the Gentile bill. In the so-called 'new provinces' and in the Aosta Valley, the consequences of this provision were limited to the introduction of 'extra hours' which were to be devoted to the study of mother tongues within the national school system. In the Aosta valley, the recently-abolished system of extra-curricular classes in French were thus re-introduced. The situation of French in the valley was, actually, therefore, slightly improved. Under the Gentile bill, village schools were replaced by the so-called *scuole sussidiate* (state subsidised schools), institutions where some tuition in French was allowed. The effectiveness of these schools was, however, seriously hampered by the cuts in their budget decided on by the Finance Minister, Alberto de Stefani.[30] The study of the mother tongue of minority groups at the primary school level was thus turned into that of a local or a second language by Gentile.

Practical implementation of the rules relative to extra hours in the new provinces encountered various official obstacles from the very beginning. In Julian Venetia, the opportunity to attend extra classes was not automatically granted to all Slovenian and Croatian pupils, but could take place only upon the presentation of a special request by the parents. The examination of such applications was deliberately made a time-consuming business by school officials. Classes were fixed with timetables which rendered attendance difficult for the children. Moreover, language teaching was limited to oral instruction, and quite often given by Italians who had a poor command of Slovenian and Croatian. No textbooks were admitted. The Slovenian member of parliament, Engelbert Besednjak, a Catholic priest, condemned the whole system of extra hours as a cheat.

The same problems occurred in south Tyrol, where classes were limited to the main centres: Bolzano, Merano, Bressanone and Brunico. In such a situation it was not surprising that the introduction of the Gentile reform was followed by impressive demonstrations and protests. In the Aosta valley, the *Ligue Valdotaine* presented Mussolini with a petition signed by 8000 heads of families. German mothers organised a big demonstration in front of the Subprefecture of Bolzano. The reaction of the Slavs in Julian Venetia was less well organised, but still quite strong. In the second half of the 1920s, illegal and violent forms of protest occurred. The south Tyrolean members of parliament, Paul von Sternbach and Karl Tinzl, maintained that the aim of the Fascist government was no longer the diffusion of Italian in the new provinces, but the suppression of minority languages. The Gentile bill was followed, in 1924, by the closing down of German and Slav kindergartens, and their replacement by Italian institutions under the supervision of a Fascist national council. In south Tyrol, the attempt to organise private *Spielstuben* (kindergarten playrooms) was hampered and nullified by the intervention of Italian police authorities.

In 1925, even this limited opportunity for study of their mother tongue was taken away from the minorities. The extra hours were abolished by a decree issued by Minister Fedele on 22 November 1925. From the report annexed to the decree, it appears that the abolition of extra classes was decided on, above all, because of the state of tension reflected in the spirit of the alloglot population in the border areas. According to Fedele their feelings were being exploited by the enemies of Italy.[31] These words make it clear Fascist policy towards minorities was determined primarily by their location at the borders of Italy and also by the problems of international policy connected with this fact.

The overlapping of these two factors affected the Fascist attitude to such an extent that, during the 1930s, Mussolini declared that the fate of the German schools would have been totally different if south Tyrol had been in Tuscany instead of in the alpine region.[32] But in Fedele's 1925 report, there were also some passages that were typical of the Fascist concept of the state and of its consequences for the regime's nationality policy. Italy, it was argued, was not an aggregate of nationalities such as the Habsburg monarchy had been. Neither was it a state *sui generis* with strong alloglot minorities, like the successor states of Austria–Hungary: Czechoslovakia, Yugoslavia or Poland. It was a geographical and ethnic whole, with well determined geographical boundaries marked by the Alps and the sea. The national government had, therefore, to ensure a linguistic and cultural unity of all those who lived within the political boundaries of the Italian motherland. These concepts were personally stressed by Mussolini in a circular letter sent to all Ministries on 1 November 1925.[33] In this he criticised the views of liberal politicians, according to which the new boundaries of Italy were, above all, based upon strategic considerations. Instead he put forward the Fascist concept of the Italian character of all the annexed territories, which was to be reaffirmed wherever it had been erased or weakened by history.

This 'reconquest' had to begin, according to Mussolini, with the diffusion of the Italian language in the areas next to the borders and, for this to occur, the exclusive use of Italian in primary schools had to be ensured absolutely. The Fascist leader thus allocated to schools an essential task in his national policy in the alloglot or mixed territories. Mussolini's words can also be seen as a proof of the fact that the Italian denationalisation policy was not a reply to widespread irredentist trends among the minority groups, but an aim in itself, based upon ideological foundations and a radical vision of the national future. The measures associated with the italianisation of schools were accompanied by provisions that drastically reduced the number of Slav and German teachers, inherited from Austria. In fact, even before the Gentile reform, a substantial number of teachers had been forced out under various pretexts, such as not being in possession of Italian citizenship or having an inadequate knowledge of the official language. The Gentile law, and the following abolition of extra classes, led, in November 1925, to a regulation imposing the duty upon all alloglot teachers of taking an examination in order to become qualified to teach in Italian. A subsequent law, dated 24 December 1925, gave the authorities the opportunity to dismiss all those civil servants who did not fulfil their duties loyally, a measure easily made applicable to employees belonging to national minorities.[34]

The combined effect of these two provisions led to the discharge of many German and Slav teachers, all the more because the examination that they had to take was made extremely difficult, in order to eliminate as many applicants as possible. The few teachers who managed to stay on in their posts were generally moved to different provinces from those where their original jobs had been. In Upper Adige, only 111 out of 745 teachers in service in 1921, remained at the end of school year 1927–8.[35] However, most of these were forced to retire or move to other areas of the peninsula from 1928–9. On the other hand, 412 Italian teachers were sent to Upper Adige in the first years of transformation of the South Tyrolean school system: 115 in 1923–4; 86 in 1924–5; 62 in 1926–7; 24 in 1927–8; and 15 in 1928–9.[36] In 1936, only 50 Slav teachers out of about 1000 in 1923 were still in their positions; and of these only ten were allowed to stay in their native territory.[37]

The italianisation of the school system was, therefore, generally followed by the dismissal of teachers who spoke the same mother tongue as their pupils. Thus alloglot children were confronted not only with being taught Italian, a language of which they were often totally ignorant, at least at the beginning of their schooling, but also with teachers who could not communicate with them. Moreover, sometimes Italian teachers attracted to the new provinces by salary, allocation of living quarters and other career incentives, felt themselves entrusted with the mission of extracting pupils from the cultural community they belonged to. The aim behind italianisation of the school system was closely connected in Fascist politics, with the moral aim of eliminating and uprooting the languages and cultures of the alloglot populations, starting with the youngest generation. The introduction of Italian as the only acceptable language of instruction, and the elimination of extra-curricular language hours, were followed by rules which forbade private tuition in minority languages (a decree issued by the Prefect of Trento on 27 November 1925 was the first step).[38] Even tuition within families was prohibited, if it was given to more than three children at the same time.

In a parliamentary speech of 14 May 1926, devoted to the problem of use of a mother tongue at school, Karl Tinzl vainly demanded for the German children the minimal right to learn a language through private tuition; a right uncontested elsewhere in Italy. Provincial and police authorities watched diligently for any form of clandestine instruction and they intervened quite frequently. Teachers were compelled to rebuke children when they chatted among themselves in their own tongue. Guido Miglia, an Istrian writer, gives a very vivid and impressive picture of this, when he compares his experience as a young primary school teacher among Croatian children with his personal fate when he had to leave his native town, Pola, in 1947.[39]

The Teaching of Religion

The teaching of religion was, equally, viewed with suspicion, because it was considered to be an instrument for defending non-Italian languages, and preserving particularistic traditions. Under Austrian rule religion had been a compulsory subject of instruction, taught by priests and not by secular teachers. In Italy, the teaching of religion was introduced into the primary school curriculum by the Gentile bill, but only later on, with the Church–State treaty of 1929, into the secondary school. Under a decree issued in 1919 by the Italian military authority, the teaching of religion in the new provinces was kept in the curriculum and was still entrusted to the clergy, but as an optional subject. In 1923, the Ministry of Education made the first attempt to italianise religious instruction under the general provisions of the Gentile bill, but this ruling was withdrawn under the pressure from the Holy See.[40]

The use of a mother tongue in the teaching of religion – not only in Julian Venetia and South Tyrol, but also in the Aosta Valley – was limited to the first three years of primary school by a decree dated

January 1924, issued by the Ministry of Education, but it was also tolerated in the higher grades. In 1926, however, bilingual catechisms and the exlusive use of Italian in oral instruction were imposed. After a certain delay, starting with the school year 1928–9, this provision was finally enforced. Many ecclesiastical catechists then moved out of the schools, to be replaced by ordinary teachers. A network of parish schools, particularly widespread in south Tyrol, was thus established for the teaching of catechism and religion. In this extra school teaching, the potential for defence of national identity and use of a mother tongue varied from region to region, depending also on the cooperation of the ecclesiastical authorities and the degree of ethnic compatibility between the clergy and the faithful.

In south Tyrol, where both clergy and believers were mostly German, parish schools played a significant role in preserving the mother tongue and, in some cases, also provided some elementary language instruction under the cover of teaching religion.[41] In Julian Venetia, where the national line of demarcation also passed through the Church itself, the chances of national resistance by Slovenes and Croats within ecclesiastical institutions were much weaker. In the Aosta valley, at the beginning of the 1930s, when an Italian nationalist prelate, Monsignore Renzo Imberti, succeeded the franco-phone and francophile bishop, Angelo Calabrese, a turning point could be observed in the attitude of the Church towards the linguistic and national problems of the valley. The defence of French was then entrusted to the lower clergy, and their initiatives.[42] This finally came to resemble the situation in Julian Venetia. Some evidence of a profound Italian penetration of the region, however, is given by the fact that by 1929, only 26 out of 86 parish priests were using French while teaching catechism to children.

Self-defence Measures taken by the Minorities

In schools, after the abolition of extra classes, the only officially recognised place devoted to the study of the languages of minorities was that of teaching the mother tongue as a foreign language, and this was possible only in secondary schools where the curriculum permitted learning a modern foreign language.[43] This was not always feasible. In the Aosta *lycee*, for instance, reinstated after its abolition in 1861, the study of German as a foreign language in place of French was introduced in 1924. In Julian Venetia, the study of Slovenian and Croatian was offered in only a few schools and its presence was further reduced by frequent interventions from schoolmasters or some Italian parents who protested against the 'shame' of teaching Slav languages. In 1931–2, the courses in Slovenian and Croatian were abolished altogether, and they were only partially restarted from 1937 on. The choice of the mother tongue also prohibited the study of any other foreign language, and this fact caused protests everywhere, especially in the tourist area of Upper Adige. Moreover, this form of teaching the mother tongue was inadequate and unsatisfactory, all the more because it was generally entrusted to Italian teachers, who did not usually possess an adequate background in, or fluent knowledge of, the language.

During the 1930s, some concessions were made by Italian authorities towards the south Tyrolean minority, in the shape of private extra school courses in German open to children enrolled in the compulsory school classes. These concessions, given for foreign policy reasons, aimed to strengthen the prestige of the friendly governments of Dollfuss and Schuschnigg in Austria.[44] The already limited scope of these measures was further weakened by the obstacles put in the way of their effective implementation. Furthermore, most local circles considered the courses organised and supervised by Italians with scepticism, and preferred the more dangerous opportunities offered by clandestine 'catacomb schools' which were oriented towards the German speaking community at a national and ideological level. Even less significant were some sporadic concessions made to Slovenes and Croats, which also aimed at a *detente* in the relationship with the government in Belgrade.

A defence of the minority group was, therefore, not really possible within the public school system and had to rely upon the self-organised capacity for resistance of the populations involved (in Upper Adige, for instance, singing groups and circles were used as a means to keep linguistic traditions alive and to spread them among the younger generation). Realistic chances of preserving a linguistic and cultural inheritance were closely related to the social and cultural level of the families themselves. For this very reason, the first line of defence was, in most cases, inadequate and had to be supplemented by some organised forms of private and clandestine tuition, on which Fascist repression concentrated. Although similar attempts were made in Julian Venetia and the Aosta valley, Upper Adige was the major centre for a widespread network of clandestine schools, the so-called 'catacomb schools'. They had a very high number of pupils and were based on an efficient organisation which allowed them to survive the many blows dealt them by the police authorities.

The ethnic compactness of the south Tyroleans, their developed social awareness, the financial and political support given by the organisations for the defence of German minorities in Europe, were all factors which explain the capacity to create an organic emergency school system in Upper Adige, one which could not be created on a systematic basis elsewhere. A recent book by Maria Villgrater gives impressive figures concerning the diffusion of the 'catacomb schools' network: an average of more than 200 teachers, mainly female and 5000 pupils were involved in the courses every year.[45] Textbooks and other teaching aids were generally smuggled into south Tyrol from Germany and Austria. Courses for the training of teachers involved were held both in Italy and outside, mainly in Austria and Bavaria. The clandestine schools had strong ties with German organisations. This inevitably brought a consequent increase in the influence upon it of German nationalist tendencies and, later on, of national socialism. This led, in the late 1930s, to considerable tensions between Catholics and National Socialist sympathisers in south Tyrol.[46]

It is necessary in this context to look at the role played by the Catholic Church, whose actual involvement varied from place to place. In Upper Adige the Church as a whole was involved. In Julian Venetia[47] and in the Aosta valley,[48] where great tensions and conflicts were to be found within the Church, which was also split up along national lines and where denationalisation pressures sometimes even affected the seminaries, it was very much in the hands of individual bishops and priests. But, on the whole, the words of an Aostan historian, Ettore Passerin d'Entrèves, who described the Church as the Noah's ark of French during the Fascist period[49] can be extended to all minorities living in the border areas of northern Italy, even if it often was the lower clergy, acting on an individual basis, and not the hierarchy who were the real protagonists in the defensive struggle.

The strong presence of the Church and of the religious orders in south Tyrolean society before and after 1918 gave rise to a flourishing network of private Catholic secondary schools for boys and girls, owned by religious orders active in the principal centres of Upper Adige.[50] Although less directly, and more slowly than the state schools, they too were affected by general regulations. In some cases these led to their suppression or induced their owners to opt either for closing down, or, in some instances, for italianisation. In those schools which continued operating, though, the teaching of German as a second language was tolerated. Four religious private schools, destined for the education of the clergy, and which kept the character of German institutions, were very important in the defence of the mother tongue. In particular, the two seminaries, one at Bressanone (Brixen) for the eponymous diocese and one at Dorf Tirol for the German part of the diocese of Trento, which were also frequently attended by pupils who did not intend to become priests but looked instead for an education in a German environment, represented important and relatively free institutions which other minority groups did not possess.

Conclusions

School policy, like all the other aspects of Fascist policy towards national minorities, though characterised by uniform direction and consistent logic, was in practice very much affected by local conditions prevailing in the different areas and, especially, by the uneven intensity of opposition to the regime.[51] In Upper Adige, the ruling class, with its aristocratic and bourgeois components, plus the political elites and most of public opinion, were all conservative in their orientation. The ideological confrontation with Fascism, therefore, was not very direct there, especially in the first years after Mussolini's seizure of power. Opposition by Catholics and liberals displayed a moderate profile and restrained attitudes. On the other hand, the lack of a local Italian element, at least until the mid 1930s, when Italian immigration into Bolzano took place, gave the national struggle in that region the character of a conflict between the state power and a minority, and not that of a struggle between two ethnic groups. Thus, the room granted for national resistance by the minority was relatively ample.

In Aosta valley, belonging politically and spiritually to the Piedmontese state first and to the Italian kingdom second, Fascist pressures gave a strong push to the already ongoing process of italianisation of the social elites. But the place of these elites which 'betrayed' their own people was taken by elements of the middle and working classes (students, primary school teachers, lower clergy, postmen) who had never felt a greater need to defend vigorously their identity than at the very moment when it was under attack.[52] Particularly in the smaller valleys and the minor centres, lacking in more acute social and national tensions, close ties with the national tradition could be safeguarded.

The most strained and violent political climate was that of Julian Venetia, where the strain between the repressive state apparatus and Slovenian and Croatian minorities grew and developed into an open conflict between the national groups living in the region.[53] This national struggle was intensified by the parallel existence of a long-standing and deeply rooted social tension, which gave rise to a politically radical clandestine opposition within which a communist component was soon to prevail. The Slav reaction therefore took a more violent form, one not found elsewhere, which ended up with actions such as setting fire to Italian school and nursery school buildings, the two most visible and hated symbols of the Italian denationalisation policy.[54] Italian repression, on its part, was extremely harsh.

The variations in political climate thus brought about, despite the uniform character of the school and linguistic policy, substantial differences in the forms of cultural defence. As already mentioned, from the very beginning, Fascism focussed on the school as the essential instrument in the policy of denationalisation. School was the place where the education of the younger generation was proceeding and the regime believed that the young, not being conditioned by the past, were more open to Italian penetration and to assimilation. Learning at school was supplemented by the activities of the regime's youth organisations, which attempted to take children and youngsters away from the influence of their families and the Church in order to italianise them more fully.[55]

In the document of May 1927, Minister Fedele identified assimilation and spiritual conquest of the new generation as the main task of Fascist educational policy. However, the violence implicit in the concept of assimilation was, in itself, in strident contrast with the idea of spiritual conquest. In trying to attain its objectives, the regime naturally did not hesitate to use all the means at its disposal in order to suppress the languages and cultural traditions of the minorities. The consequence of this violence was a reaction which produced exactly opposite results, namely the strengthening of the very identity Fascism wanted to see eradicated. The failure of its assimilation policy was openly admitted by the regime itself, at least insofar as Upper Adige was concerned. In 1934, Mussolini decided to create an industrial area in Bolzano with the hope of creating an Italian speaking majority in the region through a wave of immigration of Italian workers to the main south Tyrolean city. Later on, in 1939 the *Duce* tried to solve the still unresolved problem of the character of this area through an agreement with Germany, the so-called Options Agreement, which paved the way for the emigration of a part of the German speaking population from south Tyrol.

Also from the educational point of view, the attempt to enforce at a very early age the study of Italian, a foreign tongue, upon children from minority groups who did not understand it and only possessed an oral knowledge of their own mother tongue, ended in failure. Children did not learn their mother tongue correctly and they also learned very poor Italian, which in many cases they completely forgot once they finished the school. The method used at the same time by French authorities to introduce, or reintroduce French, in Alsace–Lorraine, starting from the mother tongue in order to outflank it and later to replace it with French, proved to be more efficient than the brutal and violent method imposed by Mussolini. The Fascist school system condemned to a double illiteracy the youngsters of the minority groups belonging to the socially weakest classes.[56] The school policy of the Fascist regime was a great human and cultural tragedy for national minorities, but it also clearly demonstrated the total failure of attempts at assimilation. The moral and physical violence Fascism used was, in turn, the cause of similar violence which so tragically affected the Italians of Istria and Fiume in 1945 and in the following years.

Notes

1. For a general overview of the ethnic and linguistic groups in Italy see Salvi.
2. Adler (1980), pp. 227–32; Brocherel; Omezzoli.
3. Vegezzi-Ruscalla. For the reactions of the French speaking population to Vegezzi-Ruscalla's proposals, see Bérard.
4. A synthesis of the educational policy in the valley up to the Credaro law is traced by Adler (1980), pp. 229–33. For the reactions to the italianization attempts of 1883, see Réan, pp. 5–16.
5. Gatterer, pp. 33; 116–18.
6. Corsini (1980), Kramer.
7. Ara (1974), pp. 9–140.
8. Kramer, Die Italiener unter der österreichisch – ungarischen Monarchie, p. 45.
9. Gatterer, pp. 109–14; see also Sestan, pp. 81–103. An Austrian official report concerning the primary school quarrel between Italians and Slovenes in Trieste, written by the Governor of the 'Küstenland', Prince Konrad Hohenlohe, on 17 January 1906, is kept in Allgemeines Verwaltungsarchiv, Vienna, Ministerrats–Präsidium, 1164/1907. A good overview of the whole school system in Trieste is given in a special issue of *Umana* (August 1958), 'Le istituzioni di cultura della Trieste moderna'. From this source are taken the figures concerning the attendance of German schools in Trieste.
10. Gatterer, pp. 136–7.
11. Sestan, p. 110.
12. Passerin d'Entrèves, p. 233.
13. For a balanced account of Liberal and Fascist policies in the new provinces, see Rusinow.
14. Gatterer, pp. 310–12; Toscano, pp. 51–54.
15. Corsini (1969); Gatterer, pp. 271–304; Silvestri.
16. Trafojer, pp. 48–51.
17. Čermelj, pp. 24–5. Čermelj's book, originally published in Slovenian in 1936, is still the standard work on Fascist denationalisation policy in Julian Venetia and was (1974) translated into Italian. The literature on this topic is substantially less conspicuous than the one devoted to the German south Tyrolese minority. For a contemporary Italian account on school policy in the new provinces see Ferretti.
18. Gatterer, pp. 315–19.
19. Villgrater, pp. 21–2.
20. For the problematic of the 'rescue policy' and the Corbino bill see Adler (1979), pp. 37–41; Ara (1987), p. 329; Trafojer, pp. 225–7; Villgrater, pp. 23–8.
21. Stuparich, pp. 163–7.
22. Ferretti, p. 102.
23. Adler (1980), pp. 238–9.
24. Archivio centrale dello Stato, Roma (hereafter A.C.S.), Presidenza del consiglio dei ministri (P.C.M.), Gabinetto, 1924, fo. 123, 1 1–11 32, official report of the Education Director of Trento, 11 August 1923; Adler (1981), p. 332.
25. Villgrater, pp. 29; 32–3.
26. Adler (1980), pp. 241–3.
27. A.C.S., P.C.M., Gabinetto, 1924, fo. 123 1 1–11 32.

28. For a general appraisal of the Gentile Reform see Bertoni Jovine, pp. 265–8. As concerns the reform's ideological approach towards national minorities and its impact on their school system see Adler (1979), pp. 65–6; Adler (1981), pp. 333–4; Čermelj, pp. 25–6; Gatterer, pp. 457–61; Klein, p. 238; Passerin d'Entrèves, p. 238.
29. A.C.S., P.C.M., Gabinetto, 1928–30, fo. 356 1 1–13 82, report of the Minister of Public Education to the President of the Council of Ministers.
30. Adler (1980), pp. 248–9.
31. A.C.S., P.C.M., *Provvedimenti legislativi*, 1925, *Istruzione*, no. 186.
32. Schuschnigg, p. 241.
33. A.C.S., P.C.M., Gabinetto, 1926, fo. 1 1–13 4539.
34. Čermelj, p. 28.
35. Villgrater, pp. 65–70.
36. These figures are taken from a document 'La politica italiana in Alto Adige', compiled in October 1945 by the office of the province of Bolzano, which is kept in A.C.S., Min. Gab. A.A. 1944–45, fo. 47, no. 3773. The whole section of the document 'La scuola nella Venezia Tridentina' has very useful, although often one sided, data concerning Italian school policy in Upper Adige in the interwar period.
37. Čermelj, p. 28.
38. *Ibid.*, p. 35; Gatterer, p. 462. I will return below to the problem of Italian attitude towards the different forms of clandestine tuition in connection with the problem of the 'catacomb schools'.
39. Miglia, pp. 18–20. The late Ladislao Mittner, the greatest Italian germanist, gave to this author an example of the difficulty of breaking through the German speaking environment of Brunico, the south Tyrolese town where he served as a secondary school teacher in the late 1920s and early 1930s.
40. Adler (1979), p. 121–30; Čermelj, pp. 26–7; A. Gruber, pp. 61–5.
41. Villgrater, pp. 271–303.
42. Passerin d'Entrèves, pp. 240–3; Soave, pp. 25–38.
43. Čermelj, pp. 33–5; Gatterer, pp. 460–1; Passerin d'Entrèves, p. 236.
44. Ara (1987), pp. 274–5; 287–8; A. Gruber, pp. 182–3.
45. Villgrater, pp. 95–270. Also see Gatterer pp. 461–4; Marzari, pp. 38–54.
46. Steurer, p. 248.
47. Čermelj, pp. 106–18; Gatterer, pp. 692–702. For the roots of the contrast see Valdevit. For the following years some observations can be found in Ara and Magris, pp. 128–9; 205; Pirjevec, pp. 25–6, 111–6; Rusinow, pp. 202–3.
48. Adler (1980) pp. 269–71; Soave, pp. 17–31.
49. Passerin d'Entrèves, pp. 252.
50. Gatterer, p. 710; Villgrater, pp. 56–9.
51. Gatterer, pp. 526–8.
52. Passerin d'Entrèves, p. 252.
53. Apih; Kacin-Wohinz, pp. 385–410. A balanced portrait of the development of the national struggle in the region is given by Sestan, pp. 105–25. On the interrelations between national conflict and school policy: Pirjevec, pp. 23, 28.
54. Rusinow, p. 204.
55. Čermelj, pp. 37–44.
56. Impressive examples in this sense are given for German children of south Tyrol in Villgrater, pp. 281–9.

Select Bibliography

Adler, Wienfried (1980), 'La politica del fascismo in Valle d'Aosta', in *Bollettino storico-bibliografico subalpino*, LXXVIII.

Adler, Wienfried (1981), 'Die Kulturpolitik des italienischen Faschismus in Südtirol', in *Quellen und Forschungen aus italienischen Archiven und Bibliotheken*, 61.

Adler, Wienfried (1979), 'Die Minderheitspolitik des italienischen Faschismus in Südtirol und im Aostatal: 1922–1929', unpublished thesis, University of Trier.

Apih, Elio (1966), *Italia, fascismo e antifascismo nella Venezia Giulia, 1918–1943*, Bari.

Ara, Angelo (1987), *Fra Austria e Italia: dalle Cinque Giornate alla questione alto-atesina*, Udine.

Ara, Angelo (1974), 'La questione dell'universitá italiana in Austria', *Ricerche sugli austro-italiani e l'ultima Austria*, Rome.

Ara, Angelo and Magris, Claudio (1987), *Trieste: un'identità di frontiera*, Turin.

Bérard, Édouard (1862), *La langue française dans la Vallée d'Aoste*, 2nd edn. 1974, Aosta.

Bertoni Jovine, Dina (1972), *La scuola italiana dal 1870 ai giorni nostri*, Rome.

Brocherel, Jules (1952), *Le patois et la langue française dans la Vallée d'Aoste*, Neuchâtel.

Čermelj, Lavo (1945), *Life-and-death struggle of a national minority: the Yugoslavs in Italy*, 2nd edn., Ljubljana.

Corsini, Umberto (1980), 'Die Italiener', Wandruszka, Adam and Urbanitsch, Peter, (eds) *Die Habsburgermonarchie, 1848–1918*, vol. III, *Die Völker des Reiches*, pt. 2, Vienna.

Corsini, Umberto (1969), 'Il Trentino e l'Alto Adige nel periodo 3–11–1918 – 31–12–1922' Idem (ed.), *Trentino e Alto Adige dall'Austria all'Italia*, Bolzano.

Ferretti, Giovanni (1923), *La scuola nelle terre redente*, Florence.

Gatterer, Claus (1968), *Im Kampf gegen Rom. Bürger, Minderheiten und Autonomien in Italien*, Vienna.

Gruber, Alfons (1975), *Südtirol unter dem Faschismus*.Bozen, 2nd edn.

Gruber Benco, Aurelia (ed.) (August 1958), 'Le istituzioni di cultura della Trieste moderna', special issue of *Umana*, Trieste.

Kacin-Wohinz, Milica (1972), 'Appunti sul movimento antifascista nella Venezia Giulia', in *Quaderni del centro di ricerche storiche di Rovigno*, II.

Klein, Gabriella (1968), *La politica linguistica del fascismo*, Bologna.

Kramer, Hans (1954), *Die Italiener unter der österreichisch-ungarischen Monarchie*, Vienna.

Marzari, Walter (1974), *Kanonikus Michael Gamper: Ein Kämpfer für Glauben und Heimat gegen Faschisten in Südtirol*, Vienna.

Miglia, Guido (1973), *Dentro l'Istria: Diario, 1945–1947*, Trieste.

Omezzoli, Tullio (1965/66), 'Conflitti di lingua e di cultura in Valle d'Aosta', unpublished thesis, 2 vols., University of Turin.

Passerin d'Entrèves, Ettore (1973), 'La lotta per l'autonomia e la difesa del francese in Valle d'Aosta', Fontana, Sandro, (ed.), *Il fascismo e le autonomie locali*, Bologna.

Pirjevec, Jože (ed.) (1983), *Introduzione alla storia culturale e politica slovena a Trieste nel' 900*, Trieste.

Réan, Anselme (1932), *La phase initiale de la lutte contre la langue française dans la Vallée d'Aoste*, Ivrea.

Rusinow, Dennison I. (1969), *Italy's Austrian Heritage, 1919–1946*, Oxford.

Salvi, Sergio (1975), *Le lingue tagliate. Storia delle minoranze linguistiche in Italia*, Milan.

Schuschnigg, Kurt von (1946), *Ein Requiem in Rot-Weiss-Rot*, Zürich.

Sestan, Ernesto, (1965), *Venezia Giulia. Lineamenti di una storia etnica e culturale*, 2nd edn., Bari.

Silvestri, Claudio (1966), *Dalla Redenzione al Fascismo. Trieste, 1918–1922*. 2nd edn., Udine.

Soave, Sergio (n.d.), *Cultura e mito dell'autonomia: La Chiesa in Valle d'Aosta, 1900–1948*, Milan.

Steurer, Leopold (1980), *Südtirol zwischen Rom und Berlin*, Vienna.

Stuparich, Giani (1921), 'Autonomia e liberismo nella Venezia Giulia', *Rivista di Milano*.

Toscano, Mario (1968), *Storia diplomatica della questione dell'Alto Adige*, Bari.

Trafojer, Karl (1971), 'Die innenpolitische Lage in Südtirol: 1918–1925', unpublished thesis, University of Vienna.

Valdevit, Giampaolo (1979), *Chiesa e lotte nazionali: il caso di Trieste, 1850–1919*, Udine.

Vegezzi-Ruscalla, Giovenale (1861), *Diritto e necessità di abrogare il francese in alcune valli della provincia di Torino*, Turin.

Villgrater, Maria (1984), *Katakombenschule: Faschismus und Schule in Südtirol*, Bozen.

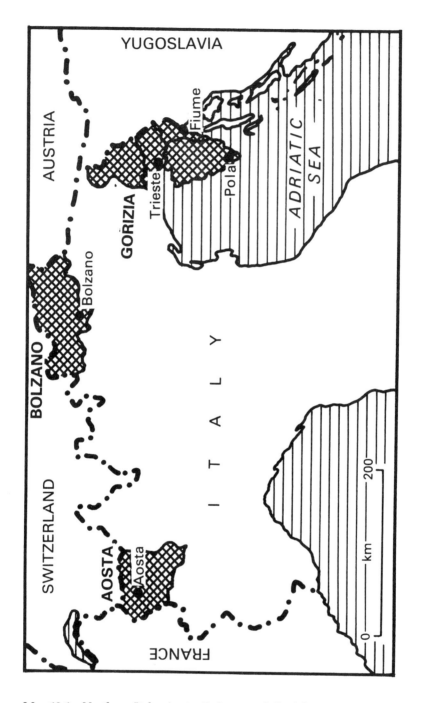

Map 12.1   Northern Italy, Aosta, Bolzano and Gorizia
Source: Encyclopedia Italiane

13 Spanish Education Policy Towards Non-Dominant Linguistic Groups, 1850–1940

JOSE LUIS GARCIA GARRIDO

Introductory Remarks

Spain is one of the oldest nation–states in Europe. Its territorial unity dates back to the end of the fifteenth century, when the ancient kingdoms of Castile and Aragon were combined into one. Since then, the territorial structure of the country has not changed substantially: the present boundaries of the Spanish state coincide basically with those already in existence by the end of the fifteenth century.

Certainly, the process of unification had begun much earlier, at the beginning of the Christian era, when a full romanisation of the Hispanic peninsula had taken place. Both the Roman domination and the subsequent occupation by the Visigoths, together with an early adoption of Christianity as a religion, gave the entire country and its inhabitants a deep sense of belonging to the European Christian community and a substantial ethnic uniformity. Until 1492, one of the most important factors behind the unification movement was the struggle against Moorish domination, through a long process known as the *Reconquista* (reconquest), or restoration of territorial as well as cultural and religious unity to the whole country.

Nevertheless, the political and religious and, to a certain degree, ethnic and cultural unity achieved during the Middle and modern ages did not encompass all linguistic areas within the Spanish territory. There were three main areas of difference: Euskadi (the Basque country) in the north, Galicia in the north west and Catalunya in the north east. Differential elements of ethnicity can be recognised in the population of these three 'historical regions', as they are usually called, particularly in the case of Galicia and, to a lesser degree, in Euskadi. But it seems clear that the main differentiating characteristic between them and the rest of the Castilian speaking Spanish state has always been their languages, which have been preserved for centuries, in spite of the constant influence and even pressure exercised by a much larger linguistic majority.

Although we will deal with the three regions separately later, some introductory information can be given here about the main characteristics of each. (For the location of the three regions in the Spanish peninsula, see Map 13.1). Catalunya, bordering the Mediterranean Sea, is closely linked to the European continent, even though the Pyrenees represent a solid barrier in most of its northern boundaries. In comparison to the rest of Spain and the other 'historical regions', Catalunya is a big territory (31 434 sq km). Also, it has always been rather densely populated, especially the coastal regions, where commerce and, since the middle of the last century, industry have given the region relative prosperity which has also been supported by a remarkable growth in agriculture. It must be remembered, furthermore, that the Catalan region comprises, at least from the linguistic point of view, some regions in the south eastern part of France and some others south of the present Catalunya, although these territories have been politically separated from Catalunya for a long time (including the entire period covered here).

In the north of the peninsula, the Basque country is a mountainous and rather small territory (7 268 sq km). Its population has grown substantially since the last century, owing to a process of industrialisation that affected mainly the large cities and attracted masses of people coming from other Spanish regions. Industrialisation caused a major development in the region's economy and greatly changed its traditional face. Before industrialisation, this region was inhabited by country people, concentrating on agricultural activities, mostly in isolated *caserios* (typical rural houses). As a people they were very fond of their traditions and their peculiar language. As in the case of Catalunya, the Basque country also extends into French territory, even though the cultural relationship between the two parts (French and Spanish) has not been very important for centuries. It must also be said that the northern part of Navarra is often considered to be part of the Basque country (in fact, Basque nationalists have always claimed the whole of Navarra, though their pretensions have seldom been accepted by the majority of the Navarran people).

In the north west of the peninsula, Galicia represents a very isolated and rather underdeveloped region, with a territory of 29 434 sq km, and with a dispersed and relatively large population (smaller, however, than that of either Catalunya or Euskadi). The inhabitants have usually been engaged in agriculture and fishing, taking advantage of the excellent resources of fish and seafood existing along the intricate coast and estuaries. But the low standard of life, and several other circumstances, have tended to favour migration to other regions of Spain and even overseas, especially to some countries of Latin America. Culturally speaking, both the proximity of Portugal and isolation from the rest of Spanish territory have had a major influence on the Galician mentality and way of life. Also, like Basques and Catalans, they have always been very fond of their traditions. Among Galician migrants, *morriña* (a melancholy feeling of homesickness) has become proverbial.

Since other aspects (religious, cultural, educational, etc.) of these groups will be dealt with in more detail later, it seems appropriate to analyse first the emergence of nationalist feelings among them.

The Cultural and Political Problem: its Rise and Evolution

In his work *España invertebrada (Invertebrate Spain)*, first published in 1922, José Ortega y Gasset wrote:

> One of the most typical phenomena of Spanish political life during the last 20 years has been the emergence of regionalisms, nationalisms and separatisms; that is to say, movements of ethnic and territorial secession. Are there many Spaniards who have realised what is the true historical nature of such movements? I am afraid that this is not the case.
>
> For the vast majority, Catalan and Basque 'nationalism' is an artificial movement, which, coming from nowhere, without any cause or deep rooted reasons, begins suddenly, a few years ago. According to this point of view, Catalunya and the Basque country were not social units different from Castilia or Andalucia before that movement. Spain was a homogeneous unit, without real continuity, without natural barriers between the different parts. To speak just about regions, about different peoples, about Catalunya or Euskadi was to cut a homogeneous block with a knife and to slice into different pieces that which was a compact volume (. . .)
>
> I could not emphasise sufficiently the extent to which I disagree with that view on the source, character, importance, and treatment of the urge towards secession.[1]

Several points can be emphasised in this perceptive text. First, Ortega's estimation that the nationalist phenomenon arose (at least as a secessionist problem) at the beginning of the twentieth century. Second, his conviction that it dealt with a problem whose true nature was misunderstood by most of the people, many intellectuals and politicians included. Third, his opinion that this misunderstanding relied on a deficient interpretation or evaluation of Spanish history. Finally, his disagreement with the generalised point of view.

Very briefly, according to Ortega, the history of Spain as a nation can be defined, first, as an early and speedy process of integration and, later (from 1580 on), as a slow process of disintegration. The integrative period had begun in the Middle Ages, and had reached its peak at the end of the fifteenth century, when Isabel de Castila and Fernando de Aragon had joined their vast kingdoms – in both of which different peoples had already been merged – in order to undertake a major policy of expansion (which Ortega calls 'the first *Weltpolitik* in history'). An assumption underlies this interpretation: that 'nations take form and live when they have a programme for tomorrow' and, consequently, when that programme has come to an end, or there is no programme, a process of disintegration becomes unavoidable. After the loss of the colonies, in the nineteenth century, a phenomenon called 'particularism' by Ortega began to emerge:

> The essence of particularism is that every group stops feeling itself as part of a whole, and consequently ceases to share the same feelings with others. . . . we can say that particularism is present today throughout Spain, even if its nature is regulated by the conditions of each region. In Bilbao and Barcelona, which consider themselves the biggest economic centres, it has taken an aggressive and well-defined character, with many rhetorical features. In Galicia, a poor land inhabited by an uncomplaining, suspicious people lacking in self-confidence, particularism seems to go underground, as an eruption which cannot break out, and it takes the form of a silent and humble bitterness.[2]

From this interpretation, it is clear that the emergence of national-isms does have roots in the past. At the same time, it figures as a problem during the period studied here.

A General Look at Educational Policy

The Spanish public education system was established rather late, compared to those of other European countries. In very general terms, we can say that its real birth took place in 1821. In that year, the *Cortes* (Spanish parliament) promulgated a *Reglamento general de Instrucción Pública* (General Regulations on Public Education), which introduced an institutional structure consisting of three grades and created a *Dirección General de Estudios* (General Study Directorate) as a centralised organ to direct this education policy. However, neither of these had their desired effect because of changes in the political sphere. In 1845, another regulation, the *Plan Pidal* (Pidal law), was approved, and, as in France, whose educational ideas and system have always had a great influence on Spain, a strong centralising process took place. One example will suffice: the rector of every university had to be directly nominated by the king and chosen from 'illustrious people', yet active professors were excluded from this group. One final point: only the University of Madrid was empowered to award a doctoral degree, causing considerable upset at, for instance, the University of Barcelona.

Another important question dealt with by the *Plan Pidal* was that concerned with the relationship between state and Church in the educational field. Until then, education had been largely the province of the Church. The new regulation aimed at the secularisation of the school system. Gil de Zarate, the main inspirer, justified the new regulation by saying that 'the essence of teaching is the essence of power', and that 'to give responsibility for teaching to the Church is to intend that people are educated for the Church and not for the state'.[3] But in the same year, a new constitution had decreed, once more, that 'the Spanish religion is Catholic, Apostolic, and Roman. The state is obliged to maintain this worship and its ministers' (article 11, 1845 Spanish constitution). As a consequence of this, reaction to the *Plan Pidal* was very strong. It was also one of the main factors behind the signing of a new *concordat* (agreement) between the Church and the Spanish state in 1851. This *concordat* included the following article:

> Teaching in the universities, colleges, seminaries and public and private schools of any kind will be in full harmony with the doctrines of the Catholic religion; and, to this purpose, no impediment will be put on the bishops and other diocesan pastors, in order to keep guard over the purity of learning about faith and morals and over the religious education of the youth, even in the public schools.[4]

A few years later, in 1857, the first comprehensive Spanish *Ley Moyano* (law on education), called after the Minister responsible came into being. The old liberal idea of planning for strong centralisation continued, and was even reinforced. It was a notion that was to last for a whole century. The sole educational administrative body envisaged was the central one, answerable to the *Ministerio de Fomento* and under the direct management of the *Dirección General de Instrucción Pública*. Some peripheral administrative organs, such as the 'university districts', headed by the rector, the provincial Board of Public Education and the municipal Board of Primary Education, were created, but these had little power.

Under the Moyano law, as in the former legislative document, no mention was made about the possible use of non-Castilian Spanish languages in the schools at any grade. On the contrary, the law established very clearly that 'the Spanish Academy of grammar and ortography will provide the compulsory and sole texts for language teaching in public education' (article 88). As far as relations between Church and state in the educational field were concerned, the law did not introduce any modifications to the agreements of the 1845 concordat. The only significant development in this direction came from some concessions given to the Church over the establishment of primary and secondary schools, especially in the qualification of the teaching staff. Of interest in this latter respect, were the regulations about the qualification of teachers in the public schools. Primary school teachers were to be trained in normal (teacher training) schools established in every province and supported by the provincial authorities (except for one central normal school which was to be supported directly by the state government). But this provision did not mean any concession of a linguistic nature for those normal schools located in the non-Castilian regions and provinces. Some years later (1849), special rules for the normal schools of public education appeared, in which the principle of complete centralisation remained unchanged. So, teacher training was made to correspond with a policy of linguistic as well as administrative centralism. Moreover, it was a policy with which all the liberal and national parties agreed.

On the question of centralism, educational policy remained basically unchanged, with very few innovations, for many years. Neither the 1868 September revolution, nor the establishment of the republic of 1873, opened new horizons in this respect, in spite of the temporary influence of some regionalist politicians such as Pi i Margall, to whom we will return later. Two new constitutions were promulgated during this period (1869 and 1873), but neither of them introduced new elements to the traditional relationship between the central power and the linguistic regions. Instead, some changes took place in the relations between Church and state, especially as a result of the passage of article 21 of the 1869 constitution, under which religious freedom was promulgated. This, and other events, aroused strong reactions from many people, and the clergy even refused to accept the constitution. Nevertheless, the revolutionaries did not push for a revival of statism. In accordance with their radical liberalism, they promulgated in October 1868 a decree in which a very open form of freedom of teaching was advanced:

> The greater the number of persons who teach, the greater the number of truths disseminated. . . . Certainly, the individual can teach error, but the state can fall into it also. . . . When the State has a monopoly on teaching, its errors are received like dogma. . . . One of the most stubborn obstacles to the evolution of new ideas has been this monopoly on teaching.[5]

The new regulation, however, did not bring about either a decentralisation of educational policy or an enthusiasm from churchmen for the facilities given to private schools. This was because freedom of teaching also meant the freedom to voice theories and opinions which could not be in agreement with the doctrine of the Church.

Anyhow, with the restoration of the monarchy in 1874, and the adoption of a new constitution in 1876, there was a return to the more traditional approach. Although the principle of freedom of teaching was retained, some amendments were made, especially ones intended to avoid promotion of theories contrary to the faith and morals of the Catholic Church. *Conservadores* (Conservatives) and *liberales* (Liberals) had alternative periods in government, but neither of them changed substantially the former *status quo* in educational matters. From 1885 to 1898, educational policy was substantially liberal, but had to follow one unlikely direction, which was in large part contrary to liberal principles, that of protecting the rights of the state to promote its own schools. The centralisation process continued. As a result the normal schools, which earlier had been supported by the provincial authorities, were now supported directly from state funds, in order to bring teacher training under the control of the state.

As far as the use of regional languages in schools was concerned, central government policy remained that of open rejection of their use for many years, in spite of the fact that the claims for them were growing more and more insistent, and not just in Catalunya and the Basque country. As an example, we can mention the case of a Valencian member of the Spanish parliament, Manuel Polo y Peyrolón, who, in 1896, asked the government to allow the use of regional languages in schools, and to permit teachers to be properly prepared for this form of instruction.

> I believe [he said] that it would be very efficient to introduce regional languages in teaching boys and girls, and to require from the teachers, as a sine qua non condition, knowledge of the regional dialect; it seems to me that a royal order from the Ministry would suffice for that. This step would generate profitable results; but the results could be better still if in the normal schools of Valencia, Barcelona, San Sebastián, Bilbao, Vittoria, Pamplona, etc. the teaching of Valencian, Catalan, Basque, etc., was done in such a way that every teacher would know both Castilian and the regional language, using the latter to teach the former and *vice versa*.

The Minister, Linares Rivas, answered the deputy's request by observing that the law could not allow this, because, according to him:

> I believe it is a great disadvantage to the fatherland, and it would be a still greater danger, to find a region or a part of Spain in which the inhabitants could not understand the authorities as well as the inhabitants of other parts of the country.[6]

A general crisis occurred at the end of the century (1889 used to be considered a key year), when an opportunity arose for a deeper discussion about education. A famous book, published by Macias Picavea in 1899 (see bibliography) laid particular emphasis on the poor quality of schools, the training and salaries of teachers, etc. On the other hand, separatist movements in Catalunya and the Basque country, with substantial cultural and educational components, began to appear on the political scene. Some well known exponents of the so called *Regeracionsim*, especially Joaquin Costa (ver I. Turin) and others, who were inspired by the ideas of the *Institucion Libre de Enseñanza*, demanded a major reform of educational policy.

In 1900, under a conservative government, a completely separate Ministry of Public Education and Fine Arts was created, which contributed to the continuance of a strongly centralised administration. In 1901, the liberal Romanones's Ministry intended to strengthen the role of the provinces (with its *Diputaciones* and *Juntas provinciales*) and even that of the *Ayuntamientos* (the municipal government). But, as Puelles Benitez commented, this policy 'failed because of the lack of economic resources'.[7] It should be added that there was, on the part of the central authorities, no desire at that time to introduce true decentralisation, as is shown by several political measures devoted to increasing the quality of public education throughout Spain. One important such measure was the inclusion of the salaries of primary teachers in the state budget. Very briefly, all actions taken to improve the school system resulted in a reinforcement of state centralism in education.

As far as the relationship between state and Church was concerned, the Romanones's Ministry gave new opportunities for deep disagreements. Religion became, once again, an optional subject, and it was required that clergymen teaching in church schools had the same qualifications as teachers in the ordinary public schools. Both of these measures were widely resisted.

In some linguistic regions, disagreements between Church and state arose over the language of teaching. For instance, the Spanish parliament reacted strongly to a pastoral letter published by the bishop of Barcelona, Dr Morgades, in which the teaching of the catechism in Catalan was recommended. In 1902, a royal decree from the Liberal Minister of Public Education, Romanones, forbade the use of Catalan for the teaching of the catechism and religion in school. Yet, the calls for decentralisation did not disappear. Because of this, a decade later, a type of decentralised government – the *Mancomunitat de Catalunya* – was allowed, although, as we shall see later, its impact may have been of little consequence in terms of educational policy. However, some important actions were taken at that time; and other linguistic movements, like those of the Basque country and Galicia, wanted to adopt similar policies. But the dictatorship of General Primo de Rivera suspended any moves in this direction, thus provoking a general feeling of frustration, especially in Catalunya.

With the arrival of the Second Republic in 1931, the situation was altered considerably. First of all, a new policy of decentralisation and regionalism was put into practice; however, the changes fell short of expectations due to the beginning of the civil war in 1936. Furthermore, the relationship between state and Church worsened from the start, and the two were on very bad terms when the new republican constitution was promulgated in which the dissolution of religious orders and the nationalisation of their properties were proposed. Both of these factors, of course, influenced the development of educational policy, which was in many aspects very rapid during this period. Unfortunately, it is not possible here to pay more attention to some of the reforms, such as the raising of the cultural and economic level of teachers, the reform of normal schools, and so on. In Catalunya, the development of its own educational system was seen as an important objective.

The Catalan system was, indeed, a pattern for other nationalist and regionalist movements, particularly in the Basque country. Nevertheless, the nature of the political scene discouraged the extension of such a programme to other regions of Spain. The civil war and Franco's dictatorship initiated a new process of centralisation in the educational field as well as elsewhere.

On the basis of this discussion, the educational evolution in practice in each of the three linguistic regions can now be highlighted.

Education in Catalunya

Sanchez Albornoz along with other historians, underlined the contribution of the Catalans to the creation of Spanish unity during the Middle Ages. But it seems clear that this consciousness of unity was persistently accompanied by an equally deep consciousness of difference. During the two centuries that followed the unification of Castile and Aragon, both these feelings coexisted peacefully among the Catalan people, who were able to preserve their language, traditions, and even an autonomous system of government up to the end of the seventeenth century. At that time, the royal absolutism of both the Bourbon kings, Louis XIV in France and Philip V in Spain, began to impose a policy of linguistic as well as political restriction on their Catalan territories. In 1716, Philip V dictated the Decree of *Nova Planta* for the *Principat de Catalunya*, which broke abruptly with the tradition of autonomy in that area. It can be said that this date marks the origin of Catalan separatist claims, which were to be repeated more intensively during the second half of the following century, especially as a consequence of the Romantic movement.

The Romantic movement increased erudite interest in the old, and always vital, Catalan language. The Aribau's ode *La patria* ('The Fatherland') has been considered as the first step by this movement and was followed, some time later, by the restoration of the medieval *Jocs Florals* (a kind of poetic exhibition in the Catalan tongue) first organised in Barcelona in 1859 and soon extended to other places. At the same time, several books on the Catalan language, grammar and history were being written. In one of these, Pers i Romona says that 'Catalan will be the national language of Catalunya, whereas the Catalan people are persuaded that the kings of Castile are only the counts of Barcelona'.[8] As a rule, however, there were no real protests against the use of Castilian as the official language of Catalunya at the time, nor any demands for political autonomy. The *Jocs Florals* movement has, thus, been considered as mere provincialism.

The second stage of the movement was of a rather more political nature. It was represented by Pi i Margall's federalism and Almirall's regionalism. Both believed that the federalist solution was the best one for both Spain and Catalunya. However, Pi i Margall had major responsibilities in the First Republican government, and, consequently, his attention was focused less on the Catalan problem than on the territorial structure of the entire republic. His plan was to return to the ancient regional division of Spain (abolished in 1835 when the 49 provinces were created), and to establish 14 autonomous regions on the basis of a federal agreement.

On the other hand, Almirall

> . . . differs from Pi i Margall, above all, in that he looks particularly and primarily at the Catalan situation, and not at the political system of Spain as a whole . . . He believes that only after solving the Catalan question is it possible to deal with the other Spanish regional questions.

Anyhow, as Hina also writes, 'the Restoration period can be marked out as the golden period of Catalan regionalism'.[9] This high point was possible in particular because of the literary movement known as the *Renaixença* (Renaissance), amongst whose members great writers such as Verdaguer, Guimera and others must be listed. At the end of the nineteenth century, when the restoration entered a critical period, other famous writers, like Maragall, contributed greatly to the prestige of Catalan literature in Catalunya, as well as in Spain and abroad. This, obviously, reinforced Catalan love for their language and traditions, and new avenues for cultural and political autonomy were opened. In 1906, Prat de la Riba, who was later to be the president of the *Mancomunitat*, wrote *La nacionalitat catalana*, an interesting book in which a new term, 'nationality', was applied to Catalunya. Thus, nationalist claims found a new theoretical basis in the works of Prat de la Riba. The Catalan language came to be considered the most important bulwark of Catalan nationality and, consequently, nationalists strove to replace the bilingualism that existed in practice with Catalan monolingualism.

However, none of these events ever penetrated the daily routine of the Catalan primary and secondary schools; the ordinary teaching language remained Castilian. The use of Catalan was reserved for family life and for some cultural and religious activities promoted by the clergy, who were always influential in the country. In fact, many of the movements against state centralism or in favour of their own cultural traditions were encouraged by the Catalan clergy. For instance, the Abbey of Montserrat, belonging to the Benedictine Order, has traditionally always been a focal point for the preservation and dissemination of the Catalan culture and language. Endowed with a deep practical sense, the Catalans have seldom presented resistance to the daily reality of bilingualism and, on the contrary, have made significant contributions to Castilian literature. So far as the development of the educational system is concerned, during both the nineteenth century and the first decades of the twentieth, Catalunya occupied an important position in the context of Spain as a whole, encouraging movements of innovation and reform in the public as well as in the private sector. Yet love for their own traditions and language did not push the Catalans to a total rejection of the Castilian school. Even in the 'rationalist schools' of Ferrer i Guardia, the language of teaching was Castilian.

However, initiatives in favour of an extension of the Catalan language, both in the cultural field and in the school, developed greatly after the end of the nineteenth century. In 1889, the *Associació Protectora de l'Ensenyança Catalana* (Catalan Teaching Protection Association) was founded; it also promoted the teaching of the language in normal schools. In 1903, the first *Congrés Universitari Catalán* (Catalan University Congress) was held, and, some years later in 1906, the first *Congrés Internacional de la Llengua Catalana* (International Catalan Language Congress) was attended by more than 3000 people. The *Institut d'Estudis Catalans* (Institute of Catalan Studies), established in 1907 by Prat de la Riba, has been the centre for some brilliant research in and promotion of the Catalan language, helped by the founding of the Library of Catalunya. Of particular interest was the *Escola de Mestres* (School for Teachers), founded in 1906 by Joan Bardina, which worked towards the spread of a new pedagogical approach. Unfortunately, after only four years the centre was closed for financial reasons.[10]

The main centre for work in the preservation and extension of the Catalan language, however, was the primary schools. This was one of the objectives pursued by the *Mancomunitat de Catalunya*, created in April of 1914. At this time, the literacy level of Catalunya was very low, although in practical fact higher than that of the rest of Spain (in 1915, the illiteracy rate in Catalunya was only 48 per cent versus the overall Spanish rate of 59 per cent). Some believed that the lack of teaching in the native language in public and private schools was one of the main causes of illiteracy in Catalunya. Puig i Cadafalch wrote in 1915:

> The imposition at school of a language that we do not speak is the reason for our backwardness. In the schools, it is the cause of illiteracy and lack of education. There is, between the teacher and student, a kind of wall which discourages sympathetic communication: the wall of pretending continually to disguise the language. Now, when we know modern methodologies, we understand what a vexation it is for children to be sentenced to school for the conquered.[11]

The *Mancomunitat* continued the policies pursued earlier by the city council of Barcelona, which from 1908, aimed to create a network of public local schools. Among them, the *Escola del Bosc*, under the direction of Rosa Sensat and inspired by the New Education movement, had a wide influence in the region. Another interesting institution was the *Consell de Pedagogia* (Council for Educational Research), which was the organiser, in 1914, of the *Escola d'Estiu* (summer school) for teachers. Briefly, the *Mancomunitat* favoured many reforms in the educational field, but these reforms were necessarily limited. As Carbonell writes:

> . . . in that period of the *Mancomunitat*, action was undertaken particularly within the public realm, and experiments could be performed. We cannot correctly speak yet of a true Catalan education system because of the great political and economic limitations of the *Mancomunitat*, but we can indeed begin to speak of public and not just private action.[12]

However, the foundation of the *Mancomunitat de Catalunya* did not change the central government's position concerning the exclusive use of the Castilian language in Catalan schools. As we have seen, some provisions for a regular use of Catalan were implemented by the *Mancomunitat*, as well as by the Barcelona local authorities, but, with few exceptions, they found the same traditional hostility among members of the Spanish parliament and central government. Nevertheless, in 1918, an extra-parliamentary commission was established to study a proposed Statute of Autonomy for Catalunya, the text of which was to include some slight concessions for the use of Catalan (alongside Castilian) in the schools. Further events, though, did not permit the completion of this project, and later, with the arrival of Primo de Rivera's dictatorship, such an agreement became impossible until after proclamation of the second republic in 1931.

A rather different supervisory direction then emerged. The first Minister of Education of the republican government was Marcellino Domino, a Catalan who had earlier fought, as a member of the Spanish parliament, for the introduction of Catalan in the schools of the *Principat*. Consequently, a few days after the proclamation of the republic, a first *Decreto* approving such an introduction was promulgated on 29 April 1931, followed by another in July, regulating the teaching of Catalan in the normal schools of the region. As Lozano says, 'the teaching of Catalan was encouraged at all levels, basically in the sense of a 'Catalan reeducation' of adults and was particularly directed at the civil servants.[13] In order to illustrate the change of direction, it seems to me interesting to quote here some words from the introduction to the April 1931 decree:

> The Catalan language, banned and fought by the dictatorship, was already, before that regime, and is today, deeply as well as widely, the language in which one of the most emotional and creative people in the Hispanic land shows its awareness and expresses its thought. The more the mother tongue becomes an instrument of its culture, the more that culture becomes effective. That is to say: even if the attention focuses on Catalunya, because the problem there is the most apparent and the wrong the most obvious, any solution should not be restricted only to Catalan as a mother tongue, but instead should also be applied to other peninsular languages which are entitled to the same rights.[14]

In 1932, a Statute of Autonomy for Catalunya was published, whereby the *Generalitat* (the regional government) could control a large sector of the public services as its own responsibility. In the field of public education, however, the responsibilities actually surrendered by the central government were less than those claimed in theory. Control of primary education continued in the hands of the central government, and Castilian continued to be the compulsory language of instruction in primary and secondary schools. At university level, 'a kind of consortium was established on the basis of an autonomous system for the University of Barcelona, which was to be headed by a board of members, with equal proportions being nominated by both the central and regional governments'.[15]

The establishment of the autonomous university was surely one of the most interesting educational achievements of the new legal situation, but it was not the only one. The *Escola Normal de la Generalitat* was now able to conduct wide-ranging innovations, as could the *Institut Escola*, the *Pavellons pro-Infància*, the *Escoles d'Estiu* and various other centres, all of them under the overall direction of the *Consell de Cultura* (Cultural Council) of the *Generalitat*. As far as the Catalan language was concerned, many schools, especially in Barcelona, could now put the real work of catalanisation into practice, depending upon the local authorities and many other cultural activities (for example, summer schools, newsletters, broadcasting, etc.).

The beginning of the civil war, in 1936, did not end the educational improvements. On the contrary, a *Comité de l'Escola Nova Unificada* (Unified New School Committee) was created, with the aim of building up a genuinely Catalan educational system. Yet, the outcome of the civil war made a realisation of these political initiatives impossible.

Education in the Basque Country

As in the case of Catalunya, the basis of Basque nationalist or regionalist claims rests on two main supports: language and history. But there are many significant differences between the two areas in relation to these supports. We will analyse the linguistic aspect first, because a sound understanding of its nature is basic for any other consideration.

The Basque language, the Vascuence or Euskera, is not only a pre-Roman language, but also a pre-Aryan one. Its historical origin has been, and continues to be, very controversial; but this need not detain us here. What is important is that, in spite of many obstacles due mainly to the process of romanisation and castilianisation, and to its own difficult linguistic nature, Euskera has succeeded in surviving into the present day, even if it is spoken by only a small portion of the population (not more than a half million). Beltza gives some data on the quantitative growth of Basque speakers (in Spanish Basque country) during the period here analysed: in 1863, there were 610 000; in 1868, 391 000; in 1931, 400 000; in 1934, 570 000; and in 1936, 700 000.[16] The numbers for 1936 represented approximately 45 per cent of the population then living in Basque country. It must be added that a significant number of Basque speakers could not then and cannot today write in the Basque language, and also that the dialectical forms are numerous and have usually been an obstacle to the unification of Euskera.

Another feature of the Basque language is that its literary heritage is not very rich. Certainly, there are ancient written survivals of the language, but they are only small fragments. As Michelena says 'the Euskera's oldest literary monuments are fragments of songs referring to events of the fourteenth and, in particular, fifteenth centuries, which have been transmitted by historians of the sixteenth and seventeenth centuries'.[17] Only a few books appeared before the eighteenth century, when Father Larramendi, a Jesuit, published some works. As a matter of fact, most of the former writers in Euskera were clergymen,[18] although some opposition to an extension of the Basque language had also come in earlier years from some ecclesiastical authorities. For instance, the establishment of a bishopric in Vittoria (capital city of one of the three Basque provinces) produced a protest from a very influential abbot, who wrote to the Spanish authorities claiming that this measure would serve to maintain a language that was already sentenced to disappear:

> . . . the establishment of a diocese embracing the three Basque provinces does not come to revive it, an objective that seems to be the main one, of this measure. The Basque people having a bishop, a chapter, and parish priests who speak their language, they will cling more and more to it, recovering the lost area and making it a national language; and if we take into account that they will also develop a greater love for their traditions, *fueros* and habits, a different national-ity will probably be helped to arise, one which will also become a foundation of political segregation later . . .[19]

These words were indeed a premonition. From then on, and even earlier, the role played by the Catholic Church and its institutions in maintaining and improving Euskera was remarkable. While school teachers tried to be understood by pupils in Castilian, the priests made use of Euskera in both pastoral actions and in teaching catechism.

As in Catalunya, the restoration period opened new horizons in the linguistic as well as the political spheres. Referring to Euskera, Arturo Campion wrote in 1876:

> The language is the nationality . . . Sometimes, the only thing which remains from the old glory is a distorted, adulterated and rotten language; but times are progressing, the human conscience is waking up and a renewed nationality is sprouting from that ruinous language.[20]

But Campion wrote these words in Castilian, and in a newsletter published in Castilian, called *La Paz*. Great writers such as Pio Baroja or Unamuno, born in the Basque country, never wrote in Euskera, but always in Castilian. Certainly, literary exhibitions like those of the Catalan *Jocs Florals* were developed in the Basque country, but their cultural significance was much less profound.

In the field of schooling, there were very few reforms. At the secondary level, a *catedra* (chair) of Euskera was created in Bilbao in 1888 by the provincial authorities, with the aim of encouraging the study of a very old language more and more threatened with extinction. Both Unamuno and Arana were applicants for the post, but the open competition was won by a third scholar, a priest, R. M. Azkue. As a rule, the Basque bourgeoisie, especially the upper middle class, remained uninterested in the introduction of the Vascuence in school. Even in the rural areas, people preferred to send their children away from home to Spanish speaking schools located in more prosperous towns in order to secure for them a better education. Euskera never received the social support enjoyed by Catalan.

Furthermore, even the founder of Basque political nationalism, Sabino Arana, an expert in Euskera grammar and history, did not consider the language as the major distinguishing factor of the Basque nation. For him, race was primary. Euskera has, of course, always been of great importance, but it has never risen above second place.

> If one is not a patriot, to know Euskera does not mean anything. Euskera will not save the fatherland; patriotism will. Spread patriotism, and with this Euskera will be spread. If you spread Euskera as a language without a fatherland, the fatherland's enemies will spread with this.

In any case, Euskera was very important as an element of difference between the Basque and the Spanish people. Arana's words sound aggressively:

> The restoration of Euskera would produce a national difference, and this would be a constant danger for Spain . . .

and

> . . . the difference of language is the great way to preserve us against the contagion of the Spaniards.[21]

In fact, Euskera was very seldom taught in school before 1936. As we have already seen, it was only on occasions that priests would use Euskera to teach the catechism, and then not without opposition. As a rule, during the eighteenth century, the Basque municipal authorities required teachers to use Castilian at school and to avoid Euskera. In the nineteenth century, the centralised nature of control over schools implied the extension of Castilian as the official language of instruction. A major step in this direction was the foundation of normal schools for teachers in the main cities. B. Marin has made a detailed study of the creation and history of the most important of these schools – the normal school of Vizcaya – between the years 1865 and 1901. From her study, it becomes apparent that the teaching of Euskera was not included in the curriculum at all.[22] This absence, of course, provoked reactions.

The most significant was, perhaps, that in which a priest Resurrección M. de Azkue, played the main part. As mentioned above, he served as a professor of Euskera in the Institute of Vizcaya. He also created a Basque primary school in Bilbao, in 1896, with the name *Ikastetxea* ('school' in Euskera). It seems that Azkue had asked permission to teach Euskera to students of the normal school but that his request had been denied by the Director. One day in October 1899, he forced open the door of the primary school annexed to the normal school and began to teach Euskera. Not surprisingly, he was denounced to the police and the state authorities, but he repeated the action on several more days. As a result of this and other actions, the teaching of the Basque language in the normal school (namely in the primary school annexed thereto) was introduced. However, despite this, the daily situation in schools had not changed very much at the beginning of the twentieth century, nor, indeed, did it do so later.

As mentioned above, the second foundation stone (the first for some) of Basque nationalism/regionalism is history. As well as including an early link with the kingdom of Castile, this history also boasts of some degree of long standing governmental autonomy. Although the historical Basque provinces were incorporated into the Castilian crown at an early date (Alava and Guipuzcoa in 1200, and Vizcaya in 1379), they enjoyed a kind of political autonomy under the form of the *fueros* (territorial charters, written or oral law codes in which the political organisation and traditions of the people were collected) until 1839. Navarra, which most nationalists also consider a Basque province (Euskera is spoken in its northern part) enjoyed the same privilege. The rise of the liberal state was seen, in the Basque provinces, as a danger to the preservation of their *fueros* and traditions. In response, a vast movement of opposition to this liberal conception of the state was organized under the leadership of Prince Carlos, a movement which was consequently named *carlismo*, and which was defeated first in 1840 after a cruel civil war, and then again in 1876. The main consequence of these defeats was the loss of the *fueros*, which had become not only political and legislative charters but also, as the Basque poet Mañagorri wrote, 'our way of life' for the Basque people.[23] The old tree of Guernica, near to which the Basque assembly met and the *Señor* swore the *fueros*, became, and remains, an important symbol.

At the very roots of the Basque problem there is, therefore, a strong component of traditionalism, and rejection of the liberal and centralist state and its demands for the industrialisation of the country. The deeply Christian–Catholic feelings of the Basque people as a whole, and of the Basque *carlistas* in particular, must also be remembered. In fact, the founder of the Basque Nationalist party, Sabino Arana (1865–1903) was a *carlista* in his youth and a fervent believer throughout his life. One of his chief principles was *Jaungoikoa eta Legi Zarra*, ('God and the ancient law'). The nationalist Aranzandi, like many other nationalist pioneers a clergyman, wrote in 1930 that 'for Arana, the religious principle was both the motive and the correct principle'.[24] In a kind of Basque nationalist syllabus which was published at the beginning of the twentieth century, it was clearly stated that the Basque Nationalist party was, first of all, a Catholic party:

> Don't have any doubt: between seeing Euskadi free, but lost from the way of Christ, and seeing it enslaved, but loyal to Christ, the Basque Nationalist party would choose the second option.[25]

It seems clear that it was between 1876 and 1936 that Basque national consciousness began to spread among several social groups, especially the middle classes. Caro Baroja has summarised this situation in the following lines:

> Against dynastic governments, a nationalist party emerges, which in part takes some ideals from the defeated *carlismo* and in part produces other ideals itself. The Basque people working in literature, arts and science have a bigger role than ever, but not within the country nor within the political groups either, but as a single personality in Spain and abroad. Within the Basque country there is, on the other hand, a great interest in knowing the language, the customs, the anthropological features better. In short . . . the Basque country lives in a kind of exuberance and self-satisfaction, with a superiority complex, like the Catalan one, in comparison with the rest of Spain.[26]

However, it was impossible to pass from the euphoric expectations to concrete policy. Though, in the political field, the Nationalist party managed to obtain some seats in the Spanish parliament (seven in 1918 and 12 in 1933), this was not sufficient to open the way quickly to autonomous government and, consequently, to implementing its own educational policy. Certainly, some private actions could be taken, like the unofficial creation of a handful of *ikastolas* (pre-primary and primary schools) and some educational programmes for adults. The first congress of Basque studies, held in 1918, served as an opportunity for reflection on the necessity of developing a different educational policy. One of the main speakers, J.L. de Urabayen, offered the following description to the participants:

The people move away, instinctively, from those who do not under-stand them. Here you have the compelling and disgraceful percent-ages of illiteracy suffered by our Basque country (Alava, 32 per cent, Gipuzcoa, 40 per cent, Vizcaya, 40.79 per cent; and Navarra, 43.41 per cent). There seem to be many reasons for this situation of cultural poverty, especially the lack of schools. But certainly not the least one is the innate mistrust of those who don't understand him, by the peasant. In places where Euskera is used, this is the only reason; the absurdity is imposed upon them by law, or with the excuse of the law, and the *Euskaldunes* (Basque people) defend themselves the only way they can – by running away from the school.[27]

At the same congress, Urabayen expressed some ideas about factors in the selection of teachers in the Basque country. These included the notion of giving priority to native Basque candidates and the implementation of a test to demonstrate mastery of the Basque language.

The most important activities in the educational field were those planned and executed by the *Diputación de Vizcaya* (the Provincial Authorities) from 1917 onwards. In that year, a board of Public Education of Vizcaya was created, under the leadership of the nationalist Ramon de la Sota. The Board planned a massive pro-gramme of schooling, based on a classification of the provincial territory according to two different types: *euskaldun* areas, inhabited mainly by a Basque speaking population, and *elderdun* areas, which were mostly Castilian speaking. On the basis of a plan presented by the provincial deputy, Juan Gallano, the Board began the construc-tion of a hundred primary schools (named *Escuelas de Barriada*) in 1920. The new schools were designed to cover the educational needs of a population of which a large portion lived in *caserios* and which was widely scattered (in 1920, more than 35 per cent of the population inhabited areas with less than ten houses). In his book written in 1930 about these schools, the supervisor, Pedro Zufia, discussed the classification of the schools into two categories – 'A' for Basque speakers and 'B' for Castilian speakers. The main language, how-ever, was to be Castilian:

> Teaching in both categories will actually be in the Castilian language; but in those of category 'A', the teacher is obliged to use the Basque language as a means or way of teaching for all the pupils who are ignorant of Castilian, while bearing in mind that his task is actually to teach the Castilian language.[28]

It seems, however, that some conflicts arose between the first regulations for these schools, in 1921, and others imposed later, during the dictatorship of Primo de Rivera.

The first rules, published in 1921, differ substantially from the following ones concerning important aspects such as the list of subject matter, the teaching of Euskera and the teaching of regional history and geography. While the rules of 1921 set up a system of teaching entirely in Euskera, at least for the schools located in the Basque zones, in the later regulations, this orientation is replaced by that of teaching in Castilian.[29]

The province of Guipúzcoa also tried to put a similar programme into practice, but later events did not facilitate the required changes. In fact, unlike the Catalan case, a Statute of Autonomy was to be given to Euskadi only in October 1936, too late for the implementation of an effective linguistic and educational policy as the civil war had begun. Its first article stated:

> *Vascuence* will be, like Castilian, the official language of the Basque country, and, consequently, official general provisions emanating from the self-governing element will be written in both languages. In relationship with the Spanish state or its authorities, Castilian will be the official language.

One year later, the Statute was abolished by the military government. However, it was not possible to abolish a vast movement which had developed over a century and had deep roots in ancient history. As Gurruchaga writes:

> General Franco's regime was faced with a socio-symbolic capital which had been created in a long historical process, a code for the social workings of the Basque country which, after the military rising and the republican–nationalist faction's defeat, had to move into exile or become silent.[30]

The Case of Galicia

Among the three 'historical regions' endowed with their own language, Galicia has been undoubtedly the one closest to Spain as an entity in both general and educational policy. Yet an examination of the non-dominant linguistic groups in Spain would be incomplete without some reference to the Galician case, even though a brief one. From the beginning of the modern age, Galicia had been permanently linked to the kingdom of Castile and had never enjoyed any kind of autonomy, political or cultural. During the Middle Ages, though, the fuedal lords sometimes remained independent and, for some short periods, the country was, in fact, a separate kingdom, the kingdom of Galicia. However, this situation did not last long. In any case, in any given period, the distinguishing feature of the Galician region was its isolation with regard to the rest of Spain and, of course, to the central government. Galicia was a rather poor land, with a system of very small rural properties divided among the population (the *minifundio* or smallholding system), and it industrialised very late and to a limited extent. Even today, it remains mostly agricultural and rural. Referring to the end of the nineteenth century, Duran offers this description:

> Everything there reveals rusticity; the urbanisation process, very slight, goes largely unnoticed by the traveller, who sees Galicia exclusively as a land of *labregos* (peasants) and *mariñeiros* (seamen).[31]

Its population has often tended to emigrate to other Spanish regions and also abroad, especially during the nineteenth century and the first decades of the twentieth, when there was movement to South America. In all areas to which they emigrated Galicians continued to maintain a deep love for their motherland, characterised as a strong feeling of *morriña*. However, in spite of their language and their individual traits, they have always felt themselves to be Spanish and have usually shown a remarkable love and concern for Spain as a whole and for Spanish affairs. In fact, many Spanish politicians have been Galicians.

This could be one reason, among others, to explain the initial lack, and the late development, of regionalist or nationalist movements like those in Catalunya and the Basque Country. It is true that in 1846 there was a military revolt demanding Galician autonomy, but it had no popular support and was crushed immediately. Since then, no other similar event has ever taken place, save for the participation of some rural groups in the actions of the *carlistas*.

Nevertheless, a regionalist movement began to appear in the last decades of the nineteenth century, the main exponent being Alfredo Brañas, who, in 1889, published a work entitled *El regionalismo* ('Regionalism'). Traditionalist and conservative, Brañas aimed at an open decentralisation and a struggle against the local bosses' *caciquismo* (despotism), one of Galician society's centuries-old problems. However, no regionalist or nationalist political party was to be created until 1929, the year which saw the creation of the *Organización Republicana Gallega Autónoma*, (the 'Galician Autonomous Republican Organisation') which was the main promoter of a Statute of Autonomy for Galicia. The Statute was prepared, submitted to a popular consultation in Galicia in June 1936, and finally presented to the Spanish parliament for approval a month later. However, the Civil War had already begun and Galicia was soon in the hands of the insurgent troops.

Like the Catalans and Basques, the Galicians have their own language, spoken by the people since the Middle Ages in spite of the strong influence of Castilian through not only the administration, but also through intellectual and ecclesiastical circles as well. However, the Galician language has always maintained a particular prestige as a language of poetry, used by minstrels and troubadours in very ancient times. However a Galician literature only began to emerge in about 1850, mainly on the basis of poetic works, such as those of Pastor Diaz and Pintos. This was the period of *rexurdimento*, which paralleled the Catalan *renaixenca*. The movement reached its peak with Rosalia de Castro, an eminent Galician and Spanish poetess of the nineteenth century. She, and others such as Pondal and Curros Enriquez, contributed much to the understanding and prestige of the Galician language. Some prose writers (Rodriguez Castelao, Risco, Otero Pedrayo, etc.) worked in a similar way at the beginning of the twentieth century. The Galician language ceased to be exclusively an oral means of communication between *labregos* and *mariñeiros*. A claim for the protection and extension of the language, especially through schooling, began to gain ground. During the debates over the statute of autonomy, Alexandro Bóveda said:

> If the linguistic coexistence principle is not recognised, every seaman and every countryman will have the same idea about the Galician language as they have had till now – it is a language which should not be used and which is inferior.[32]

The traditionally backward situation of Galician schooling in contrast to that of the rest of Spain must also be mentioned. Referring to the last decades of the nineteenth century, Costa Rico enumerates some of the main problems of the Galician primary schools. There was a very low rate of attendance (especially among girls); there were bad and inappropriate buildings; few, badly qualified and poorly paid teachers; local Boards were deficient in their operation; and there was an open lack of interest on the part of the local and national authorities. Learning was especially difficult due to the use of Castilian as the sole language of instruction.[33] The lack of interest on the part of the local authorities, in these matters was unequivocally denounced, in 1875, by the rector of the University of Santiago de Compostela, Antonio Casares, who, in his report to the national authorities, wrote:

> After the 1868 September revolution, many municipal councils decided on the dissolution of the schools as one of the first steps; and even though most of them have been reestablished, the teachers have been badly received and poorly paid.[34]

This fact emphasises the deficient cultural background of the Galician municipal authorities and the unsuitability of an education system which could not manage to be of interest to either the authorities or the people. Unfortunately, the situation did not change much in the following decades. In 1940, Galicia was still a country which had yet to find new ways for educational as well as political, social and economic development.

Some Final Considerations

To sum up, it seems appropriate to draw attention to a few comparative points which are particularly significant. The general policy of the Spanish state concerning the three linguistic groups studied here can be considered as one of assimilation, even if the nationalist movements have often denounced it as a policy of domination. Certainly, there were some differences of policy at different historical periods, but the desire to make the cultural traits of the three regions conform to a general Spanish culture prevailed throughout the period analysed here. However, the necessity of implementing a policy of integration was also considered at certain times, especially at the end of the nineteenth century, during the First World War, and during the Second Republic, when Statutes of Autonomy were given to Catalunya and the Basque country. It could be added that, among the three regions, Catalunya has undoubtedly been the most vocal in her demands for autonomy and, probably as a result, the first to receive state recognition as a different cultural region. By contrast, Galicia has always been the most forgotten area in its cultural development.

In the educational field, it does not seem accurate to speak of discrimination in the state's relations to the three linguistic regions. The development of education, during the period here analysed, has been as good or as bad as in the rest of Spain. In fact, it can be said that because of several factors (historical, economic, geographical, etc.) the educational development of Catalunya and the Basque country was more successful than that of other Spanish Castilian regions, such as, for instance, Extremadura or Andalucia. If anything, Galicia has been the least favoured region in education, as in other aspects, but certainly not because of her language. On the other hand, a preferential treatment, such as demanded by Catalan and Basque nationalists (at least in respect of self government), was not allowed either. Would the educational situation have been better if a native monolingualism (Catalan, Basque, or Galician) had prevailed? It is difficult to say.

The unification process of the Spanish regions ended at the

moment that the Spanish empire began. An imperialist mentality had consequently pervaded many aspects of Spanish history, and had also been present in the field of education, both public and private (textbooks of history and geography, school songs, and cultural manifestations, etc.). Sometimes, the concept of the Spanish language as an imperial language has also played a role on the political scene, as, for instance, in the first years of Franco's regime (from 1937 onward), especially under the inspiration of *Falange Española* (Falangist Movement of Spain). In those years, it was not unusual to find, in some cities like Barcelona, official posters recommending 'Let's speak the language of the Empire'.

However, this does not necessarily indicate an imperialist approach in the relations between the Spanish state and the linguistic regions included in it. These regions had never been considered as colonies or as territorial possessions of Castile. On the contrary, they had contributed to Spanish history on a much more equal level, in particular, to the history of education. The quarrels were provoked when, from the end of the nineteenth century, the 'particularisms' of the regions (in Ortega's words) interfered with the powerful feelings of nationalism that existed in Spain as a whole. It is because of this that the simple idea of federalism was always rejected, or presented as potentially causing a breakdown of Spain as a compact nation–state. Several nationalisms had reacted by opposing this prevalent Spanish nationalism, demanding different structures and policies, such as segregation, federalism, cultural pluralism, and so on. In all these cases, the introduction of regional languages at school was one of the main objectives.

As far as Spanish majority groups are concerned, their attitudes and reactions changed progressively throughout the entire period analysed here, from the imposition of a full educational uniformity on every region, to more moderate policies. It can be said that all social groups and sectors contributed to this evolution. There were no substantial differences among the Spanish national political parties (including even the radical ones) on this matter. In fact, all of them, when in government, put policies of a centralist tendency into practice.

For its part, the Church adopted different attitudes according to circumstances of place and time. As a rule, it had favoured the evolution of greater regional consciousness and had helped the development of regional languages and cultures. Its role was extremely important in the emergence of Basque nationalist claims, as well as in the case of Catalunya. In Galicia, by contrast it had usually adopted positions closer to the Spanish centralist point of view, even though many clergymen had promoted substantial activities there in the fields of education and culture.

Turning to teachers and other educational staff, they largely reflected the training that they had received at the normal schools, from the middle of the nineteenth century when these institutions were created. This meant that their approaches were generally centralist and uniformist, even though many of them had originally come from the linguistic regions under discussion. However, an evolution in their attitudes can also be seen, especially in Catalunya.

Concerning these three minority linguistic groups, there were important differences among them in their cultural and educational relations with the Spanish majority. In the case of Galicia, we can see an attitude of acceptance of the Spanish general, as well as cultural and educational, policy, even though apathy and indifference arose in evident connection with the slow development of education in the country.

The leading movements in the Basque country, particularly through the *carlistas* wars, expressed a rejection of the pattern of industrial development represented by the liberal state, and a desire to recover the country's traditions of self-government and religiosity, the two objectives which were fully assumed by the nationalist tendencies from the end of the nineteenth century onwards. It was at this point that Basque nationalism orientated itself towards a clear cut rejection of Spanish life and culture as a whole, and that the educational aspects (including the adoption of Euskera as the language of instruction) began to emerge.

On the other hand, the regionalist and nationalist movements in Catalunya laid enormous stress on the priority of the cultural and linguistic aspects of development and they very seldom expressed a complete rejection of the Spanish state and culture, although adopting several forms of open opposition (as a rule). Furthermore, the development of education in Catalunya was earlier and broader than in the rest of Spain, and favoured many positive innovations and new forms of educational experience.

Notes

1. Ortega y Gasset, pp. 38–9.
2. *Ibid.*, p. 47.
3. Gil de Zarate, p. 117
4. Article 2, Concordat of 1845, in *Bases documentales* II, p. 165.
5. *Colección Legislativa* (1868), p. 416 ff.
6. Quoted by Ferrer i Gironés, pp. 80–1.
7. Puelles Benítez, p. 276.
8. Pers i Ramona, p. 180.
9. Hina, pp. 157 and 154.
10. Delgado.
11. Quoted by Balcells, p. 171.

12. ICE, p. 12.
13. Lozano, p. 245.
14. *Colección Legislativa* (1931–1932), p. 132.
15. Balcells, p. 251.
16. Beltza, pp. 141–2.
17. Michelena, p. 40.
18. Sarasola, pp. 59 and 183.
19. Letter of the Abbot of Santo Domino de la Calzada to the Minister of Justice, August 1861, in García de Cortázar, pp. 119–20.
20. Quoted by Elorza, p. 28.
21. Arana, pp. 137 and 403–4.
22. Marin, pp. 116–25.
23. Fernandez Albadalejo, p. 371.
24. Quoted by Corcuera, p. 320.
25. Ibero, p. 73
26. Caro Baroja, p. 31.
27. J. L. Urabayen, 'El maestro de la escuela vasca' (A teacher for the Basque school), First Congress of Basque Studies, 1918, full text in Marin, pp. 215–27.
28. Zufia, *Las escuelas de barriada*, p. 27.
29. Arrien, p. 16.
30. Gurruchaga, p. 128.
31. Durán, p. 5.
32. Magarinos, p. 72.
33. Costa Rico, pp. 192–3.
34. Quoted by Suárez Pazos, p. 319.

Select Bibliography

Arana, S. (1965), *Obras completas* (Complete Works). Buenos Aires.
Arpal, J. (ed.) (1983), *Educatción y sociedad en el País Vasco* (Education and society in the Basque Country), San Sebastián.
Arrien, G. (1985), 'Las escuelas de barriada de la Diputación de Vizcaya' ('District schools of the Province of Vizcaya'), in *Kimu*, 9–10.
Balcells, A. (1983), *Historia Contemporánea de Cataluña* (A Contemporary History of Catalunya), Barcelona.
Beltza, E. (1976), *Historia del nacionalismo vasco* (A History of the Basque Nationalism), San Sebastián.
Caro Baroja, J. (1984), *El laberinto vasco* (The Basque Labyrinth), San Sebastián.
Carr, R. (1968), *España 1808–1939* (Spain 1808–1939), Barcelona.
Castro, A. (1954), *La realidad histórica de España* (The historical reality of Spain), Mexico.
Colección Legislativa de Instrucción Primaria (Legislative Collection of Public Instruction), 1856, 1868, Madrid.
Collección Legislativa de Instrucción Pública (Legislative Collection of Public Instruction), 1931–1932, Madrid.
Corcuera Atienza, J. (1979), *Orígenes, ideología y organización del nacionalismo vasco 1876–1904* (Origins, ideology and organization of the Basque nationalism), Madrid.
Costa Rico, A. (1983), 'Instituciones para la formación de los maestros gallegos en los finales del siglo XIX' (Centers for the training of Galician teachers at the end of the XIX century), in *Historia de la Educación*, 2.
Durán, J.A. (1976), *Agrarismo y movilización campesina en el país gallego, 1875–1912* (Agrariarism and rural mobilisation in the Galician country), Madrid.

Elorza, A. (1978), *Ideologías del nacionalismo vasco* (Ideologies of Basque nationalism), San Sebastián.

Fernández Albadalejo, P. (1974), *La crisis del Antiguo Régimen en Guipúzcoa*, Madrid.

Ferrer i Gironés, F. (1986), *La persecució política de la llengua catalana* (The political persecution of the Catalan language), 2nd edn., Barcelona.

García de Cortázar, F. and Montero, M. (1984), *Historia Contemporánea del País Vasco* (Contemporary History of the Basque country), San Sebastián.

Gurruchaga, A. (1985), *El código nacionalista vasco durante el franquismo* (The Basque nationalist statute during Franco's regime), Barcelona.

Hina, H. (1986), *Castilla y Cataluña en el debate cultural, 1714–1939* (Castile and Catalunya in the cultural debate), Barcelona.

de Ibero, E. (1906), *Ami Vasco* (Basque friend), Buenos Aires.

ICE (Institut of Educational Sciences) (1984), *L'obra pedagógica d'Alexandre Galí* (Alexandre Galí's educational work), Barcelona.

Lozano, C. (1980), *La educación republicana 1931–1939* (Republican education), Barcelona.

Macías Picavea, R. (1899), *El problema nacional: hechos, causas, remedios* (The national problem: events, causes, remedies), Madrid.

Magariños, A. (1984), *Quiénes somos los gallegos* (Who are we the Galicians), Barcelona.

Marín, B. (1985), *La Escuela Normal de Maestros de Vizcaya 1865–1901* (The Normal School for Teachers in Vizcaya), Bilbao.

Michelena, L. (1960), *Historia de la literatura vasca* (History of the Basque literature), Madrid.

Ortega y Gasset, J. (1983), *España invertebrada* (Invertebrate Spain), 1st edn. 1922, Madrid.

Pérez Vilariño, S. (1979), *Dependencia y discriminación escolar en Galicia* (School dependency and discrimination in Galicia), Madrid.

Pers i Ramona, M. (1857), *Bosquejo histórico de la lengua y literatura catalanas, desde su origen hasta nuestros días* (Historical outline of the Catalan language and literature), Barcelona.

Puelles Benítez, M. (1980), *Educación e ideología en la España contemporánea* (Education and ideology in Contemporary Spain), Madrid.

Sánchez Albórnoz, C. (1957), *España, un enigma histórico* (Spain, a historical enigma), 2 Vols, Buenos Aires.

Sarasola, I. (1976), *Historia de la literatura vasca* (History of the Basque literature), Madrid.

Suárez Pazos, M. (1983), 'El campesino gallego y su rechazo a la escuela primaria 1868–1874' (The Galician countryman and his rejection of the primary school) in *Historia de la Educación*, 2.

Vintró, E. (ed.) (1985), *L'ensenyament* (Education), Barcelona.

Zufía, P. (1930), *Las escuelas de barriada en Vizcaya* (District schools in Vizcaya), Bilbao.

Urabayen, J.L. 'El maestro de la escuela vasca' (A teacher for the Basque school). Full text collected by Mann, B. (ed.).

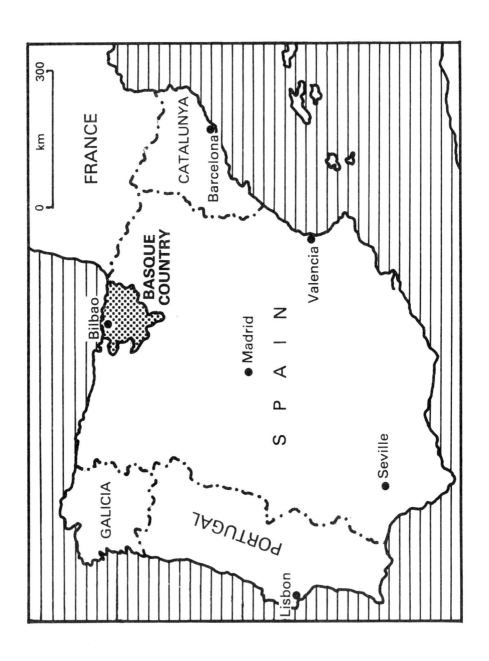

Map 13.1   Galicia, Catalunya and Basque Country

14 Education and Modernisation in a Multi-Ethnic Society: Bosnia, 1850–1918

ROBIN OKEY

The Balkan provinces of Bosnia and Herzegovina (hereafter referred to under the name of the former and larger) had close ties with other Serbo–Croat speaking provinces under alien rule in the years of this study, but their unique ethno-religious make-up and separate political status justify treatment apart. Bosnia alone in the nineteenth century passed from Ottoman to Habsburg rule which not only gave it a role in two of the great multi-national empires with which we are concerned but also meant that 1878 – the year of the transfer – in some ways saw the reversal of dominance that other European societies experienced in 1918. In *some* ways, because, as will be shown, the Bosnian Muslims were themselves subordinate to the metropolitan power in the earlier period and retained something of their privileged position in the later one. More significant for the evolution of Bosnia's cultural politics was that the Orthodox Serbs, the province's relative majority, remained unequivocally non-dominant throughout. This turning point around the year 1878 will be observed below.

Schooling in Bosnia under Ottoman rule, 1850–78

Bosnia in 1850 was reputed to be the most backward province of European Turkey. Sarajevo, the capital of this province of some 51 000 sq km lay amid mountains several days march from the Austrian frontier – Bosnia had no paved roads till 1862. Social relations appeared equally primitive. The one and a quarter million inhabitants (who rose to two million by 1911) lacked any kind of common civic spirit despite a common language and origin, but were divided into three bitterly antagonistic factions, for whom, as in the Middle Ages, religion prescribed ethnic identity. Muslims, nearly two-fifths of the population made up the free peasantry, the great bulk of urban artisans and the aristocracy, which presided over the semi-servile

319

Christian *raya* (subject class). Orthodox Serbs, just over two-fifths, had a narrow mercantile elite which distinguished them from the less numerous and poorer Catholics, whose only leaders were the Franciscan clergy. The Serbs were also distinguished by their national name. Catholics called themselves 'Latins' not Croats, while the Muslims dubbed themselves Turks or Bosniaks.

Yet around 1850 the forces of change were already beginning to lap the shores of this redoubt of traditionalism. Adjacent, in autonomous Serbia and awakening Croatia, the architects of the nation building process looked to Bosnia as a natural unit in 'national unification', whose possession would, incidentally, give either Serbs or Croats a dominant position in the south Slav world. In 1844 a secret plan of the Serbian government had made Bosnia the chief object of a network of nationalist agents in 'unredeemed' lands, often recruited among Orthodox clergy and teachers, and the prosperous merchants mentioned above. As the south Slav movement grew the Habsburg monarchy moved in to control it through consular activity, diplomatic pressure and funding of Christian, mainly Catholic, activity. Meanwhile, the defeat of autonomist Bosnian Muslim rebels in 1852 gave the *Tanzimat* (reforming, restructuring) regime in Constantinople central control over Bosnia for the first time in centuries. Between them these three interacting tendencies determined that the dominant theme in Bosnian history from the outset of our period would be the pressure to modernise. What gave the modernisation process its distinctive form in Bosnia, however, was that it had been initiated by the non-dominant Christians, not the Ottoman state, let alone the locally dominant Bosnian Muslims who, after 1852, sulkily opposed all *Tanzimat* innovation. For these innovations, which were essentially a response to European pressure and involved unfamiliar concepts of civil and religious equality, ran up against the *millet* (ethno-religious communal administrative institution) idea of the traditional Ottoman state, in which separate religious groups were left free to run their own affairs and the Muslim *millet* was more equal than others.

Education played a central role in the modernising ideology of nineteenth century Bosnian Christians. The Herderian based Romantic nationalism of the Serb and Croat movements stressed cultural development through the mother tongue. Only 'Enlightenment', its *Leitmotiv*, could raise up peasant societies from ignorance and poverty to fulfil their rightful destiny. The assumed propensity of Balkan Christians for European progress as opposed to oriental–Islamic backwardness was what legitimised these movements in their own eyes and those of western observers. Teachers were, then, by definition 'cultural workers' of the front rank. The 1840s saw the start of modern schooling among Bosnian Christians, with monastic educational traditions yielding to schools organised into separate years, with graded, often textbook material, qualified teachers, a broader syllabus; sometimes even school funds. Appearing at first in Sarajevo and the Herzegovinian capital Mostar, such schools gradually spread to the five other regional centres and to many of the 42 district towns. By 1878 there were 56 Orthodox and 54 Catholic schools in Bosnia with some 4400 boy and 1400 girl pupils. In fact, 113 Orthodox schools had been founded, more than half of them in villages, but these latter were particularly unstable and shortlived.

Few that survived were even as well organised as suggested in the model outlined above. Among Catholic schools only the nine run by the Order of Merciful Sisters from Zagreb had qualified teachers; the remainder were kept by Franciscans. Many Serbs teachers also came from outside Bosnia or were trained there, in teachers' training colleges in Belgrade, or Sombor in the Vojvodina. A training college/ *cum* seminary functioned briefly at Banjaluka in Bosnia in the 1860s. Only in Sarajevo did the Serbs have a *realka* or the first four years of a secondary school, thinly attended. Post-primary education was also available in Franciscan monasteries but only to novices who completed their training abroad. That said, the most dynamic members of the Christian enlightenment were teachers or teaching clergy: for the Catholics, men like the Franciscan Ivan Frano Jukić, editor of *The Bosnian Friend* (1850–1); and for the Orthodox, the monk Pelagić, founder of the Banjaluka college or the Dalmation born Teofil Petranović, Director of the Sarajevo Serb schools from 1865 to 1869, Serbian agent, member of the patriotic *Omladina* movement and first publisher of Bosnian folk poetry.

By contrast, the education of Muslim children remained wholly traditional, though broader based. In 1877, 917 *mektebs* (elementary religious schools) were teaching 28 000 boys and 12 000 girls to read the Koran in Arabic; about 40 *medresse* (theologically orientated secondary schools) gave a secondary education in religious subjects and Arabic grammar. Instruction was not organised into a fixed number of annual classes, but was individual and of no fixed duration. Any teaching aids were in Turkish or Arabic. Only a very few Muslims could write their mother tongue in Arabic or Cyrillic script. The 1860s, however, saw a change in government attitudes. Governor Osman Pasha, 1860–8, acting in the spirit of the *Tanzimat*, began to attend prize givings in Christian schools. A provincial printing press was launched which produced three Cyrillic textbooks. A *rüshdiye* or secondary school with mixed secular–religious syllabus on Constantinople lines was set up in Sarajevo, open to all confessions. Attempts to rationalise religious instruction in so-called Reform *Mektebs*, however, failed. In 1869 an imperial school law ordered local authorities to found state schools with modern syllabuses and Turkish as the main language of instruction. Teachers and textbooks in private schools were also to be subject to official approval. These provisions represented a total breach with the *millet* tradition. They aroused bitter protests from Bosnian Serbs when, in 1874, an imperial rescript tried to enforce them in Bosnia, particularly by challenging the role of the merchant dominated Orthodox Serb communes which, in larger places, maintained church and school, appointing the teacher and frequently the parish priest.

After 1878 Serb nationalists were frequently to contrast Austrian 'tyranny' with the cultural autonomy they had enjoyed under the Turks. As can be seen this was a half truth at best. From the 1860s a clash was already developing between the instincts of a modernising state and the aspirations of non-dominant Bosnian Christians. The impact of the clash was blurred only by the weakness of the Ottoman reform movement. Lacking an effective administrative structure, let alone a modernising social base in its Balkan provinces, it could only operate through intermittent coercion rather than as the mediator of steady socio-economic change. The incompetence of the seven governors who followed Osman Pasha between 1869 and 1874 showed the extent to which his had been personal achievements. Nevertheless, the expulsion of Petranović in 1869, the imprisonment of Pelagić and others, the transfer of a leading Serb school to a government commissioner in 1875 and the pressure on Serb schools to describe themselves and their language as Bosnian rather than Serb all showed the incompatibility between government and community views of the cultural progress wished by both. Under the altogether more systematic Austrian administration these tensions could only get worse.

Schooling in Austrian Bosnia, 1878–1918[1]

Goals and Assumptions

Austrian educational ideology in Bosnia reflected the complex nature of the Habsburg state. On the one hand, it was simply an old fashioned dynastic structure, needing Bosnia as a strategic wedge against Serbian and Montenegrin expansionism which might unduly impress its own south Slav subjects. On the other hand, this dynastic structure had developed subtle mechanisms to maintain loyalty against seemingly more potent ethnic pulls. Whereas the Ottoman state was poorly developed and, as the Turkish bias of the 1869 school law showed, not effectively multi-national, the Habsburg monarchy inherited from Josephinian enlightened despotism a formidable bureaucratic tradition, embedding multi-cultural elements that partly justified supra-national pretensions. But in 1867 it had undergone a further transformation. Yielding to Magyar nationalism it had turned itself into Austria–Hungary, the Dual Monarchy, in which Franz Joseph acknowledged two constitutional states, dominated by Austro–German liberals and Magyar gentry respectively. These three elements, the dynastic, the supra-national, and the Austro–Magyar, were together to condition the nature of Bosnian government.

The translation of these factors into governmental forms was no easy matter, particularly since Austria–Hungary's mandate at the Congress of Berlin left the Turks nominal suzerainty. Essentially, however, the decision to occupy had been the emperor's, and Bosnia was administered outside the dualist framework by the Austro–Hungarian Joint Finance Ministry, subject to provisions of Austrian and Hungarian laws of 1880. The fact that till 1910 it was governed in an absolutist manner also helped the administration to retain something of the spirit of the pre-compromise common monarchy. Between 1878 and 1918 thousands of Croat, Habsburg Serb and Slovene migrants to Bosnia, together with Czechs, Slovaks, Germans, Magyars, Poles and Ruthenians gave the province a modern administrative infrastructure and transformed the oriental appearance of the larger towns. Operating with the public in Serbo–Croat, internally in German, they provided *prima facie* justification for the 'civilising mission' by which the Dual Monarchy legitimised its presence on Bosnian soil. The Dual Monarchy's unacknowledged goal in Bosnia was therefore to frustrate south Slav, particularly Serb nationalism. However, its acknowledged goal, and the means thereto, was to win Bosnians for the Habsburg idea. 'Assimilation' or 'amalgamation' with the rest of the Dual Monarchy were terms occasionally used by the authorities. This did not mean, of course, assimilation into a dominant national culture, but adjustment to a political system having its own internal communications network and certain common values, like reverence for the dynasty, and an Austrian way of doing things. 'Integration' is the term which will be applied to the process here.

Yet the Habsburg idea had become profoundly ambiguous by 1878, as has been seen. The radical, meliorative drive of Josephinist bureaucracy, though not wholly extinguished, had long been over-laid by conservatism. The nineteenth century was an age of reform from below, not above: the impulse to change had switched from enlightened despots to mobilising nationalisms, the strongest of which had forced the dynasty to give up some of its power. Did the 1867 Compromise mean that Habsburg government's traditional claim of evenhandedness towards all its peoples was being belied in practice, even as it was used to distinguish between Turkish and Austrian performance in Bosnia? The first years of occupation to 1880, and to a lesser extent 1882, saw a covert battle between radical and conservative interpretations of the Habsburg legacy. In this earliest phase, echoes of Josephinist reforming zeal came from Croat officials, initially advantaged because of language and proximity. The deputing of non-commissioned officers to organise village schools, ambitious plans for a school law providing for a state educational system with six *Kreis* (circuit) inspectors, 60 new schools in the first year and 30 annually thereafter, were combined with Croatian motifs and frequent disregard for the sensibilities of Orthodox Serbs or Muslims in matters of script, religion and terminology. Vienna agreed only to one inspector, a Yugoslav minded Dalmatian Serb who quickly resigned when he saw his plans would not be implemented. In 1880 the post was discontinued.

Meanwhile, the provincial government in Sarajevo fought persistently for an interconfessional system of schooling against the scepticism of a clericalising Austrian government and the Education Minister in Hungary, where 80 per cent of schools were confessional. In sensitive border areas where Serb schools were being reopened after the insurrection, it sought to assimilate them to the state schools, by offering grants and teachers or simply reclassifying them as schools of the political rather than the religious commune. The leading communes of Sarajevo and Mostar complained of interference with traditional autonomies and found many of their teachers expelled. Incited by Mostar Serbs against Catholicising tendencies in the schools, the Serbs along the Montenegrin border rose into a revolt for this and other reasons, early in 1882 which took 70 000 men to put down. This was the end of Croatian-tinged reformism's unequal struggle with the more conservative interpretation of cultural mission as represented by the dominant German and Magyar elites in the empire. After all, as Foreign Minister Andrássy told British Prime Minister Disraeli in 1878, Austria was 'a conservative, non-Slav state'.[2]

The essence of this interpretation was distilled by the Serbo–Croat speaking Magyar Benjamin von Kállay who as Austro–Hungarian Joint Finance Minister had oversight of Bosnian affairs from 1882 till his death in 1903. Basically, Kállay reduced the cultural mission to two things which the Turks had patently failed to provide: confessional equality and an ordered administration. This approach had many advantages. It limited expenditure on a province which Austro–German and Magyar liberals had not wanted to occupy and which therefore was statutorily obliged to fund its administration from its own undeveloped resources. It avoided reforms like the redemption of the *kmets* (semi-servile Christian peasantry) which, besides being costly, would have undermined the position of the Muslim landowners whom Kállay saw as potentially the most important prop of his regime. (The Bosnian Muslims, or a part of them, therefore retained for a while the ambiguous status of local elite under metropolitan rule that they had had in the last decades of Turkish power.) In particular, by setting the ethnic problem in a religious context, it implied that Bosnia's ethnic groups were essentially confessional and not national bodies. The consequence, for Kállay, was that the state arrogated to itself the sphere of secular modern life and institutions. In his philosophy of history – Kállay was both an intellectual and a historian – religious exclusivism was an essentially oriental feature, entailing the orient's incapacity for state building beyond the level of oriental despotism. It was Rome which had developed the western concept of a common civil law which, in treating all alike, conferred upon them equal status.[3] The Serbian nexus between Orthodoxy and Serbdom was, therefore, for Kállay an oriental presumption which contrasted with the multi-ethnic political nationhood of his native Hungary. To this neo-liberal bow to western civic principles, albeit in highly conservative form, Kállay added an adherence to a modified economic liberalism. While preserving the Bosnian land settlement for the Muslims *Begs* (landowners), he opened up Bosnia to Austro–Hungarian capital, looking to socio-economic processes rather than direct state spending to bring about a gradual westernisation of the province.

The enduring features of the occupation's educational policy were shaped under Kállay, and subordinate to this framework. Interestingly, there was to be no school law (and was not till 1913). Kállay wished to feel his way. He combined an ultimately rigid philosophy with considerable tactical flexibililty, linked to a paternalism which eschewed bureaucratic dealings with backward people. The decision in favour of a state system of intercommunal schools alongside confessional, was relatively liberal, by contrast with British policy in Cyprus where the regime contented itself with supervising existing confessional schools. A clinching factor was that only such schools would be attended by Muslims. The fact that there were to be relatively few of these intercommunal schools was conservative, however. The late twentieth century concept of education in developing countries as a force for social mobilisation and change, while shared by Slav elements in the early Bosnian administration, was alien to the majority Austrian view. According to this, education was to service the needs of the existing society and only cautiously to anticipate them. The Bosnian administration's greatest fear was of a 'half-educated proletariat' lacking appropriate job outlets.[4] The inter-communal state school was to represent the higher Austrian civic principle, gradually leavening a society still, however, envisaged and governed in confessional terms. What did this mean in practice? The Bosnian education system was tailored to specific tasks and fashioned hierarchically, with inputs increasing at the secondary and tertiary levels, where a serviceable class of well educated Bosnians was to be produced. There was no attempt to generalise primary education. Of the 1888 budget's total expenditure of £756 356, 20 per cent went on the *gendarmerie*, three and a half per cent on education and less than one per cent on primary schools.[5] Not till 1886 was a teachers' training college established and a regular sum inserted in the annual budget for primary school buildings; not till 1892 were teachers' career circumstances regulated and arrangements made for periodic increments and pensions. Bosnia had 40 state primary schools in 1882–3, 143 in 1891–2 and 200 in 1899–1900 with 2428, 11 177 and 22 486 pupils respectively. The proportion of these to all primary school pupils rose from 31 per cent to 62 per cent to 74 per cent in these years.

These figures represented, of course, a great advance over pre-occupation circumstances and should be considered against the financial background. While in Austria primary schools were mainly a local expenditure, Bosnian poverty made regulations of 1880 to this effect impracticable and forced the provincial government to shoulder the building and salary costs, with local communities often able to pledge little more than fuel for heating. Measured against British educational expenditure in Egypt which in 1891 was budgeted only 70 000 out of 5 237 000 Egyptian pounds, the Bosnian administration appears generous. Yet this is not the most relevant comparison.

In 1905 there were still twice as many schools per head of population in Serbia as in Bosnia, and four times as many in Hungary. Fiscal reasons alone cannot explain the discrepancy. Kállay did not stint money on priorities. Nor were cultural factors decisive. In 1883 the provincial government reported that its school building programme 'would also have lively support from the native population, since the need for education and schools is already felt by them, especially among the Orthodox'.[6] By the next decade communities were waiting several years after the processing of their applications and agreement of contractual obligations before being included in the annual building programmes. The growth of state schools in the 1880s had been due in fair part to conversion of confessional schools. The fact was that the regime was not concerned to generalise primary education. It showed urgency only in connection with particular target groups of political interest to it.

Serbs under the influence of a confessional school were one of these. The provincial government's educational proposals of 1884 recommended government schools in four places where the Orthodox commune had already built one; in six others which had had confessional schools before the occupation; in a border village where children were visiting the adjacent Serbian school; and in a Herzogovinian border town where the Serb school had just ceased to function. The same pattern recurred in its 1885 proposals. By 1886 at least 29 Serb schools had become state schools or seen a state school go up beside them. In one case in the Herzegovinian border town of Gacko, the Serb school was surrounded by *gendarmes* at night and the teacher, who had planned a boarding school to undercut government competition, was led away to Sarajevo. By contrast, government schools were rarely set up in Serb areas with no schools. In 1883–4 Orthodox Serbs made up 55 per cent of all primary school pupils in the province, Catholics 35 per cent and Muslims only 5 per cent. By 1891–2 the figures were 48, 33 and 14 per cent respectively. By 1911–12 Muslims were up to 14 per cent and Catholics to 37 per cent, but the Orthodox Serbs had fallen below their share of the population to 42 per cent.

The rise in Muslim attendance owed much to official efforts to sustain this community as a counterweight to the Serbs. Kállay spoke later of the 'intrigues, persuasion and pressure' exercised on Muslims in early years to get them to school. The clever revival of the name *rüshdiye* for a special kind of elementary school, combining oriental subjects with 'the 3 Rs', that opened from 1883 on, in the major towns, was a case in point. That this was to be only a stage towards a fully western education, however, became plain through his insistence that the Reform *Mektebs* springing up in the 1890s should teach just religious subjects, not Serbo–Croat, thus serving as stepping stones and not rivals to the state primary schools. The restriction to one *Dar-ul-Muallim* (Muslim teacher training college) also showed Kállay's determination only to train people who would be sure of employment, and reluctance to be involved in reform of the Muslim *medresse*. An effectively Muslim state girls' school in Sarajevo resumed initiatives on that front. Muslim boys, however, enjoyed positive discrimination in state secondary as well as primary schools. Of 30 scholarships to the Sarajevo *gymnasium* in 1895, 20 went to the 24 Muslims among the 145 applicants.

More was spent on a new building for the Sarajevo *gymnasium*, founded in 1879, than on all primary school building throughout the 1880s. Though secondary schools took the lion's share of the education budget they were not numerous. Kállay resisted calls for a second *gymnasium*, in Mostar, till 1894 and there were still only four in 1914. Political motives again played a part. Higher girls' schools were set up in Mostar and Sarajevo to counter the Russian girls' school in Cetinje and a request for a Mostar Serb equivalent was rejected. Political motives also could be linked to vocational. The nine commercial schools, for example, were to distract Serb merchant sons from the humanistic *Gymnasiums* where they might abandon useful trade for nationalist punditry. Craft schools were a sop to the crisis caused by Austrian competition among Muslim artisans. The Sarajevo technical middle school was founded, for example, to provide prospective 'contractors, clerks, contractor supervisors, foremen, gamekeepers, head gamekeepers and in certain cases where practicable . . . forest officials in the middle ranks of the forestry service'.[7]

However, the well equipped secondary schools were also intended to win the allegiance of able young Bosnians. A relatively lavish scholarship policy induced these into Bosnia's middle schools, and thence – some 30 a year – to higher education in the Dual Monarchy. Between 1884 and 1897 the government spent 495 000K on training only 21 Bosnians to university graduation level. But a higher girls' school training, too, cost 10 000K and a technical middle school forestry student 8300K a year, in a society where the basic annual primary teacher's salary was 1000K!

For those who received this expensive education, the authorities went to great trouble to see that it was ideologically sound. Kállay scrapped plans to revamp Croatian textbooks to Bosnian use and decided to produce his own. His Sarajevo Provincial Government wrote in 1884 of the 'immense political significance of emancipating this province from Croat or Serb influence' through 'creation of a specific Bosnian self-consciousness' and its 'sanctioning in the textbooks'.[8] The effort to foster a Bosnian identity that was neither Serb nor Croat was continued for 20 years, during which time the term 'Orthodox Serb' was permitted only in a religious context. The official phrase was 'oriental Orthodox' and official forms sent also to Serb schools referred to the mother tongue as Bosnian.

It was not always easy to meet the regime's criteria. The first draft for a secondary school reading book, prepared by a Serb, was rejected by the authorities because it failed to provide a balance between passages from German and Hungarian literature and from Serbian and Croatian literature, it did not use the Arabic classics sufficiently, underplayed Bosnian themes and cited the official Serbian version of the Bible![9] Geography which bred 'love of the homeland' and a sense of it as a 'constituent part' of the Dual Monarchy, might be relatively straight-forward. History was not straightforward, desirable as it might be 'in the presentation of . . . past centuries always to stress those factors calculated to give a correct impression of the importance and influence of the monarchy, particularly in its relations with Bosnia–Herzego-vina'.[10] A history of Bosnia did not appear till 1893, and a history text on the Middle Ages not till 1901. Even then it was nearly recalled when it was discovered that proof correction had failed to remove a reference to medieval Croatia's *samostalnost* (independence) *vis-à-vis* Hungary. Officials spent anxious hours debating whether *samostalnost* might be interpreted as autonomy, rather than independence. Kállay, however, forbade extempore history lessons based on pictures in school readers before the authorised histories arrived, saying Bosnian teachers could not be relied upon.

One link with the Dual Monarchy was, of course, the German

language, teaching of which was compulsory for two hours a week in the last two years of urban elementary schools till 1891, and voluntary thereafter. In the secondary schools it was compulsory and heavily represented; on a par with Serbo–Croat at nearly four hours a week through the eight years of the classical *gymnasiums* and outweighing it in the Banjaluka *Realschule* (non-classical commercially orientated secondary school) and the higher girls' schools. There was a German language cadet school in Sarajevo, founded in 1879.

The Non-Dominant Response: the Serb and Muslim Movements for Cultural Autonomy

The most receptive of native Bosnians to the government's determined course were the once despised Catholics. In a society identifying ethnicity and religion these now felt something of the aura of dominance, swelled as they were by thousands of often high ranking migrants from the Dual Monarchy. By 1912 Catholics slightly outnumbered Orthodox in the province's *gymnasiums*. In the new circumstances Franciscans, sometimes grumpily, transferred their primary schools to the state sector in the 1880s and concentrated their educational efforts at developing two private *gymnasiums*, one each in Bosnia and Herzegovina. A third Catholic *gymnasium*, that was, however, open to all, was run with state aid by the Jesuits in Travnik. Other religious orders entered Bosnia to join the Merciful Sisters in maintaining confessional primary schools, of which there were 31 with 3164 pupils, mainly girls, in 1912–13. Educated Catholics developed a Croat rather than a Bosnian ideology, but Croat nationalism exercised the Serbs more than it did the regime.

The Orthodox Serbs, indeed, against whom government policy was mainly directed, reacted sharply. With their developing commercial elite, national awareness and the tight knit structure of their parochial 'Church and school communes', they were in a position to challenge the regime's bosnianising course. Some of the chief battles were fought out in the sphere of schooling. As the head of the Sarajevo provincial government reported in 1897:

> The sincerity owed to the respected Ministry obliges me to confess that the provincial government does not take up a favourable attitude to the oriental Orthodox confessional schools . . . Here as in all Balkan countries the oriental Orthodox school bears much less a confessional than an outspokenly national character and is in the first instance a political tool to educate the young people in a generally extreme direction determined by the leading circles.[11]

The authorities had expected that faced with the competition of efficient state schools the less well equipped Serb confessional schools would wither away, as indeed they did in Croatia–Slavonia after the Croatian school law of 1874 and as the Bosnian Franciscan primary schools did after 1878. Wretched and fluctuating as were the circumstances of most Serb rural schools, their urban schools were almost on a governmental level and exercised a leadership role.

The failure of the 1882 revolt only confirmed educated Serbs' resort to the one weapon remaining – cultural nationalism, the unspoken programme of the influential literary periodical *Bosanska Vila*, permitted to appear in Sarajevo from 1886:

Canons and guns have had their day . . .;
today peoples and countries are conquered
by far more convenient, but also
far more dangerous means – culture and
books.[12]

The argument that national culture was for the most advanced countries the tool of success – 'look how in Germany all training is put on a national footing'[13] – proved inspirational for people who felt their own identity threatened by discrimination and denationalisation. As in all nationalisms there was a paranoid element. Serb complaints about the Roman script, for instance, appeared to suggest that it was being imposed on them. In fact regulations prescribed, outside the compulsory learning of both scripts, the use of Cyrillic books for Orthodox and Roman script books for Catholics. What Serbs resented was that the neutral Muslims were allocated books in Roman script. The grievance was not so much one of discrimination as of power – Serbs were being denied an instrument of hegemony. But it worked all the same. By 1891–2 the proportion of Serb schools and pupils to intercommunal ones was rising again, and attendance was better, no doubt since it was the poorer Serbs who attended the state schools, because they were free.

Government could respond in two ways to this challenge, not necessarily mutually exclusive. But Kállay rejected the provincial government's 1894 proposal for an upswing in the primary school building programme – 150 new schools in five years – and followed instead only the path of repression. From 1892 Serb teachers required government certificates of political reliability before they could take up appointments. These were often withheld for many months so that schools remained idle. The annual concerts in honour of the Serb patron saint, Sava, held usually in Serb school halls, were ruthlessly censored. Honoraria for Orthodox priests teaching religion in state schools were stepped up to the point where their withdrawal would be a serious blow to these men of influence among a primitive people, as the provincial government put it.

The chief feature of the competition from the early 1890s, however, was Kállay's belated attempt to enforce uniform patterns of supervision on the communes and their educational activities, through the imposition of the so-called *Normalstatut*. The only effect was to drive communal leaders into a movement for cultural autonomy, on the lines of the Orthodox Serb Karlowitz patriarchate in Hungary. The struggle lasted from 1896 to 1905 and was joined in 1899 by a similar Muslim movement. Both sought to remove control of communal institutions and property from government and its allies in the hierarchy. Attendance at the Muslim girls' school and contributions for the Reform *Mektebs* fell off, the latter shadowed by their ties with the state schools. Since the urban based communal leaderships succeeded in exploiting rural discontent and in involving extra-Bosnian factors, including the ecumenical patriarchate and the *Sheikh-ul-Islam*, Kállay's successor, Burián, decided to concede many of the Serbs' demands in the autonomy statute of 1905. The rigid adherence to bosnianising ideology had already weakened in Kállay's last years.

The Serb autonomy statute had somewhat equivocal consequences. On the one hand it provided for lay dominated bodies at eparchial and all-Bosnian levels which could more effectively take in hand the building up of a Serb confessional school system. Tacitly, the authorities now left school building in wholly Serb areas largely to the Serbs; there were 70 Serb schools in 1906 and 122 in 1914. Moreover, though the state claimed that its right of supervision had been reiterated in the autonomy statute the Serbs succeeded in making these rights, as a governmental inquest after the assassination of Franz Ferdinand complained, 'a mere shadow'.[14] In particular, government objections to the lack of dynastic spirit in the teaching of history and geography were not attended to. On the other hand the experience of autonomy taught the Serbs that they lacked the resources to develop their schools as they would have wished, let alone launch into fresh fields, like a Serb *gymnasium* or male teachers' training college. They held out so strongly over history and geography because, with the Serb school syllabus modelled on the state schools, these were really the only distinctive features of the confessional system to remain. Serb teachers continued to be lost to the better paid state sector and there was frequent friction between them and priests and businessmen in the communal organisations.

On Muslim autonomy the number of Reform *Mektebs*, too, rose sharply, from 84 to 149 in two years, with 12 491 pupils. A ferment of debate on Muslim education now developed but reached no clear conclusion, because of tensions between government, Muslim conservatives and Muslim radicals as to the relation of Muslim schools to the state system, and girls' education. Decisions that religious textbooks should be printed in Serbo–Croat but in Arabic letters, and *Ulema* (Muslim learned men) opposition to a Muslim girls' teacher training college led, ironically, to calls in the Muslim press for government intervention.

Willy nilly, then, the chief responsibility for Bosnian education remained with the government. In 1906 one of its leading figures calculated that of the 120 schools earmarked for building in the accelerated programme of 1894, only 24 had materialised. The average increase in provision had remained at a lowly six or seven schools a year. This rate was now to be increased to 18, but still with ministerial admonitions to remain within the resources of the Bosnian budget. From 1906 to 1912 the number of state schools did in fact rise quite sharply, from 261 to 374. But more drastic commitments, to a school in every commune and to 'relative compulsion' (that is, compulsory school attendance where facilities existed), had to await the demands of Bosnia's first elected representatives, voiced in the *diet* set up under the constitution of 1910. Incidentally, by the definition adopted (that is, a school within 4 km) half the population enjoyed such facilities. The *diet*'s resolutions reflected discontent with official policy in other ways. The *diet* debated equal use of the Roman and Cyrillic scripts for all pupils, proportional funding of confessional institutions, defunding of the German language cadet school in Sarajevo, and abolition of the 1907 ban on non-official illiteracy courses. This latter notorious regulation, which hardly squared with a situation where 89 per cent were still illiterate and only a sixth of eligible children attended any school, showed the political difficulties bedevilling the regime's educational course, some of them, no doubt, self-imposed. Other resolutions pointed to its failure to convince Bosnians of its commitment to confessional evenhandedness. The figure of 326 Catholic teachers to 245 Orthodox in state primary schools in 1909–10, when Orthodox adherents were twice as numerous in the population as Catholics, leant *prima facie* plausibility to opposition charges that, like Turkey before it, Austria was helping its coreligionists to a position of dominance in a mixed society. Muslim teachers numbered 107, which showed the strictly limited success of earlier attempts at integration of the Muslim community. Just over a sixth of the 51 000 primary school pupils were Muslims in 1912, respectable for boys but including a mere 249 girls. Actually, even of Christian pupils only 24 per cent were girls. The fact that in 1905 attendance in the fourth and last year of state primary schools was only one third that of attendance in the first year casts further doubt on the solidity of what had been achieved. At these levels, at least, it was easier to talk of a cultural mission than to carry one out.

The Nemesis of Austrian Educational Policy: The Student Revolt

By the twentieth century total expenditure on state primary schools outstripped that on non-primary. Since half of the former sum was now met by local authorities, however, the provincial government continued to pay out the larger part of its own contribution to the secondary sector. The Bosnian Herzegovinian Institute, set up as a hall of residence for Bosnian higher education students in Vienna in 1899, was further proof of the seriousness with which the regime took this field. Yet a 1906 report on Bosnian education by a leading Joint Finance Ministry official, the historian Thallóczy, stated that since about 1887, as fading memories of Turkish misrule weakened austrophilism, growing numbers of Bosnian youths came to acquire western culture without absorbing its spirit. They thus developed into a half-educated caste, combined with a feeling of intellectual superiority and resentful of an administration which excluded them from positions of power they deemed to be their due.[15] Under Serb and Croat nationalist influence this led from about 1900 to student demonstrations in Vienna, to open letters attacking the regime, and to the drafting of radical programmes. Protests at the draconian regulations of the Bosnian Herzegovinian Institute against cafes, societies and smoking, which led to the expulsion of 26 of its 34 inmates in its first year were not the least of the causes for the unrest.

Actually, the authorities had several regular confidants among student youths. One of these tried in his reports to convince his paymasters that protest was not due to separatist feeling but to frustration at anti-Serb attitudes among Bosnian teachers and idealistic concern for speedier social development. He was wasting his time. Thallóczy's recommendations were for a restriction of the intake into Bosnian secondary schools, through the introduction of school fees and the abolition of parallel classes. The warden of the Bosnian Herzegovinian Institute was bitter about his charges – one could 'seek in vain in this section of the youth for modesty, gratitude, duty, a sense of decency; indeed, still more, they seem to exert themselves everywhere to document the reverse of these virtues'.[16] In this climate, resentments continued to smoulder. In 1908 the Director of one of Bosnia's three *gymnasiums* was dismissed for dealing poorly with the case of a mutinous Serb ex-pupil who had struck him in the street and been congratulated for heroism by a young Serb teacher at the school. As in previous disturbances in the state teachers' training college, tensions between Serb and Croat students and staff also played a role, exacerbated by the new daily press. In 1910 the first act of terrorism took place, and from 1912 a wave of secondary school strikes occurred both on public issues and on allegations of teacher discrimination. A rapid buildup of secret secondary school associations, Serb, Croat and Yugoslav in orientation, responded to the ferment of the south Slav world at a time of the Balkan wars and constitutional crisis in Croatia.

The authorities' response to all this was remarkably low key. Its main theme was that academic authorities should concern themselves more for their pupils' personal development. The discovery of inflammatory postcards sent to a Bosnian student, including one from the would be assassin of the Governor of Croatia, led to suspicions that a central revolutionary student organisation might be at large. But the Sarajevo State Prosecutor accepted the student's plea that terms like 'revolutionary Yugoslav greetings' were just jokes; 'individual bombastic expressions cannot be taken as anything more than phrases, the product of youthful phantasy', he reported.[17] A school outing to Serbia during which treasonable sentiments were expressed in a teacher's presence was not reported to Vienna. The circulars of the Sarajevo educational authorities continued to breathe an earnest humanitarianism.

In 1911 they finally decided to permit pupil associations in secondary schools. 'Every friend of healthy national development rejoices when youth is nationally minded, when it has ideals and dreams for these are the most beautiful prerogatives of youth', was how the government Chief Inspector for secondary schools began his report on disturbances in the Mostar *gymnasium* days before the assassination of Franz Ferdinand.[18] After the event, of course, commentaries were altogether more sombre. Like Thallóczy eight years earlier, they stressed the syndrome of the developing society inadequately attuned to western norms. Springing largely from poverty stricken peasant homes, with parents wholly ignorant of the requirements of education, left therefore to their own devices at a most vulnerable age, maturing early in inadequate digs in an unfamiliar urban environment, young Bosnians easily fell prey to untoward pressures. A teaching staff often mediocre because of difficulties of recruitment to backward Bosnia and lacking personal touch with the pupils could not overcome these problems.[19] The fault lay in general social and political circumstances which the school was powerless to allay.

Much in this analysis of the Sarajevo authorities is borne out by what we know of the lives of Gavrilo Princip, Nedjelko Čabrinović, Danilo Ilić and other young Bosnians. The melancholic young Princip provides a classic case study of the alienation to which sensitive youth is subject in a fitfully modernising society under imperial rule. 'My life also is full of bitterness and gall, my wrath has more thorns in it than others', he wrote to an acquaintance. Again, in the piece of poetry he underlined in a book in his last stay in Belgrade:

> Even if we have not created anything ourselves,
> We will at least have put an end to the misery of our times;
> Our grave will yet be the foundation
> Of the new life without the flaws of today.[20]

These words also bring out what is missing in the authorities' analysis: the moral earnestness and idealism pervading so much of the student community of pre-1914 Bosnia.

In Sarajevo, with a secondary school population of 900, one

bookseller alone sold in a year 1000 copies of Schopenhauer on honour; 150 copies of his *Metaphysics of Sexual Love*; 150 copies of the leading Serbian literary critics' work on Serbo–Croat nationalism; and 70 copies of Dostoevsky's *Crime and Punishment*. The Russian novelists, populists and anarchists, the Scandinavian dramatists, the German socialists, French and English positivists, and G. Mazzini: all this came within the purview of Young Bosnia. Much of it was first translated by themselves and published in *feuilletons* of the daily press or in the student journals which proliferated in the south Slav world. Danilo Ilić alone, in the period 1913–14, translated Gorky's *The Burning Heart* and *Greetings to Liberated Humanity*; Oscar Wilde's essays on art and criticism; Andreyev's *Dark Horizon*; Bakunin's *The Paris Commune and the Idea of the State*; and Camus' *Le Mensonge du Parlamentarisme*, along with several other works.

It was not to be expected that the Habsburg authorities, still overwhelmingly non-Bosnian at the upper levels, should appreciate this fervid intellectualism of Bosnian student youth. Their own concept of secondary school life was of something much more sedate. Elsewhere in the Dual Monarchy, including nearby Croatia, *gymnasiums* were largely the preserve of the professional classes, the children of those already educated. Outside the south Slav world there was almost total incomprehension of the student movement and its aims. As Moritz Benedikt commented in an editorial in his influential *Neue Freie Presse* (New Free Press) on the assassination attempt by a student on the Bosnian Governor in 1910, more in terms of bathos than anger: why shed the blood of a stranger, and on the day of the opening of the Bosnian *diet*? This was not Russia! Perhaps it was the deed 'of one of those half-educated in whose heads the elements of the time ferment without finding elaboration or clarification', or of a passionate southerner filled with Serbian anti-monarchy hate literature; or again of a would-be emulator of the heroes of the songs which women sang while spinning in the evenings.[21] In Bosnia officials had a more concrete grasp of the problems. Yet there was still a deep sense of shock in the aftermath of June 1914 at what had been hatched by products of a school system which was a 'faithful imitator' of the Dual Monarchy's, with access to all the results of decades of academic research and tradition, where 'automatic' means were to hand to organise the Bosnian secondary schools 'according to the most modern principles'.[22] Naturally, recriminations between the Joint Finance Ministry and the provincial government in Sarajevo were severe, with the latter countermanding a ministerial order to close an entire *gymnasium* and dismiss all its staff. All 143 Serb confessional schools were, however, closed for the duration, and Cyrillic was banned from textbooks and teaching except for Orthodox religious instruction. The Chief Inspector of secondary schools, a Croat *litterateur* of mildly Yugoslav sympathies, was investigated for high treason. No new schools were built in the last two years of the war and probably not in the first two either. Few 'cultural missions' have faced such embarrassing questions as did the Bosnian educational service around 1914.

Conclusions

These questions might be embarrassing, but were they damning? The great difficulties under which Bosnian administrators laboured must also be remembered in shaping a conclusion. They faced, in an awkwardly ambiguous semi-colonial context, problems which have perplexed many governments since of 'modernisation' and 'political development', namely, of stable transition between two very different states of society. It is this protean process which in multi-ethnic polities has led governments to expand their operations into cultural spheres considered autonomous by ethnic groups, and led ethnic groups to reformulate their identities in terms of the more potent concept of nationhood, both sides legitimising their strategies as the key to progress. Hence modernisation is a key concept for the European Science Foundation project.

But the discussion above also reveals the elusiveness of this concept. The fact that in Bosnia almost all parties invoked different versions of it demonstrates the degree of subjectivity it involves. The chief distinction at stake was that between the dominant state's view of modernity in terms of political order and economic progress, seen in partnership of the state and *laissez faire* capitalism, and the non-dominant groups' stress of cultural motifs, the voluntarist mobilisation of energies around the ethno-national ideal. Kállay's philosophy of history appears to a later age particularly arbitrary because he combined the dominant state view with a classification of western and oriental traits, to the latters' disadvantage, and allocated the Serbs to the oriental/non-modern sphere. This operation, characteristic of the age of imperialism – and Kállay was a proconsular figure – had the negative effect of letting him discount and contest the very Serb capacity for constructive national development which had aroused his fear in the first place. To the element of self-deception was added a certain dose of humbug. Kállay identified modernity with calm rationality and impartiality, claiming for the Habsburg state an Olympian objectivity above the squabbles of traditionalist Balkanites. Yet he bolstered the position of Muslims as much as he could and when they nonetheless defected in majority to the Serbs he dropped the exclusively Bosnian idea and leant some encouragement to the Croats. Meanwhile, he condemned the passionate protest these manoeuvres aroused in the non-dominant groups as further signs of their immaturity. The pattern can be seen elsewhere.

Yet open to misrepresentation as is the concept of modernisation, the process it labels without doubt provided the dynamic within which schooling and other aspects of the dominant/non-dominant relationship evolved. The late twentieth century is much better sensitised than was Moritz Benedikt, for instance, to the stresses and strains in developing societies that produce student nationalist militancy. To be fair, Kállay and his intellectual *alter ego* Thallóczy were also aware of the potential problem of social change in a backward environment. It underlay their gradualist approach, with its fear of an 'intellectual proletariat' and deracinated Muslims. It may be doubted, however, if they fully understood all the problems of their particular brand of neo-imperialist ideology with its mix of conservative and mildly liberal elements. The Bosnian experience showed that authority in this kind of situation faced a dual challenge from younger elements who wanted faster change and from traditionalists who resented change at all. Kállay's policy which shored up the position of Muslims on the land while allowing free play to capitalist forces to undermine the Muslim artisans provided the setting in which both traditionalist and western educated Muslims would eventually throw their weight behind the Serb movement for cultural autonomy.

There was a second and subtler issue at stake. Austrian ideology as shaped by Kállay was based on two implicitly contradictory principles: confessional equality as the key to the communal problem and arrogation of modernity to the sphere of the state. The stress on confessionalism had the not unintended consequence of highlighting the religious divisions which kept Serbs and Croats apart. But the effect of state backed capitalist modernisation, however halting, tended to weaken the power of religion and, thereby, to call in question the bases of south Slav ethnicity. By the twentieth century Serb and Croat intellectuals became increasingly uneasy about the religious aspect of their national identity, which seemed to conflict with the spirit of the age. This, together with the Herderian emphasis on language, which they had in common, increased pressures towards yugoslavism, even if it was weaker in Bosnia than elsewhere. It was a period of flux, in which Bosnian students could swing disconcertingly from the Serb–Croat feuding of the 1900s to a position of some collaboration from 1912. In the last years of peace this crisis of consciousness drove many young Muslims to opt for a Serb or Croat allegiance and, as these began to draw closer, to participate in the Yugoslav student movement. Parallels arise with contemporary Hindu–Muslim relations in the British *Raj*.

There is, of course, an element of hindsight in this critique. If Princip's shots had not led to world war, would not an Austrian Bosnia have remained in which, despite the autonomy movements, there were more Serbs in state than confessional schools, and

Muslims were abandoning the *rüshdiye* for ordinary primary schools where the ratio had been ten to one the other way in the 1880s? Austria had successfully implemented non-denominational schooling in the heart of a multi-faith society, where the British had failed in the same task in nineteenth century Ireland. Thirty per cent of Bosnian officials were now native born, and Dr Nikola Mandić, a native Catholic, became Civil Adlatus in 1913, presiding over a constitutional regime installed by Kállay's pragmatic successors. Could it be argued that the Bosnia school system had succeeded in what it had been so carefully intended to do: set European cultural standards, provide native personnel as necessary, inculcate appropriate attitudes into the broader population through the educated minority, and thereby facilitate a gradual and controlled process of modernisation?

Not really, for Princip's bullets, too, were a significant outcome of government educational policy. They cannot be dismissed merely as an aberration. While Bosnians in practice accepted the state school, for all its disproportionately Catholic/Croat staffing, they also by-and-large disliked the Bosnian administration and remained detached from the Habsburg idea. The wider realities of Bosnian life, including humiliation at political and national impotence, festering suspicions of the role of the Croat minority and the Catholic Church, and above all peasant poverty and bitterness, kept breaking through the carefully erected structures of the state educational system to impregnate the consciouness of the pupils within. Nor did education lend itself easily to control, even by an absolutist state. There was something stubbornly democratic about the nineteenth century Balkan village school, in practice so many tiny focuses of autonomous initiative in remote localities awakening for the first time to glimmering self-awareness. As to the secondary schools, their staff, largely recruited from the more liberal atmosphere of the Dual Monarchy, were poor allies in the grand design. *Gymnasium* Director Nemanjić in 1894 did not even have a list of his pupils' homes or lodgings. He granted boys leave of absence without serious enquiry into their reasons or their parents' knowledge.[23] Lilek, the province's senior history master, 'a somewhat croaticised Slovene', as Thallóczy grumbled sourly, wanted to write a history textbook eulogising Calvinism and the French Revolution![24] The whole structure of academic life, modelled on central European traditions, allowed students to transfer from one institution to another, to defer examinations, in general to work the system in a way which would be unthinkable in purportedly liberal Britain. The tradition of academic freedom as the one inviolate heritage of the Enlightenment in semi-absolutist central Europe was too deeply engrained. How otherwise could 47 Bosnian Serbs have been allowed to study in Austrian universities in 1902 on Serbian government scholarships?

In short, when the Bosnian provincial government wrote after the assassination of 1914 that the school authorities could not be held responsible for the acts of its pupils outside their gates, saying this was a matter for the police – it wrote the epitaph on its educational policies.[25] Education cannot be insulated from the broader society, even for limited purposes and selected target groups. This is the lesson of Austria's 'cultural mission' in Bosnia.

The non-dominant view of modernity in its relation to schooling cannot, however, pass without comment either. This view identified modernity with cultivation of the national spirit. It played a crucial role at the point at which ethnic consciousness was passing from the phase of peasant revolt to that of cultural self-definition. The relevance of education in this process was obvious. Yet as national consciousness strengthened and the nation became a more diverse social reality, the role of the school became less central and clear. By the constitutional era, there were at least three separately organised tendencies in Bosnian Serb life; a conservative commercial elite, a democratic professional grouping and a radical, pro-peasant wing – not to speak of Young Bosnia. The naive view of modernity which identified it, as *Bosanska vila* had done, with a society where everyone joined choral societies and professors lectured on national history to the masses, fractured in this new phase.

Hence the disputes in the Serb autonomy organs after 1906 as to how much of Serb communal resources should go on confessional education. Some deemed it a waste of money. Many now thought that the primary purpose of schooling was strictly educational, and not national. The professional journal of Serb teachers in Bosnia founded just before 1914 reflects disillusionment with their lot, resentment of the merchant elite, of the poor relations with the clergy and dismay at the material problems of the Balkan primary school teacher. With growing uncertainty about their role, Serb teachers were less prepared to make the heavy commitments to Serb associational life which were expected of them (for example, membership of choirs, church song, literacy and temperance societies etc.) than in the heady days of the 1890s when the school was the focal point of political struggle. By 1914 social motifs were in cross current with national.

Thus the experience of non-dominant Serbs, like that of the Bosnian government, demonstrated both the importance and the limitations of schooling as a political tool. Schooling was important because both sides saw that great social changes were inevitable and sought through the schools to guide their course. It had its limitations because – besides problems of lack of resources – neither side was as in tune with history as it thought, so that schooling plans came into conflict with social reality rather than expediting it. True, at the time the Serb national vision possessed more dynamism than the Habsburg idea, but its own contradictions humbled it too by 1945.

There is a warning here for the historian. As for the politician, schooling, so for the historian, the concept of modernity, has its limitations. It should not be used to suggest that what is 'modern' can be objectively agreed. Rather, it has been used here to unlock the subjective worlds of the actors studied, who all believed that their generation held the key to the future. It was this sense of living at the birth of a new age which gave education its prestige and otherwise parish pump disputes about village schools their intensity in Bosnian life in our period.

Notes

1. The discussion of schooling in the Austrian period is based on archival sources, chiefly the records of the Austro–Hungarian Joint Finance Ministry preserved in the Bosnian state archives in Sarajevo (Državni Arhiv SR Bosne i Hercegovine) and also the Šušljić MSS in the Bosnian National Library, Sarajevo, being 29 notebooks of materials on Serb schools collected by the teacher Risto Šušljić between 1930 and 1945 and drawing on the Serb press, personal correspondence and private knowledge. Additional statistical information has been taken from the works by Bogičević, Dlustuš, Invanišević and Pejanović listed in the select bibliography. A fuller treatment of a part of the period may be found in my unpublished doctoral dissertation.
2. Quoted in fra Gavranović, p. 285.
3. Benjamin von Kállay, pp. 428–89.
4. For one use of this quite common phrase, see Državni arhiv SR Bosne i Hercegovine, Joint Finance Ministry papers (hereafter DAB, JFM) BH 3086/1893 JFM-PG (Provincial Government), 10 May.
5. Public Record Office, London, Foreign Office 7/1125. Consul General Freeman to Lord Salisbury. 27 December 1887.
6. DAB, JFM BH 4791/1883 JFM-PG, 4 September.
7. Lj. Dlustuš, p. 401.
8. DAB, JFM. BH 968/1884. PG-JFM, 11 January.
9. DAB, JFM, BH 12736/1893, PG-JFM, 28 October.
10. DAB, JFM, BH 968/1184, PG-JRM, 11 January (geography); BH 3720/1895, undated memorandum (history).
11. DAB, JFM, BH Pr. (Präsidial) BH 81/1897. PG-JFM, 15 January.
12. Bosanska vila. Vol.1 (1886), p. 15.
13. Ibid., vol 6 (1891) p. 64.
14. DAB, JFM, Pr. BH 831/1915, PG-JFM, 17 July.
15. DAB, JFM, Pr. BH 1282/1904. Thallóczy's memorandum, no date, but completed in 1906.
16. DAB, JFM, KB (Kabinettbriefe) BH 13/1903. Zurunić-Kállay, 22 February.
17. DAB, JFM, Pr. BH 1600/1914, enclosing Prosecutor's opinion of (June) 1912.
18. DAB, JFM, Pr BH 705/1914. Inspector Alaupović-PG, early June.
19. See particularly DAB, JFM, Pr BH 968/1914, Äusserung des Departments 3b.
20. V. Dedijer, p. 470.
21. Neue Freie Presse, Leading article, 10 June 1910.
22. DAB, JFM, Pr BH 968/1914, Äusserung des Departments 3b.
23. DAB, JFM, Pr BH 383/1894, PG-JFM. 4 April 1894.
24. DAB, JFM, BH 14158/1892. Thallóczy comment, no date.
25. DAB, JFM, Pr BH 968/1914, PG-JFM.

Select Bibliography

Background – Administrative, Political and Cultural

Bericht über die Verwaltung von Bosnien und der Herzegowina, herausgegeben vom

Gemeinsamen Finazministerium (1906). Further reports appeared in 1907, 1908, 1911, 1913 and 1917, Vienna.

Dedijer V. (1963), *The Road to Sarajevo*.

Daković, L. (1985), *Političke organizacije Bosansko-hercegovačkih Katolika Hrvata. Dio I. Do otvaranja Sabora 1910*, (Political Organisations of the Catholic Croats of Bosnia-Herzegovina. Part I. To the Opening of the Diet in 1910), Zagreb.

Gavranović, B. (1935). *Uspostava redovite katoličke hierarhije u Bosni i Hercegovini*, (Establishment of a Regular Catholic Hierarchy in Bosnia–Herzegovina), Belgrade.

Hauptmann, F. (ed.) (1967), *Borba Muslimana Bosne i Hercegovine za vjersku i vakufsko-mearifsku autonomiju*. (The struggle of Bosnia-Herzegovinian Muslims for autonomy in religion and Waqf affairs), Documents, Sarajevo.

Kállay, B. von (1883), 'Ungarn an den Grenzen des Orients und des Occidents' in *Ungarische Revue*, vol. 3.

Kraljačić, T. (1987), *Kalajev režim u Bosni i Hercegovini 1882–1903* (The Kállay regime in Bosnia-Herzegovina 1882–1903), Sarajevo.

Madžar, B. (1982), *Pokret Srba Bosne i Hercegovine za vjersko-prosvjetnu samoupravu*. (The Movement of Bosnia-Herzegovinian Serbs for religious and cultural autonomy), Sarajevo.

Okey, R. (1972), *Cultural and Political Problems of the Austro–Hungarian Administration of Bosnia–Herzegovina, 1873–1903*. Unpublished PhD thesis, Oxford.

Palavestra, P. (1965), *Književnost Mlade Bosne* (The literature of Young Bosnia), 2 vols, Sarajevo.

Schmid, F. (1914), *Bosnien und die Herzegowina unter der Verwaltung Österreich-Ungarns*, Leipzig.

Slijepčević, P. et al, (1929), *Napor Bosne i Hercegovine za oslobodenje i ujedinjenje* (The struggle of Bosnia-Herzegovina for freedom and unification), Sarajevo.

Education – General and the Turkish Period

Bogičević, V. (1965) *Istorija razvitka osnovnih škola u Bosni i Hercegovini od 1463–1918* (History of the development of elementary schools in Bosnia–Herzegovina, 1463–1918), Sarajevo.

Ćurić, H. (1983), *Muslimansko školstvo u Bosni i Hercegovini do 1918* (Muslim education in Bosnia-Herzegovina up to 1918), Sarajevo.

Pejanović, D. (1953), *Srednje i stručne škole u Bosni i Hercegovini od početka do 1941* (Secondary and specialised schools in Bosnia-Herzegovina from their origins till 1941), Sarajevo.

Skarić, V. (1931), *Sarajevo i okolina od najstarijih vremena do danas*, (Sarajevo and surroundings from earliest times to today), Sarajevo.

Education – the Austrian Period

Dlustuš, Lj. (1894), Školske prilike u Bosnu i Hercegovini od okupacije do danas. (Educational conditions in Bosnia-Herzegovina from the occupation to today), *Školski vjesnik*, vol. (i) 1–3, 50–4, 101–6, 155–61, 223–7, 341–3, 401–4, 455–8, 531–8.

Kraljačić, T. (1984), Funkcije državnih škola u nacionalnoj politici Kalajevog režima (The functions of the state schools in the nationality policy of the Kállay regime) *Istorijski časopis* vol. 31.

Ljubibratić, D. (1959), *Gavrilo Princip*, Belgrade.

Papić, M. (1972), *Školstvo u Bosni i Hercegovini za vrijeme austrougarske okupacije 1878–1918* (Education in Bosnia-Herzegovina during the Austro-Hungarian occupation 1878–1918), Sarajevo.

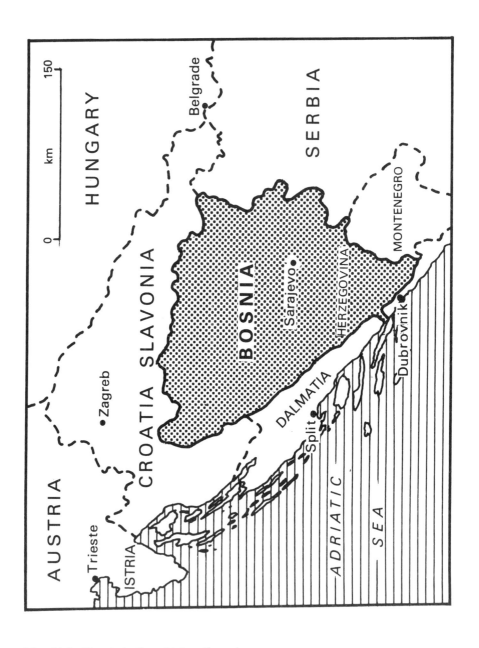

Map 14.1   Bosnia in the nineteenth century

15 The Education of the Greeks in the Ottoman Empire, 1856–1923: A Case Study of 'Controlled Toleration'

ANDREAS KAZAMIAS

This study examines the education of the Greeks, an ethno-religious non-dominant group, which was scattered in various parts of the empire, during a particular historical period: from circa 1856 to circa 1923. The specific areas of the empire, where Greek adherents to the Orthodox faith were settled during the period under study, were Anatolia (roughly the Asiatic part of present day Turkey), Istanbul and its European vicinity, Thrace and Macedonia, particularly Salonica and the surrounding region, Epirus, Thessaly, the Aegean islands and Crete. This study will not examine the education of the Greeks in Cyprus, or in other parts of the Ottoman empire.

The Ottoman educational policies and the Greek activities are examined at two levels of analysis and from two interrelated conceptual and methodological perspectives. The first of the two perspectives is predominantly theoretical. It is a model, a conceptual platform, the parameters of which are abstracted from the historical experience of the Ottoman empire prior to the nineteenth century. For our purposes here, the main characteristics of this Ottoman model include: the nature of the Ottoman empire–state; the social structure of the Ottoman society; culture, ideology, and education; and the international context of the Ottoman world.

The second perspective, which will constitute the main body of the study, is predominantly historical, contextual and particular-specific. The analysis and interpretation of the particular phenomena during the period 1856–1923 will make use of the previously mentioned conceptual platform, as well as categories from relevant macro-social or socio-educational theories.

The period 1856–1923 was chosen for several reasons. In 1856, the famous *Hatt-i Hümayun* (imperial rescript), on the reorganisation, modernisation (westernisation) and reform of the Ottoman empire, was officially proclaimed. This was an event of great importance in the incipient social and political restructuring of the Greek Orthodox *millet*, (the ethno-religious communal administrative institution, literally 'peoples') responsible for education. The year 1923 marked the disintegration of the multi-ethnic and multi-religious empire, as well as its predominantly Muslim theocratic state, and the establishment of the secular, ethnically and religiously more homogeneous Turkish nation–state. With the proclamation of the Turkish republic, the *millet* system and, by implication, the Greek Orthodox *millet*, also came to an end. Further, as part of the Peace Treaty of Lausanne between Greece and the newly formed Turkish State, a mandatory exchange of populations between the two countries was negotiated. The vast majority of the Greeks in Anatolia and eastern Thrace were transferred to the Greek mainland, and, in return, the bulk of the Moslem population in Greek lands was moved to Turkey. Lastly, the educational policies of the new Turkish state towards all remaining ethnic minorities, including the Greeks, changed substantially from those of the Ottoman Empire.

The Ottoman Empire–State, Society and Educational Policy: A Conceptual Framework

In its pre-nineteenth century ideal typical form, the Ottoman empire–state can be described as a multi-religious, multi-ethnic and polyglot social system, in which power and authority were vested in and emanated from a 'dynastic, divinely sanctioned sultan–caliph', and wielded by him through a hierarchically organised civil and religious (Muslim) bureaucracy. The sultan's authority and supervision over his multiple ethno-religious 'subjects' (especially the Christians and Jews) was carried out through the system of *millets*. According to one student of the subject, this institutional arrangement, 'provided on the one hand, a degree of religious, cultural and ethnic continuity within these (the non-Muslim) communities, while on the other it permitted their incorporation into the Ottoman administrative, economic and political system'.[1]

The Orthodox Greeks, together with the other Orthodox ethnic groups, scattered all over the empire (namely, the Serbs, the Romanians, the Bulgarians, the Vlachs, the Orthodox Albanians and the Arabs) constituted the *Millet-i Rum* (Greek Orthodox *millet*) which until well into the nineteenth century was the largest and most prominent.

In a sense, the Greek *millet* constituted a 'state within the state'. At its head sat the patriarch of Constantinople who, to the Greeks at least, combined both religious and ethnic roles and was, therefore, also known as *'ethnarch,'* the 'leader of the nation'. The patriarch's role was twofold: ecclesiastical (as the head of the Greek Orthodox Church) and political (as part of the Ottoman state apparatus and as *ethnarch*). Through a hierarchy of metropolitans, bishops and clergy, the patriarch held jurisdiction over most of the affairs of the Greek Orthodox community. These included, among others, the adjudication of civil cases (marriage, divorce, dowry and inheritance) and, most pertinently for us, educational provision.

Ottoman society was differentiated, vertically and horizontally, along political, social, cultural, religious and ideological lines. More specifically, it was divided into a privileged, politically and religiously (Muslim) dominant Ottoman, and mainly Turkish, ruling class, and the *rayas*, a non-dominant, religiously heterogeneous and politically disenfranchised subject class. Each of the two classes had clearly defined legal rights, duties/obligations, and functions: the rulers were responsible for governing, exploiting and defending the imperial wealth, and the subjects for providing the imperial wealth, as well as for catering to their own religious, social, cultural and educational needs.[2]

The subject class was, in turn, divided into Muslims and *Dimmis* (non-Muslims) and into urban and rural dwellers (peasants), again with differential status and power attached to each category. The non-Muslim groups were separated from their Muslim counterpart and from each other culturally, politically, legally and economically. Added to this, one must note the urban–rural economic and socio-cultural dichotomies as well as the geographic dispersal of the members of each *millet*, which was especially the case with the Greeks.

The Ottoman empire–state's educational policy towards the non-dominant ethno-religious groups might at best be described as *'laissez faire'* or 'controlled toleration'. In this policy arena, the Ottoman state was a 'weak' state; the Ottoman rulers neither encouraged nor, as a rule, discouraged education among the non-dominant groups. Consequently, educational provision among the Greeks, for example, was like religion, exclusively the Greek Orthodox *millet's* affair. More often than not educational initiatives were taken at the local community level, but, as a rule, they had to be sanctioned by the patriarchate which dispensed authority and exercised supervision through the metropolitans and parish priests. Schools, where they existed, were often attached to churches or monasteries and were supported by them. Children, as a popular Greek ballad goes, went to school to learn 'the Greek letters and Godly matters'. The teacher was often the local priest or monk or someone else who combined two or three callings (priest, cantor, farmer, painter, tailor, cobbler, etc.).[3]

The educational state of affairs among the Christian Greeks during the heyday of the Ottoman empire was not very satisfactory, a situation which can be attributed to several factors. First, the non-interventionist Ottoman state educational policy, when considered in conjunction with the same state's interventionist policy in the fiscal sphere (the exacting of taxes from the subject class), was an enormous drain on the financial resources of the ethno-religious communities, without the rendering of compensatory social services. Left to themselves, the *rayas* had to rely for all of their social, economic and cultural needs on their already impoverished condition. Second, the Greek Orthodox *millet* was a fragmented, isolated, non-cohesive and not clearly indentifiable socio-cultural system. As Vucinich has noted: 'the *millet* system means isolation of ethnic and confessional social entities, and isolation meant stagnation'.[4]

The educational, cultural and economic stagnation of the Greek *millet* was exacerbated further by another contributing factor, namely, the consequences (some unintended) of the Ottoman conquest. Among such consequences were the fleeing of Greek intellectuals, teachers and merchants from the Ottoman occupied areas, the dispersal of the Greek population and the resettlement of Ottoman Muslims, which resulted in radical population changes. Added to the above, one cannot discount the significance of the relative isolation (cultural, economic, political) of the Ottoman empire–state itself from the rest of the world. Lastly, the confessional organisation of the *millet* with responsibility for education and culture placed in ecclesiastical authorities headed by the patriarch, and its community structure which was headed by the *kodjabashis* (notables), provide yet another explanatory dimension for the prevalent educational conditions (the paucity of provision and the primarily religiously centred 'national' curriculum) among the non-dominant Greeks. Generally, the role of the Church was passive and highly conservative, and as noted above, its limited educational activities, where they occurred, were narrowly confessional in nature. Furthermore, it should not be forgotten that, by and large, the patriarchate, as Karpat points out, 'functioned as a faithful office of the Ottoman bureaucracy', it was 'closed to western thought', and 'it exercised a docile function as the intermediary between the sultan and the Orthodox *raya*'.[5] The community notables, in their turn, were not particularly known for their promotion of education and culture, but rather for their avarice and oppression.

Tradition and the Quest for Modernity in the Ottoman Empire–State

By the middle of the nineteenth century, the 'traditional' framework of the Ottoman polity, society and education, as conceptualised above, had begun to erode in several of its aspects as a consequence of internal and external socio-economic, political and cultural–ideological forces and factors. Attempts by certain 'modernisers' to reorganise/reorder the Ottoman institutional framework and society, and thus help maintain the viability of a transformed empire–state were not entirely successful.

The Ottoman quest for modernity can be approached from the perspective of three broad and historically overlapping multi-dimensional conceptual categories: (a) defensive modernisation; (b) ottomanism; and (c) Turkish nationalism. Here, we shall pay attention to ottomanisation and Turkish nationalism because they are more germane to the nature and the period of our study.

During the middle decades of the nineteenth century (from 1839 to 1876), a series of principles were promulgated and institutional reforms, the *Tanzimat* (restructuring or reordering) were introduced, affecting many state apparatuses (administrative, fiscal, military, judicial, educational), as well as the organisation of the *millets*. Among the basic principles of the *Tanzimat*, as embodied in the *Hatt-i Sherif* (noble rescript) of 1839 and the *Hatt-i Hümayun* of 1856, was the affirmation of religious, social, political and economic equality among all the members of the empire. In addition, the *Hatt-i Hümayun* decreed that the *millets* were to be reorganised under new constitutions; the financial and monetary system was to be over-hauled and banks were to be established; public works were to be undertaken in the provinces; communications, commerce and agri-culture were to be improved; and, generally, the empire–state would draw on 'the knowledge, the skills and the capital of Europe'.[6]

It was not just European knowledge, skills and 'capital', that is, efficiency oriented and essentially technocratic mechanisms, that were to be drawn and indeed were drawn upon during and after the *Tanzimat* period. The Euro-centred 'world system' entailed a move-ment of 'cultural capital' as well; that is, ideas, education and culture. Nineteenth century European concepts of liberalism, nation, nationality, nationalism, individual freedom, Herderian Romantic-ism, constitutionalism, equality, secularism and secular education found their way into the erstwhile relatively cloistered and tradition bound Ottoman Islamic system. In the context of the expansive European commercial capitalism and nationalism, and the attendant social, demographic and institutional changes, this traffic of 'cultural capital' contributed to the nurturing of new currents of thought and activity, some quite revolutionary, among the dominant Ottoman elites, and the creation of a politico-ideological and educational ferment that revolved around the declining condition of the empire and ways to revitalise it.

Implicit in the reformist/modernising politico-ideological developments of the period was a new conception of the Ottoman state *qua* state and a new concept of citizenship – the concept of 'ottomanism' – which was to apply equally and without distinction or prejudice to all subjects of the empire. Ottomanism and ottomanisation became the official ideology and policy of the empire–state and, in theory, remained in force until the demise of the empire.[7] Here, for the first time in Ottoman history, Christians and Jews were placed, in principle, on a par with the Muslim Turks, and all subjects of the sultan were to enjoy individual liberty, and would be 'equal in the eyes of the law'. But Islam was to remain the official religion of the state.

Within the conceptual framework of ottomanism/ottomanisation and modernisation, state activity in education became more extended and more direct. For it was believed that education was an important mechanism for the revival of a moribund empire and for the attainment of the Ottomanist political citizenship and developmental goals, which also implied the integration of the minorities and the neutralisation of their nationalist separatist aspirations. In practice, however, this involvement did not affect directly the relative educational 'autonomy' of the *millets*, which continued to be responsible for schools and for any other educational and cultural activities. In essence, as shown below, it applied to the Muslim subjects. In the *Hatt-i Hümayun*, the traditional *millet* privilege of establishing, maintaining and operating schools was reaffirmed, with the proviso that the 'method of teaching and the appointment of teachers (and headmasters) should be under the control and supervision of a mixed council of public instruction, the members of which shall be appointed by Us', meaning the sultan. In a subsequent memorandum (1867) by the Minister of Foreign Affairs to the representatives of the great powers in Istanbul on the application of the *Hatt-i Hümayun*, it was explained that the reason for such intervention by the Sublime Porte was 'to prevent, in case of need, the impropriety of the direction of the schools being given to individuals whose principles are inimical to the authority of the Imperial Government, or against public order'.[8]

The Ottoman state's policy towards the Greek Orthodox subjects therefore continued to be basically one of 'controlled toleration'. But the broader policy of ottomanism aimed, among other things, at the integration of the ethno-religious minorities into the fragmented Ottoman society. Certain educational innovations which were initiated during the *Tanzimat* period, were, in certain respects, part of the vision of integration, and therefore, merit some attention.

The most significant educational policy developments during this mid-nineteenth century period were (a) the fairly comprehensive education law of 1869, the *Maarifi Umumiye Nizamnamesi* (Regulations for General Education), which foreshadowed a new institutional framework for Ottoman education, and (b) the setting up of two important educational institutions: the *Mülkiye* (civil service school) and the *Mektebi Sultani* (imperial secondary school) at Galatasaray. The education law provided, *inter alia*, for compulsory primary education, the organisation of the administration of education, the grading of schools into *sübyan* or *iptidai* (primary), *rüshdiyes* (middle) and *idadis* and *sultanis* (secondary), and for a university in Istanbul.[9]

Although as a whole this new educational scheme applied to Muslim subjects of the state, parts of it were intended for all, including non-Muslims. This was particularly the case with the *idadis* and *sultanis* (secondary level schools), the university, and the *Mülkiye* and the Galatasaray *Lise* (two special schools). The policy was to bring Muslim and non-Muslim (Christian and Jewish) students together in the same school and to provide them with an essentially non-Muslim secular type of education, one derived from western Europe but not of an entirely distinctive national pattern. In this way it was hoped that a new generation of people would acquire the values that would ultimately bring the different ethno-religious populations closer together into a sort of Ottoman brotherhood. This goal was nowhere more apparent than in the establishment of the *Mektebi Sultani*, the Galatasaray *Lise*, in 1867.[10]

The new Ottoman educational framework did not materialise *in toto* as planned; nor can the tangible results of the aforementioned educational innovations be said to have been spectacular, insofar as ottomanism was concerned. Although the 1869 regulations provided that *sultanis* be established in all the provincial capitals, the Galatasaray *lise* was the only one that materialised, and the subsequent growth of such schools was very slow. Furthermore, when this *lise* was first opened in September 1868, true to its original charter, it registered a multi-ethnic and multi-religious group of students as follows: 147 Muslims, 48 Gregorian Armenians, 36 Greek Orthodox, 34 Jews, 34 Bulgarians, 23 Roman Catholics, and 19 Armenian Catholics. But very soon thereafter, this *lise* and similar institutions, were recruiting their students mostly from the Muslim Turkish population. They thus developed into highly selective elite upper secondary schools preparing a small number of students, mostly from the higher socio-economic strata, for further education in the universities and for high careers in the society.

Similarly, the *Mülkiye*, established in 1859 for the explicit purpose of training a select group of persons to staff the expanding civil bureaucracy, also developed into a largely Ottoman Turkish institution in its social composition. In any case, the non-Muslims, including the Greeks, did not patronise the new schools. Instead, as will be shown below, the Greeks expanded their own separate educational activities. Indeed, some of the wealthier amongst them even preferred to send their sons and daughters to some newly established, thoroughly western foreign operated schools such as Robert College in Bebek, Istanbul, and the American College for Women in Üsküdar on the Anatolian side of the Bosphorus that were almost totally non-Ottoman Muslim in their student body. Other Greeks who could afford it sent their children to Greek schools and the University of Athens.

Although ottomanism remained the 'official' ideology and policy of the Empire–state until 1918, several social, political and intellectual developments after 1876 altered the context and meaning of modernisation–westernisation. Among the European currents that were now affecting the Ottoman Turks themselves was none other than the potent force of nationalism and the kindred concepts of nationality and nation–state. Following the unsettled period of the 'constitutional' rule of the Young Turks (1909–18) and the Greco–Turkish War a different social formation and concept of the state emerged: the more socio-politically and ideologically circumscribed, and essentially monoethnic and secular nationalist, Turkish state under Kemal Atatürk.

What, if any, were the effects of these developments on Ottoman education policy towards the ethnic minorities and especially the Greeks? What were the educational reactions and activities of the non-dominant Greeks? The Ottoman state's more direct involvement outside the *millet* system continued to be extended during the Hamidian and Young Turk rule. For example, under the Young Turks, a new education law was passed (1913) and several *sultanis* (upper level secondary schools) modelled on the original such institution at Galatasaray, were established in several provincial capitals.

Such expanded state involvement was, however, practically speaking, restricted to the Ottoman Muslim Turkish subjects. The policy of 'controlled toleration' towards the Greeks continued. However, the degree of 'control', as well as of 'toleration' exercised, differed to a certain extent from region to region, and even from town to town or community to community, depending on local conditions and the relationships between the Ottoman local administration and the community lay and ecclesiastical functionaries. More often than not, as elaborated in a section below, the Greek *millet* had considerable latitude or even autonomy. But there were cases where the Ottoman authorities would refuse Greek petitions to open up a school; or where the provincial governor or local Ottoman functionary would expect that due recognition be given in the schools to the person of the sultan – this usually took the form of 'prayers' for the *Padishah's* (sultan) health and well being during special celebrations such as the Greek Letters Day celebration on 30 January, or even that Turkish be taught. Also there were cases where any activities by teachers inside and outside the schools, or by the *syllogoi* (social and cultural societies) that sought to promote pro-Greek nationalistic sentiment, would not be looked at with favour and would indeed be proscribed. At the same time, one cannot but note some interesting 'paradoxes'. Elderly Greek refugees who left Smyrna (Izmir) after the exchange of populations between Greece and Turkey in 1923 and are now living in Athens, recalled to this writer that when the Greeks celebrated Greek Independence Day on 25 March in Smyrna, the provincial and local Ottoman officials would be invited, and would attend.

A few additional comments would be pertinent here. In their vision of, and activities for, a reformed Ottoman empire–state certain Young Ottomans, notably Namik Kemal and, more so, the Young Turks, were less prone to tolerate nationalistic activities by ethnic minorities. Furthermore, in the 1890s, the teaching of the Turkish language was made obligatory in the ethnic minority schools, although this regulation was not strictly enforced. It should, nevertheless, be noted here that, as the empire–state was veering toward greater centralisation, Islamisation and turkification there seems to have been a greater tendency toward increased vigilance over and encroachment in the educational and cultural affairs of the Greek *millet*. On its part, the Greek *millet* leadership (the higher clergy, the intelligentsia and the urban bourgeoisie), was not disposed to look with favour towards any turkifying or even ottomanising state proclivities. Such a message is clearly implied in the following statement by Chrysostomos, the Greek archbishop of Drama, in 1908.

> If the Turks wish to turn us into a homogeneous nation they are attempting the impossible, and there will be very serious trouble. We must always be Greeks first and *Osmanlis* (Ottomans) afterwards. If they allow us and other nations to develop along our own lines; if they do not interfere with our own religion, our schools, our social and racial ideals, all will go well.[11]

The bipolar educational policy of the modernising Ottoman state, particularly under the Young Turk regime, when considered in conjunction with the openly stated Greek preference for a separate, autonomously provided and essentially Greek education, could not but have contributed to the widening of the social and political chasm between the dominant Ottoman Turks and the non-dominant Ottoman Greeks. Such a separatism was exacerbated in the wake of the developing restrictive Ottoman Turkish nationalism on the one hand, and the parallel developing irredentist and education related Greek nationalism, on the other. Let us, therefore, comment further on the expanding educational activities of the Greeks.

Greek Education, Modernisation and the Quest for National Identity

As with the broader Ottoman polity and society, the essentially Euro-centred process of modernisation and the associated political ideologies of nationalism, liberalism and secularism, impregnated the ethno-religious *millets*, particularly the Greek *millet*. This modernisation process was facilitated by the associated activism of an economically powerful, and in some sectors (for example, merchant shipping), dominant group of overseas Greek industrialists, merchants and financiers, as well as by certain internal demographic shifts, all of which played an important part in the structural and cultural–ideological transformation of the Greek *millet*. The hegemonic role of the Greek Orthodox patriarchate and the supportive ecclesiastical and traditional lay elites (mainly the Phanariot aristocracy in Istanbul) in the preservation, cohesion and legitimisation of the *millet* as an ethno-religious apparatus of the Ottoman state was now being challenged by modernising economic and intellectual elites who sought to promote a more circumscribed 'nationalist' *Greek* community, identity and ethnicity. Schools and certain other cultural mechanisms (for example, the *syllogoi* and other societies or clubs) were integral parts of this process of Greek ethnic transformation, in that they both contributed cultural–ideological factors and were a consequence of them. But who were these modernising Ottoman Greeks?

Demographic and Socio-Economic Characteristics of the Ottoman Greeks

After the formation of an independent Greek nation–state (1830), the population of the Ottoman Empire classified as Greek diminished. However, there were still more Greeks living in Ottoman lands (in Europe, Anatolia and the Middle East) than in independent Greece. Statistics vary according to author and sources consulted. For the middle decades of the nineteenth century, estimates have ranged from over four million to about two million. The Ottoman census of 1881/82–3 recorded the Greek population as a total of 2 332 191. By 1914, the Ottomans had lost several of their European provinces to the Greek nation–state and to the Albanians. Still, according to the 1914 Ottoman census, the Greek population stood at 1 729 657, a figure which represented about nine per cent of the total population of the Ottoman empire.[12] A demographic breakdown and a social analysis of this Ottoman sub-group reveals some noteworthy characteristics of significance for this study.

First, it is relevant to highlight the large number of Greeks who were concentrated in commercially active urban coastal centres of Anatolia and in Istanbul. In some cities, for example, Izmir (Smyrna) and Ayvalik (Kydonies) on the western coast of Asia Minor and Samsun on the northern Pontos region, the Greek population by 1920 had surpassed the Muslim Turkish. In Istanbul, the most significant centre of Hellenism outside independent Greece, of a total population of 1 059 000 in 1897, 236 000 (about 24 per cent) were classified as Greeks, surpassed only by 597 000 Turks. By 1920, according to some sources, the Greek population of Istanbul numbered somewhere between 300 000 and 400 000.

Another, perhaps more significant, modernising development was an unprecedented economic 'resurgence' or, in the words of one source, a 'Greek managed economic boom', especially in the main urban centres.[13] A conspicuous example of the dominant economic position of the Ottoman Greeks is furnished by their percentage contribution to capital investment in the Ottoman Empire in 1914. Taking all national/ethnic groups, including the Turks, the Greeks contributed 50 per cent of such investment, while investments by Turks amounted to only 15 per cent.[14]

In the rural areas of Anatolia and the European parts of the Ottoman Empire, the Greeks were engaged mostly in farming, shepherding and small scale trading. Urban Greeks continued to be involved in large numbers in the traditional petty bourgeois occupations. But what was changing was the rise into economic, political and educational prominence of an expanded urban commercial upper bourgeoisie, active in international trade and the modern sectors of the economy, such as finance, shipping, manufacturing, mechanised transport, export oriented agriculture and the free professions. The economic prominence of the Greeks of Istanbul in foreign trade, commerce and finance was especially salient. By the 1870s, the *sarrafs* (Greek bankers) controlled the four most important banking enterprises of Istanbul, namely, the *Société Générale de l'Empire Ottoman*, the *Crédit Général Ottoman*, the *Banque de Constantinople*, and the *Société Ottoman de Changes et de Valeurs*. Some of them provided financial help and advice to the sultans and thus were able to wield political power as well.[15]

Greek Educational and Cultural Awakening

Within the framework of the Ottoman government policy of 'controlled toleration' and the relative autonomy of the ethno-religious *millet*, and in the context of the nineteenth century social transformation, the Greek minority was able to organise a network of educational and cultural institutions that had many of the trappings of a western modern and, in many respects, secular system of education. The educational picture that emerges from the sources is polymorphous and quite complex from the standpoint of administration, institutions, curriculum and teaching. There were variations among geographic regions and between urban centres and rural areas, and with respect to the relative role of the Church *vis-à-vis* lay authorities. One could say that there were several interlocking institutional networks and layers of authority, operating, at one level, within a semi-autonomous and increasingly 'national', but rather loose, ethno-religious confederated civil society and, at another, under the supervisory canopy of a weak Ottoman state.

The administration, control and supervision of schools were carried out by mixed bodies – ecclesiastical and lay – at the different levels of the *millet* organisational structure. At the top stood the highest ecclesiastical and national (ethnic) authority in Constantinople consisting of the patriarch and the two bodies surrounding him, namely, the Holy Synod and the Permanent Mixed (clergy–laity) National (ethnic) Council. Locally, three levels of educational administration and control could be identified: district, community and *enories* (communal parishes). At the district level, Mixed Ecclesiastical Councils elected Education Committees, which met under the chairmanship of the ecclesiastical authority (the metropolitan), and were responsible for the 'intellectual progress' of all educational establishments in the district: that is, they approved the curriculum, the appointment of teachers and monitored what went on inside the schools. At the community level, direct administration and supervision of educational establishments was the responsibility of School Boards, elected by the representatives from the communal parishes and presided over by the metropolitan or his representative. At the parish level, schools were governed by elected School Boards whose function included, *inter alia*, the management of the financial affairs of the school, the appointment and dismissal of teachers, the introduction of new textbooks and new teaching methods, the effective implementation of the curriculum, the conduct of examinations at the proper time, and the faithful discharging of the duties and responsibilities of all personnel involved.[16]

In actual fact, the picture was not this tidy. Other structures and networks, some entirely lay and secular, could be observed whose educational and political role should not be underestimated. Among these were the *syllogoi* and the *sōmateia* or *adelphotétes* (brotherhoods). Some of them, particularly *EFEK* (the Greek literary *Syllogos* of Constantinople), were particularly influential.[17]

In the second half of the nineteenth century, *syllogoi* were established in most areas of the empire where Greeks were living (Istanbul, Smyrna, Epirus, Trabzon, Thessalonikē, Serres, Thessaly, Crete, etc). Strictly speaking, *syllogoi* were different from schools, in terms of structure, clientele and many of their activities and goals. The aim of their functions was more broadly cultural, intellectual, social and, somewhat indirectly, national–political than that of schools. The clientele of the *syllogoi* was mainly adult and their structures were less formal than those of the schools. *Syllogoi* were also more autonomous and secular, in terms of their relation to the Church, than the schools.

The *syllogoi* are relevant in this study for several reasons. In the first place, they represent a consequential socio-educational development of political significance that was related to the nineteenth century social transformation referred to above. In addition to their broad cultural activities, the *syllogoi* were directly involved in more circumscribed educational matters: they established schools, supported others in need, and oversaw their educational activities. They set up teacher training institutions; they provided financial assistance to students intending either to become teachers or to attend the University of Athens, and in many cases, they helped in securing adequate physical and human resources. The educational functions of *EFEK*, for example, were so extensive that a contemporary French–Greek writer likened this *syllogos* to a 'Ministry of Public Instruction for the Greeks of the Ottoman empire'.[18]

More politically, the *syllogoi* sought to develop cultural identity and national consciousness among the Orthodox Greeks, a political identification to complement the already established religious identification. This goal was pursued mainly through non-school cultural activities, such as public lectures and *concours* on Greek history, language and culture, cultural contacts with independent Greece, publication of the works of ancient Greek authors, the creation of libraries, and so on. However, the national–political goal was not always overt. It was expected that the sense of Greek ethnic national identity would accrue, more or less naturally, from an exposure to Greek culture and its achievements through the ages and from the cultivation of the Greek language. There was little, if any, direct, ideologically circumscribed political education or socialisation into Greek nationalism.

This was even truer in the case of schooling in general. It can be said that the role of schools *qua* schools in the development of national identity among the diaspora Greeks in the Ottoman Empire has not been carefully researched at yet, and it may indeed have been exaggerated in the existing literature.

Within the general administrative framework described above, different types of schools had developed, especially in the commercially active urban centres. The most widespread type included the numerous basic schools known variously as *dēmotika* (elementary), *koinotika* (community), *astika* (urban), *koina* (common), or, as in the case of Istanbul *katòtera* (lower) schools. In some outer regions such as rural Crete, basic Greek education was also provided in what were known as 'monastery schools'. These lower educational establishments were organised into a varied and graded number of yearly classes, ranging from three to seven. Some were coeducational but more often than not schools were single sex and proportionately there were more for boys than for girls. Schools taught a variety of subjects, for example, reading, writing, arithmetic, Greek language, Orthodox religion and catechism, geography, ancient Greek history, drawing, needlework (in girls' schools), singing etc. Their main aims were basic literacy, particularly linguistic competence, and moral development which also entailed catechism of the Orthodox Greek faith.

It is difficult to assess the extensiveness of basic schooling, among the Ottoman Greeks because of the paucity of statistical data for the whole of the Ottoman Empire, particularly in the rural areas. The information that is available is often unreliable and complicated by the fact that basic schools were often part of an institutional complex that included other types of schools: *Hellenic, pro-gymnasiums* or *semi-gymnasiums, gymnasiums* and *lyceums* (middle or lower secondary, and upper secondary), and thus were not counted separately. These caveats notwithstanding, it may be reasonably claimed that by the opening decades of the twentieth century there was considerable provision that reached a comparatively large number of school age children in most urban centres, particularly in commercially flourishing places with sizeable Greek populations.

Even in smaller towns and in villages, efforts to provide some type of basic schooling were on the increase. For example, the Greek *Calendar* of Istanbul for the year 1903–4 recorded that in that city there were 64 'lower schools' (37 for boys and 27 for girls) with 360 teachers and 11 788 pupils.[19] According to another source, in 1899–1900 there were 185 schools of all levels and kinds in the greater Istanbul area with 584 teachers and 18 571 pupils.[20] In a recent, fairly detailed study of educational provision in Macedonia, which included the *vilayets* (provinces) of Salonica and Monasterion, it is estimated that at the turn of the century there were 592 *grammatodidaskaleia* (common schools) or places where 'basic letters' where taught and 261 'boys' and girls' schools and mixed elementary schools'. In addition, there were 79 lower secondary and upper secondary schools, 82 kindergartens, five night schools, one religious seminary, 17 schools for orphans and three schools for sewing and needlework. All in all, it was estimated that in a population of 655 982 people there were 1041 'educational institutions', 1704 teachers and 67 772 students. Based on such figures, it was calculated that in the whole Macedonian region the percentage of students in the total population stood at 10.33 per cent.[21]

Moving further inland, in the heart of Anatolia, and in the Pontos region, the case of the turcophone district of Kayseri (Kaisareia) in Cappadocia is rather revealing. 'In all the villages of the region in 1905', a recent writer has noted, 'elementary schools for boys and girls were functioning', together with 'one *gymnasium* recognised throughout the Oicumene, a girls' schools, two schools for orphans and five *semi-gymnasiums*'.[22] Referring to the Pontos region, another writer has claimed: 'By the 1880s virtually every Kouroumli village boasted a new school next to its new church'.[23]

In Crete, recently assembled and mostly unpublished data indicate significant expansion of educational provision during the period 1881–1900. According to the census of 1881, in a Christian population of 202 934 people, 13 971 persons, representing about 6.88 per cent, were attending some form of school, the numbers and percentages being generally higher in the urban than in the rural areas. About 20 years later, in 1901–2, in a Christian population of 269 948 people, 27 062 and 2378 persons were attending elementary schools and *gymnasiums* respectively representing approximately 11 per cent of the said population. The participation of girls had increased from 22.7 per cent to 28 per cent and the number of teachers had increased from 341 to 418 (382 men and 36 women).[24] Putting some of this statistical information into some sort of comparative European perspective, it can be added that, according to one estimate, the percentage of the population at school on Crete was 11 per cent, while in other countries estimates were 14 per cent for France; 15 per cent for England; 13 per cent for Austria; 12 per cent for Denmark; 11 per cent for Belgium; 8 per cent for Italy; 6 per cent for Greece; 4 per cent for Portugal; and 1 per cent for Russia.

As basic schooling became more widely disseminated and more systematically organised, so did the education and preparation of teachers. One could still find priests, monks or educated laymen who also acted as teachers, especially in villages and outer regions. But generally lower school teachers had finished the level of *Hellenic* schools, *semi-gymnasiums* or *gymnasiums*, or even *didaskaleia* (normal schools or teaching training institutions) where they were exposed to both general academic and professional–pedagogical subjects. A contemporary review of the curriculum of the teacher training schools of Epirus, Macedonia, Thessaloniké, Serres, Thrace, and Istanbul shows a wide ranging and rather diverse array of such subjects including: ancient Greek, philosophy, physics, natural sciences, music, gymnastics, French, mathematics, religion, geography, calligraphy, sometimes Turkish and modern Greek culture, physiology, pedagogy, methods of teaching, and practical exercises.[25] In this connection, it is of historical interest to add that for most of the nineteenth century, the monitorial system of instruction was prevalent among Ottoman Greeks, as indeed it was among the mainland Greeks.

The monitorial system, originating in nineteenth century industrial England, provided a cheap and highly moralistic type of instruction that was believed to be appropriate for the education and socialisation of the 'lower orders' of society, especially the rapidly expanding industrial urban proletariat, within the framework of the emerging European and American capitalist socio-economic formations. In the Ottoman empire, the monitorial system was also an economical way of providing instruction to the growing numbers of Ottoman Greek children attending schools. However, both socially and ideologically, it can also be viewed as congruent with the penetration of nineteenth century European capitalism and *laissez faire* bourgeois liberalism, and all that these forces implied, into the Ottoman empire.

Lower schools were established, supported and run by local communities or parishes through their *ephories* (School Boards). The impetus for setting up these schools came from several voluntary sources: the local Community Councils (in regions such as Crete from the *démogeronties*) (Councils of Elders), individuals and the Church. The School Boards were mixed clergy–laity bodies with greater lay representation. In the archives of the metropolitan see of Pelagonia in Macedonia at the turn of the twentieth century it is recorded that at its meetings the School Board in one community discussed and acted upon such matters as the maintenance of the schools, teachers, behaviour of students, curriculum and examinations, and also the programme of activities of important annual celebrations such as that of the 'Three Hierarchs' (Basil the Great, John Chrysostom, and Gregory Naziantinos) on 30 January. In the Greek world this is both a religious holiday and a cultural event (Greek Letters Day). It is also interesting to note that the programme for this occasion in this particular community included a 'Hymn to His Majesty the Sultan'!

Also, in the minutes of the meeting of 24 February 1907, we read that at the successful ceremony in honour of the Three Hierarchs, the son of the local *gymnasium* headmaster delivered a speech with the title: 'The significance of the present celebration and the power of the language in our national (ethnic) existence and welfare'. It was further decided that the speech be printed as a pamphlet and distributed to the people.[26]

In addition to the common schools, there also developed a network of general 'lower' and 'higher' secondary schools, especially in the urban centres. Such establishments were also organised into classes and went by different names: lower institutions being the *Hellenic* schools, *progymnasiums, semi-gymnasiums or hémigymnasiums*, and higher ones including the *gymnasiums, parthenagogeia,* or *lycées/lykeia*. Of these, *Hellenic* schools, the *semi-gymnasiums* and the *progymnasiums*, which were essentially similar, were the more numerous. Normally, they consisted of three or four classes and in some areas, they formed the lower level of a six or seven year educational complex, the upper level being the *gymnasium/gymnasion* or *lycée/lykeion*. The *gymnasiums* were fewer and were to be found mainly in the urban centres. Some of them enjoyed very high reputation throughout the Hellenic world. Such was the case, for example, with the old *Hé Mégalé tou Genous Schole* (Great School of the Nation) in Istanbul, the *He Evangelike Schole tès Smyrnes* (Evangelical School of Smyrna) and the Zosimiea School of Ioannina in Epirus.

It appears however that by the end of the nineteenth century, secondary schools (lower and upper) were to be found in all major urban centres; and a considerable number of smaller towns boasted of the existence of lower secondary institutions (*semi-gymnasiums, progymnasiums* or *Hellenic* schools). The case of Mathytos in Thrace was not uncommon. From 1887, following a period of stagnation, a cultural revival seems to have taken place there. In addition to a *syllogos*, Mathytos had then established a seven year urban school for boys, a *parthenagogeion* (six year school for girls) and one kindergarten. Children finishing the first two schools could enter the second class of the *gymnasiums* in Istanbul and Smyrna. Others followed their fathers' occupation as farmers, seamen, potters or clerks in commercial enterprises; and the majority went to Istanbul to become apprentices and then master craftsmen themselves.[27]

Similarly, in the 1880s and after, Cappadocia, in central Anatolia could boast of *semigymnasiums* not only in the city of Kayseri, but also in the nearby towns of Tarsiah, Tavlusun, Kermir and Talas, as well as a full *gymnasium* housed in the Holy Monastery of John the Prodromos in the village of Zincintere. Such schools operated parallel with an extensive network of boys' and girls' elementary schools, and drew their students not only from Cappadocia but also from places farther away. They taught general subjects but also, invariably, Turkish, for this region was heavily populated by turcophone Greeks.[28]

In the province of Macedonia it has been estimated that at the beginning of the twentieth century, there were about 79 'secondary' schools of different types: 12 *semigymnasiums*, 7 *gymnasiums*, and 56 *Hellenic* or equivalent institutions. The distribution of these schools, in terms of *kaza* (district) and Greek population, was rather uneven. The seven *gymnasiums* were located in the urban centres of districts, all except one of which had populations of over 35 000 inhabitants. Two of them were in the city of Thessaloniké, the most heavily populated area. The others were in the cities of Serres, Monasteri, Korytsa, Siatista, Tsosili and Kozane (the main city in the Kozane district with a population of only 16 120 people).[29]

In the island of Crete the increased educational activity referred to above included a number of secondary schools, especially in the 1880s and 1890s (just prior to Cretan independence). This was a period of increased political, social and cultural gestation that followed a series of revolts against the Ottoman government, certain stopgap measures of limited self-government, and two educational decrees (in 1881 and 1887) for the reorganisation of the existing schools and the setting up of new ones. By 1901–2, according to several sources, two *gymnasiums* (one in Chania and the other in Heraklion), two *semigymnasiums* (in Rethymnon and in Neapolis), 17 *Hellenic*, three higher schools for girls and one teacher training school had been established.[30]

There were some variations in the type of education these general 'secondary' schools provided, depending on where they were located and on any special provisions that may have been attached to their foundation. In general, however, they provided an academic and 'classical' humanistic curriculum, that in almost all cases included ancient Greek, but also Latin, modern Greek, history, religion, mathematics, physics, and physical education. In the *gymnasiums* additional subjects such as rhetoric, philosophy, psychology and French were also taught, while in the curriculum of the higher schools for girls one also finds some economics, 'home pedagogy', music, art, and calligraphy.[31]

Interestingly and quite significantly, the Turkish language or other Ottoman Turkish subjects such as history and geography were rarely taught, if at all, in the Greek schools, except in the already cited turcophone Cappadocia. The schools of the Greek minority were thoroughly Greek and Orthodox in their curriculum and in the language of instruction. Studies in the secondary or higher schools comprised mainly secular literary subjects. But it should also be added that religion formed part of the formal and informal (that is, hidden) curriculum of all these schools. Church functionaries sat on the Boards of Governors and the Orthodox Greek patriarchate exerted considerable influence, directly or indirectly, over them, as the autocephalous Greek Church did over the schools of the Greek state. Also, in both the Greek state and the Ottoman Greek *millet*, Orthodox Christianity and Greek ethnicity or Hellenic 'national' cultural awareness were gradually coalescing into a dominant and legitimating cultural and nationalist educational ideology, known as the Helleno–Christian ideology.

However, such rather Greek idiosyncratic Orthodox religious connections should not obscure the significance of the secular modernist characteristics of the Greek minority secondary schools which bore the imprint of similar secular institutions in Greece proper. Such schools were themselves influenced by and quite similar to western European counterparts, notably the German (Prussian) *Lateinschulen* (classical secondary school) and the classical humanistic *gymnasien* as inspired by the neohumanism of Wilhelm von Humboldt (1767–1835). In short, the Greek *gymnasiums*, including those of the diaspora, were in certain respects a species of the nineteenth century European genus of secondary schooling that included, among others, the French *lycée*, the English grammar school, the Prussian *gymnasium*, and the Russian *gymnasium*. This type of schooling was primarily classical and humanistic, secular, intellectually elitist, and socially middle and upper class. But for the Greeks of the new state, as well as of the Ottoman empire, a classical humanistic and literary type of schooling was perceived to be more than a conduit for the transfer of a western European intellectual and middle class 'liberal' culture. A classical, mainly Greek, *paideia*, in association with certain aspects of institutionalised Orthodox Christianity, was believed to be an important vehicle for the development of Greek national consciousness.[32]

Education and the Neohellenic Ethno-Nationalist Revival

The educational awakening of the Ottoman Greeks during a period of European, and Greek, nationalist revival raises educational–historical questions with broader comparative and theoretical implications. What was the relationship, if any, between the educational activities of the Ottoman Greeks, and the nineteenth century neohellenic nationalism that transcended the confines of the modern Greek state and the Ottoman Greek *millet*? What role, if any, did Greek schooling play in the development of Greek national consciousness? What light does the Greek experience throw on the inter-relationship between nationalism and education?

The Ottoman Greek nationality–schooling question may be examined from two parallel angles: first, from that of the independent and essentially ethno-secular Greek nation–state in the Balkan peninsula, and, secondly, that of the dependent and essentially ethno-religious Greek Orthodox *millet*. From the Greek nation–state angle, explicit efforts were made to foster national consciousness and ethnic identity among the Ottoman Greeks through the promotion and support of Greek schools, the teaching of the Greek language, and through non-school cultural activities. In addition, the Greek state provided a great number of teachers in all parts of the empire, even in the more isolated areas of Anatolia.

From the other angle, one of the avowed aims, at least by certain groups, of the spread of schooling, particularly the teaching of the Greek language, was to 'hellenise' the *millet*. Among other things, such educational activities could act as a safeguard against plausible alien, religious or national proselytisation (Roman Catholic, Protestant, Islamic, or Slavic). But one should be cautious in the kinds of extended inferences that one can draw from the above. It is evident that the extension of Greek schooling must be seen and interpreted within the wider context of structural change and modernisation in the Ottoman empire and the Greek *millet*. The establishment of Greek schools was connected with the growth of urban commercial centres following the expansion of the Euro-centred capitalist system and with the emergence of a Greek 'cosmopolitan' commercial bourgeoisie. As with the west European 'centre', therefore, expanded schooling as a form of 'exo-socialisation', to use E. Gellner's apt terminology, was intimately connected with the developing of a new social order in the Ottoman and Greek 'periphery'.[33]

In the context of Gellner's theoretical analysis of nationalism, one may reasonably hypothesise that the expansion of Greek schooling, in association with the other social and demographic changes referred to, could not but have contributed to greater social mobilisation, communication and cohesion among the previously rather dispersed communities of the Greek *millet*. Such interrelated social characteristics and processes may be regarded as constituting 'functional prerequisites' for the fostering of a sense of group identity/affinity, itself a contributing factor in the formation and nourishment of ethno-national identity.

Perhaps an even more significant 'functional prerequisite' in this process was the Greek language. Language, according to Herder, the historian Hugh Seton-Watson, the comparative educator Nicholas Hans, and others, was an important factor in the formation of national identity and 'the building up of national character' in Europe and other parts of the world, as well as in more recent political movements 'for national independence and unity'.[34] Certainly the

Greeks placed a great deal of emphasis on the teaching of the Greek language, both the ancient form and the modern versions of it. To the nationalist elites inside and outside mainland Greece, the Greek language was an important means of communication, cultural 'integration', and ethnic awareness. Learning the Greek language could also protect the turcophone Orthodox Greeks in Anatolia and in other parts of the empire from possible Islamisation and turkification. Alternatively it could maintain and indeed strengthen the 'latent' Hellenic ethnic sentiment among the Greeks in border regions such as Macedonia and Epirus in the Balkan peninsula, where there was a real danger of Slavic conversion or annexation. Again, the cultivation of the Greek language could provide a protective shield against certain efforts at Roman Catholic proselytisation.

The possible connection between Greek schooling and ethno-nationalism among the Ottoman Greeks may further be investigated by looking at other qualitative internal aspects – either manifest or 'hidden' – of the educational process. As a general rule, the Ottoman government's policy of 'controlled toleration' set limits to activities that overtly aimed at a separatist non-Ottoman ethno-national politicisation of the Greek youth. For example, explicit ethnic national content with politically relevant values and orientations was absent from the formal curriculum of the schools. It is still plausible, however, that ethno-nationalist values and orientations were transmitted openly or 'clandestinely' by the teachers in the classroom, outside the formal curriculum, or through 'extracurricular' activities. Along these lines, it is pertinent to refer to instances such as the ones already cited where the Greeks in certain communities would celebrate national and ethno-religious events under the tolerant eyes of the Ottoman rulers. The Greek teachers, particularly those who came from mainland independent Greece, perceived their role not simply in strictly educational terms. Concurrently, they looked at themselves as ethno-nationalist Hellenists charged with the added mission of cultivating nationalist Hellenic sentiments, attitudes and loyalties. From anecdotal evidence it appears that the extent to which the Greek teachers were able to perform politico-culturally relevant educational tasks in the classroom or outside varied according to region and historical period. It appears, for example, that such efforts were more prevalent in the more thickly Greek populated coastal regions and in the large urban centres than in places like central Anatolia.[35] It is, however, more difficult to assess the degree of success that they met with than the prevalence of such activities.

The Ottoman government's response also varied according to place and time. Spasmodic efforts were made to curtail or suppress nationalist propaganda and other similar activities, especially towards the end of the nineteenth century and the ascendance to power of the Young Turks in the twentieth. But, generally, as a recent study has concluded: 'Greek attempts at "rehellenisation" met with relatively little opposition from the Ottoman authorities'.[36]

Notes

1. Karpat (1982) pp. 141–2.
2. Vryonis, pp. 46, 54–5.
3. Vacalopoulos, (1976), p. 171.
4. Vucinich, pp. 87–9.
5. Karpat (1973), p. 34.
6. Kazamias, pp. 56–61.
7. Mardin, p. 21.
8. Papastathis.
9. Kazamias, p. 63.
10. *Ibid.*, p. 65.
11. Quoted by Adanir.
12. Karpat (1985), p. 48.
13. *Ibid.*, p. 47.
14. Alexandris, p. 32.
15. Svolopoulos.
16. Papastathis.
17. Stavrou, pp. 57–78.
18. Chassiotis, p. 456. Also see Vakalopoulos, pp. 155–73.
19. *Hémerologion, 1905*, p. 205.
20. Svolopoulos.
21. Papadopoulos, pp. 214–44
22. Tsalikoglou, p. 18.
23. Bryer, p. 187.
24. Androulakis, pp. 86–8, 116, 135, 140, and 147. See also Gondikakis.
25. Chassiotis, pp. 370–441.
26. Archeio Metropoleos Pelagoneia.
27. Sitaras, pp. 156–68.
28. Tsalikoglou, pp. 9–45. See also *Xenophanés*, p.74.
29. Papadopoulos, pp. 220—3. See also Vakalopoulos, pp. 155–69.
30. Kassimatis, p. 27. See also Androulakis.
31. Kassimatis, pp. 2113–4. See also Gondikakis.
32. See, for example, Tsoukalas, pp. 345–7, and 454–6.
33. Gellner, p.38.
34. Seton-Watson, p. 10; N. Hans, pp. 40–62.
35. Clogg, pp. 197–9.
36. *Ibid.*, p. 198.

Select Bibliography

Adanir, F. 'The Macedonians in the Ottoman Empire, 1878–1912', MS.
Alexandris, A. (1983), *The Greek minority of Istanbul and Greek–Turkish relations, 1918–1974*, Athens.

Androulakis, Y. 'Hé ekpaideusé stén Krété apo to 1815–1904' (Education in Crete from 1815–1904), MS.

Archeio Metropoleos Pelagoneia, Vivlion praktikon tou synedriou tés ephoreias, Ar. 20, 1906–7, Archive of the Metropolitan See of Pelagonia, Book of the minutes of the meeting of the board, 1906–7.

Bryer, A.A.M. (1976), 'The Pontic revival of the new Greece', in Diamandouros, N.P. et al. (eds) *Hellenism and the first Greek war of liberation (1821–1830): Continuity and Change,* Thessalonika.

Chassiotis, G. (1881), *L'Instruction publique chez les Grecs depuis la price de Constantinople par les Turcs jusqu'a nos jours,* Paris.

Clogg, R. (1982), 'The Greek *millet* in the Ottoman Empire', in Braude, B., and Lewis, B., (eds) *Christians and Jews in the Ottoman Empire: The functioning of a plural society.* Vol. 1, *The central lands.*

'Ethnika Philanthropika katastémata en Konstantinoupolei', *Hémerologeion tou etous 1905* ('National philanthropic institutions in Constantinople', Calendar for the year 1905).

Gellner, E. (1983), *Nations and nationalism,* Oxford.

Gondikakis, S. 'Hé ekpaideusé stén Krété kata ten Tourkokratia' (Education in Crete during the period of Turkish rule'), MS.

Hans, N. (1949), *Comparative education: A study of educational factors and traditions.*

Karpat, K. (1982) 'Millet and Nationality', in *Braude, op. cit.*

Karpat, K. (1985), *Ottoman populations, 1830–1914,* Madison, Wisconsin.

Karpat, K. (1973), *An inquiry into the social foundations of nationalism in Ottoman state,* Princeton.

Kassimatis, P. (1953), *Historiké episkopésis tés én Krété Ekpaideuseos: Historia ton schleion tés Krétés* (An historical review of education in Crete: History of the schools of Crete), Athens.

Kazamias, A. (1966), *Education and the quest for modernity in Turkey.*

Mardin, S. (1976), *The genesis of Young Ottoman thought.*

Papadopoulos, S. (1970), *Ekpaideutiké kai koinonké drasteriotéta tou Hellénismou tés Makedonias kata ton teleutaio aiona tés Tourkokratias* (Educational and social activity of the Greeks (Hellenism) of Macedonia during the last century of the Turkish rule), Thessalonica.

Papastathis, Ch. K. (1951), *Genikoi kanonismoi peri dieuthetéseos ton ecclésiastikon kai ethnikon pragmaton tou hypo tou Oikoumenikou thronou diatelounton orthodoxon christianon hypékoon tés A. Megaliotétos tou Soultanou* (General ordinances on the regulation of ecclesiastical and national affairs of the orthodox Christian subjects of His Majesty the Sultan, who come under the Ecumenical throne).

Seton-Watson, H. (1977), *Nations and states.*

Sitaras, A. (1971), *Hé Mathytos-Polis tés Thrakikés chersonésou epi tou Helléspontou* (Mathytos – A city of the Thracian peninsula on the Hellespont), Athens.

Stavrou, T. (1967), *Ho en Konstantinoupolei Hellénikos Philologigos Syllogos* (The Greek Literary Society of Constantinople), Athens.

Svolopoulos, C. 'The Greeks in Constantinople, 1856–1908', MS.

Tsalikoglou, E. (1976), *Hellénika ekpaideutéria kai Hellénorthodoxoi Koinotétes tés peripherias Kaisareias* (Greek educational institutions and Greek Orthodox communities of the district of Kaisareia), Athens.

Tsoukalas, K. (1977), *Exartésé kai enaparagogé: Ho koinonikos rolos ton ekpaideutikon méchanismon stén Hellada, 1830–1922* (Dependence and reproduction: the social role of educational mechanisms in Greece, 1830–1922), Athens.

Vacalopoulos, A. (1976), *The Greek nation, 1453–1669, The cultural and economic background of modern Greek society,* New Brunswick, New Jersey.

Vakalopoulos, K. (1988), *Neotourkoi kai Makedonia, 1908–1912* (The New Turks and Macedonia), Thessalonica.

Vryonis, S. (1976), 'The Greeks under Turkish Rule', in Diamandourous N.P., *et. al.*, (eds.), *Hellenism and the first Greek war of liberation (1821–1830): Continuity and Change*, Thessalonike.
Xenophanés, (1896), vol. I.

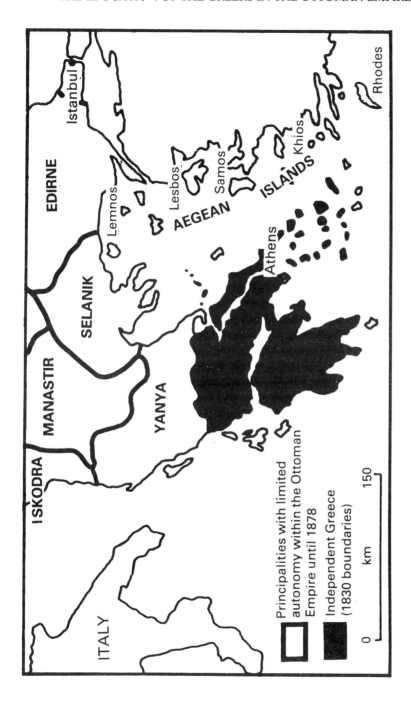

Map 15.1   European Ottoman empire before the Treaty of Berlin 1878
Source: Karpat, *Ottoman Populations (1830–1914)*

16 The Education of the Muslim Turks and the Christian Greeks in Cyprus, 1850–1905

COSTAS P. KYRRIS

Educational Provision and Types of Schools, 1850–1878

Though Cyprus had been under Ottoman occupation since 1570–71, until the mid nineteenth century very few Turkish schools existed there. When the British took over the island in 1878, only 41 Turkish schools were functioning: (a) 29 *sibyan* (elementary schools) each run by a *hoja* (teacher) who taught the Koran, the Arabic alphabet, hand writing, reading, and some arithmetic; (b) one *rüshdie* (upgraded elementary school) in Nicosia, to whose curriculum were added algebra, natural sciences, Turkish and morals: and (c) 11 middle or low level *medreses* (religious schools) which taught arithmetic, cosmography, grammar, syntax, geometry, Muslim philosophy, logic and discussion. All *medreses* were erected by *Vakf* endowments. Some of the *sibyan* schools were directly administered by the *Evcaf* foundation while the majority were administered by trustees under *Evcaf* control.

According to the High Commissioner's *Report* of 27 July 1880, the Muslim schools totalled 64, as against 76 Christian, whereas according to the May 1883 *Report of the Evcaf Properties* the number of Muslim schools was 70. Many of them were rural and rudimentary, though technically 'state' establishments, possibly founded as a result of the application of the relevant order issued by the Ottoman government in 1870, one year after the one issued for Bosnia. The number of teachers was 114. From 1862 the Turkish schools received an annual grant from the state treasury. On the other hand, Greek schools, before 1878 'were supported entirely by voluntary contributions', by Church and people, usually the wealthy notables. State aid and state

369

recognition of education were confined to the Muslim population. Despite these drawbacks, the non-dominant Greek majority (73.9 per cent as against a 24.5 per cent Muslim minority) operated 76 Christian Greek elementary schools in 1880, together with a few 'Hellenic schools' or half-*gymnasiums* in the main cities. All of these followed the models of schools on the Greek mainland and in the Greek diaspora. As of 1833, a number of schools had also been established by American Covenanter missionaries for Greek children, mainly in Larnaca, where a European community was living. When the missionaries left in 1841 their schools continued to operate.

The numerical and qualitative superiority of the Greek schools, all self-supported, was due to the numerical, economic and cultural prominence of the Greek majority. Despite occasional or frequent persecution and/or oppression by the Ottoman rulers, the Greek Christians controlled a substantial part of the local economy and political life. This came about as a result of the traditional privileged status of the Greek Orthodox Church and the class of Orthodox notables, which was reestablished after the end of Venetian rule in 1570–1. It was also furthered by the relative freedoms provided by the mid ninteenth century *Tanzimat* (reforms), although their application to Cyprus was limited and patchy. The influence of the ideology of the Enlightenment on Greek Cypriot prelates, landowners, merchants and other urban bourgeois elites, who were in close contact with the European bourgeoisie living mostly in Larnaca and with the bourgeois elites in Greece, as well as the diaspora, favourably affected Greek Cypriot education and imprinted on it a nationalist, humanist and idealist–intellectualist bias.[1]

Owing to its bureaucratic–administrative and military character, the imported Turkish Muslim elite kept aloof from the people of both creeds, Christian and Muslim. This aloofness was exacerbated by the fact that a substantial number of the 'local' Muslims, especially from rural areas, were converted Christians, who remained 'crypto-Christians' without any clear ethno-religious identity. Mostly Greek speaking, they lived in peace with their Greek neighbours and shared many common social and even religious values with them. These factors account for the low number of Muslim schools found by the British in 1878.[2]

Muslim–Turkish Education, 1878–95

Under the impetus given to educational and other developments after the British occupation, 'the leading Muslim gentlemen of Nicosia were anxious to raise the standard of their schools and desirous that really useful subjects should be taught', according to a report of the Chief Secretary to the government on *The Educational System of Cyprus between 1878 and 1902*.

A turning point in British educational policy in Cyprus was the rejection, by Lord Kimberley, the Liberal party Colonial Secretary, on 10 June 1881, of the proposals which had been submitted in 1880, as a means of checking the emerging Greek Cypriot *Enosist* movement. According to those proposals, education should be given in English, English secondary schools should be established in the three main cities and a teachers' training college be set up under an English headmaster. Kimberley considered the anglicising policy financially impossible and useless, and he extolled the excellence of Greek as a vehicle of higher learning. He advocated mere auxiliary government participation in the schools' financial and administrative burdens. Such establishments would continue to be the responsibility of the Greek and Muslim communities. He also laid great stress on the improvement of elementary education for promoting 'the welfare of the island', but did not concern himself with the development of secondary schools, which were the principal concern of the Church. However, contrary to his initial project to set up one mixed Central Board of Education for bringing the two communities together and restraining one sided tendencies, eventually the High Commisioner's proposal was accepted by him. Two separate boards were created in 1881, the Board for Greek Schools and the Board for Muslim Schools. Both Boards were presided over by the Chief Secretary and had as their secretary the Inspector of Schools, as the Director of Education was now called. The Chief Secretary would confer with the two Boards as to the distribution, after inspection, of government grants-in-aid to deserving schools and teachers, following the system of allocation according to results in force in England between 1862 and 1890. The Boards' powers were, therefore, advisory. District Schools Committees were also appointed as an intermediate authority between the Central Boards' executive and the Village School Committees' managerial authority. The latter were, like those of towns, 'elected' by the inhabitants according to an oligarchic system causing bitter conflicts between 'Old' and 'New' Muslim groups.[3]

Besides the control exercised on Muslim education by the Chief Secretary as Chairman and the Inspector of Schools as secretary of the Board for Muslim Schools, indirect government supervision was also secured through the presence on that Board of one person appointed by the two delegates of *Evcaf* (one Ottoman and the other British), both of whom were appointed by the High Commisioner. The other members of the Board (the Chief Cadi, the Mufti, and six Muslim notables elected by the District School Committees) advocated the interests of the Muslim community, but with advisory power. Since *Evcaf* continued to subsidize a number of schools, it claimed full control over them. As in the Ottoman period, maps, globes and books for the Muslim schools came from Constantinople, from where many teachers also originated, particularly for the *rüshdie* school. Greek Cypriot schools received their books and teachers mainly from Athens but also from other centres of Greek education in the Hellenic diaspora.

Direct control and support by Constantinople of a section of Muslim education was preserved in the capital, where all schools except three were entrusted to an officer appointed by the sultan. They would continue, however, to be inspected by the Inspector of Schools. The British usually adopted all or most of the suggestions of the Board for Muslim Schools as to grants-in-aid, the establishment of new schools and other topics; although sometimes they did not agree with the Board, noting with anger some of the Board's activities that went beyond its authority. There were even conflicts between *Evcaf* and the Board for Muslim Schools over funds and the control of some schools, and over efforts by *Evcaf* to prevent ignorant *hojas* from teaching in schools dependent on mosques. Cooperation, however, generally prevailed in their relations, particularly with regard to the establishment of Muslim schools in crypto-Christian rural communities.[4]

It was through the initiative of *Evcaf* and its British delegate that, in 1887, a Moslem school was founded in the crypto-Christian Greek speaking villages of Ayios Theodoros and Kokkina, in the poor area of Tillyria, under the supervision of the *mudir* of Lefka. More Muslim schools were established both before and after 1887 by the government, following the proposals of the Board for Muslim Schools in other Greek speaking 'Muslim' villages such as Louroudjina, Platani, Kornokipos, Kampyli, Vretzia, Lapithiou, Ayios Nicolaos, Kalo Khorio, Ayios Symeon, Korovia, Galinoporni, Plataniskia, Khoulou, Kilani, Ayios Ioannis, Yiallia, and Lefkara. These schools were offered grants which were gradually increased, despite the frequently contrary opinion of the Inspector of Schools. Many of them were reported 'unsatisfactory' or 'temporarily closed' and their grants were unclaimed and forfeited due to lack of interest. According to the Inspector, 'results did not justify larger grants', or any grants at all, in cases in which the Greek speaking children had to be taught in Greek for two or more years by a Greek speaking *hoja* before they could understand Turkish. On 15 December 1887 the Inspector even vainly proposed that 'a school maintained entirely by the government (and not a distinctively Muslim school) is the only thing that could have a chance of succeeding' at Ayios Theodoros and

Kokkina as well as in all other Greek speaking villages. Increased grants to crypto-Christian schools continued to be favoured by the Board for Muslim Schools and the government, contrary to the principle of grants according to results supported by the Inspector of Schools.[5]

Had the 1881 census of population adopted the distinction between 'really Muslim', so-called by the Inspector of Schools and the crypto-Christian, superficially Muslim Turkish communities, the Board for Muslim Schools would have had little or no chance to 'prescribe' Muslim schools for the crypto–Christians and insist on their complete turkification through education and religion. The motive of this 'omission' cannot have been unrelated to the 'divide and rule' policy of British colonialism and its effort through this to check the Greek Cypriot *Enosist* movement.

In this way the Muslim, or mostly half Muslim, minority was pushed to acquire or strengthen Turkish consciousness and at least to preserve its numerical importance by the local authorities and the Turkish Cypriot elite. Such an encouragement appeared 'necessary' also in view of the fact that the Muslim schools did not tend to increase in number as much as Greek schools, and were unable, or neglected, to absorb the sums allotted to them. More important still, the Greek schools were favoured by the voluntary system, which did not operate in the case of Muslims, and by liberal grants paid for their support by the Greek Cypriot communities of Egypt. In fact, the Cypriot Brotherhood of Egypt had taken a keen interest in the crypto-Christian villages in Tillyria (Ayios Theodoros) and elsewhere (Monagri in the Limassol district, Vatili, Drousha, Orini, etc.), where it subsidised the establishment of Greek schools. For unknown reasons, the Brotherhood failed in Ayios Theodoros, whereas it had more success in other places such as Pyrgos and Monagri.

In the distribution of grants, the Liberal government instituted a change that favoured Greek education. Instead of the disproportionate sums fixed for 1881–2 for Greek and Muslim schools (£598 and £875 for 3141 and 1426 pupils respectively), the Colonial Office in 1883–4, ordered that the annual grant-in-aid to primary schools be increased to £3000, out of which £2250 should go to Greek and £750 to Muslim schools, at the ratio of 3/4 to 1/4 according to population figures. To this a building grant was also added. Due to the Chief Secretary's reaction, it was decided that, from 1886–7, Christian schools would receive £2834 as grant-in-aid, plus £166 as building grant, and Muslim schools £1000 by way of temporary excess payment preserving the existing ratio.

The number of Muslim primary schools receiving grants in 1884–5 was only 59; in 1885–6, 54 to 56; and in 1886–7, 62 to 60. If we add those unaided, the total number of such schools amounted to 80. In

1887–8, the aided Muslim primary schools numbered 63 and in 1889–90, 94 with 3516 children. In the same year, there were 225 Greek schools with 10 342 children. All schools were managed to a great extent on the Lancastrian (monitorial) system, though among the Greek schools there were some monastic ones. An example of this in 1885–8 was the school run by the monastery of Makhairas with a government grant-in-aid, which, however, was discontinued because of the small number of scholars. Despite the considerable change of proportion in population figures (according to the 1891 census, there were 161 247 Christians and 44 044 Muslims) the government did not intend to 'disturb the existing allocation of the grant-in-aid'.

Meanwhile in September 1885, the system of examination of masters for (primary) Muslim schools was established by the government, declaring 'all or nearly all schoolmasters unfit' until they were trained at the *rüshdie* and passed an examination. Two years later rudimentarily applied 'new teaching methods' were slowly introduced, and some emphasis was placed on science, as demanded by progressive Muslim notables. At the same time, a relative 'modernisation' of the *rüshdie* took place through its adaptation to the needs of the British administration. Despite these developments, there were protests by some Muslims against the way Muslim schools were functioning.[6]

In the meantime, the 'new method' system of teaching was massively introduced in Greek Cypriot schools and instructors of the method were appointed, some of them after special studies in Athens. The Muslims felt that they had to take measures to make their schools at least as good as those of the Greek Cypriots. For some of them, the cause of backwardness and decline was the system of appointments to the Board for Muslim Schools, which had only advisory powers and no right to interfere with school administration, regulations and discipline. The Greeks also insisted on real educational autonomy, in particular 'that their recommendations should be final and not in need of authorisation by government'.

On 20 February 1893, the local Muslim paper *Yeni Zeman (New Time)* criticised unmethodical instruction in Muslim Cypriot schools, insufficient preparation of the pupils admitted to the *rüshdie* 'as a grant of favour', and the unsatisfactory teaching in it of geometry, geography and universal history, which was 'very slight in comparison with the requirements of present time'. It expressed 'worry at the unsuccessful efforts to establish Muslim schools in a number of Greek speaking rural areas such as Tillyria, the village of Lurugina' and others, whose inhabitants were 'Muslims (only) by name and by religion'. It proposed the amalgamation of the ten small schools of Nicosia into three or four large efficient ones, similar measures to be taken in the other towns and in large villages, and the appointment of competent masters, who should receive ample pay to be supplied by the local government, the Ottoman government and *Evcaf*. The paper also proposed that the organisation and running of schools, the preparation of their programme, and the fixing of teachers' salaries, should be entrusted to a general committee to be elected by the (Muslim) inhabitants. Finally, it was recommended that the reports of the Inspector of Schools should be taken into consideration, but that inspection should also be carried out by 'the Director of the Muslim Schools appointed from Constantinople. . . on behalf of the inhabitants'.

The issues put forward in the *Yeni Zeman* article were hotly discussed by the Muslim community. Voices were raised against unrepresentative modes of election of School Committees, insufficient teaching of secular subjects in primary schools; the miserable state of schools; and the unjust distribution of grants. These and other manifestations of the wish for absolute educational autonomy, closer educational ties with the Ottoman Empire and the increase of the funds spent on Muslim schools were parallelled by voices calling for more substantial financial contribution by the *Evcaf*. By 1891–2, explicit claims were made by Muslim notables that *Evcaf* should devote to schools the proceeds of the *menderisse vakfs*, whose properties, however, the *Evcaf* authorities declared 'lost'. But there were also efforts by the British and some Muslim notables to introduce the voluntary contribution system in their education. The Board for Muslim Schools itself was, like *Evcaf*, inclined towards introducing the voluntary system by law in limitation of the system in force in the Christian schools. This, however, was opposed by many villagers, since the funds of the grants-in-aid used for paying the teachers' salaries were raised from them as 'voluntary contributions', which were 'continually falling off', causing the reduction of salaries and leading to the appointment of inferior men as teachers. In some cases, Greek and Muslim villagers submitted joint applications, written in Greek, to the effect that 'the government should pay these salaries and raise by direct taxation the money' required for this.

The culmination of the Muslim drive for emulation of Greek progress and practices in education was the foundation, in December 1893, of the Moslem Education Beneficial Society by a group of Nicosia Muslim notables connected with the anti-*Enosist* paper *Zeman*. The principal aim of this society was to establish, through contributions, a high school and a school of arts and industry for the Muslim community. Although these aims were not achieved, the ideas of this society, like those of *Yeni Zeman*, influenced the government towards including provisions for contributions by the Muslims in support of their schools like the Greeks in the new Education law of 1895.

For their part, a committee of Greek Cypriot notables, presided over by Archbishop Sophronios, founded the Pancyprium *gymnasium* in 1893. This school, which acquired considerable eminence later on, was supported by contributions, with the lion's share being paid by the Cypriot Brotherhood of Egypt. It followed the programme of studies used by the *gymnasiums* of Greece, and it was recognised by the Greek government as equivalent to its Greek counterparts. Also, it undertook the training of elementary school teachers. The Pancyprium *gymnasium* was, until February 1893, the sole full Greek secondary school on the island, the only other such school, the private *lyceum* of T. Tsetsos at Larnaca having operated for only three years.[7]

The Education Law of 1895

The next turning point in educational policy was the Education law XVIII of 1895, passed by the Legislative Council during the tenure of office of the pro-Greek High Commissioner Sir Walter Sendall. It was introduced by the Greek members of the Legislative Council and incorporated several of Archbishop Sophronios' views on the function and power of the Greek Education Board. Officially, the Board became the policy making authority for all matters relating to Greek education. It could lay down the school curriculum. It could deal with complaints of inhabitants or teachers not settled by the District Education Committee and with appeals against those Committees' decisions. It could make decisions on complaints about the village contributions for school expenses. It could make regulations defining teachers' duties and the conditions under which they could be dismissed by the District Education Committees. It could determine the villages in which elementary schools should be established. It could consider the reports of the Inspector of Schools when referred to them by the government. Finally, it could recommend to the government the grants to be allocated to schools. The District Education Committee could recommend annually to the Greek Education Board those villages which should be compelled to support schools in the following year. Also, they could determine appeals from the Village School Committees, appoint village teachers, and fix their salaries in case the Village School Committees failed to do it. These Committees could appoint or dismiss teachers of (primary) schools, fix their salaries, divide the village education contributions between the local church or churches and the inhabitants, and inform the District Education Committee on all matters concerning education in their villages.

The Greek Education Board was to consist of the Chief Secretary to the government as Chairman, the archbishop, and nine elected members. Six of these members were to be elected by the Greek community, one from each of the six District Education Committees and three were to be chosen by the Greek members of the Legislative Council from among themselves, for a tenure of two years. The Chairman of the Board had the casting vote. The Inspector of Schools would be the Board's secretary. The District Education Committees were composed of four elected and two *ex-officio* members, who were the District Commissioner acting as its chairman, and the local bishop. The election of the four members came indirectly from the villages supporting schools in each district. All Greek members of the Legislative Council had the right to attend the District Education Committees' meetings and to vote on all matters. The Village School Committees consisted of three to five persons elected yearly by the tax paying Greek inhabitants of each village at an assembly convoked by the *mukhtar* or head of the village, who would report the results to the District Education Committee. The chairmanship of Town School Committees was reserved for the bishops, and their members were appointed by the Holy Synod from among the Town Church Committees.

Muslim education was organized in a similar manner. The Muslim Education Board was composed of the Chief Secretary as chairman, the Chief *Cadi*, the *Mufti*, a person appointed by the delegates of *Evcaf*, and six members to be elected in the same way as for the Greek system, every two years. The District Education Committee for Muslim schools consisted of the Commissioner who was chairman, the *Cadi* of the District, and four members elected by the Muslim community of the district. Village and Town School Committees were elected under the same conditions as their Greek counterparts. The law also established standards required of all teachers.

What is striking in this structure is the combination of democratic principles, leaving 'the people to a much greater extent than in the past to manage things for themselves', as an official stressed on 3 August 1886, with firm government control of at least some aspects of education through the *ex-officio* English members on the Greek Education Board, the Muslim Education Board and the District School Committees of the schools of both communities. From the administrative point of view the new system proved to be a partnership between the government and the Church, the *Evcaf* and the Greek and Muslim elites. An important feature of the system was the complete independence of the Town School Communities of the three main towns (Nicosia, Limassol, Larnaca), which were responsible for both secondary and elementary schools, the latter having been exempted from the provisions of the 1895 law in conformity with democratic principles. The Town School Committees, however, had no right to make assessments. They could only collect children's tuition fees and the Church contributions, receive the government grant and distribute it among the teachers, and appoint or dismiss the teachers of the schools managed by them. Only when two-thirds of the tax paying inhabitants of those towns so decided, could their schools be brought under the law. This balanced approach would suit the demands of the communities for autonomy in education. At the same time, it would help to check the growing *Enosist* Greek agitation on the one hand, and the recurring attachment of the Muslim elite to Ottoman values on the other. In January 1893, the *Mufti* stressed to the High Commissioner that, although satisfied with the existing administration, Cypriot Muslims considered Cyprus an integral part of the Ottoman empire.[8]

Still more important for future educational and ethnic developments was the power vested in the two Boards to determine the villages in which schools of either denomination were to be established. Such power was used most profitably by the Muslim Education Board for founding more Muslim Turkish schools in many crypto-Christian villages, to which they allocated lavish grants. This activity was often done despite the advice of the Inspector of Schools and against the will of the inhabitants, but also without the least reaction on the part of the Greek Education Board or the Church. In some cases, the British encouraged Greek children to attend Turkish courses in Muslim schools or Turkish and English in their own school, in order to increase the number of persons able to read the three languages, and 'to hasten the time when all records will be in English'. Such a development, according to the Commissioner of Nicosia, 'will facilitate the work of the English officers in the government, while placing the two communities on an equal footing'. The policy produced poor results on the linguistic level; but the idea of equalisation has been pursued systematically until today.[9]

Among the means used by the British for implementing the policy of equalisation were repeated plans to 'reform radically' Muslim education and elevate its poor quality. At the same time, until 1909, sporadic, ineffective and 'unofficial' efforts were made to check the nationalist activities of Greek teachers. Such efforts included proposals that grants-in-aid be made only to teachers 'free from the reproach' of 'weakening the people's confidence in the British government'. The reaction of the Church, which considered education its own province, and of the Greek Education Board, foiled the plans of the government, which, however, though almost always accepting the two Boards' recommendations of grants, considered their role as advisory. In 1902, the High Commissioner unsuccessfully proposed to London to deprive both Boards of even their advisory role in the distribution of grants, and with the funds saved from rejected conditional grants, 'to establish a few model central schools'.

Being unable to pay the costs of the growing number of primary schools, the Church had soon to ask for increased grants. The unconditional offer of the grants, however, was undermined by the Church's financial weakness and its internal conflicts, such as that over the Archbishop's throne in the years 1900 to 1909. This facilitated the gradual intervention of the government from 1909 onwards. This change was also the result of the insistence by the Greek Education Board in 1898, that only books printed in Greece should be used in Greek Cypriot schools. This led the High Commissioner to propose a project of 'preparing proper (school) books', some of them on practical subjects, for example, hygiene, domestic economy, and teaching methods, at government expense, to replace 'the books at present in use', which were 'undesirable and gave the children wrong impressions'. The project, which did not materialise until the 1930s, together with the English instruction vote, was intended to turn education gradually in a more practical direction, as opposed to classical studies, in accordance with the trend then prevailing in Europe. It would also have alienated the two communities from Greek and Ottoman values respectively, and attached them to a British imperial culture. British control was only imposed on the *rüshdie* and the Muslim town schools (1900), whereas the parallel repeated government efforts to impose its control on books and curriculum were defeated in the Legislative Council and temporarily abandoned.[10]

Government Policy Towards Muslim Education, 1878–98

The British concern with the improvement of Muslim Cypriot education ran parallel to the propagation of English teaching. The first example of this was the establishment of the English School for Muslim children in the Turkish quarter of Nicosia in December 1880, which, however, caused protests in a local Greek paper (*Neon Kition*) against the 'use of . . . Christian . . . money for promoting the Muslim minority's civilisation'. By contrast, there was no Greek Cypriot opposition to a private English school, established in June 1880, for all ethno-religious communities. Another school, supported by the government was the Nicosia high school, in which English was introduced. In 1882–3, the 'English grant' was withdrawn from the high schools, but, until 1885–6, English teaching grants were offered at least to some communal elementary schools to pay English born teachers upon local request. To meet the financial needs of this policy, and of communal schools in general, the government had to refuse grants to proposed private English teaching schools such as that planned by Major Osman-bey at Limassol, and the girls' school reestablished in autumn 1886 in Larnaca by American missionaries.[11]

With a constant government initiative and funds, a Muslim school for girls was founded in Nicosia, in 1888. But the constant concern of the government with the *rüshdie* dominated the 1890s, when efforts were made to reform it so as to 'serve as a training school for teachers of Muslim elementary schools'. On 30 July 1896, the Inspector of Schools commented that the *rüshdie* was 'the only educational institution that the government has absolute control over'. Thus the school could cope with the increasing need for teachers of the Muslim primary schools, whose number had risen from 74 in 1884–6 to 152 in 1904–5, as against 176 Greek schools in the former year, and 307 in the latter. The corresponding number of pupils in 1904–5 was 5180 Muslims and 18 533 Greeks.

A further British link with the *rüshdie* was the donation, in 1897, by the pro-Greek High Commissioner Sir Walter Sendal, of a substantial sum (£100), whose annual proceeds were to be distributed to the four best pupils as the 'Victoria Prize'. A much more substantial grant of £500, however, had earlier been offered by the High Commissioner (in January 1897) to the Phaneromeni Greek girls' school in Nicosia, to serve as the fund for the 'Victoria Scholarship' for the further studies of a female teacher of the school. Again in November 1897, the *rüshdie* entered a new period of reorganisation, which mainly consisted of the adoption of 'the programme observed in the superior *idadi* schools in the Turkish empire' and the approval of an examination for admission to it. Some leading Muslims, however, considered the reduction of the grants for them entailed by the heavy expenditure devoted to this school as detrimental for the rural Muslim schools. On the other hand, the disproportionate amount of the grants allocated to the *rüshdie–idadi* and the Pancyprium *gymnasium* led to Greek Cypriot protests, to which the official answer, on 13 December 1898, was:

> We took over [the *rüshdie–idadi*] at the occupation and we are liable for the whole of its expense. To the *gymnasium* we give a contribution which may be more or less . . . or cease according to the manner in which it is maintained. The two institutions are not on the same footing.[12]

The English Instruction Vote (1899) and its Reception by the Two Communities, 1899–1901

A landmark in educational policy was the approval, in September 1899, of the English Instruction Vote of £300, for the 'payment of annual bonuses', to every school 'where a certain proportion of pupils . . . receives satisfactory instruction in English'. In the Legislative Council the bonuses were described as a bribe by the Greek bishop of Kition. Though favouring the distribution of the vote among high schools as a subsidy for English teaching, the bishop opposed the introduction of English in the Greek primary schools for pedagogical reasons, and in order to prevent the anglicisation of Greek children. According to him and the other Greek leaders, this, after all, was the ultimate aim of the new policy, which revived the 1880s plans thwarted by Kimberley. Similar, if more elaborate arguments were used in articles in the local press. The newspaper *Aletheia (the Truth)* of Limassol called the new plan 'the work of the followers of imperialism blotting the liberal traditions of the English nation', while a document by the Greek teachers of Limassol repudiated 'any Greek teachers who might dare to teach it (English) in the island's elementary schools'.

Despite this, a number of teachers from both communities began to be trained in English in summer classes in 1901. To these were added civil servants, especially land registry clerks of all denominations (Armenians, Maronites, Muslims, Greeks), policemen and police-men's sons. Teachers, mainly Anglican priests of the Eastern Church Association, as a mission had existed in Cyprus since 1896, were brought over from England by the Inspector of Schools to carry out the project. Some of them were posted in the Pancyprium *gymnasium* and in other Greek secondary schools. The reception of this activity was cool and disappointing. Because of this, the government 'gave up all idea of helping in this respect' and decided instead to establish an 'independent, private, separate English school' in Nicosia in September 1900, to which it allotted the greatest part of the English Instruction Vote. A second English school was intended to be founded in Larnaca, but it never materialised because 'there has . . . been a good deal of private (English) tuition for men carried on by the minister of the American mission – though not under Government auspices'.[13]

The English school was founded and directed, until 1935, by Canon F.D. Newham, one of the priest teachers, in order 'to check the Hellenic affinities' of the *gymnasium,* as the High Commisioners put it. However, according to the first issue of the English school magazine in 1909, the school was 'founded at the request of several prominent residents of Cyprus'. Also, the same magazine noted that 'the number of (its) successful candidates for the government examination (leading often to civil service posts) has been steadily on the increase' and 'the school is appreciated by the inhabitants'. Besides the English vote, the English school received government advances and loans for its expenses, and also ten per cent of the education taxes paid by the Protestant community of Cyprus. In 1901, its director, F.D. Newham, succeeded Reverend Archdeacon I. Spencer as Inspector of Schools and was soon restyled Chief Inspector of Schools.[14]

In conclusion, it could be said that wherever the British met with little or no resistance, they tactfully imposed English teaching (in the *idadi* and the Saint Sophia school). Where there was resistance, as in the case of the Greeks, they offered material attractions such as teachers' bonuses, which were rejected by many but accepted by several, despite the continuing attacks on them by the Greek press. What, however, the British chiefly counted upon for eventual success, was the importance of English for a successful civil service career, and in the commercial and other practical domains of the developing Cypriot society. As F.D. Newham stated in his report on English teaching dated 10 July 1901:

> As the commercial and other advantages of . . . English become more appreciated . . . local difficulties may be expected to disappear, and if more funds were available for grants, the area of instruction could, through the schoolmasters, be widely extended.

Thus the 1880 anglicisation process now assumed an artful form, free of the element of compulsion, and this enabled the government to state, that it had 'never made it compulsory that English sh[oul]d be taught in schools'.[15]

Government Control and the Anglicising Influence on Muslim Secondary and Town Schools 1899–1900

A landmark in the development of Muslim education was the report prepared by a three man commission in 1900 on the administrative inefficiency and immorality of the headmaster of the *idadi*, and what was felt to be its deplorable situation. The headmaster's dismissal was followed by the adoption of the report's proposal that 'Mr. J.V. Thompson, relieved of some of the teaching in the lower classes . . . be entrusted the general discipline of the school'. Thompson's own proposals for the reform of the school were soon adopted. One such proposal was that Greek be included as a subject for regular instruction. In addition, more emphasis was to be placed on English teaching and the religious character of the *idadi* was to be minimised. Measures were also taken for the coordination of primary education with the reformed *idadi*. At least one of the Muslim leaders, Dervish *pasha*, member of the Muslim Education Board and the Legislative Council, contested such an open British interference with the *idadi*. In

June 1900, he moved an unsuccessful resolution in the Legislative Council to the effect that:

the management of the *idadi* school belonging to the Muslim inhabitants . . . be, in like manner as done in the case of the Greek *gymnasium*, put in the charge of a committee consisting of members of the Muslim Education Board, elected by the inhabitants, under the presidency of the chief Cadi.[16]

From September 1900 to September 1901, when an 'enlightened Turk' from Turkey was appointed headmaster, the school was under the *de facto* directorship of J.V. Thompson, who was careful not to give the impression of 'converting the institution into an English school'. British influence on it, however, increased further as appears in the contract signed by the new headmaster and the High Commissioner as chairman of the school's committee. The approved new programme in the contract included: English and Turkish (20 hours each per week), history, including the history of England (11 hours), Greek (12 hours), geography (15 hours), arithmetic (14 hours), geometry (six hours), algebra (three hours), Persian (nine hours), Arabic (12 hours), bookkeeping (four hours), Turkish calligraphy (two hours) and useful knowledge (two hours). In addition, however, it included religious subjects (18 hours) obviously a concession to conservative Muslim feeling. In December 1900, the Muslim Education Board's subcommittee for the *rüshdie-Idadi* was superseded by a Muslim Secondary Education Committee, under the presidency of the High Commissioner, who also appointed its members. Among the first concerns of this committee were improvement of English style sport, the acquisition of more land for the *Idadi* and the importation of 'English and Turkish wall maps . . . from England and Constantinople'. In January 1901, all Muslim town schools were placed under the charge of a commission appointed and presided over by the High Commissioner. Thus the government grip on a substantial section of Muslim education was completed, and its approval was required even for the good conduct certificates of the pupils.[17]

Government Measures to Establish an Agricultural Technical School for Both Communities 1899–1900

The Government's parallel policy to give a practical direction to the education of both communities was clearly apparent in 1899. But it failed, despite the fact that the elites of both communities were gradually feeling the need for at least some practical schools. Like the

Muslims, who in 1893 made abortive plans to establish a school of arts and industry and a high school, apparently an *idadi*, the Greek Cypriots founded a *gymnasium* in the same year. But this was done only after long discussions in the press as to its most suitable type, whether it should be practical, classical, mixed classical or religious and practical. The classical type was dictated by the chief financier, the Cypriot Brotherhood of Egypt, for both national and practical reasons: to prepare nationally minded teachers and intellectuals. The archbishop, however, stressed the need for a commercial and a science section in the *gymnasium*, according to French and German models, and in 1896–7, a short lived commercial–practical section was added to it by Mr Volonakis, the new headmaster from Greece (1896–1911). It was reestablished in 1907–8. In the meantime, a private commercial seminary was also started in Nicosia in 1899 by a self-taught accountant named C. Samuel. In 1896–7, the 'pedagogical section' of the *gymnasium* was converted into a professional teachers training school, with a curriculum that included agriculture, which Mr Volonakis considered an indispensable qualification for teachers. The school's survival was due to its support through an annual grant by the British government.

In 1899, on instructions from London, which were accompanied by an address on technical education delivered by A.J. Balfour at the Battersea polytechnic and published in *The Times* of 4 February 1899, the government decided to establish at a 'technical school' under its control 'so as to get rid of all distinction to the callings of Turk and Greek'. The school would teach 'agriculture, care of stock, arbori-culture . . . freehand drawing. . . , drawing to scale and making patterns' to all would-be elementary school teachers, who 'might receive a bonus for giving instruction in such subjects'. But law no. 447/99, passed on 30 June 1899 in the Legislative Council for the establishment of such a school 'was disallowed' until further instructions were received from the Secretary of State for the Colonies because (a) the bishop of Kition wanted it to be in his diocese and not in Nicosia, and (b) the Greek and Muslim members of the Legislative Council disagreed as to the number of Greek and Muslim members in the school's managing committee, a difficulty recurring in future years in many similar instances. Another cause of the failure was financial. In December 1902, however, a big farm to the south of Nicosia was purchased by the government for the establishment of an agricultural and technical school. But the farm functioned as an experimental agricultural centre rather than as a school. Finally, such a school was founded in 1913 but it was short-lived. Until then, the government's practical measures to promote agricultural and technical instruction were restricted to the dispatch by the Department of Agriculture of itinerant instructors to the rural areas to teach better farming methods; to occasional written instructions to potters; and to the training of juvenile delinquents in the government prison at Nicosia in shoe making and the like. In the late 1920s, lectures on practical agriculture and cooperative principles were given to teachers by the government, but the establishment of an agricultural college at Morphou, envisaged in 1930, materialised only in the 1940s.[18]

Conclusion: A General Assessment of Ottoman and British Education Policies in Cyprus 1859–78 and 1878–1905

The privileged position of the education of the Muslim minority of Cyprus in the last forty years of Ottoman rule produced poor results. This was due mainly to the bureaucratic military character of the Ottoman Cypriot ruling class and its social, racial and psychological isolation from the masses of the local Muslim population, especially from the crypto-Christian Cypriot peasants who were not willing to adopt the Islamic Turkish culture. By contrast, the education of the Greek Cypriot Christians during the Ottoman period was superior. This was due to the fact that Christians who were in the majority, controlled a great part of the local economy, while the Greek Cypriot Church also enjoyed a privileged status. Other factors that accounted for the superiority of Greek Christian education when compared to Muslim education were the partial application of the *Tanzimat*, the influence of the Enlightenment ideology, and the employment of the Greeks from the mainland and from the diaspora.

In the first 27 years of British rule, Muslim education was promoted numerically by the establishment by the Muslim Education Board, with government support, of Muslim schools in the crypto-Christian communities, despite the objections of many of them, in order to create a strong, self-conscious Muslim Turkish minority as a check to Greek Cypriot unionist nationalism. Greek nationalism was centred in the Greek schools, which, though financed mainly by voluntary contributions, profited from grants instituted by the Liberal government in London (1883–4) at a ratio of three to one. This situation coupled with the foundation, in 1893, of the privately financed Pancyprium *gymnasium*, strengthened the Turkish Cypriot elite's drive to elevate their *rüshdie* into an *idadi* and to improve their primary schools. The failure of this Turkish drive led the government to establish a Muslim girls' school in 1888, and to reform it into an *idadi* in 1897, for the purpose of producing suitable primary school teachers. The 1895 education law, which combined democratic principles with government control, mostly profited the Muslim minority.

The Muslim Education Board continued, with British encouragement, to establish Muslim schools in crypto-Christian villages. But the government failed to impose its control on the school programmes and books of the communities. In 1899, and after, the government resumed the previously unsystematic plan to propagate English language and culture among the civil servants and in the primary and secondary schools of both communities. This was done through the English instruction grant of 1899 and through bonuses to primary school teachers who taught English. On top of everything came the founding, in 1900, of the 'private' English school in order to check the Hellenic ideology of the *gymnasium* and the full government control and anglicising influence imposed on the *idadi* and all the Muslim town schools.

The Greek Cypriot reaction to the bonuses had little success, because it ran contrary to the attraction and the practical importance of English teaching for the developing local economy and society, in which trends towards commercial, agricultural and technical education began to appear. The belated effort of the government to establish its own intercommunal agricultural technical school failed owing to local jealousies, insufficiency of funds and the antagonism between Greeks and Muslims as to their share in its management. Agriculture and commercial subjects were only taught in the *gymnasium* 'teachers school' and the commercial and bookkeeping sections in the *idadi*, whereas the government gave agricultural and technical instruction through itinerant instructors and in the Nicosia prison, and occasionally by letters to potters. Despite the undoubted achievements of education in the island in the first 25 years of British rule, they were far below what the Cypriots expected from a European administration. Their chief complaints were summarised in 1902 by A. Chacallis, a Greek member of the Legislative Council, in his book *Cyprus under British Rule*. What Chacallis blamed most for this inadequacy was the insufficiency of the education grant, which, by comparison, was far smaller than that spent on Guiana, Barbados, and other British colonies, to say nothing of Crete.

Notes

1. Hill, pp. 142–268, 305, 400 ff; Kyrris (1976), pp. 127–166; Persianis, pp. 35–58.
2. Papadopoullos (1980), pp. 27–30, 334–57; Papadopoullos (1965), pp. 61–80; Georghallides, pp. 52–4.
3. *Ibid.*, pp. 45–8; Persianis, pp. 45–80, 113–30, 150–78; Public Record Office of Cyprus [PRO] SAI/1885–95.
4. PRO, SAI/1885–90.
5. *Ibid.*, SAI/1894.
6. *Ibid.*, SAI/1886–91.

7. Spyridakis, pp. 8–19.
8. Persianis, pp. 53–88; Georghallides, pp. 49–50; Weir, pp. 37–8; Suha, p.361; PRO, SAI/1896–1900, pp. 49–50.
9. PRO, SAI/1895–1901.
10. Persianis, pp. 35–44, 66–88; Weir, pp. 45–94, 84–134.
11. *The Cyprus Gazette*, June 29, 1881, p. 101; PRO, SAI/1885.
12. *The Cyprus Blue Book*, 1885–6, 1898–9, 1899–1900, 1904–5; Myrianthopoulos, pp. 38, 189, 273; PRO, SAI/1895–99.
13. PRO 1899–1901; Hill, pp. 500–3, 570–1.
14. Georghallides, pp. 72–3, SAI/1900–1.
15. PRO, SAI/1901.
16. PRO, SAI/1900.
17. PRO, SAI/1900–1.
18. Persianis, pp. 35–40, 191–9; Spyridakis, pp. 23–37; Weir, pp. 45–9, 67–74, 84–134.

Select Bibliography

Annual Report of Limassol District after the First Year of British Administration, July 1878–79, Vol 41/1.

Behçet, H. (1969), *Kibris Türk Maarif Tarihi (1571–1968), (History of Turkish Cypriot Education (1571–1968))*, Nicosia.

Chacallis, A. (1902), *Cyprus under British Rule.*

Georghallides, G.S. (1979), *A Political and Administrative History of Cyprus, 1918–1926, With a Survey of the Foundation of British Rule*, Nicosia.

Hill, G. (1952) *History of Cyprus. The Ottoman Province, The British Colony 1571–1948, Vol IV*, Cambridge.

Kyrris, C.P. (1967) *History of Secondary Education in Famagusta (1151–1955)*, (in Greek), Nicosia.

Kyrris, C.P. (1976), 'Symbiotic Elements in the History of the Two Communities of Cyprus (1570–1878)', *Proceedings of the International Symposium on Political Geography*, Nicosia.

Myrianthopoulos, Kl.I. (1946), *Education in Cyprus under British Rule, 1878–1946* (in Greek), Limassol.

Papadopoullos, Th. (1965), *Social and Historical Data on Population, (1570–1881)* Nicosia.

Papadopoullos, Th. (1980), *Consular Documents of the XIXth Century* (in Greek), Nicosia.

Persianis, P.K. *Church and State in Cyprus Education: The Contribution of the Greek Orthodox Church of Cyprus to Cyprus Education during the British Administration (1878–1960).*

Public Record Office of Cyprus, Files of the class SAI/1885–1909, Nicosia.

Spyridakis, C. (1944), *A Commemorative Album on the Fiftieth Anniversary of the Pancyprium Gymnasium, 1893–1943* (in Greek), Nicosia.

Suha, A. (1973), 'Turkish Education in Cyprus', *Proceedings of the First International Congress of Cypriot Studies* (Nicosia, 12–16 March 1969), III, 1, Nicosia.

The Cyprus Blue Book, 1885–1905, Nicosia.

The Cyprus Gazette, 1880–1881 ff., Nicosia.

Cyprus, Correspondence Respecting the Affairs of Cyprus (1881), presented to both Houses of Parliament by Command of Her Majesty, June 1881.

Weir, W.W. (1952), *Education in Cyprus, Some Theories and Practices in Education in the Island of Cyprus since 1878*, Cyprus.

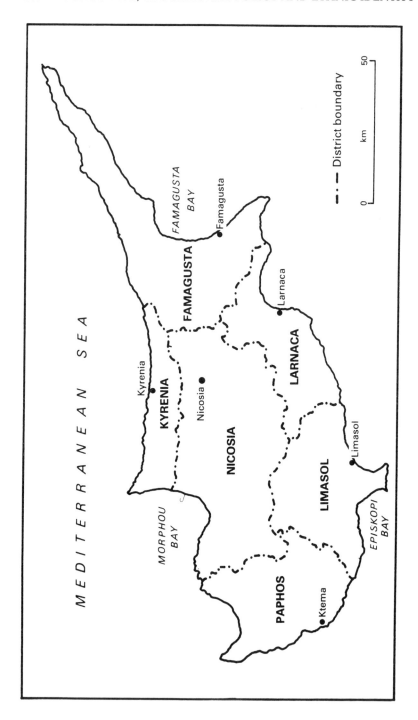

Map 16.1   Cyprus under the Turks (before 1878)

17 Governments and the Education of Non-Dominant Ethnic Groups in Comparative Perspective

KNUT ERIKSEN, ANDREAS KAZAMIAS, ROBIN OKEY and JANUSZ TOMIAK

The relations between governments and non-dominant ethnic groups in respect of education which have been surveyed in this book were played out against a background of demographic, socio-economic, political and cultural changes of very fundamental significance. The most important ones need to be underlined again here. The 'modernising' impulses already visible in 1850, and noted in the opening chapter, gathered strength throughout the period of this study. On average, populations in 1940 were at least twice what they had been in 1850; the proportion living in towns had nearly doubled; and real wages had advanced considerably. Of course, there were significant deviations from, and variations within this pattern. The population of Ireland had halved. Over much of eastern Europe rising population and limited land meant that many peasants were not necessarily better off than they – or their parents – had been before. A consistent statistic remained, however, the expansion in those that might be called the middle classes; commercial, professional, administrative and (though sometimes from a low base) industrial sectors, to which might be added the increased prosperity of at least a portion of the peasantry. To changes in social structure corresponded changes in patterns of communications which had created vastly expanded cultural networks in press, entertainment and sport, servicing largely, but by no means exclusively, the needs of the swelling urban and middle classes. These changes, which may be loosely summarised under the convenient, if problematic, label 'modernisation', loosened inherited structures and increased the proportion of people able to play an autonomous social role. It is reasonable, therefore, to assume that they had a significant role in the reshaping of relations between governments and non-dominant ethnic groups in our period.

There were other changes of equal importance. There was an

uneven, but persistent growth in secularising tendencies and a corresponding decline in religious convictions, noticeable everywhere. The influence of the Churches was in a steady decline and their power was inevitably curtailed in a wide range of culturally and socially significant activities, though the differences in the rate of change between the various countries were, in this context, as significant as the general trend and there were exceptions to this rule, particularly in central and eastern Europe and Ireland.

Most important, the concept of the role of the state in society was also undergoing constant and very fundamental changes. The autocratic and absolutist forms of government were challenged and undermined in several states, though they continued their existence elsewhere in the second half of the nineteenth century. Constitutional forms of government were instituted in some of the great empires, while representative governments offered a promise of genuine democratisation in a number of states, only to be replaced after the First World War by new versions of autocratic and dictatorial regimes. However, what mattered most was that the power of the state was everywhere rapidly gaining in importance. All its branches and all its agencies could be – and were – mobilised to promote 'modernisation'.

The introduction, at various points of time in the different states, of universal, compulsory, free and efficient education, disseminating useful knowledge, met with a considerable degree of support from all quarters, as being in the joint interest of the state and its citizens. There were, however, two issues of enormous consequence, which were bound to lead to the clash of interests in the multi-religious and multi-ethnic empires and states bent upon rigorous modernisation. They were the language of instruction and the teaching of religion. Both were inescapably bringing into confrontation the governments representing the interests of the dominant elements in society and the non-dominant ethnic groups. The phenomenon of involvement of secular state authorities in educational affairs thus contributed to provoking ethnic conflicts. In many ways the emphasis on schooling was firmly connected with the efforts to assimilate the minorities and to establish a homogeneous, or at least a politically stable state. The authorities optimistically considered the schools to be the main instrument in this process. In reality, the outcomes turned out to be only marginally significant and often even quite contrary to what had originally been intended and expected. This observation is one of the striking comparative findings of this study.

Government Policies in Respect of Non-Dominant Ethnic Groups

As our studies show, traditional barriers to the advancement of non-dominant ethnic groups remained strong over much of Europe till

1918 at least, and in many instances till 1940. The most important of these was linguistic discrimination, though the evolution of language policies varied widely. The provisions of the 1857 Spanish Education law excluding regional languages from the school remained in force throughout these years. Till the 1880s this was true, too, of the National School system established in Ireland in 1831 and that developed in Wales between 1839 and 1870. By contrast, the use of Czech in Habsburg schools and of Finnish in the Grand Duchy of Finland steadily expanded. Alongside the patterns of no change and improvement, there was also retrogression, sustained or inter-mittent, in the teaching of Polish in Russian and Prussian Poland, the non-Magyar languages of Hungary and Sami and Finnish speakers in Sweden and Norway. The cultural chauvinism of the Young Turks in the Ottoman empire's dying years and late tsarist pressures in Finland were also belated echoes of the same phenomenon.

Religion was yet another prominent marker of non-dominant ethnic identity. Indeed, for the Catholic Irish, the great majority of whom only spoke English in 1851, it was the major one. In Ireland and preponderantly Nonconformist Wales in the United Kingdom, educational institutions at secondary and higher level and the wealthiest associations promoting primary education were initially under control of the state Anglican Church, whose alleged prosely-tising goals continued to have ethnic overtones for the non-dominant groups. In the Balkans, the right to autonomous Orthodox schools was asserted as a national inheritance against Ottoman Muslim and (in Bosnia after 1878) Catholic Austrian rulers. In Russian Poland, Catholics could not become *gymnasium* directors, Orthodox schools were specially funded and, as also in eastern Finland, Orthodox minorities were pinpointed as the advance troops of russification.

The evolution of government policy in this sphere mirrored that in the language sector. While a relaxation of traditional policies of dominance could be observed in the disestablishment of the Church of Ireland in 1869 and of the Anglican Church in Wales in 1920, or in the grant of autonomy to the Orthodox Serb Church in Austro–Hungarian Bosnia in 1906, the aggressive use of Orthodoxy in the minority lands of the Russian empire, though shaken by the revolution of 1905, was not really abandoned till tsarism fell. More subtle, if less easily identifiable, were the associations of back-wardness which dominant groups continued to fix on non-dominant ones until the turning point of 1918, as noted in the case of the Irish and Welsh in the British Isles, the Flemings in Belgium, the Slavs in the Habsburg Monarchy. Even in the case of a 'historic' people, the Italians of Austria, the limited teaching of Italian history and culture in the schools could reinforce acceptance of inherited minority status.

Our surveys, therefore, reveal a great variety of experience. How have our contributors classified this experience, in terms of the concepts offered in the 'guidelines'? Interestingly, none have identified a policy of domination, a possibility considered only to be rejected in the chapter on Spain. This judgement appears correct. A policy of domination in educational terms suggests the use of the school merely to reproduce ethnic divides, with the non-dominant ethnic groups' schools providing necessary labour skills and affording no entry to state or social power. It is, therefore, suited to a system like South African apartheid rather than one such as that of centralist Spain, which discriminated negatively against non-Castilians by refusing to accept their self-valuation, but did not positively deny them upward mobility within the state. The abandonment of systems of domination in this sense in our field of study reflects the pervasive influence of the liberal concept of the citizen, endowed with civil (if not political) equality, as the foundation of the state. This concept, forced upon the Ottoman empire by the powers in 1839 and 1856, penetrated even the Russian empire; quite vigorously in Finland, but more haltingly in its Polish lands. It is here, if anywhere, that state educational policy came closest to naked domination, for though Polish products of russified schools could and did reach high positions elsewhere in the empire, it was harder for them to do so in their own homeland. But even the tsarist state, with its roots in enlightened despotism, if not liberalism, aimed, in intention at least, towards assimilation. For a system of educational domination at its purest it is necessary to look to the German Baltic barons' regimen in Latvia and Estonia, which tsarism began to dismantle from the 1880s.

A policy of *assimilation* appears the obvious option for states whose self-confidence grew with the range of their responsibilities in an expanding age. The term is used in chapters on Spain, Italy, Finland, Sweden, Norway, partitioned Poland, Hungary and Austrian Bosnia. Yet it is highly ambiguous. E.C. Thaden's distinction between administrative and cultural russification is helpful here, with the former more suitable for tsarist Finland, where Russian never became compulsory in elementary schools, and the latter for tsarist Poland between 1885 and 1905, when no other teaching language was allowed. Ottomanisation provides another example of administrative assimilation, designed to win loyalty to the Ottoman state rather than the Turkish nation and culture. Yet, distinctions remain blurred. Could administrative russification in Finland have led on to cultural russification, as had happened in the Baltic lands? Did cultural assimilation mean the acquiring of bilingualism through the knowledge of the language of state, or the eventual displacement of the mother tongue and change of ethnic identity?

In Hungary and Prussian Poland, where the government's aim was to increase the number of Magyars and Germans respectively, it seems logical to assume that the latter was the case, though, as with many magyarised Slovaks, it may have been assumed that a continued bilingualism was no bar to a Magyar heart. In the case of Russian Poland it is harder to imagine Russian authorities thought they were turning Poles into Russians. Here, if a practical goal other than obtuse nationalist ideology existed at all, monolingual Russian instruction was presumably supposed at least to habituate Polish peasants with the Russian link. Either way, the distinction is clear. Policies of russification, germanisation, magyarisation, etc. could either aim to strengthen allegiance to the state framework in which non-dominant populations lived, or could work for self-identification with the dominant nation. In subsequent discussion, for purposes of clarity, the term 'assimilation' will be used only for the second of these positions, and the term 'integration' for the first.

Integration, not assimilation in this sense, was the policy of multi-national Austria and of ottomanisation under the *Tanzimat*. It is also the term used by both contributors on the United Kingdom. This may seem surprising when it is remembered that British policies denied the Celtic languages any role in the schools and helped facilitate the linguistic anglicisation of Ireland and Wales. What underlies Dr Comerford's and Dr Okey's analyses, however, is the view that the British state cannot be identified with an English nation seeking as its primary purpose to impose its culture. The framework of reference in the United Kingdom was political and religious; Irish theories of nationality like English stressed common citizenship, religious and civil equality and free government. Integration of Ireland into the British political system required, from the perspective of London, the overcoming of the sectarian feud of Catholic and Protestant and attendant agrarian violence. An interdenominational system of education was seen as the means to this.

In both Ireland and Wales government was motivated in the first instance to respond to popular activity. Prior to integration was the need to regulate the secret or hedge schools springing up in Ireland and to keep the peace which in Wales had been disrupted by social unrest. Indeed, both Dr Comerford and Dr Okey emphasise the *laissez faire* traditions of the British state and the limited nature of direct government intervention and control in the educational sphere. In another developed society, Belgium, with its extensive system of municipal and private schools, the first function of government in the educational sphere seems even more to have been regulatory.

Two issues of particular interest emerge from this survey. First, assimilation in the sense of policy explicitly aiming to change the identity of non-dominant ethnic groups was a comparatively rare feature of government action in the years 1850–1914. Second, east

European scholars sometimes use the term assimilation to describe policies which did not really challenge the linguistic identity of non-dominant ethnic groups, while scholars from the British Isles contest this term even when policies involving systematic linguistic discrimination were involved. Underlying these differences of perception, and a finding of great significance, is the theme that the modernisation process took essentially different forms in western and eastern Europe, and that assimilationist policies as defined above were the product of the particular patterns of development in the eastern half.

In western Europe, certainly in the United Kingdom and Belgium, a powerful capitalist class, English and French speaking respectively, made systematic state intervention in the economy or in support of anglicisation or frenchification unnecessary. It was the relative failure of capitalism in Ireland which drove the British state into such interventionism as it practised. In central and eastern Europe, however, government assumed a more positive role in the modernising process: partly because German and Italian governments had first to be created; partly because in the effort to catch up with the west they tended to a more activist economic role. Moreover, under the influence of Herder's critique of a rationalistic, universalistic Enlightenment, central, and then east, European thought had stressed the significance of linguistic cultural heritage and the unique contribution all ethnic groups had to make towards the fulfilment of the potential of humanity. The politicisation of this cultural nationalism created a potent ideology in which language, culture, nation and ultimately state were conflated to an extent unknown in the west.

The nation–state became in itself a modernising principle. As German and Italian nationalism rubbed off on the Slavs, questions of language and culture became the dominant organising themes of politics. Governments like those of Hungary after 1867, or Prussia after 1873–1886, led the way in aiding the state language and culture to victories which social forces appeared too sluggish to provide. Such an atmosphere, too, could generate charges of assimilation even where, perhaps, more traditional government motives were at work. The activities of societies like the *Deutscher Schulverein* (German School Association) and its Czech equivalent in Bohemia thus assumed public importance disproportionate to the number of people affected by them. For it can be assumed that official attempts to change the ethnic identity of whole populations through educational means are fraught with such difficulties that they are more likely to be made after other means of social control are felt to have failed.

Such other means might be on the one hand the dominant groups' control of autonomous social processes, as in the economic hegemony of British anglophones or Belgian francophones. Alternatively, they might be long standing mechanisms of political integration through inculcation of dynastic loyalty, indirect rule or the bureaucratic centralisation identified by E.C. Thaden. These mechanisms had been traditional in the east European empires – indirect rule in the Ottoman *millet* system, and in Congress Poland up to 1830 and in tsarist Finland till much later; dynastic loyalty and bureaucratic centralism in Austria till 1918. None of them excluded assimilation of highly educated members of non-dominant ethnic groups. With the advancing pace of change, empires were more and more faced with the choice of dismantling instruments of elite assimilation (abandonment of German as the sole language of post-primary education in Austria from the 1850s) or of expanding assimilation to new elements (Young Turks, late tsarist Russia).

The end of the First World War brought with it the break up of the great empires which, in turn, resulted in the emergence or re-emergence of several independent states in central and eastern Europe and the redrawing of the frontiers. However, as numerous areas possessed ethnically mixed populations, the task of fixing the actual borders between any two neighbouring states proved extremely difficult. In consequence, though non-dominant ethnic groups became much smaller, with the acceptance of the principle of political self-determination and the establishment of new states in that part of Europe, ethnic tensions were bound to continue and, often, result in an open conflict. An important element in this was the fact that by that time, the national consciousness of practically all the nations and nationalities was already well developed and the different ethnic groups were by then very conscious of their rights. This consciousness included the right to education in the mother tongue, particularly under the regimes ostensibly based upon a democratic order. In general this applied equally to the small non-dominant ethnic groups in all parts of Europe, which were unable to claim political independence or, at the very least, a limited measure of political autonomy.

However, with time, a policy of assimilation was developed not only in Fascist Italy and Germany, but also in several of the new liberal democracies. This tendency, contrasting with the integration policies of some former empires, was in part a logical consequence of these states' claim to, and understanding of, nationhood. The liberal state evidently was in favour of individual rights and not necessarily group rights. In deference to liberal professions, however, assimilation was, at first, gradual or was most consistently implemented in disputed border areas *vis-à-vis* alloglot minority groups, or to small populations. In this sense, assimilation had already become the policy of Sweden and Norway towards Sami and Kvens before 1914.

These countries provided the example that farreaching national and political changes do not necessarily affect minority policies.

Italy also illustrated this pattern if in a more complex way. The liberal Italian governments of the period 1918–22 conducted a relatively moderate policy of assimilation. Yet at all levels, the educational role of Italian language and culture was increased at the expense of minorities, whose presence was considered to be an anomalous and transitional phenomenon. In the liberal period, however, individual rights were still formally granted, while collective and corporate rights were regularly set aside. Undoubtedly, a considerable measure of continuity from the earlier times can be noted. The centralisation of school system and the active suppression of 'foreign' languages and cultures starting around 1860 made it easier for the Fascist regime to intensify the policy of italianisation later. The Fascist seizure of power represented the turning point vis-à-vis the minorities in some ways. In previous years the Fascists had criticised the liberal politicians strongly for being too soft towards minorities. The policy of assimilation reached its most extreme form under the Fascist regime. Any compromise with the minorities came to be regarded as a betrayal of victory and of Italian 'sacred' interests. Thus all schoolchildren were to be taught and raised in the Italian language and spirit.

The assimilationist policy of Spanish governments undoubtedly had other roots. The minority policy of the Spanish state concerning the three regions studied by Professor Garrido was characterised by linguistic and administrative centralism. In the schools the Castilian language was compulsory and taught in all parts of the country. The gradually increasing regional claims for bilingualism were firmly rejected by the central authorities. The policy of cultural assimilation was, in substance, supported by liberal as well as conservative and Fascist parties. Even radical parties put a centralist policy into practice when in power. Only the Second Republic tried to change this course in the 1930s, but the outbreak of the Civil War prevented a more fundamental implementation of this new policy of decentralisation and of regional linguistic and educational autonomy. Under Franco's dictatorship the few moves towards a pluralist policy were promptly reversed. The slogan had become: 'Let's speak the language of the empire!'

In other states, for various reasons, a more fluctuating and complex pattern appeared. In interwar Poland one could discern a policy aiming at gradual assimilation, at least in respect of certain non-dominant ethnic groups. This policy, however, was subject to considerable opposition from various quarters. Change was by no means always consistent. In addition the various attitudes and reactions of the numerous minorities made it difficult for the Polish government to pursue a firm and uniform policy. In sum, one may observe a substantial increase in bilingual schools or schools teaching in Polish. The heightened problem for the non-dominant groups which remained under alien rule was expressed in the German mayor of Bolzen's claim to the Italian prime minister that Italy, in acquiring her south Tirolers, had ceased to be a national state. This was, of course, far from the Italian understanding and becomes more ironic, if applied to Czechoslovakia, where the number of Germans in the new, self-consciously national state, was much greater.

In general, after 1918 one could observe the scaling down of educational rights of minorities under Fascism and neoFascism and a greater willingness to respect such rights where strong democratic traditions continued.

Motives Generating and Legitimising Policies in Respect of Non-Dominant Ethnic Groups

It is important that an attempt is made to identify the different considerations which motivated the dominant groups and governments in pursuing the policies delineated above. Clearly, much depended upon the way in which the concept of modernisation was viewed in the period 1850–1914. For many individuals, peoples and systems it was a generic concept, embracing social, political, economic and cultural growth and development. From this perspective to pursue the concept was to ally oneself with the forces of progress against those of reaction. Modernisation was, therefore, a highly ideological concept which governments invoked to legitimise their policies. However, the differences between the various parts of Europe were, in this respect, of great consequence. In the west, liberalism, economic development and a political concept of the nation derived from 1789, and the industrial revolution in England, blunted the conflict between governments and non-dominant ethnic groups. Rapidly expanding opportunities for economic advancement directed the efforts of individual citizens, including those coming from the different minority groups, towards effective application of entrepreneurial, technical and labour skills in industry, trade and commerce. The material reward for individual and group integration proved a more effective catalyst than linguistic adherence and a form of historically – rather than linguistically – derived national Romanticism *à la* Walter Scott came to dominate the scene.

In central and eastern Europe where the German influences predominated, Herderian Romanticism gave the culturally derived nations a more direct role in the historical process, making the clash between government and ethnicity much harder to avoid. A question which arises in this connection is whether, since the ethnic issue was so much more important in eastern Europe than in the west, the east European experience should not be treated as the norm rather than a special manifestation. Chlebowczyk's reference, in his *On Small and Young Nations* (Warsaw, 1980) to western ethnicities as 'stagnating, vestigial local communities, incapable of development' is worth noting in this context. Yet, if our study can contribute a more balanced view, weighting as they deserve the role of the Irish, Flemings and Catalans as well as Finns, Slovaks and Serbs, it will have served its purpose. True, western non-dominant groups, unlike eastern, were relatively small, regional minorities overall, facing prestigious states, so the problem was quite different. But their nineteenth century quiescence (barring Ireland) was not just a matter of historic torpor, but also a reflection of their participation in western economic dynamism. The Basques' and Catalans' leading role in the Spanish economy is the case in point. Oversimplification of the situation by Germans and Magyars (who assumed that the Slavs were their Welsh and Bretons) entailed a disastrous miscalculation. The value of treating the European ethnic problem as a single, developmental process may, therefore, seem to make sense.

Within these parameters government policies were, of course, influenced by many particular considerations. The traditional distinction made between historic and non-historic nations is of significance here; witness the difference in treatment of the historic French and non-historic Slovene entities in post-1861 Italy. It is, none the less, clear that historic languages could suffer because their people constituted a correspondingly greater threat – hence the persecution of Polish and Russia's support of Finnish as against Swedish in 1880s, because the tsarist authorities disliked Svecoman scandinavianism. To promote modernisation in the sense of promoting economic growth, industrialisation and technical progress, ethnic and cultural uniformity was considered essential. In Norway, Sweden and Finland the new economic imperialism could be said to correspond to the colonial policy of the west – a Nordic version of the 'white man's burden'. In conflicts between Sami reindeer herders on the one side and farmers and capitalist mining companies on the other, the state authorities usually supported the allegedly more 'civilised' forms of production.

That the concept of modernisation is a tricky one is clearly illustrated by the political and ethnic conflicts within the Habsburg monarchy. All parties involved there invoked different versions of the concept. The dominant Austrians in Bosnia argued for modernity in terms of political order and economic progress. On the other hand, some of the activists acting on behalf of the non-dominant ethnic groups identified the concept with the cultivation of the national spirit in order to create a 'dynamic' cultural identity which later on could trigger off economic and political changes.

In imperial Germany modernisation embraced many more aspects of social and cultural life. Bismarck's *Kulturkampf* (cultural campaign) challenged the traditional rights of the Churches and the concepts of *Kultursprache* (civilised language) and *Kulturnation* (civilised nation) had definite national overtones, bound to affect adversely the position of Polish speaking inhabitants in the Poznań (Posen) region, Silesia and Masuria. In the Ottoman empire, as Professor Kazamias underlines, the concept of modernisation was equated with that of westernisation or europeanisation and hence with industrialisation, finance capitalism, commercial expension as well as military improvements. This had enormous consequences for reorganising the educational system, updating curricula and providing more effective teacher training.

Concepts of modernisation, because of their heavy ideological content, easily leant themselves to exploitation in notions of nationalism and cultural superiority. In Italy, Prussia (and later, the German *Reich*), Norway and Sweden these ideas, along with racist thinking (the so-called Social Darwinism) were to some extent, highly influential. One possible reason was that these states had all earlier striven themselves for independence or unification and a spirit of national pride and cultural superiority had been awakened in their populations. Many Germans tended to regard the Poles as an inferior people. In the Habsburg monarchy the Austrian authorities felt they had a 'cultural mission' to limit the influence of Balkan Muslims and Orthodox Serbs, who were seen as backward nations.

The ideology of nationalism and the widespread ideas about the struggle for existence between superior and inferior races thus provided legitimacy for ousting 'foreign' languages and cultures and absorbing the weak and so-called 'primitive races'. The aim was to make way for the homogeneous national states. In Spain and the kingdom of Italy the unification process was combined with administrative centralism and the idea that the state should necessarily be based upon a linguistic and cultural monolithism. For Mussolini the denationalisation of minorities was to promote an Italian 'reconquest' of lost territories and 'grandeur'. Italianisation of schools and other cultural institutions was an aim based on a strong ideological foundation and an extremist vision of national greatness. In Franco's regime the concept of the Spanish language as the imperial language played a major role. Very few Spanish politicians challenged the policy of monolingualism in schools and acculturation of the various regions.

In the Polish republic between the two world wars the implicit, rather than explicit, concept of the civilising mission of the Polish culture, considered as the bulwark of western civilisation, played a role in the Polish government's educational policy towards the non-dominant ethnic groups inhabiting eastern Poland. This concept, naturally rejected by the different minority groups which by that time were increasingly aware of their own identity and cultural distinctiveness, could make only limited headway under very exceptional circumstances, where there was a cultural lag in the case of a group whose evolution had been delayed through lack of opportunities for development arising out of its earlier history. This could only apply to the Byelorussians, inhabiting the north eastern part of interwar Poland, but not the other non-dominant ethnic groups living in that country.

Integral to the dominant/non-dominant relationship thus was the maintenance of the claim to superior status of a particular culture, language or state system. Whatever the particular reason for this claim, strategic, political or ideological, it was usually associated with the claim to superior modernity or efficiency. Here was the kernel of government education policy to non-dominant groups in nineteenth century Europe. However, where the state or state-dominant people were considered not to be the most advanced sector of the society, as for example in Russia or Turkey, there the government policy met the greatest difficulties.

In almost all the case studies presented here, security considerations played a major role in the introduction and development of a rigorous policy of assimilation. This could be seen as an integral part of *Realpolitik* pursued with particular vigour by the governments of the great empires in the last two decades of the nineteenth and the first fourteen years of the twentieth century. The nationalism expressed by ethnic groups, even their very existence, excited alarm. A widespread opinion among the authorities was that they could split the nation, or, if situated in the border areas, involve the government in territorial disputes with hostile neighbour states. It was often regarded essential to extinguish the language and other distinctive cultural traits of the minorities in order to protect the regime and the sovereign state in question. The opinion prevailed that cultural pluralism and tolerance could easily stimulate nationalism, separatism and fifth columnism.

As shown by many case studies, national consolidation was considered the best way of allaying the fears of the dominant groups and removing the danger of possible disintegration. The unified kingdom of Italy, for example, initiated a policy of assimilation principally in the border areas. Security considerations undoubtedly played a key role in this, as well as the almost sacred concept of a unitary and national state which developed during the *Risorgimento*. After the end of the First World War a more frenetic nationalism and policy of assimilation developed. The explicit objective was to put an end to the ethnic tensions and conflicts in the border areas, which could be exploited by the hostile neighbouring states. Mussolini in the 1930s privately indicated that the fate of German schools in south Tyrol would have been totally different if south Tyrol had been situated in Tuscany and not in the Alps.

In the Habsburg Monarchy the policy of bosnianisation was pursued to counteract separatist Serb and Croat nationalism. In Slovakia the dominant Hungarian group feared the rise of Slovak nationalism and its suspicions of a Czech–Slovak conspiracy were nourished by the Czechs' verbal support of the Slovak cause. In partitioned Poland the Russian and German empires tried to eradicate the rising tide of Polish nationalism as a means of securing the integrity of the state and ensuring full control of the key border areas and to prevent the restauration of an independent and united Poland.

Bureaucratic considerations, too, were sometimes explicitly put forward by officials and politicians as valid reason for eliminating teaching in minority languages. It was generally argued that one common language would simplify administration and reduce costs. Bilingual education in schools was opposed by administrators and most educators on the grounds of impracticality. It was time consuming and expensive, and prevented the learning of the main language. In addition it was argued that cultural uniformity was the prerequisite for economic efficiency and social mobilisation and that it was essential that the members of non-dominant ethnic groups could easily communicate with the authorities as well as the other inhabitants of the country.

Specific Policy Measures

It is important to bear in mind, while discussing the dominant governments' measures *vis-à-vis* the non-dominant ethnic groups in general, that all state institutions were intended in principle to support the processes of assimilation or integration. Throughout the period 1850–1940, however, special emphasis was attached to schooling and language policy. One reason was that state and local administrative apparatus was still in embryo in many European countries, and in certain areas it did not fully develop until well into the twentieth century. The schools and Churches were for quite a long time the only institutions with which the young of non-dominant groups had regular contact. It was, therefore, not surprising that first and foremost it was the schools that were regarded as the main instruments in the assimilation and 'civilisation' of the minorities.

The policy of assimilation through the schools was enforced in the different countries by very similar means. One important instrument used by many governments was the attempt gradually to suppress the schools of the minorities or to transform them into schools completely dominated by the language and culture of the majority population. This policy was designed both to promote internal cohesion for political reasons and to rationalise the school network.

In Italy, children were forced everywhere to attend the Italian, and not the German or Slav schools, and during the Fascist regime, ethnic schools were gradually closed or transformed into Italian ones. In Slovakia, the dominant Hungarians managed successfully to close all Slovak secondary schools, and gradually to put aside Slovak language teaching and cultural activities in primary schools. The Poles in the Prussian and Russian provinces of partitioned Poland were unable to enjoy basic civil rights and education in schools was used to speed up germanisation or russification. Even the cultural line of defence of religious instruction in Polish was eventually attacked by the state. In Bosnia the Habsburg monarchy pursued a more subtle and moderate policy by introducing non-denominational state schools. The objective was to bolster the Habsburg idea and the process of bosnianisation in order to counteract Serb separatist efforts. However, confessional schools in general were not abolished or, initially, systematically controlled.

The Polish governments in the interwar period had by contrast no consistent minority educational policy. It was however of considerable consequence here that besides creating legal and administrative obstacles, the authorities could also refuse to offer financial support to schools teaching only in the mother tongue. In some countries like Sweden and Norway a more influential measure was the building of state financed boarding schools. The rationale behind this was to reduce the cultural influence of the Finnish and Sami parents by letting the schoolchildren stay as long as possible under the influence of a purely Swedish or Norwegian learning environment.

The language of instruction in schools was regarded by most state authorities as the key educational issue. In countries with rigorous assimilationist programmes education was, from the outset, therefore, to be mainly conducted in the language of the dominant ethnic group. All or most children were to learn to read, speak and write the language of the dominant population. Previous provisions that the children were also to learn their own native language were gradually dropped in the second half of the nineteenth century. Steps were taken in both the nation–states and empires to ensure that the contents of history and geography school textbooks had the prescribed 'national' contents. Even in interwar Czechoslovakia, where the German school system enjoyed a considerable degree of autonomy, tension arose insofar as the teaching of history and geography to the German youth was concerned. Clearly, it was not an easy thing to reconcile the education of German youth in becoming loyal citizens of the Czechoslovak republic and, at the same time, cultivating in them high respect for German culture and values.

Another important consideration was the training and employment of teachers; in schools for the various non-dominant ethnic groups. Generally, the state authorities regarded the recruitment of loyal teachers as essential for the implementation of the policy of assimilation in the school system. In some countries and provinces the authorities tried to prevent the children from being educated by teachers from their own ethnic minority group. This was the case in Fascist Italy, Norway and the Polish parts of the Russian and German empires. More usual was the introduction of strict control over the education of teachers; for example, by taking rigorous examinations they had to prove a sound knowledge of the language of the dominant nationality.

As in the other fields, administrative measures were taken to ensure the desired objectives in this field. Italy provides a good example where the Minister of Education proposed in 1911 to transfer the right of appointing teachers from the municipalities to the Ministry, in order to restrict the influence of local bodies and clergymen over the selection of teachers. The Fascist state went a step further. In 1925 the Gentile law made it possible for the Fascist regime to dismiss most of the German and Slav teachers or to transfer them to other parts of the country. On the other hand, Italian teachers were encouraged to apply for jobs in the new provinces by a set of incentives. Disloyal teachers were promptly dismissed.

In Bosnia, the Austrian authorities supervised educational practices with the help of informers and loyalty tests. In Slovakia, the Hungarian authorities dismissed several Slovak teachers who were regarded as disloyal or did not prove their knowledge of the Hungarian language.

Around the turn of the century similar efforts were made in Norway to strengthen the control over educational practices. Due partly to the process of secularisation and partly to the lack of support of the policy of norwegianisation, the Church lost much of its influence over school policy. Official policy in both Norway and Sweden was complemented by economic measures directed at teachers as well as parents. For example, if a poor Norwegian teacher failed to sustain required standards, he would lose a substantial salary supplement and his chances of promotion were severely curtailed.

The Non-Dominant Ethnic Groups and the Political Spectrum

It is very difficult to single out a general conservative, liberal or socialist strategy or policy vis-à-vis ethnic minority groups cutting right across the national boundaries and valid for all countries. The pattern is too complex and diverse for this. At best, it is possible to trace a definite Fascist or Marxist–Leninist approach to the problems of nationality and ethnic minorities. The Fascist one (at its height in the 1930s in Germany, Italy and Spain) represented an extreme and violent form of nationalism and ethnic repression. On the other hand, the communist parties favoured minority rights and national self-determination in principle, but these ideals were not infrequently, however, modified by pragmatic consideration.

In Sweden and Norway particularly the assimilationist policy towards minorities was supported by an overwhelming majority of politicians of all colours. In Sweden the Conservative party was the most consistent defender of this policy; while in Norway it was the Liberal party. In neither case did the Social Democratic parties attempt the presentation of an alternative course; though when in power in the 1930s the Swedish socialists did offer a slight modification of Sweden's assimilationist attitude towards the Finns. In Spain and post-war Poland in particular attitudes were to a large extent spread along the traditional left–right political spectrum. Parties on the right favoured a policy of gradual assimilation, arguing that multi-ethnic states were not viable political structures. Parties of the left covered a range of positions, but tended to defend the right of the minorities to education in the mother tongue and their struggle for a fuller cultural and, partly, also political autonomy. The 'centre' parties advocated 'education for state citizenship', in the sense of forming positive attitudes towards the state and a willingness to defend it against all sorts of internal and external enemies. To achieve this the centre parties advocated a policy that made some gestures towards the claims of the various nationalities, though the degree to which this was carried out reflected the size, economic strength and cultural history of each nationality.

These examples clearly indicate that party ideologies and the traditional political left–centre–right continuum may directly influence the standpoints of governments, parties, officials and individuals in ethnic affairs. However, the main preliminary conclusion to be drawn from this sample of case studies is that there are considerable deviations from, and few, if any, clear cut political patterns to discern.

Responses and Reactions of the Non-Dominant Ethnic Groups

The reaction of the ethnic minority groups towards policies of assimilation were not uniform, but rather depended on four main factors: the size of the groups concerned, their ideological climate and their pattern of social mobilisation, and the political situation in which they lived. No coherent movement for mother tongue education developed among a group as small as the Sami in our period, though isolation saved many of them, particularly the nomads, from assimilation. The Welsh speaking population, some million strong, made little attempt to resist all-English education in the day schools till the 1880s and thereafter accepted only a very subordinate place for Welsh as a teaching medium, though individuals sought more thorough-going bilingualism.

Here ideology also came into play. The Welsh popular awakening of the nineteenth century owed more to Nonconformist religion, with its stress on individual salvation, than to Herderian collective values. The anglicising role of industrialisation in south east Wales illustrates a further factor. Assimilation of non-dominant groups often occurred more readily in large cities and towns, partly due to more effective administrative control and partly because acculturation opened better professional opportunities enabling the sons of the parents from minority groups to be employed in the state service. Urban centres thus remained important melting pots. In practically every ethnic minority there were at least some parents who preferred sending their children to schools with the language of the dominant group as language of instruction, keeping in mind that the latter greatly facilitated access to secondary schools, higher education and public offices.

Similarly, labour migrants and weak illiterate and isolated ethnic groups with scattered population tended to accept assimilation. This was the fate of the Finnish immigrant group in Norway, of many Polish workers employed in French coal mining industry and of the numerous group of Czech migrants in Vienna. All these groups were to a large extent assimilated to the majority populations, partly because they freely tended to accept assimilation and partly due to a consistent policy of assimilation exercised by the dominant governments over a long period of time. Most controversial in this respect was the increasing adoption of French by Flemish workers in Brussels from the late nineteenth century, for Brussels stood in traditional Flemish speaking territory. Flemish patriots argued here that assimilation was due to the pressure of dominant attitudes and sought to limit the right of Flemish parents to educate their children through French.

In direct contrast to this, large ethnic groups concentrated in clearly defined geographical areas, with a long historical tradition behind them generally resisted, with great determination, any perceived threat of denationalisation. Such groups include the minorities living in the heart of Europe and in the Nordic area, which were strongly influenced by the Herderian based Romantic nationalism stressing cultural development through the mother tongue. It turned out to be 'ahistoric' to try to assimilate peoples like the Poles, Czechs and south Slavs. Indeed, in our period such attempts were largely confined to Polish areas. Among a smaller group, like the Slovaks, lacking both state traditions and significant urban centres of their own, wavering in national allegiance might be observed in some products of state secondary schools, but realistic assimilation of primary school pupils was hardly possible.

Elsewhere, pressures on non-dominant better educated strata to conform to dominant groups triggered off protests and fuelled charges of 'denationalisation' on which nationalist movements flourished. Besides, the stronger central and eastern European non-dominant ethnic groups were often able to take advantage of late nineteenth century trends, both social and political. Social mobilisation and urbanisation in such groups could take place within a relatively homogeneous ethnic framework, so that Prague became increasingly a Czech, and Helsinki a Finnish metropolis. Nationalisation of the school network, therefore, went hand in hand with social development. The fall of the German liberals in parliamentary Austria in 1879 enabled the Czechs to trade their support of the new clerical–Slav government for concessions on a Czech language university and accelerated czechisation of secondary schools. In a different context, incidentally, consolidation of Catholic education in Ireland in this period also owed something to the increased parliamentary leverage of Irish nationalists.

Where, however, the nationalising pressures were greater, as in pre–1914 Russian and Prussian Poland and many situations between the wars, the opposition of minorities could be expressed in many ways. One widespread form of reaction was to turn the back to the state controlled schools and to concentrate on developing alternative forms of education. Much education could be obtained outside the school, in church activities, youth movements associated with political parties, in voluntary associations and clandestine societies. In oppressive states and wherever the parents found school teaching objectionable, children could be taught 'the truth' at home. Occasionally, individual parents permitted their children to drop attending school for a shorter, or even longer, period of time, especially if they felt that the school did not serve their interests.

In some countries and areas extra classes or private schools were opened, based on the mother tongue and culture of the school children. In the new Italian provinces, for example, a network of parish schools was established, especially in south Tyrol. The extra teaching done in such schools played a major role in preserving the mother tongue. Another line of defence was the study of the mother tongue as a foreign language in secondary schools or in the seminaries.

Germans in south Tyrol and south Slavs in Julian Venetia, Byelorussians in the Polish state and many Poles within the German and Russian empires established a system of self-education in clandestine schools to avoid italianisation, polonisation, germanisation or russification. In south Tyrol a widespread network of 'catacomb schools' arose, partly supported and financed by German associations for the defence of alloglot Germans. German textbooks were smuggled into the province from Germany and Austria in order to support their blood relations.

More direct action was also taken sometimes. In Italy, for example, the nationalist policies of the Fascists provoked violent Slav countermeasures. One extreme reaction was the occasional killing of Italian teachers, and another was setting fire to Italian school buildings as the most visible and hated symbols of the Italian denationalisation policy. School strikes were also organised to resist new assimilationist measures. Terrorist activities, however, were not frequent, even in Fascist Italy.

In defending their language and cultural distinctiveness, the non-dominant ethnic groups often tried to seek help from other important bodies. In most countries the Churches played a major role in education and were the institutions that represented the most fervent and consistent opposition toward the policy of assimilation. There were, however, also situations where the state and the Church moved hand in hand, or where the Church was neutral or indifferent to ethnic issues. The educational functions of many Churches were extensive, covering for example, separate church schools, religious instruction, teaching at all levels and inspection or supervision of educational practices. The general trend in the period under review for governments to seek to restrict these functions in the name of modernisation and to check clerical criticism of assimilation was itself often limited by lack of alternative resources or by caution. Confessional schools remained dominant, for example, in Slovakia and the attempt to establish an interconfessional school system in Ireland was effectively abandoned.

In practice many Churches and individual priests initiated or supported industrial, agrarian and technological changes. The evidence of the case studies indicates that in Ireland and partitioned Poland the Catholic Church had a decisive role in shaping national identity, not only as places where divine services were held, but also as cultural institutions where patriotic loyalties were taught. Ethnic protests could thus be closely linked to religious activities, making religion an important vehicle for ethnic defence. In Ireland and Poland, the religious hierarchy as well as the lower clergy protested against persecution and cultural and political discrimination, thus promoting national consciousness under foreign domination. In the Polish case the Russian and Prussian authorities reacted by removing priests from elementary schools and entrusting religious instruction to lay teachers, but the attacks on the Church only resulted in the strengthening of the ties between the Poles and Catholicism. The authorities thus found that the priest could be more dangerous outside the school, than within it.

Elsewhere the Church was more split on minority and educational issues. Local clergymen were often bound up with the people and protested vehemently against the attempts to make the Church or the teaching of religion in the schools an instrument of state interests. As religion was usually a compulsory subject of education, often taught by priests and not secular teachers, this was of considerable significance in many countries.

However, the authorities were not unaware that the teaching of religion served as an instrument for the defence of the minority languages and the preservation of ethnic identity and took steps to minimise its impact. Thus in Italy the teaching of religion was transformed from a compulsory to an optional subject in the liberal period just after the end of the First World War. The Fascist regime went further, enforcing new strict provisions to italianise religious instruction, including bilingual catechisms. In addition, clerical teachers were gradually replaced by lay catechists. In Spain the Catholic Church was split on cultural and linguistic issues, though priests generally tended to promote regional consciousness and the development of regional languages and cultures, particularly in the Basque country and in Catalunya. Slovakia saw a split also. The hierarchy of all important religious communities supported a hungarianisation policy, while the lower clergy tended to defend the Slovak culture and nationalist aspirations which was significant as most primary schools were in church hands. Yet in Belgium religion and ethnicity were not closely linked and the Catholic Church did not generally involve itself in conflicts between French and Flemish speaking groups.

The clergymen opposing dominant governments' pressures argued that the Church had first and foremost its own goals and that the main purpose of the Church was to save souls and not to denationalise their parishioners. They emphasised the necessity of addressing people in their own language, without involving the clergy in the traditional conflict between God and Caesar. The protests of many local clergymen can be explained by the fact that they themselves belonged to ethnic minority groups, or that they tended to identify themselves with the prevailing local attitudes. Some ministers of religion also argued for cultural pluralism or for a more moderate policy of gradual assimilation on pedagogical and tactical grounds. As teachers or supervisors of education, they often observed and commented on the pedagogical difficulties arising out of a rigorous policy of assimilation.

In Sweden and Norway some clergymen warned that harsh measures could have the opposite effects from what the authorities expected, leading to damaging internal clashes and even pushing minority groups into the arms of the neighbouring state. Nor was Church opposition restricted to Protestant clergymen with their traditional stress on the mother tongue. Local Catholic and Orthodox priests could also insist on preaching in the mother tongue of the congregation. In the Aosta valley in Italy, local clergymen were in the front row of the local protest against italianisation. Of course, their defence of French was partly due to a determination to defend local traditions and partly also to their opposition to the lay and anti-clerical Italian state. Yet again, under Ottoman rule the Orthodox clergy of Greece defended and cultivated the Greek language and cultural traditions, though the ecclesiastical hierarchy often played a more ambiguous role, anxious to retain its authority and the considerable degree of influence it had in the state.

It is difficult, on the whole, to identify any distinct Lutheran, Presbyterian, Catholic or Orthodox attitude to the policy of assimilation. Instead there are significant differences within all these Churches and in the shifting approaches over time from country to country and from one ethnic group to another. The split concerning ethnic and educational issues was often very noticeable. Within the Catholic Church the Pope traditionally did not intervene in ethnic issues. The lower clergy and not the hierarchy were normally the most eager defenders of the rights of the minorities, especially concerning religious instruction. The parish priests thus tended to identify themselves with local sentiments. But in Upper Adige and partitioned Poland, the Catholic Church as an entity protested against the policy of assimilation.

Although the Churches were in many instances powerful allies of many national minorities, and the case studies present a rich sample of individual Churches' protests, this observation cannot conceal the fact that the Churches as institutions also functioned in many ways as instruments of official policies of assimilation. There were numerous examples of bishops and clergymen eagerly advocating and practising a rigorous assimilationist policy, for example, in Poland under the German rule, Italy, Sweden and Norway. It is, however, necessary to add that, in this case, they were as a rule the representatives of the dominant ethnic groups placed in the position of authority by the ecclesiastical authorities.

The existence of the League of Nations was of definite consequence in the struggle of the non-dominant ethnic groups against the dominant governments' policies in the interwar period. Numerous disputes between the different countries, including disputes concerning the question of instruction in minority languages in schools or problems over appointing heads and staff of schools catering for minorities were referred to the League in the 1920s and 1930s. This was of particular importance for Poland and Germany, Austria, Czechoslovakia and Hungary. However, this form of arbitration between the contending parties could be successful only when the non-dominant group in question could rely upon its cause being taken up by a member state determined to act on behalf of its conationals living in another state. This consideration weakened the effective use of the League as a protector of national minorities in general, while major political disagreements further reduced its role in the late 1930s.

On the basis of the above evidence it is clear that the response of the ethnic groups to pressures for integration and, particularly, assimilation involved a full range of reactions. They included desperate, sporadic acts of defiance, muted opposition and determined, integrated long term resistance in which institutions like the family, Churches and voluntary associations were involved. They all played a role in strengthening the national identity of the different ethnic groups and in adding fuel to the already burning flames of nationalism, engulfing late nineteenth and early twentieth century Europe. The latter, by no means extinguished by the First World War, reappeared again in the interwar period and, despite the efforts of the League of Nations, exploded in the catastrophe of the Second World War.

Outcomes of Educational Policies *vis-à-vis* the Minorities

The consequences of educational policies pursued by dominant governments in respect of non-dominant ethnic groups varied from period to period and from state to state. They may be broadly categorised, however, according to the goals of government policy discussed above.

Policies of assimilation had as their object the establishment of state unity and cohesion. What they in fact produced was exactly the opposite, namely divisiveness and, often, open hostility between the dominant and dominated ethnic groups. There was an obvious miscalculation on the part of governments in power, when they reckoned that the attractions of good efficient education in a dominant language, combined with a consistent policy of assimilation, would inevitably result in a gradual, but a very definite weakening of the non-dominant ethnic groups and, ultimately, their extinction. What the authorities did not appreciate was the fact that, particularly in the closing decades of the nineteenth and the early twentieth century, when the pressures exerted upon the minority groups were stepped up in some of the great Empires, notably in Germany, Russia and the Hungarian part of the Habsburg empire, the strength of national feelings in such groups was already of such intensity that they were bound to resist all the attempts at denationalisation with the utmost determination.

This was, as far as can be judged, due to the fact that social processes were also drawing the masses within the orbit of the national movement on both sides of the dominant/dominated ethnic divide. On the dominant side, the governments of Germany, Russia and Hungary determined to strengthen the state from within in a political and economic sense in the age of imperialism and intensive rivalry, endeavoured to attain educational and cultural unity through insisting on teaching in the dominant language in all elementary schools. The minorities, by that time very conscious of the fact that the mother tongue was the most fundamental aspect of national identity, and its preservation was crucial for their survival, opposed teaching in an alien tongue with all the means at their disposal.

However, in the Austrian part of the Habsburg empire after 1867 and, in practice, in the Ottoman empire, with its policy of controlled *laissez faire* toleration, central government pursued a very different policy of admitting cultural pluralism and transferring educational responsibilities, to an extent, to regional or confessional authorities, hoping thus to deepen support and loyalty to the state. British policy in Ireland was not dissimilar, though here cultural pluralism took religious rather than linguistic form, since most Irish people already spoke English. Britain sought first to reduce Protestant–Catholic tensions through the non-denominational National School system; when this was criticised as secularism by the Churches, she effectively permitted the development of a powerful and self-sufficient Catholic educational sector. Again, the goal was to win commitment to a political system by relaxing cultural hegemonism.

In these more liberal schooling policies there was also miscalculation, however, or at the very least grave risk. The advantages were some defusion of tension and involvement of minority communities with some of the difficulties of decision making without, in theory, forfeiting ultimate rights of supervision and control. In practice, the risk was that freer scope for mother tongue, national religion and study of the national past could encourage non-dominant ethnic groups to sense that with the attainment of full political independence they could progress even further than had been the case so far. No doubt, educational policy was not the main reason for the secession of Czechs, Catholic Irish and Balkan Christians in the years 1912–22, but it was powerless to stop it. Imperial pluralism only whetted the appetite for national democracy.

The interwar successor states, therefore, had two failed models of educational policy to choose from. In the event most of their work was counterproductive. The Spanish and Italian governments' attempts to denationalise the non-dominant ethnic groups in these two countries were not successful and only added to the struggle of the Basques and Catalans in Spain as well as the Slavs and Germans in Italy against the dominant governments in the 1930s. The consequences of the assimilationist measures taken in the Scandinavian countries *vis-à-vis* the Lapps were equally negative. The dominant governments there consistently claimed, as in several other countries in central and eastern Europe that they were pursuing a policy of integration in respect of the smaller and economically weaker minority groups. The latter equally consistently argued that this was not really the case and that the ultimate aim was denationalisation. The exceptions constituted larger, economically stronger minorities, with fully developed cultural traditions behind them. They exploited their cultural and economic strength to their advantage and could preserve their schools and other educational and cultural institutions against the dominant governments' pressures. But it was an uneasy truce rather than positive co-operation and it did not lead to successful integration either.

The differential educational policies of the dominant governments *vis-à-vis* the non-dominant ethnic groups consisted, therefore, of measures which seemed to aim at checking the strongest, subduing the weaker and destroying the weakest of the minority groups and, as a result, entailed serious political risks, which were not clearly perceived at the time. Because of the tensions and confrontations which they produced, they often resulted in undermining the internal stability in a given region; in slowing down, rather than speeding up the process of modernisation and, therefore, producing consequences directly opposite from the ones that had been anticipated.

Apart from this, oppressive educational measures taken against many ethnic groups associated closely with a particular religious denomination, frequently resulted in cementing an intimate fusion between religious and ethnic adherence and, inevitably brought Churches into the field of political action at some level. This was yet another unintended byproduct of ill conceived educational measures, and was particularly important in partitioned Poland, Slovakia under Hungarian rule, Ireland, Wales, Italy and the Balkans. Yet it must be remembered that religious adherence did not always play a significant role in the growth of nationality movements; as when both the dominant and the dominated groups shared a common religion, or when the leadership of the national movement was firmly controlled by secular forces from within.

In terms of international politics, the policies of enforced assimilation through education brought about increased misunderstandings and accusations of unfair treatment of ethnic minorities. The feelings of injustice and denial of basic human rights caused sporadic crises in international relations, and, when ruthlessly exploited by the propaganda machines of some states, contributed to the worsening of the international situation at the beginning of the twentieth century and on the eve of the Second World War.

Insofar as the non-dominant ethnic groups as such were concerned, the policies of assimilation and integration pursued by the dominant governments produced efforts aiming at social mobilisation within particular minority groups. The effectiveness of this process was itself conditioned by numerous external influences, but it was very much enhanced by the growing feeling within various minority groups that successful resistance to denationalising pressures could best be built upon a solid basis of material prosperity, social cohesion and sound leadership. When these were also accompanied by favourable demographic trends, lasting foundations were laid for a decisive move by a particular group directed towards political action aiming at autonomy or outright independence.

Conclusions

The contributors to this volume have aimed at examining the relationship between governments and non-dominant ethnic groups in many different parts of European continent with widely differing intellectual traditions and diverse socio-political formations. The temporal dimension has been found to be equally important. It is evident that the concepts of the state and citizenship were undergoing a process of continuous evolution; with the subject of absolutism becoming the citizen of constitutionalism and, finally, the patriot of the nation–state ideal. Indeed, the studies confirm that the notions concerning the rights and duties of states and citizens *vis-à-vis* each other profoundly affected educational policies, their legitimation, substance and effectiveness. Equally, they influenced the reactions of the non-dominant ethnic groups to such policies.

Concerning the differences in the intellectual traditions with regard to questions of state and nation, the studies reveal that the most crucial one was the predominance of the German influence in central, northern and eastern Europe, expressing itself in the Herderian concept of nationality based upon language. In the remaining parts of the continent, both the French revolutionary and the English liberal traditions linked the concept of nationhood to political rather than cultural factors, though in each case cultural Romanticism was not absent, being linked, however, to the Sir Walter Scott branch of European Romanticism – in the sense of a heightened stress on ethnic historical tradition – rather than to cultural Herderianism.

In terms of the time span, a distinction must be drawn between the period 1850–1918 and 1918–40 in respect of the prevailing mode of political organisation; the former being characterised by the existence of multi-national empires, the latter by the existence of nation–states, incorporating very substantial non-dominant ethnic groups. However, certain patterns of the pre–1918 period also tended to perpetuate themselves in the interwar period, despite the fact that the relative proportions of the non-dominant ethnic groups declined in comparison with the previous period and that in several instances, what were once minority groups became majorities in the newly constituted states.

In the light of the evidence presented, an important contextual factor which affected the dynamics of ethnic identity formation and educational developments appears to have been the acceleration of social and economic change, the pressures arising out of industrialisation and urbanisation, the growing stress put upon modernisation and national development. These pressures affected both sides of the dominant/dominated divide. In the case of the former, they spurred governments on to increase their efforts to unify and strengthen states from within. In the case of the latter, they enhanced the determination of non-dominant ethnic groups to defend their own cultural and material interests and to resist what they considered to be unfair treatment and exploitation.

Within this configuration of forces the school emerged as a focal point of conflict between the state building and the nation emancipation processes. Education came to be considered an important and positive agent in the formation of politically significant values to both the dominant and non-dominant ethnic groups. Ample evidence has been given of many governments' express determination to use education as an instrument of political control in an attempt to denationalise ethnic minorities. Policies of assimilation, integration and *laissez faire* were pursued by different dominant governments and at different times. Looking back at the period 1850–1914 as a whole, one can identify the 1880s, 1890s and the period 1900–14 as years in which the policies of enforced assimilation were at their peak in Germany, Russia and Hungary. In the Austrian part of the Habsburg empire after 1867 and the Ottoman empire in the period 1850–1923, more liberal and conciliatory policies of *laissez faire* prevailed. British educational policy in Ireland and Wales caused fewer problems, as a high proportion of the people of Ireland and Wales already spoke English. In the interwar period dominant governments in many newly established states pursued what, in their view, were the policies of integration, but what the minorities often viewed as covert policies of assimilation and, therefore, resisted resolutely. Such a development was, indeed, inherent in the triumph of democratic nationalism after 1918, as long as belief in the link between modernity and nation building held sway.

The rationale underlying these policies again varied very greatly from state to state and from period to period, and included different types of ideologies such as imperialism, Social Darwinism, civilising mission, cultural pluralism, nationalism, federalism, social justice or modernisation, as well as national security, interstate and foreign relations, economic and developmental considerations and supra-national influences. A wide range of specific measures were taken in order to put the different policies into effect. They ranged from the closing of schools and classes teaching in a mother tongue, strict supervision over the training and activities of teaching personnel, to controlling the contents of curriculums and, particularly, the teaching of history. Of the other important social institutions, influencing the juxtaposition between dominant governments and non-dominant ethnic groups, the case studies have identified Churches, family and voluntary associations as potentially significant and, in some cases very consequential agencies, defending minority interests and promoting minority values through religious and grass root social and cultural activities and initiatives.

Different political outlooks, reflecting major differences in basic ideological orientations operated behind the educational policies of dominant groups and conditioned their substance, though even they were not powerful enough to make a real difference to the position of minorities in most of the states. In some instances, however, the left wing of the political spectrum was seen as being much more in favour of liberal and more acceptable policy measures than the centre or the right wing, the latter frequently pushing rigorous assimilationist policies.

On the other hand, ethnic minorities believed in the power of education for ensuring cultural–ethnic cohesion and ethnic revival, which, under certain conditions led to political demands and actions. Education was thus perceived by the dominated ethnic groups as a mechanism of political emancipation or liberation. This was true of virtually all non-dominant ethnic groups in the multi-national, polyethnic empire states. The educational activities of these groups centred mainly on a struggle for the right to instruction in the mother tongue, the teaching of religion in the mother tongue, an unbiased study of history and gaining of opportunity for unhampered artistic expression. In certain cases, for example in Poland under foreign rule or Italy, the minority groups countered oppressive policies by setting up clandestine schools, in which they cultivated their language, religion and culture.

Turning to the important question of the effectiveness of education in the processes of socialisation, cultural cohesion and national development, evidence has been gathered which indicates that policies of assimilation were not as successful as had been intended. This was partly because governments did not often have the resources to control the social process through the schools. The scale of the education provided was plainly inadequate for the wide variety of tasks which governments did expect from it. By the same token, however, education was not able to carry the full load of expectations of non-dominant ethnic groups. Here lay the logic of government policies of relative devolution and tolerance towards schooling of non-dominant ethnic groups. However, the most important factor in the failure of enforced assimilation through the school, was the determined effort to resist it, noticeable among all the minority groups after their national consciousness had been awakened.

Important questions which arise in connection with this study are: Was education a truly significant element in the overall relationship between dominant governments and non-dominant ethnic groups? Did the educational policies *vis-à-vis* non-dominant ethnic groups constitute a really important aspect of political life in multi-ethnic empires between 1850 and 1914 and multi-national states in the interwar period? The studies included in the volume suggest that in both cases the answer should be affirmative. Yet, the important thing was not what the policies achieved, but what they failed to achieve, and also what they ultimately resulted in, very much against the original expectations of those who were responsible for their formulation and implementation.

Our study suggests that in those states where the governments decided to follow a policy of assimilation through insisting upon education in the dominant language, they appeared to touch the most sensitive nerve in the consciousness of the members of minority groups. By introducing curricular patterns extolling the dominant groups' values and traditions, they provoked resistance and resentment, and the resolution to defend minority languages and cultural distinctiveness. By insisting that the dominant groups' values and traditions were, because of their very character, superior to others, they changed resistance and resentment into open defiance. By intensifying the pressure, particularly towards the end of the nineteenth and the very beginning of the twentieth century, they left the minority groups with hardly any other option than a determined striving for cultural autonomy and, if that was rejected, for outright political independence.

On the other hand, in states where more conciliatory and enlightened policies prevailed, education in the mother tongue strengthened the national consciousness and national pride and could contribute to demands for a full independence. It is only in the exceptional cases of non-dominant groups which for historical reasons had already largely lost the knowledge of their own language and the will to fight for its retention that the political consequences of educational policies were less visible. Upon this evidence rests the case for paying much greater attention to education in examining the record of the past. The study of nationalism, and, therefore, the study of modern history is incomplete and lacks an important perspective without an explicit, direct and continuous reference to education in general, and educational policies in multi-ethnic and multi-national states in particular.

Naturally, educational policy was not the only important aspect of relationship between the dominant governments and non-dominant ethnic groups. It is necessary to take into account also the findings of other researchers investigating further aspects of that relationship in order to have a complete picture and understand the full complexity of the issues involved. While the above conclusions are indicative of the importance of comparative perspective in the study of history, they also reveal how much more must be done in the future in order to obtain a more comprehensive and balanced picture of the principal forces which, by shaping the past, influence present day developments and thereby affect the shape of things to come.

Index

Aberdare Commission on Intermediate and Higher Education in Wales (1880) 42
Aberdare Report 42, 43
Aberystwyth University College 42
Alapuro, R. 88
Albornoz, S. 299
Alexander II, Tsar 90, 99
Alexander III, Tsar 97
All-Jewish Workers' Union 195
Almirall, 300
American College for Women, Usküdar 350
Ampezzo 267
Andrassy, G. 324
Andreyev, L. 335
Anglican Church in Ireland 17, 18
Anglican Church in Wales 35, 40, 41, 58
Anglican National Society 36, 40
Anglican Welsh Education Committee 43
Anschluss 226
Antwerp 117–19
Aosta valley 264–6, 270, 273, 275, 280, 281, 282, 284
Apponyi laws 254, 257
Ara, A. 263
Arana, S. 306, 308
Aranzandi 308
Aribau, B.C. 300
Arnsberg 148
Assimilation 100–5, 323, 392, 395, 396
Association of German Bürgerschule Teachers 226
Association of German Teachers at Academic Secondary Schools in the Czechoslovak republic 226
Association of German Teachers at Commercial Schools 226
Association of Teachers at Technical-Vocational Schools 226

Bakunin, M. 335
Balfour, A.J. 384
Balkan Peninsula 4
Bangor Normal College 42
Barcelona 300, 302, 304, 314
Bardina, J. 301
Baroja, Caro 308
Basil the Great 358

Basque country 292, 298, 304–10, 313–15, 398
Basque language 304
Baudelaire, C. 112
Bauer, O. 164
Beck, J. 191
Belgian Workers' party 122
Belgium 391, 394
  Act of 1914 125–9
  bilingualism 120–1
  Dutch as language of instruction 116
  Flemish Movement 121–5
  French as language of instruction 115–17
  French as second language 117–20
  frenchification process 112–29
  German occupying forces 126
  language in education 111–30
  linguistic communities 111–13
  primary education law (1914) 125
  primary schools 114–15, 123–4
  stimulation of national consciousness 113
  territoriality principle 127–9
Benedikt, M. 335, 337
Benes, E. 222, 246
Benitez, P. 298
Berchem, 117
Besednjak, E. 277
Bismarck, Otto von 136, 143, 147, 176, 399
Björnson, B. 257
Blue Books 38, 40, 51
Bobrikov, N. 102
Bohemia 217–19, 235–8, 241–9
Bosnia 319–42, 391, 398, 403
  Austrian Bosnia (1878–1918) 322–36
  Serb and Muslim Movements for Cultural Autonomy 329–32
  student revolt 332–6
  under Ottoman rule (1850–78) 319–22
Bosnian Herzegovinian Institute 332, 333
Bóveda, A. 312
Brañas, A. 311
Brandenburg 133
Bratislava 251, 252
Brecon Congregational Academy 44
British and Foreign Schools Society 37, 40
British Parliamentary Reform Act (1884) 45
Brno 235, 241, 243
Brügel, J.W. 215

419

Brussels 115, 116, 125, 127–9, 405
Budapest 257
Buls, C. 116
Bruián, 331
Burning Heart, The 335
Byelorussian National Committee 198
Byelorussians 163, 198–9, 400, 407

Čabrinović, N. 334
Calabrese, Bishop Angelo 281
Cambrian Educational Society (1846) 40
Cambrophilia 45–6
Camp of Great Poland 187
Campion, A. 305
Camus, A. 335
Carbonell 302
Carlos, Prince 307
Carpathian Germans 212, 216
Casares, A. 312
Castelao, R. 312
Catalan Teaching Protection Association 301
Catalan University Congress 301
Catalunya 291, 292, 298–304, 313–15
Catholic Church
  in Aosta valley 283
  in Bohemia 244
  in Czechoslovakia 258
  in Finland 88
  in Galicia 167–8
  in Ireland 19, 21
  in Italy 265
  in Poland 164–5, 180, 409
  in Poznań 180
  in South Tyrol 283
  in Spain 297, 305, 408
  in Upper Adige 283
Catholic emancipation 14
Catholic priests 19
Catholic University in Ireland 22
Central Welsh Board 42, 54
Central Yiddish School Organisation 197
České Budějovice 238
Chacallis, A. 386
Chief Inspectorate of Brussels 116
Chief Inspectorate of Leuven 117
Chlebowczyk, B. 398
Chrudim 235
Chrysostom, J. 358
Chrysostomos, Archbishop of Drama 351
Chrzescijańska Demokracja 187
Church Education Society 17, 19
Church of Ireland 14, 17, 22, 30
Cieszkowski, A. 142
Colonisation Commission 178
Comerford, R.V. 13, 393
Comité de l'Escola Nova Unificada 304
Commission on the State of Education in
  Wales (1846–7) 37
Committee for the protection of the French
  language in the Aosta Valley 265

Committee of Educational-Cultural Societies
  and Trade Unions 190
Committee of the Privy Council 37
Communist party of Poland 188
Congress of Berlin 323
Congress of Vienna 164
Consell de Cultura 304
Corbino law 272, 273
Corbino, M.O. 272
Corsica 275
Costa, J. 298
Cotton, D. 41
Cracow 164, 169
Credaro, L. 265
Credaro law 265
Crime and Punishment 335
Croats 263, 268, 281, 282, 320, 329, 333, 337,
  401
Croce, B. 274
Cross Education Commission (1887) 47
Cultural Committee of the Sudeten German
  Teachers' Associations 222, 226, 227–8
Cygnaeus, U. 91, 98
Cymru Fydd 46
Cyprus 369–87
  Education Law of 1895 376–9
  educational provision and types of
    schools (1850–1878) 369–70
  English Instruction Vote (1899) 380–2
  government control and anglicising
    influence on Muslim secondary and
    town schools (1899–1900) 382–3
  government measures to establish an
    agricultural technical school (1899–1900)
    383–5
  government policy towards Muslim
    education (1878–98) 379–80
  Greek schools 369–87
  Muslim schools 369–87
  Muslim-Turkish education (1878–95) 370–6
  Ottoman and British education policies
    (1859–78, 1878–1905) 385–6
  Turkish schools 369–87
  Under British Rule 370–86
Czechoslovakia 397, 402
  attitudes and reactions among Germans
    223–7
  Austrian–Hungarian heritage 213, 216,
    219–21
  Bezirksschulausschüsse 224
  Bürgerschulen 225
  Catholic Church in 258
  conflict areas between German
    representatives and state authorities
    224–6
  disciplinary actions against unreliable
    teachers 225
  educational policy 221–2
  German medium school system 216–20
  German schools in (1918–1938) 211–32
  Germans as ethnic group in 211

Landesschulräte 221
Minderheitsschulgesetz 224
multi-national character of 212
nationality problem 215, 217
Ortsschulräte 221, 224
Provincial Schools Council 219, 221, 225
relation between Czechs and Germans 214
Slovaks in 258
socio-political framework 212–16
Sprengelbürgerschulgesetz 225
teachers' associations 226
Czechs in Polish Republic 203
Czechs under Habsburg Monarchy 235–8
degree of literacy 236–7
education in early twentieth century 247–9
education in second half of nineteenth
century 241–3
educational background 238–41
elementary education 243–4
gymnasiums 241–6
illiteracy rate 237
secondary education 244–7
Czechoslovak University 258

Dalmatia 268
Danish conflict in Schleswig-Holstein 151–4
Dark Horizon 335
Darlington, T. 46
Davies, Sir Arthur 49, 52, 53, 54
Davies, Alfred 48
Davies, D.I. 47, 48
de Aragon, F. 294
de Azkue, R.M. 306, 307
de Castila, I. 294
de Castro, R. 312
de Courtenay, Jan Baudouin 190
de la Riba, P. 301
de la Sota, R. 309
Dèrer, I. 220, 221, 225, 229
de Rivera, Primo General 299, 303, 309
de Stefani, A. 277
de Urabayen, J.L. 308, 309
de Zarate, G. 295
Deutsche Nationalpartei 225
Deutsche Nationalsozialistische Arbeiterpartei
225
Deutsche Pestalozzi Gesellschaft 227
de Vroede, M. 111
de Zarate, G. 295
Diaz, Pastor 312
Die Erziehung 227
Diesterweg 91
Diwygiwr 44
Dmowski, R. 187
Dollfuss, E. 282
Dolmanyos, I. 255
Domino, M. 303
Dorf Tirol 283
Dostoevsky, F. 334
Dublin Castle 13–14
Duran, J.A. 311

Düsseldorf 148
Eastern Marches Society 146, 177
Ecclesia Cambrensis 41
Education Act 1870 26
Education Act 1902 41
Education Act 1918 49, 50
Education Nouvelle 220
Edwards, O.M. 48, 49, 51, 52, 58
EFEK 355
Emanzipationsedikt 133
Enare 80
Engman, M. 88
Enriquez, C. 312
Eriksen, K.E. 63, 88, 389
Escola Normal de la Generalitat 303
Escoles d'Estiu 304
Estonia 392
European Romanticism 414
European Science Foundation 336
Euskadi 291
Euskera 304–6
Exo-socialisation 1, 11

Falk, Minister of Culture 133, 152
Falski, M. 190
February Manifesto 101–3
Fedele, P. 277, 278, 285
Felbiger, I. 238
Fenno-Scandia 64, 65
Fennomen 90, 92, 95–7, 102
Fenyes, E. 249
Ferdinand, Franz 331, 334
Fernando de Aragon 294
Ferretti, G. 273
Finland 64, 69, 80, 82, 87–109, 398
assimilation policy 100–5
Constitutionalists 96
elementary schools 90, 93, 97–100, 105
Governor General of 106
international perspectives 106
liberalism 106–7
National Board of Education 90, 92, 97,
98, 104
Nordic perspectives 106
Orthodox Church in 100
outcomes and effects of educational policy
105–6
panSlavic movement 100, 107
period of liberalism 89–94
period of static conservatism (1809–1855)
88–9
russification policy 101
Slavic policy versus Finnish nationalism
94–100
teacher training 90
Finnish Literature Society 89
Finnish speaking population 70, 79, 81
see also Kvens
Finnmark 63, 78
Finns 66, 68, 80
Finns Fund 68

Fisher, H.A.L. 49, 58
Flamingants 121–6
Flanders. *See* Flemings
Flemings 111, 112, 113, 127–9, 391, 405
Flemish Movement 121–5
Franco, General 299, 310, 314, 396, 399
Franko, I. 171
Franz Joseph, Emperor 243, 246, 323
Französisches Gymnasium 133
Frederick the Great 138
Frederick VI, King of Denmark 152
French language, in Italy 265
Friuli 266
Froebel, F. 91

Gaelic League 24, 25
Gałecki, W. 189
Galicia (part of Poland) 164–71, 192
    Roman Catholicism in 167–8
Galicia (part of Spain) 291–3, 310–15
Galician Autonomous Republican
    Organisation 311
Gallano, J. 309
Garrido, J.L.G. 291, 396
Gatterer, Claus 269
Gellner, E. 1, 8, 55, 56, 362
Geneva Convention 191
Gentile, G. 275–7
Gentile law 275–80, 403
German Cultural Association 227
German National Association for the
    Protection of Minority Rights 200
German Pestalozzi Association 227
German School Association 394
German schools
    curricular situation in 220
    in Czechoslovakia. *See* Czechoslovakia
    in Poland. *See* Poland
    in Trieste 269
German Teachers' Association in the
    Czechoslovak State 226
Germans in Polish Republic 199–202
Germany 399
    see also Prussia
Ghent 118–19
Ghent University 122, 126
Giertych, J. 187
Giolitti 274
Gladstone, W.E. 22, 46
Gorizia-Gradisca 268
Gorky, M. 334
Governments and non-dominant ethnic
    groups 389–417
Grabski, S. 187, 193
Greek Catholicism in Galicia 167–8
Greeks
    in Cyprus 369–87
    in the Ottoman Empire 343–66
    demographic and socio-economic
        characteristics of 352–4

educational and cultural awakening 354–
    61
    quest for national identity 352
Greetings to Liberated Humanity 335
Gregor-Tajovsky, J. 257
Griffiths, J. 47
Guimera, A. 300
Guipúzcoa 310
Gurruchaga, A. 310

Habsburg empire 1, 6, 411
Habsburg monarchy 235–8, 243, 263, 269,
    320, 391, 399, 401, 402
    Italian schools within 267–9
Hanak, P. 255
Hans, N. 8, 362
Hatt-i Hümayun 344, 347, 348
Hatt-i Sherif 347
Havliček, K. 239
Havránek, J. 235
Hechter, 57
Heiden, Governor General 97
Heikkilä, M. 96
Heinemann, M. 133
Helsingfors Dagblad 89
Helsinki Daily 89
Helsinki University 89, 91, 101
Henlein, K. 223, 226, 229
Herder, J.G. 6, 337, 405
Herderian Romanticism 320, 397, 406, 414
Herzegovina, *See* under Bosnia
Hina, H. 300
Hitler, Adolf 155, 225
Hitler Youth 201
Hitlerism 82
Hobsbawm, E. 4, 7, 8
Hodza, M. 221, 225
Holy See 280
Home Rule 27
Hungarian rule, Slovaks under 249–58
Hungary 253, 392
Huysmanns, C. 126

Idria 271
Ilić, D. 334
Imberti, Monsignore R. 281
Institut Escola 304
Institute of Catalan Studies 301
Integration 393
Intermediate Education Act of 1878 21
*Internal Colonialism: the Celtic Fringe in British
    National Development* 57
International Catalan Language Congress
    301
Ireland 13–32, 391, 394
    Anglican Church in 17, 18
    Board of Commissioners 16–20, 28
    Board of Education 16
    Board of Public Works 14
    challenge to clerical dominance 25

Commissioners of National Education 15, 16, 25, 29
Conservatives 21
Department of Agriculture and Technical Instruction 27
Department of Education 27, 29
Evangelicals 19
Home Rule 28, 29
Intermediate Education Board 21, 25, 26
local government 14
model schools 20
national school system 15–20
non-vested schools 18
Presbyterian schools 18
primary education 18
protestants in 24, 28
secondary schools 20–3
teacher training 19–20
universities 20–3
Irish Catholics 13–32
Irish language 23–5
Irish National Teachers Organisation 26
Isabel de Castila 294
Istria 268, 271
Italy 263–89, 396, 399, 402, 407
'catacomb' schools 282–3
Catholic Church in 265
developments after World War I 269–74
Fascist period 270, 274–80, 284–5
French language in 265
national minorities after unification 264–7
Options Agreement 285
self-defence measures taken by minorities 281–3
teaching of history, 272, 276
teaching of religion 280–1

Jedrzejewicz, J. 189
Jesuit Order 239
Jewish People's party in Poland 195
Jews
in Bohemia 243–4
in Poland 167
in Polish Republic 194–7
in Prussia 133–6
in Slovakia 252
Jirásek, A. 249
Jirecek, K. 246
Jones, Kilsby 44, 47
Jones, Reverend W. 36
Joseph II, Emperor 238, 240, 249
Jukič, I.F. 320
Julian Venetia 263, 269, 271–4, 280–2, 284, 407
Jussila, O. 88

Kadner, O. 216
Kafka, F. 244
Kalevala 89
Kalisz 173

Karlowitz 330
Karpat, K. 345
Kay-Shuttleworth, J.P. 43, 44
Kazamias, A. 343
Kemal, N. 351
Kildare Place Society 15, 16
Kimberley, Lord 371, 381
Kindermann, F. 238
King's Academy 143
Kohn, H. 5
Kola 63, 80
Köller 153
Königliche Akademie 143
Korth, R. 142
Kortrijk 117
Kosciałkowski-Zyndram, M. 194
Kozák, J.B. 222
Kuikka, M.T. 87
Kulturausschuss der Sudetendeutschen Lehrerverbände 226
Kvens 63, 64, 68, 70, 71, 74, 76, 82
Kyrris, C.P. 369

Laestadians 71, 74, 77
Laghetti 272
Language Manifesto (1900) 101
Language Society 47, 48
Lapps, see Samis
Larramendi, Father 305
Latvia 392
League of Nations 190, 191, 410
Ledóchowski, Count 144
Leuven 117
lex Perek 247
Liberal Education Act of 1870 41
Liberalism 21, 89, 92–4, 106–7
Liberec 222, 226
Library of Catalunya 301
Lilek 338
Lingen, R.W. 39, 40, 44, 57, 58
Lipski, Wojciech 142
Lithuanians 163, 202–3
Lloyd George, D. 41, 46, 49
Local and Provincial School Councils 221
Louis XIV, King of France 299
Lowe, R. 8
Lublin 173
Lunetta, F. 214
Luther, Martin 74
Lutheran Church 87, 88, 92, 93, 99, 253
Lvov 169, 192
Lvov University 170

Maarifi Umumiye Nizamnamesi 349
Mañagorri 307
Mancomunitat de Catalunya 298, 302
Mandić, N. 338
Maria Magadalena Gymnasium 143
Maria Theresia, Empress 238
Marin, B. 306

Marks Haindorf Foundation 135
Marxism-Leninism 80
Masaryk, T.G. 215, 222, 228, 246, 249
Masuria 399
Maynooth College 21
Mektebi Sultani 349
Mensonge du Parlamentarisme, Le 335
Miąso, J. 163
Miglia, G. 280
Military Academy in Wiener Neustadt 240
Mitter, W. 211
Modeen, T. 88
Montserrat, Abbey of 301
Moravia 217–19, 235–8, 241, 242–9
Morgades, Dr., Bishop of Barcelona 298
Moyano law 295
Mühlberger, J. 229
Mülkiye 349, 350
Münster 148
Murray, Archbishop of Dublin 19
Muslims 319–22, 329–36, 337, 346, 369–87
Mussolini, Benito 274, 275, 277, 278, 279,
    284, 285, 399, 401
My People 51

Napoleon 163
Narodowa Demokracja 187
National Archive, Finland 88
National Council of Education for Wales 54
National Eisteddfod Association (1880) 42
National Society Training Colleges 41
National Union of Teachers of Wales 55
National University of Ireland 22, 25
Nationalism 65, 76, 82, 154, 180, 205, 267,
    294, 307, 314, 320, 299
Natisone valley 266
Navarra 292
Naziantinos, G. 358
Nemanjić, D. 338
Neohellenic ethno-nationalist revival 361–4
Newcastle Commission on Education 44
Newham, F.D. 381, 382
Nicholas I, Tsar 89
Non-dominant ethnic groups 389–417
    and modernisation 2–4, 6–10, 399–401,
        412, 414
    and political spectrum 404
    government policies in respect of 390–7
    motives generating and legitimising
        policies in respect of 397–401
    outcomes of educational policies
        concerning 410–13
    responses and reactions of 405–10
    specific policy measures concerning 401–3
Norrbotten 63, 70, 73
North Wales Scholarship Association 42
Northern Ireland 30
Norway 63–85, 395, 398, 399, 403, 405, 409
    church opposition to assimilation policy
        74
    Director of Schools 70, 71, 74–5, 77, 78
    education in context of other assimilation
        measures 72–3
    ethnic opposition to policy of assimilation
        76–8
    language policy 68
    minority policy in European context 80–2
    moderate assimilation period (1850–80)
        67–8
    norwegianisation (1870–1900) 68–9
    outcomes and effects of assimilation 78–9
    party consensus 75–6
    school role, in assimilation policy 71–2
    Zenith of Assimilation Policy (1900–40)
        69–71

O'Connell, D. 14
Okey, R. 4, 5, 35, 319, 389, 393
Ollivant, Bishop 41
Olomouc 235
Omladina 321
Options Agreement 285
Ortega y Gasset, J. 293, 294, 314
Orthodox Church 80, 88
    in Finland 100
    in Kingdom of Poland 173
Oslo University 76
Ostmarkenverein 146, 177
Otto, E. 230
Ottoman empire 4, 6, 7, 399
    conceptual framework 344–6
    educational policy towards non-dominant
        ethno-religious groups 345
    Greeks in 343–66
    demographic and socio-economic
        characteristics of 352–4
    educational and cultural awakening 354–
        61
    quest for national identity 352
    tradition and quest for modernity 347–52
Owen, Sir Hugh 40, 42, 47, 58

Pädagogische Rundschau 226
Pantycelyn, W. 56
Pardubice 235
Paris Commune and the Idea of the State, The
    335
Pasha, Osman 321, 322
Passerin d'Entrèves, E. 283
Pavellons pro-Infància 304
Pawlik, M. 171
Peace of Prague 152
Pedrao, O. 312
Pekař, J. 249
Pelagič, V. 322
Pelcl, F.M. 240
Perathoner, J. 270
Percy, Lord Eustace 58
Perner, J. 240

Pers i Romona 300
Pestalozzi, J. 91
Petranović, T. 321, 322
Philip V, King of Spain 299
Pi i Margall 296, 300
Piarist Order 239
Picavea, M. 298
Piłsudski, J. 188, 204
Pintos 312
Piotrków 173
Pítacco, Giorgio 269
Plzeň 235
Podrecca, A. 266
Pola 271, 280
Poland 392, 393, 396, 400, 402, 406, 407 (*see* also Polish Republic)
    Catholic Church in 164–5, 180, 409
    Communist party of 188
    Jews in 167
    Kingdom of 164, 166, 167, 171–6
    partial partition of 163
Polish constitution 190
Polish Jews. See Jews
Polish labour force, assimilation of 148–51
Polish language 139
Polish migrant labour 147–51
Polish minority in Prussia 143–51
Polish Piedmont 166
Polish Republic 185–208, 399
    Chrzescijańska Demokracja 187
    Czechs in 203
    Germans in 199–202
    Jews in 194–7
    Lithuanians in 202–3
    Narodowa Demokracja 187
    policy towards ethnic groups 204–6
    political spectrum 187–9
    population 185
    Ukrainians in 192–4
Polish Teachers' Union 189
Polish territories under Austrian, Russian and German rule (1850-1918) 163–83
Politico-ideological transformations 4
Polo y Peyrolón, M. 297
Pomerania 200
Pondal, 312
Poor Law guardians 14
Potemra, M. 255
Potsdam edict of 1685 133
Powis Commission 26
Poznań 142–7, 163, 164, 166, 176, 200, 399
Prácheň 238
Prague 235, 237, 238, 241, 244, 245, 247, 406
Prague University 240, 243, 246–7
Praski, R. 190
Preissler, G. 222, 226, 227
Presbyterians 17, 18, 21
Princip, G. 334, 337, 338
Protestants
    in Ireland 24, 28

in Kingdom of Poland 173
in Wales 36
Privincial School Council of Turin 265
Prussia 133–59, 399
    Abitur 140
    Allgemeinbildung 137
    Allgemeines Landrecht 138, 140
    Berechtigungswesen 140
    Bürgerliche Bildung 141
    cultural centralisation 136
    denationalisation of minorities 147
    elementary education 137
    extermination of Polish and Jewish culture 155
    germanisation 144, 153
    Geschäftssprachengesetz 145
    grossdeutsch 141
    gymnasium 133–6, 138–41, 143, 150–2
    High German 137, 138, 150
    Jewish minority 133–6
    Kleindeutsch 141
    Konistorien 140
    Kultursprache 140–2
    language policy towards minorities 136
    nationalist policy 136
    Nationalsprache 140–2
    Polish migrant labour 147–51
    Polish minority in 143–51
    Poznań Province 142–7
    Provinzialschulkollegien 140
    prussification 137
    Realgymasien 136
    Reichsgründung 138
    relationship between state, schools and ethnic minorities 133
    religious education 138, 144
    Schulaufsichtsgesetz 139
    Schulkompromiss 140
    science subjects 138
    secondary schools 144
    Staatspädagogik 137
    strike against germanisation 146
    teacher training 135, 139
    unifying administration reorganisation 136
    use of German language 143–4
    Volkserziehung 136
    Volksschule 136, 139–40
Puig i Cadafalch 302
Purkyně, K. 239

Queen's College Cork 22
Queen's College Galway 22
Queen's Colleges 22
Queen's University 22

Realpolitik 64–6
Rees, Reverend Thomas 45
Reformpädagogik 220
Rhineland 134

Rico, C. 312
Rieger, B. 246
Rieger, F.L. 248
Rivas, L. 297
Robert College, Bebek, Istanbul 350
Rohn, E. 225
Romanones, 298
Romanovs 6
Romish errors 18
Roudnice 235
Royal Flemish Academy for Linguistics and
    Literature 123
Royal University 22
Ruhr 147, 148, 150
Rumanians 237
Ruthenians 237

Šafarik, P.J. 241
Samis (Lapps) 63–72, 74–6, 78–80, 82, 412
Samuel, C. 384
Sardinia 263–4, 266
Savoy 264, 265
Scandinavia, See Norway; Sweden
Schiper, J. 197
Schleswig-Holstein 69
    Danish conflict in 151–4
Schneider, Dr. 152
School for Teachers 301
Schuschnigg, K. 282
Scott, Sir Walter 397, 414
Sempołowska, S. 189–90
Sendal, Sir Walter 380
Sensat, R. 302
Serbs 320, 329–36, 337, 344, 401
Seton-Watson, H. 8, 362
Seton-Watson, R. 257
Silesia 144, 200, 217–19, 235–8, 399
Sinn Féin 29
Slavia Veneta 266
Slavs 391, 394
Slovakia
    Apponyi laws 254
    educational background 252–3
    educational policy 253–5
    enforced or voluntary assimilation 255–8
    German minority in 255
    gymnasiums 254–6
    magyarisation 216, 251, 253–5
    national structure of population 250–1
    politically induced changes 251
    population in different branches of
        production 237
    school system 253
Slovaks 393, 401
    under Czechoslovak republic 258
    under Hungarian rule 249–58
Slovenes 237, 247, 263, 266, 268, 269, 281,
    282
Smith, A.D. 8, 45
Smith, Adam 7

Snellman, J.V. 102
Social Darwinism 2, 65, 76, 82, 399, 415
Social Science Section of the National
    Eisteddfod (1861) 42
Society for Byelorussian Schools 198
Society for Educational Assistance 178
Society for Popular Reading Rooms 178
Society for the Promotion of the Irish
    Language 24
Society of Cyril and Methodius 268, 271
Socio-economic transformations 3
Sophronios, Archbishop 376
South Tyrol 263, 267, 270, 273, 280–2, 401,
    407
Spain 291–317, 392, 396, 399
    Catholic Church in 297, 305, 408
    cultural and political problems 293–4
    Cultural Council 304
    educational policy 294–9
    Jocs Florals 300, 305
    Plan Pidal 294–5
Spencer, Reverend Archdeacon I. 382
Spina, F. 223, 224
Spranger, E. 222
Stablewski, Archbishop 145, 147
Stanley, E. 15
Starkie, W.J.M. 27
Statute of Autonomy for Catalunya 303
Stavrianos, L.S. 4
Stefanek, Anton 256
Stuparich, G. 273
Sudeten Germans 211, 212, 215, 222–6, 230
Svecomen 92, 95
Sweden 63–85, 395, 398, 399, 409
    church opposition to assimilation policy
        74
    education in context of other assimilation
        measures 72–3
    ethnic opposition to policy of assimilation
        76–8
    language of education 67
    minority policy 69–71, 80–2
    moderate assimilation period (1850–80)
        67–8
    outcomes and effects of assimilation 78–9
    party consensus 75–6
    school policy 70
    school role in assimilation policy 71–2
    state schools 67
    swedification (1870–1900) 68–9
Symons, Commissioner 39

T. Szewczenko Society 171
Taaffe, E. 242
Tanzimat 347, 349, 393
Taunton Commission (1868) 46
Thaden, E.C. 392, 395
Thallóczy, L. 333, 334, 337
Thirlwall, Bishop 41, 43

Thompson, F.M.L. xxii
Thompson, J.V. 382, 383
Tienen 117
Tinzl, K. 278, 280
Tolmino 271
Tolomei, E. 274
Tolstoy, D. 94
Tomiak, J. xvi, 185, 389
Tornedalen 67, 72, 81
Tractarians 19
Trentino 267, 274
Trento 267, 274, 280, 283
Trieste 268, 269, 271
Trinity College Dublin 21, 22
Troms 68, 71
Tromsø 63
Trzemeszno 143
Tsetsos, T. 376
Turin 264, 275
Turks, in Cyprus 369–87
Tvrdý, J. 222

Ukrainian Military Organisation 194
Ukrainian National Democratic Union 194
Ukrainians 163, 170
  in Polish Republic 192–4
Unamuno, M. 306
Union for Industrial Progress in Bohemia 240
Union for the Defence of German Culture Abroad 201
Union of German Teachers 201
Union of German Teachers at the German Association for Culture and Science 201
United Kingdom 13, 15, 294
University College
  Aberystwyth 42
  Ireland 22
Upper Adige 263, 272–4, 282, 284, 285
Upper Silesia 154
Ustředni Matice Školska (Central Eudcational Society) 247
Utsjok 80

Valdotaine League for the Defence of the French Language 265
Vascuence 304
Vegezzi-Ruscalla, G. 264
Venezia Tridentina 275
Verdaguer, J. 300
Victor Emmanuel III 270
Victoria, Queen of England 43
Vienna 236, 247, 248, 269, 333
Villgrater, M. 282
Vistula land 166
Volhynia 203
Volonakis 384
von Eichhorn, Minister of Culture 142
von Gossler 145, 153
von Gunther 144

von Humboldt, Wilhelm 137
von Kállay, B. 324, 325, 326, 327, 328, 330, 336, 337
von Kothen, C. 97
von Mühler 152
von Sternbach, P. 278
von Studt 146, 151
Vucinich, W.S. 346

Wales 35–61, 391, 405
  Anglican Church in 35, 40, 41, 58
  British Schools 40, 43
  Circulating Schools movement 37
  Commission of 1846–7 37–45
  Education movement 37–45, 50–5
  labour movement 55
  National Schools 40–1
  Nonconformist wing 42
  primary schools 36
  secondary schools 52
  Sunday Schools 35–7, 39, 44
  University of 42, 45
  works schools 37
Walloons 111, 112, 113, 124, 127–9
Walsh, Archbishop of Dublin 26
Warsaw 163, 164, 173
Warsaw University 147
Warta 178
Watkins, Sir Percy 58
Weber, P. 242
Weimar Republic 136–7, 140, 154
Welsh Code of 1907 48
Welsh Department 50, 52, 54
Welsh Department of the Board of Education (1907) 48
Welsh Education Committee (1845) 40
Welsh in Education and Life 53
Welsh Intermediate Education Act (1889) 42
Welsh language 35–6, 45–9, 51–4, 58
Welsh Language Society 47, 57
Welsh National Council for Education 48
Welsh National Education Council 54
Welsh Nationalist party 55
Welsh Nonconformity 50–1
Whately, R., Church of Ireland archbishop of Dublin 17, 30
Wilde, O. 335
Wilhelm II, Kaiser 146
Women's Association 102

Ylikangas, H. 93
Young Bosnia 339
Young Ottomans 351
Young Turks 350, 351

Zara 268, 271
Zentralverein der Deutschen Lehrerinnen 226
Zimmern, A. 46
Zufia, P. 309